SEPTEMBER 2004–AUGUST 2005

TARBELL'S

KJV & NRSV
Lesson
Commentary

BASED ON THE INTERNATIONAL SUNDAY SCHOOL LESSONS

EDITOR: DR. DANIEL LIOY

COOK COMMUNICATIONS MINISTRIES CURRICULUM
COLORADO SPRINGS, COLORADO/PARIS, ONTARIO

TARBELL'S KJV & NRSV LESSON COMMENTARY © 2004 Cook Communications Ministries, 4050 Lee Vance View, Colorado Springs, CO 80918, U.S.A. All rights reserved. Printed in U.S.A. May not be reproduced without permission. Lessons based on International Sunday School Lessons: the International Bible Lessons for Christian Teaching, © 2001 by the Committee on the Uniform Series.

Editorial Manager: Douglas C. Schmidt

Editor: Daniel Lioy, Ph.D.

Designer: Robert de la Peña

Cover Design by Jeffrey P. Barnes

Cover photography © 1998 by Dan Stultz

ISBN: 078144022X

CONTENTS

SEPTEMBER, OCTOBER, NOVEMBER 2004
THE COST OF CONTINUING CREATION

UNIT I: CREATED FOR A PURPOSE

UNIT II: GOD'S CREATIVITY CONTINUES

UNIT III: A NEW CREATION

DECEMBER 2004, JANUARY, FEBRUARY 2005
CALLED TO BE GOD'S PEOPLE

UNIT I: GOD CALLS A PEOPLE

UNIT II: THE CALL OF JESUS AND HIS FOLLOWERS (GOSPEL OF MARK)

UNIT III: WHOSOEVER WILL—COME

CONTENTS

Over 25 years ago I preached my first sermon at a small country church in the western part of the United States. To be honest, I remember little of what I said, but I vividly recall the song that preceded my message. It was Martin Luther's *A Mighty Fortress*. Hearing Christian voices passionately sing this hymn so moved me that I decided to get more involved in the teaching ministry of the church,

I also realized that when people fervently praise God for who He is and for what He has done, they can't help but feel they have caught a glimpse of what heaven will be like and hunger for more of that feeling. Indeed, giving glory to God not only is pleasing to Him but also nourishing to our soul.

One of the most effective ways we can honor the Lord is by teaching His Word to His people. Certainly the writers of the Old and New Testaments believed this. In fact, toward the end of his life, Paul urged Christians leaders such as Timothy to *proclaim the message* (2 Tim. 4:2). And because the apostle saw this as a vital, ongoing ministry of the church, he wanted all who taught Scripture—including each of you who will be using this year's edition of *Tarbell's*—to *be persistent whether the time is favorable or unfavorable*. Furthermore, each week as you prepare for and teach a host of Sunday school classes, you should do so *with the utmost patience.*

That God has adopted us into His family and blessed us with His Word are a couple of reasons why we can serve Him so diligently. Moreover, the Lord's purpose in creating us, inviting us to be His people, and empowering us to be effective Christians (all themes covered in this year's lesson series) is so that He may be glorified and His people encouraged in the faith. Hopefully, after we study His Word in each lesson to follow, we can exclaim, "Praise God!"

Forever in His Service,

Dan Lioy

Sunday school materials from the following denominations and publishers follow the International Sunday School Lesson outlines (sometimes known as the Uniform Series). Because *Tarbell's KJV & NRSV Lesson Commentary* follows the same ISSL outlines, you can use *Tarbell's* as an excellent teacher resource to supplement the materials from these publishing houses.

Nondenominational:

Standard Publishing—*Adult*

Urban Ministries—*All ages*

Denominational:

Advent Christian General Conference—*Adult*

American Baptist (Judson Press)—*Adult*

Church of God in Christ (Church of God in Christ Publishing House)—*Adult*

Church of Christ Holiness—*Adult*

Church of God (Warner Press)—*Adult*

Church of God by Faith—*Adult*

National Baptist Convention of America (Boyd)—*All ages*

National Primitive Baptist Convention—*Adult*

Progressive National Baptist Convention—*Adult*

Presbyterian Church (U.S.A.) (Bible Discovery Series—Presbyterian Publishing House or P.R.E.M.)—*Adult*

Southern Baptist (Baptist Sunday School Board)—*All ages*

Union Gospel Press—*All ages*

United Holy Church of America—*Adult*

United Methodist Church (Cokesbury)—*All ages*

SEPTEMBER, OCTOBER, NOVEMBER 2004

THE GOD OF CONTINUING CREATION

FROM THE DUST OF THE GROUND

Background Scripture: Genesis 2
Devotional Reading: Psalm 150

KEY VERSE: The LORD God formed man from the dust of the ground, and breathed into his nostrils the breath of life; and the man became a living being. Genesis 2:7.

KING JAMES VERSION

GENESIS 2:4 These are the generations of the heavens and of the earth when they were created, in the day that the LORD God made the earth and the heavens,
5 And every plant of the field before it was in the earth, and every herb of the field before it grew: for the LORD God had not caused it to rain upon the earth, and there was not a man to till the ground. 6 But there went up a mist from the earth, and watered the whole face of the ground. 7 And the LORD God formed man of the dust of the ground, and breathed into his nostrils the breath of life; and man became a living soul. . . .

15 And the LORD God took the man, and put him into the garden of Eden to dress it and to keep it.

16 And the LORD God commanded the man, saying, Of every tree of the garden thou mayest freely eat:
17 But of the tree of the knowledge of good and evil, thou shalt not eat of it: for in the day that thou eatest thereof thou shalt surely die.

18 And the LORD God said, It is not good that the man should be alone; I will make him an help meet for him. 19 And out of the ground the LORD God formed every beast of the field, and every fowl of the air; and brought them unto Adam to see what he would call them: and whatsoever Adam called every living creature, that was the name thereof. 20 And Adam gave names to all cattle, and to the fowl of the air, and to every beast of the field; but for Adam there was not found an help meet for him.

21 And the LORD God caused a deep sleep to fall upon Adam, and he slept: and he took one of his ribs, and closed up the flesh instead thereof; 22 And the rib, which the LORD God had taken from man, made he a woman, and brought her unto the man. 23 And Adam said, This is now bone of my bones, and flesh of my flesh: she shall be called Woman, because she was taken out of Man. 24 Therefore shall a man leave his father and his mother, and shall cleave unto his wife: and they shall be one flesh. 25 And they were both naked, the man and his wife, and were not ashamed.

NEW REVISED STANDARD VERSION

GENESIS 2:4 In the day that the LORD God made the earth and the heavens, 5 when no plant of the field was yet in the earth and no herb of the field had yet sprung up—for the LORD God had not caused it to rain upon the earth, and there was no one to till the ground; 6 but a stream would rise from the earth, and water the whole face of the ground— 7 then the LORD God formed man from the dust of the ground, and breathed into his nostrils the breath of life; and the man became a living being. . . .

15 The LORD God took the man and put him in the garden of Eden to till it and keep it. 16 And the LORD God commanded the man, "You may freely eat of every tree of the garden; 17 but of the tree of the knowledge of good and evil you shall not eat, for in the day that you eat of it you shall die."

18 Then the LORD God said, "It is not good that the man should be alone; I will make him a helper as his partner." 19 So out of the ground the LORD God formed every animal of the field and every bird of the air, and brought them to the man to see what he would call them; and whatever the man called every living creature, that was its name. 20 The man gave names to all cattle, and to the birds of the air, and to every animal of the field; but for the man there was not found a helper as his partner. 21 So the LORD God caused a deep sleep to fall upon the man, and he slept; then he took one of his ribs and closed up its place with flesh. 22 And the rib that the LORD God had taken from the man he made into a woman and brought her to the man. 23 Then the man said,

"This at last is bone of my bones
   and flesh of my flesh;
this one shall be called Woman,
   for out of Man this one was taken."

24 Therefore a man leaves his father and his mother and clings to his wife, and they become one flesh.

HOME BIBLE READINGS

Monday, August 30	Psalm 148:1-6	*Praise the Lord*
Tuesday, August 31	Psalm 148:7-13	*Let All the Earth Praise God*
Wednesday, September 1	Genesis 1:26-31	*God's Creation Is Good*
Thursday, September 2	Genesis 2:4b-9	*God Created Man*
Friday, September 3	Genesis 2:10-14	*The Garden Is Watered by Rivers*
Saturday, September 4	Genesis 2:15-20	*Man Is Placed in the Garden*
Sunday, September 5	Genesis 2:21-25	*God Creates a Helper for Man*

BACKGROUND

In 1925 the John Scopes "Monkey Trial" in Dayton, Tennessee, pitted lawyers Clarence Darrow and William Jennings Bryan against one another. The argument was between evolution and divine creation. The same argument flares up repeatedly in school districts today where explanations that challenge secular evolution must be given equal time in high school biology classes. This week you will have an opportunity to examine the biblical record.

Note that there are two accounts in Genesis of the Lord's creation of the universe. Don't be put off by the differences between the two accounts, for both describe the same event, told from two angles. The Creation account in Genesis 1:1—2:4a sounds like a solemn litany, repeating such phrases as *and God saw that it was good* and *there was evening and there was morning* and *according to their kinds.* This version of the Creation account focuses on the entire universe and all creatures in it, with humankind coming at the climax. By contrast, the second account (2:4b-25) seems to hurry to the creation of humankind. The creation of heaven and earth is described in a single phrase.

With respect to the second account, the word rendered *dust* (2:7) in Hebrew is *adamah*, and is the root of the word *adam* (or *humankind*). The Hebrew word might be translated as "earthling," since the Lord fashioned this clay figure out of moist soil of the earth. The Lord then breathed life into the clay figure. This living being is not defined at this point as either male or female, although the word *adam* is translated as "man." Many Bible scholars refer to *adam* here as "human" since specific reference to gender does not come until later in chapter 2.

The human is placed by the Lord in a state of paradise, a lovely garden. Genesis 2 insists that there were three basic facets of the human's task. (1) Vocation: The human was to care for the garden, be responsible for God's property and enhance it, and work for a living. Labor was considered part of the original order of creation. (2) Freedom: The human was not created as a robot, but was meant to enjoy and celebrate God's creation. Food, for example, was intended to sustain strength and bring enjoyment. (3) Limitation: *Knowledge of good and evil* (2:9) meant that *adam* had to accept limits to human existence. Humankind was not intended to step beyond human creatureliness.

This great Creation account concludes with God's concern for human loneliness. None of the animals was considered sufficient for the companionship needs of humans. The Lord then created two genders. The specific Hebrew word for a male is *ish* and was used at this point for the first time (2:23). The female word is *ishshah*. Woman, like man, owes her life solely to God.

In responding to the woman, the man spoke for the first time. He discovers himself as male, comes alive, and is no longer passive. True companionship comes into being as the man and the woman live as partners in a harmonious relationship with the Lord and each other. *Ish* (man) and *ishshah* (woman) are given to each other by God as a result of the Lord's special concern.

NOTES ON THE PRINTED TEXT

In the Book of Genesis we learn about the origins of humankind. Concerning Adam, God took the basic elements of the earth and fashioned the first man from the dust of the ground. Then God formed from Adam a woman named Eve to be his counterpart and companion.

As was noted earlier, Genesis 1:1—2:4a describes how God created the heavens and the earth. Then, beginning in 2:4b, Moses focused the readers' attention on what God specifically did for humankind. At this time God had not sent any rain. Thus, there were no plants growing; also, there was no one to *till the ground* (2:5). The soil, however, was not arid, for a mist emerged from the ground and kept it moist (2:6).

Two important features are emphasized in the description of the first man's creation. One is that God formed Adam from *the dust of the ground* (2:7). Like the animals that were created before Adam, he was made from elements that God had previously formed. Moreover, like the potter who shapes clay into a work of art, God took the basic elements of the earth and fashioned the first man.

The second important feature is Adam's dependence on God for life. Adam's physical form may have been derived from the soil, but it was God who gave have him the breath of life. Though Adam was much like the animals, he was also different because he was made in the image of God (see 1:26-27). Like the first man, we also owe our very existence to the Lord. It is for His glory that we live.

Prior to Adam's creation, God planted a garden called *Eden* (2:8) east of the land of Israel. Moses clearly meant for his readers to understand Eden as a real place, since he provided many geographic details (2:9-14). The garden was not only a place of enjoyment for Adam but also a place of service, for God put the man in Eden to *till and keep it* (2:15). In fact, Adam's work enabled the garden to bear fruit. Thus, the man had the responsibility of acting as a steward of God's creation.

The fact that Adam was given this assignment prior to the Fall implies that work is part of God's original design for humanity and was not one of the consequences of sin. This point reminds us that God created us to serve Him faithfully on earth.

God placed within the garden many kinds of trees, including the *tree of life* (2:9) and the *tree of the knowledge of good and evil.* Although the latter was pleasant to look at and good for food, God prohibited Adam from partaking of it (2:16-17). The Lord warned Adam that if he ate this tree's fruit, he would suffer death (physically and spiritually). The fact that Adam had so many alternatives to choose from makes his eventual disobedience of God all the more condemnable. Sorrow and loss also come to us when we disobey God.

Perhaps once Adam had begun his work, the Lord noted that it was not good for the man to live *alone* (2:18). This fact was confirmed as Adam named the animals that God had created (2:19). As a result, the Lord determined to create a counterpart, companion, and co-laborer for him (2:20). The suitability of *Eve* (3:20) lay in the fact that she was comparable to Adam. From this we see that, though Eve differed from Adam, she was not less than he was.

Now that Adam knew he needed a mate, God caused a deep sleep to come over him. The Lord first took a part of Adam's side and then closed up the spot from which the rib had been taken (2:21). Next, God made a woman from Adam's rib and brought her to him (2:22).

The phrase translated *[God] took one of [the man's] ribs* (2:21) can also be translated "[God] took part of [the man's] side." In the Old Testament, the Hebrew word for "rib" is more often translated "side." For example, in Exodus 25:12 it refers to the sides of the ark of the covenant. Such usage has led some commentators to suggest that God took more than a rib from Adam when He made the first woman. God may have taken some flesh along with the bone. If so, Adam spoke quite literally when he called the woman *bone of my bones and flesh of my flesh* (2:23).

The excitement that Adam felt at the creation of Eve is shown in the man's short poetic song. Adam now had a companion whom God had created from the man's own body. Eve was truly part of the man's own *flesh* and *bone*. In calling her *Woman*, Adam stressed that Eve not only was comparable to him but also suitable for him.

The desire for suitable companionship explains why a man leaves the household of his parents to establish a new one with his *wife* (2:24). In the case of Adam and Eve, they were married from their first moment together and remained united for life. Their marriage set a pattern for the marriages of their descendants.

The statement in 2:25 that the man and woman were both *naked* and *not ashamed* prepares the reader for the changes that would take place afterward. The entrance of sin not only disrupted Adam's fellowship with God, but also dealt a tragic blow to the unity experienced by Adam and Eve.

The creation of the first woman emphasizes our need as human beings to be in relationships. Because men and women were created for each other, they can unite in a marriage and become like one person—knowing each other's thoughts and sharing each other's hopes and dreams.

It also remains true that we need relationships beyond marriage. God made us all with the desire to be lovingly related to others. The relationships we have are gifts from God to be cared for and nurtured.

All good relationships need two main ingredients—love and truth. Sometimes, however, relationships get damaged in the process of living. These require forgiveness and healing. Other relationships may grow strained or distant through neglect. These require renewed care and attention on our part. Still other relationships are a continual joy and we hope they will never end. These require prayer for wisdom.

SUGGESTIONS TO TEACHERS

"Why was I born?" "What's the purpose of human existence?" Teenagers, unsure of their identities and feeling alone may ask the first question. Rabbis, theologians, and philosophers have discussed the second. Both queries reflect a basic human desire to find some meaning to life. Your class members undoubtedly have pondered whether God has any purpose for them. This week's lesson opens this profound topic from the point of view of Genesis 2.

1. LOVING US INTO EXISTENCE. According to the biblical account, our lives are not the result of some cosmic joke as some people might believe. The caring Creator made humankind out of the dust of the ground. Like a potter shaping a vessel, He fashioned us into human form from clay or earth. (You might want to explain that the Hebrew word *adamah*—which means "earth" or "dust"—is the basis for the word *adam*.) Earthy stuff we may be, but the Lord breathed life into us. Expressed differently, we humans are made of the ordinary stuff that everything else in nature has. But God designed us to be self-aware beings, thereby making us different from caterpillars, cats, and chimpanzees (to name a few creatures).

2. LAVISHING PROVISION. The Creator placed humanity in a world with provision to nourish bodies and beauty to nurture spirits. Talk with the class about ways we humans have spoiled our surroundings. God's provision is sufficient when we take care of the garden that is this beautiful planet.

3. LEAVING US WITH A PURPOSE. The Creator holds us humans responsible to look after this "garden," or planet Earth. Bring up the need to treat all nature with care. Christians should properly speak out against ravishing Earth's provisions or plundering its resources.

4. LIMITING HUMAN KNOWLEDGE AND ACCOMPLISHMENTS. Discuss the significance of the prohibition against eating *of the tree of the knowledge of good and evil* (Gen. 2:17). God puts boundaries on our human freedom. Contrary to popular thinking in today's society, we are not always permitted to do as we please.

5. LEARNING PARTNERSHIP. Genesis 2 opens the subject of the relationship of the genders. An entire lesson, of course, can be spent on marriage and male-female relationships. The basic point, though, is mutual caring, not domineering by either gender. The man and the woman in a marriage must consider one another as a partner.

6. LIVING IN OPENNESS. Round out this lesson by reminding the class that God's intention for us as humans is that we live in trust with Him and one another. Humility, not haughtiness, should characterize every aspect of our lives, especially our dealings with our fellow human beings.

| **FOR ADULTS** | ■ **TOPIC:** Discovering Our Value in God's Creation |
| | ■ **QUESTIONS:** 1. From where did man's physical elements come? |

2. What differentiated man from the rest of the creatures? 3. What did God expect Adam to do in Eden? 4. What was the nature of God's warning to Adam? 5. How do we know that marriage and the family were part of God's plan from the start?

■ **ILLUSTRATIONS:**

Looking Up Ancestors. Most people have at least a passing interest in who their ancestors were. For some, it becomes a near-obsession to trace family roots. Professional genealogists make their living by tracking down distant forebearers for those wanting to know names and dates.

Some people get a deep sense of satisfaction in being able to say that a relative came over on the Mayflower or fought in the American Revolution. In Germany, amidst a growing desire to trace personal histories back to a Teutonic knight at the very least, several people have announced that Frederick the Great is on their family tree. One person even insists that Charlemagne is an ancestor!

Our ultimate parentage, however, begins with God. The account recorded in Genesis of the origin of humankind is actually our claim to distinction. In fact, it is our *only* claim, for in it we see that we can trace our lineage to the hand of the Creator. Genesis and genealogy have the same root word, and the biblical account offers us our authentic sense of importance.

Partnership of Caring and Commitment. A Bible-thumping minister named Glynn ("Scotty") Wolfe married 29 times in his lifetime. Apparently Wolfe didn't read or understand the passage in Genesis where it is reported that God created man and woman to live together caringly, faithfully, and permanently in a partnership. Wolfe cast off one wife for eating sunflower seeds in bed and divorced another for using his toothbrush. Wife number 29, Linda Essex, was Wolfe's match in that she proudly claimed the record of being the world's most frequently married woman. (Her trip to the altar with Wolfe was her 23rd.) Wolfe died in June 1997, leaving Linda the opportunity of hunting for husband number 24. God did not intend people to be throwaway commodities.

Testimony from *Star Trek*'s Creator. The late Gene Roddenberry, the brilliant creator of the award-winning *Star Trek* series, is quoted as pondering the wonders of creation as he wrote the science fiction stories set in the 21st century. He particularly was struck by the conviction he held that no other intelligent forms of life exist in the world overhead. "In fact," stated this television dramatist, "everything about our sun and its planets proclaims RESERVED FOR HUMANITY. What a lovely educational arrangement for the offspring of our fertile Earth-egg planet!" —From "Open Forum" sponsored by Volkswagen, 1988.

While God made this planet for us, we know from this week's lesson that we are made for God and His purposes.

Reverence for Life. Noted philosopher and religionist Albert Schweitzer said the following: "Reverence for life . . . does not allow the scholar to live for his science alone, even if he is very useful . . . the artist to exist only for his art, even if he gives inspiration to many. . . . It refuses to let the businessman imagine that he fulfills all legitimate demands in the course of his business activities. It demands from all that they should sacrifice a portion of their own lives for others." We are reminded from John 14:6 that the One who is *life* sacrificed Himself on the cross for us so that we might be redeemed.

| **For Youth** | ■ TOPIC: Discovering Our Value |
| | ■ QUESTIONS: 1. What did God use to create the first man? |

2. What made Adam different from the rest of the creatures that God had brought into existence? 3. In what sense was Eden a place of service? 4. What did God say would happen to Adam if he ate the fruit growing on the tree of the knowledge of good and evil? 5. Why did God create a counterpart and companion for Adam?

■ **ILLUSTRATIONS:**

God's Creation. Pastor Alvin Stevens heard that little Bridgeville, California, was for sale. The entire town, 80 acres and 25 buildings, Stevens felt, was where the Lord wanted Stevens and his flock to live. Stevens drove the 330 miles north of San Francisco and looked at the land of mist-shrouded forests and trout-filled streams. He saw the place as an ideal spot to raise families and care for the elderly. The asking price was $450,000 with a down payment of $150,000.

Stevens took his dream of buying a Garden of Eden to his congregation at Stonybrook Full Gospel Temple. After a prayer meeting, five of the 70 people agreed to sell their homes and make up the down payment. Forty-eight people eventually moved to Eden, a former stagecoach stop that became a hippie commune. During the hippies' time, marijuana had been grown and continued to sprout when Stevens's people moved in. Toilets and septic tanks were broken.

Heaps of smelly garbage and abandoned electrical equipment littered the area. In addition, a high unemployment rate dampened the hopes of the new residents. Pastor Stevens's families found that the place was not the idyllic spot they'd hoped to live in. Their Eden had been spoiled.

Perhaps the story illustrates the Genesis account. God brought into existence a garden with a wonderful variety of creations. By their act of aggression humans allowed the garden to deteriorate. No amount of human effort could change that process. Only God's creation was perfect. People simply cannot recreate Eden.

What Do You Believe? July 1997 was the 50th anniversary of a weird crash in Roswell, New Mexico. The site is particularly interesting for individuals interested in UFOs (Unidentified Flying Objects) because of the alleged crash of a flying saucer. National interest reached a peak. A *Time* magazine/Yankelovich poll indicated that 34 percent of Americans believe that intelligent beings from other planets have visited the Earth. Of these, 65 percent believe a UFO crashed at Roswell, and 80 percent believe that the U.S. government knows more about extraterrestrials than it chooses to release. Some scientists assume the existence of intelligent life among the planets. Even if it is true, most theologians believe that any such species simply enlarges the creativity of the Creator. Whatever the case may be, this vast universe is proof that no one can limit God's power.

At the Beginning. Scientists examining modern human origins have utilized special genetic studies. They believe they have strong evidence that there was an ancestral "Adam" living about 188,000 years ago with a previously discovered "Eve." Certain male-specific segments of the Y chromosome (the chromosome passed from father to son) traced a common ancestor to every man on earth.

While analysis of DNA, particularly the mitochondria (the tiny structures within each cell that generates energy and is transmitted by the mother), indicated that humans have a common female ancestor who lived in Africa about 200,000 years ago, the quest for the male was more difficult. However, Michael F. Hammer and other scientists at the University of Arizona at Tucson found definitive evidence for the male. All cautioned that many males and females were living at that time and it was misleading to dub the individuals "Adam" and "Eve" and consider them the sources of all human beings.

Moses, the writer of Genesis, had no difficulty in describing the creation of a male and female. The account relates the creation of the human species from these two created beings.

Mother of Us All. In 1991, Penn State anthropologist Henry Harpending and geneticist Mark Stoneking, along with a team of other scholars, announced the discovery of a skeleton of an African woman they dated at approximately 200,000 years old. Apparently, she lived in a cave, used stone tools, and competed with lions for food. Some experts who examined the bones and the genetic material believe her to be the common ancestor of every human being. Their conclusion, dubbed the Eve Hypothesis, states that billions of people on earth are the direct descendants of this one African woman. The scholars hastened to add that their Eve was not the *single* ancestral mother of all people. Other women were having babies at the same time.

This information reminds us that many people are curious about their origins and identities. Moses, the writer of Genesis, reminded his readers that God created humankind—both male and female.

The Mouse and the Elephant. There is an old Indian legend of a mouse and an elephant who were close friends. Everywhere these huge and tiny creatures went, they walked together, side by side. One day they came upon a long, narrow bridge suspended over a deep gully. Side by side they stepped onto the bridge and walked across. When the two stepped off the other side, the little mouse said to the elephant, "Wow, we sure made that old bridge shake!"

Compared to God, we are like mice; yet, when we go with God, we can make the world shake. We must remember, however, God's greatness and our smallness before Him. We are the creatures and He is the Creator.

BEGINNING AGAIN

BACKGROUND SCRIPTURE: Genesis 6:5—9:17
DEVOTIONAL READING: Genesis 9:8-17

2

KEY VERSE: "When the bow is in the clouds, I will see it and remember the everlasting covenant between God and every living creature of all flesh that is on the earth." Genesis 9:16.

KING JAMES VERSION

GENESIS 6:5 And GOD saw that the wickedness of man was great in the earth, and that every imagination of the thoughts of his heart was only evil continually.

6 And it repented the LORD that he had made man on the earth, and it grieved him at his heart. 7 And the LORD said, I will destroy man whom I have created from the face of the earth; both man, and beast, and the creeping thing, and the fowls of the air; for it repenteth me that I have made them.

8 But Noah found grace in the eyes of the LORD. . . .

7:1 And the LORD said unto Noah, Come thou and all thy house into the ark; for thee have I seen righteous before me in this generation. 2 Of every clean beast thou shalt take to thee by sevens, the male and his female: and of beasts that are not clean by two, the male and his female. 3 Of fowls also of the air by sevens, the male and the female; to keep seed alive upon the face of all the earth. 4 For yet seven days, and I will cause it to rain upon the earth forty days and forty nights; and every living substance that I have made will I destroy from off the face of the earth.

5 And Noah did according unto all that the LORD commanded him. . . .

17 And the flood was forty days upon the earth; and the waters increased, and bare up the ark, and it was lift up above the earth. . . . 23 And every living substance was destroyed which was upon the face of the ground, both man, and cattle, and the creeping things, and the fowl of the heaven; and they were destroyed from the earth: and Noah only remained alive, and they that were with him in the ark. . . .

8:14 And in the second month, on the seven and twentieth day of the month, was the earth dried.

15 And God spake unto Noah, saying, 16 Go forth of the ark, thou, and thy wife, and thy sons, and thy sons' wives with thee. . . .

9:1 And God blessed Noah and his sons, and said unto them, Be fruitful, and multiply, and replenish the earth.

NEW REVISED STANDARD VERSION

GENESIS 6:5 The LORD saw that the wickedness of humankind was great in the earth, and that every inclination of the thoughts of their hearts was only evil continually. 6 And the LORD was sorry that he had made humankind on the earth, and it grieved him to his heart. 7 So the LORD said, "I will blot out from the earth the human beings I have created—people together with animals and creeping things and birds of the air, for I am sorry that I have made them." 8 But Noah found favor in the sight of the LORD. . . .

7:1 Then the LORD said to Noah, "Go into the ark, you and all your household, for I have seen that you alone are righteous before me in this generation. 2 Take with you seven pairs of all clean animals, the male and its mate; and a pair of the animals that are not clean, the male and its mate; 3 and seven pairs of the birds of the air also, male and female, to keep their kind alive on the face of all the earth. 4 For in seven days I will send rain on the earth for forty days and forty nights; and every living thing that I have made I will blot out from the face of the ground." 5 And Noah did all that the LORD had commanded him. . . .

17 The flood continued forty days on the earth; and the waters increased, and bore up the ark, and it rose high above the earth. . . . 23 He blotted out every living thing that was on the face of the ground, human beings and animals and creeping things and birds of the air; they were blotted out from the earth. Only Noah was left, and those that were with him in the ark. . . .

8:14 In the second month, on the twenty-seventh day of the month, the earth was dry. 15 Then God said to Noah, 16 "Go out of the ark, you and your wife, and your sons and your sons' wives with you. . . .

9:1 God blessed Noah and his sons, and said to them, "Be fruitful and multiply, and fill the earth.

Monday, September 6	Genesis 6:5-12	*The Wickedness of Humans Is Great*
Tuesday, September 7	Genesis 6:13-22	*God Has Noah Build an Ark*
Wednesday, September 8	Genesis 7:1-16	*Noah Enters the Ark*
Thursday, September 9	Genesis 7:17—8:5	*The Flood Comes*
Friday, September 10	Genesis 8:6-19	*Noah Leaves the Ark*
Saturday, September 11	Genesis 8:20—9:7	*God Blesses Noah and His Family*
Sunday, September 12	Genesis 9:8-17	*God Makes a Covenant*

BACKGROUND

The ripple effects of human disobedience brought alienation between brothers and sisters, within families, and among entire communities. Finally, the rebellion against the Lord's plans seemed to infect the entire population. Those are the sad facts we must face in Scripture.

The Book of Genesis describes what God tried to do about the shattered relationships between humanity and Himself and among humans themselves. This week's lesson is actually best understood as a three-part drama. First, God's judgment—His case against His human creation. Second, God's grief—His disappointment over the way humanity persisted in refusing to obey. Third, God's resolution—His desire to start things afresh.

The Genesis account stresses how evil humans had become. The situation was so hopeless that only God could bring about a change. The human race had sunk to such depths of depravity that God had to intervene. Human corruption and violence could not be tolerated indefinitely. This account emphasizes that God is to be taken seriously, not trifled with or ignored.

The Genesis account of the Flood has certain features in common with other flood stories in the ancient Near East, but is radically different. Although archaeologists point out that there was an enormous flood in the Tigris-Euphrates Valley leaving a strata of clay eight feet deep over a 40-mile-wide area stretching for over 400 miles, the Genesis event is not like the Gilgamesh Epic of the Babylonians or the Enuma Elish. In these, various deities act capriciously while humans are portrayed as heroes. Genesis, on the other hand, spotlights the one God, the Creator, not many gods. Also, the Flood is not an arbitrary outburst by peevish deities as in the other flood stories, but God's determined act to effect a new beginning with His creation. Moreover, the hero is not the human Noah (who goes and gets drunk after the flood subsides) but the Lord!

Most important, God insisted on making a fresh start by instituting a covenant between Himself and Noah's family and descendants. This unconditional promise, symbolized by the rainbow, meant that God would stand with His human creation even though humans might fail to keep their word to Him. Humans were not given license to sin with impunity, but were assured that God intended to preserve a people who would stand for Him.

NOTES ON THE PRINTED TEXT

The Lord saw the wickedness of humankind's deeds on the earth. In particular, He observed that their thoughts and desires, plans and intentions were continually bent on doing *evil* (Gen. 6:5). In short, every inclination was given only to evil all the time. The tragedy is that even today, people take their God-given capacities and use them to carry out wicked schemes.

The Lord was grieved and sorrowed by humankind's wicked bent (6:6). God was so angered that He decided to judge the human race. Because the Lord had created humankind, He had the moral right to wipe them from the face of *the earth* (6:7). Everything from people to animals, including creatures that move on the ground and birds that fly in the air, would be affected.

Although God condemned the human race, He was pleased with Noah (6:8). In particular, Noah found grace, or experienced *favor*, with the Lord. His kindness and mercy toward Noah was based on the righteous character of the latter (6:9). God, too, is pleased with us when we follow Him with all our heart.

The Lord decided to bring judgment on the world. He would send a flood to destroy all life, except one godly man (Noah) and his family and the animals they would gather. God gave Noah instructions for building and stocking an ark that could rise up on the floodwaters, and Noah did what the Lord had commanded (6:13-22).

Perhaps after a period of time had elapsed, the Lord commanded Noah and his household to enter *the ark* (7:1). God spared these people because only Noah, among the entire human race, was upright. His godly character serves as a positive example of how all of us should live.

The Lord also wanted Noah to bring into the ark seven pairs of every kind of clean animal, both *the male and its mate* (7:2). God had approved these creatures for eating and for sacrifice. Moreover, Noah was to bring into the ark one pair of every kind of unclean animal, both the male and the female. Furthermore, God directed Noah to bring into the ark seven pairs of every bird in the sky, both *male and female* (7:3).

God's intent in all this was to ensure that every kind of living creature would survive the worldwide flood. This deluge would engulf the world for *forty days and forty nights* (7:4). Except for the people and creatures in the ark, every living thing on the face of the earth would perish. Noah took God seriously, for he did exactly as God *had commanded* (7:5). In this way, Noah proved himself to be a genuine person of faith and obedience.

One week later, just as the Lord had forewarned (7:4), the floodwaters inundated *the earth* (7:10). Both underground waters and rain from the sky engulfed the planet (7:11). For 40 long days the earth was deluged by the *flood* (7:17). The rising water lifted the boat high above the ground.

Because Noah had obeyed the Lord in the building of the ark, this vessel floated safely on *the face of the waters* (7:18). Meanwhile, all living creatures on the earth died—from people to animals to every creeping thing and even the birds in the sky (7:23). The only exception was Noah and those with him in the ark. Only they survived the devastation of the Flood.

After about ten and a half months, the floodwaters began to recede (8:13). Two more months passed before the earth was finally *dry* (8:14). We can only imagine how relieved Noah and his household must have felt at this time. Then God spoke to *Noah* (8:15) and commanded him, his household, and the creatures in the ark to leave the vessel (8:16). Noah, in turn, obeyed the Lord (8:17-18). Like Noah, we also are wise to follow God's leading in our lives.

After Noah left the ark, he built an altar to the Lord and sacrificed ritually clean animals and birds on it (8:20). This pleased God (8:21), and He *blessed Noah and his sons* (9:1). This included God's command for Noah and his children to spread out across *the earth* (9:7). Then God confirmed His statements with an unconditional covenant between Himself and all people and animals (9:9-10).

The rainbow was the sign of God's solemn agreement never again to use water to destroy all life (9:11-13). After the traumatic experience of the Flood, Noah's family needed this reassurance. When God saw the rainbow in the clouds, He would remember the eternal covenant between Himself and every living creature on the earth (9:16).

God saw that the earth needed a new start, and He gave it one. It is true that the Flood was not an easy way to begin again, but God's grace preserved all those who trusted Him. In the same way, by grace through faith in Christ, we can realize new beginnings in all areas of our life.

SUGGESTIONS TO TEACHERS

The account of Noah perhaps brings back memories of childhood Sunday school days, where we marched toy animals two by two into a playtime ark. It also has been the source of cartoons, jokes, and skits. Who can forget Bill Cosby's monologue in which he played the part of Noah? The account of the Flood has led to pointless quibbling on the part of some critics ("How could a craft 450 feet by 75 feet by 45 feet hold such a huge cargo and also supplies of food and water for 40 days?" and "What happened to the fish during the Flood?") The point of this lesson is not to argue about details in the Genesis account. Rather, it must center on God's response to our wicked ways, and the covenant God has made to be faithful to us in spite of our failure to respond to His love.

1. GOD'S REGRETS. The Genesis account reminds us that God is not aloof. Nor is He passive and insensitive. God has feelings. God responds to what we do or don't do. The Flood narrative depicts the Lord as grieving over human depravity. Discuss what the Lord's feelings must be with respect to the way your church members live.

2. NOAH'S RELATIONSHIP. *Noah found favor in the sight of the LORD* (Gen. 6:8) may lead you and the class to consider what may be done to find favor with the Lord in these times. What most pleases God, according to Scripture?

3. HUMANITY'S RUIN. Sin has consequences. God, indeed, does judge His people. God holds every person responsible to live according to the ways He has disclosed. What are some examples in our day where refusal to live responsibly before God has brought misery?

4. HEAVEN'S RAIN. Don't spend lesson time discussing relatively unimportant details, such as the provisions for the animals on the ark, or the recent attempts to locate the remains of the ark in Turkey on Mount Ararat. The main point is that God decided to cleanse the earth for a fresh start with humans.

5. GOD'S REMEMBERING. The Lord does not forget His faithful followers. Just as God was mindful of Noah and his family as they were swept amidst the swirling waters, He remembers us today (see 1 Pet. 3:20-22).

6. COVENANT'S RAINBOW. Remind your class that God entered into a covenant with Noah and his family, which has been renewed through the history of the people of God. The climax is the covenant through the death and resurrection of Jesus Christ. From the earliest, when the rainbow symbolized that first covenant, so the Cross tells of a greater covenant God has made with us.

FOR ADULTS	■ **TOPIC:** Beginning Again

■ **QUESTIONS:** 1. Why did the Lord decide to wipe out the human race? 2. Why did the Lord decide to spare Noah? 3. Why was the family of Noah permitted to enter into the ark with him? 4. Why is God's designation of clean and unclean animals to Noah significant? 5. How did God protect Noah and his family from the floodwaters?

■ **ILLUSTRATIONS:**

The Rainbow Sign. It was many years ago, in January 1882, that George Matheson's beloved hymn "O Love That Wilt Not Let Me Go" first appeared in *Life and Work,* the official paper of the Church of Scotland. You may recall that the third stanza of the hymn pursues the theme of the rainbow. It is interesting that in the original version Matheson wrote: "I climb the rainbow in the rain." Someplace along the line this was improved with the line we know: "I trace the rainbow through the rain." But first of all the blind poet was climbing the rainbow!

This may be shades of Judy Garland—"Somewhere Over the Rainbow"! But Matheson's "pot of gold" at the end of the rainbow was his faith that "the promise is not vain, that morn shall tearless be." This is a far cry from the easy optimism that at the end of the rainbow is some human hope. At the end of Matheson's rainbow was the biblical hope, and this was the "joy that seekest me through pain."

There is more to Noah's rainbow than even that. It is the eternal promise that never again will God destroy the earth and its inhabitants. Under the threat of nuclear war, it seems a fatuous hope, one that we might by our own foolishness deny. But God is still in control, and that's what the rainbow sign means.

Wrong Direction. Starting in 1982, several expeditions have struggled up the steep, icy gorges of Mount Ararat, the great volcanic cone that dominates the frontiers of eastern Turkey, Armenia, and Iran. Scores of groups from the United States, France, Germany, Japan, and Turkey have been granted permits to seek traces of Noah's ark on the glaciers and passes surrounding the 16,946-foot peak. The favorite location for finding the remnants of Noah's ark is a vast chasm known as the Ahora Gorge, which is covered by a glacier and clouds. Reports have been given of a large rectangular form in the ice.

At least one person has admitted to misleading the public by owning up to passing off a fragment of wood which supposedly came from the ark. George Jammal, an Israeli actor, admitted to the press in October 1993 that he had made up the story that he had discovered a piece of wood from the ark. Earlier, CBS had canceled two other programs which were in development to feature "In Search of Noah's Ark," on CBS television, February 20, 1993. Jammal stated that the piece of wood he claimed came from the ark was actually a piece of California pine from some railroad tracks in Long Beach, California. He hardened it by frying it on his kitchen stove, and even made a videotape of himself doing it. Jammal also admitted that he had never been in Turkey.

All the fuss over the wood and the ark are beside the point. God's people need to search for the meaning of the ark, not for remains of wood of a craft built by Noah. So let's focus on God's Word to us through the scriptural account. In there we will find eternal truth for our lives.

Truth from Noah. Truth one from the Noah account: wickedness will eventually—and inevitably—be swept away in judgment. The flood image, the giant flood that wipes out everything sinful and wrong, to me represents God's moral law that is always at work. For a time, evil may grow and spread. But evil can't survive indefinitely on this planet. The whole universe is against it. In fact, at the moment of evil's greatest power and expansion—even then—the forces of good are welling up to sweep it out of the world, just as Noah's world was swept clean by the waters of the flood.

The Lord has designed the universe in such a way that evil cannot survive long within it. Consider Adolph Hitler. At the peak of his power in 1943, Hitler was master of nearly all of Europe except the British Isles. His armies had conquered nearly half of the Soviet Union. Hitler promised the German people a Thousand Year Reich. But just two years later, in utter defeat, Hitler committed suicide in his Berlin bunker to avoid being captured by the Russians. The evil of the Nazi empire was widespread and vicious. For a time it seemed nearly invincible. But the forces of good welled up and swept it away. The Noah account reminds us that, in the universe God has created, evil is always temporary. Evil cannot last.

■ **TOPIC:** Starting Over

■ **QUESTIONS:** 1. What did God observe about the people who were alive at the time of Noah? 2. Why did Noah experience God's favor? 3. What was God's intent in having a variety of creatures enter into the ark? 4. How did Noah prove himself to be a genuine person of faith and obedience? 5. What was included in the blessing of God to Noah and his sons?

■ **ILLUSTRATIONS:**

Is Proof Necessary? Mount Ararat is a 16,946-foot heap of volcanic rubble in eastern Turkey. Since 1961, there have been 37 expeditions seeking to locate Noah's ark. Searchers risked death from the difficult weather or arrest from Turkish officials since the mountain lies in a security zone along the border of the former Soviet Union. Why do people search? One searcher, Henry Morris, wants to prove the event of the Flood. He hopes to catalyze a spiritual renaissance. As a doubting Thomas needed the proof of the Resurrection, so too the discovery of the ark would prove the veracity of the first 11 chapters of Genesis, Morris claimed.

Flood of Data. As the *Sojourner* left the *Mars Pathfinder* probe on the surface of Mars in July 1997, it began to send color photographs and other data concerning the red planet. The shapes and colors of rocks on the bone-dry planet, the surface textures, crystal splotches of ancient puddles with salty residues, and the undulating low ridges and valleys all led scientists to infer that the Plain of Ares Vallis, where the spacecraft had landed, had been scoured by water. The tilt of rocks and the tail of debris behind the pebbles all suggested that a flood came from the southwest. Michael Malin, a geologist and head of Malin Space Science Systems of La Jolla, California, estimated that a huge deluge that only Noah could appreciate, some hundreds of miles wide, hundreds of feet deep, flowing for thousands of miles, flooded the planet about one to three billion years ago.

While the Mars landing yielded a mountain of data on the ancient deluge, the real point of the Flood in Genesis is God's saving love. The Lord cared enough for His creation to preserve humanity.

Missed Point. John Baumgardner was a lab scientist profiled in *U.S. News & World Report.* He developed a computer program called "Terra." Now used worldwide in geophysics, Baumgardner, a devout Christian, developed "Terra" to prove the Flood really could have happened. Baumgardner has shown that the Genesis account of the Flood was a historic event. But the rebirth of the world through God's saving care and love is what is most important in the account.

GOD RAISES UP A DELIVERER

BACKGROUND SCRIPTURE: Exodus 3—4
DEVOTIONAL READING: Exodus 3:13-17

KEY VERSE: "I will send you to Pharaoh to bring
my people, the Israelites, out of Egypt." Exodus 3:10.

KING JAMES VERSION

EXODUS 3:1 Now Moses kept the flock of Jethro his father in law, the priest of Midian: and he led the flock to the backside of the desert, and came to the mountain of God, even to Horeb. 2 And the angel of the LORD appeared unto him in a flame of fire out of the midst of a bush: and he looked, and, behold, the bush burned with fire, and the bush was not consumed. 3 And Moses said, I will now turn aside, and see this great sight, why the bush is not burnt. 4 And when the LORD saw that he turned aside to see, God called unto him out of the midst of the bush, and said, Moses, Moses. And he said, Here am I. 5 And he said, Draw not nigh hither: put off thy shoes from off thy feet, for the place whereon thou standest is holy ground. 6 Moreover he said, I am the God of thy father, the God of Abraham, the God of Isaac, and the God of Jacob. And Moses hid his face; for he was afraid to look upon God.

7 And the LORD said, I have surely seen the affliction of my people which are in Egypt, and have heard their cry by reason of their taskmasters; for I know their sorrows; 8 And I am come down to deliver them out of the hand of the Egyptians, and to bring them up out of that land unto a good land and a large, unto a land flowing with milk and honey; unto the place of the Canaanites, and the Hittites, and the Amorites, and the Perizzites, and the Hivites, and the Jebusites. 9 Now therefore, behold, the cry of the children of Israel is come unto me: and I have also seen the oppression wherewith the Egyptians oppress them. 10 Come now therefore, and I will send thee unto Pharaoh, that thou mayest bring forth my people the children of Israel out of Egypt.

11 And Moses said unto God, Who am I, that I should go unto Pharaoh, and that I should bring forth the children of Israel out of Egypt? 12 And he said, Certainly I will be with thee; and this shall be a token unto thee, that I have sent thee: When thou hast brought forth the people out of Egypt, ye shall serve God upon this mountain.

NEW REVISED STANDARD VERSION

EXODUS 3:1 Moses was keeping the flock of his father-in-law Jethro, the priest of Midian; he led his flock beyond the wilderness, and came to Horeb, the mountain of God. 2 There the angel of the LORD appeared to him in a flame of fire out of a bush; he looked, and the bush was blazing, yet it was not consumed. 3 Then Moses said, "I must turn aside and look at this great sight, and see why the bush is not burned up." 4 When the LORD saw that he had turned aside to see, God called to him out of the bush, "Moses, Moses!" And he said, "Here I am." 5 Then he said, "Come no closer! Remove the sandals from your feet, for the place on which you are standing is holy ground." 6 He said further, "I am the God of your father, the God of Abraham, the God of Isaac, and the God of Jacob." And Moses hid his face, for he was afraid to look at God.

7 Then the LORD said, "I have observed the misery of my people who are in Egypt; I have heard their cry on account of their taskmasters. Indeed, I know their sufferings, 8 and I have come down to deliver them from the Egyptians, and to bring them up out of that land to a good and broad land, a land flowing with milk and honey, to the country of the Canaanites, the Hittites, the Amorites, the Perizzites, the Hivites, and the Jebusites. 9 The cry of the Israelites has now come to me; I have also seen how the Egyptians oppress them. 10 So come, I will send you to Pharaoh to bring my people, the Israelites, out of Egypt." 11 But Moses said to God, "Who am I that I should go to Pharaoh, and bring the Israelites out of Egypt?" 12 He said, "I will be with you; and this shall be the sign for you that it is I who sent you: when you have brought the people out of Egypt, you shall worship God on this mountain."

Monday, September 13	Exodus 3:1-6	*God Speaks to Moses*
Tuesday, September 14	Exodus 3:7-12	*God Calls Moses to Lead*
Wednesday, September 15.	Exodus 3:13-22	*God Gives Moses Instructions*
Thursday, September 16	Exodus 4:1-9	*God Gives Moses Special Powers*
Friday, September 17	Exodus 4:10-17	*Moses Still Feels Inadequate*
Saturday, September 18	Exodus 4:18-23	*Moses Returns to Egypt*
Sunday, September 19	Exodus 4:24-31	*The Israelites Believe Moses*

BACKGROUND

This week we fast-forward the narrative of God's people to the time of Moses. Let's back up a bit and note that Jacob and his family settled in Egypt around 1876 B.C. At this time, his son Joseph was the prime minister of Egypt, being the second-in-command next to Pharaoh (Gen. 41:41-43). Jacob died in 1859 B.C., and Joseph died in 1805 B.C. For the next four centuries, the Israelites lived in Egypt (Exod. 12:40). But by the time Moses was born in 1526 B.C., a new king had come to the throne, and he knew nothing about Joseph or what he had done (1:8). This ruler was possibly Ahmose, who founded the 18th dynasty and expelled a group of foreigners named the Hyksos from the land.

The next pharaoh, Thutmose III, told his people that the large number of Israelites living in Egypt were becoming a threat to the nation. He therefore ordered that they be enslaved and placed into labor gangs under harsh Egyptian taskmasters (1:9-11). Moses, who by now had become a prominent member of Pharaoh's court (Acts 7:22), reacted angrily at the cruelty of an Egyptian brutally beating an Israelite laborer, and he thus murdered the Egyptian. Moses then fled for his life and sought asylum among the Midianite people (Exod. 2:11-15).

Moses married Zipporah (the daughter of a Midianite priest named Reuel), started a family, and spent the next 40 years as a sheepherder (2:16-22). During this time, Thutmose III died and was succeeded by his son, Amunhotep II. Meanwhile, the Israelites groaned beneath their burden of slavery, and God responded to their cries for help (2:23-25). He did so by revealing Himself to Moses and commanding him to return to Egypt to lead the Israelites to freedom (3:1-12).

NOTES ON THE PRINTED TEXT

After meeting Jethro in the land of Midian and marrying one of his daughters, Moses had tended sheep for his father-in-law for a number of years (Exod. 3:1). The last thing Moses ever planned on doing was to return to Egypt. But God had other plans for the shepherd.

One day, as the octogenarian wandered alone in the desert near Mount Horeb, he might have thought that God had forgotten about him and the Hebrews reeling in their bondage in Egypt. The Lord, however, had heard His people's cries and came to get Moses involved in His plan to deliver them. Leading sheep through the wilderness had been good training for the man God was about to call to shepherd His people. Even today God prepares His people for the ministries to which He calls them.

The heavenly being who appeared to Moses was no ordinary angel. *The angel of the LORD* (3:2) was probably God Himself. Moses was amazed by the sight of flames engulfing but not consuming a bush. We are left with the impression that Moses was drawn by curiosity. That is why he turned away from his flock to investigate the scene before him (3:3).

Once Moses came close to scrutinize the miraculous fire, God called out to him. Moses, perhaps sensing the divine nature of the fire and call, responded *"Here am I"* (3:4). This reply shows trust and availability. The Lord directed Moses to take off his sandals, an act that showed respect and submission (3:5). In Bible times, people removed their footwear before entering a house because they did not want to dirty the home of the respected host. Similarly, Moses was entering the presence of the Lord. The ground He chose to inhabit was holy because He was there at that time.

Just as dirt shows up best on white clothing, so our spiritual and moral uncleanness shows up best when measured against the purity of God's holiness. If we measure our uprightness by the standards of the world, we may come out looking fairly clean; but measured against the absolute holiness of God, our sinfulness comes into sharp focus—thus pointing to our need for a Savior.

Besides revealing His holiness to Moses, God also revealed His faithfulness. The mention in 3:6 of *Abraham*, *Isaac*, and *Jacob* brought to mind the covenant God had made with these men. God still honored that covenant and would rescue His people because of it.

At this point Moses realized that he was talking with God Himself and hid his face out of shame and fear; but just as the bush was not destroyed, neither was Moses consumed by the Lord's presence. Here we see that, besides being holy, God is also merciful and full of grace toward us.

God may not have responded as quickly to the Hebrews' cries as they would have liked, but He was concerned with and involved in their struggles (3:7). Because of what He saw in Egypt, the Lord came down to Mount Horeb to reveal Himself to Moses and to rescue His people. God spoke with compassion for His people, carefully noting their mistreatment and cries for help.

God's plan was to lead the people out of their suffering and slavery to a land that was both good (in terms of quality) and large (in terms of size; 3:8). The description of Canaan as *flowing with milk and honey* underscored the abundance and prosperity of the region, which was then occupied by a variety of peoples.

Here the Israelites would enjoy freedom and the Lord's gracious provision; and God, not Moses, would deliver them from their harsh slave drivers (3:9). God's plan of action, though, included Moses (3:10). He would go to Egypt, confront *Pharaoh*, and lead the Hebrews out of that land of bondage.

When Moses was younger, he was confident and impulsive; but now that he was older, the greatness of the task before him made him unsure. The aged shepherd, now feeling overwhelmed and insufficient, in honest humility questioned God's choice (3:11).

The Lord did not enter into a debate with Moses; instead, God pledged that He would be with the octogenarian (3:12). Moses did not have to fear because it was ultimately the Lord who was rescuing His people. As a sign of His pledge to Moses, God promised that when Moses and the Israelites left Egypt, they would worship and serve Him together at that very *mountain*.

We should not be surprised to find God working through human instruments. For example, the Lord sometimes works through physicians when someone is praying for the healing of an illness. God sometimes works through a preacher when someone is praying for a better understanding of the Word. God sometimes works through a comforting friend when someone is praying for relief from depression.

The idea is that the Lord often works through people just like us. He is not bound by the restrictions of time and happenstance; instead, He sees the broader contours and works in our lives to bring about His will. When we keep looking to Him in faith, we will experience a peace and happiness that surpass all understanding (Phil. 4:6-7).

SUGGESTIONS TO TEACHERS

Anyone becoming a naturalized citizen of the United States is required to learn the basic history of the nation. Citizenship means knowing and appreciating the events that brought the U.S. into existence. The same is true with our faith. To be members of God's family, we must understand the account of His dealings with His people. For example, Israel's departure from Egypt was a pivotal event. Although we will be discussing Moses as the key human leader in this great drama, we should remember that God was the central character.

1. INEXPLICABLE REVELATION. Moses' encounter with the Lord through the burning bush cannot be explained away by stating that it was a species of brilliant thornbush found in Sinai or the reflection of the sunlight on the bush. No, Moses had met the living God, and His holy presence defied explanation. Ask your students to share why they think God's presence in their lives sometimes is beyond explanation.

2. UNEXPECTED ROLE. God said that He was sending Moses to Pharaoh to lead the Israelites out of Egypt. This suggests that God's encounters with us usually include a call to serve. The tasks that He gives us to do sometimes are not what we might expect or desire. Discuss with the class members some of the unexpected jobs God has had them do in the past.

3. UNDERSTANDABLE RELUCTANCE. Moses had no wish to go back to Egypt, where he was a wanted fugitive for murdering an Egyptian official. At times, we might drag our feet or plead that we are unable to carry out what the Lord wants us to do. But God sweeps aside our excuses!

4. UNMISTAKABLE REALIZATION. When Moses balked at appearing before Pharaoh, the Lord reassured him that he would not be alone. Regardless of how difficult or unpleasant the situation might get, God would give him success. Let the students know that God continues to help believers to do His will. With His strength and companionship, they can serve Him with confidence!

FOR ADULTS

■ **TOPIC:** Power for Deliverance

■ **QUESTIONS:** 1. How did God make His presence known to Moses, and what was unusual about it? 2. In what way did Moses' initial response show that he wanted to hear and heed the Lord? 3. Why do you think Moses felt inadequate when God directed him to appear before Pharaoh and liberate the Israelites? 4. What are some things God has called you to do, and how have you typically responded? 5. How can the promise of God encourage you to do tasks for Him that seem too difficult to handle?

■ **ILLUSTRATIONS:**

Unexpected Call. A number years ago in Atlanta, a young businessman named Jack Stephens got a call from a friend heading a local boys' club. The man asked Jack to drive a youngster and his mother to the hospital. Jack agreed, and met the mother and her boy at their house, which was not far from his home. (Jack learned that the boy had leukemia and that the disease was in its final stages.) Early the next day as the three rode to the hospital, the boy was stretched out on his mother's lap, and his feet extended over to Jack. Jack glanced down at the child, and their eyes met.

"Are you God?" the boy asked. Though startled by the question, Jack answered, "No, son. Why do you ask?" The boy responded, "My mother said that God would come and take me away with Him." Jack was shaken by the reply. Even more distressing was the fact that a week later, the boy went home to be with the Lord.

Despite the sadness of the boy's death, Jack Stephens found himself drawn to God in a way that he had not expected. The question, "Are you God?" was like a voice from the "burning bush" in Jack's life. He realized that he had to do more for the Lord with his life. Eventually, Jack became the Director of the Joseph B. Whitehead Memorial Boys' Club in Atlanta, Georgia.

Perhaps the voice of God is calling from the "burning bush" in your life. The Lord might be summoning you to do more than just enjoy a life of ease with other believers in your church. God might be calling you to be His representative to those in this world who are suffering and spiritually lost. Perhaps the Lord wants you to be His agent among the helpless and forgotten, whom He remembers.

Do you feel overwhelmed by such a prospect? You don't need to be, for God will remain with you every step of the way.

God's Name. In Exodus 3:14, God revealed Himself as *"I AM WHO I AM."* This could also be rendered, "I AM WHAT I AM" or "I WILL BE WHAT I WILL BE." Scholars struggle over the precise meaning of the Hebrew phrase. Some say this name for God points to His self-existence and eternality.

Albert Van Den Heuvel offers another interpretation. He says that the original should be translated, "I WILL BE WHO I WAS" and that God intended this phrase to instill hope in His people down through the ages. For example, the Lord was saying to Moses, "I will be to you who I was to Abraham." Jesus was saying to Peter, "I will be to you who I was to Abraham and Moses." And today this same Lord is declaring to us, "I will be to you who I was to Peter and those Galilean fisherman, and to Moses and to Abraham and to the prophets, as well as to Paul and Silas, to Matthew and Mark and Luke and John, to Luther, to Calvin, to Wesley, and to all the host of the family of faith."

Burning but Not Consumed. Many of our Protestant forebears in Europe identified closely with God's call to Moses to serve Him obediently. In fact, many in the Reformed tradition—such as the Scots, the Irish, the Huguenots, and the Magyars—depict a burning bush on their church's official seal or insignia. It often has the Latin inscription, *Nec Tamen Consumebatur.* This means, in effect, "burning but not consumed." The phrase refers to the Lord's mysterious call to His people and His holy, indescribable presence among them. God's fire was understood to burn on without end, and continued to confront them. As Hebrews 12:29 says, *our God is a consuming fire.*

FOR YOUTH ■ **TOPIC:** Help Is on the Way
■ **QUESTIONS:** 1. In what ways do you think Moses' experience as a shepherd in the wilderness humbled him? 2. How would you have responded if God revealed Himself to you in a burning bush? 3. What difficult tasks has God called you to do, and how have you responded? 4. What do you think it means to serve God obediently? 5. What are some ways that God cares for believers today?

■ **ILLUSTRATIONS:**

Sense of Call. When Laura Hannant was four years old, she went to Nepal and met Mother Teresa. Now 12, Laura stood before an assembly of juniors and seniors at Pittsburgh's Baldwin High School and spoke about the evils of child labor.

Laura said that she was the daughter of a Canadian television newsman. She noted seeing firsthand in India children living in virtual slavery. Laura related that at four, she accidentally wandered into a sweatshop in India. She recalled her and her father watching the children run and hide as the owner screamed at them. Laura told the audience that she later heard about a child who had tried to escape the 14-hour work days and the regular beatings, only to be caught and killed in front of the other children as a warning. Laura said that some of the children she saw in India had the skin on their fingers split open from working on carpet looms while chained by their ankles to the machinery.

Laura explained that her experiences in India prompted her to become active in "Free the Children," which is an organization that campaigns against the exploitation of child labor. (The poised and confident speaker does not consider herself too young to support the eradication of child labor around the globe.) When someone in the audience asked why she felt called to do this job, she said, "Standing up for people's rights was something that my parents once did, and now it's something that students must do."

Laura felt called to speak for the children of the world as much as Moses felt called by the Lord to speak for Him and the Israelites. At some point, you too will sense God's call and claim on your life to serve Him.

Sacred Ground? Tourists pass at a rate of 1200 people per hour. Often they leave flowers or teddy bears and—much to the chagrin of the caretakers—even peel the bark off of nearby trees where they write messages in red ink. The spot is the bronze plaque marking Elvis Presley's grave at Graceland. Karen Christ of Canton, Ohio, called the ground "sacred." Fay Mathany of Richmond, Virginia, feels close to Elvis at this spot.

When Moses stood before the burning bush, he was filled with awe, but not because he was near the spot where a dead person had been buried. Rather, he knew that he was in the presence of the holy and living God. The ground was sacred because God had made His presence known there. At different times in your life you will sense God's holy presence. In those moments, you should show Him respect, sincerity, and reverence.

Special Spot. The Air Force wanted to build a 50-foot dark aluminum star to honor the war dead from the youngest service branch of the United States. The dedication was supposed to take place on September 18, 1997, which was just in time for a fiftieth anniversary celebration.

Oddly enough, the largest foe of the memorial was the Marine Corps. Why? Because the spot the Air Force had chosen was just downhill from the 78-foot high Marine Corps Memorial, which features the images of the five marines and one sailor raising the American flag on Mount Suribachi, Iwo Jima, during World War II. The Marines countered that a second memorial was too much for the two-acre park. Former Marine and New York Representative Gerald Solomon spoke for many when he declared that the area was sacred ground.

In contrast, note the attitude of Moses concerning the spot where *the angel of the Lord appeared to him in a flame of fire out of a bush* (Exod. 3:2). Moses never set aside this area as special, and he never built any shrine to mark the spot. Why? Because he knew that the ground was sacred, or special, due to God's presence there. Holy ground may be found in a church building, at a church camp, in a funeral home, or in many other places. It will be special to you because you sense God's presence there and His call on your life to serve Him.

BECOMING GOD'S PEOPLE

BACKGROUND SCRIPTURE: Deuteronomy 29:1-29
DEVOTIONAL READING: Deuteronomy 30:15-20

KEY VERSES: Enter into the covenant of the LORD your God, . . . in order that he may establish you today as his people. Deuteronomy 29:12–13.

KING JAMES VERSION

DEUTERONOMY 29:2 And Moses called unto all Israel, and said unto them, Ye have seen all that the LORD did before your eyes in the land of Egypt unto Pharaoh, and unto all his servants, and unto all his land; 3 The great temptations which thine eyes have seen, the signs, and those great miracles: 4 Yet the LORD hath not given you an heart to perceive, and eyes to see, and ears to hear, unto this day. 5And I have led you forty years in the wilderness: your clothes are not waxen old upon you, and thy shoe is not waxen old upon thy foot. 6 Ye have not eaten bread, neither have ye drunk wine or strong drink: that ye might know that I am the LORD your God. 7 And when ye came unto this place, Sihon the king of Heshbon, and Og the king of Bashan, came out against us unto battle, and we smote them: 8 And we took their land, and gave it for an inheritance unto the Reubenites, and to the Gadites, and to the half tribe of Manasseh. 9 Keep therefore the words of this covenant, and do them, that ye may prosper in all that ye do.

10 Ye stand this day all of you before the LORD your God; your captains of your tribes, your elders, and your officers, with all the men of Israel, 11 Your little ones, your wives, and thy stranger that is in thy camp, from the hewer of thy wood unto the drawer of thy water: 12 That thou shouldest enter into covenant with the LORD thy God, and into his oath, which the LORD thy God maketh with thee this day: 13 That he may establish thee to day for a people unto himself, and that he may be unto thee a God, as he hath said unto thee, and as he hath sworn unto thy fathers, to Abraham, to Isaac, and to Jacob. 14 Neither with you only do I make this covenant and this oath; 15 But with him that standeth here with us this day before the LORD our God, and also with him that is not here with us this day.

NEW REVISED STANDARD VERSION

DEUTERONOMY 29:2 Moses summoned all Israel and said to them: You have seen all that the LORD did before your eyes in the land of Egypt, to Pharaoh and to all his servants and to all his land, 3 the great trials that your eyes saw, the signs, and those great wonders. 4 But to this day the LORD has not given you a mind to understand, or eyes to see, or ears to hear. 5 I have led you forty years in the wilderness. The clothes on your back have not worn out, and the sandals on your feet have not worn out; 6 you have not eaten bread, and you have not drunk wine or strong drink—so that you may know that I am the LORD your God. 7 When you came to this place, King Sihon of Heshbon and King Og of Bashan came out against us for battle, but we defeated them. 8 We took their land and gave it as an inheritance to the Reubenites, the Gadites, and the half-tribe of Manasseh. 9 Therefore diligently observe the words of this covenant, in order that you may succeed in everything that you do.

10 You stand assembled today, all of you, before the LORD your God—the leaders of your tribes, your elders, and your officials, all the men of Israel, 11 your children, your women, and the aliens who are in your camp, both those who cut your wood and those who draw your water— 12 to enter into the covenant of the LORD your God, sworn by an oath, which the LORD your God is making with you today; 13 in order that he may establish you today as his people, and that he may be your God, as he promised you and as he swore to your ancestors, to Abraham, to Isaac, and to Jacob. 14 I am making this covenant, sworn by an oath, not only with you who stand here with us today before the LORD our God, 15 but also with those who are not here with us today.

BACKGROUND

Leviticus, Numbers, and Deuteronomy are the third, fourth, and fifth books of the Pentateuch—also known as the book of the law, or the Torah. Together, they describe events occurring from the time the Israelites continued their encampment at the foot of Mount Sinai to the death of Moses. The laws, purposes, and character of God are intriguingly portrayed in the these three books. Through a study of them, we can learn how God blessed and admonished those whom He had chosen to be His representatives to the rest of the world. In fact, these books have much to teach us as we strive to be God's people in the world today.

These three books show that for the Lord it was not enough to deliver the Israelites out of the cruel hands of the Egyptians; He also wanted them to thrive as His chosen people. Of course, their new freedom did not mean that they could do whatever they wanted. Rather, God's will for them was to follow His sacred laws, to serve His divine purposes, and to be a reflection of His character to the people around them.

God pledged to protect the Israelites as long as they remained faithful to Him. Recorded in Leviticus, Numbers, and Deuteronomy are details of how the Israelites were to be the Lord's consecrated people. By obeying the laws and regulations that God wanted them to observe, the Israelites would be prepared to flourish in the promised land.

With respect to the fifth book of the Torah, the word *Deuteronomy* means "repetition of the law," and this book is called such because it recites the law of Moses a second time. Covering the period from about a month before to a month after Moses' death, the Book of Deuteronomy contains Moses' reminders to the Israelites about their covenant with the Lord. It also records Moses' transferring his leadership responsibilities to Joshua.

In this book the Israelite leader recorded a series of sermons to the Israelites about how they were to conduct themselves when they entered the promised land. Hoping to make them ready for the challenge of the future, Moses urged them to recall the laws and experiences of their past. He emphasized those laws that were especially needed for the people to make a successful entrance into Canaan. Tradition has always accepted another writer (presumably Joshua) as the author of Deuteronomy 34, which describes Moses' death.

NOTES ON THE PRINTED TEXT

The laws, purposes, and character of God are intriguingly portrayed in the Books of Leviticus, Numbers, and Deuteronomy. Through a study of these books, we can learn how God blessed and admonished those whom He had selected to be His representatives to the rest of the world. In fact, these books have much to teach us as we strive to be God's people in the world today.

The *covenant* (Deut. 29:1) was the basis for the intimate relationship between God and His chosen people. In it, the Lord pledged to protect the Israelites as long as they remained faithful to Him. Recorded in Deuteronomy are details of how the Israelites were to be the Lord's consecrated people. By obeying the laws and regulations that God wanted them to observe, the Israelites would be prepared to flourish in Canaan.

At *Horeb,* or Mount Sinai, the Lord had entered into a covenant with the generation of Israelites whom He had freed from Egypt; but because that generation had disbelieved and disobeyed the Lord, they wandered in the desert for 40 years and eventually died (see Heb. 3:16-19).

Moses now summoned a new generation of Israelites in the land on the east side of the Jordan River. He reminded them of all the Lord had done for them in freeing them from slavery. God had triumphed over Pharaoh, all his servants, and the entire *land of Egypt* (Deut. 29:2). On the Israelites' behalf, the Lord performed great signs and miracles (29:3). God continued to manifest His greatness in the Israelites' wilderness wanderings and in the land of Moab.

In order for the people to grasp and appreciate what they had seen and heard, they needed a transformed heart that was dependent on God (29:4). When the Israelites responded in faith and obedience, this corporate awareness would be fully realized. Even today God wants us to trust in Him fully and follow His will wholeheartedly.

Moses reminded the Israelites that God had led and cared for them during their *forty years in the wilderness* (29:5). During that time, neither their shirts nor their *sandals* wore out. While they might not have enjoyed some of the so-called finer things of life, the Israelites never went without food, for the Lord graciously provided it to them (29:6). We, too, must recognize that God is the ultimate source of our food, clothing, and shelter.

God moreover protected His people during their sojourn in the wilderness. As they journeyed through the land on the east side of the Jordan, King Sihon of Heshbon and King Og of Bashan attacked them; and the Israelites were able to defeat their foes because the Lord intervened (29:7). He also enabled His people to distribute the conquered land as an inheritance to the tribes of Reuben and Gad and to *the half-tribe of Manasseh* (29:8).

In accordance with the terms of the covenant, the Lord had remained faithful to His people. Now Moses called on them to pledge their faithfulness to God. If they willingly and consistently kept the terms of the covenant, they would prosper in all they did (29:9). God is also pleased when we heed His Word.

Moses was officiating a solemn occasion in which the tribal leaders and officials as well as parents and children were gathered (29:10); also included were foreigners living in their encampment who chopped their wood and hauled their *water* (29:11).

The intent was for the current generation of people to enter into the same covenant as the previous generation. The Lord was pledging to be the covenant God of Israel, and He confirmed it with *an oath* (29:12). Likewise, the covenant meant that the Israelites belonged to the Lord (29:13). This is the same God who had affirmed His commitment to *Abraham*, *Isaac*, and *Jacob* centuries earlier. He is also the One whom we worship and serve through faith in Christ.

Moses noted that the current generation of Israelites was not the only group with whom the Lord was entering into a covenantal relationship (29:14). The privileges and obligations associated with the covenant applied to all future generations of Israelites (29:15).

Although God has lavished on us every spiritual blessing in Christ (Eph. 1:3), His foremost intent is for us to remain faithful to Him. As long as we are humble in spirit and thankful in heart, we will continue to enjoy His unfailing love. We also have the responsibility to tell others how they too can become partakers of His grace.

SUGGESTIONS TO TEACHERS

At the beginning of the American Revolution, George Washington's Continental Army was a motley collection of untrained, inexperienced, and poorly armed farmers and laborers. After being driven from New York in a series of disastrous defeats, Washington's rag-tag force retreated to the winter snows at Valley Forge, Pennsylvania. Gradually, through the patience and genius of Washington's leadership, what had been not much more than an armed rabble became welded into a lean and effective fighting force.

1. DISOBEDIENT AND DEFEATED. The Israelites also had to endure the pain of being forged into a cohesive and obedient strike force. Without consulting God, some impetuously took matters into their own hands and tried to mount an assault on the Canaanites. Their ill-planned act of disobedience brought total defeat. The Israelites had to submit to God's chastening. They needed to learn to be dutiful before the Lord. Let the class members know that God's people are called to serve in His spiritual army. Our term of enlistment is for life. As Christians, we should be prepared to go through God's "basic training" and constantly keep ourselves ready as the Lord's frontline defense against the forces of evil.

2. DIRECTED AND DUTIFUL. In accordance with God's leading, a new generation of Israelites emerged to penetrate and conquer the promised land. As Christians, we are called to *overcome evil with good* (Rom. 12:21).

3. DISCIPLINED AND DETERMINED. Gradually the Israelites were welded by God into a dedicated and disciplined fighting force. And eventually, the critics and complainers died off. The new generation of God's chosen people were hardy and ready to heed His commands. Take this opportunity to discuss with the students how their congregation can become a trained and dedicated group of believers who are ready to fight against the forces of darkness.

4. DECLARATIONS OF ASSURANCE. Moses told the Israelites that God's work would not end just because there would be a change in leadership from Moses to Joshua. Moses assured them that Joshua would continue what God had called His people to do. In the face of unsettling conditions, Moses brought hope and confidence.

<table>
<tr><td>

FOR ADULTS

</td><td>

■ TOPIC: Becoming God's People

■ QUESTIONS: 1. How had God displayed His unwavering commitment to His people? 2. What would enable the Israelites to

</td></tr>
</table>

grasp and appreciate what they had seen and heard? 3. What was God's intent in providing for His people's needs? 4. What did Moses' recounting of the Israelites' historical experiences underscore? 5. In what sense was the covenant more than a matter of heeding certain regulations?

■ ILLUSTRATIONS:

Life-Saving or Museum Tending? Many years ago an acquaintance named Bert, who was studying in Scotland, went to an interesting area with an old building that had flowers growing around it. It was obviously a lifesaving station. Being interested in the sea and boats, Bert asked if he could see the building. The curator rather reluctantly took Bert up to it. The scene was rather austere and the atmosphere very businesslike.

There were rails running down from the building to the water. The windows had curtains hanging in them. There were people bustling around the inside, polishing the brass. The lifesaving boat itself, a big vessel mounted on a dolly, was painted beautifully. It was all most interesting and quaint.

Inside there was an odor of gasoline from a pair of powerful outboard motors, and the smell of oilskins. Bert happened to notice, though, that the huge doors that opened into the railway on which the lifeboat would be launched into the sea had big bars across that were bolted shut. The door's bars were painted over and obviously the doors had not been opened for many years.

This puzzled Bert. Finally he asked one of the people puttering around to explain how they got the lifeboat out. "Oh," the person quipped, "we don't do that sort of thing here anymore!" Bert was startled by the man's reply. It turned out this lifeboat station was actually a sort of hobby for a few enthusiasts who liked to play and pretend at lifeboat maintenance. In a way, the building was a type of museum.

Consider this. We who believe in Christ belong to His spiritual body and are commanded to reach the lost with His lifesaving message. Are the churches we occupy simply being prettied up for our own comfort? Do we regard ourselves as hobbyists or enthusiasts, puttering around with religious affairs?

Proud Tradition to Maintain. A British friend of mine who served in the famous regiment, The King's Own Scottish Borderers, often pointed out the sense of continuity he and others felt through enlistment in this renowned military outfit. He proudly recounted that since 1689, this regiment has existed and won countless honors, including coveted permission to parade through Edinburgh with fixed bayonets. He told about the bond he has with members who passed away generations before, and the deep sense of obligation to pass on the heritage to future Scots. One day, after a worship service, he solemnly commented that this is the way Christians should feel about maintaining community in the church.

Critical of God. Like the Israelites, we sometimes become impatient and critical of God. Our inclination to think that we know better is reminiscent of the story about a farmer named Nasr-ed-Din Hodja, who lived in the Near East. One day Hodja sat irritably in the sun under a walnut tree while looking at his pumpkin vines. Perhaps the heat had disrupted his thinking when he said to himself, "How foolish God is! He has made such silly mistakes. Here He puts a great big heavy pumpkin on a tiny vine without strength enough to do anything but lie on the ground. And He puts tiny walnuts on a big tree whose branches could hold the weight of a man. If I were God, I could do better than that!"

Just then, a breeze dislocated a walnut in the tree, and it fell on the head of skeptical Nasr-ed-Din Hodja, who rubbed his head, now a sadder and a wiser man. "Suppose," he mused, "there had been a pumpkin up there, instead of a walnut. Never again will I try to plan the world for God. From here on, I will thank God that He has done so well!"

FOR YOUTH

■ TOPIC: We Belong

■ QUESTIONS: 1. What did God pledge in His covenant with the people of Israel? 2. Why did an entire generation of Israelites wander in the desert for 40 years and eventually die there? 3. Why did a new generation of Israelites need a transformed heart that was dependent on God? 4. In what ways had God protected His people during their sojourn in the wilderness? 5. Who was present at the solemn occasion that Moses was officiating?

■ ILLUSTRATIONS:

We Belong. We are members of God's covenant community through faith in Christ. It's a bit like being a member of a great relay team. One believer runs a lap and then passes on the baton to another. The runner receiving the baton is called upon to exert every effort to carry it forward for the sake of the team, and then relinquish it to another teammate. Each believer knows that it is the victory of the team that is paramount, not one's own personal glory. In God's work, each of us is responsible for our lap in God's race.

God's Word reminds us that the Lord's redemptive plans will be accomplished. Moses was granted a look at the promised land from the top of Mount Nebo and assured that the Israelites would be settled there under Joshua. The new leader would guide the people and urge them to remain faithful to the Mosaic covenant.

Scripture reassures us that God's plan of redemption will be fulfilled. We may not live to see all the Lord's plans carried out, just as we will not live to see all our own hopes and dreams fulfilled. The most important matter is that our desires coincide with God's will for us. Our foremost goal should be to glorify the Lord through our thoughts, words, and actions. If we can say that we did this in life, then we know that we have done things of eternal significance.

Promoter. Ninth-grader Zachary Quinto was a member of the Youth Advisory Council of the Youth Volunteer Corps, a series of Boys and Girls Clubs in Western Pennsylvania. Concerned with youth at risk, Zachary planned and coordinated an event that paired 50 second, third, and fourth grade inner-city children each with a high school volunteer. Zachary's hope was to prevent the high rate of school failure by building the children's self-esteem with positive activities and good role models. The adolescent continued to watch and monitor the growth and development of the project.

Zachary offered one positive alternative to those tempted to make an unwise choice of friends or role models. Long before Zachary, God used Moses to challenge Israel to make a positive choice. Moses summoned the nation, as God's people, to live in obedience to the Lord. How wise are your choices?

No Direction. On Tuesday, December 23, 1997, actor-comedian Chris Farley died. The gifted comic had a successful five-year career with *Saturday Night Live* before moving to movies and completing such films as *Tommy Boy, Black Sheep,* and *Beverly Hills Ninja.*

Despite wealth and popularity, Farley seemed to lack direction. He regularly attended church and had practically every creature comfort anyone could want. But he seemed to have a void in life that he yearned to fill. In his attempt to do so, he succumbed to drugs, alcohol, gluttony, and anxiety. Farley aimlessly wandered through the vast desert of his life searching for contentment and meaning.

It's tragic that Farley failed to trust God for leadership, wisdom, and joy. His life reminds us that apart from God there can be no true meaning or satisfaction. It is only when we trust in Christ and thereby become part of the community of faith that life will have real direction and purpose for us.

Long-Term Consequence. The police stopped young Craig's car. It was initially a routine Friday night traffic stop. However, the law enforcement officers discovered that Craig had been drinking. They thus charged him with driving under the influence of alcohol and underage drinking. Craig was convicted, and he lost his driver's license until he was 21.

An action committed early can have long-term negative consequences. The Israelites learned this hard lesson, and it prevented an entire generation from entering the promised land. When we are unfaithful to God, it might adversely affect our life for years to come. It's always better to follow God's will than to recklessly move forward with our sinful plans.

CREATING A NEW DYNASTY

BACKGROUND SCRIPTURE: 2 Samuel 7
DEVOTIONAL READING: 2 Samuel 7:10-17

KEY VERSE: Your house and your kingdom shall be made sure
forever before me; your throne shall be established forever. 2 Samuel 7:16.

5

KING JAMES VERSION

2 SAMUEL 7:18 Then went king David in, and sat before the LORD, and he said, Who am I, O Lord GOD? and what is my house, that thou hast brought me hitherto? 19 And this was yet a small thing in thy sight, O Lord GOD; but thou hast spoken also of thy servant's house for a great while to come. And is this the manner of man, O Lord GOD? 20 And what can David say more unto thee? for thou, Lord GOD, knowest thy servant. 21 For thy word's sake, and according to thine own heart, hast thou done all these great things, to make thy servant know them. 22 Wherefore thou art great, O LORD God: for there is none like thee, neither is there any God beside thee, according to all that we have heard with our ears. 23 And what one nation in the earth is like thy people, even like Israel, whom God went to redeem for a people to himself, and to make him a name, and to do for you great things and terrible, for thy land, before thy people, which thou redeemedst to thee from Egypt, from the nations and their gods?
24 For thou hast confirmed to thyself thy people Israel to be a people unto thee for ever: and thou, LORD, art become their God. 25 And now, O LORD God, the word that thou hast spoken concerning thy servant, and concerning his house, establish it for ever, and do as thou hast said. 26 And let thy name be magnified for ever, saying, The LORD of hosts is the God over Israel: and let the house of thy servant David be established before thee. 27 For thou, O LORD of hosts, God of Israel, hast revealed to thy servant, saying, I will build thee an house: therefore hath thy servant found in his heart to pray this prayer unto thee. 28 And now, O Lord GOD, thou art that God, and thy words be true, and thou hast promised this goodness unto thy servant: 29 Therefore now let it please thee to bless the house of thy servant, that it may continue for ever before thee: for thou, O Lord GOD, hast spoken it: and with thy blessing let the house of thy servant be blessed for ever.

NEW REVISED STANDARD VERSION

2 SAMUEL 7:18 Then King David went in and sat before the LORD, and said, "Who am I, O Lord GOD, and what is my house, that you have brought me thus far? 19 And yet this was a small thing in your eyes, O Lord GOD; you have spoken also of your servant's house for a great while to come. May this be instruction for the people, O Lord GOD! 20 And what more can David say to you? For you know your servant, O Lord GOD! 21 Because of your promise, and according to your own heart, you have wrought all this greatness, so that your servant may know it. 22 Therefore you are great, O LORD God; for there is no one like you, and there is no God besides you, according to all that we have heard with our ears. 23 Who is like your people, like Israel? Is there another nation on earth whose God went to redeem it as a people, and to make a name for himself, doing great and awesome things for them, by driving out before his people nations and their gods? 24 And you established your people Israel for yourself to be your people forever; and you, O LORD, became their God. 25 And now, O LORD God, as for the word that you have spoken concerning your servant and concerning his house, confirm it forever; do as you have promised. 26 Thus your name will be magnified forever in the saying, 'The LORD of hosts is God over Israel'; and the house of your servant David will be established before you. 27 For you, O LORD of hosts, the God of Israel, have made this revelation to your servant, saying, 'I will build you a house'; therefore your servant has found courage to pray this prayer to you. 28 And now, O Lord GOD, you are God, and your words are true, and you have promised this good thing to your servant; 29 now therefore may it please you to bless the house of your servant, so that it may continue forever before you; for you, O Lord GOD, have spoken, and with your blessing shall the house of your servant be blessed forever."

Monday, September 27	Psalm 86:8-13	*God's Steadfast Love Is Great*
Tuesday, September 28	2 Samuel 6:1-5	*David Moves the Ark of God*
Wednesday, September 29	2 Samuel 6:11-15	*David Brings the Ark to Jerusalem*
Thursday, September 30	2 Samuel 7:1-9	*God Sends a Message to David*
Friday, October 1	2 Samuel 7:10-17	*God Makes a Covenant with David*
Saturday, October 2	2 Samuel 7:18-22	*David Prays to God*
Sunday, October 3	2 Samuel 7:23-29	*David Seeks God's Blessing*

BACKGROUND

The books of 1 and 2 Samuel recount the great transition in the development of God's kingdom in the Old Testament era. As a boy Samuel was summoned to serve as prophet, priest, and judge to guide Israel into the monarchy, that is, a system of government under one king. Under his leadership Israel's loose association of tribes developed into a nation with a strong centralized government.

In preparation for the nation's move into the new era, Samuel was called to repair the moral fabric and restore the spiritual vitality of a people who had drifted far from God. Samuel finished the work of the judges and launched the monarchy, not by human strength and intuition, but by the power of God through prayer.

Along with establishing the monarchy, Samuel aided in launching an order of the prophets (1 Sam. 19:20) so as to bring God's Word to His people. From Samuel's time onward, the prophets promoted the spiritual life of Israel and were the channels through whom God made His will known to both king and commoner.

The first person Samuel appointed to be king, Saul, was a moral and spiritual failure. He constantly compromised God's commands and brought Israel to the brink of ruin. He ended his life tormented by evil spirits. In contrast, his successor David is described as a *"man after [God's] own heart"* (13:14). Though imperfect in his personal life and kingly reign, David stood out as a leader known for his single-minded devotion to the God of Israel.

With respect to chapter-by-chapter content, 1 Samuel gives an account of Israel's transition from the period of the judges to the monarchy. A summary of Samuel's judgeship is found in chapters 1—8, while chapters 9—15 relate Saul's coronation and early years as king. The stormy relationship between David and Saul is covered in chapters 16—30. First Samuel comes to a close with the death of Saul and his sons in chapter 31.

Second Samuel chronicles the history of David's reign as king. It begins with an account of his rule over the southern kingdom of Judah (chaps. 1—4), then goes on to tell about his expansion of the kingdom and his rise as a powerful and popular monarch. Although David was a man of deep faith, his human failings and often ruthless drive to get what he wanted resulted in great distress for himself and his family.

God promised to give an eternal dynasty, an eternal throne, and an eternal kingdom to David. Then, after the king's death, the Lord would allow his son (Solomon) to sit on his throne; and God would be merciful and fair in His dealings with David's successor. The Lord would also give permanence to David's rule. Though David and his descendants would pass away, the reign of his greatest descendant—Jesus Christ—would be unbroken (2 Sam. 7:11-16).

David, in response to the good and gracious promises God had made, went into the tent that housed the ark of the covenant and sat before the presence of *the Lord* (7:18). The king saw himself as the servant of the all-powerful God of Israel and reflected this attitude in his prayer.

David began by acknowledging that the sovereign Lord had shown His special favor on the king and his family by bringing them to a pivotal place in Israel's history; but God did not stop there, for He pledged to give David and his posterity a lasting dynasty (7:19). The king realized that this was not the usual way God dealt with *people*.

David acknowledged that the all-powerful Lord knew the heart of His *servant* (7:20). There thus was nothing more the king could say about the special recognition and treatment he and his posterity had received. We, too, are left speechless at the grace and kindness God has displayed toward us in Christ (Eph. 2:1-7).

David was not the ultimate reason God had established a covenant with the king. The Lord would fulfill His promises and thereby accomplish His purposes to glorify His name (2 Sam. 7:21). It was pure grace that He chose David and revealed His plan to the king.

As David reflected on these truths, he realized how great Israel's God, the all-powerful Lord, really was (7:22). Everything that God had done on behalf of His people and revealed to them underscored that there was *no one like* Him, whether in heaven or on earth. From this we see that Yahweh alone is God, and all other so-called gods are sham deities.

The superlative character of God is evidenced by His choosing and redeeming Israel. They alone were freed from slavery in Egypt to be God's special people. The Lord's name, or reputation, was magnified by His trouncing such nations and false gods as those associated with Egypt (7:23). In short, as David's words in 7:24 attest, the sovereign Lord made *Israel* His *people*, and He, in turn, became *their God*. Even Yahweh's promises to David were ultimately for the benefit of the Israelites.

The king petitioned God to do as He had promised concerning the king and his family. In particular, David wanted the Lord to establish his house as a perpetual dynasty (7:25). By doing this, God would magnify His name, or reputation, among the nations.

People would acknowledge that almighty God ruled over Israel and that He had chosen and established David's descendants as the nation's kings (7:26). We, too, can give God the praise for His marvelous plan of redemption.

The promise revealed to David was the reason he had prayed so confidently to the all-powerful Lord, Israel's God. The king was especially cognizant of God's intent to establish in His presence an unending Davidic dynasty (7:27). The king realized that only *God*, the sovereign LORD, could fulfill such a plan; and David was sure that God would bring to pass the good things He had pledged to His *servant* (7:28). We, too, can know that God's promises are true and assured of being fulfilled.

David brought closure to his prayer by asking God to bless the dynasty of His *servant* (7:29). By enabling the house of David to stand permanently before Him, the Lord would glorify His name before the nations of the world. God's fulfillment of His pledge to David would magnify the reputation of the divine.

Because the all-powerful Lord had spoken, David accepted by faith God's extraordinary and irrevocable promises. David was convinced that, by blessing the dynasty of His servant into the future, the Lord's eternal plan of redemption would ultimately be accomplished.

David's life and witness remind us that a seeker of God is likely to experience His blessings. When we let God's concerns rank higher in importance than our own (as David did), our character changes, and we are more likely to experience kindness and favor from the Lord.

This does not mean that service earns blessings or erases problems. Even David faced significant problems in his life; but he did see the greater purposes of God for which he worked—the building of the nation of Israel—become fruitful. We also must be careful not to dictate to God just what our blessings should be; instead, our goal is to serve God and let Him decide on how and when and where the blessings will come.

Perhaps some of us will be blessed by seeing people we have been teaching really grasp what God is about. Another possibility is that we will witness someone advance whom we have helped get a job. Imagine how exciting it would be for us to receive a positive report from a missions agency that we have supported for years! All these things are possible as we continually seek to please God in every area of our lives.

SUGGESTIONS TO TEACHERS

This week's lesson is based on the time in history when David was at his most glorious. His nation, spanning the area from modern Iraq through Syria in Egypt, stood tall and secure. But David was troubled by the fact that while he lived in a magnificent home, the ark of God was housed in a tent. The king thus decided to build a temple for the Lord.

As we read in 2 Samuel 7, however, God did not want the king to do this for Him. Perhaps at first David was saddened by the Lord's decision. But then David could take comfort in knowing that God was using him to unify the nation and subdue Israel's enemies. Likewise, God would give David a lasting dynasty.

1. DAVID'S DECISION. What finer desire could there be than to build a beautiful temple for the Lord! David's motive was noble and his plan was commendable. Our intentions sometimes seem to fit in with what we imagine God would have us to do. But for various reasons, we are not able to accomplish what we had planned. Encourage the students to share personal episodes of disappointment and how they handled them.

2. NATHAN'S DECLARATION. David and Nathan had assumed that it would be proper for the king to build a temple in Jerusalem to house the ark of the covenant. However, neither David nor Nathan had consulted the Lord. Thankfully, when God revealed to Nathan His real intent for David, the prophet had the courage to declare the same to the king.

3. DAVID'S DEVOTION. Rather than lash out in anger, David graciously accepted God's word through Nathan. David learned that God did not want him to build a temple for the ark. Though he would not have the honor of completing this project, he had other enormous tasks to finish as Israel's king.

4. GOD'S DECREE. God had accomplished significant things through David. He had given David a great name. The Lord had also given Israel a place of rest. Moreover, God had given David peace from all his enemies. In addition to these, God declared that the king's descendants would become an enduring dynasty over Israel.

The New Testament reveals that God's promises to David are fulfilled in Christ. Through Jesus' death and resurrection, we have the hope of eternal life. We can count on God to keep His promises to us. Regardless of our current problems, God's love for us remains unshakable.

FOR ADULTS

■ **TOPIC:** Leaving a Legacy

■ **QUESTIONS:** 1. What did God promise in His covenant with David? 2. As David reflected on the Lord's gracious promise, what did the king recognize about God? 3. How had the Lord underscored His greatness to the surrounding nations? 4. What emboldened David to ask God to make His pledge a permanent reality? 5. Why was the courage the king displayed in his response proper?

■ **ILLUSTRATIONS:**

An Enduring Legacy. Arthur Ashe, the champion American tennis player, acquired AIDS (Acquired Immunodeficiency Syndrome) through a blood transfusion at the time he underwent heart surgery. The medical personnel in the hospital did not suspect or inspect the unit of H.I.V. (Human Immunodeficiency Virus) contaminated blood.

Ashe did not realize that he was infected with the dreaded virus until five years later when he first suffered numbness and then growing paralysis in his playing arm. The diagnosis was a brain tumor. This stay in the hospital for surgery revealed that he had contracted AIDS. After being released from the hospital, the seventh-ranked tennis star had to face rumors about his condition as well as deal with retirement from his beloved sport.

Arthur Ashe resisted the temptation to be angry at the Lord. In 1992, he addressed the students at the Niagara County Community College and testified that despite having his disease, his trust in God was firm. Ashe knew that regardless of the outcome, God would remain with him in his ordeal. He has left an enduring legacy of faith.

Challenge of a Promise. Ricky Hoyt has cerebral palsy. He is confined to a wheelchair. His disability is classified technically as a spastic quadriplegic. He cannot even talk, and has to communicate through a voice synthesizer. Nonetheless, Ricky Hoyt has been able to compete in over 600 sports events, including 111 triathlons, a 45-day cross country odyssey in 1992, and nearly 20 Boston Marathons. He can do these things because of his father's promise and the way he has kept his pledge.

Ricky's father, Dick, is a retired military officer who has devoted himself to compete with Ricky to fulfill his son's dreams. Ricky is the heart and his father is the body. Together they compete. Dick pushes the wheelchair, fulfilling his promise to his son to let him participate even in big-time marathons.

How much more does God fulfill His promises to those who trust Him? Believers know that the Lord will remain faithful to them and accomplish all that He has planned.

Commitment to God's Promise. Habitat for Humanity has provided affordable housing for millions throughout the world. But few know the story of its origins. A young millionaire named Millard Fuller had amassed a fortune by the age of 29, and was able to buy anything he fancied. However, he discovered that his marriage had collapsed because of his greed and attention only to business.

Shocked at having his wife, Linda, leave him, Fuller began to take stock of his life. He located Linda in New York and listened to her tell him that she didn't care about having him buy her things. He heard her describe how her life was barren of meaning with a materialistic way of living. They talked and wept together. Then they knelt and prayed.

That night in a hotel room in New York City, the couple promised God and each other that they would stop living merely for themselves and commit their lives to helping the oppressed and homeless. The Fullers' promise has been fulfilled in ways they never anticipated. For example, countless chapters of Habitat for Humanity now exist in North American communities and in many developing countries around the world.

■ **TOPIC:** God's People Forever

■ **QUESTIONS:** 1. How did David see himself before the presence of the God of Israel? 2. How had the sovereign Lord shown His special favor on the king and his family? 3. What was the ultimate reason God would fulfill His promises and thereby accomplish His purposes? 4. How would God magnify His name, or reputation, among the nations? 5. How did David bring closure to his prayer?

■ **ILLUSTRATIONS:**

Lost Tradition. Judith Martin, better known as Miss Manners, noted that contemporary houses contain a room with a large table that is usually set with a 500 piece jigsaw puzzle or is used as a desk. The space, which once was called the family dining room, is now often used for other purposes. This suggests that modern society has deemphasized the importance of the traditional practice of the family meal.

Many would acknowledge that the family meal has been helpful in keeping households together. It is a time when relationships are built, especially as news of each member's day is exchanged, manners are taught, and social skills are developed. Miss Manners laments that family members often eat by themselves, and then they wonder why they feel alone.

David saw the temple as a way of bringing the people of his nation together. He wanted to expand and reinforce a tradition of worship so that God's people would become a strong and united faith community. Though the Lord did not allow David to build the temple, He did affirm the king's idea by allowing Solomon—David's son—to do the job.

Ingredient for Traditional Family. A strong economy providing employment and money positively affects the family structure. Research conducted by Gail M. Johnson, a sociologist at Penn State University, demonstrates a correlation between economic status and the family structure. Johnson's findings showed that job loss resulted in higher divorce rates and out of wedlock births, and this in turn changed the family concept and structure. The percentage of families headed by women with children grew, while married couples with families declined.

According to Johnson, 42 percent of white children and 86 percent of black children will spend part of their lives in a female-headed household. In 1960, the figure was 5.1 million. In 2003, the number of children living only with their mother had tripled to 15.6 million. Female headed households are also more likely to be poor because women are forced to take lower paying jobs.

Johnson says that unemployment is the leading cause of female-headed households. Women tend to marry men who have a good job. In contrast, they tend to avoid marrying men who are unemployed. Clearly, when the economy is good, there are many more employed men than unemployed men who are married.

Strangely, one ingredient is missing from Johnson's research. Scripture teaches that God is supposed to be a part of family life. Consider David. The king had palaces, prestige, power, and wealth. Stability existed throughout his kingdom. But he also sensed the importance of God being present in his life and in the lives of his family members.

Traditional Family Changes. The so-called traditional family image is gone. In previous generations the mother would have been a full-time homemaker and the father would have been the major wage earner. The norm would have been for them to stay married to each other for life and have children. Now, only 10 percent of the families in the United States fit that mold, according to Danielle Lichter, Director of Penn State University's Population Institute. The traditional family has been replaced by single parent families.

The kind of family in which we live is not the most important factor from God's point of view. Of greater concern is whether He reigns supreme among all the family members. Regardless of how many possessions a family may have, The Lord wants to see healthy relationships being cultivated in which the love of Christ is displayed through all the circumstances of life among God's people forever.

CREATING A REDEEMED PEOPLE

BACKGROUND SCRIPTURE: Isaiah 43
DEVOTIONAL READING: Isaiah 42:5-13

KEY VERSE: Do not fear, for I have redeemed you;
I have called you by name, you are mine. Isaiah 43:1.

6

KING JAMES VERSION

ISAIAH 43:1 But now thus saith the LORD that created thee, O Jacob, and he that formed thee, O Israel, Fear not: for I have redeemed thee, I have called thee by thy name; thou art mine. 2 When thou passest through the waters, I will be with thee; and through the rivers, they shall not overflow thee: when thou walkest through the fire, thou shalt not be burned; neither shall the flame kindle upon thee. . . .

10 Ye are my witnesses, saith the LORD, and my servant whom I have chosen: that ye may know and believe me, and understand that I am he: before me there was no God formed, neither shall there be after me. 11 I, even I, am the LORD; and beside me there is no saviour. 12 I have declared, and have saved, and I have shewed, when there was no strange god among you: therefore ye are my witnesses, saith the LORD, that I am God. 13 Yea, before the day was I am he; and there is none that can deliver out of my hand: I will work, and who shall let it? . . .

18 Remember ye not the former things, neither consider the things of old. 19 Behold, I will do a new thing; now it shall spring forth; shall ye not know it? I will even make a way in the wilderness, and rivers in the desert.

NEW REVISED STANDARD VERSION

ISAIAH 43:1 But now thus says the LORD,
he who created you, O Jacob,
he who formed you, O Israel:
Do not fear, for I have redeemed you;
I have called you by name, you are mine.
2 When you pass through the waters, I will be with you;
and through the rivers, they shall not overwhelm you;
when you walk through fire you shall not be burned,
and the flame shall not consume you. . . .
10 You are my witnesses, says the LORD,
and my servant whom I have chosen,
so that you may know and believe me
and understand that I am he.
Before me no god was formed,
nor shall there be any after me.
11 I, I am the LORD,
and besides me there is no savior.
12 I declared and saved and proclaimed,
when there was no strange god among you;
and you are my witnesses, says the LORD.
13 I am God, and also henceforth I am He;
there is no one who can deliver from my hand;
I work and who can hinder it? . . .
18 Do not remember the former things,
or consider the things of old.
19 I am about to do a new thing;
now it springs forth, do you not perceive it?
I will make a way in the wilderness
and rivers in the desert.

Monday, October 4	Isaiah 40:25-31	*Our God Is the Everlasting God*
Tuesday, October 5	Isaiah 42:5-13	*Give Glory to God*
Wednesday, October 6	Isaiah 43:1-7	*Israel Is Redeemed*
Thursday, October 7	Isaiah 43:8-15	*God Is Our God and Savior*
Friday, October 8	Isaiah 43:16-21	*God Will Bring Salvation*
Saturday, October 9	Isaiah 43:22-28	*Israel Is Still on Trial*
Sunday, October 10	Isaiah 44:1-8	*The One God Blesses Israel*

BACKGROUND

The Book of Isaiah is a compilation of history, predictions, warnings, and promises relayed from God, through Isaiah, to the people of Judah. Throughout his long ministry, Isaiah preached about God's righteousness, warned about judgment for sin, and proclaimed God's love and forgiveness. He also prophesied the glory that awaits those who remain faithful to God.

Among Christians, the Book of Isaiah is one of the best-loved portions in the Old Testament. The primary reason for this is that Isaiah contains more prophecies of the Messiah, Jesus, than any other Old Testament book. John 12:41 says that Isaiah *saw [Jesus'] glory and spoke about him.*

That Isaiah wrote the prophecy attributed to him is confirmed by the appearance of his name 16 times throughout the book. Isaiah (whose name means "the Lord saves") was born and reared in Jerusalem in days of prosperity. It seems that Isaiah's family was an affluent one and that he was well educated.

Jewish tradition holds that Isaiah's father, Amoz, was a brother of King Amaziah. If so, then Isaiah was a grandson of King Joash and a first cousin of King Uzziah. Certainly Isaiah spent much time in the company of royalty. He even gave advice on foreign affairs to King Hezekiah. According to 8:3, Isaiah was married to a *prophetess*. This word may mean that she carried on a prophetic ministry of her own, or it may simply mean that she was the wife of a prophet. She and Isaiah had two sons, whose names were symbolic (7:3; 8:3).

Isaiah received his call to ministry in the year of King Uzziah's death, that is, 740 B.C. His ministry continued through the reign of Hezekiah, who died in 686 B.C. (1:1). According to tradition, Isaiah was martyred during King Manasseh's reign (697–642 B.C.) by being sawed in half inside a hollow log. Possibly Hebrews 11:37 refers to this event.

When Isaiah began his ministry in 740 B.C., the northern kingdom of Israel was near collapse due to political, spiritual, and military deterioration. Things were going from bad to worse. In 723 B.C., the weakened northern kingdom finally fell to the Assyrian Empire, which had been expanding steadily for the past century and a half.

The southern kingdom, Judah, was heading for a similar fate. Under the leadership of wicked King Ahaz, Judah was ripe for a fall. The nation had become corrupt socially, politically, and religiously. It was during this time that Isaiah delivered his messages to the people of Judah.

Isaiah called Judah to repent of idolatry and moral degeneracy. But then, failing to turn the nation Godward, Isaiah informed the people of Judah that their rebellion would lead to captivity at the hands of the Babylonians. Isaiah also foretold that, following the captivity, God would restore His people. God's declaring all this in advance (through Isaiah) was intended to highlight His sovereignty in contrast to the powerlessness of false gods.

Isaiah also foretold the ministry of the Servant of the Lord, who would redeem not just Judah but the whole world. About 700 years later, the suffering Servant, Jesus Christ, died for sinners as prophesied by Isaiah.

NOTES ON THE PRINTED TEXT

While God had promised that He would exile His rebellious people to Babylon, Isaiah 43 was written as if the exile were already near its end and the prophet could now see beyond the terrible time to a day of God's blessing that awaited the faithful remnant. That day was so certain that it is as if it had already arrived. Accordingly, this week's lesson text primarily deals with the restoration of God's people to the land of promise.

Isaiah 43:1 begins with *the* LORD making an authoritative and trustworthy declaration to His people. God first referred to them as *Jacob*, whom He had created. The Lord then called His people by the name of *Israel*, whom He had formed. God reminded His chosen people that He would redeem and protect them. This remained true despite the storms of life they encountered. Even when their circumstances seemed overwhelming, they would still remain His, for He had called them *by name*. This truth spotlights the Lord's intimate relationship with the Israelites.

The Israelites, as a nation and as a people, had gone through harrowing experiences that challenged their faith and hope; but even in such difficult moments as the exodus from Egypt and the crossing of the Jordan River, God was with them. This would continue to be true as they anticipated their eventual restoration to the promised land. The message for believers today is not much different. At times we might feel weighed down by circumstances; but we need not fear, for God is with us in every situation. He is the sovereign Lord who created all things.

God declared that, when the Israelites passed through difficult waters, He would be with them (43:2); and when they had to cross seemingly impassible *rivers*, they would not be overwhelmed. The Lord would prevent them from being consumed by the flames of oppression as they made their journey to their homeland.

The abiding truth for us is that God has never failed in His promise to strengthen us in difficult times. Pleasures and powers of this world may offer temporary comfort, but they fade like flowers (see 40:6-8). God's love and care for us are everlasting. Let us bless the Lord for His comfort to us!

In 43:3-9, we learn that the Lord is the *Savior* of *Israel* and the Judge of all humankind. In particular, 43:9 declares that the false gods worshiped by the pagans could not foretell Cyrus' future deliverance of Israel from Babylon.

The situation was far different, however, for the Israelites. As a nation they had experienced the great works the Lord did on their behalf. They thus were a logical choice to be God's witnesses; and it was reasonable to expect them to serve their Maker (43:10).

Consider what the Lord had done for His people. He rescued them from Egypt and enabled them to conquer Canaan. Why, then, should the Israelites not come to know, believe, and understand that Yahweh alone is the true, living, and eternal God?

Even more explicit is 43:11 concerning the uniqueness of Israel's God. He alone is *the LORD*. Likewise, there is no deliverer besides Him. In fact, only He could free His people from exile under Babylon.

No other entity worshiped among the nations surrounding Israel could make the claim of foretelling and then bringing to pass Israel's deliverance (43:12). Only *the LORD* could rightfully make this assertion; and His people were His *witnesses* that He, the only true and living God, and saved them.

Before time ever began, the Lord eternally existed as God; and He will eternally remain as such long after time ends (43:13). In light of this, no creature in heaven or on earth could ever oppose what Yahweh decreed He would do. In the case of Israel, He would redeem and restore the nation. No entity would be able to thwart or reverse His plan.

What a great comfort it is to have God as our Lord. He is eternal, unchanging, and as mighty today as He was in the day of Creation. He does not grow weak with the passing of time, and He is not tired from having to sustain the universe; and most remarkable of all, we can trust the Lord to give us strength for His purpose in our lives.

In the past, God allowed powerful nations to overrun His people. Now, in a comforting gesture, He urged them to let the past evils go. In light of the glorious prospects awaiting Israel, God urged His people to no longer think about the past prophecies of judgment (43:18).

The command of Cyrus for the Jewish exiles to return to their homeland is the *new thing* (43:19) being referred to here. From the eternal perspective of the Lord, the fall of Babylon and the restoration of Israel had already begun.

When the promised act of deliverance occurred, God's people were to recognize it as such. At the prophesied moment, the Lord would give the exiles a free and clear route back to the promised land. It would be as if God created a pathway for His people to travel and a river for them to refresh themselves along the journey.

When we come to faith in Christ, it does not mean all our troubles go away; yet, even in difficult times, the Lord upholds and comforts us.

SUGGESTIONS TO TEACHERS

In the context of God's chosen people being notoriously prone to look anywhere but to Him for strength, Isaiah 43 stresses that God alone would free His people and restore them to the promised land. The all-powerful Lord of Israel stands in sharp contrast to the powerless and lifeless idols of Babylon. A key theme in this regard is God's loving plans for His people, which are fulfilled when believers offer a committed response to Him. Many in our world today—and in our churches—need to remember that God is still at work in His world.

1. PLEA FOR REMEMBERING. Isaiah called upon God's people to remember the Lord's goodness in their lives in the past. Remembering God is important. During times of apparent hopelessness, God's people can recall instances of His goodness and guidance in their lives.

Invite your group members to tell about times when remembering God's workings in the past helped them get through difficult days. Then remind them of the words inscribed on many altars and communion tables, "Do this in memory of me." Recalling the death and resurrection of the Savior is the central act of worship in every Christian congregation.

2. PREDICTION OF RETURN. Isaiah assured his hearers that God would enable them to return to Judah. He based his confidence in God's Word, contrasting his insight to that of astrologers, fortunetellers, and all others who claimed special wisdom. God's people may rest assured that the Lord will bring new beginnings because of His faithfulness. While many look for guidance in the occult or through so-called "psychics," we need to hear Isaiah's words ringing out clearly.

3. PROMISE OF REBUILDING. Jerusalem would be rebuilt and the temple restored. In other words, God's purposes would be fulfilled. God bestows hope upon those who trust and serve Him. He introduces a future in the worst of circumstances for those who are committed to Him.

4. PREPARATION OF A RULER. Isaiah stated that Cyrus, the powerful ruler of Persia and conqueror of Babylon, would be God's instrument in history. Cyrus was a pagan. Nonetheless, he was used by the Ruler of all history.

With God-given insight, the prophet realized that his Lord could call the most unlikely persons and employ them as His agents. Cyrus would be the leader to carry out God's purposes and permit the exiles to rebuild. God's intentions will not be thwarted forever. He remains in charge of the world, despite the grim destruction of human violence, greed, and rebelliousness.

FOR ADULTS

■ TOPIC: Recreating Community

■ QUESTIONS: 1. Who does the all-powerful Lord of Israel stand in sharp contrast to? 2. Why were the Israelites to respond in faith to God's promises, rather than be frightened? 3. In an imaginary courtroom scene, what did the Lord urge Israel and the nations to consider? 4. Why were the

Israelites a logical choice to be God's witnesses? 5. Why is it that no creature could ever oppose what Yahweh decreed He would do?

■ **ILLUSTRATIONS:**

Comfort for the Raging. Two shoppers in a supermarket got in a fistfight over who should be first in a newly opened checkout lane. An airline flight returned to a major American city after a passenger was accused of throwing a can of beer at a flight attendant and biting a pilot. One father in an eastern state beat another father to death in an argument over rough play at their sons' hockey practice. A high school baseball coach in the South turned himself in to face charges that he broke an umpire's jaw after a disputed call. All these events were reported by *USA Today* over the span of a few months.

"Bad tempers are on display everywhere," wrote reporter Karen S. Peterson. The media is constantly reporting incidents of road rage, airplane rage, biker rage, surfer rage, grocery store rage, and rage at youth sporting events. This has led scientists to say the United States is in the middle of an anger epidemic. This epidemic rattles both those who study social trends and parents who fear the country is at a cultural precipice.

"We have lost some of the glue holding our society together," Peterson quoted one parent as saying. "We have lost our respect for others. The example we are setting for our kids is terrible."

Experts searching for causes blame an increasing sense of self-importance, the widespread feeling that things should happen "my" way. Other factors, they say, include too little time, overcrowding, intrusive technology, and too many demands for change in a society hurtling into the twenty-first century. In the midst of our rage, we are desperately in need of comfort—and of a Comforter.

God at Work. Two men were forced to accept early retirement from their company. George and Henry both felt hurt and angry at being terminated unexpectedly after 30 years' faithful service. Both were also concerned about their finances in the days ahead.

George, however, was a man of faith. Certain that even an unforeseen early retirement could be used by God for good, he faced the future knowing that God was still in control. Henry, on the other hand, grew increasingly bitter. When George tried to share about his trust in the Lord, Henry snapped, "Don't give me any of that God stuff! What does God or anyone care?"

Although George faced over nine months of uncertainty, he started his own business by buying a carpet-cleaning franchise. Now, seven years later, he looks back on his life and sees that God had been involved more than he ever suspected. Henry, however, has become more bitter, brooding over "my bad breaks" and complaining about "the unfair system." Henry's wife is concerned that his attitude and inactivity are affecting his health.

Do you rely on God even in the toughest times? Countless people like George can testify: God cares and stays close—no matter what the situation.

Comfort for the Needy. In an attempt to bring comfort to Vietnamese children without parents, Christian workers are running an orphanage under difficult conditions in Vietnam. The religious group opened a home for children from the minority Cham population, according to Zenit, a Christian news agency. Bethany House, northeast of Ho Chi Minh City, houses 50 boys three- to nineteen-years old, many of whom have lost both parents. Cham fathers normally abandon their children and remarry if the mother dies, according to the news agency.

The orphans attend school and also are instructed in the faith. The Christian workers often are confronted by local authorities, since the Cham people embrace their own traditional religion, a local version of Hinduism, according to Zenit. However, some Cham adults have converted to Christianity and been baptized.

Predictions. French physician and astrologer Michel de Notredame is better known by his Latin name, Nostradamus. In the fifteenth century he penned a book of rhymed prophecies entitled *Centuries*. The book is chiefly known for correctly predicting the manner in which Henry II of France would die. Many people, though, have credited Nostradamus for predicting various events in European history, including the rise of Adolf Hitler. Yet the predictions are extremely vague and open to a variety of interpretations.

Contrast this with a true prophet! Isaiah's prophecies would find historical fulfillment. God was working for the sake of Israel, and not one word was spoken in vain.

FOR YOUTH

■ **TOPIC:** Living Securely

■ **QUESTIONS:** 1. What did God promise to do for His people as they made their journey to their homeland? 2. What had the Israelites, as a nation, experienced from the Lord? 3. In what way is Isaiah 43:11 explicit about the uniqueness of Israel's God? 4. Why could no other entity worshiped among the nations surrounding Israel make the claim of foretelling and then bringing to pass Israel's deliverance? 5. What did the Lord, in a comforting gesture, urge His people to do?

■ **ILLUSTRATIONS:**

Comfort through Redemption. A year after brutally attacking a pastor, a gang member became a Christian. Patrick Shikanda Lokhotio apologized for attacking Timothy Njoya, pastor of a large Presbyterian church in Nairobi, Kenya, *Ecumenical News International* reported. Lokhotio beat Njoya with a wooden club outside the Parliament building on June 10, 1999, as the pastor led a political protest.

Lokhotio sought forgiveness from Njoya and his congregation in an address to the church July 3, 2000. Njoya publicly forgave him months earlier and asked the authorities to stop criminal proceedings against him. Lokhotio said he was ashamed for "beating up a man of God," and promised to live a Christian lifestyle.

Lokhotio's change "shows God's miracles have worked in this church," Njoya said. Lokhotio had been a member of a youth gang. During his talk, he introduced six members of the gang who also have pledged to mend their ways. About 100 other members of the gang have said they will come to the church.

Wary and Worried. Consider the romantic view of the life of a college freshman: four years of stimulating academic growth—and enjoyable parties—should prepare him or her for entry into the adult world. But is that how it really is?

Actually, today's freshmen feel great stress and anxiety. The American Council on Education surveyed two hundred thousand college freshmen. The majority of respondents indicated a growing anxiety about the cost of attending college. They were afraid they wouldn't be able to finish college because of tuition costs and expressed hopelessness about the potential job market. These 18-year-olds are wary and worried.

Isaiah spoke to a similar group of people. He urged them to have hope and promised them a blessed future. His message speaks to anyone worried about the next four years—or even the next day.

His-Story. Michael Jackson's album *His-Story* featured a retrospective look at his music. The sales initially flagged until he shot a video that included an inappropriate scene. Then sales skyrocketed.

Though many liked Jackson's music, we should recognize that the title His-Story really belongs to God. His story—the story of the Lord of the Universe—is found in the Bible and describes His restoration of His people. It is the greatest story ever, culminating in the gift of Himself for the world's salvation. This Lord has called each of us to place all of our hope in him. We will not be disappointed.

CREATING A NEW COVENANT

BACKGROUND SCRIPTURE: Jeremiah 29:1-14; 31:31-34
DEVOTIONAL READING: Jeremiah 30:18-22

KEY VERSE: This is the covenant that I will make with the house of Israel after those days, says the LORD: I will put my law within them, and I will write it on their hearts; and I will be their God, and they shall be my people. Jeremiah 31:33.

KING JAMES VERSION

JEREMIAH 29:10 For thus saith the LORD, That after seventy years be accomplished at Babylon I will visit you, and perform my good word toward you, in causing you to return to this place. 11 For I know the thoughts that I think toward you, saith the LORD, thoughts of peace, and not of evil, to give you an expected end. 12 Then shall ye call upon me, and ye shall go and pray unto me, and I will hearken unto you. 13 And ye shall seek me, and find me, when ye shall search for me with all your heart. 14 And I will be found of you, saith the LORD: and I will turn away your captivity, and I will gather you from all the nations, and from all the places whither I have driven you, saith the LORD; and I will bring you again into the place whence I caused you to be carried away captive. . . .

31:31 Behold, the days come, saith the LORD, that I will make a new covenant with the house of Israel, and with the house of Judah: 32 Not according to the covenant that I made with their fathers in the day that I took them by the hand to bring them out of the land of Egypt; which my covenant they brake, although I was an husband unto them, saith the LORD: 33 But this shall be the covenant that I will make with the house of Israel; After those days, saith the LORD, I will put my law in their inward parts, and write it in their hearts; and will be their God, and they shall be my people. 34 And they shall teach no more every man his neighbour, and every man his brother, saying, Know the LORD: for they shall all know me, from the least of them unto the greatest of them, saith the LORD: for I will forgive their iniquity, and I will remember their sin no more.

NEW REVISED STANDARD VERSION

JEREMIAH 29:10 For thus says the LORD: Only when Babylon's seventy years are completed will I visit you, and I will fulfill to you my promise and bring you back to this place. 11 For surely I know the plans I have for you, says the LORD, plans for your welfare and not for harm, to give you a future with hope. 12 Then when you call upon me and come and pray to me, I will hear you. 13 When you search for me, you will find me; if you seek me with all your heart, 14 I will let you find me, says the LORD, and I will restore your fortunes and gather you from all the nations and all the places where I have driven you, says the LORD, and I will bring you back to the place from which I sent you into exile. . . .

31:31 The days are surely coming, says the LORD, when I will make a new covenant with the house of Israel and the house of Judah. 32 It will not be like the covenant that I made with their ancestors when I took them by the hand to bring them out of the land of Egypt—a covenant that they broke, though I was their husband, says the LORD. 33 But this is the covenant that I will make with the house of Israel after those days, says the LORD: I will put my law within them, and I will write it on their hearts; and I will be their God, and they shall be my people. 34 No longer shall they teach one another, or say to each other, "Know the LORD," for they shall all know me, from the least of them to the greatest, says the LORD; for I will forgive their iniquity, and remember their sin no more.

Monday, October 11	Jeremiah 29:10-14	*God Will Restore the Exiles*
Tuesday, October 12	Jeremiah 30:2-9	*After Judgment Will Come Freedom*
Wednesday, October 13	Jeremiah 30:18-22	*Restoration Will Bring Abundance and Happiness*
Thursday, October 14	Jeremiah 31:1-6	*God Is Always Faithful*
Friday, October 15	Jeremiah 31:7-14	*The Exiles Will Return with Joy*
Saturday, October 16	Jeremiah 31:23-30	*God Restores All Who Are Responsible*
Sunday, October 17	Jeremiah 31:31-34	*God Makes a New Covenant*

BACKGROUND

Jeremiah is known as the "weeping prophet" because of his deep sadness and grief over Israel's refusal to repent, even in the face of certain and imminent destruction. Though Baruch, the prophet's companion and scribe, penned this longest book of the Bible, the words of the prophecies belong to Jeremiah.

Jeremiah was a member of a priestly family, namely, that of Hilkiah. His hometown was Anathoth, a city set aside by Joshua for those of Levitical descent. Jeremiah may have been a descendant of Abiathar, a priest of Anathoth banished by Solomon for his lack of loyalty. In that case, the prophet did not have a sterling heritage.

No biblical writer revealed more of his soul than Jeremiah. Through his often brash and pointed complaints to God, we see the exasperation of his heart. He was commanded by God to never marry and have children. He preached for years, only to be rebuked, insulted, and banished by leaders who hated him. Unlike other Old Testament prophets, Jeremiah did not have the benefit of miracles to validate his message.

One of the most obvious features of the Book of Jeremiah is that its messages aren't arranged chronologically. With the exception of chapter 13, the first 20 chapters of Jeremiah probably come from the period between the prophet's call by God (626 B.C.) and a critical battle between Egypt and Babylon (605 B.C.). Most of the material in chapters 21—39 appear to date from the reigns of kings Jehoiakim and Zedekiah. Within those broad boundaries, the prophetic messages cluster by topic or theme.

Like Ezekiel, Jeremiah placed a strong emphasis on individual responsibility. Judah fell as a nation because it was made up of individuals who chose not to obey God in their daily lives. The mystery of the new covenant is introduced in Jeremiah 31, where God would relate to His people directly and personally rather than through the rituals and sacrifices of the Mosaic law. Jeremiah made it clear that the temple, the ark of the covenant, and the abundance of sacrifices paled in significance when placed next to the attitude of a person's heart. Through the words of Jeremiah, God calls the hearts of all people to repentance, reconciliation, and restoration.

NOTES ON THE PRINTED TEXT

Jeremiah 29 records the letter of the prophet to the people of Judah in Babylonia. In the document, Jeremiah urged the exiles to live peacefully in the foreign land, knowing that God would one day restore them to Judah. The hope of restoration—both physical and spiritual—is underscored in the promise of the new covenant found in 31:31-34. Through these words of the prophet, God called His people to repentance, reconciliation, and restoration.

Some had falsely prophesied that the Babylonian captivity would be short in duration (Jer. 29:8-9). The Lord, however, declared to the exiles that the people of Judah would remain in captivity until the 70 years of Babylonian rule had been *completed* (29:10). Then God would once again *visit* His people with consideration and kindness. He particularly noted His intent to fulfill His gracious *promise* of restoring His people to their homeland.

The exiles, as they languished in captivity, would struggle with discouragement; but God reassured them that He was well aware of His plans for them. He pledged to prosper, not harm them, and to give them a future filled with *hope* (29:11). At times we can feel despondent over our circumstances. In those moments, we can look to God for inner, lasting peace.

The Lord urged the exiles to commune with Him in prayer, assured that He would hear and respond to their requests (29:12). When they sought God in prayer, they would find Him immediately available to them. His continual presence, in turn, would prompt them to seek Him with all their *heart* (29:13).

Prayer is just as important for believers today as it was in Bible times. Of course, when we pray to God, we should not see it as a method of creating a positive mental attitude in ourselves so that we are able to do what we have asked to be done; instead, prayer creates within us a right attitude with respect to God's will.

The Lord not only pledged to make Himself available to His humble and repentant people, but also to reverse their status as captives in a foreign land (29:14). God pledged to regather the exiles from all the nations and bring them back to their homeland. This promise extends beyond the return of the Jews to Jerusalem to the Second Advent of the Messiah.

The promise of a future messianic age serves as a thematic link between Jeremiah 29:10-14 and 31:31-34. By saying in 31:31 that *the days are surely coming*, the Lord indicated that the *new covenant* will be part of this future time of blessing. Moreover, God would establish a new covenant with His chosen people because of the limitations associated with the old one. Both *the house of Israel and the house of Judah* were included in this promise.

Under the old covenant God had made with the ancestors of the Jews, He had to take the people by the hand (so to speak) and lead them out of *Egypt* (31:32). The tragedy is that the Israelites continually violated the stipulations of the old *covenant*. This remained true, even though God was like a faithful and devoted husband to His people.

The Lord pledged that, after He planted His people back in their homeland, He would establish a new covenant with the entire nation (31:33). God promised that at that time He would put His *law* within them and *write it on their hearts* and minds; also, the Lord would be the *God* of the Jews, and they would be His chosen *people*.

Here we see that the new covenant involves the inner life (the hearts and minds) of God's people. It also involves their relationship with the Lord. We know from the teaching of the New Testament that we are the heirs of the spiritual blessings associated with the new covenant. The Lord truly is our God, and we really are His people.

Note that 31:34 carries forward these truths by declaring that the people would no longer need to *teach* their neighbors and relatives to know *the LORD* in an intimate and personal way. The reason is that, under the new covenant, all of them—from the least important to the most important—would truly *know* the Lord.

The New Testament reveals that Jesus fulfilled Jeremiah's prophecy of the coming new covenant. The Messiah did so through His death on the cross. The Savior's atoning sacrifice made redemption and forgiveness of sins possible. All are now invited to partake of what He has done. In short, those who put their faith in Christ are forgiven and receive everlasting life (John 3:16).

SUGGESTIONS TO TEACHERS

Judah could not escape God's judgment for a national lifestyle of rebelliousness that had persisted for centuries. Even as the Babylonian armies starved Jerusalem into surrender, God sent a promise through Jeremiah that He would restore His people in the future. Sin brings discipline, but God does not abandon His people. He corrects them so that they can enjoy eternal blessings.

1. HOPE FOR A NEW START. The Lord assured His people in the face of judgment that they had a future. They would survive because they belonged to Him. Even Israel, though no longer a nation, would be restored in the end. The chastening of the Lord is never pleasant, but it can lead in time to a new beginning, one that is free from the burden of sin that brought about God's discipline.

2. HOPE FOR A NEW BLESSING. Israel and Judah's new beginning would be more than a shoestring survival of hard times. God would abundantly bless His people. When God is done chastening one of His children in response to a persistent sin, He doesn't treat them as second-class citizens in His kingdom. He blesses them with eternal riches and joy.

3. HOPE FOR A NEW ATTITUDE. In Jeremiah's day the people of Judah felt destined to judgment because of the sins of their ancestors. They had distorted the idea that sin has generational consequences. God's people need to accept personal responsibility for their sins. This attitude carries with it the glad expectation that when those sins are forgiven, God welcomes His people back into His favor.

4. HOPE FOR A NEW HEART. Through Jeremiah, the Lord revealed that a whole new arrangement was needed between Him and His people to deal with their inability to keep the terms of Mosaic law. God promised a new covenant that would give His people new hearts capable of keeping their commitment to Him. The new covenant was initiated by Jesus through His death as a sacrifice for sins.

5. HOPE FOR A NEW RELATIONSHIP. Since the new covenant would be written on the hearts of the restored people, they would truly know the Lord. Teachers may not be needed to introduce new covenant people to God, but they are needed to help believers deepen their relationship with Him. New covenant people also know complete forgiveness of all their sins. Old covenant sacrifices for sin were temporary measures, but the new covenant sacrifice of Jesus for sins is an eternal solution (Heb. 10:11-14). To know God intimately and enjoy His complete forgiveness is the basis of a wonderful relationship.

FOR ADULTS	■ **TOPIC:** Creating a New Covenant

■ **QUESTIONS:** 1. What was God's long term goal with respect to the exiles? 2. What truth encouraged the exiles to call out to God in prayer? 3. How extensive is God's promise to His people of restoration? 4. What did the Lord promise to do for His people in the new covenant? 5. What is the basis for God establishing such a profoundly different covenant with His people?

■ **ILLUSTRATIONS:**

Hope for a Fresh Start. A teenaged girl wandered into the kitchen after dinner one Mother's Day and was horrified to see her mom at the sink starting to wash dishes. "Oh, Mom," she said, "you shouldn't have to do dishes on Mother's Day." Her mother was touched and took off her apron and handed it to her daughter.

"They'll keep till tomorrow," the girl remarked over her shoulder, never seeing the offered apron.

For a moment, this mother thought her daughter had made a fresh start as a responsible young woman. Too often our intentions to make fresh starts are about as meaningful as this teenager's concern for her mother. God, however, is committed to conforming our lives to the image of His Son. By the Lord's grace we can make genuinely fresh starts, even after the most discouraging failures.

Hope for a Transformed Heart. It was Stewardship Sunday at church and the richest man in town had volunteered to "share" his thoughts with the congregation about giving to the Lord. He bellowed, "I'm a millionaire, and I credit all my wealth to the rich blessing of God. It all started with a moment of faith. I had just earned my first dollar, and I went to church that evening with that dollar folded in my pocket. The speaker was a missionary who told about his work."

The boastful man continued, "I only had that dollar. I had to give it all to God's work or give nothing at all. So at that moment I decided to give my whole dollar to God. I believe God blessed that choice to give Him all I had, and that's why I'm a wealthy man today."

There was an awed silence in the church as the millionaire swaggered to his seat. As he settled in, an elderly woman in the same pew leaned over and whispered loudly, "I dare you to do it all again!"

That challenge was a good test of the millionaire's heart. If he had a new covenant heart, and God (not the elderly woman) wanted him to give all his money to Christian work, would he do it again? How would we respond?

Hope for a New Relationship. James Boswell, the famous eighteenth century biographer of Samuel Johnson, liked to tell a story about going fishing when he was a boy with his father. The day was fixed in his adult mind like a videotape he could play over and over. He remembered several pointers about fishing that he father had given him that day.

Years later a friend thought it would be interesting to find out what Boswell's father had thought of that day. The father's journals had become available for research, so the scholar in question found the pertinent journal ledger for Boswell's red letter fishing trip. The scholar read the following entry, written in the father's firm handwriting: "Gone fishing with my son today; a day wasted."

No new covenant children of God need ever worry that their heavenly Father will consider time with them "a day wasted." The new covenant is one based on relationship and forgiveness. Thus, a day with our heavenly Father deepens our relationship with Him and our appreciation of the forgiveness He offers.

FOR YOUTH

■ **TOPIC:** A New Agreement

■ **QUESTIONS:** 1. How did God reassure the exiles, who were languishing in captivity? 2. What would prompt the exiles to seek God with all their heart? 3. Why would God establish a new covenant with His chosen people? 4. What was necessary for God to do under the old covenant He had made with the Jews' ancestors? 5. Under the new covenant, who will know the Lord?

■ **ILLUSTRATIONS:**

Hope for a New Start. "Open up! This is the police!" voices shouted. For an instant Mike thought the television was on really loud downstairs. The next instant he was flushing crack cocaine down the toilet. When the police burst through his door, Mike was high but his apartment was clean.

"Stand up!" one officer ordered. "Get on the floor," another barked.

Slowed by the drugs, Mike just stared. An officer threw him to the floor. Another hit him in the face with his gun. Mike thought he was going to die. Then the thought crossed his mind—*no one would care*.

The police left with no drugs and no arrest. Mike sat shaking. It was time for a change. He walked downtown to the mission and asked a chaplain to lead him to Christ. Then Mike signed on for a drug rehabilitation program. It doesn't take long to detoxify, but it can take several years to break an addiction.

That's a true story from a major Midwestern city. At last check, Mike was clean. He hit bottom but dared hope for a new start in Jesus Christ.

Who's to Blame Here? The story is told of a man who went out in the forest to hunt a bear. He wanted to make a fur coat from the pelt. Hours into the woods, the man saw a huge brown bear ripping apart a dead tree and eating termites. The man raised his rifle and prepared to shoot the animal.

Just then the bear glanced up from its work and saw the hunter. "Hold on," the bear called out calmly. "Let's talk this over. Surely there must be some way to deal with this without resorting to gunplay. Come over here and sit with me on this rock and tell me what you really want."

The hunter was so surprised that he did what the bear said. "Well," the hunter began, "what I really want is a fur coat."

"That seems reasonable," the bear replied. "What I was after here was lunch. Let's see if we can hit on a plan that gets us both what we want."

Soon the hunter and the bear were deep in conversation. The hunter leaned his gun against a tree so that he could gesture freely. Not much later the bear waddled away deeply gratified. The animal had gotten a better lunch than termites, and it figured if one looked at the incident in the "correct" way, the hunter had a fur coat, too!

Can you blame the bear in this fictitious story? After all, the hunter was responsible for ending up as the animal's lunch. The moral is that we shouldn't blame parents or school or friends for our poor choices and our sins.

Hope for a New Heart. Four ladies were playing bridge in the day room of a retirement home when a white-haired gentleman shuffled in and looked around absently. Conversation at the card table stopped. Each of the women thought, "This must be a new resident!"

"Hello there. You must be new," chirped the first lady.

The man smiled and nodded. "I just moved in this morning."

"Where did you live before coming here?" chimed in the second lady.

"San Quentin," the man answered. "I was just released after 20 years."

"Oh, really," gasped the third lady. "What did you do?"

"I murdered my wife," the man flatly replied.

The fourth lady sat up suddenly and purred, "Oh, then you're single!"

Twenty years in San Quentin did not make this man a good boyfriend for the fourth lady unless God had changed the man's heart in jail. The Babylonian captivity of Jerusalem and Judah would mean little unless it led to a profound change in the hearts of the people in exile. If you have trusted in Jesus as your Savior, God wants to change your heart through the work of His Spirit in you.

CREATING A NEW HOPE

BACKGROUND SCRIPTURE: Ezekiel 37
DEVOTIONAL READING: Ezekiel 37:24-28

KEY VERSE: "I will put my spirit within you, and you shall live, and I will place you on your own soil; then you shall know that I, the LORD, have spoken and will act." Ezekiel 37:14.

KING JAMES VERSION

EZEKIEL 37:1 The hand of the LORD was upon me, and carried me out in the spirit of the LORD, and set me down in the midst of the valley which was full of bones, 2 And caused me to pass by them round about: and, behold, there were very many in the open valley; and, lo, they were very dry. 3 And he said unto me, Son of man, can these bones live? And I answered, O Lord GOD, thou knowest. 4 Again he said unto me, Prophesy upon these bones, and say unto them, O ye dry bones, hear the word of the LORD. 5 Thus saith the Lord GOD unto these bones; Behold, I will cause breath to enter into you, and ye shall live: 6 And I will lay sinews upon you, and will bring up flesh upon you, and cover you with skin, and put breath in you, and ye shall live; and ye shall know that I am the LORD. 7 So I prophesied as I was commanded: and as I prophesied, there was a noise, and behold a shaking, and the bones came together, bone to his bone. 8 And when I beheld, lo, the sinews and the flesh came up upon them, and the skin covered them above: but there was no breath in them. 9 Then said he unto me, Prophesy unto the wind, prophesy, son of man, and say to the wind, Thus saith the Lord GOD; Come from the four winds, O breath, and breathe upon these slain, that they may live. 10 So I prophesied as he commanded me, and the breath came into them, and they lived, and stood up upon their feet, an exceeding great army. 11 Then he said unto me, Son of man, these bones are the whole house of Israel: behold, they say, Our bones are dried, and our hope is lost: we are cut off for our parts. 12 Therefore prophesy and say unto them, Thus saith the Lord GOD; Behold, O my people, I will open your graves, and cause you to come up out of your graves, and bring you into the land of Israel. 13 And ye shall know that I am the LORD, when I have opened your graves, O my people, and brought you up out of your graves, 14 And shall put my spirit in you, and ye shall live, and I shall place you in your own land: then shall ye know that I the LORD have spoken it, and performed it, saith the LORD.

NEW REVISED STANDARD VERSION

EZEKIEL 37:1 The hand of the LORD came upon me, and he brought me out by the spirit of the LORD and set me down in the middle of a valley; it was full of bones. 2 He led me all around them; there were very many lying in the valley, and they were very dry. 3 He said to me, "Mortal, can these bones live?" I answered, "O Lord GOD, you know." 4 Then he said to me, "Prophesy to these bones, and say to them: O dry bones, hear the word of the LORD. 5 Thus says the Lord GOD to these bones: I will cause breath to enter you, and you shall live. 6 I will lay sinews on you, and will cause flesh to come upon you, and cover you with skin, and put breath in you, and you shall live; and you shall know that I am the LORD."

7 So I prophesied as I had been commanded; and as I prophesied, suddenly there was a noise, a rattling, and the bones came together, bone to its bone. 8 I looked, and there were sinews on them, and flesh had come upon them, and skin had covered them; but there was no breath in them. 9 Then he said to me, "Prophesy to the breath, prophesy, mortal, and say to the breath: Thus says the Lord GOD: Come from the four winds, O breath, and breathe upon these slain, that they may live." 10 I prophesied as he commanded me, and the breath came into them, and they lived, and stood on their feet, a vast multitude.

11 Then he said to me, "Mortal, these bones are the whole house of Israel. They say, 'Our bones are dried up, and our hope is lost; we are cut off completely.' 12 Therefore prophesy, and say to them, Thus says the Lord GOD: I am going to open your graves, and bring you up from your graves, O my people; and I will bring you back to the land of Israel. 13 And you shall know that I am the LORD, when I open your graves, and bring you up from your graves, O my people. 14 I will put my spirit within you, and you shall live, and I will place you on your own soil; then you shall know that I, the LORD, have spoken and will act, says the LORD.'"

Monday, October 18	Ezekiel 36:16-22	*God's Name Was Profaned*
Tuesday, October 19	Ezekiel 36:23-32	*God Will Give a New Heart*
Wednesday, October 20	Ezekiel 36:33-38	*The People Shall Know God*
Thursday, October 21	Ezekiel 37:1-6	*Ezekiel Sees the Dry Bones*
Friday, October 22	Ezekiel 37:7-14	*The Dry Bones Live and Breathe*
Saturday, October 23	Ezekiel 37:15-23	*Two Nations Shall Become One*
Sunday, October 24	Ezekiel 37:24-28	*God Will Bless the New Nation*

BACKGROUND

Little biographical information is known about Ezekiel, but there is almost uniform agreement among scholars that he was the sole author of the book bearing his name. The writer is identified as a *priest . . . [the] son of Buzi* (Ezek. 1:3). Ezekiel, meaning "God strengthens," is mentioned along with Jeremiah and Zechariah as the only prophet-priests in Scripture. All three prophesied either during the period of Israel's exile or in the period immediately after.

Ezekiel spent his early years in Jerusalem. As his writing shows, he was very familiar with the city and its temple. After he was taken captive to Babylon, the prophet lived in his own house in a village near Nippur on the Kebar (or Chebar) River. Apparently a person of some stature among the leaders of his people, Ezekiel's home became a central meeting place (8:1; 14:1; 20:1). We know that the prophet was married. But 10 years into the exile his wife died suddenly, perhaps of the plague (24:16-18). The couple was apparently childless.

The date of writing and span of Ezekiel's ministry can be established by the numerous dates given in the book (1:1-2; 8:1; 20:1; 24:1; 26:1; 29:1, 17; 30:20; 31:1; 32:1, 17; 33:21; 40:1). The prophecies of Ezekiel are presented in chronological order (two exceptions are found in 29:1, 17). The prophecies began with *the fifth year of the exile* (1:2), and concluded with *the twenty-fifth year of our exile* (40:1). Based on these chronological pegs, it is possible to deduce that Ezekiel's ministry began on July 31, 593 B.C., probably when he was 30 years old (1:1-2). His ministry ended around March 26, 571 (29:17). By this reckoning, Ezekiel prophesied for approximately 22 years, from age 30 to 52.

In Ezekiel, at least two major structural features are evident. The first of these are the chronological presentation of significant events, visions, and oracles. But this chronological arrangement is paralleled by a presentation of the material based on content. The central theme of chapters 1—24 is the judgment of Judah, while that of chapters 33—48 speak of Judah's future restoration. Between these two major focal points, in chapters 25—32, Ezekiel pronounced God's judgment upon other nations.

The content of Ezekiel's prophecies was delivered through a variety of literary means. These included symbolic actions, allegories or parables, and most importantly, visions. In broad outline, the first vision focused on the presence of God's glory in Babylon (1—3), the second on the judgment of Jerusalem (8—11), and the third (37) and fourth visions (40—48) on the future restoration of Judah.

NOTES ON THE PRINTED TEXT

Ezekiel 37 contains one of the book's major visions. Many experts think Ezekiel, already in exile in Babylonia, had this vision sometime after the fall of Jerusalem to the Babylonians in 586 B.C. God, through this vision, wanted to show in a powerful way what He would do to the exiled Jews. Although their nation was dead, He would raise it to life again. The valley of bones was transformed into a battlefield covered with God's mighty army.

Ezekiel related that the power of the Lord took control of him and transported him by the Spirit to the middle of a valley or plain that was *full of bones* (37:1), perhaps the same plain where he had seen his earlier visions. God had Ezekiel walk among the bones in every direction so that he might get the full impact of the horrifying scene (37:2). As 37:9 indicates, these were the remains of those who had been *slain* in battle.

The Lord asked whether the multitudes of bones could ever live again (37:3). Humanly speaking, the answer was no. Ezekiel, however, was wise enough to acknowledge that the *Lord God* could make the bones *live*, if He so desired. In their fallen state, the unsaved are a little like spiritual zombies. By every natural indication they appear to be alive. From God's perspective, however, there is no eternal life. A radical change must take place in order for things to be different. Such is only possible through faith in Christ.

The Lord told Ezekiel to announce to the bones certain truths He wanted them to *hear* (37:4). God promised He would cause breath to enter the bones so that they would *live* (37:5). He would give them tendons, flesh, skin, and breath—everything they needed to exist (37:6). In this way, it would be known that *the LORD,* Israel's covenant God, alone had the power to impart and sustain life.

The world might scoff at the idea of receiving new life in Christ. Believers know from God's Word, however, that it is a reality. In the new birth, the Spirit replaces the sinners' fallen human nature with a new one. Thus, their relationship with God is restored, their rebelliousness and unbelief are supplanted by obedience and dependence, and their hatred is exchanged for unconditional love.

Ezekiel declared all that God had *commanded* (37:7). As the prophet did, he heard a *rattling* noise, created by the *bones* as they *came together*. Bones joined bones, then *sinews* and *flesh* appeared where there had been none. Finally, *skin* covered the bodies of bones (37:8). There was one essential element missing, however. No breath of life was present in the recreated bodies. Therefore, the Lord told Ezekiel to make a declaration to the wind, or breath of life (37:9). As a sign of His power, God would command *breath* to come from every region of the globe and *breathe* new life into the dead bodies.

Ezekiel, as a faithful servant, declared what the Lord *commanded* (37:10); and as the prophet did so, the *breath* of life entered the bodies scattered all over the valley. Every last one of them stood up, enough to make a large army.

The exiled Jews were familiar with the destruction and death that the cruel Babylonians could inflict on an imposing army. The Jews also knew that the enemy could fill an entire valley with the bones of soldiers who had fallen in battle. Although it appeared as if there was no future for God's people, the Lord would demonstrate through Ezekiel's vision that there still was hope.

With both Judah and Israel desolate and the people exiled, the entire house of Israel was as politically and spiritually dead as the remains of the fallen soldiers (37:11). In particular, the exiles felt as if they had no *hope* for the future; but the sovereign Lord, through Ezekiel, declared that He would open up the graves of His people, raise them from their graves, and restore them to *the land of Israel* (37:12). The point of Ezekiel's vision was that in a future day God would bring His people back to the land He had promised to their ancestors. At that time the united people of Israel and Judah would no longer worship idols or do other things that made them unacceptable to God.

When God opened the graves of His people and raised them from these graves, they then would know that He was *the LORD* (37:13). In that future day of restoration, God promised to put His life-giving Spirit within His people and cause them to rest in their homeland (37:14). When God both spoke and acted on His promises, His people would *know* that He was Yahweh, *the LORD*. Because the people of Israel were spiritually dead, they needed to be restored to life, both individually and as a nation. As the people looked to the Lord in faith, they would receive and abide in the new life He offered through His Son.

We, as believers, also need to recognize that true life exists only in communion with Christ. In fact, abiding in the new life He offers is a matter of faith. We realize that it is important to do, and we depend on the Lord for the strength to abide in Him. We should not take abiding in Christ lightly. If we allow ourselves to drift away from Him, we will become spiritually barren. It is only as we draw close to the Lord and live in vital union with His Son that we will spiritually grow.

SUGGESTIONS TO TEACHERS

Even great church leaders become depressed and find it hard to maintain hope. The famous Joseph Butler, Dean of St. Paul's Cathedral and later Bishop of Durham, turned down his appointment to be the archbishop of Canterbury, explaining that there was no hope for the future of the Church or the Christian faith in England. Reformer John Calvin also had his dark times of despair, once crying, "The future appalls me," and questioning whether God could bring any good to what appeared a hopeless situation in his life. You and your students perhaps have also asked where God was during a period of suffering or distress. This lesson from Ezekiel provides a vision of the future with God.

1. SCENE OF HOPELESSNESS. In this gruesome vision, Ezekiel saw the aftermath of a great battle. Here the remains of the slain armies have been dismembered, picked apart by the jackals and vultures, and scattered over a wide valley. The scene depicts total hopelessness. In the light of the Holocaust, the Cambodian killing fields, the carnage in Bosnia and Rwanda, and the terrorist attacks on the World Trade Towers and the Pentagon, many persons only see hopelessness today. Can God do anything in the face of such devastation? Ask your students to talk about the basis for their hope in the future.

2. SPIRIT OF VITALITY. Ezekiel, ordered by the Lord to prophesy to the skeletons, discovered that God confers new life. And in the startling vision, Ezekiel watched as the bones were knit together with new sinew and finally constituted into a great army again. God is able, greater than death itself. This vision of the Lord bestowing life in "death valley" has been enacted in real life, time and time again, but especially when the Father raised up His Son after the crucifixion. Discuss what spiritual renewal means in practical terms for believers today.

3. SYMBOL OF RENEWAL. Ezekiel, of course, was using this image to tell the exiles that God had a new beginning in mind for them. This account also declares that during those times when we may feel all is lost, God offers us a bright future. Perhaps some in your class can share about times when the Lord gave them a renewed vision during a tough time in their lives.

4. STATEMENT OF ASSURANCE. Spend significant time on Ezekiel 37:26-27, and let the message there sink in. God still covenants with His people. Through Jesus Christ, our God assures us that His purposes are peaceful and He wants us to be in a relationship of peace with Him and with each other. When we live in such ways of caring and harmony, we become aware that He truly does dwell with us.

FOR ADULTS	■ **TOPIC:** Looking for Hope

■ **QUESTIONS:** 1. As Ezekiel looked around, what was the startling and memorable image he saw? 2. What would the people of Israel understand when they heard the name of the Lord? 3. What would the Lord command the wind, or breath of life, to do? 4. What did the Lord reveal about the bones? 5. What was the point of Ezekiel's prophecy?

■ **ILLUSTRATIONS:**

Saints in Circulation. For a short time in the seventeenth century, England was not a monarchy. A Puritan army overthrew and executed Charles I, and Oliver Cromwell became the Lord Protector of England. During his administration, the government ran low on silver for coins. Cromwell sent his agents to investigate a local cathedral to see whether there were any precious metals on the premises.

After scouring the cathedral, Cromwell's officers reported, "The only silver we could find is in the statues of the saints standing in the corners." To which straitlaced old Oliver Cromwell, Lord Protector of the British Isles, is reported to have said, "Good! We'll melt down the saints and put them in circulation!"

God told His people through the prophet Ezekiel that He would one day restore them to their homeland, renew their hearts and spirits, and bless them tremendously. All of this would bring great glory to His holy name. Perhaps more important than Israel's dwelling in the land of promise was their relationship with God. He had chosen them to be joined to Him in love and obedience. He wanted them to be devoted and faithful to Him. In the future day of restoration, the former exiles would truly be God's people, and the Lord would genuinely be their God. Such a relationship would be characterized by intimacy and joy, loyalty and integrity. Even today, the Lord intends that His new covenant people be active in His service—saints in circulation, if you will.

Art in the Blots. The great poet and educator of some years back, Sir Rabindranath Tagore, was also an artist of sufficient distinction to merit an exhibition of his drawings in London. He discovered his talent for art somewhat late in life in a rather unusual way.

Tagore was primarily a writer whose poetry and prose won a Nobel Prize for literature in 1913. He wrote of the everyday life of the people who lived close to India's sacred river, the Ganges.

One day while writing, Tagore spilled an ink blot on the sheet of paper near the bottom. His first impulse was to tear up the sheet and throw it away, but paper was not as plentiful in India then as it is in America today. The stain was too deep to erase and no chemical eradicator was available. There was only one thing left to do—change the blot from a blemish into a decoration.

It was in his efforts to do this that Rabindranath Tagore discovered a latent talent for art. Of course, there were many hours of hard and often frustrating work between the blot on the paper and the exhibition of his drawings in London.

We may see only "blots" in our lives—the ugly stains of our mistakes. But the Lord can take those stains and create something beautiful. After all, He is working in us the character qualities of His Son, Jesus.

You Can't Do the Job Alone. From his hospital bed a man wrote his insurance company the following letter: "Dear Sirs, I am writing this in response to your request for more information concerning my entry in box three of my insurance claim form where I printed 'Trying to do the job alone' as the cause of my accident.

"I was working on Saturday, the fifth of last month, repairing a chimney on the rooftop of a six-story building. Upon completing the job, I had approximately 185 pounds of bricks left over, which I needed to remove from the roof. I mention the weight of the bricks, because you will notice in box two of my claim form that my weight is 135 pounds. The difference in these two weights is important.

"Because I was trying to do the job alone, I tied a length of rope sufficient to reach the ground to a large wooden barrel, which I set on the edge of the roof, while I threaded the rope over a pulley mounted on the parapet. I went down to the ground and securely tied the rope to a hook on the side of the building.

"Then I ascended the six flights of stairs to the roof, pushed the barrel from the edge so that it hung from the pulley, and loaded all 185 pounds of bricks into the barrel. I descended the six flights of stairs to the ground and loosened the rope from the hook on the side of the building to lower the bricks to the ground. I call your attention again to box two where my weight is listed as 135 pounds.

"When I was hoisted off the ground by the weight of the rapidly descending barrel, I lost my composure and failed to let go of the rope. As I made a rapid ascent up the side of the building, in the vicinity of the third floor, I met the rapidly descending barrel of bricks and sustained the concussion noted on my insurance form.

"The barrel and I continued in opposite directions. It struck the ground about the time my fingers buried up to the first knuckle in the pulley at the top of the building. Fortunately, this time I kept my composure and did not let go of the rope.

"Unfortunately, the bottom broke out of the barrel, spilling the 185 pounds of bricks. The empty barrel weighed about 50 pounds, and if you refer once again to my weight in box two, you will understand why I suddenly began a rapid descent down the side of the building. In the vicinity of the third floor, I met the barrel ascending rapidly, which explains the two broken ankles.

"When I landed on the pile of bricks, fracturing five vertebrae, I regret to say that I once again lost my composure and let go of the rope. The barrel began a rapid descent down the side of the building, breaking both my legs on impact.

"And so you see, returning to box five on my insurance claim form, why I reported that I received my injuries, because I was 'Trying to do the job alone.'"

The life God wants for His spiritual children cannot be lived alone. The Holy Spirit makes our hearts and lives new so that we will desire to live for the Lord, and He provides the power to follow through on our motivation to obey God. If you try to live for the Lord in your own strength, you might end up with spiritual bumps and bruises.

■ **TOPIC:** Brought Back to Life

■ **QUESTIONS:** 1. What truths did God want Ezekiel to announce to the bones? 2. How would God make known that He alone had the power to impart and sustain life? 3. What set of events took place when Ezekiel declared all that God had commanded? 4. What did God say would happen when Ezekiel made a declaration to the wind, or breath of life? 5. What was the main point of Ezekiel's vision?

■ **ILLUSTRATIONS:**

Life from Death. Over the course of the Civil War, the armies of the North and South marched up and down the Shenandoah Valley. The battles were fierce, burials hasty. In one campaign a Union soldier wrote of discovering a human skull in which a field bird had laid its speckled eggs. From what was dead emerged new life.

Ezekiel also experienced new life emerging from the lifeless. God's creative power was at work around the prophet restoring vitality to fallen warriors. You, too, will experience God's restoration and energizing power within your life through the Holy Spirit. Ask Him to work in you today.

Revitalization. The Green Bay Packers played in the Super Bowl in 1968. After that year, the fans waited. Winning only occasionally, Green Bay, with its name of "Titletown, USA," became a joke. The city was seen by other NFL players as too isolated and too small. Coaches threatened to trade players to Green Bay unless they shaped up and performed better.

In 1992, however, the team once again came alive. Reggie White came to town wanting to go to the Super Bowl. The new quarterback, Brett Favre, told him that he could make a difference. The two took a liking to each other and found a common purpose. They succeeded. They missed the 1996 Super Bowl by losing the NFC Championship game to Dallas in the game's final moments. However, on January 26, 1997, the Green Bay Packers defeated the New England Patriots to win Super Bowl XXXI.

A dynamic and skilled individual can revitalize a team. If a human being can accomplish this kind of transformation, how much more can God revitalize a nation! The vision of the valley of the dry bones demonstrates that even the deadest force in history can rise up and, with power, praise God.

New Beginnings. Leo Durocher, manager of the old New York Giants, spoke with a weeping rookie named Willie Mays after Mays had gone 1 for 16 in his major-league debut. Durocher encouraged him, saying, "Tomorrow's another day, kid, and you're going to be playing center field tomorrow." Of course, Willie Mays went on to have more than a few excellent "tomorrows." But who knows how much influence Durocher had with just a few kind words at a critical time?

God has the same kind of vision for His people as Durocher had for Mays. So the Lord offers each of us another opportunity. He gives His people new beginnings and new starts.

CREATING A RENEWED TRUST

BACKGROUND SCRIPTURE: Psalm 73
DEVOTIONAL READING: Psalm 91:1-10

KEY VERSE: My flesh and my heart may fail, but God is
the strength of my heart and my portion forever. Psalm 73:26.

KING JAMES VERSION

PSALM 73:1 Truly God is good to Israel, even to such as are of a clean heart. 2 But as for me, my feet were almost gone; my steps had well nigh slipped. 3For I was envious at the foolish, when I saw the prosperity of the wicked. . . .

12 Behold, these are the ungodly, who prosper in the world; they increase in riches. 13 Verily I have cleansed my heart in vain, and washed my hands in innocency. . . .

16 When I thought to know this, it was too painful for me; 17 Until I went into the sanctuary of God; then understood I their end. 18 Surely thou didst set them in slippery places: thou castedst them down into destruction. . . .

21 Thus my heart was grieved, and I was pricked in my reins. 22 So foolish was I, and ignorant: I was as a beast before thee. 23 Nevertheless I am continually with thee: thou hast holden me by my right hand. 24 Thou shalt guide me with thy counsel, and afterward receive me to glory. 25 Whom have I in heaven but thee? and there is none upon earth that I desire beside thee. 26 My flesh and my heart faileth: but God is the strength of my heart, and my portion for ever.

NEW REVISED STANDARD VERSION

PSALM 73:1 Truly God is good to the upright,
  to those who are pure in heart.
2 But as for me, my feet had almost stumbled;
  my steps had nearly slipped.
3 For I was envious of the arrogant;
  I saw the prosperity of the wicked. . . .
12 Such are the wicked;
  always at ease, they increase in riches.
13 All in vain I have kept my heart clean
  and washed my hands in innocence. . . .
16 But when I thought how to understand this,
  it seemed to me a wearisome task,
17 until I went into the sanctuary of God;
  then I perceived their end.
18 Truly you set them in slippery places;
  you make them fall to ruin. . . .
21 When my soul was embittered,
  when I was pricked in heart,
22 I was stupid and ignorant;
  I was like a brute beast toward you.
23 Nevertheless I am continually with you;
  you hold my right hand.
24 You guide me with your counsel,
  and afterward you will receive me with honor.
25 Whom have I in heaven but you?
  And there is nothing on earth that I desire other
    than you.
26 My flesh and my heart may fail,
  but God is the strength of my heart and my portion
    forever.

9

HOME BIBLE READINGS

BACKGROUND

Muslims claim that the Koran was delivered by Allah to Muhammad in its entirety exactly as it reads in Arabic today. While the Bible—as God's Word—is fully inspired, its writings were set down by people over a long period of time. The Old Testament, for example, is a collection of many kinds of literature written in many different places and periods of history.

The Bible's literary pieces reflect the various situations in which God's people found themselves. Scholars point to at least three kinds of writings in our Old Testament, showing three distinct types of writers.

One is the priestly writings. These show the approach of those engaged in the impressive ceremonies at the Jerusalem temple. The priests found worship to be the most significant expression of doing God's will.

A second form is the prophetic. This type of literature presents the oracles or sermons of the brave spokespersons for God who dared to call for repentance in Israel. The prophets' writings showed that they were more concerned with justice than with observing the niceties of ritual.

The third genre of writings in the Old Testament is called "wisdom literature." By "wisdom" we mean more than mere intellectual knowledge. Rather, wisdom in the Scriptures meant ordering one's personal life so that the Lord would be known, honored, and served. Some of the Psalms, as well as the books of Proverbs, Job, and Ecclesiastes, are known as Wisdom Literature.

Consider Psalm 73. It describes how a person wise in the ways of God will see the hand of the Lord, even in the face of suffering and adversity. The wise person will not give up on God or quit on life because he or she knows that the Lord remains supreme. The psalms were to be repeated, and Psalm 73, like each of the 150 in our collection of Psalms, was used as a means of affirming God's goodness.

NOTES ON THE PRINTED TEXT

The best-known author of psalms was David. More psalms—nearly half of the book—are attributed to David than to any other author. Furthermore, historians recorded that David not only was the *favorite of the Strong One of Israel* (2 Sam. 23:1, or as the NIV puts it, "Israel's singer of songs"), but also that he organized the sanctuary's music program (1 Chron. 15:3-28). Of the

Psalter's several authors, only David is represented in each of the book's major divisions.

With respect to Psalm 73, Asaph is said to be its author. The Bible mentions an Asaph who was the son of Berrachiah (1 Chron. 6:39; 15:17) and one of the three leaders of music in David's organization of the tabernacle service (16:4-5). Asaph was appointed to sound the cymbals in the temple choir and was a composer of sacred lyrics. This Asaph is credited with writing Psalms 50 and 73—83.

At the time King Hezekiah restored worship in the temple, he ordered the Levite choirs to sing the songs of David and Asaph (2 Chron. 29:30). It seems that Asaph's descendants were involved in the temple choir and carried on the tradition of his musical ministry (2 Chron. 35:15; Ezra 3:10).

Asaph began Psalm 73 by noting God's goodness to the nation of Israel (73:1). The Lord was especially kind to those who maintained *pure* motives. Asaph came to this conclusion after wrestling with the problem of evil. The psalmist described his experience as one in which he almost slipped and fell in his walk of faith (73:2). The reason is that he grew envious of the proud and foolish person who seemed to prosper despite his or her life of wickedness (73:3).

Envy is the unhealthy desire to have something that someone else has. The danger of envy is that it can harm our relationships with others; also, it is difficult for us to be involved in an open, caring relationship with someone while secretly resenting that person's successes. By its very nature, envy promotes self-pity and blinds us to the good things in our lives.

The hidden dangers of envy are numerous. It can harm relationships with others; also, it's difficult to be involved in an open, caring relationship with someone while secretly resenting that person's successes. And envy can harm our view of ourselves. By its very nature, envy promotes self-pity and blinds us to the good things in our lives.

As Asaph observed how the wicked lived, he was vexed at how they enjoyed increasing prosperity and *ease* (73:12). The psalmist became so embittered that he wondered whether it was in vain that he kept his heart pure and maintained a virtuous lifestyle (73:13). The more Asaph tried to fathom how it was possible for the wicked to prosper, the more onerous the task seemed (73:16).

As we reflect on Asaph's experience, we see that envy negatively affects our relationship with God. Trusting Him for our daily bread is not consistent with deciding that He failed by giving something to another person what He should have given to us.

According to 73:17, Asaph's attitude began to change when he went into the *sanctuary of God* for a time of worship and prayer. As the psalmist considered the *end* of the wicked, he realized that God placed them on a slippery path whose end was gloomy (73:18). In fact, their downfall was certain.

Eventually Asaph realized how embittered he had become in his heart and soul due to the prosperity of the wicked (73:21). He was unreasonable in his thinking and lacking in insight in his understanding. Before God, Asaph was as senseless as *brute beast* (73:22).

Throughout this ordeal, Asaph continually remained with God, whom Asaph metaphorically described as holding his *right hand* (73:23). The psalmist was assured that the Lord would keep on guiding him with His wise *counsel* (73:24). Asaph was also confident of a future time when God would vindicate his faith by bringing the wicked to justice. Beyond that, the psalmist looked forward to being taken into the Lord's glory.

Asaph regarded God as the sole object of his desire and worship, whether it was *in heaven* or *on earth* (73:25). Although at times the psalmist's mind and body might grow weak, he looked to God for stability and *strength* (73:26).

Asaph not only unveiled his own personal struggle through this poignant psalm; he also dramatically described the type of internal conflicts that have plagued believers throughout history. Through Asaph's struggle, we can more fully appreciate the deceptive power and danger of allowing envy a foothold in our lives.

Asaph, instead of denying his sinful attitude, confessed. Then—instead of demanding that God correct the unfair situation—the psalmist asked that God correct his short-sighted attitude. Such an approach will also allow us to appreciate the blessings that God gives each of us every day.

SUGGESTIONS TO TEACHERS

People who base their faith on the Bible's message gather and sing together. This contrasts with most other religions. Jews and Christians participate in congregational singing as an integral part of their worship. And for three millennia, the psalms have been the foundational form of congregational music. This week's lesson takes up this important portion of the Old Testament.

Start by reminding your students that the psalms were originally sung or chanted. As the hymnbook of the Bible, these songs expressed every kind of human emotion, from anger and despair to thanks and praise. Many are part of what is known as "wisdom literature." Psalm 73 shows a believer singing his faith in God, despite life's apparent undeserved suffering.

You may want to open or close your class session by singing the paraphrase of Psalm 73 known as "In Sweet Communion, Lord, with Thee," which appears in many church hymnals. Or you could read the verses aloud together, then cover these points about the psalmist:

1. AFFIRMS GOD'S GOODNESS. The psalmist opened his conversation with us and the Lord by affirming that God is good to those who live uprightly. The bedrock belief of Old Testament writers was a trust in the goodness of God.

2. ADMITS PERSONAL TESTING. The psalmist angrily noted that proud and arrogant persons seem successful and powerful while showing no respect toward the Lord. The writer asked why he should live responsibly before God, since there was no apparent reward for goodness. With a surprising frankness, the psalmist bitterly complained to God. The psalms offer a healthy openness of dialogue between a person and God. There's no pretending or hiding, just a blunt acknowledgment of anger and a frank questioning of God's ways. Here is the way of honest prayer. Ask your students: When has your belief in God's goodness been most severely challenged? How did you cope?

3. APPROPRIATES GOD'S PERSPECTIVE. Here is where worship is vital. While standing before the Lord in worship, the psalmist began to understand God's version of reality. The psalmist finally realized that God has the last say in life and will allow the rebellious and insolent people to *fall into ruin* (73:18). Impress upon your students the need for regular worship.

4. ANNOUNCES GOD'S SUFFICIENCY. As the song progresses, the crucial point becomes clear: God's presence is what we need most. Have your class members consider 73:25 together. God is sufficient for whatever we may suffer. If we have an awareness of the Lord, what more do we need?

5. ACKNOWLEDGES PURPOSE TO FAITH. The psalmist concluded his hymn-meditation by stating the reason for trusting in God: that he may tell of all of God's works. What a tremendous summary of faith's results!

FOR ADULTS	■ **TOPIC:** Creating a Renewed Trust

■ **QUESTIONS:** 1. What was the nature of the crisis of faith Asaph was experiencing? 2. What aspect of the wicked did the psalmist envy? 3. Why did Asaph lament having kept his heart cleansed and his hands washed? 4. What did Asaph feel was the outcome of his decision to live uprightly? 5. What brought about a change in the perspective of Asaph?

■ **ILLUSTRATIONS:**

Empty Hymns. In England, state-supported schools open each day with hymns and prayers. However, the most popular hymn sung by schools as part of their legally required daily act of worship mentions neither God nor Christ. Called *One More Step,* it is published by the BBC in *Come and Praise,* a book widely used in primary schools. Here are the lyrics:

> One more step along the world I go,
> One more step along the world I go,
> From the old things to the new
> Keep me traveling along the world with you.

The chorus is:

> And it's from the old I travel to the new,
> Keep me traveling along with you.

Similarly devoid of distinctly Christian content is *When I Needed a Neighbour*—written by a Mr. Carter—

When I needed a neighbour, were you there, were you there?
When I needed a neighbour, were you there?

The chorus is:
And the creed and the colour and the name won't matter, were you there?

Richard Wilkins, the general secretary of the Association of Christian Teachers, said: "Such theologically empty ditties don't do anyone any good. If the children who sing them think they're taking part in an act of Christian worship, they've been badly misled."

Arts in God's Service. "That it is good and God-pleasing to sing hymns is, I think, known to every Christian; for everyone is aware not only of the example of the prophets and kings in the Old Testament who praised God with song and sound, with poetry and psaltery, but also of the common and ancient custom of the Christian Church to sing Psalms. St. Paul himself instituted this in 1 Corinthians 14:15 and exhorted the Colossians (3:16) to sing spiritual songs and psalms heartily unto the Lord so that God's Word and Christian teaching might be instilled and implanted in many ways.

"Therefore, I, too, in order to make a start and to give an incentive to those who can do better, have with the help of others compiled several hymns, so that the holy gospel which now by the grace of God has risen anew, may be noised and spread abroad.

"Like Moses in his song (Exodus 15:2), we may now boast that Christ is our praise and song and say with St. Paul, in 1 Corinthians 2:2, that we should know nothing to sing or say, save Jesus Christ. . . .

"Nor am I of the opinion that the gospel should destroy and blight all the arts, as some of the pseudo-religious claim. But I would like to see all the arts, especially music, used in the service of God, who gave and made them."—Martin Luther, in the Preface to *The Wittenberg Hymnal,* 1524.

Face the Music. How did the expression "face the music" originate? In the 17th century, during the Cromwell era in England, church organs were considered profane and thus destroyed. By the time of the Restoration, when the monarchy came back, no organs remained in churches. Therefore, other musical instruments were used. Galleries were provided for the instrumentalists. When the time came to sing psalms and hymns, the congregation was instructed to turn toward the gallery and to "face the music."

Today the expression has come to denote a confrontation. Three centuries ago, though, "face the music" held a note of hope and joy. For Christians, when times of suffering or questioning come, celebrating God's constant care and guidance through worship—facing the music in the original sense—is the best way to find strength.

<table>
<tr><td>FOR YOUTH</td><td>■ TOPIC: That's Not Fair!
■ QUESTIONS: 1. How did Asaph describe his struggle with the problem of evil?</td></tr>
</table>

■ **TOPIC:** That's Not Fair!

■ **QUESTIONS:** 1. How did Asaph describe his struggle with the problem of evil? 2. Why did Asaph wonder whether it was in vain that he kept his heart pure? 3. What happened when Asaph went into the temple of God for a time of worship and prayer? 4. What did Asaph conclude as he considered the end of the wicked? 5. What kind of future did Asaph look forward to?

■ **ILLUSTRATIONS:**

What's Your Philosophy? A 1999 study by UCLA and the American Council of Education compared the attitudes of 9 million college freshmen over 30 years. In 1967, 82 percent of entering students felt it was essential to develop a meaningful philosophy of life, and they made that their top goal. Now that objective ranks sixth, endorsed by only 42 percent of students.

In contrast, less than half of the 1967 incoming students said that making money was important to them. Now 74 percent have made that their top goal. Materialism and idealism have traded places. Money and wealth are the all-important objectives today.

Youth see and admire prosperity. While the psalmist saw the prosperity of others, he claimed that he desired nothing more than God's presence. Living an upright and pure life were sufficient for him.

Cynical Icon. Most children have heard or read the stories of Tom Sawyer and Huck Finn. They are classics by Mark Twain, a man who made the world laugh. During the early 1900s, he became one of the most prominent celebrities of his time, famous enough that he claimed he was the "most conspicuous person on the planet." Few realized, though, that his humor padded a moralizing motive. In later years, Twain took off the gloves and produced biting satire.

In one of his books, *The Mysterious Stranger,* Twain insisted that humans drop all religious illusions and depend only upon themselves, not God, to make a better world. His philosophical treatise, *What Is Man?* was considered so irreverent that his daughter, Jean, refused to even type it! In his autobiography Twain wrote in despair and bitterness that humans are of no consequence and achieve nothing. They are a foolish mistake. They leave no sign that they ever existed in this world and are thus forgotten.

Contrast Twain's belief with another writer named Asaph. The psalmist may have questioned God, but he came to a different conclusion about life. He rejoiced in God's presence and in a personal relationship with his Lord that would last beyond the grave.

Sang about Feelings. The Beatles were considered the greatest rock band the world has seen. Their uniqueness and brilliance still shines after more than 40 years. The reason is that their music continues to capture young people's feelings.

The band of 1964 that played *I Want to Hold Your Hand* began to come of age several years later, singing about the *Taxman* or urging young people to *Think for Yourself.* The gloominess of youth was also captured in *Norwegian Wood* and *In My Life.* Individuality emerged, and by 1969 it was obvious who wrote what songs and that serious tensions existed within the band. Drugs and religious gurus could not heal the conflict.

Long before the Beatles, young people were expressing their deepest feelings through music and poetry. The psalmist shared his feelings in poetry and penned words that expressed his hope in God. They are words that have endured and stood the test of time. Have you found them true in your own life?

A NEW APPROACH

BACKGROUND SCRIPTURE: Matthew 5
DEVOTIONAL READING: Matthew 5:1-12

KEY VERSE: "Do not think that I have come to abolish the law or
the prophets; I have come not to abolish but to fulfill." Matthew 5:17.

KING JAMES VERSION

MATTHEW 5:17 Think not that I am come to destroy the law, or the prophets: I am not come to destroy, but to fulfil. 18 For verily I say unto you, Till heaven and earth pass, one jot or one tittle shall in no wise pass from the law, till all be fulfilled. . . .

21 Ye have heard that it was said by them of old time, Thou shalt not kill; and whosoever shall kill shall be in danger of the judgment: 22 But I say unto you, That whosoever is angry with his brother without a cause shall be in danger of the judgment: and whosoever shall say to his brother, Raca, shall be in danger of the council: but whosoever shall say, Thou fool, shall be in danger of hell fire. . . .

27 Ye have heard that it was said by them of old time, Thou shalt not commit adultery: 28 But I say unto you, That whosoever looketh on a woman to lust after her hath committed adultery with her already in his heart. . . .

31 It hath been said, Whosoever shall put away his wife, let him give her a writing of divorcement: 32 But I say unto you, That whosoever shall put away his wife, saving for the cause of fornication, causeth her to commit adultery: and whosoever shall marry her that is divorced committeth adultery.

33 Again, ye have heard that it hath been said by them of old time, Thou shalt not forswear thyself, but shalt perform unto the Lord thine oaths: 34 But I say unto you, Swear not at all; neither by heaven; for it is God's throne: 35 Nor by the earth; for it is his footstool: neither by Jerusalem; for it is the city of the great King. . . .

38 Ye have heard that it hath been said, An eye for an eye, and a tooth for a tooth: 39 But I say unto you, That ye resist not evil: but whosoever shall smite thee on thy right cheek, turn to him the other also. . . .

43 Ye have heard that it hath been said, Thou shalt love thy neighbour, and hate thine enemy. 44 But I say unto you, Love your enemies, bless them that curse you, do good to them that hate you, and pray for them which despitefully use you, and persecute you.

NEW REVISED STANDARD VERSION

MATTHEW 5:17 "Do not think that I have come to abolish the law or the prophets; I have come not to abolish but to fulfill. 18 For truly I tell you, until heaven and earth pass away, not one letter, not one stroke of a letter, will pass from the law until all is accomplished. . . .

21 "You have heard that it was said to those of ancient times, 'You shall not murder'; and 'whoever murders shall be liable to judgment.' 22 But I say to you that if you are angry with a brother or sister, you will be liable to judgment; and if you insult a brother or sister, you will be liable to the council; and if you say, 'You fool,' you will be liable to the hell of fire. . . .

27 "You have heard that it was said, 'You shall not commit adultery.' 28 But I say to you that everyone who looks at a woman with lust has already committed adultery with her in his heart. . . .

31 "It was also said, 'Whoever divorces his wife, let him give her a certificate of divorce.' 32 But I say to you that anyone who divorces his wife, except on the ground of unchastity, causes her to commit adultery; and whoever marries a divorced woman commits adultery.

33 "Again, you have heard that it was said to those of ancient times, 'You shall not swear falsely, but carry out the vows you have made to the Lord.' 34 But I say to you, Do not swear at all, either by heaven, for it is the throne of God, 35 or by the earth, for it is his footstool, or by Jerusalem, for it is the city of the great King. . . .

38 "You have heard that it was said, 'An eye for an eye and a tooth for a tooth.' 39 But I say to you, Do not resist an evildoer. But if anyone strikes you on the right cheek, turn the other also; . . .

43 "You have heard that it was said, 'You shall love your neighbor and hate your enemy.' 44 But I say to you, Love your enemies and pray for those who persecute you."

Monday, November 1	Matthew 5:1-12	*Jesus Teaches about Blessings*
Tuesday, November 2	Matthew 5:13-20	*We Are to Obey God's Will*
Wednesday, November 3	Matthew 5:21-26	*A Teaching about Anger*
Thursday, November 4	Matthew 5:27-32	*Teachings about Adultery and Divorce*
Friday, November 5	Matthew 5:33-37	*A Teaching about Taking Oaths*
Saturday, November 6	Matthew 5:38-42	*A Teaching about Nonviolent Resistance*
Sunday, November 7	Matthew 5:43-48	*A Teaching about Loving Enemies*

BACKGROUND

Jesus is King! The Gospel of Matthew introduces us to the King of all the earth, showing us His humble beginnings, proclaiming to us His teachings, and convincing us with His miracles. Of course, the Old Testament prophets had foretold that a Messiah, or "anointed one," would come to deliver the people of Israel.

As the Jews languished under the strict rule of the Roman Empire, they longed for the appearance of this promised redeemer. Then during the reign of Herod the Great, God fulfilled His Word by sending His Son, Jesus Christ, to be born on earth as a human being. The first verse of Matthew announces this great event: *An account of the genealogy of Jesus the Messiah, the son of David, the son of Abraham.*

Many Jews thought the prophesied Messiah would deliver them from their Roman overlords and set up a glorious kingdom in a strictly political sense. In reality, Jesus came to experience rejection and death as a suffering Servant. By dying on the cross, this teacher from Nazareth not only brought spiritual deliverance to His followers, but altered the course of world history as well.

Readers of this beautiful Gospel discover how Jesus chose the Twelve, why He was rejected by the religious leaders, and what led to His crucifixion. The book powerfully demonstrates that Jesus' death, although tragic, is the means by which God provides salvation for the whole world.

Matthew wrote his Gospel to address the needs of the early Christian church members, especially those from a Jewish background. He wanted to establish that Jesus truly was the promised Messiah of the Hebrew Scriptures (for examples, see Matt. 16:15-16; 27:37). Since Matthew wanted to prove that Jesus fulfilled all the Old Testament predictions about the Messiah, he referred at least 12 times to the ancient prophecies (key examples: 1:22-23; 21:4-5; 26:55-56). In addition, Matthew quoted or alluded to the Old Testament Scriptures more than 90 times.

NOTES ON THE PRINTED TEXT

The Gospel of Matthew places a special emphasis on the teaching of Jesus, and it does so in a way that is unique. One of the interesting features of Matthew's writing is that he grouped Jesus' teaching into five distinct sections. The Sermon on the Mount (chapters 5—7) is the first of these sections. The second section appears in chapter 10, in which Jesus instructed His disciples about their mission of spreading the Gospel. The third section appears in chapter 13, in which Jesus told parables about the kingdom of God. The fourth section appears in chapter 18, in which Jesus taught about life in the Christian community. And the fifth section appears in chapters 23—25, in which Jesus taught about His second coming and judgment.

A straightforward reading of Matthew 4:1-25 gives the impression that Jesus taught the Sermon on the Mount during the first year of His public ministry. Likewise, a straightforward reading of 5:1—7:29 suggests that Jesus delivered His sermon at one time in one location.

Despite this impression, the relation between the Sermon on the Mount recorded in Matthew and the Sermon on the Plain recorded in Luke 6:17-49 remains unclear. Only a portion of the first appears in the second, and 34 of the verses in Matthew's sermon occur in different contexts in Luke. Apparently Jesus repeated some of His weightier sayings in different forms, with varied application, to meet the need of the situation.

Observations such as these have led some to argue that the Sermon on the Mount is a compilation of various teachings that were given on different occasions in several places. According to this view, Luke presented an abbreviated version of the longer sermon recorded in Matthew. Matthew either took a single sermon and expanded it with other relevant teachings of Christ, or he took numerous teachings of Jesus and wove them into a coherent, thematically related unit.

Those who say the Sermon on the Mount and the Sermon on the Plain are the same argue that the differences between the two discourses can be accounted for or harmonized. It is also maintained that the similarity of the beginnings, endings, and subject matter strengthens the impression that the two passages represent the same discourse.

Despite the differences of opinion, there are some broad conclusions that can be drawn. First, an examination of Matthew 5:1—7:29 reveals that it is not a mere patchwork of isolated and unrelated sayings. Rather it reads as a seamless whole. Thus, one should study the passage as a complete literary unit. Second, one should consider the sermon to be an accurate and reliable account of what Jesus taught. This remains true regardless of whether this discourse was given at one time or represents material He repeated numerous times under a variety of circumstances.

Jesus' discourse is called the Sermon on the Mount because He delivered this series of messages on one of the gently sloping hillsides at the northwest corner of the Sea of Galilee, probably not far from Capernaum. As Jesus' popularity soared, huge crowds began to follow Him (5:1-2). His disciples could easily have been tempted to feel proud, prestigious, and possessive. Perhaps that's why Jesus warned them about the challenges they faced. He told them that instead of expecting fame and fortune, they should expect to mourn, face hunger, and be persecuted. And though their reward may not come in this life, Jesus assured them that they would reap rich heavenly rewards for embodying certain spiritual qualities (5:3-12).

Tragically, some misunderstood the reason for Jesus' coming to earth. They incorrectly assumed that His intent was to abolish the law of Moses and the writings of the prophets (Matt. 5:17). The Savior, however, declared that His goal was to *fulfill* the Hebrew Scriptures. Jesus, in fact, noted in 5:18 that until *heaven and earth* ceased to exist, not the smallest *letter* or *stroke* in a Hebrew character would vanish *from the law* until God had achieved what He had foreordained.

It was Jesus' intent to clarify the true meaning and proper application of the law. For instance, He cited the ancient biblical teaching against murdering and that murders must be brought to trial (5:21). Christ, however, assured His followers that if they were angry against someone without a cause, they were worthy of *judgment* (5:22). Another example, noted by Jesus, involved calling someone *"You fool."* He explained that this infraction was worthy to be tried by the Jewish supreme court of His day. Moreover, those who called other people worthless fools were liable to hell's eternal *fire*.

In 5:27, Jesus cited the ancient biblical teaching against committing *adultery*. Then, in 5:28, He declared that if a man gazed at a woman with lustful intentions, he had *already committed adultery with her in his heart*. Christ wanted virtue, not vice, to undergird the lives of His followers.

In 5:31, Jesus mentioned Deuteronomy 24:1-4, which authorized a husband to issue a certificate of divorce to his wife. Jesus brought corrective and needed balance to the topic by stating that divorce for any reason other than sexual immorality caused the rejected spouse to commit adultery. Likewise marriage to an improperly divorced person was an act of *adultery* (Matt. 5:32).

In 5:33, Christ mentioned the ancient teaching that it was important to heed, rather than violate, one's sworn pledge to *the Lord*. Tragically the religious leaders had brought hypocrisy and abuse to oath taking. To eliminate these wrongs, Jesus declared that no oath should be made whatsoever (5:34). His preference was to abolish oaths, especially if these became occasions for lying and deceiving, rather than encouraging truthfulness.

Christ declared that *heaven*, the *throne* room of God, that *earth*, the *footstool* of His feet (see Isa. 66:1), and that Jerusalem, the city of the great King (see Ps. 48:2), were not to be cited as witnesses to any type of pledge, especially false ones. When a person appealed to any of these objects while making an oath, these became as binding as if the individual had invoked the name of the Lord. Even oaths made against a person's head were to be avoided, for no person but God could control the lightness or the darkness of one's *hair* (Matt. 5:35-36).

Jesus' comment about *"an eye for an eye and a tooth for a tooth"* (5:38) actually referred to the law regarding retaliation. God wanted the punishment to fit the crime. Therefore, civil authorities were supposed to set limits, according to the crime committed, as to what punishments they could impose on their citizens.

Sadly, many used this law as a guideline for what they should do in all their relationships. Jesus wanted to correct this problem and go even further by urging His followers not to seek revenge, but instead to put others first and be generous beyond expectations. For instance, believers who were slapped on the right cheek were told to also offer the other *cheek* (5:39).

Some religious leaders had rationalized away Leviticus 19:18 by defining *neighbor* narrowly. Others even added the stipulation to hate one's enemies. Jesus, however, called His followers to love, bless, and pray for their enemy as well as their *neighbor* (Matt. 5:43-44).

SUGGESTIONS TO TEACHERS

Jesus' command for us to *"be perfect"* (Matt. 5:48) is both a directive and a reminder. We are told to have the same kind of love for our fellow human beings that is described in 5:38-47. *"Be perfect"* is also a reminder that God loves all people without partiality. Of course, we'll never be perfect in the sense that God is, but we should strive to love everyone as He does. Also, obedience to such a command requires the transforming work of the Holy Spirit. We cannot love others as Jesus does apart from the grace of God.

1. TO OBEY IS TO HAVE THE RIGHT ATTITUDE. First Samuel 15:22-23 records the prophet Samuel's words to Saul after the king had chosen to offer ritual sacrifices instead of obeying a direct command from the Lord: *"Has the LORD as great delight in burnt offerings and sacrifices, as in obeying the voice of the LORD? Surely, to obey is better than sacrifice, and to heed than the fat of rams. For rebellion is no less a sin than divination, and stubbornness is like iniquity and idolatry."* Jesus longs for our loving obedience far more than our absent-minded religious formalities and ceremonies. It's not so much that these activities are unimportant as it is that we have the proper reasons and attitudes for performing them.

2. TO OBEY IS TO HELP OTHERS OBEY. God wants us to go beyond telling and encouraging others to obey Him. He wants us to help others obey Him by obeying Him ourselves and by being an example of obedience.

3. TO OBEY IS TO LOVE GOD. Real obedience cannot happen apart from our love for God. In fact, our obedience demonstrates our love for Him. It's no wonder that Jesus said, *"They who have my commandments and keep them are those who love me; and those who love me will be loved by my Father, and I will love them and reveal myself to them"* (John 14:21).

4. TO OBEY IS TO BE GOD-CENTERED. The religious leaders of Jesus' day obeyed God outwardly, but they did so because it would enhance their status among the people. Their obedience was self-centered. Jesus said our obedience should be God-centered, based on our reverence for Him. We're to follow His will, not seek the approval of those who may be watching us.

5. TO OBEY IS TO LIVE BY THE PRINCIPLES BEHIND THE LAW. Jesus' teaching went beyond a ritualistic obedience to the law. He taught that we should obey the "spirit of the law," namely, the principles behind the law and the purpose for which God gave the law.

6. TO OBEY IS TO TRUST GOD. We are not left to our own devices when it comes to obeying God. The Lord, through His Spirit, helps us to obey Him. We cannot obey by ourselves; rather, our obedience comes from God working in us.

FOR ADULTS

■ TOPIC: Living by New Rules

■ QUESTIONS: 1. What was Jesus' purpose with respect to the law and prophets? 2. In what ways did Jesus fulfill the law? 3. How did Jesus' teaching on anger differ from that of the religious leaders of His day? 4. How did Jesus go far beyond the common understanding of the commandment concerning adultery? 5. What did God originally intend for the law of retaliation?

■ ILLUSTRATIONS:

Love Your Enemies. On the morning of November 8, 1987, Gordon Wilson took his daughter Marie to a parade in the town of Enniskillen, Northern Ireland. As Wilson and his 20-year-old daughter stood beside a brick wall waiting for English soldiers and police to come marching by, a bomb planted by terrorists exploded from behind, and the brick wall tumbled down on them.

The blast instantly killed six people and pinned Gordon and Marie beneath several feet of bricks. Gordon's arm and shoulder were severely injured. Unable to move, he felt someone take hold of his hand. It was Marie. "Is that you, Dad?" she asked. "Yes, Marie," Gordon answered. Though her voice was belabored, he could hear her over the screams of several people. "Are you all right?" Gordon asked her. "Yes," she said.

As Gordon felt his daughter's grip beginning to loosen, again and again he asked if she was all right. Each time she said yes. Finally, Marie said, "Daddy, I love you very much." Those were her last words. Four hours later she died in the hospital of severe spinal and brain injuries.

Later that evening, a British Broadcasting Company reporter requested permission to interview Gordon. After Gordon described what had happened, the reporter asked, "How do you feel about the guys who planted the bomb?" "I bear them no ill will," Gordon replied. "I bear them no grudge. Bitter talk is not going to bring Marie back to life. I shall pray tonight and every night that God will forgive them."

Many asked Gordon, who later became a senator in the Republic of Ireland, how he could say such a thing, how he could forgive such a horrendous act. Gordon explained, "I was hurt. I had just lost my daughter. But I wasn't angry. Marie's last words to me—words of love—had put me on a plane of love. I received God's grace, through the strength of His love for me, to forgive." And for years after this tragedy, Gordon continued to work for peace in Northern Ireland.

Pray for Them Who Despitefully Use You. A woman called the pastor's office, asking the minister to come to her home to pray for her ill husband. The pastor didn't recognize her voice, so he asked her name.

"This is Orlean Weathers," she said. "Mrs. Weathers," the pastor said, "I'm sorry, but I don't believe I know you. Have you attended our church?" "Oh, no," she said. "I attend Reverend Morgan's church over on the other side of town." "Well," the pastor responded, "don't you think you ought to call Reverend Morgan to come and pray with your husband?" "No, sir. I couldn't do that," she said. "What my husband has is contagious."

But I Say unto You. In 1777, George Washington's army faced a winter of cold and bleak inactivity on a small mountain near Morristown, New Jersey. The general sensed the restlessness of his men, and so he ordered a stockade built around the encampment immediately. He also doubled the perimeter guard. Work started right away and rumors abounded about how near the enemy might be and whether the stockade would be finished on time.

In the spring, even though the fortifications were not finished, Washington ordered a move. Thinking they were about to be overrun by the enemy, the soldiers did a rapid deployment. Leaving the unfinished fortification, they marched—not to defeat—but to victory over nearby English forces. It was only history that gave the unfinished fort its name: Fort Nonsense.

God, in His inscrutable wisdom, sometimes sends us to do tasks that we don't fully understand, that don't make a lot of earthly sense. But He asks us to work at them, not for the immediate necessity of their completion, but for the good of our character and the good of our souls, especially as He leads us on to higher things.

FOR YOUTH

■ TOPIC: It's about Attitude and Actions

■ QUESTIONS: 1. What did Jesus underscore through His work on the cross? 2. What were Jesus' followers worthy of if they became angry against someone without a cause? 3. How did Jesus stress that He wanted virtue, not vice, to undergird our lives? 4. How had some religious leaders rationalized away Leviticus 19:18? 5. How can we become reflectors of God's virtue and holiness?

■ ILLUSTRATIONS:

Pray for Them Who Persecute You. Chris Carrier of Coral Gables, Florida, was abducted when he was 10 years old. His kidnappers, angry with the boy's family, burned him with cigarettes, stabbed him numerous times with an ice pick, shot him in the head, and left him to die in the Everglades. Remarkably, the boy survived, though he lost sight in one eye. No one was ever arrested.

Finally, 22 years later, a man confessed to the crime. Chris, by then a youth minister at a nearby church, went to see him. He found the man, a 77-year-old ex-convict, frail and blind, living in a Miami Beach nursing home. Chris began visiting often, reading to the ex-convict from the Bible and praying with him. The ministry of Chris opened the door for the man to make a profession of faith in Jesus Christ.

No arrest was forthcoming, for the statute of limitations on the crime was long past. And the statute of limitations had also run out on Chris's hatred and bitterness. He said, "While many people can't understand how I could forgive my kidnapper, from my point of view I couldn't *not* forgive him. If I'd chosen to hate him all these years, or spent my life looking for revenge, then I wouldn't be the man I am today, the man my wife and children love, the man God has helped me to be."

I studied intently the photograph, in *Leadership Journal*, of Chris holding his kidnapper's hand and praying with him as he lay in a nursing home bed. When I think about the absence of hatred, when I think about the presence of forgiveness, and when I think about Jesus' command to love your enemies, I think about that picture.

I'm Diving In! I recently ran across the anonymous quote, "We're not in this to test the waters; we are in this to make waves." What an excellent idea for the believer who wants to fulfill Christ's call to impact this world. We're not called to be like everybody else. We're not called to go with the flow. We are called to be different, to act different, and to talk different. We shouldn't resign ourselves to simply testing the waters. We should do what Steven Curtis Chapman's hit song of 1999 says:

I'm diving in, I'm going deep in over my head, I want to be
Caught in the rush, lost in the flow, in over my head, I want to go
The river's deep, the river's wide, the river's water is alive
So sink or swim, I'm diving in!

Be Careful! One day Francis of Assisi and Brother Leo were out walking together. Suddenly Brother Leo called out, "Brother Francis!"

"Yes, I am Brother Francis," came the reply.

"Be careful, Brother Francis! People are saying remarkable things about you! Be careful."

And Francis of Assisi replied, "My friend, pray to the Lord that I may succeed in becoming what people think I am."

A NEW BODY

BACKGROUND SCRIPTURE: 1 Corinthians 15:1-11
DEVOTIONAL READING: 1 Corinthians 15

KEY VERSE: "Where, O death, is your victory?
Where, O death, is your sting?" 1 Corinthians 15:55.

KING JAMES VERSION

1 CORINTHIANS 15:42 So also is the resurrection of the dead. It is sown in corruption; it is raised in incorruption: 43 It is sown in dishonour; it is raised in glory: it is sown in weakness; it is raised in power: 44 It is sown a natural body; it is raised a spiritual body. There is a natural body, and there is a spiritual body. 45 And so it is written, The first man Adam was made a living soul; the last Adam was made a quickening spirit. 46 Howbeit that was not first which is spiritual, but that which is natural; and afterward that which is spiritual. 47 The first man is of the earth, earthy: the second man is the Lord from heaven. 48 As is the earthy, such are they also that are earthy: and as is the heavenly, such are they also that are heavenly. 49 And as we have borne the image of the earthy, we shall also bear the image of the heavenly. 50 Now this I say, brethren, that flesh and blood cannot inherit the kingdom of God; neither doth corruption inherit incorruption.

51 Behold, I shew you a mystery; We shall not all sleep, but we shall all be changed, 52 In a moment, in the twinkling of an eye, at the last trump: for the trumpet shall sound, and the dead shall be raised incorruptible, and we shall be changed. 53 For this corruptible must put on incorruption, and this mortal must put on immortality. 54 So when this corruptible shall have put on incorruption, and this mortal shall have put on immortality, then shall be brought to pass the saying that is written, Death is swallowed up in victory. 55 O death, where is thy sting? O grave, where is thy victory? 56 The sting of death is sin; and the strength of sin is the law. 57 But thanks be to God, which giveth us the victory through our Lord Jesus Christ.

NEW REVISED STANDARD VERSION

1 CORINTHIANS 15:42 So it is with the resurrection of the dead. What is sown is perishable, what is raised is imperishable. 43 It is sown in dishonor, it is raised in glory. It is sown in weakness, it is raised in power. 44 It is sown a physical body, it is raised a spiritual body. If there is a physical body, there is also a spiritual body. 45 Thus it is written, "The first man, Adam, became a living being"; the last Adam became a life-giving spirit. 46 But it is not the spiritual that is first, but the physical, and then the spiritual. 47 The first man was from the earth, a man of dust; the second man is from heaven. 48 As was the man of dust, so are those who are of the dust; and as is the man of heaven, so are those who are of heaven. 49 Just as we have borne the image of the man of dust, we will also bear the image of the man of heaven.

50 What I am saying, brothers and sisters, is this: flesh and blood cannot inherit the kingdom of God, nor does the perishable inherit the imperishable. 51 Listen, I will tell you a mystery! We will not all die, but we will all be changed, 52 in a moment, in the twinkling of an eye, at the last trumpet. For the trumpet will sound, and the dead will be raised imperishable, and we will be changed. 53 For this perishable body must put on imperishability, and this mortal body must put on immortality. 54 When this perishable body puts on imperishability, and this mortal body puts on immortality, then the saying that is written will be fulfilled:

"Death has been swallowed up in victory."

55 "Where, O death, is your victory?

Where, O death, is your sting?"

56 The sting of death is sin, and the power of sin is the law. 57 But thanks be to God, who gives us the victory through our Lord Jesus Christ.

11

Monday, November 8	1 Corinthians 15:1-11	*Paul Reviews the Resurrection Tradition*
Tuesday, November 9	1 Corinthians 15:12-19	*Doubts Concerning Resurrection*
Wednesday, November 10	1 Corinthians 15:20-28	*The Significance of Christ's Resurrection*
Thursday, November 11	1 Corinthians 15:29-34	*Arguments to Support Belief in Resurrection*
Friday, November 12	1 Corinthians 15:35-41	*Paul Deals with Physical Resurrection*
Saturday, November 13	1 Corinthians 15:42-50	*Paul Explains the Spiritual Body*
Sunday, November 14	1 Corinthians 15:51-58	*Have Confidence in the Resurrection*

BACKGROUND

The first-century A.D. church at Corinth was still young when problems like divisions, immorality, immaturity, and instability began to crop up. To address these problems, the apostle Paul, who had founded the church about five years earlier while on his second missionary journey, wrote a letter to believers instructing them to live godly lives.

Because Paul dealt with a number of practical issues facing the church, this letter is highly relevant to Christians today. In fact, as you study the principles taught by the apostle Paul, you may find more than a few similarities between the church at Corinth and the church of the early twenty-first century. You're also likely to discover a number of resemblances between the society of first-century A.D. Corinth and our society today.

One of the most immediate problems facing the people of the church was division within its ranks. So Paul, in the early part of his letter, told the church to strive for unity. But there were other issues to be dealt with as well. Among these were a growing laxity for discipline, a surge of lawsuits being brought before non-Christian judges, and a spreading propensity for sexual immorality. There was probably also some opposition to Paul in the church.

Perhaps while Paul was in the process of writing this letter, Corinthian believers sent him a letter in which they asked his advice on a variety of moral and social matters (7:1). This gave rise to the apostle's instruction about maintaining stable marriages, about discontinuing less than ethical actions, about what to do and what not to do in public worship, and about the reality of Jesus' resurrection. It may have taken Paul days or weeks to write this letter. The time was probably about A.D. 55, when Paul was near the end of his three-year ministry at Ephesus and at the midpoint of his third missionary journey

It should come as no surprise that Jesus' resurrection was the cornerstone of Paul's faith. The apostle had built his ministry on knowing that the Father had raised the Son from the dead after His crucifixion. In fact, Paul had endured all sorts of hardship because of his commitment to the risen, living Lord. Therefore, the apostle was dismayed that some in the fledgling church at Corinth were denying the bodily resurrection of the dead.

Greek philosophy offered little hope to humans after death. The wispy idea of immortal souls provided no comfort in the face of the finality and tragedy of death. Most in that society resigned themselves to the notion that they would cease to exist after they died. Life must have seemed short and cheap for the bulk of the population.

Most in the Corinthian church believed that Christians, after death, live on forever in heaven as spirits. But to some of them the idea of one's soul being rejoined with one's body was distasteful. It's clear that this distorted thinking reflected the mindset of the culture in which the members of the Corinthian church lived. Imagine the feelings of despair and hopelessness that overwhelmed some in the congregation when they heard others deny the reality of the Resurrection.

Paul sensed the need to correct this erroneous thinking. He began his argument by establishing common ground with his readers. They all believed that God had raised Jesus from the dead. In fact, Christ's resurrection signified that He had conquered death and sin.

Paul called the Corinthian believers back to the central truths of their faith. He reminded them that apart from the good news of Christ's resurrection their hope was in vain, that they were still mired in guilt, and that life was futile. Of course, if Jesus was still dead, then Paul's preaching and the Corinthians' faith were both useless. Without the Resurrection, the Gospel was not worth spreading or believing. Thankfully, Paul firmly asserted that Christ was raised. In fact, He serves as a pledge that more resurrections will one day follow.

NOTES ON THE PRINTED TEXT

Paul, after pointing out the implications of denying the doctrine of the resurrection, focused on describing the nature and implications of the believers' resurrection body. Here, it seems, he got at the core of the Corinthians' objection. They did not like the idea of a physical body's coming back to life. Paul insisted that believers will have bodies at the resurrection, but he also explained how a resurrection body differs from an earthly body.

The apostle noted that the believers' earthly bodies are subject to death and decay; but they are raised incorruptible and *imperishable* (1 Cor. 15:42). The earthly body, which is sown in dishonor and weakness, is resurrected to glory and *power* (15:43). The natural body will one day give way to a *spiritual body* (15:44).

In 15:45, Paul quoted from Genesis 2:7 to stress that, while Adam (the first man) became a living person, Christ (the last Adam) became a life-giving spirit. This means that, after His resurrection, Jesus' body took on a spiritual or glorified body.

The divine order is for the natural body to precede the spiritual body (1 Cor. 15:46). In the case of Adam, he was made from the dust of the earth, whereas Christ is *from heaven* (15:47); also, whereas all people have an earthly body like Adam's, the heavenly bodies of believers will be like Christ's (15:48). Thus, just as believers now bear the image of Adam, the man of dust, in the resurrection they will bear the image of Christ, *the man of heaven* (15:49). There are times when we feel powerless and ineffective. We can find comfort in knowing that when Christ returns, our bodies will be transformed.

Paul summarized his previous thoughts by revealing that our earthly human bodies cannot inherit the *kingdom of God* (15:50). The reason is that former are subject to decay, whereas the latter will last forever.

Paul next explained a mystery to his readers, namely, that living as well as dead believers will have their bodies transformed at Christ's return (15:51). This will happen instantaneously—in a mere moment, in the blinking of an eye—when the consummation of history occurs (15:52).

At the sound of the last trumpet, deceased believers will be raised and they, along with Christians who are alive at that time, will be changed. Both groups will be given transformed, imperishable bodies. It is necessary for perishable bodies to be changed into imperishable ones in order for believers to inherit the kingdom of God (15:53).

At the present moment, the earthly bodies of believers are subject to death and decay; but at the resurrection, they will be transformed into imperishable heavenly bodies (15:54). Then *death* will be swallowed up in victory (see Isa. 25:8), and the sting of death will be eliminated forever (1 Cor. 15:55; see Hos. 13:14).

Paul explained that death gives sin its sting; also, sin derives its power from *the law* (1 Cor. 15:56). All of that will be changed in the resurrection. Then Jesus will give His followers victory over sin and death. That is why God should be given unending praise and *thanks* (15:57).

Let us not overlook this key truth. Christ conquered death so that we can live with Him in heaven. Our new life will be replete with a new spiritual body to dwell in the splendor of God's presence. Thus, because we are in Christ, we can replace fear with rejoicing that some day we will be reunited with all of our brothers and sisters in the Lord.

SUGGESTIONS TO TEACHERS

Is the Bible reliable? Are the writings in the New Testament merely "pious legends" as one critic claims? Some people have even dismissed the scriptural reports about Jesus, declaring them to be stories of a "fictitious" character. This week's lesson is a good opportunity to review the way the good news of Jesus was revealed, and to reflect on the trustworthiness of the reports in the New Testament.

1. EYEWITNESS REPORTS. Have the class look at the opening verses in Luke and 1 John. Impress on the class that these two individuals, as well as other writers of our New Testament, searched out eyewitnesses or were eyewitnesses of Jesus themselves. Luke and John were scrupulously careful reporters. Each intended to give an *orderly account* (Luke 1:1). The Scriptures should never be classified as fiction.

2. ESSENTIAL RELIANCE. The New Testament was not put together merely as a report on Jesus, as a biographer might collect material on an interesting subject. Every portion of every one of the 27 "books" was intended to strengthen the faith of hearers or readers. Paul in 1 Corinthians 15 put it plainly: everything he told his readers was meant for them to *hold firmly to the message that I proclaimed to you* (1 Cor. 15:2). The purpose of the Bible is to bring into being a community that will rely on the Lord and strive to practice the reality of His realm in every area of life.

3. EFFECTIVE RELEASE. The good news of Christ to earlier believers and to us remains the same: Jesus' death and resurrection bring liberation from the bonds of guilt, anxiety, and futility. Have the class focus on 15:1-4, emphasizing that the Messiah died for our sins. Suggest to the class that a list be made of what that death on the cross may mean to people today. Note how significant the experience of the risen Lord was to Paul.

4. ETERNAL RELATIONSHIP. Finally, have the class take a good look at the words in the opening verses of 1 John. This reporter of the good news of Jesus Christ rejoiced in knowing he and all those trusting in the Gospel had an unbroken friendship with God for all time. That truly is good news! In the face of all the bad news in the nightly newscasts or morning newspapers which threaten to make us despair, the report of God's great gift of Jesus Christ brings new life.

FOR ADULTS

■ **TOPIC:** Live with Confidence

■ **QUESTIONS:** 1. In what ways do our earthly and resurrection bodies differ? 2. What is the difference between Adam and Christ? 3. What was the nature of the mystery that Paul wanted to explain to the Corinthians? 4. What will happen to the bodies of believers when Jesus returns at the consummation of history? 5. How did Paul describe the long-anticipated defeat of death?

■ **ILLUSTRATIONS:**

The Evidence. A father was explaining to his five-year-old son how Jesus died and then revisited His followers after rising from the dead. "That's what we believe," the father said. "That's how we know Jesus is the Son of God, because He came back from the dead just as He said He would." "Do you mean like Elvis?" the boy observed.

We have no evidence that Elvis ever came back from the dead, but there is a great deal of evidence for Jesus' resurrection. Perhaps some of the greatest evidence is the fact that Christ lives in the hearts of believers today. For Christians, the resurrection of Jesus is at the core of their faith.

Without the resurrection, every word of Jesus is transformed into a lie, every belief we hold is undermined, and everything the church has accomplished for almost 2,000 years is pointless. But of course Christ did rise from the dead. Our preaching, believing, and hoping have not been in vain. That's why on Easter, throngs of people crowd the church. They know that Easter is the most glorious day of the year, and they know why that is true. It's Resurrection Day!

Triumph of the Risen Lord. For over 75 years, the Soviet Union had repressed the church by closing congregations, shooting or imprisoning religious leaders, seizing Bibles and other religious literature, and forbidding any public proclamation of the good news of Jesus' resurrection. The powerful government promoted atheism. In fact, religion was said to be "the opium of the people" (a statement originally made by Karl Marx).

In a prominent location in Moscow, a poster had printed on it, "Glory to the Communist Party!" A number of years ago, a visitor was walking through that city with a Russian acquaintance when they came to the place where the poster had hung. "Look at that!" the Russian said, pointing to a large banner fluttering in the chill breeze of a Russian spring. "KHRISTOS VOSKRESE!" the banner proclaimed in swooping old Cyrillic letters. In other words, CHRIST IS RISEN!

The wonderful news of the Resurrection has outlasted all revolutions, all ideologies, and all empires. The risen, living Christ triumphs over all forever!

Our Experience as Well. D. T. Niles once said, "The resurrection that awaits us beyond physical death will be but the glorious consummation of the risen life that we have in Christ." I like the way F. B. Meyer said it in a sermon title: "Death— A Parenthesis in Life." He knew that Jesus' resurrection means that believers can conquer death through faith in Him. The resurrection of Christ means that believers don't have to fear death. We also don't have to be entombed in doubt, anxiety, loneliness, or guilt. By defeating death, Christ also broke death's power to hold us captive to sin.

FOR YOUTH

■ TOPIC: New Life in a New Body

■ QUESTIONS: 1. How will the believer's earthly body differ from the body to be received in the resurrection? 2. What point was Paul underscoring by quoting Genesis 2:7? 3. Why is it that our earthly bodies cannot inherit God's kingdom? 4. What was the nature of the mystery that Paul explained to his readers? 5. When will death be swallowed up in victory?

■ ILLUSTRATIONS:

Failed Experiment. It was billed as *Elvis—The Concert!* Advertisements promised to bring Elvis (live through the "magic" of video) along with his original band of James Burton, Glen D. Hardin, Jerry Scheff, Ron Tutt, and J. D.

Sumner. The original back-up female and male touring group for Elvis was also to be present.

However, on March 18, 1998, fewer than 4,000 fans paid $25 to see Elvis. The music roared and Elvis stepped onto the stage's main screen. The response? Mostly everyone yawned. Those who attended agreed that Elvis was still dead. What was billed as the "beyond death experiment" had failed. Fans agreed and said that it was like watching television or a haunting music video complete with musicians who seemed like ghosts. One girl named Hilda said, "You almost think he's here, but then it's sad to look down at the stage and see that he's not." Despite all the hype, Elvis was still dead.

Paul assured the Corinthian Christians that there was life after physical death for them. God would one day give believers a resurrection body. Because of Jesus' rising from the dead, they had proof that the hope of eternal life is an absolute certainty.

Death, Where Is Your Sting? A small boy was allergic to bee stings. The allergy was so severe that physicians warned the family that a single bee sting could produce anaphylactic shock. This is a severe medical emergency that could kill the child by preventing him from breathing.

One day, a bee landed on the boy's cheek. The child was almost paralyzed with fright. Calmly the father allowed the bee to walk onto his own finger. The father agitated the bee and then allowed it to sting him. The bee flew back to the boy, but this time the child was unafraid. Death had been robbed of its power!

This story illustrates Paul's point to the Corinthian believers. They did not need to fear death, for Christ had removed its sting through His resurrection. And through faith in Christ, they could conquer death.

Looking for Hope. On the early morning of March 22, 1998, fire raced through a mountain cabin. Eight students from Line Mountain High School and three college students from Lititz, all from Herndon, Pennsylvania, were killed as they slept inside. They had come to camp to enjoy spring break.

As news of the tragedy spread, the high school opened to provide counseling and support to students looking for hope. It remained open through the night and the following day. Classes were canceled Monday as students came to the school, talked, cried, and hugged. Flags flew at half staff in the tight-knit community in Miles Township. Throughout the day, students wrote notes in which they spoke about their love, pledged to support the survivors of the fire, and promised to organize a reunion sometime later. That night, a prayer service led by local clergy was held in the gym, and a candlelight vigil followed in the school's stadium. The efforts were to soothe the souls of those in the community.

Paul understood such grief and loss. However, the apostle also knew about God's promise of the resurrection. Paul declared that for those who have trusted in Christ, eternal life awaited them in heaven with God!

Abundant Information. Almost two-thirds of all public schools are now on the Internet. The Internet is the world's largest computer network and the closest thing to an information superhighway. The Internet is, in reality, a global network of networks that link together large computer-communication services. Although only about 20 percent of all classrooms have connections, most libraries and computer labs are connected to the Net. The United States government would like to have every American classroom wired to the Internet by the year 2006.

The reason for this is that there is a world of information on the Net from NASA, *National Geographic,* the Public Broadcasting Service, Scholastic On-line Education, and Network America. All are considered by educators to be top resources. The Net is simply an information superhighway, as most claim.

Youth live in a world where information is plentiful. However, they also live in a world where meaning is scarce. The Bible provides not only information about the Savior but also a wealth of material as to His meaning and significance in history.

A New Creature in Christ

BACKGROUND SCRIPTURE: 2 Corinthians 5:11-21
DEVOTIONAL READING: 2 Corinthians 4:16—5:5

KEY VERSE: If anyone is in Christ, there is a new creation: everything old has passed away; see, everything has become new! 2 Corinthians 5:17.

KING JAMES VERSION

2 CORINTHIANS 5:11 Knowing therefore the terror of the Lord, we persuade men; but we are made manifest unto God; and I trust also are made manifest in your consciences.

12 For we commend not ourselves again unto you, but give you occasion to glory on our behalf, that ye may have somewhat to answer them which glory in appearance, and not in heart. 13 For whether we be beside ourselves, it is to God: or whether we be sober, it is for your cause. 14 For the love of Christ constraineth us; because we thus judge, that if one died for all, then were all dead: 15 And that he died for all, that they which live should not henceforth live unto themselves, but unto him which died for them, and rose again.

16 Wherefore henceforth know we no man after the flesh: yea, though we have known Christ after the flesh, yet now henceforth know we him no more.

17 Therefore if any man be in Christ, he is a new creature: old things are passed away; behold, all things are become new. 18 And all things are of God, who hath reconciled us to himself by Jesus Christ, and hath given to us the ministry of reconciliation; 19 To wit, that God was in Christ, reconciling the world unto himself, not imputing their trespasses unto them; and hath committed unto us the word of reconciliation. 20 Now then we are ambassadors for Christ, as though God did beseech you by us: we pray you in Christ's stead, be ye reconciled to God. 21 For he hath made him to be sin for us, who knew no sin; that we might be made the righteousness of God in him.

NEW REVISED STANDARD VERSION

2 CORINTHIANS 5:11 Therefore, knowing the fear of the Lord, we try to persuade others; but we ourselves are well known to God, and I hope that we are also well known to your consciences. 12 We are not commending ourselves to you again, but giving you an opportunity to boast about us, so that you may be able to answer those who boast in outward appearance and not in the heart. 13 For if we are beside ourselves, it is for God; if we are in our right mind, it is for you. 14 For the love of Christ urges us on, because we are convinced that one has died for all; therefore all have died. 15 And he died for all, so that those who live might live no longer for themselves, but for him who died and was raised for them.

16 From now on, therefore, we regard no one from a human point of view; even though we once knew Christ from a human point of view,we know him no longer in that way. 17 So if anyone is in Christ, there is a new creation: everything old has passed away; see, everything has become new! 18 All this is from God, who reconciled us to himself through Christ, and has given us the ministry of reconciliation; 19 that is, in Christ God was reconciling the world to himself, not counting their trespasses against them, and entrusting the message of reconciliation to us. 20 So we are ambassadors for Christ, since God is making his appeal through us; we entreat you on behalf of Christ, be reconciled to God. 21 For our sake he made him to be sin who knew no sin, so that in him we might become the righteousness of God.

12

HOME BIBLE READINGS

BACKGROUND

Paul's "problem church" was the Corinthian congregation. Like a loving parent, the patient apostle grieved over the divisions which tore apart this church. From a reading of 2 Corinthians, we learn that Paul made a quick visit to Corinth. Instead of the reconciliation Paul longed for, however, the trip was *painful* (2:1). At least one critic continued to malign Paul. But eventually wiser heads prevailed, and the Corinthians censured the troublemaker.

Paul wrote this second letter to the Corinthians not to justify himself but to clarify his mission. Throughout this letter he emerged as a person who was so deeply committed to Jesus Christ that the apostle had little concern for what others might have thought about him.

NOTES ON THE PRINTED TEXT

When our nation sends an ambassador to another country, it is as though all our citizens are reaching out into a new realm. That is how the Bible describes God's outreach to the world. He stretches out His arms through us, His ambassadors, with the message of reconciliation to Him.

Paul was such an ambassador. He had a reverential fear of God, and this prompted the apostle to labor diligently to persuade people. Paul urged the lost to trust in Christ for salvation; and the apostle—whose conscience was clear before God—underscored to the believers at Corinth the sincerity of his motives and integrity of his ministry (2 Cor. 5:11).

This was not another occasion in which Paul bragged about himself to the Corinthians; rather, the apostle wanted to give them an opportunity to be proud of all that Paul and his colleagues had done for the cause of Christ (5:12). It would also enable the Corinthians to respond to those who took pride in *outward appearance,* rather than what is *in the heart.*

Some of Paul's opponents evidently accused him of being crazy. In response, the apostle declared that everything he did was intended to glorify God and benefit Christians (5:13). The Savior's love for the lost motivated Paul to evangelize the lost (5:14).

The apostle related that Jesus *died* on the cross for all people. While the unsaved remain dead in their sins, the redeemed have *died* to their sins through faith in Christ. Thus, believers no longer live to please themselves, but for Jesus. He was crucified and resurrected *for them* (5:15).

Paul's teaching underscores two reasons for us to witness for Christ. One is our anticipation of our lives being evaluated by God. The second is the love of Christ shown in His atoning sacrifice for us. Because of all that Jesus has done for us, we should seek to herald His message of salvation to the lost.

Paul declared that he no longer evaluated people from an outward point of view. The apostle, in fact, admitted that he once mistakenly thought about Christ in this way. Thankfully, Paul no longer regarded Jesus as just another person (5:16). The apostle's main point is that we who trust in Christ become a *new creation* (5:17). God radically transforms our sinful lives—in a sense, recreating us—so that what is *old has passed away* to make room for what is *new*.

God took the initiative to give us newness of life; and the work of the Son on the cross is the reason the Father can reconcile us to Himself (5:18). (This refers to a change of relationship in which enmity is replaced by harmony and fellowship.) Moreover, God has *given us the ministry* of urging the lost to experience God's forgiveness and peace.

Paul explained that it was in and through Christ that God made reconciliation with the world possible; and the wonderful message Paul and others declared is that, when the lost trust in Christ, God no longer counts their trespasses against them. This is the essence of the gospel message the Lord had entrusted to Paul (5:19).

The apostle, in turn, went out as an ambassador for Christ. God, through Paul, urged people to make peace with the Lord (5:20). This is possible because God treated Jesus—who is the sinless One—as if He were a sinner. The Father did this so that He could make us acceptable to Him (5:21).

Because we have been spiritually transformed in Christ, we have a vastly different approach to life. That includes devoting ourselves to reaching the lost with the good news of salvation.

SUGGESTIONS TO TEACHERS

Frequently, we are content to follow the same programs within our congregations that we've had for years without giving any thought about their place in Christ's work. Or we race ahead with the creation of new programs without first considering whether these programs are in accord with the purpose of the Church. More than a few churches spend more time talking about cash shortages or the softball team or painting the nursery or when to hold the rummage sale than about God's overarching dreams for His community of faith.

This week's lesson starts with a brief look at Paul's work in the face of criticism and continues with his great sense of purpose for Christ's spiritual body. Paul's place in that purpose sustained and guided him through all his difficulties. Likewise, Christians today will be supported in their problems by this vision. Let us look for what we can learn from Paul's situation.

1. CONTROLLED BY THE LOVE OF CHRIST. Paul's actions were sometimes misperceived. Apparently some thought he boasted about himself. Others thought he was unimpressive. Still others felt he was overly enthusiastic and excitable. Paul brushed aside all the criticisms by claiming that his main purpose was to promote the reconciling work of God through Christ. The apostle stated that he was controlled by the *love of Christ* (2 Cor. 5:14). Sniping remarks by others, therefore, did not stop Paul from doing God's work. Let this section generate some class comments on ways to handle critical comments when believers are trying to serve the Lord.

2. CONVINCED BY THE DEATH OF CHRIST. Paul also wrote that because of the death of Christ, he had already gone through the death experience. The old Saul "died" on the Damascus road! Paul was given a new viewpoint. Because of Christ, the apostle was able to see all others from the Savior's perspective. Use 5:14b-16 to assist those in the class to catch a new sense of the meaning of Jesus' death for them in their daily living.

3. CONVERTED TO THE LIFE OF CHRIST. Paul used bold words in 5:17 to convey what it means to know Jesus Christ: *a new creation*! Has the "old" personality been allowed to pass away so that the "new" brought by Christ may flower into being in the lives of those in your class? You might pass out slips of paper and have each person indicate ways in which he or she has become a new person in Christ. Or have each person list areas in his or her daily life that he or she feels Christ wants to make "new."

4. CREATED FOR RECONCILIATION THROUGH CHRIST. Don't skimp on lesson time when you get to the part on the great manifesto for the Church in 5:18-20. Each word must be pondered. Because God has reconciled us to Himself, we are called to bring reconciliation to the world. This is our ministry. We are Christ's ambassadors. In what situations will we be called to minister reconciliation in the Master's name? In what areas of your community are the ambassadorial duties of your congregation most needed?

FOR ADULTS

■ **TOPIC:** New Beginnings

■ **QUESTIONS:** 1. What is the background to Paul's words in 2 Corinthians 5:11-21? 2. What did the Corinthian church people accuse Paul of doing? 3. How does the term *ambassadors* apply to us as Christ's people? 4. In what parts of your community is reconciliation most needed? 5. What does reconciliation with God through Christ and also with others mean?

■ **ILLUSTRATIONS:**

Broken Relationships. Fred Craddock once described a pathetic interview he had had on a flight to the West Coast. There was one seat next to him. His seatmate, whom he had not met previously, began to cry. Craddock tried to pay no attention and concentrate on his book. But the woman next to him continued weeping. Finally he turned his head and said something about being sorry that she was upset. The woman blurted out that she was on the way to her father's funeral. Craddock offered condolences. The tears continued, and Craddock commented, "You and your father were obviously very close."

"Oh, no. Just the opposite."

After Craddock expressed surprise, the woman continued. "I haven't seen my father or talked to him or written to him since I left home 17 years ago. That was the night I flung my napkin onto my dinner, got up, and walked out. Just before I slammed the door, I screamed at him to go to hell. That was the last contact I had with him."

Isn't this the situation in our world? Behind the seething anger and militant actions of those in the Middle East are the hurts and broken relationships between the Arab world and the West going back to the Crusades and even to Roman times. The standoff between terrorists and the United States is in part a reaction to the ways they and others feel that we have failed to respect them and others. Whatever the place, whether war-torn northern Ireland, Palestine, or almost any inner-city neighborhood in any of America's large cities, the brokenness is obvious.

A Mended Relationship. Even when we may be the ones who are wronged and hurt, we are called to be in partnership with God in mending the broken relationship. Jack's father walked out on the family when Jack was 12. Jack's mother was forced to find work to support the family, and Jack took part-time jobs to help out too. Meanwhile, the father lived comfortably, but never took any interest in Jack or his former wife. For a couple of years, Jack would hear from his father at Christmas in the form of a card with a dollar bill enclosed. Then the Christmas cards stopped. Eventually Jack graduated from high school, then put himself through college. Then, after answering the call to ministry, Jack went to seminary.

Finally, the time came for Jack to be ordained. On the night of his ordination, Jack's father turned up uninvited and obviously half drunk. It was the first time Jack had seen his father since he had walked out 15 years earlier. The situation was awkward as the father went around introducing himself in a loud voice as "this boy's proud father." Jack was furious, but said nothing.

When his father sidled up to Jack at the reception, he apparently sensed the coolness on the part of his son. "Oh, so now you're religious and uppity, are you?" the father said. "Another wise guy, phony preacher, that's what you are. Well, Jackie boy, I want no part of you." And he marched out.

After that, Jack's church work seemed ineffective. His sermons seemed to be scoldings. People found it hard to warm to him. Even the woman back in Chicago at the seminary whom he had been dating told him she wasn't interested in seeing Jack anymore because things just weren't quite right between them.

Finally, Jack sought professional help. A sensitive therapist soon put his finger on Jack's problem: his father and the hurt the older man had inflicted. After agonizing for months, Jack resolved to go to the man who had hurt him so deeply. He found his father finally, living in Tucson, where he had just lost his job because of a chronic drinking problem. Jack finally blurted, "Dad, I've been mad at you for 20 years for all that you've done to me. We've not been in touch. After the scene at my ordination three years ago, I felt I never wanted to see you again. But I've finally discovered that we simply must be reconciled. Dad, I want you to know I really do forgive you. And I want you to come and visit me."

The old man looked as if he had been struck. Suddenly both began to weep. Then they embraced. Jack found a father. And the father found a son. Both men began new lives. Jack's preaching seemed to lose its scolding tone, and his ministry took on a caring quality.

That day of reconciliation with the father convinced Jack that he'd given life back to his dad and to himself. A corner of the torn fabric of creation was mended. Two angry men discovered that they were opening themselves to God as He repaired creation.

Each of you is called to be such a partner with God. You may not be able to do much about the war-torn areas of the world , but you can work with God in mending the relationships around you.

FOR YOUTH

■ **TOPIC:** New and Improved
■ **QUESTIONS:** 1. What does the word *reconciliation* mean? 2. How does Christ reconcile the world? 3. How have you become a "new creation"? 4. What "old" things have passed away within you? 5. What can you do to be a genuine ambassador for Christ?

■ **ILLUSTRATIONS:**

Temporary Reconciliation. In late 1914 during World War I, two armies stood on the steps of their trenches facing one another. Both British and German infantry soldiers were cold, wet, and hungry. Month after month they had listened to the deafening roar of shelling and gunfire and watched the dogfighting airplanes overhead.

On Christmas Eve, everything became quiet. Small Christmas trees with candles appeared on the German side and a chorus of "Silent Night" was sung. The British soldiers responded with a chorus of "O Come, All Ye Faithful." The moon shone brightly like the star of Bethlehem over the battlefield.

On Christmas morning a single German soldier entered the no-man's-land between the two armies. He had a Christmas tree in his hands. A British soldier walked out and the two shook hands. Others came out and shook hands. They agreed to bury the dead together on the "halfway line." A German barber began giving haircuts to the British soldiers. Gifts were exchanged. The two armies played soccer in the snow. No referees participated, nor were any scores kept. Men, tired of killing and war, simply reconciled and played together. That night, after supper and a carol service, the soldiers said goodnight to each other.

The following day the officers were furious. How would the soldiers fight? Although forbidden to leave the trenches, soldiers continued their meetings and gift giving. Reconciliation grew. Differences were forgotten. Two more days passed. Then the Germans warned their new British friends that their general was coming to the front. They would have to keep their heads down while the Germans shot at them.

Several days later the friendly German soldiers from Saxony were withdrawn and replaced by fresh troops from Prussia. Reconciliation had ended. The war and the killing began once again. However, for one brief and glorious period, two armies lived Paul's message of reconciliation.

Drawn Together. On March 11, 1996, J. T. Snow of the San Francisco Giants was at bat during a spring training game. Randy Johnson of the Seattle Mariners suddenly threw a 100-MPH pitch that hit Snow's left wrist and ricocheted into his left eye. The fastball broke his left-eye orbit. The following day, Snow called his mother but not to talk about himself. He wanted to see how she was doing.

Snow had not spoken with his parents for 30 months. The reasons behind the rift remain private and Snow refused to share them. As a result, though, the family had separated. An ocean of silence kept them apart.

Snow learned, however, that his mother had cancer. Twenty-five percent of her scapula had been removed because of a growing tumor. She also had undergone 35 days of radiation and was preparing for chemotherapy.

Snow regretted those months of not speaking and being a family. Ultimately, it did not matter who was right or wrong. He just wanted them to be together again, since life was so short. As a result, the family reconciled.

This is the type of reconciliation Paul speaks of to his readers. As Christ has drawn near to us, we are to draw near to one another.

A NEW RELATIONSHIP

BACKGROUND SCRIPTURE: Ephesians 2:11–21
DEVOTIONAL READING: Ephesians 2:4-10

KEY VERSES: You are no longer strangers and aliens, but you are citizens with the saints and also members of the household of God. Ephesians 2:19.

KING JAMES VERSION

EPHESIANS 2:11 Wherefore remember, that ye being in time past Gentiles in the flesh, who are called Uncircumcision by that which is called the Circumcision in the flesh made by hands; 12 That at that time ye were without Christ, being aliens from the commonwealth of Israel, and strangers from the covenants of promise, having no hope, and without God in the world: 13 But now in Christ Jesus ye who sometimes were far off are made nigh by the blood of Christ.

14 For he is our peace, who hath made both one, and hath broken down the middle wall of partition between us; 15 Having abolished in his flesh the enmity, even the law of commandments contained in ordinances; for to make in himself of twain one new man, so making peace; 16 And that he might reconcile both unto God in one body by the cross, having slain the enmity thereby: 17 And came and preached peace to you which were afar off, and to them that were nigh. 18 For through him we both have access by one Spirit unto the Father. 19 Now therefore ye are no more strangers and foreigners, but fellowcitizens with the saints, and of the household of God; 20 And are built upon the foundation of the apostles and prophets, Jesus Christ himself being the chief corner stone; 21 In whom all the building fitly framed together groweth unto an holy temple in the Lord:

NEW REVISED STANDARD VERSION

EPHESIANS 2:11 So then, remember that at one time you Gentiles by birth, called "the uncircumcision" by those who are called "the circumcision"—a physical circumcision made in the flesh by human hands— 12 remember that you were at that time without Christ, being aliens from the commonwealth of Israel, and strangers to the covenants of promise, having no hope and without God in the world. 13 But now in Christ Jesus you who once were far off have been brought near by the blood of Christ. 14 For he is our peace; in his flesh he has made both groups into one and has broken down the dividing wall, that is, the hostility between us. 15 He has abolished the law with its commandments and ordinances, that he might create in himself one new humanity in place of the two, thus making peace, 16 and might reconcile both groups to God in one body through the cross, thus putting to death that hostility through it. 17 So he came and proclaimed peace to you who were far off and peace to those who were near; 18 for through him both of us have access in one Spirit to the Father. 19 So then you are no longer strangers and aliens, but you are citizens with the saints and also members of the household of God, 20 built upon the foundation of the apostles and prophets, with Christ Jesus himself as the cornerstone. 21 In him the whole structure is joined together and grows into a holy temple in the Lord.

13

HOME BIBLE READINGS

Monday, November 22	Ephesians 1:3-12	*We Have Received Grace through Christ*
Tuesday, November 23	Ephesians 4:1-6	*One in Christ*
Wednesday, November 24	Ephesians 4:11-16	*Growing Together in Christ*
Thursday, November 25	Ephesians 2:4-10	*Alive Together with Christ*
Friday, November 26	Ephesians 2:11-16	*Once Apart, Now Together*
Saturday, November 27	Ephesians 2:17-22	*No Longer Strangers and Aliens*
Sunday, November 28	Ephesians 3:14-19	*Rooted and Grounded in Love*

BACKGROUND

The general nature of Ephesians makes it difficult to determine the specific circumstances that gave rise to the epistle. Nevertheless, it is clear that the recipients were Gentiles (3:1) who were estranged from citizenship in the kingdom of Israel (2:11). Now, thanks to the gracious gift of God, they enjoyed the spiritual blessings that come through faith in Christ.

It is likely that Priscilla and Aquila first brought the Gospel to Ephesus (Acts 18:26), and that Paul most likely left them there as he continued on his second missionary journey (18:18-19). The city was located at the intersection of several major trade routes and became a vital commercial, political, and educational center of the Roman Empire. Ephesus was perhaps best known for its magnificent temple of Artemis, or Diana, one of the seven wonders of the ancient world.

Most importantly, Ephesus figured prominently and dramatically in early church history, for Paul used the city as a base for his missionary work in that region. In fact, on the apostle's third missionary journey, he spent three years there (20:31). So many people in Ephesus turned to Christ and renounced their pagan ways that some local craftsmen started a riot because the Gospel threatened their trade of making and selling idols (see chap. 19). Paul's affectionate ties with this church are evident by his farewell speech to its elders (20:16-38).

The letter that Paul subsequently wrote to the Ephesians has been called "The Heavenly Epistle" and "The Alps of the New Testament." In it the apostle takes the reader from the depths of ruin to the heights of redemption. And the focus of this letter is the mystery of the church. (A mystery is a previously unrevealed divine truth that God has now disclosed in Christ; 3:5, 9).

One learns from Ephesians that the church is a community where God's power to reconcile people to Himself is experienced and shared in transformed relationships (2:1-10; 4:1-16; 4:32—5:2; 5:22—6:9). It is a new temple, a building of people, grounded in the sure revelation of what God has done in history (2:19-22; 3:17-19). The church is an organism where power and authority are exercised after the pattern of Christ (1:22; 5:25-27), and its stewardship is a means of serving Him (4:11-16; 5:22—6:9). The church is an outpost in a dark world (5:3-17), looking for the day of final redemption. Above all, the church is the bride preparing for the approach of her Lord (5:22-32).

When Paul wrote the Letter to the Ephesians, he was no longer an evangelist on the move; he was a prisoner in Rome. Also, the church he was now writing to was not opposing him and his teaching. It was a basically sound church that was ready to receive advanced teaching in theology and ethics.

Ephesians contains two distinct, though related, parts. Chapters 1—3 remind the readers of their privileged status as members of Christ's body, the church, which occupies an important place in God's plan for the universe. Chapters 4—6 appeal to the readers to live in a way consistent with their godly calling, rather than conform to the ungodly society in which they lived.

Paul had reminded the Ephesians of their former need for God to raise them from spiritual death to spiritual life by His grace (2:1-10). Then Paul reminded them of their former disadvantages in contrast with the Jews (2:11-13). The Jews' privilege was due solely to God's grace in making a covenant with them; but many Jews identified their privilege with their circumcision, which was merely a sign of the covenant. They called themselves *"the circumcision"* (2:11) and used the insulting term *"uncircumcision"* of Gentiles, such as the Ephesians.

Paul stated the use of this contemptuous term without himself meaning any contempt. In fact, the apostle affirmed that, under the Gospel, circumcision holds no spiritual significance. As he said elsewhere (see Rom. 2:29), true circumcision is of the heart.

Many Jews went too far in evaluating their privileges; nevertheless, it is true that Gentiles—such as those living in Ephesus—were under some disadvantages. Paul thus described the Ephesians' condition before they were saved. First, they had been *without Christ* (Eph. 2:12). The promises of the coming Redeemer had been made to the Jews, and so Gentiles did not expect Him.

Second, Paul's readers had been alienated from the citizenship of *Israel* and strangers to the *covenants of promise*. While membership in the covenant community of Israel was not a guarantee of salvation, it was of significant value, for God had made promises of blessing to the physical descendants of Abraham and Isaac.

Third, the Ephesians previously had *no hope* and were *without God in the world*. Though God had not forgotten the Gentiles, most of them knew nothing about Him. Their pagan religious practices did not put them in touch with Him, and so left them with no hope of finding peace and immortality.

Though the Gentiles were once far away from the divine kingdom, Christ's atoning sacrifice made it possible for them to be brought into spiritual union and intimacy with Him (2:13). In fact, the Savior broke down the walls of prejudice and hostility that separated Jews and Gentiles (2:14). He also reconciled them as believers to God and united them into one spiritual body, the church.

God had given the law of Moses to the Jews, and because of that many of them felt superior to Gentiles; but with Jesus' sacrifice, He became the means of salvation for all people. He superseded the law by abolishing it in His flesh (2:15). Whereas hostility existed between Jews and Gentiles, now through faith in Christ *peace* exists between them.

Jesus' redemptive work enables both groups to be reconciled and united (2:16). Also, the gospel of peace enables Gentiles who were once far away and Jews who were near to come to the Father through the Spirit (2:17-18). Christ enables us to look beyond the barriers of race, economic status, gender, and so on, to embrace the unity we have in Him.

Paul used the analogy of a house to describe the spiritual unity that believers enjoy (2:19). The church is like a building whose foundation is the New Testament *apostles and prophets* (2:20). Through their witness, preaching, and teaching, many have come to faith; nevertheless, Jesus' Himself is the *cornerstone*, or keystone, of the church. In ancient times architects would place a large stone at the corner of a building, then line up the rest of the structure to it. The idea is that Jesus is the standard of truth by which the church exists.

Paul next described the church as a temple, probably like Herod's temple in Jerusalem. The apostle noted that God has carefully joined believers together to make them His *holy temple* (2:21). In Paul's time construction workers would shape and move huge blocks of stone until they fit each other perfectly. Similarly, through faith in Christ, Gentiles are joined together with Jews to form a dwelling where God lives by His Spirit (2:22).

These truths remind us that we are members of Christ' body, the church. We are also reminded of how closely Jesus identifies with His people's service. When we minister to others, it is as if Christ Himself is ministering through us; and as we exercise our spiritual gifts in the power of Christ, God will be given glory (see 1 Pet. 4:10-11).

SUGGESTIONS TO TEACHERS

After experiencing the bickering among choir members and listening in the women's group to the constant criticisms of the minister's performance, Pam quietly quit the church. An intelligent, sensitive young speech therapist, she had joined the congregation with great expectations for Christian fellowship and spiritual nurture. Now, instead of worshiping on Sundays, Pam started participating in a hiking club. When members of her church asked why she no longer took part, Pam replied, "Well, I guess the church is no different from any other organization. It's full of pettiness and politics. So what else is new?" Many of us have had similar feelings at some time. And those in your class surely know people like Pam. We need to take seriously Paul's words from Ephesians that form the basis for this week's lesson.

1. NOW ALIVE. Paul stated that we were once spiritually dead, but now have been given new life in Christ. In a sense, we are the Easter people! We are not among those obsessed by destruction or resigned to hopelessness. Because of Christ's resurrection, we have the hope of one day being raised from the dead.

2. NOW ACCEPTED. Once we were separated from Christ and alienated from God. Formerly we were strangers to the covenants and promises of the Lord. But now through Christ we are accepted and affirmed as God's beloved.

3. NOW ALLIED. Have the class consider some of the ways Paul described the new oneness they have in Christ: the walls of hostility dividing us have been broken; there is one new humanity instead of two; and we are members of God's household. Christ's people should never see each other as adversaries but as allies.

4. NOW AFFECTED. Through Christ, believers become a living temple housing God's presence. Do others in your community see the corporate life of your congregation as a manifestation of Christ's goodness?

FOR ADULTS

■ **TOPIC:** Becoming One Family

■ **QUESTIONS:** 1. What was the reason for the change in status of the Ephesians? 2. What is the basis for spiritual unity between believing Jews and Gentiles in the church? 3. What is the basis for the enmity between people and God being removed? 4. In what sense were the Ephesians no longer outcasts? 5. In what sense is Jesus the cornerstone of the church?

■ **ILLUSTRATIONS:**

The Healthy Forest. We sometimes mistakenly imagine a great hardwood sending down roots deep into the soil. But naturalists point out that a healthy tree is one whose roots go sideways, not deep down. And the roots don't just protect that one tree, but rather are woven together with the roots of other trees in order to hold up the entire forest. Like a healthy growth of trees in a forest, Christ's people do not consider merely protecting themselves. They realize that the loneliness, meaninglessness, and alienation in the world stem from the refusal of people to relate to God and to one another. Indulging in self-interest and self-preservation produces an unstable person who, like a poorly rooted tree, will be weak and easily toppled. Believers must be rooted together in Christ!

Door of Reconciliation. In the ancient cathedral of Saint Patrick, in Dublin, Ireland, the Medieval Chapter House has an old door with a strange hole in it. Visitors to the west end of the nave of the cathedral see the hole in the door of the Medieval Chapter House, and wonder why it is there. It seems that in 1492, two noblemen, the Earl of Ormond and the Earl of Kildare, were sworn enemies. The Earl of Ormond, feeling that his life was in danger, fled to the cathedral and took refuge in the Medieval Chapter House behind the great bolted door.

The Earl of Kildare finally realized that he would have to take the initiative and offer reconciliation. He went to the door and called to the man with whom he had been alienated. Finally, to prove that he meant as a Christian to live in peace with the Earl of Ormond, the Earl of Kildare cut a hole in the door and stretched his arm out through the hole to grasp the hand of the man within the Chapter House who was separated from him. The two became reconciled. The door is known as "the door of reconciliation." God broke through the barriers separating us from Him and one another. He calls us, in turn, to be agents of reconciliation with all from whom we are separated.

Reunited. Ken Burns, in his book entitled *The Civil War*, notes that in 1913, the Federal government held a fiftieth anniversary reunion at Gettysburg. It lasted three days. Thousands of survivors camped in the old battlefield, swapped stories, and looked up comrades.

The climax of the gathering was a reenactment of Pickett's Charge. Thousands of spectators gathered to watch as the Union veterans took their positions on Cemetery Ridge, and waited as their old adversaries emerged from the woods on Seminary Ridge and started forward toward them across the long, flat fields. Philip Myers, who witnessed the event as an 18 year old, wrote, "We could see not rifles and bayonets but canes and crutches. We soon could distinguish the more agile ones aiding those less able to maintain their places in the ranks."

As the men neared the northern line, they broke into one final, defiant rebel yell. At the sound, "after half a century of silence, a moan, a sigh, a gigantic gasp of unbelief" rose from the Union men on cemetery Ridge. "It was then," wrote Myers, "that the Yankees, unable to restrain themselves longer, burst from behind the stone wall, and flung themselves upon their former enemies . . . not in mortal combat, but reunited in brotherly love and affection."

This is a wonderful example of the love and forgiveness that can exist among believers in Christ.

FOR YOUTH

■ TOPIC: Together in Christ

■ QUESTIONS: 1. What were two ways Paul's Gentile readers had experienced alienation from the Jews? 2. What made it possible for believing Gentiles to be brought into spiritual union and intimacy with God? 3. What enables Jews and Gentiles to come to the Father through the Spirit? 4. If the church is like a building, what is its foundation? 5. What was Paul's point in calling Jesus the cornerstone of the church?

■ **ILLUSTRATIONS:**

Call for Unity. In the spring of 1997, Pope John Paul II journeyed to Poland for an 11-day trip. In Gniezno, the Pontiff spoke to the presidents of seven central and east European countries. After describing the tragic breakup of Yugoslavia, the Albanian crisis, and the massacres in Bosnia, the pope called upon the leaders to push for unity. The "invisible wall" of fear, aggressiveness, and prejudice had to be destroyed, he announced. Centuries earlier the apostle Paul spoke about a wall being destroyed and called for unity and harmony among believers in Christ.

God's Grace. In an interview with *Today's Christian Woman*, author Gwen Shamblin told this story:

> The girls at the horse barn next door are sweet, but they kept wanting our collies, Chaucer and Virginia, to come over. I told them, "I don't know about letting them come across the fence 'cause they might get confused. But as long as you don't feed them, it's fine." Soon I had no dogs. They were over at the barn every day, living the high life. I'd call them home, but they wouldn't come. . . . Eventually I realized the problem was that our dogs no longer knew who their master was. So a silent war was declared that day. I had to lift Chaucer and carry him home from the barn. We put our dogs on leashes. Then I fussed at Chaucer and Virginia when they were over there, and loved them when they were at home. Then we'd unleash them, test them, find them back over at the barn, and have to repeat the process. But finally we got their hearts back home. . . . Did I want those dogs because of their work? No! They bark at the wrong people. They bark at cars leaving, not coming. They slobber all over me and my company. They're completely in the way. They steal the cat food. They're trouble, but they're still precious to me, and I adore them.

We're precious in God's sight, and He pursues us. This is the nature of His grace toward us in Christ.

Drastic Changes. When Phil and Florence became engaged in 1961, a friend spoke with Phil to offer 10 reasons why he should not get married. The first reason was that Florence was black and that Phil was white. Even the pastor of Phil's church had said that God disapproved of his interracial union. Phil's mother cried. Despite all the pressure, Phil and Florence married and thus joined a group of interracial couples who made up less than one percent of the population in the 1960s. The marriage of Phil and Florence has endured, for it is based on commitment to the Lord and to one another. They have a loving, stable union. In fact, they say that they feel closer to each other now than when they were married nearly 40 years ago.

Today, decades later, a dramatic change has occurred in our nation, according to a 2000 U.S. Census Bureau report. Over 4 percent of marriages are interracial. The most telling statistic is the public's acceptance of mixed-race marriages. Now interracial couples thrive. Few now draw stares or disparaging remarks. Another wall—a racial one—has crumbled in America.

A Sign That Divides. A group of young boys decided to build a clubhouse. They gathered together some odd pieces of lumber and built a shack in the woods. Their last act was to hand paint a sign that read, "For Boys Only!"

A few months later one of the boys wanted to widen the club's membership by admitting a girl. He argued that she played Little League baseball and seemed like a pretty good kid. After much debate, the group allowed the girl to join. The sign was taken down, and inclusion triumphed over exclusiveness.

Jesus came to take down the signs that divide us as people. He came to build a community of love and support. He calls us, as members of this faith community, to work to take down those signs and not erect them. Because He invites all people into fellowship with Him, He wants us to do the same.

CALLED TO BE GOD'S PEOPLE

A CALL TO FOLLOW GOD

BACKGROUND SCRIPTURE: Genesis 11:27—12:9
DEVOTIONAL READING: Jeremiah 1:4-10

KEY VERSE: Now the LORD said to Abram, "Go from your country and your kindred and your father's house to the land that I will show you." Genesis 12:1.

KING JAMES VERSION

GENESIS 11: 27 Now these are the generations of Terah: Terah begat Abram, Nahor, and Haran; and Haran begat Lot. 28 And Haran died before his father Terah in the land of his nativity, in Ur of the Chaldees. 29 And Abram and Nahor took them wives: the name of Abram's wife was Sarai; and the name of Nahor's wife, Milcah, the daughter of Haran, the father of Milcah, and the father of Iscah. 30 But Sarai was barren; she had no child. 31 And Terah took Abram his son, and Lot the son of Haran his son's son, and Sarai his daughter in law, his son Abram's wife; and they went forth with them from Ur of the Chaldees, to go into the land of Canaan; and they came unto Haran, and dwelt there. 32 And the days of Terah were two hundred and five years: and Terah died in Haran.

12:1 Now the LORD had said unto Abram, Get thee out of thy country, and from thy kindred, and from thy father's house, unto a land that I will shew thee: 2 And I will make of thee a great nation, and I will bless thee, and make thy name great; and thou shalt be a blessing: 3 And I will bless them that bless thee, and curse him that curseth thee: and in thee shall all families of the earth be blessed.

4 So Abram departed, as the LORD had spoken unto him; and Lot went with him: and Abram was seventy and five years old when he departed out of Haran. 5 And Abram took Sarai his wife, and Lot his brother's son, and all their substance that they had gathered, and the souls that they had gotten in Haran; and they went forth to go into the land of Canaan; and into the land of Canaan they came.

6 And Abram passed through the land unto the place of Sichem, unto the plain of Moreh. And the Canaanite was then in the land. 7 And the LORD appeared unto Abram, and said, Unto thy seed will I give this land: and there builded he an altar unto the LORD, who appeared unto him. 8 And he removed from thence unto a mountain on the east of Bethel, and pitched his tent, having Bethel on the west, and Hai on the east: and there he builded an altar unto the LORD, and called upon the name of the LORD. 9 And Abram journeyed, going on still toward the south.

NEW REVISED STANDARD VERSION

GENESIS 11: 27 Now these are the descendants of Terah. Terah was the father of Abram, Nahor, and Haran; and Haran was the father of Lot. 28 Haran died before his father Terah in the land of his birth, in Ur of the Chaldeans. 29 Abram and Nahor took wives; the name of Abram's wife was Sarai, and the name of Nahor's wife was Milcah. She was the daughter of Haran the father of Milcah and Iscah. 30 Now Sarai was barren; she had no child.

31 Terah took his son Abram and his grandson Lot son of Haran, and his daughter-in-law Sarai, his son Abram's wife, and they went out together from Ur of the Chaldeans to go into the land of Canaan; but when they came to Haran, they settled there. 32 The days of Terah were two hundred five years; and Terah died in Haran.

12:1 Now the LORD said to Abram, "Go from your country and your kindred and your father's house to the land that I will show you. 2 I will make of you a great nation, and I will bless you, and make your name great, so that you will be a blessing. 3 I will bless those who bless you, and the one who curses you I will curse; and in you all the families of the earth shall be blessed."

4 So Abram went, as the LORD had told him; and Lot went with him. Abram was seventy-five years old when he departed from Haran. 5 Abram took his wife Sarai and his brother's son Lot, and all the possessions that they had gathered, and the persons whom they had acquired in Haran; and they set forth to go to the land of Canaan. When they had come to the land of Canaan, 6 Abram passed through the land to the place at Shechem, to the oak of Moreh. At that time the Canaanites were in the land. 7 Then the LORD appeared to Abram, and said, "To your offspring I will give this land." So he built there an altar to the LORD, who had appeared to him. 8 From there he moved on to the hill country on the east of Bethel, and pitched his tent, with Bethel on the west and Ai on the east; and there he built an altar to the LORD and invoked the name of the LORD. 9 And Abram journeyed on by stages toward the Negeb.

Monday, November 29	Isaiah 6:1-8	*God Calls Isaiah*
Tuesday, November 30	Jeremiah 1:4-10	*God Calls Jeremiah*
Wednesday, December 1	Luke 5:4-11	*Jesus Calls the First Disciples*
Thursday, December 2	Acts 9:1-9	*God Calls Saul*
Friday, December 3	Genesis 11:27-32	*Abram and Sarai Live in Haran*
Saturday, December 4	Genesis 12:1-9	*God Calls Abram*
Sunday, December 5	Genesis 15:1-6	*God Makes a Covenant with Abram*

BACKGROUND

Genesis is the book of beginnings. In this book we find the beginnings of the material universe, human life, human sin, divine judgment on human sin, covenant promises, and the Israelite tribes—to name just a few. Genesis provides a foundation for a great deal of what we can know about life and our Lord.

The Bible's first book has not always been called "Genesis." Following the tradition of naming a book after its opening word or words, the Hebrew title of the book was "In the Beginning." The current title comes from the word *geneseos* (found in the Greek translation of Gen. 2:4 and 5:1), which means "birth" or "genealogy" or "history of origin."

Genesis is the first of five books forming a group of their own at the beginning of the Old Testament. Together, Genesis through Deuteronomy are usually called the "Torah" (meaning "law" or "teaching") or the "Pentateuch" (literally, "fivevolumed [book]"). Genesis provides the background for the Exodus and the wilderness settings of the other four books.

In terms of the structure of Genesis, perhaps the best clue is a recurring phrase: "These are the generations of . . ." (Gen. 2:4; see also 5:1; 6:9;10:1;11:10, 27; 25:12,19; 36:1; 37:2). Some Bible scholars take this phrase, in each case, to be a summary of the preceding section. Many other scholars, however, take the phrase to be an introduction to the following section. Put another way, the phrase is a signal to the reader that the narrative is about to detail what became of the individual mentioned in the heading. If this view is correct, then the Book of Genesis has a prologue and 10 sections.

Genesis can also be looked at as having two main parts: chapters 1—11 and chapters 12—50. The first 11 chapters cover the time from Creation to the birth of Abraham. Although in these chapters we meet certain key individuals, such as Adam and Noah, the scope takes in all humanity. But in the book's final 38 chapters, the time span covered is much shorter: about 300 years. Also, the focus has narrowed to one family whom God called to receive and transmit His blessings.

From start to finish, Genesis is a book of history, and its historical account is trustworthy because it was inspired by God. But we should not expect the book to provide a complete or systematic history of time from its origin until the

Hebrews' Egyptian sojourn. The author's concern was not history for history's sake. He used true historical figures and events to teach truths about God and humankind. We should read Genesis, the book of beginnings, in that light.

NOTES ON THE PRINTED TEXT

Many years after the Flood and the Tower of Babel, God began a new approach in His dealings with humanity. He began to devote special attention to one family (later to become a nation) that would bear His name before all the world's peoples. Then, from out of this nation, He would raise up the Messiah, who would achieve salvation for all who would believe in Him.

Genesis 11:27, in particular, is the start of a detailed account of what happened to the family of *Terah*, especially after several of them left their homeland and began the lengthy journey to Canaan. The biblical text reveals that Terah fathered *Abram, Nahor, and Haran*, and that the latter had a son named *Lot*. Then 11:28 briefly notes that *Haran died* while still in *Ur of the Chaldees*. The city of Ur was a thriving commercial center in Abram's day. It had a population of several hundred thousand people; and excavations done at the site of the city suggest that it was noted for having high cultural standards.

While the family of Terah was still there, Abram married *Sarai* (11:29), whom 11:30 reveals was not able to have children. God would use this circumstance to mature the faith of Abram and Sarai. Abram's brother Nahor married a woman named Milcah. Such background information helps to prepare readers for upcoming events discussed in Genesis.

To set in motion His grand plan, God needed one man to become the progenitor of a holy nation (Israel), and He chose Abram of Ur for that role. We cannot be sure why God called this person and not someone else; but from later events in Abram's life, we know he had many fine qualities. This does not mean he was perfect; in fact, Joshua 24:2 reveals that at the time Abram was living in Ur, his family was worshiping false gods.

The initial journey to Canaan included Terah, his son Abram, and Terah's daughter-in-law Sarai, and Terah's grandson Lot (Gen. 11:31). When the group reached the village of *Haran*, they apparently stayed for a while. The biblical text does not state the reason for this. Maybe Abram's father, *Terah*, was too weak to travel farther; or maybe Terah decided not to leave this outpost of the Chaldean culture, which the family was used to. At any rate, Haran was the place where Terah *died* (11:32).

We next learn in 12:1 that *the LORD* told *Abram* to leave his *country*, his people, and his father's household. The patriarch was to go to a land he did not know (see Acts 7:2-3); in other words, Abram was to be lifted out of the familiar and placed in the unfamiliar. This circumstance must have seemed painful and risky to the patriarch; nevertheless, along with Abram's call came a blessing that surely acted as a powerful incentive for him to obey God. The blessing came in the form of a series of seven promises (Gen. 12:2-3; in Scripture, seven was often viewed as the symbolic number of perfection.)

In particular, the Lord pledged to make the patriarch a great nation with many descendants. God promised to give to Abram honor and make him a source of blessing to others. Through Abram and his descendants, God would pour out great blessings for all humanity. We now can see how God has fulfilled His Word. We understand how His promises reached their climax in Jesus Christ; but Abram had to accept the blessing and obey the call totally by faith (Heb. 11:8-10).

Abram, despite the ambiguities that lay ahead, called for his family to set out on the second stage of their journey. It was about another 400 miles (out of 700 total) to Canaan. The patriarch was part of a family in the lineage of Shem, the son of Noah. Abram presumably left behind many of his relatives when he headed west for Canaan in obedience to God's call. As Genesis 12:4 reveals, the patriarch was *seventy-five years old* at this time. According to 12:5, he took with him *Sarai* (his wife) and *Lot* (his nephew). Abram also took with him considerable *possessions*, slaves, and hired servants.

We know, of course, that apart from God's revelation Abram would not have abandoned the safety and wealth of his homeland; but when God called, Abram responded in trust, believing that God was able to do what He had promised. Thus, as Abram traveled through the land from north to south, he stopped at Shechem, Bethel, and the Negev area (12:6).

At this time the land was thinly populated by a variety of peoples who had descended from Canaan, the grandson of Noah. Nomadic tribesmen moved through the hill country and valleys. Some urbanization had begun to take place at fortified cities; but generally, the area was far behind the standard of civilization Abram had left behind.

According to 12:7, while Abram was at Shechem, *the LORD appeared* to him and promised to give the land of Canaan to his descendants. To our knowledge, this was the first time God had explicitly made this pledge to Abram. The promise must have meant a lot to the patriarch, now that he could see the land of Canaan all around him.

In response to the Lord's appearance, Abram *built* an *altar* at Shechem and offered sacrifices to *the LORD*. This act of devotion showed that the patriarch believed the Lord and was thankful for what He would do for him. At Bethel, Abram built another altar and again *invoked the name of the LORD* (12:8). Then he continued south, where he settled for awhile (vs. 9).

The biblical account concentrates on just a few of Abram's activities in Canaan, including pitching tents and building altars. The patriarch did not establish a permanent settlement in Canaan, but lived as a nomad, moving large flocks from place to place to find food and water. More importantly, the altars he built to worship God also served as a witness to the pagan inhabitants of the land of the patriarch's abiding faith in the Lord.

SUGGESTIONS TO TEACHERS

Try to imagine how Abram and Sarai must have felt upon hearing the call of God. They realized they would leave loved ones and tear themselves loose from the safety net of a supportive clan. They had to turn their backs on the pleasant, sheltered life in the most sophisticated civilization in that time. How could they know where they were going? To leave kinfolk and homeland for Abram and Sarai would have been as upsetting as for you to suddenly understand you were ordered by the Lord to pack up and wander in the general direction of the Gobi desert—but with no certain destination or assurance that you'd succeed in such a journey.

Despite the uncertainties that lay ahead, Abram and Sarai set off. The call of God was their reason. This journey was not their doing. Abram was not a religious genius, nor was Sarai a woman of special spiritual insight. They set off in faith. God also commands each of us to live this way.

1. THE PLIGHT OF THE PILGRIMS. Abram and Sarai set out as pilgrims with only God's promise. Living as pilgrims means realizing there is no permanence. After all, a tent is about as impermanent a shelter as one can find. As pilgrims for God, we must not put personal interests ahead of God's call.

2. THE PROMISE OF A PEOPLE. Abram and Sarai had been childless. But part of God's call to them was that they would have a son, and that they would be the founders of a great people belonging to the Lord. Such a promise seemed absurd to them. But they trusted God anyhow, and took Him at His word. Faith means trusting the Lord despite a lack of proof.

3. PERSISTENCE WITHOUT PROOFS. Abram did not hesitate to obey God's command. Like the patriarch, we must persist in obeying God's call even though there may be no immediate payoffs. We can count on God's assurance of the ultimate triumph of His plans and the assurance of His continuing presence with those who trust and obey Him.

4. PERSEVERANCE AND PIETY. Abram and his family had a long, arduous journey to Canaan. Perhaps they were tempted to turn back. Maybe they complained at times. But Abram *built an altar to the LORD and invoked the name of the LORD* (Gen. 12:8). Worship strengthened the patriarch's resolve to continue the journey.

FOR ADULTS

■ **TOPIC:** The Call to Follow God

■ **QUESTIONS:** 1. What was Sarai's condition at this time and why was that a significant detail? 2. What was there about God's call to Abram that must have made it difficult to obey? 3. What was there about God's promises that must have made them seem especially difficult for Abram to accept? 4. Why would Abram leave his homeland to go to Canaan? 5. What did the Lord promise to Abram when He appeared to him at Shechem?

■ ILLUSTRATIONS:

Ted's Surprising Adventure. Ted Boontheung Rasakham grew up in Laos in southeast Asia. Like everyone else in his family, Rasakham was a devout Buddhist. His spiritual journey led him to become a Buddhist monk. Then wartime forced him to flee the country. Rasakham sought haven across the border in northeastern Thailand. There he languished in a large, crowded refugee camp. During that period, Rasakham heard the news of Jesus for the first time. Rasakham was so affected by the good news of God in the person of Jesus that he turned over his life to the Lord and was baptized as a Christian. Many were upset, but the new convert faithfully agreed to go where God led him.

Eventually, Rasakham was able to emigrate to the United States. His adventure in faith led him to study for the Christian ministry. After years of hardship and study, Rasakham was called to the Lao United Church of Christ in Lowell (the only Laotian congregation in the United Church of Christ) and ordained on February 23, 1997, as a Christian pastor. By the grace and guidance of God, this man, like Abram, discovered that faith is a surprising adventure.

A Willingness to Go. A young clergyman in the Church of England was assigned a parish in a blighted area that had a reputation for problems. The young vicar was not happy about the notice to go to this parish. He made an appointment to discuss the matter with the insightful William Temple, who at this time was the Archbishop of Canterbury.

The young clergyman objected strenuously and pleaded to be relieved of the assignment. Temple sat patiently, listening to the young vicar's excuses. Finally the young man whimpered, "If I go there, it will kill me!" With a pleasant smile on his face, Temple quietly replied, "Well, now, you and I do not mind a little thing like that, do we?" Faith means being willing to sacrifice, even as Jesus Himself did.

The Call. Bill Forbes was a full-time dentist and taught courses in anatomy and pathology at the University of Maine. For years, Forbes has also been an active member of his American Baptist congregation. In 1989, he enrolled part time at Bangor Theological Seminary to take a class after more than 25 years in dentistry. At first, it was to increase his understanding of the Bible and the Christian faith. But a quote and an incident had such an impact on Forbe's life that he now regards these as God's "call" on him to enter the seminary and become a pastor.

The quote is from Tony Campolo, who said, "Are you going to tiptoe through life so you can arrive safely at your death?" The more Forbes reflected on this the more he began to wonder about what he would be thinking on his deathbed. He said quietly, "There's got to be more to life than making sure everything is in order when you die."

The incident occurred during a mission trip Forbes took to Honduras a number of years ago as a dentist. He saw a little girl who lost her eye due to an infection which "could have been treated for the price of a fastfood hamburger." Forbes said, "Her face will stay with me forever. I was never the same person after that trip."

In June 1997, after eight years of courses at Bangor Seminary, Forbes completed his theological studies. That same month, he sold his dental practice and said that he didn't know exactly what he'd do. While waiting for God to lead him on the next step of his adventure in faith, he and his wife, Gerri, acknowledged that they were both "excited and terrified" about the future and what it might hold for them. That's the adventure of faith!

| **FOR YOUTH** | ■ **TOPIC:** Abraham's Call |

■ **TOPIC:** Abraham's Call
■ **QUESTIONS:** 1. Who were Abram's various family members, and which ones journeyed with him to Canaan? 2. Where did Abram first stop before continuing his journey southward? 3. What specific promises did God make to Abram after commanding him to leave his homeland? 4. Who was living in the land of Canaan at the time of Abram's call to journey there? 5. How did Abram respond to the summons of God?

■ **ILLUSTRATIONS:**

A Need for a New Focus. Six-year-old Jamil Arafat Hamisjun was killed by Israeli soldiers. While the Israelis claimed that a soldier's gun accidentally went off, the Palestinians maintained that the soldier fired deliberately. Little Jamil was part of a group of Palestinian protesters gathered on Israel's West Bank. The people were upset by a huge contingent of Gush Emunin (the Group of the Faithful) who marched 24 miles from Jericho to Jerusalem.

The Orthodox Jews (who take God's commandments with great literalness) marched under a large banner that read: "The Lord said to Abraham . . . arise, walk through the land in the length of it and the breath of it; for I will give it to you." They claimed that as Jews and Abraham's descendants, God had given them the birthright to the West Bank of the Jordan River. Therefore, they had the right to build settlements on the West Bank.

Jamil and his family had argued that they too were descendants of Abraham. Standing with Palestinian Liberation Organization (PLO) flags and signs that read, "No Settlement in Palestine," the two groups squared off with tragic results.

How can peace come to two different groups who see themselves as descendants of Abraham? Perhaps the two should share the land and a new focus in a relationship with God through faith in Christ. If all of Abraham's descendants merged together, a truly great nation could develop.

Roots. As a young boy John grew up looking up at an old photograph of a man wearing the uniform of a Union Army lieutenant. His parents told him that he had been named for the man in the picture. Later, John was given a certificate of the man's Civil War induction notice.

At college, John discovered some resources that enabled him to learn about his namesake's regiment and the military action that he had experienced. When John's grandfather died, copies of dozens of letters written by his namesake during the Civil War describing his encounters at Camp Curtin, Fredericksburg, and Chancellorsville were found in an old file cabinet.

John began to take an interest in his namesake and his life as well as his other descendants. He began to explore his family roots. He wrote up reports about them for his relatives so that they might contribute their memories and learn about their ancestors.

Israel was also interested in its family roots. The account of Abram and his family is the tracing of the roots of God's people.

New Light on Abram. In 1964, Paolo Matthiae, a young professor of Near East Archaeology at the University of Rome, began to explore a series of mounds in northwestern Syria at Tell Mardikh. The area was thought not to be very promising because it lay midway between the two ancient superpowers of the day, Assyria and Egypt.

Work progressed slowly as Matthiae dug. In the fourth year a statue was discovered with an inscription by the king of the city of Ebla. Finally, in the tenth year of digging, more than 40 tablets were unearthed, each covered with cuneiform wedge-writing. The following year, 7,000 tablets were found as part of a library. What made these tablets so important was that the "five cities of the plain" were listed in the same order as Genesis 14. For those who often see Genesis as nothing more than a story without any historical basis, this was a shock!

A CALL TO LEAD FAITHFULLY

2

BACKGROUND SCRIPTURE: 1 Samuel 16:1-4b, 6-13; 2 Samuel 7:8-16
DEVOTIONAL READING: 2 Samuel 7:18-29

KEY VERSE: "The LORD does not see as mortals see; they look on the outward appearance, but the LORD looks on the heart." 1 Samuel 16:7.

KING JAMES VERSION

1 SAMUEL 16:1 And the LORD said unto Samuel, How long wilt thou mourn for Saul, seeing I have rejected him from reigning over Israel? fill thine horn with oil, and go, I will send thee to Jesse the Bethlehemite: for I have provided me a king among his sons. 2 And Samuel said, How can I go? if Saul hear it, he will kill me. And the LORD said, Take an heifer with thee, and say, I am come to sacrifice to the LORD.
3 And call Jesse to the sacrifice, and I will shew thee what thou shalt do: and thou shalt anoint unto me him whom I name unto thee. 4 And Samuel did that which the LORD spake, and came to Bethlehem. And the elders of the town trembled at his coming. . . .

6 And it came to pass, when they were come, that he looked on Eliab, and said, Surely the LORD's anointed is before him. 7 But the LORD said unto Samuel, Look not on his countenance, or on the height of his stature; because I have refused him: for the LORD seeth not as man seeth; for man looketh on the outward appearance, but the LORD looketh on the heart. 8 Then Jesse called Abinadab, and made him pass before Samuel. And he said, Neither hath the LORD chosen this. 9 Then Jesse made Shammah to pass by. And he said, Neither hath the LORD chosen this. 10 Again, Jesse made seven of his sons to pass before Samuel. And Samuel said unto Jesse, The LORD hath not chosen these. 11 And Samuel said unto Jesse, Are here all thy children? And he said, There remaineth yet the youngest, and, behold, he keepeth the sheep. And Samuel said unto Jesse, Send and fetch him: for we will not sit down till he come hither. 12 And he sent, and brought him in. Now he was ruddy, and withal of a beautiful countenance, and goodly to look to. And the LORD said, Arise, anoint him: for this is he. 13 Then Samuel took the horn of oil, and anointed him in the midst of his brethren: and the Spirit of the LORD came upon David from that day forward. So Samuel rose up, and went to Ramah.

NEW REVISED STANDARD VERSION

1 SAMUEL 16:1 The LORD said to Samuel, "How long will you grieve over Saul? I have rejected him from being king over Israel. Fill your horn with oil and set out; I will send you to Jesse the Bethlehemite, for I have provided for myself a king among his sons."
2 Samuel said, "How can I go? If Saul hears of it, he will kill me." And the LORD said, "Take a heifer with you, and say, 'I have come to sacrifice to the LORD.'
3 Invite Jesse to the sacrifice, and I will show you what you shall do; and you shall anoint for me the one whom I name to you." 4 Samuel did what the LORD commanded, and came to Bethlehem. The elders of the city came to meet him. . . .

6 When they came, he looked on Eliab and thought, "Surely the LORD's anointed is now before the LORD." 7 But the LORD said to Samuel, "Do not look on his appearance or on the height of his stature, because I have rejected him; for the LORD does not see as mortals see; they look on the outward appearance, but the LORD looks on the heart." 8 Then Jesse called Abinadab, and made him pass before Samuel. He said, "Neither has the LORD chosen this one." 9 Then Jesse made Shammah pass by. And he said, "Neither has the LORD chosen this one." 10 Jesse made seven of his sons pass before Samuel, and Samuel said to Jesse, "The LORD has not chosen any of these." 11 Samuel said to Jesse, "Are all your sons here?" And he said, "There remains yet the youngest, but he is keeping the sheep." And Samuel said to Jesse, "Send and bring him; for we will not sit down until he comes here." 12 He sent and brought him in. Now he was ruddy, and had beautiful eyes, and was handsome. The LORD said, "Rise and anoint him; for this is the one." 13 Then Samuel took the horn of oil, and anointed him in the presence of his brothers; and the spirit of the LORD came mightily upon David from that day forward. Samuel then set out and went to Ramah.

Monday, December 6	Psalm 3	*God Will Protect*
Tuesday, December 7	Psalm 5:1-8	*God Makes the Way Straight*
Wednesday, December 8	Psalm 18:1-6	*God Is a Rock and Fortress*
Thursday, December 9	1 Samuel 15:10-19	*God Rejects Saul as King*
Friday, December 10	1 Samuel 16:1-5	*Samuel Visits Jesse and His Sons*
Saturday, December 11	1 Samuel 16:6-13	*David Is Anointed King*
Sunday, December 12	1 Samuel 16:14-23	*David Joins Saul's Court*

BACKGROUND

Samuel was the last major judge in the roughly 350-year period of the judges. Accordingly, 1 Samuel picks up approximately where the Book of Judges ends. Samuel appeared on the scene during a time of pervasive, cyclical decline in Israel. Even the priesthood—under Eli's corrupt sons—was being used for personal gain and profit rather than the divine purposes for which it was intended. Israel was disintegrating morally, spiritually, and politically. But God, ever attentive to the cries of the godly, responded to Hannah's prayers and gave her a son, both to answer the desires of her heart for a child and to meet the needs of the nation.

Samuel issued the call for spiritual revival in Israel. Under his capable leadership in the offices of prophet, priest, and judge, stability came to the beleaguered nation. Regrettably, when Samuel's tenure as Israel's leader was almost at an end, it was clear that his corrupt sons were unfit to succeed him. Under these circumstances the elders of Israel requested a king as the nation's new ruler.

Though the elders' request for a king was not wrong, the motive behind their request dishonored God. They were rejecting the power of God's kingship over Israel and placing their hope in a human leader who would *"go out before us and fight our battles"* (1 Sam. 8:20). Even so, God granted their request and guided Samuel in the selection of Saul as Israel's first king. In this way, the monarchy was established in Israel.

Thus, 1 and 2 Samuel relate the history of Israel from the birth of Samuel in about 1080 B.C. to the end of David's reign in about 950 B.C., a period of roughly 130 years. First Samuel gives an account of Israel's transition from the period of the judges to the monarchy. A summary of Samuel's judgeship is found in chapters 1—8, while chapters 9—15 tell the account of Saul's coronation and early years as king. The stormy relationship between David and Saul is covered in chapters 16—30. First Samuel comes to a close with the death of Saul and his sons in chapter 31.

Second Samuel chronicles the history of David's reign as king. It begins with an account of his rule over the southern kingdom of Judah (chaps. 1—4), then goes on to tell about his expansion of the kingdom and his rise as a powerful and popular monarch. Although David was a man of deep faith, his human failings and often ruthless drive to get what he wanted resulted in great distress for himself and his family.

NOTES ON THE PRINTED TEXT

The books of 1 and 2 Samuel tell an account of great transition in the development of God's kingdom in the Old Testament era. As a boy Samuel was summoned to guide Israel into the monarchy, that is, a system of government under one king. Under his leadership Israel's loose association of tribes developed into a nation with a strong centralized government.

In preparation for the nation's move into the new era, Samuel was called to repair the moral fabric and restore the spiritual vitality of a people who had drifted far from the Lord. Samuel finished the work of the judges and launched the monarchy, not by human strength and intuition, but by the power of God through prayer.

Along with establishing the monarchy, Samuel aided in launching an order of the prophets (1 Sam. 19:20) so as to bring God's Word to his people. From Samuel's time onward, the prophets promoted the spiritual life of Israel and were the channels through whom God made His will known to both king and commoner.

The first person Samuel appointed to be king, Saul, was a moral and spiritual failure. He constantly compromised God's commands and brought Israel to the brink of ruin. He ended his life tormented by evil spirits. In contrast, his successor David is described as a *"man after [God's] own heart"* (1 Sam. 13:14). Though imperfect in his personal life and kingly reign, David stood out as a leader known for his single-minded devotion to the God of Israel.

Given what has been said, we can see why the Lord regretted making Saul king over Israel (15:35). We also discover that Saul's repeated failure to be a godly monarch deeply distressed Samuel, who had been serving as a judge and prophet of the nation for many years. In fact, Samuel persistently *grieved over* Saul's unqualified failure to lead the Israelites.

How long Samuel persisted in mourning for Saul is unclear; but when a sufficiently long enough period of time had elapsed, the Lord directed him discontinue doing so (16:1). God explained that Samuel's excessive sorrow for Saul's situation was inconsistent with the Lord's rejection of him as Israel's *king*.

In short, it was time for Samuel to implement the next stage in God's plan for the nation. Thus, the Lord directed Samuel to take a ram's horn, fill it with olive oil, and go to Bethlehem (16:2). In this small town about five miles north of Jerusalem, Samuel would find a man named Jesse who was living there. God had chosen one of his sons to be the replacement monarch for Israel.

As Samuel reflected on what God intended to do through him, the prophet became alarmed. He feared that, if Saul became aware of this plan to anoint a new king, he would have Samuel executed. In response, God directed Samuel to take a *heifer* with him to Bethlehem so that he might *sacrifice* it to *the LORD*. Samuel was also to invite Jesse to the event so that God could indicate which of his sons was to be anointed (16:3).

Despite whatever misgivings Samuel may have felt, he put those aside and did as God had directed; but when the prophet arrived in Bethlehem, the elders in the town became alarmed. Some think they were concerned that Samuel had come in his capacity as judge (see 7:16), and was there to punish them for some offense. Thus, when the elders of Bethlehem asked Samuel whether he came *peaceably* (16:4), the prophet said yes. He then explained that he had come to offer a *sacrifice to the Lord* (16:5).

Samuel next instructed the town leaders to go through the necessary purification ritual to get themselves prepared for the event. He also invited Jesse and his sons to the sacrifice and got them ready to participate in it.

When Jesse and his sons had arrived, Samuel spotted Eliab and concluded that this was the person the Lord had chosen to be *anointed* (16:6). God, however, directed Samuel not to make a snap judgment just because Eliab may have been handsome and tall, for the Lord had not chosen him to be Israel's next king (16:7). Moreover, God explained that, while people made assessments based on outward *appearance*, He looked at a person's *heart*, namely, one's thoughts and intentions.

When Jesse next had his son Abinadab walk before Samuel, the prophet said this person was not the one God had chosen as Israel's next king (16:8). In fact, Samuel declared that the Lord had not chosen any of the sons of Jesse who were then present (16:9-10).

Samuel next asked whether all of Jesse's sons were present (16:11). Jesse noted that his *youngest* son was not there, for he was out in the countryside tending the family *sheep*. Samuel then directed that the lad be brought immediately to the event; in fact, no one would be permitted to sit down and eat until Jesse's youngest son had arrived.

In Old Testament times it was rare to find a family that did not own at least a few sheep; and where there were sheep, there must have been a shepherd. In some instances, the whole family helped tend the flock. Such was the case with Jacob's sons (Gen. 37:2; 46:33-34); but often, shepherding duties fell to the junior male member of the family.

Since David was the youngest of Jesse's sons and therefore last in the family's pecking order, Jesse probably thought that whatever Samuel had come for, it could not possibly involve an insignificant shepherd boy. This episode reminds us that youth is not a barrier to having an exceptional character.

As directed, Jesse promptly sent for David; and 1 Samuel 16:12 reveals that he was *ruddy*, with attractive *eyes* and a *handsome* appearance. *Ruddy* probably referred to reddish hair and complexion. These features stood out in a land where dark hair and complexion were the norm.

Upon David's arrival, the Lord revealed to Samuel that this was the person whom He wanted to be anointed. It was the common practice in Bible times to anoint persons and things that were consecrated, or set apart, for service to God. Prophets (1 Kings 19:16), priests (Lev. 8:12), and kings (1 Sam. 9:16; 10:1; 16:13; 1 Kings 1:34) were all anointed with olive oil to signify their special separation for service to the Lord.

A prophet spoke to the people on God's behalf, while the priest represented the people before God; and it fell to the king to act as the executor of God's law. As the holder of all three offices—prophet, priest, and king—Jesus was indeed the Messiah, the Anointed One (see John 20:30-31).

As David stood among his brothers, Samuel poured the olive oil on the lad's head (1 Sam. 16:13). Then *the spirit of the LORD* came upon David and remained in control of him from *that day forward*. After that, Samuel returned to his hometown of *Ramah* in Ephraim.

SUGGESTIONS TO TEACHERS

Saul made many wrong choices, and these eventually cost him his kingship. Basically, his choices showed that he refused to follow God's directives. When charged by Samuel to obey God, and when challenged to choose God's ways, Saul repeatedly failed the Lord, the Israelites, and himself. This week's lesson points out the challenge of choosing to follow God throughout our lives.

1. DISOBEDIENCE. Saul tried to excuse his disobedience to God by claiming that he had spared the captured livestock in order to make a special sacrifice (1 Sam. 15:9, 14-15). Samuel, of course, saw through the king's lame explanation. No matter how clever we may be in trying to evade God's will, He recognizes our efforts for what they really are, namely, disobedience.

2. INSINCERITY. When questioned further, Saul continued to insist that his decision to disobey God was acceptable. But, as Samuel declared, obedience is far more important to God than sacrifice (15:17-23). We are foolish if we try to cover up our disobedience to God by insincere acts of piety.

3. REJECTION. Saul's continued acts of disobedience deeply saddened and upset Samuel. The Lord told His trusted servant, *"I regret that I made Saul king, for he has turned back from following me, and has not carried out my commands"* (15:10). And Samuel later declared to Saul, *"The LORD has torn the kingdom of Israel from you this very day, and has given it to a neighbor of yours"* (15:28). Here is a reminder to us as God's chosen people to obey Him in all that we do.

4. SELECTION. Samuel, knowing that God had rejected Saul as king, anointed young David as Israel's next ruler. Samuel knew that he was placing himself in danger by selecting David while Saul was still the nation's king. Nevertheless, Samuel accepted the risk out of his loyalty to God. This reminds us that some of our choices are difficult because of the risks involved in being a Christian. We can accept the risks, for our eyes are on the heavenly reward (Heb. 11:24-28).

■ **TOPIC:** Leadership Qualities

■ **QUESTIONS:** 1. How did Samuel initially respond to God's rejection of Saul as king? 2. What mistake did Samuel make in evaluating which of Jesse's sons God had chosen to be Israel's next king? 3. How was God's standard of selection different from that of Samuel? 4. Why did Jesse hesitate to tell Samuel he had one other son? 5. What happened to David immediately after he was anointed as Israel's next king?

■ **ILLUSTRATIONS:**

Morning-Glory Fizzle. A "fizzle" often happens in many realms of life. For example, in professional baseball coaches talk about the "morning-glory" syndrome. That name is given to young recruits who perform marvelously in spring practice in Florida or Arizona. But then as they travel north and experience the lengthy season, they begin to wilt like a morning-glory flower. By June their batting average drops to an unacceptable level. And by July they are released from their team.

The reign of Saul was like a "morning-glory" plant. At first, he seemed to have everything going for him as Israel's new king. After all, he was tall, handsome, and seemingly humble. But the promise of being a great leader was not fulfilled. He lacked the patience, fortitude, and willingness to remain obedient to God. Consequently, he fizzled out in his service. It's important for us to consider how we can prevent this from happening in our life of service to the Lord.

Silly Choice. The last time a full eclipse of the moon occurred, a survey revealed that more people in Washington, D.C., chose to view the dramatic event on their television screens than go outside their homes and see the phenomenon firsthand. The opportunity to personally witness such a rare event was available to them. But instead they chose the convenience of a picture tube.

There seems to be a spiritual lesson here. We often choose to experience life indirectly through radio and television broadcasts and the movies, rather than directly in one-to-one encounters with others. And tragically we prevent ourselves from being influential servants of God in a variety of daily events and activities.

Challenge, Choice, and Change. The Methodist movement began when John Wesley overcame his high church prejudices and brought himself to proclaim the Gospel in the open air before the common people. Wesley began preaching the message of Christ to a group of people who had assembled on Haddam Mount, which is outside Bristol, England.

Wesley later wrote in his *Journal* for March 31, 1739: "I have been all my life (till very lately) so tenacious of every point relating to decency and order, that I should have thought the saving of souls almost a sin, if it had not been done in a church." When Wesley went out to preach on the afternoon of April 2, 1739, he later noted in his *Journal:* "At four in the afternoon, I submitted to be more vile, and proclaimed in the highways the glad tidings of salvation, speaking from a little eminence in a ground adjoining to the city, to about three thousand people."

Such was Wesley's initial feeling about preaching in the open air. Nevertheless, despite his misgivings, he saw it as an opportunity for ministry and decided to change his ways. He made the right choice, for he saw many people trust in Christ for salvation. Wesley was willing to submit himself to the will of God, and the Lord greatly blessed him in his ministry.

| FOR YOUTH | ■ **TOPIC:** David's Call |
| | ■ **QUESTIONS:** 1. Why had the Lord rejected Saul as Israel's king? |

2. Why had the elders of Bethlehem become afraid when Samuel arrived? 3. In what way was Samuel mistaken in his assessment of Jesse's first seven sons? 4. What job was David assigned to do within the family of Jesse? What did this indicate about David's status? 5. What physical attributes and character qualities did David have?

■ **ILLUSTRATIONS:**

Run Your Lap in Life's Relay Race! Only one person has ever lived who could conclude His life by knowing that all His God-given plans were fulfilled. That person is Jesus Christ. Only He was able to say before dying, *"It is finished"* (John 19:30), which means that He had accomplished His redemptive work.

We are members of God's covenant community through faith in Christ. It's a bit like being a member of a great relay team. One believer runs a lap and then passes on the baton to another. The runner receiving the baton is called upon to exert every effort to carry it forward for the sake of the team, and then relinquish it to another teammate. Each believer knows that it is the victory of the team that is paramount, not one's own personal glory. In God's work, each of us is responsible for our lap in God's race.

God's Word reminds us that the Lord's redemptive plans will be accomplished. Saul turned out to be a great disappointment as Israel's first king. But the baton of leadership (so to speak) was passed on (through the intervention of Samuel) to David. The new leader would have the opportunity to guide God's people and urge them to remain faithful to the decrees of the Mosaic covenant.

Scripture reassures us that God's plan of redemption will be fulfilled. We may not live to see all the Lord's plans carried out, just as we will not live to see all our own hopes and dreams fulfilled. The most important matter is that our desires coincide with God's will for us. Our foremost goal should be to glorify the Lord through our thoughts, words, and actions. If we can say that we did this in life, then we know that we have done things of eternal significance.

Called to Lead. Brandon Williams, the running back for Valley High School, stood in the Bible Way Christian Fellowship Church in New Kensington, Pennsylvania, and announced that he would attend the University of Pittsburgh. The January 23, 1997, news conference ended months of recruiting for one of the nation's top 20 running backs. The college won over such finalists as Notre Dame, UCLA, Ohio State, and Syracuse.

Landing Williams was a huge victory for the University of Pittsburgh. The struggling football program had hired new coach Walt Harris in 1997. He guided the team to its first winning season and a Liberty Bowl appearance. However, the team was largely seniors. The program needed new and younger players to replace many of the departing players. Brandon wanted to be part of that new team and its leadership. That was part of the promise he received from former University of Pittsburgh great and NFL leader, Tony Dorsett, who reminded Brandon that he had been part of the rebuilding of a program years earlier.

Brandon is an example of a youth who has been called to lead a new project. David was a similar example. After being chosen by God, he accepted the opportunity to lead the Israelites into an era of peace and godliness.

Minor Flaws: Tests on iron rivets retrieved from the sunken liner *Titanic* have indicated that all of them had an unusually high slag content. William Garzke, the chief scientist of the *Titanic* investigation, announced this startling information while at the national meeting of the American Chemical Society.

Slag is an impurity that can contaminate forged iron. Normally, high quality rivets contain about three percent slag. But the Titanic's 3,000,000 rivets showed a level of nine percent. This made them especially weak and more likely to snap after the liner hit an iceberg. While stronger rivets would not have prevented the liner from sinking, the theory is that the vessel would have floated longer, allowing enough time for all the passengers on board to be rescued.

From this we see that even a minor flaw can cause devastating effects. For example, Saul's moral blemishes eventually caught up with him, and led the Lord to reject him as king and select another person to lead Israel.

Fame's Fifteen Minutes. The late artist of junk culture, Andy Warhol, once bellowed, "In the future, everybody will be famous for at least fifteen minutes!" In other words, fame is shortlived. It suddenly elevates people before the public. And then as quickly, they fade away. Consider Saul. For the moment he commanded power and prestige as Israel's king. But then he rebelled against God. As a result, the Lord rejected him, and he faded off the scene of history. What a tragic end!

Dry Rot. When the *U.S.S. Constitution* ("Old Ironsides") was restored in 1997, one suspicion was confirmed—dry rot existed in the vessel. While saltwater prevents decay, fresh water rots wood. The salt water had prevented decay below the waterline of the ship, but rain water had brought in wood hungry organisms like marine borers. Rain also collected in the dark, warm crannies and compartments, which allowed air borne fungi to attack the wood and produce dry rot.

People go through spiritual "dry rot." Events weaken them, sap their strength, and speed up the moral decay within them. Saul is an outstanding example of this phenomenon. Only the grace of God can spare us from experiencing something similar in our lives.

A CALL TO RESPOND

BACKGROUND SCRIPTURE: Matthew 1
DEVOTIONAL READING: Luke 1:26-32

KEY VERSE: When Joseph awoke from sleep, he did as the angel of the Lord commanded him; he took her as his wife. Matthew 1:24.

KING JAMES VERSION

MATTHEW 1:17 So all the generations from Abraham to David are fourteen generations; and from David until the carrying away into Babylon are fourteen generations; and from the carrying away into Babylon unto Christ are fourteen generations.

18Now the birth of Jesus Christ was on this wise: When as his mother Mary was espoused to Joseph, before they came together, she was found with child of the Holy Ghost. 19Then Joseph her husband, being a just man, and not willing to make her a publick example, was minded to put her away privily. 20 But while he thought on these things, behold, the angel of the Lord appeared unto him in a dream, saying, Joseph, thou son of David, fear not to take unto thee Mary thy wife: for that which is conceived in her is of the Holy Ghost. 21And she shall bring forth a son, and thou shalt call his name JESUS: for he shall save his people from their sins. 22Now all this was done, that it might be fulfilled which was spoken of the Lord by the prophet, saying, 23Behold, a virgin shall be with child, and shall bring forth a son, and they shall call his name Emmanuel, which being interpreted is, God with us. 24Then Joseph being raised from sleep did as the angel of the Lord had bidden him, and took unto him his wife: 25And knew her not till she had brought forth her firstborn son: and he called his name JESUS.

NEW REVISED STANDARD VERSION

MATTHEW 1:17 So all the generations from Abraham to David are fourteen generations; and from David to the deportation to Babylon, fourteen generations; and from the deportation to Babylon to the Messiah, fourteen generations.

18 Now the birth of Jesus the Messiah took place in this way. When his mother Mary had been engaged to Joseph, but before they lived together, she was found to be with child from the Holy Spirit. 19 Her husband Joseph, being a righteous man and unwilling to expose her to public disgrace, planned to dismiss her quietly. 20 But just when he had resolved to do this, an angel of the Lord appeared to him in a dream and said, "Joseph, son of David, do not be afraid to take Mary as your wife, for the child conceived in her is from the Holy Spirit. 21 She will bear a son, and you are to name him Jesus, for he will save his people from their sins." 22 All this took place to fulfill what had been spoken by the Lord through the prophet:

23 "Look, the virgin shall conceive and bear a son,
and they shall name him Emmanuel,"

which means, "God is with us." 24 When Joseph awoke from sleep, he did as the angel of the Lord commanded him; he took her as his wife, 25 but had no marital relations with her until she had borne a son; and he named him Jesus.

BACKGROUND

Matthew's Gospel has been called the bridge between the Old and New Testaments because it helps us understand the relationship between the old and new covenants. For instance, several times Matthew refers to some historical fact by making a statement similar to this: *Then was fulfilled what had been spoken through the prophet* (2:17). This suggests to us that the birth, death, and resurrection of Christ fulfilled the Old Testament prophecies concerning God's plan for the salvation.

Ancient Jewish writers, such as Matthew, believed that the best way to begin to tell the account of a person's life was to present his or her genealogy. Matthew thus began his Gospel with the statement, *An account of the genealogy of Jesus the Messiah, the son of David, the son of Abraham* (1:1).

The incarnation of Jesus—namely, God the Son coming to earth as a human being—is the central event of the opening chapter of Matthew's Gospel. He related the account of Jesus' miraculous conception and birth in a simple but heart-gripping style. Reading 1:18-25 will reassure a believer that the writer of these words was totally convinced that every detail of Jesus' incarnation was factual. Matthew did not attempt to throw a veil of mystery around Jesus' birth. Certainly there is a great mystery involved in what took place in the humble home of a young woman in Nazareth; yet Matthew's faith in the utter truth of the event was such that there was no shadow of doubt in his words.

Concerning ancient Jewish marriages, they consisted of three steps. First, a man and a woman became engaged when their two families agreed to the arrangement. The second step came when a public announcement was made and the couple became betrothed (*engaged*, 1:18). This formal agreement between couples planning to be married was taken much more seriously than modern-day engagements. It was considered legally binding and could be broken only by death or divorce. The relationship would not be physically consummated until after the couple was married. This comprised the third and final step in the process.

We can only imagine what Joseph must have felt when Mary *was found to be with child* (Matt. 1:18). Joseph initially did not know that Mary's offspring was *from the Holy Spirit*. According to Jewish law, if a woman broke the second step of the betrothal process by being intimate with another man, she faced serious consequences. The fiance had a right to divorce her, and the religious authorities could have the lawbreakers stoned to death (Deut. 22:23-24).

Joseph was faced with the social stigma attached to what he thought Mary had done; but Joseph, *being a righteous man* (Matt. 1:19), was *unwilling to expose [Mary] to public disgrace*. Joseph thus *planned to dismiss her quietly.* However, before Joseph could enact his plan, God miraculously intervened.

Thus, *just when [Joseph] had resolved* (1:20) to end his betrothal to Mary, *an angel of the Lord appeared to [Joseph] in a dream.* Angels are spirit beings created by God to serve Him and to function as His messengers (Heb. 1:14). In addition to good angels, there are also fallen ones. The latter are under Satan's control and do his bidding. In the case of Joseph, a good angel appeared to him. Joseph's attitude toward Mary was reversed when the angel revealed to him that *the child conceived in [Mary] is from the Holy Spirit* (Matt. 1:20).

NOTES ON THE PRINTED TEXT

Matthew began his Gospel by recording *the genealogy of Jesus* (1:1). Matthew then presented the actual historical facts concerning how Jesus was miraculously conceived and born. The Gospel of Luke also discusses this event. Together the accounts of both Gospels provide the clear facts about the incarnation of the Messiah. Upon their records this great doctrine of Christianity has been established.

In 1:17 we note that Jesus' genealogy, as Matthew presented it, comprises three sections of 14 generations each. Not every ancestor of the Savior appears in the list; yet as the descendant of Abraham and David—two of Israel's most esteemed ancestors—Jesus unquestionably qualifies as the nation's Messiah. Matthew wanted to show that the progress of biblical history had reached its fulfillment with the coming of the Savior.

Matthew's emphasis is on the manner in which Jesus was born. His birth took place *in this way* (Matt. 1:18). Because He was *the Messiah,* His coming to earth as a human being would be unique. The way in which Adam came into the world was awesome (Gen. 2:7); but Jesus' entrance upon the human scene was far more amazing.

Matthew was not writing to those who knew nothing about Jesus' birth. The fact of His virginal conception apparently was already well known and fully accepted among the early believers. Matthew thus mentioned neither the exact time nor place of this event. However, we can infer from Luke 1:26 that the locale was *a town in Galilee called Nazareth.*

Mary and Joseph decided to enter into a legally binding arrangement by becoming *engaged* (Matt. 1:18). If Mary and Joseph were of the ages typical for marriage in their time and place, she was in her early teens and he was somewhat older. The couple must have dreamed about what their life together would be like; yet neither of them could have imagined the extraordinary privilege and responsibility that would be theirs—the rearing of God's Son.

Matthew clearly stated that Mary became pregnant before she and Joseph *lived together*. Mary evidently did not tell Joseph that she had conceived a child *from the Holy Spirit*. Mary learned this from *the angel Gabriel* (Luke 1:26). He also revealed that Mary's *relative Elizabeth in her old age has . . . conceived a son* (1:36).

Upon learning this, Mary *set out and went with haste* (1:39) to visit with Elizabeth and share her good news. Mary left the matter of her pregnancy in God's hands and thus showed her total reliance upon Him. This was all the more courageous on Mary's part, for she had no way of proving her faithfulness to Joseph or to anyone else in Nazareth. Also, Mary surely knew that she could face social stigma for her pregnancy.

Joseph was *a righteous man* (Matt. 1:19), and this guided him in his decision making. Perhaps like Zechariah and Elizabeth, Joseph was *living blamelessly according to all the commandments and regulations of the Lord* (Luke 1:6). The Greek word translated *righteous* (Matt. 1:19) described Joseph's heart as well as his conduct. Out of devotion to God, Joseph decided not to consummate his marriage vows with Mary when he discovered that she was pregnant. Joseph's response to this discovery tells us something else about him. Apparently there was no outburst of anger. Joseph's love for Mary was such that he refused *to expose her to public disgrace*; instead, Joseph *planned to dismiss her quietly*.

The Lord miraculously intervened by dispatching His *angel* (1:20). This celestial being would help Joseph understand the importance of what had taken place. Whereas the angel appeared to Joseph *in a dream* (1:20), Luke states that an angel *came to* (Luke 1:28) Mary, delivered his message, and *departed from* (1:38) Mary.

The angel addressed Joseph as the *son of David* (Matt. 1:20). Matthew's genealogy listed Joseph as a descendant of the royal house of David. Now Joseph must prove himself to be a true son of David, who would have faith to believe that the promise of a Messiah was about to be fulfilled.

The angel's message to Joseph removed all of his concerns. The angel's statement, *"for the child conceived in her is from the Holy Spirit,"* explained in the clearest way the great mystery of the Incarnation. Notice that the angel did not attempt to discuss the scientific details of how the virginal conception of Jesus took place. This is the way of divine inspiration. Truths the human mind could never completely fathom are expressed in direct and completely adequate terms.

The angel was careful to tell Joseph that Mary would *bear a son* (1:21). Zechariah had also been told that Elizabeth would bear him a son (Luke 1:13), and Abraham moreover learned that his wife Sarah would bear him a son (Gen. 17:19).

This child Mary would bear was not Joseph's offspring; nevertheless, he was *to name him Jesus, for he will save his people from their sins* (Matt. 1:21). Joseph would be the legal father of this child. Incidentally, the name *Jesus* means "The

Lord saves." This observation reminds us that the Father would redeem the lost through His Son.

Matthew not only described the virgin birth, but also provided scriptural support for this unique event. It ultimately fulfilled what Isaiah the prophet had foretold long ago (1:22). Verse 23 quotes Isaiah 7:14, which says *the young woman is with child and shall bear a son, and shall name him Immanuel.* When translated, *Emmanuel* (Matt. 1:23) means *"God is with us."* This implies that the sovereign, eternal Lord would be miraculously conceived in *the virgin*, and thereby become human and dwell among people.

When Joseph awoke from his dream, he acted immediately to carry out the angel's orders (1:24). Despite what others in Nazareth might think, Joseph took Mary to be *his wife.* Joseph abstained from marital relations with her until the child was born, *and he named him Jesus* (1:25) as the angel had commanded.

SUGGESTIONS TO TEACHERS

The English word "promise" comes from a Latin term that means "to send forth." This suggests that a promise given, either written or orally, becomes the basis for expecting something to develop or happen. For instance, God promised that humanity, through the Second Adam (Rom. 5:12-20)—Jesus Christ—would triumph over the forces of sin, death, and Satan (Gen. 3:15; Rom. 16:20). Through the long centuries, that promise was kept alive. Though people often break promises, God is faithful to keep His pledge (Heb. 6:13-17). He did so when, in a most unusual and unexpected way, He sent His Son, *Emmanuel* (Matt. 1:23), to be *"God . . . with us."*

1. THE DILEMMA OF A RIGHTEOUS MAN. Being a devout, upright Jew, Joseph possibly embraced the hope of his people for a Messiah to deliver them from the bondage they had experienced from Rome. Joseph was not prepared for the way God would choose to keep His promise to send a Savior. Nevertheless, Joseph was willing to obey God's instructions. Often God chooses to accomplish His purposes in our lives in unusual and unexpected ways.

2. THE MESSAGE OF THE ANGEL. The angel first addressed Joseph's fear. He most likely was afraid of the social stigma and other negative consequences that could befall Mary, whom Joseph deeply loved. The angel's explanation was opposed to human logic and reason, yet Joseph accepted by faith what he could not fully comprehend within himself. The angel told Joseph all he needed to know in order to fulfill the purpose God had planned for him, Mary, and her unborn child.

3. THE FULFILLMENT OF PROPHECY. Matthew confirmed the message of the angel by referring to Isaiah's prophecy that *"the virgin shall conceive and bear a son, and they shall name him Emmanuel"* (Matt. 1:23). This was yet another evidence that God keeps His promise. The waiting period may at times seem long and dark, but God's promises to us will never be broken.

■ **TOPIC:** When the Unexpected Happens

■ **QUESTIONS:** 1. How did the Jews view the engagement period between a man and woman? 2. How did Matthew discuss the miraculous conception of Jesus? 3. In what ways did Joseph demonstrate his upright character in the situation involving Mary? 4. How did Matthew link the virgin birth to the Old Testament? 5. How can Christians be involved in the fulfillment of God's promise to provide a Savior to redeem the lost from their sin?

■ **ILLUSTRATIONS:**

The Unseen Player. Many years ago the *London Observer* carried the following fictitious story. A family of mice lived all their lives in a large piano. In their piano world came the music of that instrument, filling all the dark spaces with sound and harmony.

At first, the mice were impressed by the music. They drew comfort and wonder from the thought that there was someone who made the music, though the music-maker was invisible to them. Yet whoever he was, he was above them, yet close to them. The mice loved to think of this person as the Great Player whom they could not see.

Then one day a daring mouse climbed up inside the piano and returned to his fellow mice. He had found out how the music was made! Wires were the secret. Tightly stretched wires of different lengths trembled and vibrated. The mice thus had to revise all their old beliefs. None but the most conservative of them could believe in the Unseen Player.

Later another mouse explorer discovered hammers that danced up and down on the wires. This was a more complicated theory, but it proved that they lived in a purely mechanical world. Thus the Unseen Player came to be thought of by the mice as only a myth. Despite all that, the pianist, the Unseen Player, continued to play.

This is the way it has been through the ages concerning the miraculous birth of Jesus. Critics have tried to destroy the credibility of His virginal conception, claiming that it is only a lovely myth, a story with much symbolism, but no literal truth. Yet today the light of God's truth shines brighter than ever on our Lord's amazing birth and on the sinless life He lived in order to redeem us from our sins.

God's Signature. H.B. London, in his newsletter, *The Pastor's Weekly Briefing,* told about the death of a close friend named Carl Gaede, an outstanding architect. He had won many prestigious awards for his church buildings across the country. Because of his creative skills, he was able to leave his "signature" behind him. People who never knew Gaede personally see his buildings, worship in the sanctuaries he designed, and are blessed by the beauty and uniqueness of those structures.

Our signature is that unique something about us that causes others to remember us. It is the legacy we leave behind us. God the Son left His signature in the world when, in the fullness of time, He stepped out of heaven and, in the form of a little baby, became Immanuel, "God with us." His signature was His everlasting love poured into flesh and blood that never knew sin.

Making Preparation. When our orthodox Jewish friends celebrate Passover, they set a place at the table for Elijah, for they expect him to return to earth at any time to announce that the Messiah is coming. Thus, with the greatest care, they make preparation for the Savior's advent.

What kind of preparation are we making to celebrate the marvelous fact that the Messiah has, indeed, already come? Has our preparation consisted only of festive decorations and the placing of gifts under a tree? What about our spiritual preparation? Do we understand something of the fantastic preparations God made from eternity past for the coming of His Son? Have we prepared our hearts and minds to properly celebrate His birth?

FOR YOUTH

■ **TOPIC:** Jospeh's Call

■ **QUESTIONS:** 1. How did Mary's engagement to Joseph differ from a couple's engagement today? 2. What did Joseph's decision not to expose Mary to public disgrace tell us about him? 3. What did the angel tell Joseph about the baby conceived in Mary's womb? 4. Why did Matthew think it was important to include a prophecy from Isaiah in his account of the conception of Jesus? 5. How has God proven faithful to you in the keeping of His promises?

■ **ILLUSTRATIONS:**

Someone to See and Touch. A little boy was afraid to sleep alone. He did not like the darkness, and he could not stand the idea that he was in his bed, his room, all by himself. His mother tried to console him by reminding him that he was not alone and that God would be with him to protect him at all times. The little boy thought about this truth for a while. Then he said, "But I need somebody in here who has skin on him!"

God knew that we would be that way and that we could never conceive the fact He is *Spirit* (John 4:24). The Lord also knew that we could never feel secure with the reality of His presence until His Son appeared in time "with skin on him" (in a manner of speaking).

The First Creche. A legend has it that in December of 1223, Francis of Assisi was on his way to preach in the village of Greccio, Italy. As he walked, he pondered how he could bring home to the poor illiterate peasants the real meaning of Christmas. He wanted the account of the Savior's birth to live in their hearts.

Suddenly Francis had an idea. He would recreate the manger scene for his audience. First, he went to a friend in the village, and between them they fashioned the first creche, or nativity scene. Then, when the peasants came to the church on Christmas eve, they stopped in amazement and fell on their knees in adoration. There they saw a live donkey and ox. They also noticed real people playing the parts of Joseph, Mary, and the shepherds. Moreover, in a crude manger lay a representation of the infant Jesus.

Francis proceeded to tell the onlookers the wonderful account of the birth of Christ. This enabled the peasants to feel as if they were actually in ancient Bethlehem. This experience helped them never to forget the message of hope and gladness they heard that night.

Failing to See the Obvious. For most of us, celebrating Christmas has been a part of our lives from our earliest memory. Year after year we trim Christmas trees, affix garlands and wreaths throughout the house, sing the beloved carols, and exchange gifts. Sometimes, however, in the midst of our annual festivities, we pass by the obvious. We miss the miracle of the holiday.

Several years ago, in the fall of the year, my son took me in his car to the top of a small mountain just east of our town. I had passed this mountain for years and knew that it was there, but never paid any attention to it. The leaves were every shade of scarlet and yellow and brown.

My son said, "Let's get out of the car, Dad." He pointed across the valley below, and the many lush colors nearly took my breath away. Every fall this fabulous splash of color had been there, but I had not seen it! Let's not lose the miracle of Christmas beneath the tinsel and lights and wrapping paper.

A CALL TO HOPE

BACKGROUND SCRIPTURE: Luke 2:22-38
DEVOTIONAL READING: Psalm 71:1-8

KEY VERSE: "My eyes have seen your salvation, which you have prepared in the presence of all peoples." Luke 2:30-31.

KING JAMES VERSION

LUKE 2:22 And when the days of her purification according to the law of Moses were accomplished, they brought him to Jerusalem, to present him to the Lord; 23 (As it is written in the law of the Lord, Every male that openeth the womb shall be called holy to the Lord;) 24 And to offer a sacrifice according to that which is said in the law of the Lord, A pair of turtle-doves, or two young pigeons.

25 And, behold, there was a man in Jerusalem, whose name was Simeon; and the same man was just and devout, waiting for the consolation of Israel: and the Holy Ghost was upon him. 26 And it was revealed unto him by the Holy Ghost, that he should not see death, before he had seen the Lord's Christ. 27 And he came by the Spirit into the temple: and when the parents brought in the child Jesus, to do for him after the custom of the law, 28 Then took he him up in his arms, and blessed God, and said, 29 Lord, now lettest thou thy servant depart in peace, according to thy word: 30 For mine eyes have seen thy salvation, 31 Which thou hast prepared before the face of all people; 32 A light to lighten the Gentiles, and the glory of thy people Israel. 33 And Joseph and his mother marvelled at those things which were spoken of him. 34 And Simeon blessed them, and said unto Mary his mother, Behold, this child is set for the fall and rising again of many in Israel; and for a sign which shall be spoken against; 35 (Yea, a sword shall pierce through thy own soul also,) that the thoughts of many hearts may be revealed. 36 And there was one Anna, a prophetess, the daughter of Phanuel, of the tribe of Aser: she was of a great age, and had lived with an husband seven years from her virginity; 37 And she was a widow of about fourscore and four years, which departed not from the temple, but served God with fastings and prayers night and day. 38 And she coming in that instant gave thanks likewise unto the Lord, and spake of him to all them that looked for redemption in Jerusalem.

NEW REVISED STANDARD VERSION

LUKE 2:22 When the time came for their purification according to the law of Moses, they brought him up to Jerusalem to present him to the Lord 23 (as it is written in the law of the Lord, "Every firstborn male shall be designated as holy to the Lord"), 24 and they offered a sacrifice according to what is stated in the law of the Lord, "a pair of turtledoves or two young pigeons."

25 Now there was a man in Jerusalem whose name was Simeon; this man was righteous and devout, looking forward to the consolation of Israel, and the Holy Spirit rested on him. 26 It had been revealed to him by the Holy Spirit that he would not see death before he had seen the Lord's Messiah. 27 Guided by the Spirit, Simeon came into the temple; and when the parents brought in the child Jesus, to do for him what was customary under the law, 28 Simeon took him in his arms and praised God, saying,

29 "Master, now you are dismissing your servant in peace,
according to your word;
30 for my eyes have seen your salvation,
31 which you have prepared in the presence of all peoples,
32 a light for revelation to the Gentiles
and for glory to your people Israel."

33 And the child's father and mother were amazed at what was being said about him. 34 Then Simeon blessed them and said to his mother Mary, "This child is destined for the falling and the rising of many in Israel, and to be a sign that will be opposed 35 so that the inner thoughts of many will be revealed—and a sword will pierce your own soul too."

36 There was also a prophet, Anna the daughter of Phanuel, of the tribe of Asher. She was of a great age, having lived with her husband seven years after her marriage, 37 then as a widow to the age of eighty-four. She never left the temple but worshiped there with fasting and prayer night and day. 38 At that moment she came, and began to praise God and to speak about the child to all who were looking for the redemption of Jerusalem.

HOME BIBLE READINGS

Monday, December 20	Psalm 71:1-8	*You, O Lord, Are My Hope*
Tuesday, December 21	Isaiah 42:1-9	*New Things I Now Declare*
Wednesday, December 22	Luke 2:1-7	*Jesus Is Born*
Thursday, December 23	Luke 2:8-14	*Angels Appear to the Shepherds*
Friday, December 24	Luke 2:15-20	*The Shepherds See Jesus*
Saturday, December 25	Luke 2:22-26	*Jesus Is Taken to the Temple*
Sunday, December 26	Luke 2:27-38	*Simeon and Anna Praise God*

BACKGROUND

In this week's lesson we read about two elderly individuals, Simeon and Anna. Simeon was a devout Jew who encountered the infant Jesus when Joseph and Mary brought Him to the temple to be circumcised (Luke 2:25-35). Under the inspiration of the Spirit, Simeon recognized Jesus as the Messiah of Israel and the Savior of all humankind. Simeon also uttered prophecies concerning both Jesus and Mary.

Simeon is perhaps best known for his song, which has been called the *Nunc Dimittis*, a title that comes from the opening phrase in Latin, "*now you are dismissing*" (2:29; in other words, "now permit [me] to die"). The idea is that Simeon could die in peace because he had seen the Messiah.

The song bears many of the essential characteristics of Hebrew praise. For instance, it rejoices in the goodness of God, states the reason for that rejoicing, and expands poetically on that statement. Simeon's song is also filled with allusions to the Old Testament.

Anna was a widow, the daughter of Phanuel of the tribe of Asher, and thus a Galilean. The mention of Anna's lineage indicates that she came from a family of some distinction. She was living in Jerusalem at the time of Jesus' birth. In fact, she could be found in the temple courtyards day and night worshiping God through fasting and prayer (2:36-38).

Anna, like Simeon, was familiar with the period of war and national oppression that her nation had gone through in the not too distant past. (The reign of Herod the Great was especially characterized by much violence and bloodshed.) This undoubtedly is one reason why Anna had an intense longing for the redemption promised through the Messiah. This hope of national deliverance sustained her through many years of patient waiting. In the birth of Jesus, Anna's faith was abundantly rewarded, and she became a grateful and continual witness of the spiritual deliverance that had come to Israel.

Sadly, Anna's testimony as a woman would have counted for little in Jewish courts of the day. But thankfully Luke included her witness in his Gospel, perhaps to highlight one of the changes that Jesus the Redeemer wanted to bring about among His followers. No longer would they regard women as untrustworthy witnesses, but as full members of a new community of faith in Christ (Gal. 3:28).

NOTES ON THE PRINTED TEXT

Mary and Joseph were careful to fulfill the requirements of the Mosaic law. In the case of Jesus, while He was God's Son, He was not born above the law. Thus it was fitting for Jesus' family to observe its customs. Accordingly, eight days after Jesus' birth, Mary and Joseph had Him circumcised (Lev. 12:3; Luke 2:21). Circumcision symbolized the Jews' unique relationship with God. It was also customary for Jewish boys to be named when they were circumcised.

A woman who had given birth to a male child was considered to be ceremonially unclean for seven days (Lev. 12:2). Then for 33 days more she was not to touch any sacred thing, nor was she to enter the sanctuary (12:4). After 40 days, she was required to go to the temple to be purified in the prescribed manner (Luke 2:22-24).

The woman's purification included the offering of a sacrifice. According to Leviticus 12:6, this offering was to be a year-old lamb for a burnt offering and a young pigeon or a dove for a sin offering; but the law also said that if the woman could not afford a lamb, two pigeons or doves would suffice (vs. 8). Mary evidently choose the second option due to her modest financial situation (Luke 2:24).

According to the Mosaic law, the woman's firstborn son was considered holy and thus had to be dedicated to the Lord in service (Exod. 13:2, 11-16; Luke 2:23). This requirement went back to that night in Egypt when the firstborn sons were saved from death by blood applied to the doorposts (Exod. 12:12-13); but since the entire tribe of Levi was chosen for service, a firstborn son could be released from service by a payment of a ransom (Num. 3:11-13; 18:15-16).

This act of buying back, or redeeming, the child from God was performed during a presentation ceremony at the temple, probably at the same time as the mother's purification ceremony (Luke 2:22). A sacrificial offering was the means by which the ransom was paid. In this way the parents acknowledged that their firstborn belonged to God, who alone had the power to give life.

In summary, when the time of Mary's purification had ended, she and her husband took Jesus to the temple in Jerusalem to present Him to the Lord. In the midst of the fulfillment of legal requirements, God put the stamp of approval on His Son with the unusual but blessed ministries of Simeon and Anna.

At the time of Jesus' birth, there was a pious Jew named Simeon who lived in Jerusalem (2:25). His devotion to God was evident in the way in which he observed the law of Moses. His upright way of living, however, went far beyond a mere external heeding of various rules and regulations. Simeon was also filled with (or controlled and guided by) the Holy Spirit.

Another interesting fact about Simeon is that he was *looking forward to the consolation of Israel*. In other words, he eagerly expected the Messiah to come and rescue His people. Undoubtedly Simeon was well acquainted with the Old Testament and its many prophecies that spoke of the Messiah bringing spiritual peace and rest (Isa. 9:6-7).

The Spirit had disclosed to Simeon that before he died he would see the Christ (Luke 2:26). The title *Christ* comes from a Greek word meaning "anointed one." It is equivalent to Messiah, a word derived from Hebrew. The Jews believed that a man would appear as the Lord's anointed prophet, priest, and king to bring salvation to the people of God. Sadly, most of them failed to recognize Jesus, who fulfilled the most comprehensive definition of the Messiah (John 1:10-11).

While Joseph and Mary were in the temple precincts with the infant Jesus, the Spirit led Simeon there as well. The couple allowed the elderly man to take the child in his arms. He then offered praise to God (Luke 2:27-28).

In Simeon's song, he thanked the Lord for letting him see the Redeemer. Simeon noted that the child would be a light to all peoples, whether Jew or Gentile (2:29-32). Many Jews knew of God's promises to bless their nation. But sadly they did not always give equal attention to the prophecies saying that God would bring salvation to the entire world (Isa. 49:6). Simeon, however, knew that Jesus had come to save all who believe.

Mary and Joseph were *amazed at what was being said about [Jesus]* (Luke 2:33). Simeon told them that Jesus would be rejected by many in Israel and that this would lead to their downfall. Nevertheless, He would be a source of joy to others (2:34). As a result, *"the inner thoughts of many will be revealed"* (2:35). The idea here is that a person's reasonings and motives would be exposed by the way in which he or she responded to the Savior. Even Mary herself would experience anguish and suffering because of what would happen to Jesus.

Luke noted that a prophetess named Anna was also in the temple (2:36-37). While Simeon was talking with Mary and Joseph, Anna came along and began praising God. She also talked about the infant Jesus to everyone who had been waiting for the *redemption of Jerusalem* (2:38).

SUGGESTIONS TO TEACHERS

Several years ago *Unplug the Christmas Machine* was the startling title that appeared in bookstores. The main idea behind the book was that the day after Christmas, people are no longer caught in the gears and pulled by the levers of a commercialized holiday. This week's lesson may be the first opportunity your students have to pause and recognize the true significance of the Christ.

1. SIGNIFICANT NAME. Luke 2:21 says that the newborn babe *was called Jesus.* This is the Greek form of Joshua, which means "the Lord saves." Take a few moments to discuss what it means to be saved. Be sure to go beyond the pat answers to talk seriously about how Jesus liberates us from relying on violence and revenge, and from living in destructive ways. Likewise, Jesus liberates us to serve others and promote justice. Trusting in Jesus means, for starters, that we recognize Him as our only Savior from sin.

2. SACRED OBSERVANCES. Note how Mary and Joseph observed the traditions of their faith both before and after Jesus was born. Our religious practices are also important to us, and they can have a tremendous positive effect on our children. Likewise, regular times of worship are essential to our spiritual health. Have your students discuss some religious traditions they find uplifting.

3. SIMEON'S FULFILLMENT. God lavished His mercy and grace on Simeon by allowing him to see the infant Jesus. From Simeon we learn three important truths. First, Jesus is a gift from God. Second, Jesus is the Messiah promised in the Old Testament. And third, Jesus is a light of salvation and truth to the entire world.

4. SOLEMN PRONOUNCEMENT. Simeon realized that in seeing the infant Jesus, he was privileged to behold the fulfillment of God's promise of the heaven-sent Deliverer. We have a similar opportunity when we look to Jesus with the eyes of faith. We can smile at whatever might happen to us in the future, for we know that in Christ we have the hope of eternal life.

5. SENIOR'S DISCERNMENT. End the class time by having your students examine Anna's joyful response to meeting Jesus. She both gave thanks and spoke about Him *to all who were looking for the redemption of Jerusalem* (2:38). Here is a good summary of how one responds to Jesus—with praise and testimony!

FOR ADULTS	■ TOPIC: Searching for Hope in the Right Places ■ QUESTIONS: 1. What characterized Simeon's relationship with the Spirit? 2. What specific information did Simeon share with

Mary and Joseph about Jesus? 3. What was the hope to which Anna clung? 4. What are some ways we can demonstrate our devotion to God? 5. What are some ways you have seen Jesus transform the lives of other believers?

■ **ILLUSTRATIONS:**

The XMAS of Christmas. A chaplain friend of mine noted that when people use Xmas, they really mean Xhaustion, Xcuses, Xchanges, Xcesses, Xtravagances, Xasperations, Xhibitions, and worldly Xcitement. How much better it is to make Jesus the center of our Christmas observances and thereby know the joy, happiness, sharing, and contentment found only in Him.

The Open Door. Each year at Christmastime, radio commentator Paul Harvey tells a story that wonderfully illustrates the necessity of the incarnation of Jesus. One Christmas Eve a devout mother dressed her children and asked her nonbelieving husband if he would attend the special holiday service with them. He said *no*, stating that he'd rather read the paper and enjoy the evening at home.

Shortly after his family had gone, the man noticed a repeated sound on one of his house windows. He put down his paper and found a small flock of birds shivering in the falling snow and attempting to hurl themselves through his window.

Feeling compassion for the birds, he dressed and headed outside to open the door to his warm barn, where the birds could weather the storm. The birds, however, refused to enter.

Frustrated because of all his attempts to encourage the birds had failed, the man heard himself saying, "If only I could become one of them and lead them to where it's warm and safe." Just as the words left his lips, he heard the church bells ring out, "O Come, O Come, Emmanuel." He immediately sank to his knees in the snow.

For centuries people have wondered why it was necessary for Christ to become human. Harvey's story is a clear illustration of Jesus' purpose, namely, to redeem the lost.

Time to Recognize Jesus' Presence. A researcher named Michael Fortino has made a careful study of hundreds of people across North America for over a year. By using a stopwatch, he has clocked the ways persons use their time. He has also reported the cumulative effects of these ways.

Fortino states that most people spend five years of their lives waiting in lines. Other totals of time include six months sitting at traffic lights, one year searching for misplaced objects, six years eating, eight months opening junk mail, four years doing housework, and two years trying to return telephone calls to people who never seem to be available.

This week will conclude the span of time called the year 2004. Also, we will have a new measure of 365 days to use during 2005. In light of this, let's commit ourselves to recall each day in the coming year that Christ lives in us and is a foremost part of our lives.

FOR YOUTH

■ **TOPIC:** Simeon's and Anna's Call

■ **QUESTIONS:** 1. What kind of person was Simeon? 2. What was Simeon's view of the Messiah? 3. What did Anna do when she saw the Savior? 4. How can you help your friends understand Jesus better? 5. If you had the opportunity, what are some things about Jesus you would want to share with others?

■ **ILLUSTRATIONS:**

Two Portraits. "Madonna and Child" the headline read, proclaiming the news of a birth that ended months of anticipation and national interest that bordered on obsession. Readers were treated to a story that began with conception and ended with a cesarean section.

The crowds before the hospital were huge, and the media attention was enormous as word of Lourdes Maria Ciccone's birth was released. The little 6-pound, 9-ounce girl was born on October 14, 1996, in Los Angeles to singer-entertainer

Madonna and her personal trainer, Carlos Leon. Hundreds of thousands of dollars were offered for a photograph of Madonna and her child.

What a contrast this is to another portrait, similarly titled "Madonna and Child." This one is by Crivelli, a fifteenth-century artist. It depicts a quiet barn, some shuffling animals, and a pair of reverential parents. In this painting there are no crowds, no media satellite dishes, just a simple view of the incarnation of Jesus depicted in medieval fashion and grandeur.

Perhaps this second portrait highlights the essence of the Advent, namely, that God has come in the form of a baby. God touches each of us through this humble birth in Bethlehem. As a citizen of heaven, you can join countless other believers in praising God for sending His Son.

True Homage. Audrey Wetherell Johnson (1907–1984) had been raised in England in a Christian home. Under a skeptical tutor in France, however, she came to the conclusion as a young person that she "no longer believed in the bodily resurrection of Jesus, nor in His virgin birth." She penned: "My attitude of agnosticism resulted in months of desperation as I considered the meaninglessness of life without any philosophy in which I could believe."

After returning to England, Wetherell finally arrived at a psychological crisis point. She desperately prayed that God would give her "some philosophy that makes reasonable sense." As a result of her desperate plea, "in a mysterious way that Wetherell could not explain even years later, God met her, and with tears of joy Wetherell worshiped Jesus as Savior and Lord" (Susie Hilstrom in *Worldwide Challenge*). Later she became responsible for Bible Study Fellowship, a Christian group that would eventually flourish in over 20 countries with 17,000 leaders.

Filling Father's Shoes. Thomas Watson, Jr., the man who built International Business Machines (IBM) into a computer giant, spent much of his early life worrying about filling his father's shoes. Tortured by self-doubts, Thomas was a depressed child. He was also upset that his sister, Jane, was his father's favorite.

Thomas spent much of his younger years pulling pranks, drinking, dancing, and challenging authority. After a stint in the armed forces, he began to work in the company that his father ran. Thomas succeeded by building the company into what it is today, an industrial powerhouse. At the same time, Thomas has far outgrown the shadow of his demanding father.

Perhaps like Thomas Watson, you know what it is like to grow up frustrated and unable to live up to the expectations of others. After going to the temple courts, both Joseph and Mary must have left with huge expectations for Jesus. The record of Scripture, though, indicates no frustration of His part. He simply trusted God for the future, and this enabled Jesus to do great things for the Lord. This can also be true of you!

God's Unseen Purposes. Texas evangelist James Robison has a deep heart of compassion for disadvantaged and abused women. His organization has done countless deeds of mercy to help those who have been victimized by the traumas of unwanted pregnancies. Though Robison's organization offers many services, from counseling to crisis-pregnancy support, his concern is not merely the outcome of what he has observed in others. He believes that God has a destiny for others that is often unseen by human eyes.

While others debate the technical aspects of a controversial subject, Robison feels it on a personal level. He'll be the first to tell you how thankful he is that one woman decided to keep a child that was conceived from the pregnancy that resulted from a violent rape. Robison knows that he wouldn't be here today if his mother had chosen otherwise.

Doing Something with the Good News. When we discover something that is of great value to us, don't you think that it should be shared with others, especially if, by our sharing, our own portion is enhanced, rather than reduced? The story is told of a missionary physician working in the interior regions of mainland China. One day a patient of his was cured by a simple cataract procedure.

The man was overjoyed, for he had been blinded by this condition for several years. He left the compound, and the physician continued in his daily routine for many weeks, only to be astonished by an event that occurred one day.

The blind man who had been healed of his cataracts returned to the physician's compound. But unlike the first time he had arrived, this time he was not alone. He came dragging a long rope, and holding on to this long rope were more than 50 men, women, and children—yes, they were all blind. Some had come from as far as 250 miles away, journeying through the wilderness, holding on to the rope for their guidance.

Don't ever forget that your world is filled with spiritually blinded people. Maybe it will be the rope of the Gospel that you offer that will lead them to the light of Christ.

JESUS BEGINS HIS MINISTRY

BACKGROUND SCRIPTURE: Mark 1:14-28
DEVOTIONAL READING: Matthew 4:18-25

KEY VERSE: Jesus said to [the fishermen], "Follow me and I will make you fish for people." Mark 1:17

KING JAMES VERSION

MARK 1:14 Now after that John was put in prison, Jesus came into Galilee, preaching the gospel of the kingdom of God, 15 And saying, The time is fulfilled, and the kingdom of God is at hand: repent ye, and believe the gospel. 16 Now as he walked by the sea of Galilee, he saw Simon and Andrew his brother casting a net into the sea: for they were fishers. 17 And Jesus said unto them, Come ye after me, and I will make you to become fishers of men. 18 And straightway they forsook their nets, and followed him. 19 And when he had gone a little further thence, he saw James the son of Zebedee, and John his brother, who also were in the ship mending their nets. 20 And straightway he called them: and they left their father Zebedee in the ship with the hired servants, and went after him. 21 And they went into Capernaum; and straightway on the sabbath day he entered into the synagogue, and taught. 22 And they were astonished at his doctrine: for he taught them as one that had authority, and not as the scribes.

23 And there was in their synagogue a man with an unclean spirit; and he cried out, 24 Saying, Let us alone; what have we to do with thee, thou Jesus of Nazareth? art thou come to destroy us? I know thee who thou art, the Holy One of God. 25 And Jesus rebuked him, saying, Hold thy peace, and come out of him. 26 And when the unclean spirit had torn him, and cried with a loud voice, he came out of him. 27 And they were all amazed, insomuch that they questioned among themselves, saying, What thing is this? what new doctrine is this? for with authority commandeth he even the unclean spirits, and they do obey him. 28 And immediately his fame spread abroad throughout all the region round about Galilee.

NEW REVISED STANDARD VERSION

MARK 1:14 Now after John was arrested, Jesus came to Galilee, proclaiming the good news of God, 15 and saying, "The time is fulfilled, and the kingdom of God has come near; repent, and believe in the good news."

16 As Jesus passed along the Sea of Galilee, he saw Simon and his brother Andrew casting a net into the sea—for they were fishermen. 17 And Jesus said to them, "Follow me and I will make you fish for people." 18 And immediately they left their nets and followed him. 19 As he went a little farther, he saw James son of Zebedee and his brother John, who were in their boat mending the nets. 20 Immediately he called them; and they left their father Zebedee in the boat with the hired men, and followed him.

21 They went to Capernaum; and when the sabbath came, he entered the synagogue and taught. 22 They were astounded at his teaching, for he taught them as one having authority, and not as the scribes. 23 Just then there was in their synagogue a man with an unclean spirit, 24 and he cried out, "What have you to do with us, Jesus of Nazareth? Have you come to destroy us? I know who you are, the Holy One of God." 25 But Jesus rebuked him, saying, "Be silent, and come out of him!" 26 And the unclean spirit, convulsing him and crying with a loud voice, came out of him. 27 They were all amazed, and they kept on asking one another, "What is this? A new teaching—with authority! He commands even the unclean spirits, and they obey him." 28 At once his fame began to spread throughout the surrounding region of Galilee.

BACKGROUND

The Gospel we call "Mark" does not identify its author. But church leaders in the years following the first century A.D. agreed that John Mark wrote this book. One man, Papias, writing around A.D. 140, gave this information. First, John Mark knew Peter well, and heard many of the apostle's sermons about Jesus. Second, John Mark collected material he received from Peter and arranged it into its present form. Some scholars think Mark was the first to write his Gospel, while others think either Matthew or Luke wrote their works first.

Mark would have been a young man, perhaps even a teenager, during Jesus' earthly ministry. Some speculate that the anonymous young man who fled from the scene of Jesus' arrest may have been Mark (14:51-52).

By name, Mark first appears in Scripture in Acts 12:12. After Peter was miraculously released from prison, he decided to go to *the house of Mary, the mother of John whose other name was Mark*, where the church was gathered for prayer. This fact has led some to speculate that this home, evidently a common meeting place of the church, may have held the upper room used by Jesus and His followers. If so, then Mark might have encountered Jesus many times.

Later, Mark traveled as a helper to Barnabas and Paul during the early part of their first missionary journey (13:5). But then Mark left the team to return home (13:13). Paul and Barnabas argued over whether to take Mark on a second missionary journey (15:36-39). Paul and Barnabas went separate ways, with Barnabas continuing to mentor Mark. But years later, Paul complimented Mark for his faithful service (Col. 4:10; 2 Tim. 4:11).

None of the four Gospels attempts to be a full-scale biography of Jesus. Mark's Gospel in particular has been called a passion narrative (meaning, the account of Jesus' last week) with an extended introduction. The Gospels summarize the events the key eyewitnesses felt best portrayed who Jesus was and what He had done to provide redemption for the lost.

Mark 1:1 starts with *the beginning of the good news of Jesus Christ*. These words could indicate that what follows was the good news about Jesus. In other words, He was the main focus of the narrative. Thus, the concern is not with history for its own sake, but rather with salvation through faith in Christ.

What factors distinguish Mark's Gospel? Compared to the other three, this one is much more action packed. It devotes much less space to Jesus' teaching and offers a simple fast-paced account of events. For instance, *immediately* (and similar terms) appears frequently throughout the narrative.

Although Mark wrote the briefest of the four Gospels, he spared no words as he painted a compelling portrait of the Savior serving others. In fact, the tone of the book is practical, written in such a way that the material would appeal to the Roman mind. These next weeks, as you study and teach Mark's accounts, may the truth about Jesus brighten the lives of those who hear and believe!

NOTES ON THE PRINTED TEXT

Our Scripture text relates the beginning of Jesus' public ministry, as well as how Jesus called Peter, Andrew, James, and John to be His disciples. John the Baptist's ministry was a precursor to these events. He was many things, but a diplomat was not one of them. He boldly confronted evil, no matter who was involved. For speaking out against sins committed by the ruler Herod Antipas, John was *arrested* (Mark 1:14).

With John locked up, Jesus assumed His position as the prominent spiritual leader. In Galilee He introduced His ministry with the words "*The time is fulfilled*" (1:15). The idea is that, with His proclamation of the good news of the divine kingdom (1:14), a new era had begun; and when that era reaches it completion, *the kingdom of God* (1:15) will have come in all its fullness.

It is essential to our Christian hope that we keep a good sense of history. Past events do not represent the unbroken grip of evil. Satan is powerful and active now, but his doom is certain. Neither is history moving in pointless cycles, with all things being as they always have been and always will be. The Father through the Son is moving all things toward a just conclusion.

Like John, Jesus preached repentance; yet He took His listeners beyond repentance to faith in Himself. This is the distinctively Christian message. Next, after announcing the start of a new era, Jesus set out to call His disciples. Here we see that Jesus did—and still does—eternal work through human hands.

First, the Messiah called Simon (Peter) and Andrew (1:16). These brothers certainly were not perfect; but Jesus did not summon them because of who they were. He called them because of who they could become. Such people are the raw material with which Christ builds His kingdom.

Jesus spoke to the brothers in language they could understand. They knew how it felt to catch fish—the thrill of hauling in a full net. Now they were being summoned to a task that offered deeper fulfillment: fishing *for people* (1:17). It is a call to make a difference in the world, one every believer in Christ should find challenging.

Jesus' words went straight to the hearts of Peter and Andrew. Perhaps the Savior presented to them what they had been longing for. The brothers thus immediately followed Jesus, laying aside the nets they had used in their daily work as fishermen (1:18). This indicated they were leaving their livelihood for a new call-ing as followers of Jesus. We must do the same with everything that would keep us from following Christ. Nets are not evil, and neither are possessions or career aspirations; but we must cast aside everything that hinders us from following the Messiah.

Jesus continued walking until He found James and John at work with their father, *Zebedee* (1:19). Jesus called this pair of brothers too and they *followed him* (1:20). Zebedee had the help of hired servants, and therefore presumably was able to maintain his fishing business without his sons.

We should note that, in calling the first disciples, Jesus required radical com-mitment. He did not suggest that they express an occasional interest in Him and His teachings. He commanded them to follow Him unreservedly. From this we see that following the Messiah part-time is not enough. Some people, of course, believe that Christian faith can be just one among several interests in life; but, in fact, following Jesus must come first all the time. Then the other interests can assume their proper places in one's life.

One Sabbath day Jesus entered the synagogue in *Capernaum* (1:21), His Galilean headquarters. Since it was customary for synagogues to invite visiting teachers to address the worshipers, this synagogue's leaders asked Jesus to speak. We do not know what Jesus said, but the people were *astounded at his teaching* (1:22); specifically, they were impressed by the *authority* with which Jesus taught.

In that day religious teachers tried to validate their instruction by naming respected scholars who agreed with their position; but Jesus offered no such val-idation. He spoke as though what He said mattered simply because He said it. Immediately, it was clear to everyone that this was not just another teacher.

While the worshipers were still buzzing about Jesus' teaching, something hap-pened to astonish them even more. Jesus used this incident to demonstrate His authority in a powerful way.

A man in the synagogue was possessed by an *unclean spirit* (1:23). The demon recognized Jesus and called out, identifying Him and proclaiming Him to be the "*Holy One of God*" (1:24). The evil spirit did not say this to praise Jesus but rather to gain control of Him, in keeping with the ancient belief that to know a person's name gave one power over him; but the attempt was futile.

Jesus rebuked the evil spirit and ordered it to be quiet (1:25). Then Christ told the demon to leave the man. The entity obeyed; it had no choice. Before depart-ing, however, the evil spirit screamed and threw its victim into a convulsion (1:26).

This brief incident deepened the amazement of the spectators (1:27). They were astonished by Jesus' *new teaching* (which was like nothing they had heard before), the authoritative manner in which He spoke, and His ability to demand obedience, even from *unclean spirits*. As a result of this and similar events, Jesus' fame spread throughout the entire *region of Galilee* (1:28).

SUGGESTIONS TO TEACHERS

Mark chose memorable incidents that would introduce Jesus to the lost. These events, from the beginning, let us know that we are not dealing with any ordinary ancient teacher. In this week's lesson (and in the coming weeks), as you and your class members meet Jesus once again, try to encounter Him as if you were hearing about Him for the first time. Catch the excitement as you imagine what took place. Also, be sure to ask, who is this person?

1. THE ONE WHO IS FAR ABOVE US. Jesus was someone whom God unconditionally praised. God willingly adopts us as His children, but only through grace. Jesus is different. He is God's Son by nature, not adoption.

2. THE ONE WHO KNOWS AND CARES ABOUT US. No matter what He did for us, Jesus would deserve our praise for who He is. But even as someone who stands infinitely above us, He reaches down to us. He knew the four fishermen. In subsequent accounts, we come to know the weaknesses that Jesus may have known from the beginning. Yet He invited people He encountered to be His companions. Jesus (for example) could easily have rejected or ignored the man plagued by the demon. Yet Jesus reached out to him and to other needy people with the saving truth of the Good News.

3. THE ONE WHO BECAME ONE OF US. Jesus was not a phantom or apparition. Rather, He was truly human as well as truly divine. In the realm of His physical existence, Jesus was as vulnerable to wild animals as we are. And He allowed Himself to be tempted by Satan, who tempts us all. But despite Jesus' constant victory over Satan, He still identified with us in our spiritual need. Also, at Jesus' baptism, the entire Trinity was involved. The initiative of the Father, the atoning work of the Son, and the enabling power of the Spirit were all present.

FOR ADULTS	■ **TOPIC:** Spreading the Good News ■ **QUESTIONS:** 1. What was the nature of the gospel proclamation that Jesus made throughout Galilee? 2. Why was repentance a nec-

essary part of believing in Jesus? 3. What was significant about the decision of Simon and the others to follow Jesus? 4. What was the demon trying to do in referring to the Messiah personally by name? 5. How did Jesus demonstrate His supreme authority over the evil spirit?

■ **ILLUSTRATIONS:**

Lures. To aid you as you speak this illustration, you could ask an appropriate member of your class to bring in a variety of fishing lures. Holding several where the class can see them, remind the students that most lures don't look at all like food a fish would enjoy. They merely offer shiny or colorful surfaces that catch a fish's attention. Attracted by the novelty, the fish swims over to investigate. The fisherman knows there's nothing for the fish in his lures but danger and potential death. But the fish is not smart enough to figure that out. Satan's temptations are like fishing lures. They catch our attention. But we end up getting hurt, sometimes seriously.

Follow the Leader. Charles Colson undoubtedly felt great pride when the new president of the United States invited him to serve on his staff. Few people ever receive this privilege—to have the opportunity to work in the White House, perhaps to impact the history of the nation or world. Colson did receive fame, but not in the way he intended, for the path down which he followed Richard Nixon. Colson ended up in prison for his part in the Watergate scandal. But in jail, Colson found a new and far superior leader to follow. Colson's Prison Fellowship organization has done far more to impact eternity than any act for which any presidential advisor ever could hope.

Making Prayer Work. Robert had been a pastor for 20 years. He had done well, at least by some standards. His church had grown. He poured himself into the work, hoping for more success. In the process, his family received little of his time. When Robert's son, in his late teens, developed a deep fear that developed into schizophrenia, Robert took time to reflect.

Hoping for help, Robert began reading a book written by a woman known for her God-given power in prayer. Robert discovered this woman lived in his own city. He visited her. She was blunt. "You preachers know all about prayer except how to make it work." She became Robert's mentor in prayer.

Together the two prayed over Robert's son, who found healing from his mental illness. When Robert subsequently suffered a heart attack (likely caused by his stressful lifestyle), he learned that prayer (and a changed lifestyle) brought healing where medical science by itself could not. Now at age 70, Robert's ministry continues to bear fruit.

FOR YOUTH

■ **Topic:** Good News

■ **Questions:** 1. What was the heart of the message Jesus proclaimed in Galilee? 2. What did Jesus call Simon and Andrew to do and how did they respond? 3. What was significant about James and John immediately leaving their father when they heard the call of Jesus? 4. Why were the synagogue attenders in Capernaum amazed at Jesus' teaching? 5. What did the incident involving the demon-possessed man reveal about Jesus?

■ **Illustrations:**

Reward or Punishment? Picture yourself as a second string member of your school's varsity basketball team. You have been practicing hard and improving your skills. How would you feel if your coach rewarded you by sending you back to the junior varsity squad so that you could play easy games against younger opponents? Even if the coach said, "Here's your reward for hard work. I will make your life easier for a while," you would not feel rewarded but punished.

No, you would expect your coach to give you more varsity playing time or possibly even move you into the starting five. But if he did that, then you would face even more challenges than before. But through more game time, even against tough teams, you would continue to increase your abilities.

In the same way, when God wants us to grow, He does not give us an easy stretch, but allows us to face temptations that will challenge us. As we face those challenges and defeat them, we grow stronger.

A New Adventure. By the time, she was seven, Elizabeth had lived on three different continents. Her parents, in Christian ministry, had taken her around the world. This gave her a hunger to see more of the world and to serve people facing all kinds of needs.

As she approached her teen years, Elizabeth begged her parents, on an international flight, to stop over in a third world country. During high school, Elizabeth took a short term mission trip to Russia. Travel with a college group took her to Honduras. She's planning toward an entire semester in Tanzania. These adventures have "bitten" her. She now plans a career in international missions and relief work. Following God's way can offer the greatest of adventures!

Who's Your Mentor? Andrew, a Bible college student, served part-time as a youth pastor. One of the members of his youth group was Peter. Andrew saw gobs of potential in Peter and gave him all the attention he could. Peter responded well and grew in his relationship with God. In time, he too felt a call to ministry.

Peter followed Andrew's steps to the same Bible college and also into youth ministry. Today Peter both pastors a local church and serves as a regional director of youth ministry for his denomination. In ministry effectiveness, Peter may now have surpassed Andrew, but Andrew doesn't mind. He was glad for the opportunity to pour himself into his younger friend.

Do take time to thank those adults who are giving time to you. You may not realize the impact they are having on your development.

JESUS CALLS LEVI (MATTHEW)

BACKGROUND SCRIPTURE: Mark 2:13-17
DEVOTIONAL READING: Ephesians 4:25-32

KEY VERSE: "I have come to call not the righteous but sinners." Mark 2:17.

KING JAMES VERSION

MARK 2:13 And he went forth again by the sea side; and all the multitude resorted unto him, and he taught them. 14 And as he passed by, he saw Levi the son of Alphaeus sitting at the receipt of custom, and said unto him, Follow me. And he arose and followed him.
15 And it came to pass, that, as Jesus sat at meat in his house, many publicans and sinners sat also together with Jesus and his disciples: for there were many, and they followed him. 16 And when the scribes and Pharisees saw him eat with publicans and sinners, they said unto his disciples, How is it that he eateth and drinketh with publicans and sinners? 17 When Jesus heard it, he saith unto them, They that are whole have no need of the physician, but they that are sick: I came not to call the righteous, but sinners to repentance.

NEW REVISED STANDARD VERSION

MARK 2:13 Jesus went out again beside the sea; the whole crowd gathered around him, and he taught them. 14 As he was walking along, he saw Levi son of Alphaeus sitting at the tax booth, and he said to him, "Follow me." And he got up and followed him.
15 And as he sat at dinner in Levi's house, many tax collectors and sinners were also sitting with Jesus and his disciples—for there were many who followed him. 16 When the scribes of the Pharisees saw that he was eating with sinners and tax collectors, they said to his disciples, "Why does he eat with tax collectors and sinners?" 17 When Jesus heard this, he said to them, "Those who are well have no need of a physician, but those who are sick; I have come to call not the righteous but sinners."

6

Monday, January 3	Mark 1:40-45	*Jesus Heals a Leper*
Tuesday, January 4	Mark 2:1-5	*Jesus Forgives a Paralytic*
Wednesday, January 5	Mark 2:6-12	*The Paralytic Stands Up and Walks*
Thursday, January 6	Mark 2:13-17	*I Have Come to Call Sinners*
Friday, January 7	1 John 2:9-17	*Love and Live in the Light*
Saturday, January 8	1 John 4:7-21	*Love One Another*
Sunday, January 9	Ephesians 4:25-32	*We Are Members of One Another*

BACKGROUND

As Mark continued telling his account about Jesus' ministry, he turned next to a collection of incidents involving conflict. Several of them appear in the broader context of Scripture connected with this week's lesson (Mark 2:1—3:6). Some of the interesting contrasts among these incidents include how the opponents approached Jesus and how they responded at the conclusion of the encounters. For instance, when Jesus forgave a sick man's sins, Jesus' opponents (in this case, the scribes) questioned this action. After Jesus physically healed the man, they evidently joined the crowd in amazement (2:1-12).

When Jesus ate with sinners, the scribes and the Pharisees went beyond silent questioning. Behind the scenes, they asked Jesus' disciples about His actions. In this case, Mark did not record how the opponents received the disciples' answer (2:13-17). Then, when Jesus' opponents saw that His disciples did not follow their customary practices regarding fasting, the religious leaders went directly to Jesus to ask why (2:18-22).

The religious leaders' opposition intensified gradually. The next confrontation involved the disciples picking grain on the Sabbath. It appears that by the time of this incident, antagonists were following Jesus and looking for actions of His to criticize. How else would they have been near a grain field on the Sabbath, unless they were watching while Jesus' disciples picked a bit of grain? After seeing Christ's followers break the rules, the opponents again asked Jesus what was happening. The response of the opponents was perhaps silence (2:23-28).

Then in the last of these incidents involving conflict, Mark noted that Jesus' opponents were watching Him so that they might bring a charge against Him. When, on the Sabbath, Jesus healed the man with a withered hand, the Pharisees no longer marveled, and they no longer remained silent. Instead, they began to plot how they would murder Jesus (3:1-6).

In each of these episodes, Jesus or His disciples acted in a way that displeased the religious leaders. Note the progression both in the way Jesus' opponents expressed their concern and in their final response. At first the antagonists appeared somewhat reluctant even to mention the problems they saw. But as the narrative progressed, they became rabid in their opposition. By the last incident, they were ready to pounce on Jesus.

How did the religious leaders become so critical? Today we easily picture them as the bad guys in the Gospel accounts. But it may help to know that the scribes and Pharisees developed out of a revival movement within Judaism.

During the time between the events recorded in the Old and New Testaments, some among God's people wanted to insure that they were paying adequate attention to God and His law. The last thing they wanted was for God to send them off into another exile. To insure that they did not break the law, they placed a "hedge" (so to speak) around it.

For example, the law instructed that the nation should honor the Sabbath. The reformers decided that people should know precisely what that meant. So they said, "Even if you were hungry, you should not pick enough grain for a small meal on the Sabbath" (the thinking behind 2:24); or, "unless the situation meant life or death, no one should give or receive medical care on the Sabbath" (the thinking behind 3:2).

If these humanly-devised regulations were stricter than God intended, the Pharisees thought that, in following them, at least everyone would be safe. People who did not break the overly strict rules certainly would not be breaking God's less strict laws.

This thinking was flawed because ordinary people needed to earn a living and raise a family. They did not have time to keep all the additional regulations. That apparent failure gave the wealthier, more legalistic members of society even more reason to look down on their poorer neighbors. Those who were keeping all the law fell into the deep sin of pride. Also, since it was easier to regulate external actions (as opposed to inner attitudes), the Pharisees focused their laws on visible actions, rather than on a person's heart.

Jesus never spoke against the law as God intended it. In contrast, He upheld it (Matt. 5:17-20). However, Jesus had no qualms about breaking the humanly devised commandments the Pharisees cherished. Likewise, Jesus condemned the way their traditions contradicted God's Word.

NOTES ON THE PRINTED TEXT

Until this time Jesus had selected only four disciples. They were not especially impressive men; yet they were at least respectable in the eyes of the religious leaders. Jesus' next choice was bound to raise questions. While Christ was walking along the shore of the Sea of Galilee, He taught a crowd of people who had gathered around Him (Mark 2:13). According to 2:14, He then continued on His way and came across *Levi*, the son of a man named *Alphaeus*.

Both Mark and Luke in their parallel accounts of this incident call the tax collector Levi. In Matthew 9:9, however, this person is identified as Matthew; also, in Mark's list of the Twelve, he mentions a Matthew, but no Levi (Mark 3:16-19). It is possible that Levi was the disciple's given name, while as an apostle he was called Matthew, which means "gift of God." Another such disciple was Peter, whose given name was Simon but whom Jesus renamed Peter.

As far as we know, Levi was an honest man; but as a tax collector he was a member of a profession notorious for attracting thieves. As long as the taxes came in, government officials did not ask many questions. Thus tax collectors often grossly overcharged people, pocketing the extra. It is not surprising that the Jews despised tax collectors.

Levi was even more unpopular than some other tax collectors because he was Jewish. His cooperation with the Romans made him an outcast among his own people. He was probably not permitted to worship in the synagogue. He would not have been allowed to serve as a judge or witness in court. His whole family would have been viewed as disgraced.

Thankfully, Jesus looked beyond Levi's reputation, recognizing his potential as a member of the Twelve. Jesus said, *"Follow me"* (Mark 2:14), and Levi did. He was willing to give up everything to serve Jesus. In our modern culture, we often become possessed by our possessions because we think we have to have them; and so they occupy more and more of our time and energy. Jesus, however, told the people of His day that they must give up all those things in order to be His disciple.

It clearly was not Jesus' purpose to make discipleship sound easy; indeed, He warned would-be followers that they should consider and count the cost of being His disciple prior to making a lifelong commitment. In essence, Jesus asked His would-be followers, "Will your discipleship be abandoned after a little while because you did not count the cost of commitment to Me?"

Levi expressed his gratitude to Jesus by inviting Him and His disciples to a dinner at the tax collector's home. Luke 5:29 indicates that this was a large feast. Probably Levi wanted to celebrate joining Jesus' disciples.

Levi invited many of his friends to share the joy of the occasion. This included his fellow tax collectors and many others whom the religious leaders would have considered notorious *sinners* (Mark 2:15). They were regarded as such because they did not have the time or inclination to follow the strict traditions of the scribes and Pharisees.

Jesus' presence at the banquet troubled the religious leaders. They questioned how Jesus, whom many people regarded as a true Jewish rabbi, could allow Himself to be defiled by the dregs of society (2:16). The *scribes* and *Pharisees* were implying that Jesus must be of questionable character Himself; otherwise, He would not be seen in such company.

Jesus justified His presence at the banquet with a medical analogy (2:17). He declared that healthy people did not need a *physician*; rather, the *sick* did. Christ said He had come to call *sinners* to repentance, not those who were *righteous*.

In this analogy, Jesus was the physician and the tax collectors and sinners were the spiritually sick. Jesus was at the banquet because these people needed Him. The spiritually healthy were the scribes and Pharisees. They were not actually righteous, but they saw themselves that way. Jesus was not ministering to them because they, unlike the tax collectors and sinners, had not admitted their infection with sin.

SUGGESTIONS TO TEACHERS

The Lord Jesus offered Himself to several different groups of people in first century Palestine. The paralytic of Mark 2:1-12 and the tax collector (Levi) of 2:13-17 are two noteworthy examples. The barriers that separated them from Jesus and one another meant nothing to Him. He wanted to break down those barriers with the message of grace and redemption. The standards by which some saw themselves as superior meant little to Him. Some received Him with joy, at least for a while. Some stayed with Him in the long term. And some ultimately helped murder the Son of God. Nothing has changed. Our communities and even our churches are full of these same types of people today.

1. THE NEEDY ONES. In one account, a man was paralyzed by his body. In another episode, Levi likely struggled to escape his self-serving greed. When Jesus offered freedom, both rejoiced to move on into new life.

2. THE FRIENDS OF THE NEEDY ONES. In both accounts, associates (the four who carried the paralyzed man, as well as those who attended Levi's banquet) likely rejoiced as their friends entered new freedom. What changes might have occurred in their lives as they watched Jesus act?

3. THE DISCIPLES. At least Simon, Andrew, James, and John had been following Jesus for a period of days or weeks. They had already watched Him perform astounding miracles. What would they have felt during the two incidents recorded in Mark's Gospel? Continued amazement? Pride in their association with Jesus?

4. THE CROWDS. At this point in Jesus' ministry, there were lots of people who accompanied Him. His amazing abilities to teach and heal attracted them to Jesus. They listened and watched. They gladly received. But were they ready to commit themselves to Jesus? Perhaps not in any depth.

5. THE OPPONENTS. Members of this group could not help but marvel at all Jesus said and did. But they wished that He would play the game by their rules. Forgiving sins? Eating with sinners? They saw these things as questionable behavior. They also wished to restrict Jesus. He supposedly should do nothing that violated their expectations.

FOR ADULTS

■ **TOPIC:** Sharing God's Hospitality

■ **QUESTIONS:** 1. What happened to Jesus as He was walking along the shoreline of the Sea of Galilee? 2. Why do you think Jesus chose to summon a despised tax collector such as Levi to be His disciple? 3. How did Levi respond to Jesus? 4. How did the religious leaders respond to Jesus? Why? 5. For what reason did Jesus say He had come?

◼ ILLUSTRATIONS

A Librarian's Investment. When I moved from a small elementary school to a much larger junior high, I looked for friends, both among my peers and the school staff. The librarian, Mrs. Houser, looked friendly, so I joined the Library Club, volunteering a bit of study hall time to help out with small tasks. Two years later, during my last year in that school, I was spending hours each day helping out in the library.

If God had not called me to pastoral ministry, I would have become a librarian. Why? Because Mrs. Houser took special interest in me, a chubby seventh grader. I and other members of the Library Club may have been as much of a bother as a help, but Mrs. Houser invested herself in me. We remained friends, corresponding regularly. Years later, while serving as a missionary overseas, I heard that she had died. I'm so glad I had taken many opportunities to thank her for all the friendship she had offered me.

She Can See! David McGuire could have said a quick prayer and moved his attention to the next person. While offering baked beans and buttered bread to Romanian refugees, Elvira, a gypsy woman, asked the missionary to pray for her infant daughter, Elisabeta. David did not let racial, social, or economic differences prevent him from listening to Elvira. He soon learned that the baby held in her mother's arms was blind. He took special interest in the child. Along with a friend, he paid for an optical implant, a medical procedure performed in a nearby city. But that effort failed and all but destroyed one of Elisabeta's eyes.

David refused to give up. He contacted a church in the United States, where people began raising money. He wrangled with governments to arrange visas. An airline donated seats to get mother and daughter to the state of Washington. Paul Shenk, a surgeon, offered his expertise. During the operation, he said he "felt as if the Great Physician Himself were helping me." In the food line months before, Elisabeta's situation looked grim. Today, with the help of God and lots of people, she can see.

I've Forgotten. Craig Brian Larson tells the following story. After several years of marriage, Bert and Mary were still childless. They decided to adopt a boy they named John. Within months, Mary found herself pregnant. She gave birth to Larry.

Some years later, a supposed friend was visiting the home. As the two women chatted, the visitor inquired, "Now which of these boys is yours, Mary?"

"Both of them," she quickly replied.

The friend was not satisfied. "Which of them did you adopt?"

In an answer that demonstrated overwhelming love for both her sons, Mary responded, "I have forgotten."

God, in adopting us as His children, forgave our sins. In heaven, we may ask

God about one of our less desirable choices, asking how He could have forgiven that one. He may say, "Did you really do that? I don't remember that at all."

FOR YOUTH	■ **TOPIC:** Jesus Calls Me

■ **TOPIC:** Jesus Calls Me
■ **QUESTIONS:** 1. Who was Levi, and why would his fellow Jews have despised him? 2. How did Levi respond to Jesus' call to discipleship? 3. What kinds of people did Levi invite into his home? 4. Why did the religious leaders question Jesus' decision to associate with tax collectors and other sinners? 5. What was the meaning of Jesus' response to the religious leaders?

■ **ILLUSTRATIONS:**

Dad's Concern. As a child, I regularly attended church with my parents. Dad was the pastor; only occasionally, when visiting another church, did I have the opportunity to sit next to my dad.

As a little guy, I often did what some of you may have done in church. I got tired of listening! I would yawn. If I began to lean toward my father, what would he do? My father would raise his arm. To do what? To shake me back into an alert state? No, he offered grace. He raised his arm so that I could cuddle against his side and rest comfortably.

When we come to Jesus, sometimes not in the best of shape, He never pushes us away. He does not seek to shake us up. He receives us as we are. He offers His forgiveness and love, that is, if we will lean on Him.

A Difference. Several years ago, Trevor, a 12-year-old boy, traveled with his family from Philadelphia's suburbs into the city. When he encountered homeless people, he felt shocked. Perhaps you've already heard the end of this story. With the help of others, this young man established Trevor's House, a ministry to homeless families. Trevor was only one sixth grader, but he decided that he could make a difference.

Ruth, another teen, works a part-time job at a coffee shop near her home. She chose to tithe her earnings to help the poor of the world. When she entered a web site that enabled her, from a distance, to purchase essentials for less well-off people around the world, she ended up joyfully giving far more than 10 percent. She bought a goat for a family trying to establish their farm, and a bicycle and books for a new pastor in Ghana. Ruth was even able to help purify the water supply for an entire Indian village.

Experienced a Turnaround. Elizabeth Eckford and Minnijean Brown Trickey were students entering Central High School in Little Rock, Arkansas. What made their entrance different from yours is that they were two of the nine black students, who, in 1957, brought about the beginning of the end of organized resistance to school integration.

At the 40th anniversary of the event, the former students gathered to recall their experiences. They had seen discrimination in schooling, neighborhoods, restaurants, and travel facilities. They had observed the differences between the white and black communities. Segregation seemed unfair and unjust. Those concerned students chose to turn the situation around. Armed caravans of angry whites gathered at the school and sales of weapons increased. The Arkansas National Guard was brought into the school to turn the nine students away. Mobs followed them, all the while shouting at and threatening them. A famous photograph, which was made by Will Counts, shows a white woman sneering at Eckford.

At the anniversary, Eckford related that the woman contacted her in the late 1960's to apologize and to ask forgiveness. Her conscience had bothered her, and she wanted to make peace.

Like Elizabeth Eckford and Minnijean Trickey, you might experience unfair and unjust treatment. You also might face criticism and perhaps even opposition. However, you too should turn the situation around and allow the grace of God to show through your acts of kindness and compassion.

JESUS SENDS OUT THE TWELVE

BACKGROUND SCRIPTURE: Mark 3:13-19; 6:6b-13
DEVOTIONAL READING: Luke 9:1-6

KEY VERSE: [Jesus] appointed twelve, whom he also named apostles,
to be with him, and to be sent out to proclaim the message. Mark 3:14.

KING JAMES VERSION

MARK 3:13 And he goeth up into a mountain, and calleth unto him whom he would: and they came unto him. 14 And he ordained twelve, that they should be with him, and that he might send them forth to preach, 15 And to have power to heal sicknesses, and to cast out devils: 16 And Simon he surnamed Peter; 17 And James the son of Zebedee, and John the brother of James; and he surnamed them Boanerges, which is, The sons of thunder: 18 And Andrew, and Philip, and Bartholomew, and Matthew, and Thomas, and James the son of Alphaeus, and Thaddaeus, and Simon the Canaanite, 19 And Judas Iscariot, which also betrayed him: and they went into an house. . . .

6:6 And he went round about the villages, teaching.

7 And he called unto him the twelve, and began to send them forth by two and two; and gave them power over unclean spirits; 8 And commanded them that they should take nothing for their journey, save a staff only; no scrip, no bread, no money in their purse: 9 But be shod with sandals; and not put on two coats. 10 And he said unto them, In what place soever ye enter into an house, there abide till ye depart from that place. 11 And whosoever shall not receive you, nor hear you, when ye depart thence, shake off the dust under your feet for a testimony against them. Verily I say unto you, It shall be more tolerable for Sodom and Gomorrha in the day of judgment, than for that city. 12 And they went out, and preached that men should repent. 13 And they cast out many devils, and anointed with oil many that were sick, and healed them.

NEW REVISED STANDARD VERSION

MARK 3:13 [Jesus] went up the mountain and called to him those whom he wanted, and they came to him. 14 And he appointed twelve, whom he also named apostles, to be with him, and to be sent out to proclaim the message, 15 and to have authority to cast out demons. 16 So he appointed the twelve: Simon (to whom he gave the name Peter); 17 James son of Zebedee and John the brother of James (to whom he gave the name Boanerges, that is, Sons of Thunder); 18 and Andrew, and Philip, and Bartholomew, and Matthew, and Thomas, and James son of Alphaeus, and Thaddaeus, and Simon the Cananaean, 19 and Judas Iscariot, who betrayed him. . . .

6:6 Then he went about among the villages teaching. 7 He called the twelve and began to send them out two by two, and gave them authority over the unclean spirits. 8 He ordered them to take nothing for their journey except a staff; no bread, no bag, no money in their belts; 9 but to wear sandals and not to put on two tunics. 10 He said to them, "Wherever you enter a house, stay there until you leave the place. 11 If any place will not welcome you and they refuse to hear you, as you leave, shake off the dust that is on your feet as a testimony against them." 12 So they went out and proclaimed that all should repent. 13 They cast out many demons, and anointed with oil many who were sick and cured them.

7

HOME BIBLE READINGS

BACKGROUND

The content of Mark 6:1-13 offers several windows into first-century culture. A quick look at these reminds us that Jesus lived in a world quite different from ours. To begin, religious teachers (rabbis) commonly moved around the countryside offering their knowledge to whomever would listen. Also, leaders of local synagogues often invited these traveling ministers to speak in their worship services. Individuals who wished to receive more intensive training followed a rabbi as his disciples. In this sense, the ministry of Jesus fit right into a pattern familiar to Jews of His day.

English translations of 6:3 call Jesus a *"carpenter."* That particular occupation would have included woodworking, but also much more. Most people in small villages such as Nazareth lived as poor peasants. Nearly all residents made their living off the land. They raised crops, tended animals, or both. Also, each village would have had at least one handyman. He would build and repair houses, pieces of furniture, tools, kitchen utensils, and almost any of the simple implements of first century life.

The people of Nazareth referred to Jesus as *"the son of Mary"* (6:3). Had Joseph still been alive, they might have mentioned that Jesus was his son. Mary was undoubtedly a widow. In ancient times, adult men often married girls who were still teenagers or even younger. That, combined with low life expectancy, contributed to the high percentage of women who lived as widows. When a father died, the eldest son took responsibility of caring for his mother and younger siblings. That likely offers one explanation why Jesus began His public ministry when He was 30 years old. By that time, His younger brothers were old enough to take responsibility for managing the home.

Why would the disciples have thought about wearing *two tunics* (6:9)? It's because peasants in this period wore two garments. The inner one (a tunic) was little more than a feed sack with holes for head and arms. The outer garment (a cloak) was heavier and perhaps a bit more tailored. At night, one took off the outer garment and used it as a blanket. A second tunic served as insurance. If a peasant ever had to sleep outdoors, a second tunic would serve as a second blanket. Jesus, in forbidding a second tunic, instructed His disciples to trust God to provide homes in which to stay.

Expecting to receive hospitality would not have been a large gamble. After all, people of ancient eastern cultures freely welcomed guests, even strangers, into their homes. Refusing to offer guests food to eat and a place to sleep was considered the height of rudeness.

What was the meaning of shaking *"off the dust that is on your feet"* (6:11)? This practice was a reminder of the racial distinctions that existed in first-century Palestine. When Jews crossed an area inhabited by Gentiles, their last action before leaving was to shake off the dust off their feet. That symbolically represented the fact that Jews had nothing to do with Gentiles. It was as if soil from Gentile regions would contaminate the Jewish homeland. So, when Jesus commanded His disciples to shake dust off their feet when leaving a Jewish community, the Savior made a strong statement. He was telling them to view those who had rejected them as if they were pagan Gentiles.

One last detail gives us additional insight into first-century life. As the disciples traveled two by two, they *anointed with oil many who were sick* (6:13). In that day, this practice was seen as a medicinal act. Oil also had a religious use. It represented the Holy Spirit. When a king or other person was anointed with oil, this symbolized an anointing of the Holy Spirit. With respect to Jesus' disciples, they most likely anointed the sick for religious purposes. It was a way of saying, "Not we but God will heal you."

NOTES ON THE PRINTED TEXT

The Gospel of Mark was probably the first Gospel to be written; all but 31 verses of Mark are quoted in the other two Synoptic Gospels (namely, Matthew and Luke). Of the four Gospels, Mark's is the one that reads most like a series of newspaper accounts. Information about Jesus' activities take prominence in this Gospel, especially as the writer described one event in quick detail and then moved on to the next, often introducing the upcoming action with words like *Again he entered* (3:1), *Jesus departed* (3:7), *He left that place and came* (6:1), and *Then he went about* (6:6).

With respect to this week's Scripture text based on Mark's Gospel, we learn that Jesus had been ministering throughout Galilee when He decided to pause from His activity (3:13). He went up on an undisclosed *mountain* and summoned those whom He wanted to join Him; and they responded by doing so.

Instead of selecting a large group to work with Him, Jesus kept the number to a modest size, namely, 12 disciples (3:14). The Savior's intent was that this group would spend quality time with Him. This would enable them to get to know Him, see how He operated, and learn from Him in a more intimate, personal way.

The Twelve would be Jesus' representatives as they went out heralding the good news of the kingdom. They would complement their preaching by healing the sick and driving out *demons* (3:15).

Jesus had a unique strategy for winning people to Himself. He would not do it by capitalizing on the sensation of His miracles; instead, He would do it by pouring His life into the lives of a few, who in turn could pour their lives into others. Then, as the cycle repeated, the Gospel would reach to the ends of the earth. This gives us a clue about how we should continue the Lord's work today. Our first priority should be spending time with Jesus; but beyond that we must devote ourselves to others, cultivating the love of God in their hearts.

Mark 3:16-19 give the names of *the twelve*. There was Simon, whom Jesus renamed Peter, which means "rock." Through God's grace, he would become as stable and reliable as a rock in his prominent role as a leader in the early church. Jesus nicknamed James and John the *Sons of Thunder*, perhaps due to their fervent disposition and boldness.

The Twelve also included Andrew, Philip, Bartholomew (Nathanael), Matthew (Levi), Thomas, James (the son of Alphaeus), Thaddaeus, and Simon the Cananaean. Some think the latter individual is more properly understood to be Simon the Zealot. This name would underscore his zealous temperament. Judas Iscariot is the last named person among the Twelve. He was notorious for his later betrayal of Jesus.

For months the disciples had watched Jesus minister from village to village in Galilee. Now it was time for them to try their own hands at ministry. Jesus sent them to the Jews (Matt. 10:5-6), telling them to preach repentance and perform miracles, such as casting out evil spirits.

Jesus moreover sent out the 12 disciples in six pairs (Mark 6:7). One reason for this provision may have been the law that a minimum of two witnesses was needed to establish truth (Deut. 19:15). Ministering as partners also provided companionship and support.

The Savior's specific instructions to the Twelve regarding what to take and how to act may seem strange to us (Mark 6:8-9); but there were good reasons for each instruction. The disciples were to carry only minimum supplies because God would provide for their needs; for instance, an extra tunic (used for sleeping outdoors) would not be needed because God was going to provide a warm place for them to sleep every night. Moreover, the short time spent in equipping for these mission excursions emphasized their urgency.

Jesus directed the Twelve that, when they were welcomed as a guest in the home of a village, they were to remain there until they left for other towns (6:10). After all, it would be an insult to their hosts if they were to search for a more comfortable place to lodge. In addition, the focus of the Twelve was on proclaiming the truth, not on finding the most luxurious accommodations.

Jesus prepared His disciples for the possibility that some people may not welcome or listen to them (6:11). In this case, the Twelve were instructed to *shake off the dust* of their *feet as a testimony against* the village. By this practice the Twelve would indicate that a town was no better than a heathen place in the eyes of God. In fact, on judgment day the village would be worse off than Sodom and

Gomorrah, which were the embodiment of wickedness.

Some people have said that the disciples' mission trips provide the model for Christians who are trying to obey the Great Commission (Matt. 28:19-20); but that is probably a mistake. Jesus sent His disciples on limited, temporary missions. They traveled for a few days among the towns of Galilee to introduce the Jewish people to the Messiah; in contrast, the Great Commission applies to all peoples and is relevant until Jesus returns.

Like the disciples, we are all called to minister while depending on God; and the world urgently needs our ministry too. If the Lord someday calls you to the mission field, you are wise to consider the need for money and provisions. Often well-prepared ministers have the most powerful long-term impact.

As the Twelve went out, they preached that all should repent of their sins and trust in Christ for salvation (Mark 6:12). In addition, the disciples cast out many demons as well as anointed many sick people with olive oil and *cured them* (6:13). Through such deeds and words of the Twelve, Jesus multiplied His ministry to many more people.

SUGGESTIONS TO TEACHERS

We have tended to regard Jesus' disciples (except for Judas) either as a crew of super-Christians or as a collection of bearded look-alikes in medieval art. Probably few in your class can name more than a couple of the Twelve. Use the opportunity afforded by this week's lesson to reintroduce your students to them.

1. CALLING THE COMMON TYPES. Jesus neither selected the brainiest from the groves of Athens' academe nor the most pious from the precincts of the Jerusalem temple. Jesus bypassed the wealthy from Alexandria and the powerful from Rome. Instead, He chose a group of moral outcasts. Look at the backgrounds of these men. What an unlikely group to carry out the work that Jesus wanted them to perform! Remind the class that Jesus calls ordinary persons like us, just as He called fishermen and tax collectors, to do His work.

2. CONFOUNDING THE CRITICS. Have your students take a close look at Matthew (Levi), the tax collector whom Jesus chose to be one of the Twelve. Jesus' opponents criticized Him for associating with such dubious people as Matthew. The religious leaders were more concerned with their own appearance of holiness than with helping people. But God is concerned with all people, including those who are sinful and hurting. That's why Jesus insisted on reaching sinners. Discuss the implications of Jesus' calling someone such as Matthew and the way He replied to His critics.

3. CONFERRING AUTHORITY. Explain that Jesus conferred extraordinary authority on ordinary people to do His work. Then let your students know that we serve the same Messiah today. He can use anyone, no matter how insignificant he or she might appear to be.

4. COUNTING THE CREW. The Twelve weren't drafted or forced into service. Rather, Jesus chose each disciple to serve Him in a special way. Likewise, Jesus wants every member of your class to follow Him and be committed to doing His will. He doesn't twist their arms to get them to submit. Instead, He wants them to respond willingly to His summons.

FOR ADULTS	■ TOPIC: Preparing for the Job ■ QUESTIONS: 1. What did Jesus want the Twelve He appointed to do in His name? 2. What is significant about the name that Jesus

gave to Simon? 3. What instructions did Jesus give the Twelve before sending them out in pairs? 4. What did Jesus mean by the action of shaking off the dust from one's feet? 5. What sorts of activities did the Twelve do in Jesus' name?

■ **ILLUSTRATIONS:**

Healing Attitudes. In April of 2000, the Far East Broadcasting Company reported how a witch doctor in Uganda had become a Christian. The man had warned Walter Karanja, an engineer who started a church among his co-workers in Masindi, to stop talking about Christ.

Finally the witch doctor burst wild-eyed into the church while Karanja was preaching. "Jesus of Walter, do not kill me!" he screamed. When Karanja asked him why he was so afraid, the witch doctor said that he and his followers had hated the church. "I have told them to use their powers to destroy you," he said.

"I know," Karanja replied, "but I am still here."

"Why is your power stronger than mine? Why have you and your God not killed me?" the witch doctor asked.

Karanja explained that his God, "the God of the universe," not only is all-powerful but also loving. When the man asked to know more, Karanja presented the Gospel to him. The witch doctor became a Christian and changed his name to John. A few days later he was baptized, and then he burned his witchcraft paraphernalia. News spread quickly, for he had been a prominent and feared leader. Clearly, the Gospel has the power to heal attitudes as well as bodies!

Unexpected Hospitality. In an article in *Christianity Today*, former televangelist Jim Bakker, after his release from prison, offered this praise to the family of Billy Graham.

"During the last weeks of my sentence, Franklin Graham (Billy's son) offered to help me find a job, a place to live, and a car. I tried to convince Franklin that those acts of kindness might hurt the family ministries. Franklin refused to be put off. 'Jim, you were my friend in the past and you are my friend now. If anyone rejects me for helping you, then that's their problem.'

"After my release from prison, the Graham family fulfilled Franklin's promise and gave me that help. My first Sunday out, Ruth Graham even invited me to go to church with them. They wanted me, recently freed inmate 07407-058, to sit in their family pew. And even that wasn't enough. They invited me home for dinner.

"In prison, we were not allowed to carry wallets. We all used envelopes to carry money and papers. When Ruth discovered that an envelope was the only wallet I had, she gave me one of Billy's."

Jesus sent the disciples out two by two, instructing them to depend on the generosity of faithful people. Hopefully what they received measured up to what the Grahams offered Jim Bakker.

Called to Commitment. The Calvary Chapel association has caught the essence of Jesus' call to His original disciples by training lay persons to live out their Christian commitment. Founded in 1965 by Chuck Smith, Calvary Chapel now claims over 600 congregations in the United States and another hundred worldwide, including the former Soviet bloc. Chuck Smith and his fellow pastors stress strong lay leadership, and they plant new churches by sending these lay people as a small core from parent churches. The leadership often quote the following slogan: GOD DOES NOT CALL THE QUALIFIED; HE QUALIFIES THE CALLED.

FOR YOUTH

■ **TOPIC:** I Have Something to Share
■ **QUESTIONS:** 1. Why did Jesus appoint 12 people to be His disciples? 2. What would later distinguish Judas Iscariot from the rest of the Twelve? 3. Why did Jesus send the Twelve out in pairs? 4. How were the Twelve to respond to those who rejected their message? 5. What was the point of the Twelve anointing with oil many sick people?

■ **ILLUSTRATIONS:**

Committed. Maura Donohue and Carla Sherred were juniors at Thomas Jefferson High School in Pleasant Hills, Pennsylvania. Both took a day off from school to board buses and ride to Washington, D.C., to participate in an important religious rally. They joined a group at a church at 5:30 A.M. to worship and then ride to the nation's capital. The two said they had a strong passion for their organization's moral cause. Maura and Carla are two youth committed to making a difference in their community.

Jesus called people to become His disciples and commit themselves to His cause. You also have been called to discipleship. Support it as much as these two young people have chosen to support their religious group's cause.

Showcased. There are good paying jobs for high school and college graduates, especially those competent in math and English. Sadly, many young people do not meet potential employers in person. In January, 1998, Century III Mall in

Pittsburgh hosted an Employee Showcase in order to bring the two groups together. Students from six school districts participated in the event. Many of these students had already participated in individual Career Days programs at their respective high schools, which had enabled them to explore various vocational options.

Jesus made the effort to meet potential disciples in person. He then called several fishermen to follow Him. He also called others such as Matthew, who was a tax collector, to be His disciples. Each willingly accepted the challenge to learn from Jesus and tell others about Him.

Devoted. On March 25, 1997, Amy Stolar, 18, and Jamie Huwar, 16, were preparing to attend the National Honor Society induction ceremony at Ambridge High School in Ambridge, Pennsylvania. A few hours before the ceremony, Principal Dave Perry approached the two girls and five others and ordered them to go home and change their clothes. He claimed that, according to "tradition," the young women had to wear dresses. All of the girls were in pants suits. Stolar and Huwar said that the request was sexist and refused. The girls were sent to gym class and not allowed at the induction ceremony.

The young women went to the school board. They pointed out that all seven girls were honor students, and that this ceremony was to praise them for their leadership and their character. They also pointed out that no dress codes had been established. They questioned the discrimination, especially since the letter that had been mailed stated that students were to wear "dress clothes."

The board agreed and ordered the ceremony to be repeated with everyone in attendance. Principal Perry was forced to praise the girls' devotion to their cause and show respect for their choice.

If these two young women could be so devoted to a cause such as the attire they would wear at a ceremony, how much more should you actively support and demonstrate your dedication to Jesus? He has called you to follow Him wholeheartedly. You should do so with equal enthusiasm and devotion.

JESUS CALLS FOR TOTAL COMMITMENT

BACKGROUND SCRIPTURE: Mark 8:27-38
DEVOTIONAL READING: Matthew 16:24-28

KEY VERSE: [Jesus] said to them, "If any want to become my followers, let them deny themselves and take up their cross and follow me." Mark 8:34.

KING JAMES VERSION

MARK 8:27 And Jesus went out, and his disciples, into the towns of Caesarea Philippi: and by the way he asked his disciples, saying unto them, Whom do men say that I am? 28 And they answered, John the Baptist: but some say, Elias; and others, One of the prophets. 29 And he saith unto them, But whom say ye that I am? And Peter answereth and saith unto him, Thou art the Christ. 30 And he charged them that they should tell no man of him. 31 And he began to teach them, that the Son of man must suffer many things, and be rejected of the elders, and of the chief priests, and scribes, and be killed, and after three days rise again. 32 And he spake that saying openly. And Peter took him, and began to rebuke him. 33 But when he had turned about and looked on his disciples, he rebuked Peter, saying, Get thee behind me, Satan: for thou savourest not the things that be of God, but the things that be of men. 34 And when he had called the people unto him with his disciples also, he said unto them, Whosoever will come after me, let him deny himself, and take up his cross, and follow me. 35 For whosoever will save his life shall lose it; but whosoever shall lose his life for my sake and the gospel's, the same shall save it. 36 For what shall it profit a man, if he shall gain the whole world, and lose his own soul? 37 Or what shall a man give in exchange for his soul? 38 Whosoever therefore shall be ashamed of me and of my words in this adulterous and sinful generation; of him also shall the Son of man be ashamed, when he cometh in the glory of his Father with the holy angels.

NEW REVISED STANDARD VERSION

MARK 8:27 Jesus went on with his disciples to the villages of Caesarea Philippi; and on the way he asked his disciples, "Who do people say that I am?" 28 And they answered him, "John the Baptist; and others, Elijah; and still others, one of the prophets." 29 He asked them, "But who do you say that I am?" Peter answered him, "You are the Messiah." 30 And he sternly ordered them not to tell anyone about him.

31 Then he began to teach them that the Son of Man must undergo great suffering, and be rejected by the elders, the chief priests, and the scribes, and be killed, and after three days rise again. 32 He said all this quite openly. And Peter took him aside and began to rebuke him. 33 But turning and looking at his disciples, he rebuked Peter and said, "Get behind me, Satan! For you are setting your mind not on divine things but on human things."

34 He called the crowd with his disciples, and said to them, "If any want to become my followers, let them deny themselves and take up their cross and follow me. 35 For those who want to save their life will lose it, and those who lose their life for my sake, and for the sake of the gospel, will save it. 36 For what will it profit them to gain the whole world and forfeit their life? 37 Indeed, what can they give in return for their life? 38 Those who are ashamed of me and of my words in this adulterous and sinful generation, of them the Son of Man will also be ashamed when he comes in the glory of his Father with the holy angels."

Monday, January 17	John 6:41-51	*Whoever Believes Has Eternal Life*
Tuesday, January 18	John 6:52-59	*Eat My Flesh, Drink My Blood*
Wednesday, January 19	John 6:60-69	*This Teaching Is Difficult*
Thursday, January 20	Matthew 16:13-20	*Who Do You Say I Am?*
Friday, January 21	Matthew 16:24-28	*Let Them Deny Themselves*
Saturday, January 22	Mark 8:27-30	*You Are the Messiah*
Sunday, January 23	Mark 8:31-38	*Take Up Your Cross, Follow Me*

BACKGROUND

The Scripture passage selected for this week's lesson makes reference to two significant titles for Jesus. A clear understanding of these titles enriches our understanding of Jesus' earthly ministry. The first title comes in Peter's confession of Jesus as *"the Messiah"* (Mark 8:29). Jesus freely accepted this title and praised Peter for his openness to this spiritual insight (Matt. 16:17-18). Yet Jesus rarely, if ever, referred to Himself as the Messiah.

Why didn't Jesus more boldly announce Himself as the Messiah? It's because He intended to be the Messiah in a way the Jews of His day would struggle to accept. Peter himself could not comprehend how Jesus, as the Messiah, could be crucified. For Peter and others, those two ideas were incompatible. From this point on, Jesus needed to reeducate His disciples. He helped them grasp a concept of a suffering Messiah, along the lines of Isaiah 52:13—53:12.

How did the Jews picture the Messiah? They correctly saw themselves as God's chosen people. They read their sacred writings and affirmed the prophecies concerning a glorious future for Israel (2:1-4). They combined that vision with other promises of a great king, following the model of David, who would lead Israel to great power (9:6-7).

During the time between the writing of the Old and New Testaments, the Jews added more pieces to their picture of the Messiah. They felt that, while the nations of the earth could gather to attack or oppress God's people, the Messiah would come as a great military leader. He and His armies supposedly would smash the other nations, establish God's rule over the whole world, and bring in a lasting era of peace and prosperity for all. Many Jews in Jesus' day were eager for the Messiah to arrive. In fact, they hoped the Roman Empire was the last in a line of foreign nations to hold Israel under its thumb.

Had Jesus brashly announced Himself as the Messiah, all kinds of problems could have arisen. People would want Him to act as military leader, and that was not His agenda (John 6:15; Acts 1:6-7). The Romans, who carefully watched for any hint of rebellion, would have brought in their armies and squashed such a movement. Jesus, then, would not be able to offer the ministry He intended.

Consequently, Jesus preferred to refer to Himself as the *Son of Man* (Mark 8:31), who *must undergo great suffering*. Daniel had used this phrase to describe a future figure of heavenly power and glory (Dan. 7:13-14). Because *Son of Man* (Mark 8:31) did not carry the same national and military connotations, Jesus could more easily fill this title with the meaning He intended. As the Messiah, the Son of Man would ultimately bring victory. But Jesus' victory would come through apparent defeat. And the victory He won would be offered to all people.

NOTES ON THE PRINTED TEXT

On the way to *Caesarea Philippi* (Mark 8:27), Jesus had a talk with *his disciples.* This city's second name distinguished it from another nearby Caesarea on the Mediterranean Sea, the home of Herod Antipas and the Roman governor, Pilate. In Caesarea Philippi, which was a center of pagan worship, the Savior chose to query His disciples.

Jesus had demonstrated His divine nature through His teachings and miracles. Now He came directly to the question of identity. He asked His followers who people said He was. The opinions then were much as they are today among unbelievers (8:28). People viewed Jesus as a great reformer (*John the Baptist*), or a great miracle worker (*Elijah*), or a great teacher (one among *the prophets*). Those having such views of Jesus today usually imagine they are holding Him in high esteem, when in reality they have misunderstood Him altogether.

In short, Jesus did not receive an encouraging report; but He expected better from the Twelve, so He put the question directly to them. Who did they think He was (8:29)? Peter, speaking for the rest of the disciples, declared that Jesus is *the Messiah.*

The title *Messiah* comes from a Hebrew word meaning "anointed one." It is equivalent to *Christ*, a word derived from Greek. Jews believed that a man would appear as God's anointed prophet, priest, and king to bring salvation to God's people. The Jews, however, had defined salvation mostly in political terms. Perhaps that is why most of them failed to recognize Jesus, who fulfilled the most comprehensive definition of the Christ.

Jesus accordingly urged His disciples to keep quiet regarding His identity (8:30). The popular idea of a Jewish Messiah would stir ideas of revolution and a glorious earthly kingdom. Jesus' followers needed to understand the suffering aspect of His work before they would be ready to proclaim the good news of the Messiah's arrival.

It is no coincidence that, after the height of Peter's confession that Jesus is the Christ, came the depth of Jesus' declaration regarding His own death (8:31). Once Jesus' identity was clear in the minds of His disciples, He moved swiftly to tell them why He had come to this world. The Messiah came to die.

This was Jesus' first specific teaching about His death. It was not a brief speech. It gave specific facts surrounding His crucifixion. Jesus made four points about His future: (1) He would suffer; (2) He would *be rejected*; (3) He would *be killed*; and (4) He would *rise* from the dead.

Peter was so shocked by the first three points that the fourth point apparently did not mean anything to him. Jesus had violated all Peter understood about the mission of the Messiah. Along with the majority of Jews, Peter evidently was looking for a Messiah who would defeat Rome and establish Israel as the dominant world power. In consequence, Peter took upon himself the role of counselor. He began to rebuke the One he had just called the Messiah (8:32). Peter's disbelief and dissatisfaction were quite strong (see Matt. 16:22).

Jesus, however, did an amazing thing in the midst of Peter's rebuke. The Savior turned and declared that Peter's words were satanic (Mark 8:33). *Satan* was using Peter to tempt Jesus to abandon the Father's will. Peter's ideas about the career of the Messiah were worldly, not godly, in nature. Jesus' reference to Satan reminds us that he is a real, personal, and supernatural being. Revelation 12:9 makes it clear that the devil is the archenemy of God and His people.

Peter had modeled the wrong response to Jesus' messiahship. It was left to Jesus to explain the proper response; and this is something everyone should know. Jesus thus addressed the crowd as well as the Twelve.

Jesus said He was not the only person who would need to take up a cross. Anyone who followed Him would also have to take up a *cross* (Mark 8:34). In some cases this means literally dying for Jesus' sake; but in all cases it means dying to selfishness. Believers must unashamedly live for Christ.

Jesus furthermore said that people who tried to keep their lives for themselves were eternally lost; in contrast, those who surrendered their lives for the sake of Jesus and the Gospel were eternally saved (8:35).

Here we see that giving ourselves to Jesus is the only way we can hope to be saved; of course, the life we save is not our physical existence in this world. Saving the soul (that aspect of us that reasons, feels, and wills) for eternity is infinitely more important than lengthening our life in this world. Thus those who gain the whole world without Christ still *forfeit their life* (8:36). They have traded the joy of eternity with Jesus for the fleeting pleasures of the world (8:37).

The shame of the cross may cause some people to avoid Jesus and not want to be identified with Him (8:38). They prefer this *adulterous and sinful* world more than the Savior and His teachings. Accordingly, they will have to face His rejection when He, the *Son of Man*, comes in *"the glory of His Father with the holy angels."*

SUGGESTIONS TO TEACHERS

Jesus remains the Messiah, just as He was two millennia ago. Today He issues the call to potential disciples just as He did outside Caesarea Philippi. Why not use this week's lesson to encourage your students to adopt a fresh view of Jesus and renew their desire to follow Him?

1. THE SUFFERING MESSIAH. Peter could not picture these two concepts together. Today it is common knowledge that Jesus was crucified, but all need to be reminded of the significance of that event. It was as the suffering Savior that

Jesus most clearly revealed Himself as God's unique representative, atoning for the sins of the lost.

2. THE GLORIOUS SON OF GOD. The scene of the Transfiguration caught Peter equally off guard. He did not know what to do as he saw Jesus in His kingly glory. People today would be just as shocked to see the heavenly Jesus. Nevertheless, to truly understand Jesus, we need to regard Him both at the lowest point a person could go—dying on a cross for us—and also at the peak of all humanity—the Son of God.

3. THE CALL TO SUFFERING. When Jesus spoke about taking up one's cross daily and following Him, His hearers knew just what He was referring to. When the Romans crucified people, they often forced the condemned to carry the horizontal beam of their own crosses to the place of execution (John 19:17). Every day, believers must be willing to follow the Lord's will even if it leads to pain and death.

4. THE CALL TO SURRENDER. Jesus explained in Mark 8:35 that if we try to keep, or preserve, our physical lives for ourselves, we will ultimately lose them. However, if we surrender our lives for the sake of Jesus and the Gospel, we will find true life. The questions appearing in 8:36 and 37 drive home the point that there is no benefit in losing what is of eternal value to gain what is of temporal value. Eternal life is of much more value than success, prosperity, or even a long earthly life. The one who wins without Jesus still loses in the end.

FOR ADULTS

■ TOPIC: Giving Your All

■ QUESTIONS: 1. What response did Jesus receive from His disciples when He asked them about popular opinions concerning His identity? 2. Why did Jesus warn the disciples not to tell anyone about Him? 3. How did Jesus respond when Peter began to rebuke Him? 4. What does it mean to deny oneself? 5. What will be the ultimate result of feeling ashamed of Jesus and His words?

■ ILLUSTRATIONS:

Give Me Your Faith. An old legend describes a monk who found a valuable diamond. A few days later, a traveler passed through that region. He was hungry and asked the monk for a coin with which to buy some food. The monk opened his money bag, and inside it the traveler saw the precious stone. With nothing to lose, the traveler asked the monk if he could have the diamond. As a man of God, the monk followed Jesus' words and gave the stone to the one who had asked for it.

A few days passed, and the traveler came back. He wanted to see the monk again. He caught the monk by surprise by giving back the previous jewel. But the traveler had another request. "This time I want something even more valuable. Please give me the faith in God that enabled you freely to give this diamond!"

An Example of Self-Denial. Wayne, a Christian from the United States, was about to travel into mainland China. In Hong Kong, a friend asked him first to visit another Christian who had only recently been released from a Chinese prison. Wayne feared that the Chinese man would want him to carry Bibles back to the mainland. Desiring to avoid any risk, Wayne did not want to break the law. He hoped his rationalization would be an adequate explanation for why he chose not to smuggle Bibles across the border.

Wayne arrived at the home of the Chinese man. Inside the door stood an older person smiling deeply despite his poor health. His back kept him nearly bent over. Soon a Chinese woman the same age came in with tea and small cookies. Wayne quickly observed their attraction to each other. They were continually reaching out to each other and lovingly looking at each other. As they watched Wayne watching them, they started to giggle.

Wayne turned to the friend who had brought him to this house. The friend explained, "They're newlyweds." Wayne then heard the story of how they had been engaged years before, around the time of the Communist Revolution. The day before they were to be married, Chinese Communists seized the seminary where the man was studying. Along with his peers, the groom had been taken off to a prison where he spent decades in hard labor.

Once a year, the prisoner's fiancée was permitted to visit him. At the conclusion of their visit, the officer in charge made this offer. "If you will renounce your Christian faith, you are free to go and marry her." Each year the officer heard the simple but definite answer, "No." After 30 years of repeating this ritual, the Chinese freed the man on the condition that he and his aging bride leave the country. Wayne compared his own fears with the self-denial of his Chinese friends and realized he had much to learn from them.

FOR YOUTH

■ **TOPIC:** I'm Yours, Jesus

■ **QUESTIONS:** 1. What was the popular opinion concerning Jesus' identity? 2. What did Peter declare about Jesus? 3. Why did Peter rebuke Jesus? 4. Why did Jesus then rebuke Peter? 5. What does it mean to take up one's cross?

■ **ILLUSTRATIONS:**

Commitment to the Boss. John Kenneth Galbraith, a famous economist, devoted a page in his autobiography to a faithful housekeeper named Emily. There Galbraith described how, after a tiring day, he asked Emily to keep anyone from interrupting him. Galbraith wanted to take a nap. A few minutes later the phone rang. President Lyndon Johnson was calling from the White House.

The voice on the other end said, "This is Lyndon Johnson. Get me Ken Galbraith."

"I'm sorry, Mr. President, but Dr. Galbraith is sleeping. He instructed me not to disturb him."

"Well, wake him up. I need to speak to him now on an urgent matter."

"No, Mr. President. I work for him, not you."

Later that evening, Galbraith called the President back. Was Johnson upset? No, he too praised Emily. "I need someone with that level of commitment here in the White House."

Take Time for People! People across the country are spending more and more time staring at computer monitors. The time we spend staring at those screens takes up time we can't spend with other people. Residents of college dorms often find it easier to e-mail a friend rather than walk four doors down the hall to ask a question.

Students at Seattle Pacific University decided to attack this problem—at least for a week. For that week, students were encouraged to turn off their computers unless they were needed for school-related work. Instead, special "Live Chat Rooms" were set up in each dorm, where many rediscovered the joy of carrying on extended conversations with friends they could see. These students made only a small sacrifice, but found their enriched relationships made it worthwhile.

Let Go. David Seamands tells the story of a conversation with Ed, a college student. Ed had listened to Seamands preach a sermon on giving Jesus control of one's life. Ed, a gymnast, used this picture to describe his struggle. "It's as if I had grabbed the bar in order to work out on it. But then, somehow the bar is raised to the gym ceiling and beyond. I find myself looking down on the clouds when I hear God's voice, 'Ed, let go.' I can't let go. I don't know where I will end up." At that time, Ed couldn't let go, but much later, he learned the simple lesson that when God asked him to let go, He would always be there to catch him.

Willingness to Sacrifice. The legend is told of how an ancient king's army captured a prince and his family. When the imprisoned royal family was brought before their captor, he asked the prince, "What will you give me in exchange for your freedom?" "Half of my wealth," he quickly replied. "What if I release both you *and* your children?" "Everything I own." "And what if I just release your children and your wife?" "Your Majesty, for that I would give myself."

The king was so moved by the prince's willingness to sacrifice himself that he freed the entire family, asking for nothing in return. As the family began their trip home, the prince remarked to his wife, "Wasn't that a spectacular palace?" Filled with gratitude to her husband, she answered, "I didn't even notice. All I could see was you—one who was willing to give himself for me."

JESUS DEFINES TRUE GREATNESS

BACKGROUND SCRIPTURE: Mark 10:13-45
DEVOTIONAL READING: Matthew 20:20-28

KEY VERSES: Whoever wishes to become great among you must be your servant, and whoever wishes to be first among you must be slave of all. Mark 10:43b-44.

KING JAMES VERSION

MARK 10:32 And they were in the way going up to Jerusalem; and Jesus went before them: and they were amazed; and as they followed, they were afraid. And he took again the twelve, and began to tell them what things should happen unto him, 33 Saying, Behold, we go up to Jerusalem; and the Son of man shall be delivered unto the chief priests, and unto the scribes; and they shall condemn him to death, and shall deliver him to the Gentiles: 34 And they shall mock him, and shall scourge him, and shall spit upon him, and shall kill him: and the third day he shall rise again. 35 And James and John, the sons of Zebedee, come unto him, saying, Master, we would that thou shouldest do for us whatsoever we shall desire. 36 And he said unto them, What would ye that I should do for you? 37 They said unto him, Grant unto us that we may sit, one on thy right hand, and the other on thy left hand, in thy glory. 38 But Jesus said unto them, Ye know not what ye ask: can ye drink of the cup that I drink of? and be baptized with the baptism that I am baptized with? 39 And they said unto him, We can. And Jesus said unto them, Ye shall indeed drink of the cup that I drink of; and with the baptism that I am baptized withal shall ye be baptized: 40 But to sit on my right hand and on my left hand is not mine to give; but it shall be given to them for whom it is prepared. 41 And when the ten heard it, they began to be much displeased with James and John. 42 But Jesus called them to him, and saith unto them, Ye know that they which are accounted to rule over the Gentiles exercise lordship over them; and their great ones exercise authority upon them. 43 But so shall it not be among you: but whosoever will be great among you, shall be your minister: 44 And whosoever of you will be the chiefest, shall be servant of all. 45 For even the Son of man came not to be ministered unto, but to minister, and to give his life a ransom for many.

NEW REVISED STANDARD VERSION

MARK 10:32 They were on the road, going up to Jerusalem, and Jesus was walking ahead of them; they were amazed, and those who followed were afraid. He took the twelve aside again and began to tell them what was to happen to him, 33 saying, "See, we are going up to Jerusalem, and the Son of Man will be handed over to the chief priests and the scribes, and they will condemn him to death; then they will hand him over to the Gentiles; 34 they will mock him, and spit upon him, and flog him, and kill him; and after three days he will rise again."

35 James and John, the sons of Zebedee, came forward to him and said to him, "Teacher, we want you to do for us whatever we ask of you." 36 And he said to them, "What is it you want me to do for you?" 37 And they said to him, "Grant us to sit, one at your right hand and one at your left, in your glory." 38 But Jesus said to them, "You do not know what you are asking. Are you able to drink the cup that I drink, or be baptized with the baptism that I am baptized with?" 39 They replied, "We are able." Then Jesus said to them, "The cup that I drink you will drink; and with the baptism with which I am baptized, you will be baptized; 40 but to sit at my right hand or at my left is not mine to grant, but it is for those for whom it has been prepared."

41 When the ten heard this, they began to be angry with James and John. 42 So Jesus called them and said to them, "You know that among the Gentiles those whom they recognize as their rulers lord it over them, and their great ones are tyrants over them. 43 But it is not so among you; but whoever wishes to become great among you must be your servant, 44 and whoever wishes to be first among you must be slave of all. 45 For the Son of Man came not to be served but to serve, and to give his life a ransom for many."

HOME BIBLE READINGS

BACKGROUND

The Gospel of Mark presents Jesus as the suffering Servant of the Lord (10:45). Mark focused more on the deeds of Jesus than on His teaching, placing a particular emphasis on service and sacrifice. This makes sense when we realize that the original readers of this Gospel were facing persecution.

Mark omitted the lengthy discourses found in the other Gospels, often relating only brief excerpts to give the gist of Jesus' teaching. Mark also demonstrated the humanity of Christ more clearly than any of the other Gospel writers. For example, Mark emphasized Jesus' human emotions (1:41; 3:5; 6:34), His human limitations (4:38; 11:12; 13:32), and other small details that accent the human side of the Son of God (7:33-34; 8:12; 9:36; 10:13-16).

In light of the above, it should come as no surprise that Mark originally wrote his Gospel to strengthen and guide Roman believers through a time of terrible empire-wide persecution. Mark told his readers that Jesus not only suffered and died, but also that He triumphed over the grave. The suffering Servant was also the Son of God (1:1, 11; 14:61; 15:39), the Son of Man (2:10; 8:31; 13:26), the Messiah (8:29), and the Lord (1:3; 7:28). At decisive points in Mark's Gospel, we learn that Jesus shared a unique relationship with the Father (1:11; 9:7). Demons even testified that Jesus exercised divine authority and power (1:24; 3:11; 5:7).

For Mark, faith and discipleship have no meaning apart from following the suffering Son of God. As the Son of Man served in self-abasement, so too must His disciples serve (10:42-45). In fact, true discipleship with Christ leads to self-denial and suffering (8:34). Mark furthermore depicted Jesus as the true Israelite whose life demonstrated the necessity of submitting to the Word of God (1:13; 12:35-37). Mark emphasized the importance of preaching and teaching the Gospel, not just as theological truth but also as the power of God over evil and sickness (1:27; 12:24; 16:15-18). And Mark showed Jesus' interest in the Gentiles and the validity of the church's mission to them.

NOTES ON THE PRINTED TEXT

Jesus and His disciples were on their last journey to *Jerusalem* (Mark 10:32). Something in the Savior's appearance or manner astonished the Twelve. Everyone had a sense of impending disaster.

Jesus took the Twelve aside and explained that, once they were in Jerusalem, He would be betrayed into the hands of *the chief priests and the scribes* (10:33). They would *condemn him to death* and *hand him over to the Gentiles*. The Romans would mock Him, spit on Him, and flog Him severely before crucifying Him (10:34). Victory for Jesus would come on the third day when He rose from the dead.

Jesus' remarks seem to have been fuller and more specific than those that came before. The end was at hand. He had said most of this before, but now it had a deepened intensity.

While Jesus was focused on His death, the disciples were ambitious for success. James and John made a special appeal for position and power in Christ's kingdom (10:35). Their motive was the same as the other disciples' motive for objecting to their asking. All wanted to be first, and all wanted to be served.

In response to Jesus (10:36), James and John asked to be seated in the places of honor next to Him when He ruled in *glory* (10:37). Jesus noted that the two did not fully grasp the significance of their request. Were they prepared to drink from the bitter cup of sorrow He was about to experience? Were they able to be baptized with the suffering He was about to endure (10:38)?

James and John replied that they were able to do what Jesus stated (10:39). He, in turn, assured them that they would share in His sorrow and suffering. Only the Father, though, would decide who would occupy the places of honor in Jesus' kingdom. God had prepared those positions for the ones He had chosen (10:40).

The other 10 disciples were upset at the request of James and John, probably because they too coveted positions of greatness in the kingdom (10:41). Jesus capitalized on the occasion by reaffirming His teachings on servanthood.

Christ explained that the world's leaders ruled as tyrants and exploited the masses (10:42); but the citizens of Jesus' kingdom did not try to oppress others. They, instead, looked for ways to serve (10:43). Likewise, those who wanted to be first had to give up personal rights (like a slave would) for the sake of others (10:44).

Mark 10:45 is a key verse of the second Synoptic Gospel. Jesus had already said He would die. Here He said why He would do so. He would give His *life* as a *ransom for many*, to pay for the sins of all who repent. When we trust in Jesus, we receive pardoning for sins and cleansing for our consciences (see Isa. 1:18). To experience true forgiveness, we must understand that Christ freed us from the weight of our guilt and our slavery to sin. He alone ransomed Himself at the cross so that we can serve Him with our entire being.

Jesus, of course, was the ultimate servant. Despite the glories of heaven, He came to earth as a human being. Through His atoning sacrifice, He turned greatness on its head, reversing the relationship between serving and being served. By Jesus' definition, the lower we stoop to serve others, the higher God's estimation of us as people of importance in His kingdom.

SUGGESTIONS TO TEACHERS

The healing of blind Bartimaeus (Mark 10:46-52) comes directly after Jesus' prediction of His death and resurrection and the request of James and John for positions of greatness in the divine kingdom. As time permits, consider exposing the class members, even briefly, to the account involving Bartimaeus. By drawing comparisons and contrasts between the demand of James and John (as well as the response of the other 10 disciples) and the request of Bartimaeus, you can help your students grasp some essential biblical truths.

1. BOTH ACCOUNTS INVOLVE REQUESTS. James, John, and Bartimaeus all made the right choice in taking their honest, heartfelt desires to Jesus, the Messiah.

2. BOTH ACCOUNTS INVOLVE FAITH. These individuals believed that Jesus could give them what they requested.

3. JESUS DENIED ONE REQUEST BUT GRANTED THE OTHER. Two of Jesus' disciples asked a favor and He essentially said, "No." A stranger similarly asked for help and received a positive response. Have your students discuss what made the difference.

4. JESUS DENIED THE GREEDY REQUEST. James and John asked for a gift to be squandered only on themselves and to place themselves ahead of others. Jesus had no choice but to refuse such a selfish demand.

5. JESUS GRANTED THE NEEDY REQUEST. Bartimaeus also asked for something. Yet his desire was not to surpass others, but simply to be made whole. Perhaps Bartimaeus would have gladly wished Jesus' gift of sight for all blind people. When we approach Jesus with our requests, what motivates us? If we are as eager that God would grant our requests for all His people, then we may more likely receive that for which we ask.

FOR ADULTS

■ **TOPIC:** Moving toward Greatness

■ **QUESTIONS:** 1. What possibly amazed the disciples about Jesus' resoluteness to head to Jerusalem? 2. What did Jesus foretell about what He would encounter in Jerusalem? 3. What was the essence of the request that James and John made to Jesus? 4. What was Jesus stressing by the cup and baptism analogies? 5. How did Jesus respond to the assertion made by James and John?

■ **ILLUSTRATION:**

God Loves Them All. The crowds tried to push Bartimaeus away. That's because people of ancient cultures made few allowances for the handicapped. Generally, they were shoved off to the sidelines of society. Tragically, despite improved attitudes toward the disadvantaged, this prejudice still appears today.

Every Friday evening, people gather for a special musical interdenominational service in Seattle's beautiful cathedral. Named for a Christian community in France, these events are called Taize services. During most of the service, worshipers repeatedly sing a distinctive variety of prayer choruses.

I don't attend often, but when I do, I always head for the same set of seats. Sitting there, I wait for my friends. From a nearby home, caretakers accompany a group of mentally disabled adults. They sit in my section; more accurately, I sit in their section. One of them occasionally speaks out during a quiet moment, but that doesn't happen often.

These adults show as much respect for the cathedral and the God to whom we sing as anyone there. One young man kneels during a major part of the hour. An older woman, who is even more handicapped, tries to sing with the others. In most cases, I cannot recognize her words, but I appreciate her spirit. As we prayed the Lord's Prayer together, she could remember only the first three lines. She spoke those words clearly, "Our Father, who is in heaven, hallowed be Your name." The last time I attended, we closed with the simple chorus, "Jesus, remember me when You come into Your kingdom." She knew those words. I could hear her heart as she sang.

I could just as easily sit in another part of the cathedral. But sitting with my friends has become part of the Taize experience for me. They remind me that Jesus does not listen to me pray because of anything I do for Him. Rather, He loves my challenged friends every bit as much as He loves me. Also, it wouldn't surprise me if God gave two of them the honored spots on Jesus' right and left in His glorious kingdom.

FOR YOUTH ■ TOPIC: Who Is the Greatest?
■ QUESTIONS: 1. Why did James and John request special places in Jesus' kingdom? 2. What did Jesus say would come with such places of honor? 3. What sort of greatness would Jesus' disciples attain? 4. How did Jesus say the Gentiles defined greatness? 5. How did Jesus, as the Son of Man, model true greatness?

■ ILLUSTRATIONS:

A Difficult Choice. Would you rather be Oscar the Grouch or Big Bird? That's the choice that Caroll Spinney faces when he heads for work. You guessed it. He works on the set of Sesame Street, where at various points in a day, he may be called upon to play both roles.

How did Big Bird become such a likable character? It's because one experience helped Spinney see the value of kindness. After work one day, Spinney was heading home. Walking down the sidewalk, minding his own business, Spinney passed an older man who looked drunk. Something told Spinney to go back and offer help. The man was not drunk, but merely in poor health. The man hoped someone would help him across a busy street. Reflecting back on that small deed, Spinney said, "Ever since, seeing how easy it is to help, we've had Big Bird doing good deeds."

If only James and John had learned from Jesus or even from Big Bird! If only they had learned that it's better to serve others than to grasp for themselves!

Service over Reputation. Justin Trudeau is the son of a popular former Canadian prime minister. When his father died, Justin presented the eulogy at the funeral. He received national attention for his words.

Perhaps, building on that good experience, Trudeau could have jumpstarted a political career of his own. Instead he wrote, "I'm not relishing being in the limelight. My primary responsibility is to try to live up to the chances I've been given, the strengths I have. Which means, for me, teaching."

Trudeau said that he was passionate about politics, but wanted no part of that world. "So much of politics is posturing and playing for the crowd, playing for the cameras. It's not something I feel any interest in." Instead, Trudeau gives himself to young people, wanting to help them too to become all they were meant to be.

The Problems of Greed. Americans make up only five per cent of the world's population, but our machines use one quarter of the oil the world refines each year. Per person, we go through far more water and own many more cars than the people of any other nation on earth. Per person, we waste more food than many Africans eat.

Because of how the media portrays the American lifestyle, people around the world now want to live at American levels of comfort. Everyone is competing for more. This worldwide greed may lead to major problems at some point when the supply of some necessary resource runs out. James and John fell into this trap two millennia ago, wanting the best only for themselves.

It's Not Fair. The disciples became angry when James and John asked for special treatment. How much better if the group's members had all supported one another! Contemplate an older sister in a large family remembering a key incident from her childhood.

Back home in the autumn, for the annual ritual of canning apples for winter, Mom sat the whole family down. That included us six kids and Dad, too. Equipped with knives, it was our task to reduce a mountain of fruit to pots full of peeled apples. No one ever competed with anyone else. We made hard work into a family party. We all worked as hard as we could, knowing the winter's pies depended on that day's work.

My youngest brothers probably didn't accomplish much. They spent more time eating apples and throwing apple cores at each other. But at the end of the day, my father always bought the same reward for each of us—the largest ice cream cone the corner store sold.

Was it fair? Shouldn't those who peeled more apples have received more ice cream? No, this was a family, not a competition. In fact, one year the store ran out of ice cream and my youngest brother ended up with only a popsicle. All the rest of us felt sorry for him despite the fact that he had already eaten all the apples he'd peeled that day—both of them.

God wants all of us to serve to the best of our capacity, and then to reward us all. Isn't that the way it should be?

OVERCOMING GRIEF

BACKGROUND SCRIPTURE: Ruth 1
DEVOTIONAL READING: Psalm 31:9-15

KEY VERSE: Ruth said, "Do not press me to leave you or to turn back from following you! Where you go, I will go; Where you lodge, I will lodge; your people shall be my people, and your God my God." Ruth 1:16.

KING JAMES VERSION

RUTH 1:3 And Elimelech Naomi's husband died; and she was left, and her two sons. 4 And they took them wives of the women of Moab; the name of the one was Orpah, and the name of the other Ruth: and they dwelled there about ten years. 5 And Mahlon and Chilion died also both of them; and the woman was left of her two sons and her husband.

6 Then she arose with her daughters in law, that she might return from the country of Moab: for she had heard in the country of Moab how that the LORD had visited his people in giving them bread. 7 Wherefore she went forth out of the place where she was, and her two daughters in law with her; and they went on the way to return unto the land of Judah. 8 And Naomi said unto her two daughters in law, Go, return each to her mother's house: the LORD deal kindly with you, as ye have dealt with the dead, and with me. . . .

14 And they lifted up their voice, and wept again: and Orpah kissed her mother in law; but Ruth clave unto her. 15 And she said, Behold, thy sister in law is gone back unto her people, and unto her gods: return thou after thy sister in law. 16 And Ruth said, Intreat me not to leave thee, or to return from following after thee: for whither thou goest, I will go; and where thou lodgest, I will lodge: thy people shall be my people, and thy God my God: 17 Where thou diest, will I die, and there will I be buried: the LORD do so to me, and more also, if ought but death part thee and me. 18 When she saw that she was stedfastly minded to go with her, then she left speaking unto her.

NEW REVISED STANDARD VERSION

RUTH 1:3 But Elimelech, the husband of Naomi, died, and she was left with her two sons. 4 These took Moabite wives; the name of the one was Orpah and the name of the other Ruth. When they had lived there about ten years, 5 both Mahlon and Chilion also died, so that the woman was left without her two sons and her husband.

6 Then she started to return with her daughters-in-law from the country of Moab, for she had heard in the country of Moab that the LORD had considered his people and given them food. 7 So she set out from the place where she had been living, she and her two daughters-in-law, and they went on their way to go back to the land of Judah. 8 But Naomi said to her two daughters-in-law, "Go back each of you to your mother's house. May the LORD deal kindly with you, as you have dealt with the dead and with me. . . .

14 Then they wept aloud again. Orpah kissed her mother-in-law, but Ruth clung to her.

15 So she said, "See, your sister-in-law has gone back to her people and to her gods; return after your sister-in-law." 16 But Ruth said,

"Do not press me to leave you
    or to turn back from following you!
Where you go, I will go;
    where you lodge, I will lodge;
your people shall be my people,
    and your God my God.
17 Where you die, I will die—
    there will I be buried.
May the LORD do thus and so to me,
    and more as well,
if even death parts me from you!"
18 When Naomi saw that she was determined to go with her, she said no more to her.

10

Monday, January 31	Psalm 6:1-7	*I Am Weary with Weeping*
Tuesday, February 1	Psalm 31:9-15	*My Life Is Spent with Sorrow*
Wednesday, February 2	Psalm 77:1-10	*My Soul Refuses to Be Comforted*
Thursday, February 3	Ruth 1:1-5	*Naomi Loses Her Husband and Sons*
Friday, February 4	Ruth 1:6-11	*Go Back to Your Home*
Saturday, February 5	Ruth 1:12-17	*Orpah Goes, Ruth Stays*
Sunday, February 6	Ruth 1:18-22	*Naomi and Ruth Travel to Bethlehem*

BACKGROUND

The account of familial love that takes place in the Book of Ruth probably occurred during the latter part of the period of the rule of the judges (1375–1050 B.C.). This was a time when *all the people did what was right in their own eyes* (Judg. 17:6; 21:25) and violence and chaos predominated without a central king to rule the people. The account of Ruth—with its rural setting and wholesome yet believable characters—is presented in stark contrast to these dark days for the nation of Israel.

Moab was the land east of the Dead Sea, opposite the tribal land of Judah to the sea's west. Moab was one of the nations that oppressed Israel during the period of the judges; in fact, King Eglon of Moab had forced much of Israel into being subservient to him for 18 years. And even though Israel eventually defeated Moab under Ehud's leadership (Judg. 3:12-30), there still would have been tense hostility between the two nations. Thus the famine in Israel must have been quite severe for Elimelech to make the decision to move his family to Moab (Ruth 1:1-2). The journey into Moab from their home in Bethlehem would have taken the family at least 70 miles through the Israelite tribal lands of Benjamin and Reuben, over the northern tip of the Dead Sea, and across the Jordan River.

As the head of his household, Elimelech would have maintained rights to ancestral property in Bethlehem, even after having moved to Moab. But when both he and his two sons died, the only ways Naomi could regain the property were through two legal customs: the "levirate" law and the "redemption of the land" law.

The levirate law—sometimes called the "levirate marriage"—was the custom of a widow marrying her dead husband's closest male relative, usually his brother (Deut. 25:5-10). Any offspring born from this union would carry both the name and the inheritance of the former husband. (In Naomi's case—since she was beyond childbearing years—her daughter-in-law, Ruth, became her substitute in marriage and bore a son to perpetuate the family name.)

The "redemption of the land" law was a way to get back land that had been sold because of bad crops or because the owner couldn't pay his bills. His nearest relative could redeem—or buy back—that land from its new owner. Of course, if the first owner became prosperous again, he had the right to redeem it for himself.

This enabled the Israelites to keep land in the original family. (In Naomi's case, Boaz legally cleared Elimelech's land of future claims and accepted the dual responsibility of both brother-in-law and kinsman-redeemer.)

NOTES ON THE PRINTED TEXT

This four-chapter book is named for Ruth, its chief character; but the story line is actually about how the desperate plight of Naomi and her tragic experiences and circumstances eventually ended with her gaining both abundance and happiness. The circumstances involving Ruth occurred during the time of the judges. A severe famine had struck the land; and it prompted Elimelech, who was from Bethlehem in Judah, to relocate with Naomi, his wife, and Mahlon and Chilion, his sons, to *the country of Moab* (Ruth 1:1-2).

Sometime after that, Elimelech died, leaving Naomi *with her two sons* (1:3). They decided to marry Moabite women. One was named Orpah, while the other was named Ruth (1:4). Then, when Naomi had been in Moab about 10 years, her two sons died. With Naomi's husband and sons now gone, she must have felt all alone (1:5).

According to 1:6, while Naomi was still in *Moab*, she received news that *the LORD* had blessed His people with fertile harvests. This information prompted Naomi to leave Moab with her daughters-in-law and return to Bethlehem.

Naomi, Orpah, and Ruth thus left the place where they had been staying and began the journey *back to the land of Judah* (1:7); but perhaps before the three had gone very far, Naomi asked whether her daughters-in-law would prefer to go back to their own mothers (1:8).

Naomi realized that Orpah and Ruth had been kind to Elimelech and his sons, Mahlon and Chilion, as well as to Naomi. It was Naomi's wish that the Lord would be just as kind to Orpah and Ruth.

Naomi expressed her hope that God would give Orpah and Ruth other husbands and a home of their own (1:9). The three then *wept* together; but despite the insistence of the daughters-in-law to remain with Naomi (1:10), the latter reasoned that it would be best for them to stay behind in Moab (1:11-13).

The three wept together again; then Orpah kissed her mother-in-law goodbye and returned to her home of origin (1:14). This is a case of Orpah showing practical concern for herself; thus her decision to remain in Moab was not a reproach on her character.

Ruth's feelings for Naomi evidently went much deeper than Orpah's, for Ruth *clung* to her mother-in-law. The latter, in turn, tried to persuade Ruth to follow Orpah's example in returning *to her people and to her gods* (1:15); but Ruth cared more for Naomi than for her own future.

In her pledge of loyalty (1:16-17), Ruth said she would leave the comforts of home to travel across the desert; live where Naomi lived, even in poverty; identify herself with Naomi's people, even though Ruth knew they might reject her;

commit herself to the God of Israel; and die and be buried in the same place as Naomi.

Ruth's oath in the name of the Lord might be paraphrased, "May a severe judgment fall on me if I am not true to this vow." From this Naomi not only realized that Ruth was determined to follow her no matter what perils lay ahead, but also Naomi saw that Ruth had a deep faith in the God of Israel. Thus Naomi no longer tried to persuade her daughter-in-law to remain in Moab (1:18).

SUGGESTIONS TO TEACHERS

In a very few verses, several character traits and attitudes are portrayed by one Israelite woman—Naomi—and two Moabite women—Ruth and Orpah. As we take a look at how these three women expressed these traits and attitudes, we would do well to strive to emulate them in our lives as followers of the Lord Jesus Christ.

1. BE KIND. Naomi thanked Ruth and Orpah for the kind way they had treated her husband, her sons, and herself. Indeed, the two younger women were in no way legally bound to Naomi, but they had grown to love her and respect her deeply, and thus they dealt with her in a kind manner. May we, too, treat others with kindness, sensitivity, and compassion.

2. BE THOUGHTFUL. Ruth and Orpah, though widowed themselves, realized that Naomi's circumstances were more grave than their own. Naomi, in one sense, was somewhat stranded in a foreign country. Being thoughtful of Naomi's needs, they did not discourage her from returning to her homeland, but rather began escorting her on her way home. May we, too, be thoughtful of the needs of others.

3. BE CONSIDERATE. Naomi felt that it would be in the best interest of her daughters-in-law to remain in their home country. And even though she would be alone on a dangerous journey, she was considerate enough of her daughters-in-law to encourage them to stay home while she braved the trek home. May we, too, be considerate of the best interests of others—even if it means we may have to face part of our journey alone.

4. BE LOYAL. Both Ruth and Orpah expressed intense loyalty to their mother-in-law. Though Naomi was not of their native land, their native family, their native culture, or their native religion, the two daughters-in-law continually expressed their love and loyalty to their mother-in-law. May we, too, express and act upon our loyalty to our families, church, employers, friends, and (especially) our God.

5. BE COMMITTED. No amount of explanation could convince Ruth to turn away from her mother-in-law. In fact, *Ruth clung to her* (Ruth 1:14). Ruth's commitment to her mother-in-law could not be dissuaded or deterred. And even if Naomi could only offer Ruth more tragic and desperate circumstances, the young woman was committed to stay with her mother-in-law. May we, too, never be dissuaded or deterred from our commitments.

■ **TOPIC:** Overcoming Grief

■ **QUESTIONS:** 1. What type of personal disasters wreaked havoc on Naomi's life? 2. How would these tragic and desperate circumstances make you feel if you were Naomi? 3. What would you have done if you were Naomi—stay in Moab or return to Judah? Explain your answer. 4. Do you think you would have been more like Orpah, who was finally convinced to return to her own home, or more like Ruth, who could not be discouraged from her commitment to Naomi? Explain your answer. 5. When you've had to cross over to another ethnic or cultural group, were you able to assimilate or did you remain a stranger "in their land"?

■ **ILLUSTRATIONS:**

Commitment Is the Key. "When I was a boy, my father, a baker, introduced me to the wonders of song," tenor Luciano Pavarotti relates. "He urged me to work very hard to develop my voice. Arrigo Pola, a professional tenor in my hometown of Modena, Italy, took me as a pupil. I also enrolled in a teacher's college. On graduating, I asked my father, 'Shall I be a teacher or a singer?'

"'Luciano,' my father replied, 'if you try to sit on two chairs, you will fall between them. For life, you must choose one chair.'

"I chose one. It took seven years of study and frustration before I made my first professional appearance. It took another seven to reach the Metropolitan Opera. And now I think whether it's laying bricks, writing a book—whatever we choose—we should give ourselves to it. Commitment: that's the key. Choose one chair."

Faithful to the Commitment. A young businessman was rushed to a hospital in serious condition. A physician thought that he might die. Not a religious man at the time, he did, however, turn on a radio and heard a Christian song being played: "God Will Take Care Of You." He said that he couldn't get that song out of his mind.

The young businessman began to pray and, as he did, he reported a sense of energy flowing in. It was near Christmas, a Sunday morning. He heard a group of nurses having a brief worship service in a nearby room and struggled up out of bed and joined them. While there, he committed his life to Christ. That man recovered. Thereafter, for the rest of his life, he remained faithful to his commitment.

That man referred every business and every personal decision to God and was resolute in his ethics, living by the teachings of Jesus. You've heard about this man, who told all about this in a book concerning his life. His name was J. C. Penney. He, too, insisted throughout his life that the apostle Paul was quite right in promising divine help for those in whom Christ's Spirit lives.

■ QUESTIONS: 1. What crises was Naomi facing after losing her husband and two sons? 2. In what ways was Naomi considerate of the needs of her daughters-in-law? 3. In what ways were Ruth and Orpah considerate of the needs of their mother-in-law? 4. How did Ruth go beyond expressing her loyalty to Naomi to expressing her deeper commitment to Naomi as well? 5. How does Christ's love motivate us to be loyal to other believers?

■ ILLUSTRATIONS:

Relatives Relieve Rifts. In the mid-1950s, author William Faulkner spoke to a University of Mississippi writing class. He told the class that author Ernest Hemingway lacked courage and was afraid to take chances in his fiction. However, by the time Faulkner's comment was printed, he was quoted as saying that Hemingway had a yellow streak when it came to danger. That caused a lot of hard feelings and a rift between the two authors that extended into their immediate families and relatives.

In March 1993, author-publisher Dean Faulkner Wells, niece of William Faulkner, worked together with Jack Hemingway, Ernest's son, to judge a literary competition in Los Angeles. At that time these two members of the feuding families learned that poor shorthand and editing had led to the misquote over 40 years earlier. They decided to work on bringing an end to the rift that had existed between the two families.

Here were two individuals who worked to terminate the differences that existed between their families and to reconcile the two families to each other. The two had become ambassadors who were living and enacting human reconciliation.

Don't Leave Home without Commitment. It has been said that "People cannot discover new oceans unless they have the courage to lose sight of the shore." It has also been said that "Conductors cannot direct the orchestra without turning their backs on the audience."

Found Greater Happiness. John Frank spent five years with the San Francisco 49ers. He had played in two Superbowl games and was entering his athletic prime at the age of 27. He had once dreamed of becoming a physician, but had postponed that goal to make big money in professional football; yet Frank discovered that money could never be the main purpose in life. He also learned that a sense of compassion can bring a person to a deeper joy.

The turning point in John Frank's career came the day when he rushed over to the side of an opponent who appeared to have suffered a serious injury—only to be chewed out by his coach for "giving aid and compassion to the enemy." That was the event that made Frank decide to go full-time to medical school. Frank is now a physician. Walking away from pro football seemed silly to everyone, but Frank says he is happier now in serving the hurting. He has no regrets about giving up fame and fortune in the pro ranks.

Happiness in a Capsule? She was a pretty 16-year-old. However, she was heavily into drugs. Although she was only 16, she had been in and out of hospital psychiatric units and detoxification programs.

One day, during the chaplain's visit, she asked him if he believed in God. He affirmed that he did. She asked if this God was the force who held everything together. "Yes," he responded. "Does this God have a name?" she continued. "Jesus Christ," came the chaplain's reply. The girl looked shocked, apparently unsure whether to believe the chaplain, even though she desperately needed something to hold on to in her life.

God came to earth as Jesus and lived as a human being. This realization filled the 16-year-old with hope, and she trusted in Christ for salvation. She got her life together. Today, many years later, she is a happily married woman, a mother who is continuing to discover each day how God is involved in her life.

OVERCOMING PRIDE

BACKGROUND SCRIPTURE: 2 KINGS 5
DEVOTIONAL READING: Mark 7:17-23

KEY VERSES: His servants approached and said to him, "Father, if the prophet had commanded you to do something difficult, would you not have done it?" . . . So he went down and immersed himself seven times in the Jordan. 2 Kings 5:13-14.

KING JAMES VERSION

2 KINGS 5:1 Now Naaman, captain of the host of the king of Syria, was a great man with his master, and honourable, because by him the LORD had given deliverance unto Syria: he was also a mighty man in valour, but he was a leper. 2 And the Syrians had gone out by companies, and had brought away captive out of the land of Israel a little maid; and she waited on Naaman's wife. 3 And she said unto her mistress, Would God my lord were with the prophet that is in Samaria! for he would recover him of his leprosy. 4 And one went in, and told his lord, saying, Thus and thus said the maid that is of the land of Israel. 5 And the king of Syria said, Go to, go, and I will send a letter unto the king of Israel. And he departed, and took with him ten talents of silver, and six thousand pieces of gold, and ten changes of raiment. . . .

9 So Naaman came with his horses and with his chariot, and stood at the door of the house of Elisha. 10 And Elisha sent a messenger unto him, saying, Go and wash in Jordan seven times, and thy flesh shall come again to thee, and thou shalt be clean. 11 But Naaman was wroth, and went away, and said, Behold, I thought, He will surely come out to me, and stand, and call on the name of the LORD his God, and strike his hand over the place, and recover the leper. 12 Are not Abana and Pharpar, rivers of Damascus, better than all the waters of Israel? may I not wash in them, and be clean? So he turned and went away in a rage. 13 And his servants came near, and spake unto him, and said, My father, if the prophet had bid thee do some great thing, wouldest thou not have done it? how much rather then, when he saith to thee, Wash, and be clean? 14 Then went he down, and dipped himself seven times in Jordan, according to the saying of the man of God: and his flesh came again like unto the flesh of a little child, and he was clean.

15 And he returned to the man of God, he and all his company, and came, and stood before him: and he said, Behold, now I know that there is no God in all the earth, but in Israel.

NEW REVISED STANDARD VERSION

2 KINGS 5:1 Naaman, commander of the army of the king of Aram, was a great man and in high favor with his master, because by him the LORD had given victory to Aram. The man, though a mighty warrior, suffered from leprosy. 2 Now the Arameans on one of their raids had taken a young girl captive from the land of Israel, and she served Naaman's wife. 3 She said to her mistress, "If only my lord were with the prophet who is in Samaria! He would cure him of his leprosy." 4 So Naaman went in and told his lord just what the girl from the land of Israel had said. 5 And the king of Aram said, "Go then, and I will send along a letter to the king of Israel."

He went, taking with him ten talents of silver, six thousand shekels of gold, and ten sets of garments. . . .

9 So Naaman came with his horses and chariots, and halted at the entrance of Elisha's house. 10 Elisha sent a messenger to him, saying, "Go, wash in the Jordan seven times, and your flesh shall be restored and you shall be clean." 11 But Naaman became angry and went away, saying, "I thought that for me he would surely come out, and stand and call on the name of the LORD his God, and would wave his hand over the spot, and cure the leprosy! 12 Are not Abana and Pharpar, the rivers of Damascus, better than all the waters of Israel? Could I not wash in them, and be clean?" He turned and went away in a rage. 13 But his servants approached and said to him, "Father, if the prophet had commanded you to do something difficult, would you not have done it? How much more, when all he said to you was, 'Wash, and be clean'?" 14 So he went down and immersed himself seven times in the Jordan, according to the word of the man of God; his flesh was restored like the flesh of a young boy, and he was clean.

15 Then he returned to the man of God, he and all his company; he came and stood before him and said, "Now I know that there is no God in all the earth except in Israel.

BACKGROUND

God's people had wanted a king. Thus followed Saul, David, and Solomon before the divided monarchy, which consisted of 10 northern tribes (henceforth known as Israel) and two southern tribes (called Judah). For the 600 years between the establishment of the kingdom and the rebuilding of Jerusalem after the Babylonian Exile, a series of prophets appeared on the scene.

The term "prophet" to us often means someone who predicts the future. Although the Old Testament prophets sometimes did make predictions about what was coming, they were hardly crystal-ball gazers or clairvoyants. They were primarily preachers who lived close to the Lord and dedicated themselves to preserving the covenant between God and His people. A prophet spoke out as a deeply involved citizen, making pronouncements always in the context of a specific situation. Thus the message was much more than a collection of noble devotional truisms for any age.

The best-known prophets, Elijah and Elisha (see 1 Kings 17—2 Kings 10), were each called "man of God." They had a firsthand knowledge of God's plans and presence. Yet kings and other leaders often did not want to hear their messages.

Our Scripture passage deals with Elisha, successor to the great Elijah. Elisha's ministry extended through the reigns of Ahab, Ahaziah, Jehoram, Jehu, Jehoahaz, and Jehoash—a period of over 50 years (850–800 B.C.). After Elijah was taken up into heaven on a chariot of fire, Elisha assumed the prophetic role of his mentor. Several miracles are associated with Elisha, including the cleansing of the irrigation water at Jericho, the bear attack of the mockers at Bethel, the miraculous production of oil for an indebted widow, the healing of Naaman, and the recovered ax head. It's no wonder Elisha, as a man of God, was respected as a worker of wonders and a personage of great wisdom.

This week's lesson examines the fascinating event involving Naaman, a mighty Aramean (Syrian) general, who went to the king of Israel and demanded the cure of his leprosy. The account has touches of humor. The Israelite king, terrified of the consequences of failure, relied on Elisha for help.

Elisha's prescription was for Naaman to bathe seven times in the Jordan River. Enraged at what seemed to be demeaning treatment, Naaman was ready to depart for Aram (Syria) before he was urged by his staff to wash as Elisha had suggested. The mighty Naaman found his cure and learned to respect the God of Israel.

NOTES ON THE PRINTED TEXT

Naaman was the commander of the Aramean army of King Ben-Hadad II, who lived about 860–841 B.C. Naaman was noted in history for his courage and success in battle (2 Kings 5:1); in fact, Jewish legend says he was the one who killed Ahab in the battle with the Arameans at Ramoth Gilead (1 Kings 22:34). The Arameans were moreover noted for their brutality in battle.

Naaman was also a leper. "Leprosy" is a term used in Scripture to describe several types of infectious skin diseases, not just the condition we identify as leprosy today (Hansen's disease). White skin, one symptom of these ailments, is mentioned several times in Scripture as covering the afflicted person but not disabling him or her (Exod. 4:6; Num. 12:10).

Second Kings 5:27 implies that Naaman's skin was white from leprosy, for Elisha's servant Gehazi turned as *white as snow* when he was stricken with the officer's disease. During the time Naaman had the condition, he seems to have been able the exercise the functions of a commander in the Aramean *army* (5:1); thus his was probably not a disabling or contagious skin disease.

The account concerning Naaman may be as much about the courage of a young Israelite slave girl as it is about the life change of the Syrian commander. Although the girl is mentioned only in the beginning of the account, without her willingness to speak up, Naaman would never have known about Elisha.

This young girl from Israel was captured by a raiding party (possibly under Naaman's command) and then placed in the service of *Naaman's wife* (5:2). The servant girl probably had seen her family murdered by her captors; in the least she had been separated from her family.

Something compelled the servant to return good for evil. She had no obligation to be concerned with her master's illness; yet she chose to move beyond social barriers and tell Naaman's wife that the commander could be healed. This confidence in Elisha was only outdone by the servant's courage to speak (5:3).

What began as a personal gesture by the slave girl quickly became political; rather than go directly to Elisha, Naaman went to King Ben-Hadad and gathered a letter of introduction, 750 pounds of silver, 150 pounds of gold, and 10 new sets of clothing to take to *Israel* (2 Kings 5:4-5). Ben-Hadad certainly considered Naaman worthy of such an incredible gift and such an important trip.

Naaman most likely assumed that King Joram of Israel would simply command Elisha to cure the Aramean commander. Naaman thus went directly to the *king* (5:6); however, when Joram read the letter from Ben-Hadad, Joram ripped his clothes in intense anxiety and distress (5:7).

The king had no power to heal Naaman, and he had only distaste for Elisha, who constantly opposed him because of his ungodliness. Joram assumed that

Ben-Hadad was trying to pick a fight with him, as he had done with Ahab, Joram's father (see 1 Kings 20:1-3).

Elisha heard about Joram's distress and sent word for Naaman to come to him (2 Kings 5:8). The army commander thus came with his horses and chariots and stood in the doorway of *Elisha's house* (5:9). The prophet responded by sending out his servant, who told Naaman to dip himself seven times in the Jordan River to be cured (5:10). The prophet himself was not the healer, nor was there anything magic about the waters of the river. God alone would bring about this miracle of healing.

Naaman *became angry* (5:11), probably for two reasons. One was the thought of washing in the insignificant, dirty river. Naaman knew of two rivers near his home in Damascus that he considered purer than the Jordan (5:12).

The *Abana* flowed from a deep blue pool in high mountains down into a fertile valley filled with lakes and orchards. The oasis the Abana created gave prosperity to Damascus, which sat along its banks. The *Pharpar* was the major stream running across the Damascus plain south of the city. Its cool waters, fed in the spring by snowmelt from Mount Hermon, would also have been more alluring than the sluggish Jordan River.

A second reason for Naaman's anger was that Elisha had treated him with dishonor by refusing to talk directly to him or provide some sort of immediate cure for the army commander. Naaman believed Elisha would almost come at his command. Naaman thought his wealth and stature made him worthy of Elisha's time and trouble; but the prophet did not fulfill Naaman's expectations about how he would be cured, so Naaman was ready to head home to *Damascus*.

Although Naaman's anger and pride had short-circuited his thoughts, his servants reminded him that he still had his leprosy. Would not he have done far more if the prophet had asked him to? It certainly would cost Naaman nothing to follow Elisha's instructions and try washing (5:13).

Naaman realized the wisdom in this advice (5:14). We do not know if he checked his skin after each time he dipped himself in the river, though human nature would suggest that he did. What is clear is that after the seventh time, God worked a miracle. The result was not only that Naaman was cured of his disease, but also that his skin became like that of a *young boy*.

The commander and his entire entourage next returned to Elisha. As Naaman stood before the prophet, he declared his conviction that the God of Israel was the only true deity in all the earth (5:15). The officer then made a strange request. He asked that Elisha give him as much dirt as two mules could carry back to Damascus (5:17). That request makes sense only in the context of Naaman's culture. People in a culture with many gods believed that the deity of another country could not be worshiped apart from its own land. Naaman's commitment to worship only Yahweh was sincere; however, in his mind the only way he could properly accomplish that was if he brought soil from Israel with him.

SUGGESTIONS TO TEACHERS

Some Scripture passages are like a many-faceted precious gem, with each face reflecting light and beauty. This week's selection from 2 Kings 5 is similar to that. We see not just one main point but many important lessons gleaming in this portion of the Bible. Here, then, are several key ideas you may offer your students.

1. A SLAVE GIRL WHO REMEMBERED. The testimony of a young Hebrew captive brought the mighty Naaman to Israel for treatment. The slave girl had faith in the man of God. Despite being separated from her own people, she never forgot the Lord. Furthermore, she shared her faith. Naaman—and all readers of the account—owe a debt of gratitude to this nameless young girl.

2. THE GENERAL WHO SUFFERED. The proud Naaman was likely used to bullying, buying, and bribing to get his way and carried a fortune to find a cure for his ailment. Illness also strikes the rich and powerful, and sometimes money fails to get results. But note this: God was interested in a Aramean military commander. The Lord moreover has a concern for all sufferers, no matter who they are or where they may be. How can this affect our perspective today?

3. A KING WHO TREMBLED. Israel's king was understandably frightened when a contingent of the Aramean army arrived. Was this a threat? A trick by the Aramean king to set up a pretext for invading or demanding reparations? After all, Israel's king had no way of curing Naaman. Even world leaders discover they have limits to their power. Ask your class members to share about times when their own resources fell far short. When have they hit "rock bottom" (in a manner of speaking)? What did they do then?

4. THE CURE THAT SURPRISED. Elisha rather casually sent word to Naaman to wash seven times in the Jordan River. Naaman, insulted by Elisha's lack of respect toward him as a V.I.P (Very Important Person!), was incensed. Dunk himself in a muddy little creek? But sometimes the seemingly insignificant thing is the most important thing, after all. God's ways may appear hopelessly ineffective and not worth trying. Take forgiveness, for instance. Why bother? There must be better ways of handling guilt and hurt. But the ways of the Lord, no matter how foolish or unproductive they may appear, always bring healing. Can you think of modern-day examples?

5. THE CURED OFFICER WHO PRAISED. Naaman had reluctantly obeyed Elisha's prescription. Then, experiencing his cure, Naaman praised the God of Israel. Each day we have healing and hope in our lives through Christ. The obvious response is praise and gratitude.

FOR ADULTS

■ **TOPIC:** Overcoming Pride

■ **QUESTIONS:** 1. How did Naaman find out about a possible cure for his leprosy? 2. What did Naaman take with him to Israel when he went to seek a cure? 3. What did Naaman expect Elisha to do to cure him? 4. What reasons did Naaman give for refusing to wash in the Jordan River? 5. What argument did Naaman's servants use to convince him to do as Elisha instructed?

■ ILLUSTRATIONS:

Intellectual Virtues. J. P. Moreland, in *Love Your God With All Your Mind: The Role of Reason in the Life of the Soul*, wrote the following (italics his):

> *Humility* and the associated traits of *open-mindedness, self-criticality,* and *nondefensiveness* [are] virtues relevant to the intellectual life. We must be willing to seek the truth in a spirit of humility with an admission of our own finitude; we must be willing to learn from our critics; and we need to learn to argue against our own positions in order to strengthen our understanding of them. I once heard a Christian college professor tell a group of parents that the purpose of a Christian college is to challenge the students' faith. I piped up in disagreement and argued that the purpose (among other things) was to strengthen and develop their faith, and one way to do this was to face questions honestly. The purpose of intellectual humility, open-mindedness, and so forth, is not to create a skeptical mind that never lands on a position about anything, preferring to remain suspended in midair. Rather, the purpose is for you to do anything you can to remove your unhelpful biases and get at the truth in a reasoned way. A proper development of this group of virtues can aid in that quest.

Healing from Rejection. I have never been in a war, but I know people who have. They tell me that sometimes, even years or decades after the war, they still have flashbacks to the tragedy and horrors they experienced. There is even a clinical term—post-traumatic stress syndrome (PTSS)—for people who experience such extreme trauma and have flashbacks and other symptoms that just don't seem to go away.

Sometimes when we experience injustice—in relationships, at work, or in the legal system—it is hard to let go of those memories. We dwell on our anger and our feelings of being wronged. Recently, I heard an author speak on our need to be healed from hard things that have happened in our past. He talked about people who have flashbacks to a painful childhood or a challenging time. "That's why the flashbacks come," he said, "because it's your time to be healed."

Jesus Christ knew about injustice. He was rejected by the very people He came to love and save. He was crucified though He was innocent. Yet *the stone that the builders rejected has become the very head of the corner* (1 Pet. 2:7). The cornerstone of a building offers stability, completeness, and reassurance.

Through Jesus' rejection, crucifixion, and resurrection, we can find safety and healing. As we live out the Christian life, we are like living stones being built into a spiritual house. *Come to him, a living stone, though rejected by mortals yet chosen and precious in God's sight, and like living stones, let yourselves be built into a spiritual house* (2:4-5). Is there a past hurt or rejection in your life? Perhaps it's your time to be healed.

Heeding the Warning. A Christian, as he entered a barbershop, heard a man say, "I was born a sinner. It was no responsibility of mine. It would be unjust for God to judge or condemn me for what I had no responsibility for, no matter what the Bible or preachers say!" The Christian pointed out that the Bible does not say God will condemn us just because we are born sinners. Rather, He does so if we remain sinners, rejecting the Savior, by whom He has opened the way of escape for us.

The believer used this illustration: "Suppose someone has occasion to pass your door at midnight, and notices that fire has broken out in your house. You are asleep, unaware of the danger you are in; the alarm is given and you are awakened. In this circumstance, what would your responsibility be?"

"Well," the man answered, "surely I would be responsible to heed the warning and escape as quickly as possible."

"But suppose you were to answer the one who warned you, 'I didn't set my house on fire, and have no responsibility for it,' and so remain in the house. What then?"

"In that case," he said, "I would be a fool, and responsible if I lost my life."

When we are privileged to hear the Gospel, we are accountable to receive its truth. God has given us warning of His coming judgment and the promise of His salvation for those who believe. It is our responsibility to heed the Bible's call and run to the safety of faith in Christ.

■ **TOPIC:** Pride and Prejudice

■ **QUESTIONS:** 1. Who was Naaman? 2. Who was Elisha? 3. What physical ailment did Naaman have, and why did he go to Elisha for help? 4. What are the simple, clear instructions Elisha gave Naaman? 5. Why did Naaman give praise to the God of Israel?

■ **ILLUSTRATIONS:**

Carrying the Weight. An old Arabian story tells how a royal prince once seized the land of a poor widow and made it part of his palace garden. The destitute woman complained to the chief judge of the country and asked for justice. The judge was sympathetic and fair, but he faced a very difficult situation. How could he condemn the rich and powerful prince who ruled the land?

However, the judge had courage, and he was a staunch champion of the right. He decided on a daring step. He came to the palace of the prince with a large sack in his hand. To the amazement of the prince, the judge asked permission to fill his sack with earth from the palace garden. Mystified, the prince agreed and the judge laboriously filled the huge sack to the brim. Then the judge asked the prince to lift the sack to his shoulder. The prince protested that the sack was much too heavy for one man to lift.

"This sack," the honest judge firmly replied, "which you think too heavy to bear, contains only a small portion of the land that you took from the rightful owner. How then, at the day of judgment, will you be able to support the weight of the whole?"

We Are Not the Judge. A woman in an airport bought a book to read and a package of cookies to eat while she waited for her plane. After she had taken her seat in the terminal and gotten engrossed in her book, she noticed that the man one seat away from her was fumbling to open the package of cookies on the seat between them. She was so shocked that a stranger would eat her cookies that she didn't really know what to do, so she just reached over and took one of the cookies and ate it. The man didn't say anything but soon reached over and took another. Well, the woman wasn't going to let him eat them all, so she took another as well. When they were down to one cookie, the man reached over, broke the cookie in half, and got up and left. The lady couldn't believe the man's nerve, but soon the announcement came to board to plane.

Once the woman was aboard, still angry at the man's audacity and puzzling over the incident, she reached into her purse for a tissue. It suddenly dawned on her that she really shouldn't judge people too harshly—*for there in her purse lay her still-unopened package of cookies*!

Like the woman in the airport, we need to remember that it is up to God, not us, to judge people. As Paul tells us in 1 Corinthians 4:5, *Therefore do not pronounce judgment before the time, before the Lord comes, who will bring to light the things now hidden in darkness and will disclose the purposes of the heart. Then each one will receive commendation from God.* We are responsible for communicating truth and telling others about God's coming judgment. But only God knows the hearts and intentions of all. Ultimately judgment and reward are His decision.

Jesus, See Me! Lilias Trotter served as a missionary in Muslim North Africa in the nineteenth century. In her writings, she includes a story of a girl named Melha. One day Lilias watched Melha go up to her nearly blind father and point to one of the pictures on the wall—of the Lord calling a little child to Him.

Melha turned to her father and said, "Look at Jesus!"

"I have no eyes, O my daughter—I cannot see," her father answered.

Melha lifted her head and eyes to the picture and said, "O Jesus, look at father!"

As Lilias concludes, "Was not that a bit of heavenly wisdom?" Even when we feel lost, unseen, and insufficient to know God's grace, God sees us and offers us healing. He cares when we are in pain or hurt by others. Though we often face injustice in this world, God's healing and compassion will prevail for eternity.

OVERCOMING UNCERTAINTY

BACKGROUND SCRIPTURE: John 3:1-21
DEVOTIONAL READING: John 3:17-21

KEY VERSE: For God so loved the world that he gave his only Son, so that everyone who believes in him may not perish but may have eternal life. John 3:16.

KING JAMES VERSION

JOHN 3:1 There was a man of the Pharisees, named Nicodemus, a ruler of the Jews: 2 The same came to Jesus by night, and said unto him, Rabbi, we know that thou art a teacher come from God: for no man can do these miracles that thou doest, except God be with him. 3 Jesus answered and said unto him, Verily, verily, I say unto thee, Except a man be born again, he cannot see the kingdom of God. 4 Nicodemus saith unto him, How can a man be born when he is old? can he enter the second time into his mother's womb, and be born? 5 Jesus answered, Verily, verily, I say unto thee, Except a man be born of water and of the Spirit, he cannot enter into the kingdom of God. 6 That which is born of the flesh is flesh; and that which is born of the Spirit is spirit. 7 Marvel not that I said unto thee, Ye must be born again. 8 The wind bloweth where it listeth, and thou hearest the sound thereof, but canst not tell whence it cometh, and whither it goeth: so is every one that is born of the Spirit. 9 Nicodemus answered and said unto him, How can these things be? 10 Jesus answered and said unto him, Art thou a master of Israel, and knowest not these things? 11 Verily, verily, I say unto thee, We speak that we do know, and testify that we have seen; and ye receive not our witness. 12 If I have told you earthly things, and ye believe not, how shall ye believe, if I tell you of heavenly things? 13 And no man hath ascended up to heaven, but he that came down from heaven, even the Son of man which is in heaven. 14 And as Moses lifted up the serpent in the wilderness, even so must the Son of man be lifted up: 15 That whosoever believeth in him should not perish, but have eternal life. 16 For God so loved the world, that he gave his only begotten Son, that whosoever believeth in him should not perish, but have everlasting life.

NEW REVISED STANDARD VERSION

JOHN 3:1 Now there was a Pharisee named Nicodemus, a leader of the Jews. 2 He came to Jesus by night and said to him, "Rabbi, we know that you are a teacher who has come from God; for no one can do these signs that you do apart from the presence of God." 3 Jesus answered him, "Very truly, I tell you, no one can see the kingdom of God without being born from above." 4 Nicodemus said to him, "How can anyone be born after having grown old? Can one enter a second time into the mother's womb and be born?" 5 Jesus answered, "Very truly, I tell you, no one can enter the kingdom of God without being born of water and Spirit. 6 What is born of the flesh is flesh, and what is born of the Spirit is spirit. 7 Do not be astonished that I said to you, 'You must be born from above.' 8 The wind blows where it chooses, and you hear the sound of it, but you do not know where it comes from or where it goes. So it is with everyone who is born of the Spirit." 9 Nicodemus said to him, "How can these things be?" 10 Jesus answered him, "Are you a teacher of Israel, and yet you do not understand these things?

11 "Very truly, I tell you, we speak of what we know and testify to what we have seen; yet you do not receive our testimony. 12 If I have told you about earthly things and you do not believe, how can you believe if I tell you about heavenly things? 13 No one has ascended into heaven except the one who descended from heaven, the Son of Man. 14 And just as Moses lifted up the serpent in the wilderness, so must the Son of Man be lifted up, 15 that whoever believes in him may have eternal life.

16 "For God so loved the world that he gave his only Son, so that everyone who believes in him may not perish but may have eternal life.

Monday, February 14	1 Peter 1:18-23	*You Have Been Born Anew*
Tuesday, February 15	1 John 2:29—3:5	*Born of God, Children of God*
Wednesday, February 16	1 John 5:1-5	*Born of God, Conquer the World*
Thursday, February 17	John 3:1-5	*How Can I Be Born Again?*
Friday, February 18	John 3:6-10	*How Can These Things Be?*
Saturday, February 19	John 3:11-16	*God So Loved the World*
Sunday, February 20	John 3:17-21	*Jesus Came to Save the World*

BACKGROUND

For many Christian people the Gospel according to John is the most precious book in the New Testament," says Bible scholar William Barclay. "It is the book on which above all they feed their minds, and nourish their hearts, and in which they rest their souls."

John's Gospel is priceless both for the sinner in the process of coming to Christ and for the believer who has walked with Him for many years. This Gospel satisfies the spiritual seeker and refreshes the Christian servant. Its fascination is immediate and enduring. Its message is simple and profound.

Though John's account of the life, work, and teachings of Jesus Christ lacks many of the features of the other three Gospels, it does include unique elements that enrich our understanding of who Jesus was and help us to understand the implications of His atoning work. Absent are key biographical events in Jesus' life, such as His birth, baptism, and ascension. Absent also are Jesus' popular parables and His interpretations of historical events. John probably excluded these because his primary intent was to defend the faith, not to present a purely chronological or historical account of Christ's life. John chose events in Jesus' ministry that demonstrated His supernatural origin and power. If every one of them had been written down, the author supposed, the whole world would not be able to contain the number of necessary books (John 21:25). What did get recorded was sufficient to lead people to a saving knowledge of Christ.

There is no doubt that this Gospel was written by an eyewitness of the events he described. The Gospel's details about the topography of Palestine and the towns that relate to Jesus are all on target. The author's familiarity with Jewish customs and religious practices are also dramatically evident in this Gospel.

Most importantly, however, the Gospel of John provides us with unparalleled insights into Jesus Christ. It is only in this account that we hear about the marriage feast at Cana (2:1-11), the Lord's discussion with Nicodemus (3:1-21), the raising of Lazarus (11:1-44), the washing of His disciples' feet (13:1-17), and the great "I am" declarations (6:35; 8:12, 58; 9:5; 10:7, 9, 11; 11:25; 14:6; 15:5). John also gave memorable glimpses of Thomas (11:16; 14:5; 20:24-29), Andrew (1:40-41; 6:8-9; 12:22), and Philip (6:5-7; 14:8-9).

The Gospel according to John stands as a living testimony of our Lord and

Savior Jesus Christ. John affirmed that Jesus was the Messiah and the Son of God. According to John, Jesus was not merely a human being, a man possessed with a type of Christ spirit, or a spirit being who merely appeared human. He was God who came in the flesh and now rules in heaven. John's Gospel was intended to convince people to place their trust in Jesus Christ as the Son of God who had died for their sins and is coming again.

NOTES ON THE PRINTED TEXT

Nicodemus was a member of the Jewish elite for his time (John 3:1). The Pharisees were renowned for their righteousness and strict observance of the law. As a member of the Sanhedrin, Nicodemus was one of 70 men who ran the religious affairs of the nation and had religious authority over all Jews living at that time.

Perhaps Jesus' miracles and teaching had impressed Nicodemus and brought him to this "*teacher . . . from God*" (3:2). Nicodemus had seen the signs as the Lord's seal of approval on *Jesus*. Perhaps Nicodemus felt that with all his self-righteousness, something was still missing; or perhaps Nicodemus was questioning Jesus on behalf of some members of the Sanhedrin. The night visit may mean that Nicodemus did not want to be publicly seen talking with Jesus; or it may mean that Nicodemus wanted a long conversation, which would be more possible at the end of the day.

Jesus sensed a spiritual hunger in Nicodemus but replied to him in a terse manner. In effect, Jesus told Nicodemus he was wasting his time if he thought he could enter the kingdom of God in his current condition, without being "*born from above*" (3:3). This respected religious leader needed to be radically transformed if he expected to see God's *kingdom*.

Nicodemus asked Jesus how it was possible for people to be reborn when they are *old* (3:4). The religious leader then noted that it was impossible for someone to reenter the *womb* of his or her mother and *be born* a second time. The response of Nicodemus to Jesus can be viewed in at least two ways: either Nicodemus did not understand Jesus; or Nicodemus did not like where the conversation was headed and chose to be ignorant of Jesus' true meaning. In either case, Nicodemus was searching for more information from Him.

Jesus explained that the rebirth was spiritual, not physical, and could only be accomplished by the Holy Spirit (3:5). It is not entirely clear what Jesus meant by "*of water and Spirit,*" and there are at least three prominent views.

Some think Jesus was referring to the meaning behind baptism. Since Jesus' ministry came shortly after that of John the Baptist, John's baptism of repentance was on everyone's minds. Thus Jesus' reference was to baptism, which signified repentance; in other words, Nicodemus needed to repent and be born of the Spirit to see God's kingdom. Others believe the reference is to water associated with the birth of a child. Jesus was thus referring to both physical and spiritual births. Still others note that Nicodemus, as a scholar, should have known Ezekiel 36:25-26, where *water* (as cleansing) and *spirit* are both mentioned.

Jesus' main point, of course, was that entrance into the divine kingdom could not be obtained by keeping the law or by belonging to the right race or people. He explained that what is born of physical heritage is physical (namely, weak and mortal in nature); in contrast, what is born of the Spirit is spiritual (namely, eternal and immortal in nature; John 3:6).

Jesus urged Nicodemus not to be amazed that the new birth was a necessity for anyone to enter God's kingdom (3:7). Jesus then compared the work of the Spirit to the *wind* (3:8). In fact, in both Hebrew and Greek the same word can mean "spirit" or "wind." One cannot see the wind or understand its origin, but its effects can be seen. In the same way, we cannot see the Spirit at work within a person's heart, but we can watch the dramatic changes in that person's life. Just as we cannot control the wind, so the Spirit does as He pleases.

Nicodemus admitted that he did not understand Jesus' words (3:9). The religious leader's reply should probably be taken as a sincere plea for help, not as a sarcastic questioning of Jesus' response. Nicodemus wanted to know how he could experience this new birth. Jesus was surprised that Nicodemus did not *understand* the concept of the new birth (3:10). As a prominent teacher, he should have been familiar with Old Testament passages that speak of a new life and a new heart (for example, Jer. 31:33).

Jesus noted that He spoke about what He knew and testified about He had seen. Sadly, though, many of Nicodemus' peers did not accept Jesus' *testimony* (John 3:11). If they did not believe what Jesus said about things that happen on earth, they would have much more difficulty in believing what He said about things that happen in heaven (3:12).

Thankfully for Nicodemus, he was talking with someone who could speak with authority in heavenly matters. While the Jews possessed God's revelation, no one had ever gone into heaven or come back to describe it; but because the *Son of Man* (3:13) came from there, He could reveal its nature to humanity. He revealed things that cannot be discovered by experience or logic, including how it is possible to be saved.

In the wilderness, after the Israelites had sinned and were facing God's judgment, they were delivered from death by looking at the bronze snake Moses held up on a pole (Num. 21:4-9). In Jesus' reference to this passage, the word translated *lifted up* (John 3:14) can mean both lift up (as on a cross) and exalt (as to heaven). The idea is that Jesus' death also became the stepping stone to His exaltation.

The good news is that, because of Jesus' work at Calvary, we are saved when we look to Him in faith (3:15). The Father's sacrifice of the Son highlights both the extent of God's love for humankind and the manner in which He chose to express that love (3:16); and while all believers are children of God, Jesus is God's *Son* in a unique, one-of-a-kind sense.

Thus, all who trust in Christ will not *perish*; instead, they will have *eternal life*. The fact that salvation is for all who believe implies judgment for those who do not. While John emphasized that Jesus came to offer eternal life, he could not ignore the end of those who reject the Savior.

SUGGESTIONS TO TEACHERS

Have you ever pondered what the purpose of life is? Have you ever wondered how a person could get some understanding of what the Almighty is like? Heavy questions like these may get pushed aside for a time but seem to creep back into our consciousness at some point. Maybe the occasion is a serious illness, or the loss of a loved one, or some other crisis. We struggle to make some sense of life. John 3 offers insights to us (and anyone) seeking answers to life's big questions.

1. QUERY FROM A RESPECTED LEADER. It's fun to speculate for a few moments why Nicodemus came to Jesus. Was Nicodemus deputized by the Sanhedrin to speak privately with Jesus? Or did Nicodemus just want to talk with Jesus for himself? Did this leader hope to head off a fatal confrontation between the authorities and Jesus? Obviously, Nicodemus was impressed with Jesus.

2. KEY TO AN AWARENESS OF GOD'S REALM. Devote class time to discuss the meaning of the second birth about which Jesus spoke. Point out that the Greek word *anothen* can be translated "born anew" or "born from above." Also note that the phrase *born-again Christian* is more than a cliché.

3. QUESTION ABOUT STARTING OVER. Nicodemus's question about the new birth hints that he felt his best years were behind him. If some in your class are going through a midlife crisis, a job search, forced retirement, continuing health problems, or old age, Nicodemus's query should provoke some soul-searching conversation at this point.

4. CALL FOR A SPIRITUAL REBIRTH. Jesus' admonition to Nicodemus is relevant to the members of your class, whether they are old or young. Nicodemus was so caught up in religion that he failed to know the Spirit. Until an individual personally is sensitive to the nudges of the Spirit, mere religion may seem sufficient.

5. CLAIM OF JESUS' COMING. Spend time on John 3:16-21 to let the impact of the news of God's love sink into your thoughts in a new way. Note that God did not send Jesus to condemn the world. Those clinging to notions of a vengeful deity will discover these verses to be liberating. Talk about what it means to have eternal life. Such starts here, and implies a new existence with God now.

FOR ADULTS

■ TOPIC: Overcoming Uncertainty

■ QUESTIONS: 1. Why did Nicodemus visit Jesus? 2. Why did Jesus say Nicodemus needed to be born again? 3. What role does the Holy Spirit serve in the new birth? 4. Why should Nicodemus have understood what it meant to be born again? 5. What is God's plan for the redemption of the lost?

■ ILLUSTRATIONS:

Faith Requests God's Presence. Jed Harris was a successful producer of plays some 70 years ago. He may be best known for staging the original production of Thornton Wilder's *Our Town*. In the midst of a season of endless days filled with the pressure of countless details, Harris started losing his hearing. He couldn't hear people standing next to him, and he was missing vital information.

Harris went to a noted hearing specialist who listened patiently to the producer's sad tale of diminished hearing. At the end of this narration, the audiologist pulled a fine gold pocket watch from his vest and held it to Harris's ear. "Can you hear the ticking of this watch?" the physician asked.

"Of course," Mr. Harris replied.

The physician walked to the door of his office and held up his watch. Harris concentrated and said, "Yes, I hear it quite plainly."

The specialist stepped into the adjacent room and called out, "Can you hear anything now?"

Jed Harris was astounded. "Yes, I still hear it!"

The physician came back into the room and pocketed his watch. "I see this occasionally with busy, successful people. There's nothing wrong with your hearing, Mr. Harris. You've simply quit listening."

Sometimes in the hustle and bustle of life, we lose touch with God. He's still there, but our spiritual "hearing" and "vision" switch off. It's then that we, like Nicodemus, need to have a fresh, awe-inspiring encounter with Him that leads us to trust in His Son for mercy and grace.

Faith Knows God Has the Answers. A *Time* magazine reporter asked Russian-born novelist Ayn Rand, "Ms. Rand, in a sentence, what's wrong with the modern world?" The novelist replied, "Never before has the world been clamoring so desperately for answers to crucial problems, and never before has the world been so fanatically committed to the belief that no answers are possible. To paraphrase the Bible, the modern attitude is 'Father, forgive us for we know not what we are doing and please don't tell us.'"

Rand didn't get it in one sentence, but she did capture an important concept. When things fall apart, we need to look to God for explanation, for refuge, and for strength. If we don't, we will be full of despair.

Faith Looks to God for Protection. In 1942, Eddie Rickenbacker ditched a B-17 airplane, which had been carrying a crew of seven on an inspection flight some 600 miles north of Samoa in the Pacific. No one knew what happened, whether anyone survived, or where they were. For eight days the men bobbed in a raft. Food and water were gone.

That afternoon the men prayed and went to sleep to conserve their strength. As Rickenbacker dozed with his cap over his eyes, something landed on his head. He insisted ever afterwards that he knew without looking that it was a seagull, even though he reckoned his crew was hundreds of miles from land.

Rickenbacker snatched blindly at the bird and caught it. Each airman got a mouthful of raw seagull. Its innards became bait to catch fish, which yielded food, fluids, and more bait. The eight men survived sixteen more days until the raft was spotted from the air and they were rescued.

Years later after retiring, Rickenbacker went once a week at sunset to a Florida pier with a bucket of shrimp and fed the gulls. He was thanking them and God, who had sent one of them.

FOR YOUTH

■ **TOPIC:** When God's Spirit Is Not Our Spirit

■ **QUESTIONS:** 1. Who exactly was Nicodemus? Why did he choose to visit Jesus? 3. What did Jesus mean by telling Nicodemus that everyone needed to be spiritually reborn? 4. Why is the Holy Spirit important to the new birth? 5. In what way did God show His love for the world?

■ **ILLUSTRATIONS:**

Keep in Touch with God. Tom Brokaw got his start in the television news business in Omaha, Nebraska. From there he rose rapidly through anchor spots in Los Angeles and Washington, D.C., to become co-host of the "Today" show in New York. Shortly after that promotion, Brokaw was picking up some items in Bloomingdale's when a tourist spotted him.

The out-of-towner pointed his finger and said, "Tom Brokaw! Right?"

"Right," said the newsman.

"You used to do the morning news on KMTV in Omaha. Right?"

"Right again," said Brokaw, getting ready for some fan adoration.

"I knew it the minute I spotted you," the tourist said. "Say, whatever happened to you?"

Sometimes we treat God like that tourist treated Tom Brokaw. We may have had an encounter with God at camp last summer and think that's all there is to Him. But there's a Bible filled with truths about God and a lifetime in which to interact with Him. Let's get started!

Whom Do You Trust? At the west end of Constitution Avenue in Washington, D.C., screened from the street by a grove of elm and holly trees, sits a bronze statue of Albert Einstein. Einstein's figure is 21 feet tall. He's seated on a three-step base of white granite. The physicist is depicted in a baggy sweater, wrinkled corduroy trousers, and sandals. His shock of hair is in familiar disarray.

At Einstein's feet is a map of the universe—a 28-foot square slab of granite in which 2,700 small metal studs are embedded. Each stud represents the location in the sky of a planet, major star, or familiar celestial body at noon on April 22, 1979 —the time the memorial was dedicated.

The expression on the face of Einstein's statue is a mixture of wisdom, peace, and wonder. The face reflects the serenity of a man who believed a divine mind had conceived the universe he spent his life trying to understand. He would tell his colleagues who believed in a random universe, "God does not play dice."

Einstein was not a Christian. He put his confidence in an impersonal deity. You can go beyond Einstein by trusting in the personal God of the Bible, Jesus Christ, to bring you safely through any difficulty of life.

Who Loves You? An old man died, leaving one child—a son—as his sole survivor. The father had been hard to know. The son remembered a respectful but formal relationship. Suddenly he was alone in his father's house looking through all the items kept in all the places a child never looks when his or her parents are alive.

The big stuff was easy to deal with—property, life insurance, and bank accounts. It was the personal stuff that was hard to handle. Finally the son came to the bureau drawers in the bedroom. Here were carefully sorted socks. There were several small boxes and a cigar tin. One box held military insignia, another tie tacks and foreign coins. This one had miscellaneous keys. That one held his mother's wedding ring and a lock of her hair.

In the cigar tin was a yellowed index card wrapped in tissue paper. Tiny teeth were glued to the card. A date was jotted under each tooth in his father's neat handwriting. His father had been the tooth fairy. The son always assumed it was his mother.

God loves you in ways you've never imagined. He isn't distant and uncaring, though you may think so. He has been looking out for you all your life. You can depend on Him to keep doing so forever. He isn't going to leave you an orphan, like the son in the story. Be sure your relationship with your heavenly Father is closer than the relationship in the story. *God wants it that way.*

OVERCOMING PREJUDICE

BACKGROUND SCRIPTURE: John 4:1-42
DEVOTIONAL READING: John 4:35-42

KEY VERSE: There is no longer Jew or Greek, there is no longer slave or free, there is no longer male and female; for all of you are one in Christ Jesus. Galatians 3:28.

KING JAMES VERSION

JOHN 4:7 There cometh a woman of Samaria to draw water: Jesus saith unto her, Give me to drink. 8 (For his disciples were gone away unto the city to buy meat.) 9 Then saith the woman of Samaria unto him, How is it that thou, being a Jew, askest drink of me, which am a woman of Samaria? for the Jews have no dealings with the Samaritans. 10 Jesus answered and said unto her, If thou knewest the gift of God, and who it is that saith to thee, Give me to drink; thou wouldest have asked of him, and he would have given thee living water. . . .

19 The woman saith unto him, Sir, I perceive that thou art a prophet. 20 Our fathers worshipped in this mountain; and ye say, that in Jerusalem is the place where men ought to worship. 21 Jesus saith unto her, Woman, believe me, the hour cometh, when ye shall neither in this mountain, nor yet at Jerusalem, worship the Father. 22 Ye worship ye know not what: we know what we worship: for salvation is of the Jews. 23 But the hour cometh, and now is, when the true worshippers shall worship the Father in spirit and in truth: for the Father seeketh such to worship him. 24 God is a Spirit: and they that worship him must worship him in spirit and in truth. 25 The woman saith unto him, I know that Messias cometh, which is called Christ: when he is come, he will tell us all things. 26 Jesus saith unto her, I that speak unto thee am he.

NEW REVISED STANDARD VERSION

JOHN 4:7 A Samaritan woman came to draw water, and Jesus said to her, "Give me a drink." 8 (His disciples had gone to the city to buy food.) 9 The Samaritan woman said to him, "How is it that you, a Jew, ask a drink of me, a woman of Samaria?" (Jews do not share things in common with Samaritans.) 10 Jesus answered her, "If you knew the gift of God, and who it is that is saying to you, 'Give me a drink,' you would have asked him, and he would have given you living water." . . .

19 The woman said to him, "Sir, I see that you are a prophet. 20 Our ancestors worshiped on this mountain, but you say that the place where people must worship is in Jerusalem." 21 Jesus said to her, "Woman, believe me, the hour is coming when you will worship the Father neither on this mountain nor in Jerusalem. 22 You worship what you do not know; we worship what we know, for salvation is from the Jews. 23 But the hour is coming, and is now here, when the true worshipers will worship the Father in spirit and truth, for the Father seeks such as these to worship him. 24 God is spirit, and those who worship him must worship in spirit and truth." 25 The woman said to him, "I know that Messiah is coming" (who is called Christ). "When he comes, he will proclaim all things to us." 26 Jesus said to her, "I am he, the one who is speaking to you."

13

HOME BIBLE READINGS

Monday, February 21	Colossians 3:11-17	Christ Is All and in All
Tuesday, February 22	John 4:1-6	Jesus Travels to a Samaritan City
Wednesday, February 23	John 4:7-12	Jesus Speaks About Living Water
Thursday, February 24	John 4:13-18	The Samaritan Woman Wants Living Water
Friday, February 25	John 4:19-26	I Am the Messiah
Saturday, February 26	John 4:27-34	Come and See the Man
Sunday, February 27	John 4:35-42	Many Samaritans Believed Jesus' Word

BACKGROUND

Because the Jews of Jesus' day regarded the Samaritans as half-breeds, they did not *share things in common with* (John 4:9) them. When the Assyrians took the northern kingdom of Israel captive, they brought in a wide variety of people to replace the Jews they had removed from the land (2 Kings 17:24). It is a matter of debate as to what extent these foreigners intermarried with the Jews whom Assyria left to take care of the land.

The hostility continued for centuries. After the Exile, the Jews captured the city of Samaria and caused much destruction in it. John Hyrcanus, a Jewish leader, destroyed the Samaritan temple in 128 B.C.

The animosity persisted during the time of Jesus' ministry. The Jews that lived north of Samaria often traveled east of the Jordan River to avoid going through Samaria on their way to Jerusalem. Also, to be called a "Samaritan" was the worst form of insult (see John 8:48). In fact, some religious leaders would not even say the name "Samaritan" (see Luke 10:37).

NOTES ON THE PRINTED TEXT

Jesus left Judea, where He had been ministering, and returned to Galilee (John 4:1-3). He decided to travel through Samaria and eventually came to Sychar, a village near the field that Jacob had given to his son Joseph (4:4-5). A well that Jacob had dug long ago was there (4:6). *It was about noon* when Jesus sat beside *the well*, for He was *tired* from walking.

While Jesus was at Jacob's well, an unnamed *Samaritan woman came to draw water* (4:7). Prior to this, the Twelve had gone into town to purchase supplies and presumably had taken the water bucket with them (4:8); and because Jesus was thirsty, He asked the woman to give Him a drink. This request so shocked the woman that she questioned why Jesus—a Jew—would ask her—a Samaritan woman—for a *drink* (4:9).

Jesus deftly avoided getting embroiled in the longstanding dispute that existed between the Jews and Samaritans of His day; instead, He drew attention to the gift of salvation that He, the Messiah, was offering the Samaritan woman. Jesus noted that if she truly grasped what He was saying, she would be asking Him for the water that gives eternal life (4:10).

The word translated *living* is used in Greek of flowing water. This led to the woman's misunderstanding recorded in 4:11-12. She thought Jesus was referring to some unknown source of drinkable water. The Messiah explained that He offered eternal life, which He compared to a perpetual spring flowing within believers (4:14).

The idea of an unending supply of water intrigued the woman, who pictured it as something that would replace her daily trips to and from the well carrying a heavy pot. She took Jesus literally and focused on personal convenience rather than anything spiritual (4:15).

In the continuing dialogue, Jesus showed the Samaritan women that He knew all about her personal life. He correctly noted, for instance, that she had had five husbands; and she was not married to the man she was currently living with (4:16-18). Jesus' statement made the woman realize that there was something special about Him. The woman concluded that Jesus was *a prophet* (4:19), namely, a divinely inspired person with supernatural knowledge; but then the woman cleverly tried to evade the issue of her adulterous relationship by throwing out the question of proper worship.

Many similarities existed between the faith of the Jews and the Samaritans. Both practiced circumcision as a religious rite and looked for the Messiah. Like the Jews, the Samaritans believed in a final judgment with the Messiah handing out rewards and punishments. By Jesus' day they had also forsaken all idolatry, as had the Jews.

As noted by the woman, the chief difference in the theology between the Jews and Samaritans concerned the place to worship God (4:20). The Samaritans insisted that God had to be *worshiped* on Mount Gerizim rather than in *Jerusalem*. That was the mountain where the Israelites had gathered to hear blessings read when they entered the promised land (Deut. 27:12; Josh. 8:33). Thus the Samaritans considered themselves to be the true worshipers of the Lord.

Jesus refused to get mired in this ancient debate; instead, He spoke about a future time when it would not matter whether believers' worshiped the Father on Mount Gerizim or in *Jerusalem* (John 4:21). Jesus then noted that the Samaritans, despite their sincerity and devotion, did not really know the One they worshiped. The Jews, in contrast, did know the God they worshiped, for salvation came *from the Jews* (4:22). In fact, through one of their own—the Messiah—God would make redemption available to the lost.

Jesus then made a profound statement about the true nature of worship (4:23). He declared that an *hour* was *coming*—and in fact was already *here* as a result of His advent—when the *true worshipers* venerated the Father *in spirit* (rather than in the flesh) and in *truth* (rather than in falsehood). Jesus moreover stated that the Father sought such people to be His worshipers.

It is clarifying to note that the Samaritan woman had been concerned about *where* people ought to worship, while Jesus was concerned about *who* people ought to worship. Because God is spirit (namely, immaterial in His existence), believers worshiped Him in the power of the Spirit and according to the truth of His Word (4:24).

The Samaritan woman started to wonder whether Jesus was more than just a prophet. The woman thus voiced the hope of both Samaritans and Jews, namely, that the Messiah would come. (Both the Greek term rendered "Christ" and the Hebrew word translated "Messiah" mean "the one who has been anointed.") In Bible times it was commonly believed that whenever Christ came, He would explain all the mysteries of life (4:25). At this point, Jesus directly told the Samaritan woman that He was the Messiah (4:26).

That the woman left her water pot at the well probably shows the favorable impression Jesus made on her (4:28). She forgot about her main purpose for coming to the well in her effort to tell others in the village about the stranger (4:29); as a result, the Samaritans came out to see Jesus (4:30). Many thereupon believed the woman's report and put their faith in the Messiah (4:39-42).

SUGGESTIONS TO TEACHERS

The void that exists in the lives of each of us can be filled only by Jesus Christ. When we invite the living Messiah to come into our hearts, He supplies the freeing power from the bondage of evil and sin's oppression. That is why this week's lesson, based on the fascinating encounter of Jesus and a Samaritan woman with a shady past, provides an excellent way of pondering God's good news for each of us.

1. REFUSAL TO LISTEN. This is one of those Sundays in which the biblical material seems to unfold so neatly that you don't have to struggle to put together a lesson. Provide a few details, but let the account itself unfold. Jesus was thirsty. A woman from the village arrived at the well to draw water. Her banter with Jesus showed her to be somewhat coquettish. The Samaritan, after refusing to heed Jesus' words, tried to play games with Him. But Jesus didn't go along with her evasions and pretense. The Savior wanted her to take Him seriously.

2. RELUCTANCE TO ACCEPT. Jesus was patient in the face of the Samaritan woman's persistent refusal to come clean before Him and to accept His gracious offer of new life. Even when Jesus pinpointed the woman's unsavory reputation, she still tried to get the upper hand (in a manner of speaking). Switching topics, she tried to sidetrack the conversation by introducing the ancient dispute of worship on rival mountains. Discussions on "religion" and speculation about the divine may be interesting, but can never take the place of coming to grips with reality—God's version of it.

3. REALIZATION OF JESUS' IDENTITY. Jesus brushed aside the woman's attempts to pull Him into irrelevant debates. When the woman raised the topic of the Messiah, Jesus boldly told her who He was. Jesus revealed to this woman of Samaria that she was face-to-face with her Redeemer. Your class members should be reminded that Jesus' identity is disclosed to them in order that they be offered new life.

4. RESPONSE TO SHARE. The woman at the well was so excited that she left her water pot and rushed back to her village. Up until then, she may have been ashamed and afraid of being with others; but the good new of Jesus could not be kept to herself.

FOR ADULTS	■ TOPIC: Overcoming Prejudice

■ **QUESTIONS:** 1. Why was the Samaritan woman surprised when Jesus asked her for a drink? 2. What was the gift of God to which Jesus referred? 3. Why did the woman raise the issue of proper worship? 4. What did Jesus mean when He spoke of worshiping God in spirit and in truth? 5. What did the woman eventually learn about Jesus' identity?

■ **ILLUSTRATIONS:**

Believe Now. Nearly 200 years ago, the great Charles Finney was the best-known American evangelist. Once during a series of meetings in Rochester, New York, Finney had a strange experience. The chief justice of the supreme court of New York sat in one of the upper balconies of the church. As he listened to Finney preach, he thought, *That man is speaking the truth. I ought to make a public confession of Jesus Christ.*

Another voice in his head told him he was an important person who didn't need the humiliation of going forward like an ordinary sinner. The attorney knew he would talk himself out of doing what he should if he sat there very long. So he left his seat, went down the stairs, and headed down the aisle—all while Finney kept preaching away. The judge stepped onto the platform, tugged on the evangelist's sleeve and announced, "If you will call for decisions for Christ now, I am ready to come." Right now is the time for us to have our spiritual thirst quench by the water of life Jesus offers through faith in Him.

True Repentance. The great mathematician Copernicus revolutionized the thought of humankind about the universe. His famous treatise, *The Revolution of the Heavenly Bodies*, was printed just in time to be placed in his arms as he lay dying in the spring of 1543.

Amazingly, this person, who had given to humanity a new conception of the universe, saw himself before God, not as an astronomer or a scholar, but as a sinner. Today, on his grave you can read the epitaph that he chose for himself: "I do not seek a kindness equal to that given to Paul; nor do I ask the grace granted to Peter; but that forgiveness which Thou didst give to the robber—that I earnestly pray." May that this statement be an expression of our heart desire to drink freely from the well of everlasting life our Savior offers to everyone.

FOR YOUTH

■ **TOPIC:** When God's People Are Not Our People

■ **QUESTIONS:** 1. Why is it surprising that Jesus would ask a Samaritan woman for a drink of water? 2. At first why did the woman banter with Jesus instead of taking Him seriously? 3. What was the reaction of the Samaritan woman to Jesus' announcement that He was the Messiah? 4. How does Jesus satisfy the deepest thirst of your life? For what do you think most people are thirsting?

■ **ILLUSTRATIONS:**

Soul, Not Silver. The good news for Palestinians living near the well that the Samaritan woman once used is that brief periods of peace bring tourists. The bad news is that most tourists do not spend a lot of money. Although the "Jesus industry" is heavily promoted, sales tend to be low. Merchants hawk olive wood ornaments, rosaries, Bible covers, wooden camels, and crucifixes. They sit among sachets of earth and vials of well water. The scene was a far cry from the group brought by the woman to meet Jesus. These early "pilgrims" were interested in their souls and salvation, not silver and souvenirs. They came to encounter not a passing tourist, but the One who could disclose to all people their very souls and give them eternal life.

Searching for Meaning. Tom Lehman was a PGA Tour Champion and a runner-up several times in the Masters tournament. He was also the 1996 Player of the Year. He tells that as a child he grew up in a religious family. However, he believed that if he somehow "messed up" or made a mistake, God would punish him. Although he enjoyed sports, especially golf, life seemed meaningless.

A high-school friend invited Tom to a meeting of the Fellowship of Christian Athletes. The speaker described a personal relationship with Jesus and the inability of individuals to win God's favor. Tom realized that, while he was good, he was not good enough. Like the woman at the well, Tom wanted a closer relationship with God that would produce true peace. This true peace enabled Tom to compete through 10 years without winning a championship until 1996, when he won the British Open.

Visible Reminders. Most of the people of the world drink contaminated water. Over 1.2 billion people are without fresh, easily accessible drinking water. Water-related diseases claim 25 million lives a year. Church missions are providing fresh, drinkable, living water to people in drought-striken lands. They are also providing a visible reminder of the One who provides all of us with the eternal living water to drink.

GOD'S PROJECT:

EFFECTIVE CHRISTIANS

ALL HAVE SINNED

BACKGROUND SCRIPTURE: Romans 1:16-20; 3:9-20
DEVOTIONAL READING: Psalm 59:1-5

KEY VERSE: "There is no one who is righteous, not even one." Romans 3:10.

KING JAMES VERSION

ROMANS 1:16 For I am not ashamed of the gospel of Christ: for it is the power of God unto salvation to every one that believeth; to the Jew first, and also to the Greek. 17 For therein is the righteousness of God revealed from faith to faith: as it is written, The just shall live by faith. 18 For the wrath of God is revealed from heaven against all ungodliness and unrighteousness of men, who hold the truth in unrighteousness;

19 Because that which may be known of God is manifest in them; for God hath shewed it unto them. 20 For the invisible things of him from the creation of the world are clearly seen, being understood by the things that are made, even his eternal power and Godhead; so that they are without excuse. . . .

3:9 What then? are we better than they? No, in no wise: for we have before proved both Jews and Gentiles, that they are all under sin; 10 As it is written, There is none righteous, no, not one: 11 There is none that understandeth, there is none that seeketh after God. 12 They are all gone out of the way, they are together become unprofitable; there is none that doeth good, no, not one. 13 Their throat is an open sepulchre; with their tongues they have used deceit; the poison of asps is under their lips: 14 Whose mouth is full of cursing and bitterness: 15 Their feet are swift to shed blood: 16 Destruction and misery are in their ways: 17 And the way of peace have they not known: 18 There is no fear of God before their eyes.

19 Now we know that what things soever the law saith, it saith to them who are under the law: that every mouth may be stopped, and all the world may become guilty before God. 20 Therefore by the deeds of the law there shall no flesh be justified in his sight: for by the law is the knowledge of sin.

NEW REVISED STANDARD VERSION

ROMANS 1:16 For I am not ashamed of the gospel; it is the power of God for salvation to everyone who has faith, to the Jew first and also to the Greek. 17 For in it the righteousness of God is revealed through faith for faith; as it is written, "The one who is righteous will live by faith."

18 For the wrath of God is revealed from heaven against all ungodliness and wickedness of those who by their wickedness suppress the truth. 19 For what can be known about God is plain to them, because God has shown it to them. 20 Ever since the creation of the world his eternal power and divine nature, invisible though they are, have been understood and seen through the things he has made. So they are without excuse. . . .

3: 9 What then? Are we any better off? No, not at all; for we have already charged that all, both Jews and Greeks, are under the power of sin, 10 as it is written:

"There is no one who is righteous, not even one;
11 there is no one who has understanding,
there is no one who seeks God.
12 All have turned aside, together they have become
worthless;
there is no one who shows kindness,
there is not even one."
13 "Their throats are opened graves;
they use their tongues to deceive."
"The venom of vipers is under their lips."
14 "Their mouths are full of cursing and bitterness."
15 "Their feet are swift to shed blood;
16 ruin and misery are in their paths,
17 and the way of peace they have not known."
18 "There is no fear of God before their eyes."

19 Now we know that whatever the law says, it speaks to those who are under the law, so that every mouth may be silenced, and the whole world may be held accountable to God. 20 For "no human being will be justified in his sight" by deeds prescribed by the law, for through the law comes the knowledge of sin.

HOME BIBLE READINGS

Monday, February 28	Psalm 14:1-6	*No One Does Good*
Tuesday, March 1	Psalm 10:1-6	*The Wicked Won't Turn to God*
Wednesday, March 2	John 8:1-9	*Sinners Can't Accuse Others*
Thursday, March 3	Romans 1:16-20	*The Gospel Has Saving Power*
Friday, March 4	Romans 3:9-14	*We Are All Sinful*
Saturday, March 5	Romans 3:15-20	*We Are All Guilty*
Sunday, March 6	1 John 1:5-10	*We Have All Sinned*

BACKGROUND

Paul's Letter to the Romans is both the deepest and most important of his epistles. Many Bible scholars agree that Romans has had more influence on the development of Christian theology and the growth of the church than any other New Testament book. Many believe that Romans presents the most systematic and comprehensive exposition of the Gospel of any other New Testament book. Indeed, we need only consider some of the important roles Paul's Letter to the Romans has played throughout the history of the church to realize its vast and continuing impact.

As Augustine struggled with his own sinfulness and lack of belief in the garden at Milan, he heard someone say to him, "Take up and read! Take up and read!" And it was the Book of Romans that he eventually took up and read, bringing about in him a personal change that would also transform the face of the church. As Martin Luther brooded over the theological beliefs and religious practices of his peers, it was his reading of the Book of Romans that enabled him to discover the truth of justification by faith. Subsequently, the Protestant Reformation was born! At Aldersgate Street, John Wesley listened carefully to a reading of Luther's preface to Romans and his heart was "strangely warmed," igniting in him a fire that would eventually spread a revival of faith across several continents. And even as late as the twentieth century, Karl Barth rocked the theological world with his first edition of *Romerbrief*, a theological treatise based on Paul's Letter to the Romans.

Like the rest of Paul's letters to first-century believers, he intended Romans to be read aloud before a congregation of worshipers. But with the exception of Colossians, Romans is unlike the apostle's other letters in that it was written to a majority of believers who had not yet even met Paul in person. This fact may help to explain why the apostle's salutation is so extraordinarily long and complex to read. (In the Greek text, the first seven verses are a single compound-complex sentence, and these verses are translated as such in both the NRSV and the KJV.) Thus, as Paul introduced himself (as well as his faith and his gospel message), he did not mince any words. With the initial words of his letter—one that would become a theological treatise for centuries to come—Paul told his readers not only about his mission, but also about the nature of the Gospel and about the one person in whom that Gospel is centered: Jesus Christ.

In the first three chapters of Romans we are in a great courtroom, and the entire human race stands trial. The Judge is almighty God, whose character makes Him eligible to weigh all the evidence, hear all testimony, and to act with absolute justice. The charge is that people have consistently broken the laws of God. When all the evidence is examined, no one is found to be innocent of wrongdoing.

In Romans 1:1-7, we discover that Paul was an apostle of Jesus Christ and that he proclaimed the good news of salvation. Then, in 1:8-15, Paul expressed his strong desire to visit the believers living in Rome. Humanity's lost condition motivated the apostle to make the trip to the capital of the empire. Paul viewed Rome as the great prize to be won, and he anticipated his visit with eagerness.

The apostle's goal on such a journey was to proclaim *the gospel* (1:16). Paul was not *ashamed* of the Good News, for the Lord powerfully used it to bring the lost to *salvation*. It did not matter whether a person was an unbelieving Jew or Gentile. This same gospel revealed *the righteousness of God* (1:17).

The Gospel also explained how unrighteous people could receive an upright standing before a holy God. A right standing with God came by faith and appealed to faith. This truth is revealed in Habakkuk 2:4. Paul quoted this verse to show that the good news about Christ had its roots in the Old Testament. Habakkuk's words confirm Paul's point that righteousness comes through faith.

In Romans 1:18-20, Paul analyzed human depravity by commenting on pagan culture. (The term "pagan" refers to Gentiles who are irreligious.) The apostle argued that the heathen were completely destitute of those qualities that characterized God's righteousness. Human experience and national history supply ample evidence that God's anger burns hot against all ungodliness—that is, irreverent and impious attitudes—which sinners express toward Him (1:18). Ungodliness takes many forms, chief of which is a deliberate stifling of divinely revealed truth. Sinful people bury the truth under the weight of their iniquities (1:19).

Verse 20 states that, from the beginning of time, *creation* has given people sufficient evidence of God's existence. His work in creation is a clear indication of His wisdom, goodness, *power*, eternity, majesty, infinity, immortality, and authority. Pagans cannot legitimately claim that God never gave them any revelation of His existence. Thus, their lapse into idolatry renders them guilty before God.

In Romans 3, Paul emphasized that all people—Jews and Gentiles alike—are guilty and condemned before God. The apostle Paul was willing to acknowledge that Jews had more spiritual advantages than Gentiles; but in the final analysis Jews were no better off morally before God (3:9). To substantiate his point, Paul strung together a series of quotes from the Old Testament. Much of what the apostle wrote in 3:10-18 came from the Psalms. Paul showed that the Old Testament condemned the conduct of all people, *both Jews and Greeks* (3:9).

We learn from the Hebrew sacred writings that no one by nature measured up to God's perfect standard of righteousness (3:10). Everyone was completely ignorant of spiritual truth (3:11). No one sought God with their whole heart for the purpose of loving, trusting, and serving Him. The entire human race had lost its way and deliberately turned from the path of righteousness (3:12).

The throat of humankind was like an infected and putrid grave (3:13-14). At the slightest provocation, their feet ran swiftly to commit murder (3:15). People worked hard to afflict and destroy others (3:16). They promoted quarrels, riots, revolution, and revenge (3:17). The knowledge that they would one day meet the God of vengeance did not hinder them from their crimes against humanity (3:18).

Paul next affirmed that the pronouncements of the law are for all those who are *under the law* (3:19). His readers were under the law in the sense that they were obligated to obey and heed it. They were accountable to the law because of their accountability to God Himself. The purpose of the law was to silence *every mouth* and hold the whole world *accountable to God.* The law effectively and inarguably points to God's righteous and holy standards, and points to our utter inability to measure up to it. No one is in a position to argue sin away or make excuses, for the law invalidates all rationalizations.

Paul brought closure to his discussion about the sinfulness of humanity by pointing out in 3:20 that *the law* was never provided as a means of attaining righteousness or of being pronounced righteous before God (see Acts 13:39; Gal. 2:16; 3:11); rather, the law was given to make people aware of their sin. It is through the law that human beings become conscious of sin and see their need for a solution to the problem. In this light the law is an instrument of condemnation, not justification. The law, written on the hearts of all, shines the spotlight on our desperate need for a Savior.

SUGGESTIONS TO TEACHERS

The theme of Romans is stated in 1:16, *For I am not ashamed of the gospel; it is the power of God for salvation to everyone who has faith.* Every word of this verse seems like an attempt by Paul to acknowledge and strengthen the faith of the believers at Rome. May we, too, do all within our sphere of influence to acknowledge and strengthen not only our own faith, but also the faith of those around us.

1. WHERE WE WENT WRONG. Romans 3:9-20 shows us that one of the purposes of the Old Testament law was to reveal to us where we went wrong. The law discloses to us that we have failed to live up to God's precepts and that He judges all people. This truth helps us understand that no amount of good works or deeds can take away our sinfulness or the penalty for our sinfulness. Where shall we turn for salvation?

2. JUSTIFIED BY GRACE. We cannot turn to ourselves for salvation, nor can we turn to anything that we might do (that is, any pious deed we might perform). Not even obeying the Mosaic law would help, for through it comes the knowledge of sin (3:20). God, in His grace, declares sinners righteous when they trust in Christ for salvation. Salvation is a free gift that God can offer to all people because His Son died on the cross for them.

3. FREED THROUGH REDEMPTION. Though we were held captive by our own sinfulness, we have been ransomed; we have been redeemed; we have been delivered; we have been freed. We could not purchase our own freedom, but the perfect Son of God, Jesus Christ, could and did. When we put our faith in Him, He frees us from the penalty of our own sinfulness and the bondage of sin ruling and dictating our lives.

4. SALVATION BY FAITH. God's offer of salvation to us is free. The price for this gift has already been paid by someone else—Jesus Christ. All that is left for us to do is accept God's gracious offer. We do so by faith. We demonstrate our acceptance of God's grace by placing our wholehearted trust in Jesus and in His sacrifice of atonement by His blood (3:25).

FOR ADULTS

■ TOPIC: None Is Righteous

■ QUESTIONS: 1. Why was Paul not ashamed of the Gospel? 2. In what sense is God's power displayed and righteousness made available through the Gospel? 3. What did Paul mean in Romans 3:9 when he said that all people are under sin? 4. How did the apostle substantiate the point he made in 3:9? 5. Why is it that doing the works of the law cannot justify anyone in God's sight?

■ ILLUSTRATIONS:

If Faith Had Been Encouraged. Carl Jung, the famous analytical psychologist of the twentieth century, wrote the following in his book *Memories, Dreams, Reflections:*

> Several times my father had a serious talk with me. I was free to study anything I liked, he said, but if I wanted his advice I should keep away from theology. "Be anything you like except a theologian," he said emphatically. By this time there was a tacit agreement between us that certain things could be said or done without comment. He had never taken me to task for cutting church as often as possible and for not going to Communion any more. The farther away I was from church, the better I felt. The only things I missed were the organ and the choral music, but certainly not the "religious community." The phrase meant nothing to me at all, for the habitual churchgoers struck me as being far less of a community than the "worldly" folk. The latter may have been less virtuous, but on the other hand they were much nicer people, with natural emotions, more sociable and cheerful, warmer-hearted and more sincere. I was able to reassure my father than I had not the slightest desire to be a theologian.

What might Carl Jung's assessment of the church have been had the believers encouraged each other in the faith, if they had truly lived by faith?

Passing the Faith Along. My grandmother—I called her "Mammaw"—was one of the best horticulturists that I've ever known. Her springtime and summertime flowers down in Center Point Hollow were the subject of many photographs, not to mention the number of people who slowed down or stopped just to look. She didn't know the names of all her flowers because she often made Pappaw stop along the roadside for her to dig up some wildflower that she thought was especially pretty.

And Mammaw didn't limit herself to flowers either. Her garden was always something special, too. Perhaps the most special item to ever come out of her garden was her purple-hulled green beans. These were beans that were purple until you cooked them, and then they turned green. After cooking them, you couldn't tell them from any other green beans. Mammaw gave me some seeds years ago, and we grew a fair crop at the parsonage. This year my father is growing several rows, as well as having a few rows to produce more seed.

I recently learned that those variety of beans are called Royalty Purple Pod beans, and they were developed by Elwyn M. Meader. Meader introduced more than 60 varieties—from beets to peaches to kiwi fruit to chrysanthemums. At least half of his introductions came after he "retired" from a distinguished 18-year career as a plant breeder at the University of New Hampshire. He could have gotten rich from royalties on all his releases, but instead he gave them away "as payment for his space on the planet." As a man of faith, Meader's dedication and unselfishness in sharing germplasm ideas with colleagues throughout the world may have been an even greater contribution than his varieties.

Mammaw liked to pass plants and seeds on to others, too. Several friends have recently mentioned to me, again, how Mammaw was responsible for many of the flowers in their yards and the plants in their gardens. Others throughout Stewart County still have some of Mammaw's flowers and plants growing in their gardens. Like Mammaw, Elwyn Meader passed on his ideas and his plants. By the way, Meader credited his development of the Royalty Purple Pod bean to his wife's suggestion that it would be easier to pick beans if the pod color differed from the vine color. Now you know the rest of the story!

Mammaw and Elwyn Meader were both a little like Paul. They, too, wanted to pass along their Christian faith. In that Paul desired to build up the faith of the believers living in Rome, he was "passing the faith along." May we seek to do the same!

Sins's Gulf. The great reformer Martin Luther said that "sin is essentially a departure from God." In other words, sin creates an interminable gulf between God and us. It is a gulf we have intentionally created, yet over which we are unable to build a bridge ourselves.

	■ **TOPIC:** All Are in the Same Mess
FOR **YOUTH**	■ **QUESTIONS:** 1. What happens to sinners when they believe the

Gospel? 2. What did Paul say the unsaved try to do to the truth of
God? 3. What did Paul mean when he declared that no one is righteous before
God? 4. What are some key truths evident in Romans 3:10-18? 5. Why is it impossible to be justified in God's sight by keeping the law?

■ **ILLUSTRATIONS:**

Live by Faith? In June of 1998, a constitutional amendment that would allow prayer in public places was proposed before the Congress of the United States. *Time* magazine reported, briefly, that the number of congressional members who voted in favor of this amendment was 224. *Time* also noted that the number of congressional members who were present on the House floor for opening prayer on the three days preceding the vote was 18, 8, and 18, respectively!

From Basketballs to Saints. For just a moment or two, think of yourself as a basketball. Think about your purpose, about what it is that you're supposed to do. Think about how you can best serve your purpose, about how big you should be and how round you should be. Also think about what your outlook on life should be.

If you are a basketball, your whole purpose for existence is first, to represent the sport that bears your name, and second, to bring enjoyment to those you were created to serve. On the one hand, if you're overinflated, you are going to bounce too high and shots will ricochet like bullets off the rim of the basket. On the other hand, if you are underinflated, you won't bounce. Either way, the game is going to suffer and the participants' enjoyment will be hampered. Also, either way, the purpose for your existence will be diminished.

So if you're a basketball, the right amount of air pressure makes all the difference in successfully achieving your purpose. If you had the ability to do so, you would do everything possible to keep yourself properly inflated. You would avoid having too much or too little air.

Well, the same is true for us as Christians. If we undervalue ourselves, we are less fit to encourage the faith of others; and if we overvalue ourselves, we are less fit to allow the faith of others to encourage us.

Okay, now you can stop thinking of yourself as a basketball. Now think of yourself as being a saint. Now think about your purpose, about what it is that you're supposed to do. Think about how you can best achieve your purpose. Finally, think about how being a saint should affect your morals, your lifestyle, your outlook on life.

GOD'S JUDGMENT IS JUST

BACKGROUND SCRIPTURE: Romans 2:1-16
DEVOTIONAL READING: Psalm 50:1-15

KEY VERSE: God, through Jesus Christ, will judge the secret thoughts of all. Romans 2:16.

KING JAMES VERSION

ROMANS 2:1 Therefore thou art inexcusable, O man, whosoever thou art that judgest: for wherein thou judgest another, thou condemnest thyself; for thou that judgest doest the same things. 2 But we are sure that the judgment of God is according to truth against them which commit such things. 3 And thinkest thou this, O man, that judgest them which do such things, and doest the same, that thou shalt escape the judgment of God? 4 Or despisest thou the riches of his goodness and forbearance and longsuffering; not knowing that the goodness of God leadeth thee to repentance? 5 But after thy hardness and impenitent heart treasurest up unto thyself wrath against the day of wrath and revelation of the righteous judgment of God; 6 Who will render to every man according to his deeds: 7 To them who by patient continuance in well doing seek for glory and honour and immortality, eternal life: 8 But unto them that are contentious, and do not obey the truth, but obey unrighteousness, indignation and wrath, 9 Tribulation and anguish, upon every soul of man that doeth evil, of the Jew first, and also of the Gentile; 10 But glory, honour, and peace, to every man that worketh good, to the Jew first, and also to the Gentile: 11 For there is no respect of persons with God. 12 For as many as have sinned without law shall also perish without law: and as many as have sinned in the law shall be judged by the law; 13 (For not the hearers of the law are just before God, but the doers of the law shall be justified. 14 For when the Gentiles, which have not the law, do by nature the things contained in the law, these, having not the law, are a law unto themselves: 15 Which shew the work of the law written in their hearts, their conscience also bearing witness, and their thoughts the mean while accusing or else excusing one another;) 16 In the day when God shall judge the secrets of men by Jesus Christ according to my gospel.

NEW REVISED STANDARD VERSION

ROMANS 2:1 Therefore you have no excuse, whoever you are, when you judge others; for in passing judgment on another you condemn yourself, because you, the judge, are doing the very same things. 2 You say, "We know that God's judgment on those who do such things is in accordance with truth." 3 Do you imagine, whoever you are, that when you judge those who do such things and yet do them yourself, you will escape the judgment of God? 4 Or do you despise the riches of his kindness and forbearance and patience? Do you not realize that God's kindness is meant to lead you to repentance? 5 But by your hard and impenitent heart you are storing up wrath for yourself on the day of wrath, when God's righteous judgment will be revealed. 6 For he will repay according to each one's deeds: 7 to those who by patiently doing good seek for glory and honor and immortality, he will give eternal life; 8 while for those who are self-seeking and who obey not the truth but wickedness, there will be wrath and fury. 9 There will be anguish and distress for everyone who does evil, the Jew first and also the Greek, 10 but glory and honor and peace for everyone who does good, the Jew first and also the Greek. 11 For God shows no partiality.

12 All who have sinned apart from the law will also perish apart from the law, and all who have sinned under the law will be judged by the law. 13 For it is not the hearers of the law who are righteous in God's sight, but the doers of the law who will be justified. 14 When Gentiles, who do not possess the law, do instinctively what the law requires, these, though not having the law, are a law to themselves. 15 They show that what the law requires is written on their hearts, to which their own conscience also bears witness; and their conflicting thoughts will accuse or perhaps excuse them 16 on the day when, according to my gospel, God, through Jesus Christ, will judge the secret thoughts of all.

Monday, March 7	Psalm 7:6-17	*God Is a Righteous Judge*
Tuesday, March 8	Psalm 50:1-15	*God Himself Is Judge*
Wednesday, March 9	Romans 2:1-5	*Do Not Judge Others*
Thursday, March 10	Romans 2:6-11	*God Will Judge All*
Friday, March 11	Romans 2:12-16	*Doers of the Law Are Justified*
Saturday, March 12	Romans 2:17-24	*Do Jews Follow the Law?*
Sunday, March 13	Romans 2:25-29	*Real Jews Obey the Law*

BACKGROUND

When Paul wrote his letter to the church at Rome, he was longing to make his way to the great city of the empire. His desire was not so much fueled by a wish to see the capital as it was by a longing to meet and visit with the Christians who lived there, about whom he had heard so much.

Paul wrote Romans toward the end of his third missionary journey. It was shortly before his visit to Jerusalem, in which he carried the gift from the Gentile congregations (Acts 24:17; Rom. 15:25). Internal indications suggest that at this time Paul was a resident of Corinth. These intimations include the reference to Phoebe, a member of the church at Cenchrea (the port of Corinth; Rom. 16:1-2), the references to Gaius as Paul's host (Rom. 16:23; 1 Cor. 1:14), and the reference to Erastus (Corinth's financial officer; Acts 19:22; Rom. 16:23; 2 Tim. 4:20).

Thus, the time of writing was probably during Paul's three months in Greece, which is described in Acts 20:2-3. It is known that Gallio (before whom Paul appeared; 18:12) was proconsul (normally a one-year appointment) in Achaia in A.D. 52. Paul was in Corinth during the period of A.D. 51–53 (20:18). He then sailed to Ephesus for a brief visit, and went to Caesarea and probably Jerusalem as well as Antioch (20:22). The earliest possible date for Paul's writing of Romans would be towards the end of A.D. 54. But a later date leaves more leeway for the apostle's many activities. Thus, the epistle is best dated in the early spring of A.D. 57.

Paul perceived his ministry to be at a turning point when he wrote Romans. He sensed that he had fulfilled his evangelistic ministry in the eastern Mediterranean (Rom. 15:17-23) and that the time was ripe to move west and proclaim the Gospel in Spain (15:24). He hoped to visit the Roman Christians on the way, fulfilling his longtime ambition. He also may have wanted to receive their assistance as a supporting church. In light of these considerations, it was essential for Paul to present his apostolic credentials so that his fellow believers in Rome might recognize the authenticity of his ministry. He may also have thought it necessary to defend his ministry from the false insinuations of his opponents (3:8).

Paul seemed deeply concerned that the church become a united fellowship of believing Jews and Gentiles. This emphasis is clear from the importance the apostle attached to the Gentiles' love-gift to the Jerusalem church. This concern also surfaces throughout Romans in a consistent argument made by Paul, namely, the unity of Jew and Gentile in sin through Adam and through grace in Christ (5:12-21). The saving righteousness of God, as revealed in the Gospel, is needed by both, for all have sinned (3:23). And justification can be received by both, for it comes through faith in Christ (3:24-26). The outworking of God's saving righteousness in history is the clue to His ultimate purposes for both Jew and Gentile. This saving righteousness is also to be expressed in the lives of both groups, whether personally, socially, or communally.

NOTES ON THE PRINTED TEXT

Not all people are as immoral as the pagans mentioned in Romans 1:18-32. These upstanding folks tend to be self-righteous and self-sufficient as well as critical of the actions of others. Perhaps you know some people like this who outwardly seem to be very moral.

Paul directed his comments toward individuals such as these who passed judgment on others. The apostle declared in 2:1 that even the most morally upstanding people had *no excuse* for what they did. In fact, those who judged others were condemning themselves in that they were guilty of the same sorts of misdeeds. In contrast, God is fair and impartial in His judgment of people, for His evaluation is in "*accordance with truth*" (2:2).

Paul wanted to correct the thinking of those who believed they would *escape the judgment of God* (2:3). If they were guilty of a misdeed, God would hold them responsible for what they had done. To think otherwise indicated the presence of contempt for the Lord's *kindness and forbearance and patience* (2:4). The apostle no doubt thought back to his own experience as a Jew. At one time he considered himself righteous because of his law-keeping efforts. On the road to Damascus, he discovered the futility of his thinking.

Those who remained unmoved by Paul's statements were stubborn and unrepentant in their hearts (2:5). Such ingrates were *storing up* God's *wrath* against them in the future *day* when all the wicked would be judged. In 2:6 Paul quoted from the Old Testament (see Ps. 62:12; Prov. 24:12) to make his point that God will judge all people according to what they have done. Though God did not always punish sin immediately, judgment was still coming.

Those who persist in doing what is good show they are regenerate and thus the rightful recipients of *eternal life* (Rom. 2:7). They likewise show by their actions that in eternity they desire to receive *glory and honor and immortality* from God. In contrast, He will pour out His wrath on those who live for themselves, reject the truth, and promote evil (2:8). Paul was not saying good works can save a person. The apostle stated later in his letter that no one can be declared righteous by observing the law (see Rom. 3:20; Eph. 2:8-9; Titus 3:5). Good works do not result in salvation; they simply attest to the salvation that has already been received by faith.

In Romans 2:9-10, Paul reiterated these thoughts. It did not matter whether the person was a *Jew* or *Greek*. If anyone did what was wicked, they would reap *anguish and distress.* Oppositely, Jews and Gentiles who did what was good would, in eternity, experience *glory and honor and peace* from God. Here we can see that, as Paul states in 2:11, *God shows no partiality* with people.

Paul did not mince any words when he declared in 2:12 that God will punish Gentiles for what they do wrong, even though they never had the written *law* of Moses. It should come as no surprise, then, that Jews, who have the Mosaic law, will be punished by God when they sin. In short, He holds all people accountable for their actions.

The apostle explained that just hearing the law was insufficient to be declared righteous in God's sight. Both trusting God and obeying His Word were paramount. Likewise, it was the regenerate, who gave evidence of their salvation by obeying the law, who were declared righteous by God (2:13).

Even the unregenerate have an inner awareness of moral right and wrong. It is true that they may not have the written law of God; but there are times when they instinctively heed *what the law requires* (2:14). In this way they confirm the reality of God's law written within them. This is especially true with respect to their conscience. At times it tells them they are doing what is proper; and on other occasions it accuses them of doing what is improper (2:15).

God will judge all of humanity (Jews and Gentiles), the agent of His judgment will be Jesus Christ, and His evaluation will focus on secrets of people's hearts (2:16). Sometimes people do good things that are actually rooted in selfish intentions. Other times people may appear guilty of a wrongdoing when there was no bad intention. Sometimes people internalize blame for the sins of others. Regardless of the situation, the Lord will act accordingly. On the great day, all that is hidden will be revealed. There will be no second-guessing when it comes to motives. God's judgment will be impartial, perfect, and absolutely just.

SUGGESTIONS TO TEACHERS

It is sobering to realize that our lives, apart from Christ, do not match up to God's perfect moral standard. This is because our thoughts, words, and deeds ultimately are flawed by sin. It thus does not matter how moral we are in the eyes of the world. We cannot merit the love and favor of God. If we want to be right with Him, we must trust in Christ. Only He can rescue us from our moral dilemma and secure us a place in heaven.

1. ACCEPT THE TRUTH. All of us stand guilty as sinners before God. Regardless of the excuses we might make, none of us can justify our rebellious condition. All we can do is humbly acknowledge our sin and receive God's mercy through faith in Christ.

2. ACKNOWLEDGE HUMAN DEPRAVITY. Sin is all around us. Drug dealing, sexual immorality, robbery, and murder are just a few of the horrible crimes that plague our society. When we think about the plight of the human race, we can easily become filled with sadness and anger. When God looks at the depravity of humankind, He also recoils against sin's progressive deterioration.

3. AFFIRM THE GOSPEL'S IMPORTANCE. The Gospel is a declaration of God's righteousness. The Good News explains how people can get right and stay right with the Lord. Tragically, this information is of little interest to people who think they are already acceptable to God. That is why Paul endeavored to show how far short all people come from the Lord's standard of righteousness.

4. WALK BY FAITH. Let us make walking by faith a life habit. In order for this to be true, we must continually practice walking by faith at times when we'd rather indulge our fears and doubts. But don't do it! May we practice living out our faith in the midst of disappointments, trials, temptations, and even sorrows, remembering that "*the one who is righteous will live by faith*" (1:17).

5. LIVE UPRIGHTLY. It takes a lot of courage for Christian adults to live uprightly among peers who hold to degenerate ways of thinking and acting. Encourage your students to remain firm in their commitment to Christ and the high moral standards embodied in His life, ministry, and teaching.

FOR ADULTS

■ TOPIC: God Judges All People

■ QUESTIONS: 1. Why were those who judged others ultimately condemning themselves? 2. Why was it incorrect for people to assume that they were exempt from God's judgment? 3. Who were storing up God's wrath against them in the future day when all the wicked would be judged? 4. What were Paul's basic points in Romans 2:9-10 concerning the righteous and the wicked? 5. What role does conscience serve in the things that people do, whether proper or improper in nature?

■ ILLUSTRATIONS:

No One Is Exempt. At the mission he ran, Bob (not his real name) quoted Romans 2:11 frequently, *For God shows no partiality*. But not too long ago that Scripture verse became more personal—and very public. Bob consented to be quoted in a local newspaper concerning his addiction to prescription depressants.

Bob had been a pillar in the Christian community: kind, innovative, a real "go-getter" for Christ. Now Bob was going public with his admission and his choice to slow down. His Christian walk had taken a toll on both his physical and spiritual life. He planned to take another position that would allow him time to mend and would give him greater accountability.

Can Christian leaders sin? Yes. Do they? This week's Scripture clearly answers that; and so do our life experiences. God abhors all sin and will one day judge it. Like Bob, we must consciously seek God's forgiveness and diligently work to uproot the source of stumbling in our lives.

Lost Communications. In the 1990s, NASA began its first concerted effort to explore Mars. Teams of scientists worked diligently in both the government and private sector to build a Mars lander that would effectively film and explore the red planet.

Rockets successfully launched the small, unmanned capsule into outer space. After a long period of space travel, the capsule began circling the planet, then was signalled to land. As the scientists listened carefully for the response codes from the Mars lander, they began to feel a bit queasy. Soon the planet rotated out of line-of-sight, disabling communication attempts. Now they would have to wait several hours before the lander was again in position to communicate.

All subsequent attempts, however, failed. An investigation committee later concluded that a single, yet tiny problem ruined the entire space mission and wasted billions of dollars. God's just judgment against sin is that even the smallest infraction against Him also brings disaster. The most diminutive sins are able to cut off the communication of life between us and God.

FOR YOUTH

■ **TOPIC:** God's Judgment Is Just

■ **QUESTIONS:** 1. Why are those who pass judgment on others without excuse before God? 2. What are some examples of ways in which God has manifested His kindness to you and others? 3. Why was it important for Paul to stress that God shows no partiality when He judges humankind? 4. In what sense are the doers of the law just in the sight of God? 5. What role does a person's conscience serve in God's judgment of one's actions?

■ **ILLUSTRATIONS:**

Turn to Jesus. William had long believed that Christians were weak people who needed a crutch to get through life. He was a self-made millionaire, having put himself through college and law school, eventually becoming a full partner with a high-profile law firm. When he retired, he had wealth that most people only dream about. He also had a devoted wife, four successful adult children, and seven grandchildren, whom he doted over.

Yet, one sultry afternoon, Ashley, his eight-year-old granddaughter, asked William if he had Jesus in his heart. When he said he didn't, Ashley pleaded with him to invite Jesus into his heart because she wanted William to be in heaven when she got there.

William's body was not as strong and robust as it had been most of his life; he could feel piercing aches in different parts of his body. Worst of all, he felt tired most of the time. Recently, he had questioned whether all his possessions and accomplishments had really given his life meaning and value. The more he struggled with this question, the more he knew that they had not.

Now Ashley's question and pleading made William feel even more lost. With tears in his eyes, he turned to Ashley and saw the light in her loving eyes to light his way. She took his hand in hers, and he prayed for Jesus to come into his heart. He turned to the Lord, and the Lord welcomed him with open arms.

We all need Jesus. And those who reject Him will face God's just judgment. Perhaps the Lord might use you this week to lead a friend or relative to the Savior.

Saved by Grace. A Japanese gangster who became a Christian is converting other criminals. Hiroyuki Suzuki takes the Christian message to railway stations and public squares, using his notoriety to grab attention, according to the *Times of London.* He has numerous tattoos and several amputated fingers attesting to his previous allegiance to the *yakuza* organized crime organization.

Suzuki, 44, is the founder of Mission Barabbas, a group of reformed gangsters who have embraced evangelical Christianity. His ministry includes fervent preaching and singing. The *yakuza,* in contrast, includes 80,000 gang members involved in extortion rackets, prostitution, and gambling, and bloody shoot-outs on the streets are frequent.

Christianity is considered a mysterious sect by most Japanese, and only 1.5 percent of the population is Christian. But Suzuki's church in Tokyo overflows on Sundays and attracts converts by targeting his former colleagues and apprentice hoodlums. In four years, he has baptized seven members of crime syndicates and persuaded them to leave the underworld.

Suzuki dates his conversion to a point when he was deep in debt, taking drugs, and plagued by illness. He put a gun to his temple but didn't have the nerve to pull the trigger. His estranged wife had been an ardent churchgoer and, out of desperation, he sought refuge in a church.

"I told the minister I was a gangster who had done time, deserted his wife and child, and was beyond redemption. But the minister talked to me about God's love and the meaning of the cross," Suzuki told the *Times.* He returned to his family and was accepted immediately. "That made me believe in the existence of unconditional love and the fact that people can start over again."

WE ARE JUSTIFIED BY FAITH

BACKGROUND SCRIPTURE: Romans 5:1-11, 18-21
DEVOTIONAL READING: 2 Corinthians 3:4-11

3

KEY VERSE: Since we are justified by faith, we have
peace with God through our Lord Jesus Christ. Romans 5:1.

KING JAMES VERSION

ROMANS 5:1 Therefore being justified by faith, we have peace with God through our Lord Jesus Christ: 2 By whom also we have access by faith into this grace wherein we stand, and rejoice in hope of the glory of God. 3 And not only so, but we glory in tribulations also: knowing that tribulation worketh patience; 4 And patience, experience; and experience, hope: 5 And hope maketh not ashamed; because the love of God is shed abroad in our hearts by the Holy Ghost which is given unto us.

6 For when we were yet without strength, in due time Christ died for the ungodly. 7 For scarcely for a righteous man will one die: yet peradventure for a good man some would even dare to die. 8 But God commendeth his love toward us, in that, while we were yet sinners, Christ died for us. 9 Much more then, being now justified by his blood, we shall be saved from wrath through him. 10 For if, when we were enemies, we were reconciled to God by the death of his Son, much more, being reconciled, we shall be saved by his life. 11 And not only so, but we also joy in God through our Lord Jesus Christ, by whom we have now received the atonement. . . .18 Therefore as by the offence of one judgment came upon all men to condemnation; even so by the righteousness of one the free gift came upon all men unto justification of life. 19 For as by one man's disobedience many were made sinners, so by the obedience of one shall many be made righteous. 20 Moreover the law entered, that the offence might abound. But where sin abounded, grace did much more abound: 21 That as sin hath reigned unto death, even so might grace reign through righteousness unto eternal life by Jesus Christ our Lord.

NEW REVISED STANDARD VERSION

ROMANS 5:1 Therefore, since we are justified by faith, we have peace with God through our Lord Jesus Christ, 2 through whom we have obtained access to this grace in which we stand; and we boast in our hope of sharing the glory of God. 3 And not only that, but we also boast in our sufferings, knowing that suffering produces endurance, 4 and endurance produces character, and character produces hope, 5 and hope does not disappoint us, because God's love has been poured into our hearts through the Holy Spirit that has been given to us.

6 For while we were still weak, at the right time Christ died for the ungodly. 7 Indeed, rarely will anyone die for a righteous person—though perhaps for a good person someone might actually dare to die. 8 But God proves his love for us in that while we still were sinners Christ died for us. 9 Much more surely then, now that we have been justified by his blood, will we be saved through him from the wrath of God. 10 For if while we were enemies, we were reconciled to God through the death of his Son, much more surely, having been reconciled, will we be saved by his life. 11 But more than that, we even boast in God through our Lord Jesus Christ, through whom we have now received reconciliation. . . .

18 Therefore just as one man's trespass led to condemnation for all, so one man's act of righteousness leads to justification and life for all. 19 For just as by the one man's disobedience the many were made sinners, so by the one man's obedience the many will be made righteous. 20 But law came in, with the result that the trespass multiplied; but where sin increased, grace abounded all the more, 21 so that, just as sin exercised dominion in death, so grace might also exercise dominion through justification leading to eternal life through Jesus Christ our Lord.

BACKGROUND

The first four chapters of Paul's Letter to the Romans introduces and expounds upon the concept of justification by grace through faith. Then in chapter 5, the epistle turns a corner. In many respects, this chapter is a point of transition for the apostle's entire letter.

Just as in the first four chapters Paul discussed how we are saved (the means by which God gives us salvation), in chapter 5 Paul began to write about how believers are supposed to live once they have come to salvation through faith in Christ. Thus the apostle turned his thoughts toward how to live out the spiritual life, what it means to be a Christian, and who we are supposed to be as those who have received God's gift of grace. Clearly, then, the new focus of Paul's Letter to the Romans, beginning with chapter 5, is the tension between grace and good works, especially in regard to how a Spirit-filled Christian life should be lived out.

Although chapter 5 initiates a new section of this letter to the church in Rome, it continues to build on what the apostle had written in the previous four chapters. Indeed, the first four chapters provide a foundation for Paul's writing, beginning in chapter 5, about the ways in which endurance, character, and hope affect the lives of those living out the Christian faith.

In the first 11 verses of chapter 5, the apostle demonstrated how the spiritual life finds its foundation in and is lived out by the fact that we are justified by grace through our faith in Jesus Christ. Through the gracious gift of Jesus Christ, we are now able to be in a right relationship with God; and thus, our justification is the gift that provides the background for all other spiritual gifts in the Christian life.

NOTES ON THE PRINTED TEXT

Having described for his readers the concept of justification by grace through faith, Paul began in Romans 5 to describe the benefits of justification for those who believe in Christ. The apostle wanted his readers to not only acknowledge these benefits, but also to live them out in their daily lives. Paul impressed upon them that these benefits should affect every fiber of their being—physically, mentally, emotionally, and spiritually.

The first benefit that the apostle mentioned is that *we have peace with God through our Lord Jesus Christ* (5:1). Paul was not merely referring to peaceful feelings such as calmness or tranquility. Rather, he was talking about being reconciled with God. Because of Jesus' death and resurrection, God's wrath toward us because our sins has been taken away. We need no longer fear being eternally condemned because Jesus died on the cross for us and, through Jesus, we have been ushered into a peaceful relationship with God.

The second benefit the apostle referred to is that *we have obtained access to this grace in which we stand* (5:2). God has poured out to us His unmerited favor; He has granted to us something extremely good that we do not and cannot deserve. This grace is a pure gift, and it puts us in a place of highest privilege, for it has enabled us to be adopted as the sons and daughters of God.

The third benefit Paul revealed to his readers is *our hope of sharing the glory of God* (5:2). Once again, the apostle noted what believers—whether Jews or Gentiles—should and should not boast about! Through Paul's explanation of why our justification is so desperately needed, the apostle had shown his readers that humanity had fallen short of the glorious destiny God had originally intended for it. Now, because of justification by grace through faith, redeemed humanity finds itself confidently expecting that glorious destiny, which involves, foremost, communion with God.

The fourth benefit Paul disclosed to his readers may not, on the surface, seem like a benefit at all. The apostle encouraged his readers to acknowledge and *boast in our sufferings* (5:3). Like the other benefits, these sufferings come as a result of our justification by grace through faith. Paul urged us to boast in them because they help us to realize that God is using the difficulties of life to strengthen us and build us up. When we, by God's help, face these sufferings, the trials will produce endurance, *and endurance produces character, and character produces hope* (5:4).

The fifth benefit the apostle unveiled to his readers may be considered the greatest one of all. Again, because of justification by grace through faith, *God's love has been poured into our hearts through the Holy Spirit that has been given to us* (5:5). It is because God has already shown His love toward us—through the sacrifice of His own Son—that we can be sure that He will grant us our hope of eternal life with Him. But the Holy Spirit goes beyond filling our lives with the love of God; He also enables us to live by His power.

Having told his readers about these benefits of justification by grace through faith, Paul next expounded upon the sixth benefit, giving more details about how God's love has been poured out to us. The apostle explained that *while we were still weak* (5:6)—when we were without strength to do anything good—*Christ died for the ungodly.* He took upon Himself the consequences of our own sin, and by doing so, made a way for us to be reconciled to God (5:7). It is in this way that *God proves his love for us in that while we still were sinners Christ died for us* (5:8).

The apostle reiterated that all of humanity was in a state of lostness, that it was in line to receive both the judgment and the wrath of God, that it was altogether helpless to save itself, and that we were enemies of God (5:10). But because of the sacrificial death of Jesus, *we have been justified by his blood, [and] will be saved through him from the wrath of God* (5:9). Thus, justification confirms both our salvation from God and our reconciliation with Him. Once more, the apostle returned to his theme about what believers—whether Jews or Gentiles—should and should not boast about, by saying *we even boast in God through our Lord Jesus Christ, through whom we have now received reconciliation* (5:11).

To show that Christ's saving work is extended to Jews and Gentiles alike—indeed, to all who would believe in Jesus—Paul compared the disobedience of Adam to the obedience of Christ. Whereas sinful humanity finds its demise in Adam, justified humanity finds its salvation through faith in Christ—*just as by the one man's disobedience the many were made sinners, so by the one man's obedience the many will be made righteous* (5:19). The sinful nature of humanity led to death; but those who are justified through faith in Christ receive a new life of righteousness—*so one man's act of righteousness leads to justification and life for all* (5:18).

In the midst of explaining how justification, salvation, and reconciliation come through faith in Christ, Paul further explained how and why the law came into play. The law *came in, with the result that the trespass multiplied* (5:20). The presence of the law led to an increase of sin, for the law showed clearly the wicked nature of sin. In other words, what was inherently wrong became formally and explicitly wrong once the law was revealed. Nevertheless, as people sinned more and more, God's wonderful grace became more abundant. On the one hand, sin ruled over all people and brought them to *death* (5:22). On the other hand, divine grace rules over the redeemed, giving them a right standing with God and *leading to eternal life through Jesus Christ our Lord.*

SUGGESTIONS TO TEACHERS

Being justified by grace through faith in Christ brings us wonderful and eternal benefits. Although these benefits have been described in the previous section of this week's lesson, it would be altogether proper for us to rehearse them again. This time, however, let's apply them to how we live out our faith, especially now that we have been justified by grace.

1. PEACE WITH GOD. We have peace with God because of the reconciling work of Jesus. It is not an external peace, but rather an inner peace that comes from knowing that Jesus has made us right with God, that we are in a right relationship with Him, and that no matter what else may happen to us, our lives—and our very souls—are committed to His tender care.

2. ACCESS TO THIS GRACE. We have access to God's grace because of what Jesus did for us on the cross. He took our sin and guilt and shame upon Himself and died in our place. What a picture of divine grace! The whole human race is offered this unmerited favor from God, and those who willingly accept it—

those who receive it by faith—will be eternally saved.

3. OUR HOPE. From the beginning, God has wanted us to be with Him in eternity. However, because of our sinful nature, and because He cannot allow sinfulness into His presence, we were forever separated from God. But because God loves us so much, He provided a way, through the sacrificial death of His Son, for us to be reconciled to Him. And because we are reconciled to Him, our hope of living out our destiny with Him for all eternity is assured.

4. OUR SUFFERINGS. All humanity lives through some degree of suffering. But as believers, we realize that our suffering has a purpose. God promises to use the problems and trials that we experience to help us grow in endurance, which in turn will help us to grow in character, which in turn will help us to grow in hope. Through all our experiences, God is watching over us and is ready to use those experiences to strengthen us spiritually.

5. THE HOLY SPIRIT WHO HAS BEEN GIVEN TO US. According to Romans 5:5, the Holy Spirit carries out at least a dual work in our lives. First, He convinces us of God's love for us, and the Spirit encourages us by letting us know that God's love is being *poured into our hearts*. Second, the Spirit enables and empowers us to live like people who have been justified by grace through faith. Just as we cannot live up to the standards of the law by ourselves, neither can we live as witnesses to God's love by ourselves. We must have the infilling help and power of the Spirit to truly live like Christians.

■ **TOPIC:** Justified by Faith

FOR ADULTS

■ **QUESTIONS:** 1. What does it mean to be justified by grace through faith? 2. In what ways does the believer have peace with God? 3. What is our role in obtaining *access to this grace in which we stand* (Rom. 5:2)? 4. What does it mean to share God's glory? 5. How would you explain to an unbeliever that you can rejoice in your sufferings?

■ **ILLUSTRATIONS:**

The Ladder of the Law. The *Life Application Study Bible* describes a person's attempt at keeping the law by using the analogy of a ladder that leads to God. As a sinner, separated from God, we see His law from below, as a ladder to be climbed to get to God. Perhaps we have repeatedly tried to climb it, only to fall to the ground every time we have advanced one or two rungs. Or perhaps the sheer height of the ladder seems so overwhelming that we have never even started up. In either case, what relief we should feel to see Jesus offering with open arms to lift us above the ladder of the law, to take us directly to God! Once Jesus lifts us into God's presence, we are free to obey—out of love, not necessity, and through God's power, not our own. We know that if we stumble, we will be caught and held in Christ's loving arms.

Message of Hope and Peace. Johann Sebastian Bach has struck a chord in Japan. The eighteenth-century German composer's music is conveying Christian teachings and concepts to a large and growing audience in the Asian nation, where less than one percent of the 127 million people belong to a Christian church, *First Things* magazine reported in 2003.

The nation's elite are drawn to the musical genius, and many have their first contact with Christianity through Bach's music. As many as 200 Bach choirs have started around the country in the past 10 years, and organist Masaaki Suzuki founded and conducts the Bach Collegium Japan.

Many Japanese have lost their allegiance to Buddhism and Shintoism and are attracted to the message of hope and peace they find in Bach's music. It is uncertain how many people actually have converted to Christianity.

Suffering with a Purpose. In Isaac Asimov's *Treasury of Humor*, the author confessed to having gambled only once in his life. It was, he says, "shortly after I had married; my wife left to visit her folks. I was at loose ends, and I was lured into a poker game with the boys.

"When it was all over, my conscience smote me, for I had been brought up by a puritanical father to eschew gambling in all its forms (and I had never rebelled). All I could do was confess.

"On my next trip home, I said with all the casualness I could manage, 'I played a game of poker with the boys, Papa. For money.'

"My father stared at me in astonishment and said, 'How did you make out?'

"I said, 'I lost fifteen cents.'

"And he said, 'Thank God. You might have won fifteen cents!'"

And so Asimov's father reminded him that his "sufferings" served a purpose—to discourage him from ever gambling again!

■ TOPIC: Relationships Mended

FOR YOUTH

■ QUESTIONS: 1. What does it mean to be justified by grace through faith? 2. Why did Jesus have to die for us? 3. In what ways have you suffered in the past, and what good has God brought about because of that suffering? 4. How would you define the term "reconciliation"? 5. In what ways has the Spirit enabled you to live like a Christian?

■ ILLUSTRATIONS:

Saving Humanity. A few years ago, when the movie *Saving Private Ryan* came out, a debate arose among those who had fought in World War II. One group criticized the movie for failing to acknowledge the noble purpose of World War II. Another group praised the movie, which had as its plot a squadron of soldiers risking their lives and dying in order to pull one man out of combat to be sent home. The second group said that if the public would take Private Ryan as a symbol of the rest of us who were saved by the sacrifices of those who died in Normandy, then producer Steven Spielberg's "war is hell" message was not inconsistent with believing that this war saved humanity.

Just like the squadron of soldiers in the movie, Jesus died, shedding His own blood, to save people for all eternity. His sacrifice enables our broken relationship with God to be mended.

Demonstration of Love. Writing in a 1992 issue of the *Wesleyan Christian Advocate,* Vance B. Mathis described how baseball legend Babe Ruth was playing one of his last full major league games. The Boston Braves were playing the Reds in Cincinnati. The old veteran wasn't the player he once had been. The ball looked awkward in his aging hands. He wasn't throwing well. In one inning, his misplays made most of the runs scored by Cincinnati possible. As Babe Ruth walked off the field after making a third out, head bent in embarrassment, a crescendo of boos followed him to the dugout.

A little boy in the stands couldn't tolerate it. He loved Babe Ruth, no matter what. With tears streaming down his face, the boy jumped over the railing and threw his arms around the knees of his hero. Babe Ruth picked up the boy, hugged him, set him back on the ground, and gently patted his head.

The rude booing ceased. A hush fell over the park. The crowd was touched by the child's demonstration of love and concern for the feelings of another human being. Such a story can remind us of God's love for us and desire to be in relationship with us: *God proves his love for us in that while we still were sinners Christ died for us* (Rom. 5:8).

Live Such a Life. There's an old Indian proverb that says, "When you were born, you cried, and the whole world rejoiced. Live such a life that when you die, the whole world cries, and you rejoice."

WE HAVE VICTORY IN CHRIST

BACKGROUND SCRIPTURE: John 20:1-10; Romans 6:1-14
DEVOTIONAL READING: Romans 6:15-23

4

KEY VERSE: We know that Christ, being raised from the dead, will never die again; death no longer has dominion over him. Romans 6:9.

KING JAMES VERSION

JOHN 20:1 The first day of the week cometh Mary Magdalene early, when it was yet dark, unto the sepulchre, and seeth the stone taken away from the sepulchre. 2 Then she runneth, and cometh to Simon Peter, and to the other disciple, whom Jesus loved, and saith unto them, They have taken away the Lord out of the sepulchre, and we know not where they have laid him. 3 Peter therefore went forth, and that other disciple, and came to the sepulchre. 4 So they ran both together: and the other disciple did outrun Peter, and came first to the sepulchre. 5 And he stooping down, and looking in, saw the linen clothes lying; yet went he not in. 6 Then cometh Simon Peter following him, and went into the sepulchre, and seeth the linen clothes lie, 7 And the napkin, that was about his head, not lying with the linen clothes, but wrapped together in a place by itself. 8 Then went in also that other disciple, which came first to the sepulchre, and he saw, and believed. 9 For as yet they knew not the scripture, that he must rise again from the dead. 10 Then the disciples went away again unto their own home. . . .

ROMANS 6:1 What shall we say then? Shall we continue in sin, that grace may abound? 2 God forbid. How shall we, that are dead to sin, live any longer therein? 3 Know ye not, that so many of us as were baptized into Jesus Christ were baptized into his death? 4 Therefore we are buried with him by baptism into death: that like as Christ was raised up from the dead by the glory of the Father, even so we also should walk in newness of life. 5 For if we have been planted together in the likeness of his death, we shall be also in the likeness of his resurrection: 6 Knowing this, that our old man is crucified with him, that the body of sin might be destroyed, that henceforth we should not serve sin. 7 For he that is dead is freed from sin. 8 Now if we be dead with Christ, we believe that we shall also live with him: 9 Knowing that Christ being raised from the dead dieth no more; death hath no more dominion over him. 10 For in that he died, he died unto sin once: but in that he liveth, he liveth unto God. 11 Likewise reckon ye also yourselves to be dead indeed unto sin, but alive unto God through Jesus Christ our Lord. . . . 13 Neither yield ye your members as instruments of unrighteousness unto sin: but yield yourselves unto God, as those that are alive from the dead, and your members as instruments of righteousness unto God.

NEW REVISED STANDARD VERSION

John 20:1 Early on the first day of the week, while it was still dark, Mary Magdalene came to the tomb and saw that the stone had been removed from the tomb. 2 So she ran and went to Simon Peter and the other disciple, the one whom Jesus loved, and said to them, "They have taken the Lord out of the tomb, and we do not know where they have laid him." 3 Then Peter and the other disciple set out and went toward the tomb. 4 The two were running together, but the other disciple outran Peter and reached the tomb first. 5 He bent down to look in and saw the linen wrappings lying there, but he did not go in. 6 Then Simon Peter came, following him, and went into the tomb. He saw the linen wrappings lying there, 7 and the cloth that had been on Jesus' head, not lying with the linen wrappings but rolled up in a place by itself. 8 Then the other disciple, who reached the tomb first, also went in, and he saw and believed; 9 for as yet they did not understand the scripture, that he must rise from the dead. 10 Then the disciples returned to their homes. . . .

ROMANS 6:1 What then are we to say? Should we continue in sin in order that grace may abound? 2 By no means! How can we who died to sin go on living in it? 3 Do you not know that all of us who have been baptized into Christ Jesus were baptized into his death? 4 Therefore we have been buried with him by baptism into death, so that, just as Christ was raised from the dead by the glory of the Father, so we too might walk in newness of life.

5 For if we have been united with him in a death like his, we will certainly be united with him in a resurrection like his. 6 We know that our old self was crucified with him so that the body of sin might be destroyed, and we might no longer be enslaved to sin. 7 For whoever has died is freed from sin. 8 But if we have died with Christ, we believe that we will also live with him. 9 We know that Christ, being raised from the dead, will never die again; death no longer has dominion over him. 10 The death he died, he died to sin, once for all; but the life he lives, he lives to God. 11 So you also must consider yourselves dead to sin and alive to God in Christ Jesus. . . .

13 No longer present your members to sin as instruments of wickedness, but present yourselves to God as those who have been brought from death to life, and present your members to God as instruments of righteousness.

BACKGROUND

The Resurrection is the key miracle of the Bible that confirms all the others. Belief in the resurrection of Christ helps us see beyond the physical evidence of this world. When we believe in Jesus' resurrection, we begin to glimpse the evidence beyond this world; and we begin to understand the supernatural power of God.

Many have examined the evidence of the Resurrection without believing. They have explored the historical records, the eyewitness accounts, and the transforming impact left by the Resurrection on society. They have seen the truth with their eyes and heard it with their ears, but their hearts have yet to be touched by the truth. They have not yet heard Jesus call their name. Mary saw and heard the risen Lord, but it was not until a more personal encounter that Mary finally recognized her Savior. She heard Jesus call her name.

We need to know more than external facts. We need to know a Person. We need a personal encounter with Jesus, the risen Savior. We need to hear Him speak in a personal way to our hearts. We need to open the eyes of our hearts to the supernatural depths of His love for us.

NOTES ON THE PRINTED TEXT

It was early Sunday morning, before the crack of dawn, when a devoted follower of Jesus named *Mary Magdalene* (John 20:1) ventured to *the tomb* where the Savior's body had been placed. Upon Mary's arrival, she was startled to find that *the stone had been removed* from the tomb's entrance.

Perhaps fear and agitation prompted Mary to run from the scene (20:2). When she found *Simon Peter* and John (*the other disciple*), Mary exclaimed that the body of the Lord had been removed from the tomb and that she could not find the corpse. Peter and John responded by running to the tomb, with John outrunning Peter and reaching the site first (20:3-4).

John, in turn, stooped down to peer inside the tomb (20:5). He saw the strips of *linen* that had been used to cover Jesus' body, but the disciple did not enter the chamber. When Peter arrived, he entered the tomb, saw the linen strips, and spotted the cloth that had been placed around *Jesus' head* (20:6-7). The cloth, however, was rolled up in a place by itself. These details indicate that thieves had not stolen Jesus' body, for it is unlikely that anyone who had come to remove the corpse would have bothered to unwrap it before removing it.

Next, John went inside the tomb. After examining the chamber, he believed that Jesus had risen from the dead (20:8); yet he and the rest of the disciples still did not understand the Scripture concerning the Resurrection (20:9). Once Peter and John were done checking out the scene, they went back to *their homes* (20:10).

Paul's Letter to the Romans affirms the truth of Jesus' resurrection. Moreover, in Romans it becomes clear that God is concerned with more than just our status with Him (justification—being declared righteous). The Lord is also concerned about our behavior (sanctification—becoming holy). Thus, beginning in 6:1, the apostle indicated that God has a plan for dealing with the power of sin in our lives. Paul asked whether we should *continue to sin* so that grace might increase. The answer, of course, was no (6:2). Since the Christian has died to sin, he or she cannot adopt a sinful way of life just to enjoy the benefits of God's grace.

Paul noted that Christians were baptized into Jesus' *death* (6:3). Hence, we identify with Jesus in His death and burial so that we might also identify with Him in His resurrection, which is the key to our *newness of life* (6:4). Scholars have debated whether the *baptism* is water baptism or the baptism of the Spirit. Though some think this verse refers to water baptism, it would in that case seem to teach that water baptism is necessary for salvation. Eternal life, however, hinges solely on believing in Christ.

The fact that Christ was actually buried points to the absolute reality of His death. In like fashion, the fact that Christians are buried with Jesus in baptism points to the reality that they died with Him to their former sinful ways. Just as Christ was raised from the dead, so believers are raised to newness of life. Just as Jesus' resurrection body had a newness never seen before, so the new life of the believer is one of spiritual vitality.

In 6:5, Paul emphasized that since *we have been united* with Christ in His death, we will also be united with Him in His *resurrection*. The apostle was not referring to our future bodily resurrection; rather, he described our present identification with Christ. This is made clear in 6:6, where Paul argued that the believer's death and resurrection with Christ are to be understood (respectively) as the believer's death to *sin* and newness of life toward God.

Paul moreover said that our *old self*—our preconversion state of existence—*was crucified* with Christ. God's intent was that the absolute power sin exercised over our bodies might be broken, so that we no longer would be *enslaved to sin*. Paul was not saying that the human body is intrinsically evil or sinful. He was simply referring to the flesh as controlled or dominated by rebellion—the vehicle through which sin is accomplished.

Prior to trusting in Christ, the sinner was enslaved to the pull of sin; but now the unregenerate self has been crucified with Christ. Thus, the believer is freed from sin's absolute power. Sin no longer has any legal right to exercise its control in the life of the believer. The bondage has been broken. The power is rendered inoperative (6:7).

Paul affirmed that, because of our identification with Christ in His death and resurrection, the believer is raised to a new quality of life in the here and now (6:8). At the moment of salvation—the moment we trust in Christ and are born again—we begin to share in the resurrection life of Christ.

Since Christ was *raised from the dead* (6:9), He will never die again, and death has no *dominion* over Him. In His humanity, Jesus experienced death *once* (6:10) and then was forever removed from its sphere of influence. This is an important point. Unless we can be sure that Christ conquered death once *for all*, our own confidence of victory over death through Christ is undermined. Unless we can be sure on this point, then our union with Christ carries little significance.

On the one hand, Paul affirmed that Christ died for sin once for all. On the other hand, He is now alive, and He lives only for God. Based upon Christ's everlasting life, Paul drove home his main point: believers—recognizing our identity with the crucified and resurrected Christ—are to consider ourselves dead in regard to sin and *alive to God* (6:11).

Christians moreover are no longer to put any part of their body at sin's disposal, as an implement for doing wrong; instead, they are to place themselves at God's disposal. Through their identification with Christ, believers have been raised from death to life. Thus, they are to yield their bodies to God as implements for doing good (6:13).

SUGGESTIONS TO TEACHERS

There are three aspects of the death, burial, and resurrection of Jesus that Paul seized upon to teach his readers in Rome. Perhaps it would be beneficial if we, too, seized upon the apostle's teaching and retraced the steps in which we are justified by grace through faith.

1. BAPTISM INTO DEATH. Paul pointed out that Christians were baptized into Jesus' death (Rom. 6:3). We identify with Jesus in His death and burial so that we may also identify with Him in His resurrection, which is the key to our new life (6:4). In other words, believers—in our identification with Christ—have spiritually died to sin and have been raised to newness of life. Paul went on to say, *So you also must consider yourselves dead to sin and alive to God in Christ Jesus* (6:11). The transforming power of God's grace will help us to think of our old, sinful way of life as dead and buried; we can treat the sinful yearnings and temptations of the old nature as if they were dead.

2. WALK IN NEWNESS OF LIFE. The apostle explained that *just as Christ was raised from the dead by the glory of the Father, so we too might walk in newness of life* (6:4). Since we no longer live under sin's power, and are no longer slaves to our sinful nature, we can now choose to live for Christ *in newness of life.* Because we have been united by faith with Him in His resurrection life, we have an unbroken relationship with the Father Himself—a relationship that brings us love, joy, and peace. We are *a new creation: everything old has passed away; see, everything has become new!* (2 Cor. 5:17). We live a fresh, new life in Christ!

3. RESURRECTION LIKE HIS. Just as Christ was raised from the dead, so believers are raised to newness of life. In fact, Jesus' death, burial, and resurrection give believers a picture of their old self dying, being buried, and resurrected to new life.

FOR ADULTS	■ **TOPIC:** Victory over Death ■ **QUESTIONS:** 1. What was the essence of the message Mary conveyed to Peter and John? 2. What impact did the empty tomb have

on John? 3. Why would it be incorrect to conclude that we should continue in sin so that God's grace may abound? 4. What did Paul mean when he declared that our old self was crucified with Christ? 5. Why should believers consider themselves to be dead to sin?

■ **ILLUSTRATIONS:**

Changed Lives. One of the best snapshots from the World War II era is a photograph of King George VI inspecting a bombed out section of London. In the picture, he stops to talk with a little boy who is sloppily dressed and has his cap on crooked. The king is bending on one knee and looking directly into the face of the child. And even though the picture profiles the king, you can see that he is gazing with compassion at the lad. Surely that child's life was changed. If he lived to be a hundred, he wouldn't forget that day.

The same is true of Jesus; once one truly looks into His eyes, it is difficult to turn away. "If you don't believe that," writes Brett Blair, "then ask a long parade of witnesses." Ask Mary Magdalene. She looked into Jesus' face and became a pure woman. Ask Matthew. He too looked into Jesus' face, and became an honest man. Ask Paul. When he encountered the Savior, he was changed. Paul's zeal for the law became a zeal for love. Ask Peter. Change, you ask? Oh yes, he changed. After he met Jesus, he had to wrestle with his prejudices against the Gentiles. All of these people—and all of us—represent broken men and women. Our need is to be healed, changed, repaired, and forgiven.

Born Again. In their book entitled *Born Again,* Charles Colson and Billy Graham describe what new birth in Christ really means. They note that it is literally to begin all over again, to be given a second birth.

The one who is born again doesn't all of a sudden get turned into a super-Christian. To be born again is to enter afresh into the process of spiritual growth. It is to wipe the slate clean. It is to cancel your old mortgage and start again. In other words, you don't have to be always what you have now become. Such an offer is too good to be true for many, and confusing for most; but for those who seek to be other than what they are now, who want to be more than the mere accumulation and sum total of their experiences, the invitation, "You must be born again," is an offer you cannot afford to refuse.

<table>
<tr><td>

FOR YOUTH

</td><td>

■ **TOPIC:** Life over Death!

■ **QUESTIONS:** 1. What did Mary discover when she reached the tomb? 2. What did Peter and John see when they entered the tomb?

</td></tr>
</table>

3. What does it mean to be baptized into Christ? 4. What does it mean to be dead to sin? 5. Why should believers offer themselves in service to God?

■ **ILLUSTRATIONS:**

No Future? While some youth have little hope for the future, apparently many more are optimistic. When polled by TIME/CNN and asked what happens after death, 61 percent of Americans felt that they would go to heaven. Joni Eareckson Tada, a quadriplegic since she was 17, trusts in full-body resurrection and the glorification of the body in heaven. Believers around you highlight the biblical account and announcement. Jesus rose from the dead! Death has been conquered!

An Empty Egg and an Empty Tomb. Jeremy Forrester was born with a twisted body and a slow mind. At the age of 12 he was still in second grade, seemingly unable to learn. His teacher, Doris Miller, often became exasperated with him. He would squirm in his seat, drool, and make grunting noises. At other times, he spoke clearly and distinctly, as if a spot of light had penetrated the darkness of his brain. Most of the time, however, Jeremy just irritated his teacher.

One day Doris called Jeremy's parents and asked them to come in for a consultation. As the Forresters entered the empty classroom, Doris said to them, "Jeremy really belongs in a special school. It isn't fair to him to be with younger children who don't have learning problems. Why, there is a five-year gap between his age and that of the other students." Mrs. Forrester cried softly into a tissue, while her husband spoke. "Miss Miller," he said, "there is no school of that kind nearby. It would be a terrible shock for Jeremy if we had to take him out of this school. We know he really likes it here."

Doris sat for a long time after they had left, staring at the snow outside the window. Its coldness seemed to seep into her soul. As she pondered the situation, guilt washed over her. *Here I am complaining when my problems are nothing compared to that poor family*, she thought. *Lord, please help me to be more patient with Jeremy.* From that day on, Doris tried hard to ignore Jeremy's noises and his blank stares. Then one day, he limped to her desk, dragging his bad leg behind him. "I love you, Miss Miller," he exclaimed, loud enough for the whole class to hear. The other students snickered, and Doris's face turned red. Doris stammered,

"Wh-why that's very nice, Jeremy. N-now please take your seat."

Spring came, and the children talked excitedly about the coming of Easter. Doris told them the account of Jesus, and then to emphasize the idea of new life springing forth, she gave each of the children a large plastic egg. "Now," she said to them, "I want you to take this home and bring it back tomorrow with something inside that shows new life. Do you understand?"

"Yes, Miss Miller," the children responded enthusiastically—all except for Jeremy. He listened intently; his eyes never left her face. He did not even make his usual noises. Had he understood what she had said about Jesus' death and resurrection? Did he understand the assignment? Perhaps Doris should call his parents and explain the project to them.

That evening, Doris's kitchen sink stopped up. She called the landlord and waited an hour for him to come by and unclog it. After that, she still had to shop for groceries, iron a blouse, and prepare a vocabulary test for the next day. She completely forgot about phoning Jeremy's parents.

The next morning, 19 children came to school, laughing and talking as they placed their eggs in the large wicker basket on Miss Miller's desk. After they completed their math lesson, it was time to open the eggs.

In the first egg, Doris found a flower. "Oh yes, a flower is certainly a sign of new life," she said. "When plants peek through the ground, we know that spring is here." A small girl in the first row waved her arm. "That's my egg, Miss Miller," she called out. The next egg contained a plastic butterfly, which looked very real. Doris held it up. "We all know that a caterpillar changes and grows into a beautiful butterfly. Yes, that's new life, too." Little Judy smiled proudly and said, "Miss Miller, that one is mine." Next, Doris found a rock with moss on it. She explained that moss, too, showed life. Billy spoke up from the back of the classroom, "My daddy helped me," he beamed.

Then Doris opened the fourth egg. She gasped. The egg was empty. Surely it must be Jeremy's, she thought, and of course, he did not understand her instructions. If only she had not forgotten to phone his parents. Because she did not want to embarrass him, she quietly set the egg aside and reached for another.

Suddenly, Jeremy spoke up. "Miss Miller, aren't you going to talk about my egg?" Flustered, Doris replied, "But Jeremy, your egg is empty." Jeremy looked into Doris's eyes and said softly, "Yes, but Jesus' tomb was empty, too." Time stopped. When Doris could speak again, she asked Jeremy, "Do you know why the tomb was empty?" "Oh, yes," Jeremy said, "Jesus was killed and put in there. Then His Father raised Him up."

The recess bell rang. While the children excitedly ran out to the schoolyard, Doris cried. The cold inside her melted completely away.

Three months later, Jeremy died. Those who paid their respects at the funeral home were surprised to see 19 eggs on top of his casket—*all of them empty*!

LIFE IN THE SPIRIT

BACKGROUND SCRIPTURE: Romans 8:1-17
DEVOTIONAL READING: Romans 7:1-6

KEY VERSE: All who are led by the Spirit of God are children of God. Romans 8:14.

KING JAMES VERSION

ROMANS 8:1 There is therefore now no condemnation to them which are in Christ Jesus, who walk not after the flesh, but after the Spirit. 2 For the law of the Spirit of life in Christ Jesus hath made me free from the law of sin and death. 3 For what the law could not do, in that it was weak through the flesh, God sending his own Son in the likeness of sinful flesh, and for sin, condemned sin in the flesh: 4 That the righteousness of the law might be fulfilled in us, who walk not after the flesh, but after the Spirit. 5 For they that are after the flesh do mind the things of the flesh; but they that are after the Spirit the things of the Spirit. 6 For to be carnally minded is death; but to be spiritually minded is life and peace. 7 Because the carnal mind is enmity against God: for it is not subject to the law of God, neither indeed can be. 8 So then they that are in the flesh cannot please God. 9 But ye are not in the flesh, but in the Spirit, if so be that the Spirit of God dwell in you. Now if any man have not the Spirit of Christ, he is none of his.

10 And if Christ be in you, the body is dead because of sin; but the Spirit is life because of righteousness. 11 But if the Spirit of him that raised up Jesus from the dead dwell in you, he that raised up Christ from the dead shall also quicken your mortal bodies by his Spirit that dwelleth in you. 12 Therefore, brethren, we are debtors, not to the flesh, to live after the flesh. 13 For if ye live after the flesh, ye shall die: but if ye through the Spirit do mortify the deeds of the body, ye shall live. 14 For as many as are led by the Spirit of God, they are the sons of God. 15 For ye have not received the spirit of bondage again to fear; but ye have received the Spirit of adoption, whereby we cry, Abba, Father. 16 The Spirit itself beareth witness with our spirit, that we are the children of God.

NEW REVISED STANDARD VERSION

ROMANS 8:1 There is therefore now no condemnation for those who are in Christ Jesus. 2 For the law of the Spirit of life in Christ Jesus has set you free from the law of sin and of death. 3 For God has done what the law, weakened by the flesh, could not do: by sending his own Son in the likeness of sinful flesh, and to deal with sin, he condemned sin in the flesh, 4 so that the just requirement of the law might be fulfilled in us, who walk not according to the flesh but according to the Spirit. 5 For those who live according to the flesh set their minds on the things of the flesh, but those who live according to the Spirit set their minds on the things of the Spirit. 6 To set the mind on the flesh is death, but to set the mind on the Spirit is life and peace. 7 For this reason the mind that is set on the flesh is hostile to God; it does not submit to God's law—indeed it cannot, 8 and those who are in the flesh cannot please God.

9 But you are not in the flesh; you are in the Spirit, since the Spirit of God dwells in you. Anyone who does not have the Spirit of Christ does not belong to him. 10 But if Christ is in you, though the body is dead because of sin, the Spirit is life because of righteousness. 11 If the Spirit of him who raised Jesus from the dead dwells in you, he who raised Christ from the dead will give life to your mortal bodies also through his Spirit that dwells in you.

12 So then, brothers and sisters, we are debtors, not to the flesh, to live according to the flesh— 13 for if you live according to the flesh, you will die; but if by the Spirit you put to death the deeds of the body, you will live. 14 For all who are led by the Spirit of God are children of God. 15 For you did not receive a spirit of slavery to fall back into fear, but you have received a spirit of adoption. When we cry, "Abba! Father!" 16 it is that very Spirit bearing witness with our spirit that we are children of God.

5

Monday, March 28	Romans 7:1-6	*New Life of the Spirit*
Tuesday, March 29	Romans 7:7-13	*Sin Brings Death*
Wednesday, March 30	Romans 7:14-19	*The Struggle with Sin*
Thursday, March 31	Romans 7:20-25	*Captive to the Law of Sin*
Friday, April 1	Romans 8:1-5	*Live According to the Spirit*
Saturday, April 2	Romans 8:6-11	*You Are in the Spirit*
Sunday, April 3	Romans 8:12-17	*Led by the Spirit*

BACKGROUND

Scholars are unsure of who founded the church at Rome. Some suggest it may have been established by people from the city who were converted on the Day of Pentecost. (Acts 2:10 makes reference to visitors from Rome; these visitors may have been among the 3,000 converts that day). Others say it may have been founded by converts of Paul or one of the other apostles, who then moved to Rome.

Many believe that the church at Rome was predominantly made up of Gentile believers (Rom. 1:5, 13; 11:13; 15:15-16). However, there was also a strong minority of Jewish believers (2:17; 9—11). The Jews had been expelled from Rome by Claudius in about A.D. 50, so the church of Rome would have been entirely Gentile for a period. Many of those Jews, however, had returned to Rome by the time Paul wrote this letter to the church. Others have suggested that the church was predominantly Jewish with a Gentile minority. They argue that because Paul referred to Abraham, and because he cited the law so many times, he must have intended the letter primarily for Jewish readers.

A number of factors argue against this. For example, Paul began his letter with an explicit recognition that his Roman readers were Gentiles (1:13). The fact that Paul cited Abraham (4:1) does not argue against a Gentile audience. Indeed, Paul informed us that Abraham is the father of all who believe, not just the Jews (4:11). Paul's frequent citation of Jewish law does not argue against a primarily Gentile audience. Other letters he wrote to Gentiles, such as Galatians and 1 and 2 Corinthians, often cite the law. Thus we can be relatively sure that the church at Rome was mostly Gentile. Regardless of the percentages, there was obviously tension between the two groups, which Paul addressed directly.

NOTES ON THE PRINTED TEXT

When sin beckons us, there are times when we feel like putty in its hands. Nearly two millennia ago, Paul endured the same struggles we experience, but he worked through these struggles. What the Lord taught Paul, he passed on to others. In fact, Paul instructed the Jewish and Gentile believers in Rome as to how they could live a triumphant Christian life. What the apostle taught them can help us in our Christian walk.

For instance, as Paul stated in Romans 7:24, a life dominated by sin leads to misery. It is only Christ who can set us free from this dilemma (7:25). Moreover, those who trust in Him for salvation are forgiven and thus need not fear being punished by the Lord in the future day of the condemnation of the wicked (8:1).

In 8:2, Paul used the word *law* twice to describe controlling powers. For example, there is the controlling power of *sin* and *death*, from which the controlling power of *the Spirit* sets us *free*; also, because of our union with Christ, the indwelling Spirit gives us new *life*.

In Paul's day, some people thought that keeping the law of Moses could save them. This was impossible for the law was weakened through our *flesh* (8:3), or sinful nature; but God, in His grace, enacted a different plan for our salvation. His own Son came to earth in the *likeness* of *sinful* humanity. This means that Jesus, though having a body like ours, was sinless. Through Christ's atoning sacrifice, God *condemned sin* and destroyed its control over us.

When a person becomes a Christian, a miraculous exchange occurs. The new believer's sinfulness is transferred to Christ on the cross and His perfect righteousness is transferred to the new believer. Through this exchange the requirements of the law are met in full. Christ's righteousness in the believer enables that person to consistently live *according to the Spirit* (8:4).

As a result, two options exist for believers. They can allow the Spirit to control them, or they can choose to be dominated by the sin nature. The second option leads to further sin, while first option is Christ-centered and God-honoring (8:5). The decision to be controlled by sin results in *death* (8:6), whereas being Spirit-led results in *life and peace*. This is because the sinful nature continuously fights against the will of God and always refuses to heed His commands (8:7). Understandably, then, those who follow their sinful desires *cannot please God* (8:8).

Paul affirmed his conviction that his readers were not controlled by the sinful nature; instead, they allowed *the Spirit of God* (8:9) living in them to control them. This was a wise decision, for only those who were indwelt by the Spirit were truly Christians. In brief, the Spirit is the sign and seal that a person is a believer.

Paul said that because Christ is in us, our spirits are spiritually reborn and enjoy an upright status with God. This remains true even though our mortal bodies are slowly dying as a result of our *sin* (8:10). Despite our mortality, however, we have the hope of a physical resurrection (8:11). The same *Spirit* who *raised* Christ from *the dead* will also one day raise our *mortal bodies* from the grave.

Before getting saved, we were slaves to sin. Moreover, we were, in a sense, under obligation to do whatever our sinful nature demanded; but now that we belong to Christ, we do not have to live in this way (8:12). Thus, if we choose to satisfy our sinful impulses, it will be a harbinger of death for us; oppositely, if *by the Spirit* (8:13) we *put to death* the misdeeds of *the body*, this will be an indication of life.

The choice, then, is between the Spirit and life or sin and death. Motivation for choosing the first option is found in the realization that only those who are *led by the Spirit of God* (8:14) are truly *children* of the Father. Furthermore, belonging to God's family carries many privileges and responsibilities. As sons and daughters of God, believers are called to live in a manner that reflects their new family relationship.

Because we are God's children through faith in Christ, we should not relate to the Lord as terrified, cowering slaves; instead, we should consider ourselves as welcomed and loved members of His family. After all, the indwelling Spirit has brought about our adoption as sons and daughters (8:15).

This truth is significant, for in the Roman culture an adopted family member enjoyed all the rights and privileges of a natural-born family member. Hence, believers need not be fearful about approaching God, but can boldly come to Him and say, *"Abba! Father!" Abba* is an Aramaic term that denotes the close relationship between God and believers.

Assurance of salvation comes from the Holy Spirit's connection with the spirit of believers (8:16). The Spirit provides an inner sense that Christians truly belong to God. By virtue of the new birth and adoption, believers are called *the children of God* (see John 1:12-13; 1 John 3:1-2).

SUGGESTIONS TO TEACHERS

This week's lesson is from the eighth chapter of Romans, which is the climax of the whole book. In 6:1—8:17, Paul discussed sin and the law, the Spirit-filled life, and becoming a child in God's family. The aim of this lesson is to encourage the students to follow the Spirit, rather than the sinful nature.

1. BEING INDWELT BY THE SPIRIT. At first the biblical notion of the Spirit's indwelling ministry might seem vague and abstract to the students. You can make things more concrete and meaningful for them by framing the discussion in terms of personal sin. While sin can take on many forms, it might be helpful to address the issue in terms of thoughts, feelings, and actions.

2. HANDLING LIFE'S UPS AND DOWNS. In the flow of the discussion, focus on the way the students deal with frustrations and disappointments in their lives. By operating in the flesh, they will transgress God's Word in the decisions they make, the people they spend time with, and the values they embrace; in contrast, by operating in the Spirit, they will dwell upon what is virtuous, enjoy the peace of God's presence, and treat others with consideration and kindness.

3. ACKNOWLEDGING THE RAGING BATTLE WITHIN. Be sure to share how much of a struggle it can be at times to renounce the things of the flesh and opt for the things of the Spirit. Compare it to a battle in which either sin or the Spirit dominates our lives. When the students yield to the Spirit's control, they will enjoy the fullness of eternal life offered by God. The Father will be pleased with them, and they will enjoy sweet communion with Him.

FOR ADULTS	■ **TOPIC:** Life in the Spirit

■ **QUESTIONS:** 1. Why is there no condemnation for those who are united to Christ by faith? 2. How is it possible for the righteous requirement of the law to be fulfilled in us? 3. What does it mean to walk in the Spirit, and why is it important to understand this concept? 4. How can operating in the Spirit be a truly freeing experience for believers? 5. On a personal level, what does it mean to cry out *Abba! Father!* (Rom. 8:15) to the sovereign Lord of our lives?

■ **ILLUSTRATIONS:**

Accepted. As the Gospel was being presented to a woman, she explained she had tried her best to please God. Then she added, "But I'm afraid God will never accept me." The Christian talking with her said, "I agree with you. He never will." A look of astonishment came over the woman's face, for she had not expected such a response. The believer then explained, "No, He never will, but God has accepted His Son, and if you join yourself to Him through faith, you will find God's favor!"

Many people have been deceived into thinking they must somehow earn acceptance in the eyes of God. The Bible, however, tells us that there is nothing in us, nor in what we do, that can in any way merit God's love and favor (Rom. 3:28; Eph. 2:1-5). Our salvation is rooted in the Father's mercy and the Son's sacrificial death for us (Eph. 1:4-7). Through faith in Christ, we can have new life in the Spirit.

Complete Salvation. John Newton, author of the well-known hymn *Amazing Grace*, was a miserable man at the age of 23. He had been involved in an immoral lifestyle and was engaged in the heartlessly cruel African slave trade. But he was fed up with his sinful way of life.

A crisis came on March 10, 1748, on board a ship that was caught in a violent storm. Thinking all was lost, Newton cried out in terror, "Lord, have mercy on us!" Suddenly the word *mercy* struck him with great force. If anybody needed it, he did. At that moment he trusted in Christ and experienced new life in the Spirit. God forgave Newton's sins and began to break the power of his wicked lifestyle.

Paul referred to both the mercy and the grace of God in salvation. The apostle declared that it is by God's grace we are justified and delivered from the guilt of our sins (Titus 3:7). But Paul also said it is God's mercy through the indwelling Spirit that delivers us from a lifestyle that the apostle described as *foolish* (3:3). Let's thank God daily for His grace and His mercy. Together they provide for us a complete salvation.

From Rags to Riches. During the Great Depression, a man named Mr. Yates owned a huge piece of land in Texas where he raised sheep. Financial problems had brought him to the brink of bankruptcy. Then an oil company, believing there might be oil on his land, asked for permission to drill.

With nothing to lose, Mr. Yates agreed. Soon, at a shallow depth, the workmen struck the largest oil deposit found at that time on the North American continent. Overnight, Mr. Yates became a billionaire. The amazing thing, though, is that the untapped riches were there all along. He just didn't know it!

Are you a spiritual "Mr. Yates" who is unaware of the riches you already own in Christ? When Paul wrote his Letter to the Ephesians, he revealed hidden treasure by preaching *the boundless riches of Christ* (3:8). Paul's goal was to make all Christians see how wealthy they actually are (Rom. 8:18).

FOR YOUTH

■ **TOPIC:** What Is Real Living?

■ **QUESTIONS:** 1. From what has the Spirit of life in Christ Jesus set us free? 2. By what means are the requirements of the law fulfilled in us? 3. Why is it important for our minds not to be set on the sinful nature? 4. What happens when we allow ourselves to be controlled by the Spirit? 5. What does the Spirit testify to us concerning our relationship to God?

■ **ILLUSTRATIONS:**

Receptive to the Gospel. A former heavy-metal rocker saw the 2000 Olympics in Sydney, Australia, as a time to tell people about finding new life in Christ. David Soesbee, who was voted in his high school as the most likely to be incarcerated or dead before the age of 30, was in Sydney to preach the message of life, Sydney's Wesley Mission reported. The then 34-year-old musician was among 230 Christians from 150 churches in the United States taking part in Reach-Out 2000 Sydney through Lay Witnesses for Christ, International.

In six hours of door-to-door evangelism during the first week of the Olympics, Soesbee prayed with 43 people who put their faith in Christ. "The people of Australia are very receptive to the gospel message," Soesbee said. "They have a yearning to fill that God-spaced emptiness in their lives."

Soesbee, a resident of Asheville, N.C., runs Touch Ministries, an organization that brings the Gospel to young people. A couple of years ago he traveled with a Christian band as well as ministered to musicians in several other bands.

The Passion in God's Heart. A Brazilian praise singer continues to donate all the proceeds of two CDs to help free child prostitutes in Bombay, India. Ana Paula Valadão, 24, and the worship team she leads, had sold more than 350,000 copies of their two CDs in the first year-and-a-half after they were released in 1999. All of the proceeds go to help rehabilitate children trapped in the illicit trade in Mubai, as Bombay is now known, Dallas-based Christ for the Nations reported. India Before the Throne, the ministry Ana and her pastor/father Marcio Valadão founded, helps get young girls off the streets and experience real living, the singer said.

Pastor Valadão dreamed about helping the children after witnessing their plight on a 1997 missions trip to Mubai. He learned that many of the dilapidated buildings on Falkland Street were brothels for child prostitutes. He was told that more than 20,000 girls from Nepal and India's country villages live as slaves, many of them sold by their starving parents for less than $20. To pay off their bondage, the girls, some as young as six, were forced to have relations with as many as 45 men a day. Most of the girls would die of AIDS or tuberculosis before they reached 20. Many would leave behind illegitimate children with no one to care for them. The pastor was moved with compassion to help the children find better lives.

Ana Paula's dream was to see the Body of Christ grow in intimacy through worship. As her father was returning from his trip, she was returning from a music conference "with my heart burning to record our church." Ana leads congregational worship at 12,000-member Igreja Batista da Logoinha in Belo Horizonte. Because "the Lord was doing awesome things through our worship," she and the church began Exalted, a 50-member worship and orchestral recording team. Sales of their first CD, which featured original Scripture-based songs, skyrocketed and a second release sold as well. The Brazilian government music industry awarded Ana Paula for the high sales, which she said are a blessing from God.

Their visions joined in building rehabilitation homes for the former prostitutes with the musical ministry profits. "If you think that these girls are lost forever, we can tell you they're not!" Ana Paula said. Although the outreach is fairly new, already girls are finding healing for their bodies, minds, and spirits.

"We knew God wanted us to do this," Ana Paula said. "His promises were that great things would happen, but we are always amazed at what the Lord is doing through this ministry." She said they receive hundreds of letters and e-mails about their music, sales continue to climb, and more girls in India will learn about Jesus. "The mission field won't lack anything because God's people understand that reaching the nations is the passion in God's heart."

SALVATION IN CHRIST

BACKGROUND SCRIPTURE: Romans 10:5-21
DEVOTIONAL READING: Hebrews 5:5-10

KEY VERSE: If you confess with your lips that Jesus is Lord and believe in your heart that God raised him from the dead, you will be saved. Romans 10:9.

KING JAMES VERSION

ROMANS 10:5 For Moses describeth the righteousness which is of the law, That the man which doeth those things shall live by them. 6 But the righteousness which is of faith speaketh on this wise, Say not in thine heart, Who shall ascend into heaven? (that is, to bring Christ down from above:) 7 Or, Who shall descend into the deep? (that is, to bring up Christ again from the dead.) 8 But what saith it? The word is nigh thee, even in thy mouth, and in thy heart: that is, the word of faith, which we preach; 9 That if thou shalt confess with thy mouth the Lord Jesus, and shalt believe in thine heart that God hath raised him from the dead, thou shalt be saved. 10 For with the heart man believeth unto righteousness; and with the mouth confession is made unto salvation. 11 For the scripture saith, Whosoever believeth on him shall not be ashamed.

12 For there is no difference between the Jew and the Greek: for the same Lord over all is rich unto all that call upon him. 13 For whosoever shall call upon the name of the Lord shall be saved. 14 How then shall they call on him in whom they have not believed? and how shall they believe in him of whom they have not heard? and how shall they hear without a preacher? 15 And how shall they preach, except they be sent? as it is written, How beautiful are the feet of them that preach the gospel of peace, and bring glad tidings of good things! 16 But they have not all obeyed the gospel. For Esaias saith, Lord, who hath believed our report? 17 So then faith cometh by hearing, and hearing by the word of God.

NEW REVISED STANDARD VERSION

ROMANS 10:5 Moses writes concerning the righteousness that comes from the law, that "the person who does these things will live by them." 6 But the righteousness that comes from faith says, "Do not say in your heart, 'Who will ascend into heaven?'" (that is, to bring Christ down) 7 "or 'Who will descend into the abyss?'" (that is, to bring Christ up from the dead). 8 But what does it say?

"The word is near you,
    on your lips and in your heart"

(that is, the word of faith that we proclaim);9 because if you confess with your lips that Jesus is Lord and believe in your heart that God raised him from the dead, you will be saved.10 For one believes with the heart and so is justified, and one confesses with the mouth and so is saved. 11 The scripture says, "No one who believes in him will be put to shame." 12 For there is no distinction between Jew and Greek; the same Lord is Lord of all and is generous to all who call on him. 13 For, "Everyone who calls on the name of the Lord shall be saved."

14 But how are they to call on one in whom they have not believed? And how are they to believe in one of whom they have never heard? And how are they to hear without someone to proclaim him? 15 And how are they to proclaim him unless they are sent? As it is written, "How beautiful are the feet of those who bring good news!" 16 But not all have obeyed the good news; for Isaiah says, "Lord, who has believed our message?" 17 So faith comes from what is heard, and what is heard comes through the word of Christ.

HOME BIBLE READINGS

Monday, April 4	Hebrews 5:5-10	*Christ, the Source of Eternal Salvation*
Tuesday, April 5	Romans 10:1-8	*On Your Lips, in Your Heart*
Wednesday, April 6	Romans 10:9-13	*Christ Is Lord of All*
Thursday, April 7	Romans 10:14-21	*Faith Comes Through Christ's Word*
Friday, April 8	Romans 11:1-6	*Israel Is Not Lost to Christ*
Saturday, April 9	Romans 11:13-18	*Gentiles Also Receive Salvation*
Sunday, April 10	Romans 11:19-23	*All Will Be Grafted Together*

BACKGROUND

In his *Commentary on Romans*, the reformer Martin Luther described the contents of Romans 10 this way: "The apostle intercedes for the Jews and shows that the righteousness which makes us worthy of eternal life comes alone from . . . faith in Christ." Surely Paul was disappointed that so many fellow Jews in Rome depended solely on adherence to the law for their salvation rather than on faith in Christ. As we read Paul's words, we can sense both the sadness and the urgency he must have felt. This was based on the fact that many of his fellow Jews had not yet accepted the truth of the Gospel.

Thus Paul, building upon what he had already written in regard to the Jews' pride and boasting in their heritage, embarked on an appeal for them to understand what constitutes true righteousness. Referring to several Old Testament passages, the apostle returned to the overriding theme of the letter: justification by grace through faith. Salvation cannot be earned—not by acts of righteousness, not by correct living, and not even by adherence to the law. Salvation is a gift from God that is given because people—whether Jew or Gentile—put their faith in Jesus Christ.

Paul wanted the Jews to understand that the era of the law had come to an end, while the era of Christ had come into being. This was, in fact, the same message that the apostle had driven home in his letter to the Galatians, in which he also clarified the true purpose of the Mosaic law. Though the law could not make people righteous—and thus, could not save them—it did reveal God's will so that they might recognize their sinfulness. And once they recognized their sinfulness, they would realize their need for forgiveness and justification. Acquittal and righteousness could come only through the sacrifice of one perfect, sinless being. That person was none other than Jesus Christ.

NOTES ON THE PRINTED TEXT

Paul began Romans 10 with an expression of his desire for Israel's salvation. The Israelites failed, said the apostle, because they did not understand the true nature of God's own righteousness. Such is made available only through faith in Christ. Since the Jews were ignorant of the kind of righteousness God both gives and requires for acceptance by Him, they naturally did not submit to it; instead, they attempted to create a righteousness of their own (10:1-3).

In Scripture, the concept of righteousness is closely linked to being virtuous. The idea is of acting in harmony with the character of God Himself. When this is done, one maintains a proper relationship with God.

Paul revealed the reason the Jews were confused about the nature of God's righteousness. It centered on Christ as the end, or goal, of *the law* (10:4). Here Paul emphasized two truths. First, the purpose of the law culminates or is accomplished in *Christ*. Second, because Jesus fulfilled the law, He made righteousness possible for anyone who believes. Christ assumed the debt owed to God for the broken law and for the penalty of sin (see Col. 2:13-14).

Tragically, the Jews failed to realize that if they were to attain righteousness by means of lawkeeping, they would have to be perfect in their conduct (Rom. 10:5). This is the essence of Moses' comment in Leviticus 18:5. This kind of righteousness is unavailable, for no one can measure up to the law's requirements.

In Romans 10:6-8, Paul loosely quoted Deuteronomy 30:12-14, where Moses addressed the Israelites who were about to enter the promised land. God's people had His message near them, on their lips and in their hearts, and therefore needed no one to bring it from afar. Paul used these words to emphasize a similar truth. Jesus had already come down to earth in the incarnation and had been raised from the dead. The gospel message, the *word of faith* (Rom. 10:8) that Paul was proclaiming, was readily available to his readers.

Paul's message called for two responses from those who heard it. First, it involved a verbal confession that *Jesus is Lord* (10:9), that He is truly God in the flesh. Second, it required the heartfelt belief that Jesus triumphed on the cross because *God raised him from the dead*. Confession with *the mouth* (10:10) is an indicating, outward expression of one's inward conviction about the truth of the Gospel. This is the basis for salvation.

Those who believe in Christ will never be *put to shame* (10:11; see Isa. 28:16). It does not matter whether one is a Jew or Gentile. God is impartial. Jesus is not the Lord of one group only, but is *Lord of all* (Rom. 10:12). Both Jews and Gentiles who call upon Him find themselves receiving rich blessings from Him (10:13; see Joel 2:32). To call on the Lord's name is to pray in faith for the salvation He offers.

After Paul explained the nature of salvation through Christ, the apostle answered a series of questions an unbeliever might raise regarding how a person might call upon the name of the Lord. How can the lost call on Jesus before they have believed in Him; and how can they believe in Him without first hearing the Gospel; and how can they hear the Good News unless someone announces it to them; and how can there be proclamation without those who preach being sent to do so (Rom. 10:14-15)?

In summary, Paul said there can be no calling without belief, no belief without hearing, no hearing without proclamation, and no proclamation without heralds being sent. Furthermore, when they deliver to the lost the message of salvation, *the feet* of the heralds are said to be *beautiful*, for they are bringing the *good news* of redemption. Paul was alluding to Isaiah 52:7, where a messenger delivered the good tidings that God had ended Judah's Babylonian exile.

Although the good news of salvation was proclaimed to all Israel (and to all the Gentiles as well), not everyone who heard responded to it (Rom. 10:16). Paul quoted Isaiah 53:1, from the passage on the suffering Servant, to emphasize that many Jews had not heard or understood the message of the Messiah, who had already come to suffer and die for their sins.

The fault is not the message, but in the hearing of those who do not respond; regardless of the way in which hearers of the Gospel responded, it remains true that saving faith can only result from hearing the message, the Good News *through the word of Christ* (Rom. 10:17).

SUGGESTIONS TO TEACHERS

God did not make the means of receiving His salvation complicated or difficult; rather, He made it clear and straightforward. We are saved through faith in Christ; there is no other means of salvation. Paul, knowing this, noted four unsophisticated and unpretentious steps one should follow in order to be justified by grace through faith.

1. CONFESS WITH YOUR LIPS. First comes the call to express what your mind has accepted. You've examined the facts, you've heard all the evidence you need to hear, you've realized your need for salvation, and you've recognized that Christ is your only source of salvation. Thus you express that He is the Lord who rose again, the Savior of your soul, and your Redeemer. Of course, confession made out loud represents a confirmation of what you have already accepted inside.

2. BELIEVE IN YOUR HEART. Second comes the belief that begins growing in your heart and never ceases to grow for the rest of your life. This belief becomes the center of your being; it is your complete trust in Christ and in Him alone. It is your sole hope for life that never ends. It is your conviction that God raised Christ from the dead, and that someday He'll raise you, too, to be with Him forever.

3. EMBRACE YOUR SALVATION. Third, with confession and belief comes an assurance of salvation. You have been saved from the guilt and penalty of sin. You have been saved from the dominion of sin in your life. By embracing your salvation, you are affirming the truth of the Gospel.

4. PROCLAIM THE SAVIOR. Fourth, in return for this great gift of salvation, God asks us to love Him so much and to love others so much that we spread the Good News. Proclaim God's love for all humanity. Tell others how He has saved you—and what He has saved you from. Tell people that God gave His Son so that salvation could be offered as a free gift. Tell the lost how God yearns for all to find and accept their salvation in His Son.

■ **TOPIC:** Affirming Christ as Lord

■ **QUESTIONS:** 1. What was Paul's point in Romans 10:5 about practicing a form of righteousness that is based on the law? 2. Why are heroic efforts not needed when it comes to salvation in Christ? 3. What does it mean to confess Jesus as Lord and believe in one's heart that God raised Him from the dead? 4. Why would God make salvation equally available to both Jew and Gentile? 5. Why is it important for the Gospel to be spread by word and deed to the lost?

■ **ILLUSTRATIONS:**

Preach the Gospel. It was Francis of Assisi who told his fellow believers the following: "Preach the Gospel at all times. And if necessary, use words." According to Acts 11:14, words are important, but a godly life that affirms Christ as Lord is the attracting magnet.

Spreading the Gospel. Five hundred people were baptized by fire hose on a hot New York City street over an August weekend in 2000. They arrived from the neighborhood and by bus from Washington, Boston, and Philadelphia and, dressed in white, gathered in the middle of an East Harlem street to be sprayed, according to *The New York Times.*

S. C. Madison, national leader of the United House of Prayer for All People, a nondenominational church, led the ceremony, which included music from four gospel brass bands. A church official turned on the hose, attached to a city hydrant, and water shot high into the air, raining down in a cool spray for 15 minutes. Some congregants danced to music, while others dropped to the ground praying.

The church has held the mass baptisms each summer since 1937. There are 3,000,000 congregants in 28 states, and in some cities as many as 2,000 people are baptized in a river or a pool. The New York congregation uses the municipal water supply because access to rivers is limited and pools are hard to find.

Passing On a Torch. In the book *Chicken Soup for the Unsinkable Soul,* Paul Karrar tells how the tired ex-teacher edged closer to the counter at Kmart. Her left leg hurt and she hoped she had taken all of her pills for the day: the ones for her high blood pressure, dizziness, and a host of other ills. *Thank goodness I retired years ago,* she thought to herself. *I don't have the energy to teach these days.*

Just before the line to the counter formed, the teacher spotted a young man with four children and a pregnant wife or girlfriend in tow. The teacher couldn't miss the tattoo on his neck. *He's been to prison,* she thought. The teacher continued checking him out. His white T-shirt, shaved hair, and baggy pants led the teacher to surmise, *He's a gang member.*

The teacher tried to let the man go ahead of her.

"You can go first," she offered.

"No, you go first," he insisted.

"No, you have more people with you," said the teacher.

"We should respect our elders," parried the man. And with that, he gestured with a sweeping motion indicating the way for the woman.

A brief smile flickered on the teacher's lips as she hobbled in front of him. The teacher in her decided she couldn't let the moment go and she turned back to him and asked, "Who taught you your good manners?"

"You did, Mrs. Simpson, in third grade."

Ultimately, we're all teachers; we're all teaching our own generation or the generation before us or the generation after us. We're all examples of something. We're all passing on a torch. The question is this: What kind of torch are you going to pass on?

FOR YOUTH

■ **TOPIC:** Good News for All

■ **QUESTIONS:** 1. What was the righteousness based on faith mentioned by Paul? 2. What was the word of faith that Paul declared? 3. What is necessary for someone to be saved? 4. What distinction does God make with respect to Jews and Gentiles when it comes to salvation? 5. Why is it important for the lost to hear the Word of God proclaimed?

■ **ILLUSTRATIONS:**

To Go Where the Gospel Has Never Gone Before. Native missionaries in India are taking the Gospel where it never has gone before. Workers in the Hindu strongholds of central and northern India have visited dozens of villages where people have never heard about Jesus Christ, Christian Aid Mission reported.

A Hindu leader became a Christian and has asked to be baptized, according to the Virginia-based evangelistic group. His profession of faith has caused an uproar among Hindus in the area, but many others are more open to hearing the Gospel. In another village, two Muslim young people became Christians and are facing persecution from their community.

Gold Medal Gospel. A gold medal wasn't the only prize that U.S. Olympian Sheila Taormina sought in Sydney, Australia, back in 2000. Taormina, who won a gold medal in swimming in 1996, returned to the Games because they gave her opportunities to tell others about her faith in Christ.

Taormina thought she was finished with Olympic competition after winning in Atlanta as part of the 800-meter freestyle relay swimming team, according to Beliefnet. But as she traveled afterward telling her story, she began to see her celebrity as providing an opportunity to talk about God. "The more I spoke to people, the more I began to wonder if I had stepped away from the Olympics too soon," she said.

Taormina hesitated to return to the rigorous training schedule that Olympic competition demands. She explained, "You have to become very selfish with your time. There are days when I think I could better spend my time working with the youth groups at my local church."

In Sydney, Taormina competed in the women's triathlon, involving swimming nine-tenths of a mile in the ocean, biking 24.8 miles, and running 6.2 miles. Her training regimen and enthusiasm helped her qualify for the team, and she finished sixth in Olympic competition with a time of 2 hours, 2 minutes, and 45 seconds.

"My treasure isn't another gold medal, or even returning to the Olympics again," Taormina said. "It's how I share this experience with others. It's what I bring back to them that can help them with their lives."

Your Gospel Legacy. Psychologist William James said, "The great use of life is to spend it for something that outlasts it." If you were to die today, what would be your legacy? What kind of torch would you have passed on?

Secret Service Proclamation. An advertisement in the classifieds offered a "retired" police dog for sale for $25. A woman who lived alone thought a police dog might make a good watchdog as well as a companion, so she quickly called the station and sent her check.

Later, a police officer delivered a mangy, pitiful looking creature. When the woman protested the dog's appearance and said she wanted the dog to guard her and the house, the officer replied: "Now, ma'am, don't let this dog's looks deceive you. He's in the Secret Service."

How many of us Christians are in the "Secret Service" when it comes to proclaiming the Gospel? God doesn't want secret servants!

MARKS OF THE TRUE CHRISTIAN

BACKGROUND SCRIPTURE: Romans 12:1-21
DEVOTIONAL READING: Romans 12:3-8

KEY VERSES: Let love be genuine; hate what is evil, hold fast to what is good; love one another with mutual affection; outdo one another in showing honor. Romans 12:9-10.

KING JAMES VERSION

ROMANS 12:1 I beseech you therefore, brethren, by the mercies of God, that ye present your bodies a living sacrifice, holy, acceptable unto God, which is your reasonable service. 2 And be not conformed to this world: but be ye transformed by the renewing of your mind, that ye may prove what is that good, and acceptable, and perfect, will of God. . . .

9 Let love be without dissimulation. Abhor that which is evil; cleave to that which is good. 10 Be kindly affectioned one to another with brotherly love; in honour preferring one another; 11 Not slothful in business; fervent in spirit; serving the Lord; 12 Rejoicing in hope; patient in tribulation; continuing instant in prayer; 13 Distributing to the necessity of saints; given to hospitality. 14 Bless them which persecute you: bless, and curse not. 15 Rejoice with them that do rejoice, and weep with them that weep. 16 Be of the same mind one toward another. Mind not high things, but condescend to men of low estate. Be not wise in your own conceits. 17 Recompense to no man evil for evil. Provide things honest in the sight of all men. 18 If it be possible, as much as lieth in you, live peaceably with all men. 19 Dearly beloved, avenge not yourselves, but rather give place unto wrath: for it is written, Vengeance is mine; I will repay, saith the Lord. 20 Therefore if thine enemy hunger, feed him; if he thirst, give him drink: for in so doing thou shalt heap coals of fire on his head. 21 Be not overcome of evil, but overcome evil with good.

NEW REVISED STANDARD VERSION

ROMANS 12:1 I appeal to you therefore, brothers and sisters, by the mercies of God, to present your bodies as a living sacrifice, holy and acceptable to God, which is your spiritual worship. 2 Do not be conformed to this world, but be transformed by the renewing of your minds, so that you may discern what is the will of God—what is good and acceptable and perfect. . . .

9 Let love be genuine; hate what is evil, hold fast to what is good; 10 love one another with mutual affection; outdo one another in showing honor. 11 Do not lag in zeal, be ardent in spirit, serve the Lord.
12 Rejoice in hope, be patient in suffering, persevere in prayer. 13 Contribute to the needs of the saints; extend hospitality to strangers.

14 Bless those who persecute you; bless and do not curse them. 15 Rejoice with those who rejoice, weep with those who weep. 16 Live in harmony with one another; do not be haughty, but associate with the lowly; do not claim to be wiser than you are. 17 Do not repay anyone evil for evil, but take thought for what is noble in the sight of all. 18 If it is possible, so far as it depends on you, live peaceably with all. 19 Beloved, never avenge yourselves, but leave room for the wrath of God; for it is written, "Vengeance is mine, I will repay, says the Lord." 20 No, "if your enemies are hungry, feed them; if they are thirsty, give them something to drink; for by doing this you will heap burning coals on their heads." 21 Do not be overcome by evil, but overcome evil with good.

7

Monday, April 11	Colossians 4:2-6	*Instructions for Living*
Tuesday, April 12	1 Thessalonians 4:1-12	*Live a Life Pleasing to God*
Wednesday, April 13	1 Thessalonians 5:12-22	*Hold Fast to What Is Good*
Thursday, April 14	2 Thessalonians 3:6-13	*Do What Is Right*
Friday, April 15	Romans 12:1-5	*Members One of Another*
Saturday, April 16	Romans 12:6-13	*Marks of the True Christian*
Sunday, April 17	Romans 12:14-21	*Overcome Evil with Good*

BACKGROUND

Near the conclusion of each of Paul's letters to various churches is a discussion of practical duties that arise from the biblical truths he expounded. Though he stringently taught that justification comes by grace through faith, he also taught that grace and faith should manifest themselves in the believer's life. Salvation should affect the Christian's thoughts, actions, and behaviors. For Paul, what we believe should impact how we behave.

Just as we cannot earn our salvation on our own, neither can we perform good works on our own. Again, we need divine help. And the apostle wrote that we receive that help from the Spirit, who empowers us not only to do good deeds and follow the will of God, but also gives us special abilities to carry out our work for the Lord.

Paul was writing to a church in which there were both Jewish and Gentile Christians. As they increasingly associated together, there was plenty of room for jealousies, competition, and self-interest. Rather than these vices prevailing, Paul's desire was that there be unity and cooperation among different groups of believers. Thus the apostle told the church that God has given each of us the ability to do certain things. These spiritual gifts were to be used in service to each other and for the glory of God.

To use our spiritual gifts effectively, we should recognize that all of them come from God. Though each person in the church has different special abilities, they are all valued by the Lord and needed for the growth of His people. When we know who we are and what we do best, we will be more willing to dedicate our gifts to God's service and not to our personal success. Instead of holding back anything from God's service, we will want to utilize our gifts wholeheartedly.

NOTES ON THE PRINTED TEXT

In Romans 11, Paul declared that not all his fellow Jews had rejected God's message of salvation. There were still a faithful few. The apostle made it clear that God's plans for His people would be fulfilled, and that in the process many Gentiles would come to saving faith.

Then, in chapter 12, Paul exhorted the Jewish and Gentile Christians living in Rome to commit themselves wholeheartedly to God. The apostle told them to present themselves—physically, mentally, emotionally, and spiritually—*as a living sacrifice, holy and acceptable to God, which is your spiritual worship* (12:1). There is no room for a self-important ego in committing ourselves to God. It involves the totality of our being. To make such an offering involves a decisive act of our own will—a positive involvement in becoming part of God's plan toward holiness. The Lord views this as an act of worship, for it is our most appropriate response to all that His Son, Jesus Christ, has done for us, having freed us from the power and presence of sin.

Paul knew that when we truly present ourselves to God, we will no longer want to be *conformed to this world* (12:2). Indeed, as Christ, through the Holy Spirit, begins living His life in and through us, we will develop an attitude of resistance to all the unsavory values of the world, especially those that pressure us to accept and live by unwholesome standards. We become transformed people because our thought patterns are changed from their old ways and renewed toward God's ways. This renewing of our minds enables us to *discern what is the will of God—what is good and acceptable and perfect.*

Within any group of people there exists the possibility for pride. Perhaps that's why Paul urged the members of the congregation at Rome *not to think of yourself more highly than you ought to think* (12:3). The apostle especially did not want any individuals or groups thinking themselves better than others within the church because of their cultural background or religious heritage. Every member of the congregation had value, and that value was based in their spiritual identity in Christ. Thus Paul told his readers to think with *sober judgment*, and to evaluate themselves honestly, humbly, and prayerfully *according to the measure of faith that God has assigned.*

After the apostle's explanation of the presence and use of spiritual gifts (12:4-8), verse 9 begins what many Bible scholars term the "practical section" of the chapter. Undergirding everything else that Paul taught in these verses is the command to *Let love be genuine* (12:9). This love is not merely an emotion; it also requires action. It is in no way hypocritical or self-serving or pretending. It is real love put into action that the apostle was writing about here. And if love is the foundation of our actions, then we will *hate what is evil, hold fast to what is good.* To further describe this love, Paul said to *love one another with mutual affection; outdo one another in showing honor* (12:10).

Where unconditional love is flourishing, other attitudes will also sprout up and prosper. For instance, Paul told his readers *Do not lag in zeal, be ardent in spirit* (12:11). Creativity, motivation, and excitement should be clear external marks of our Christian service. We are to *serve the Lord* as though it is the most important activity of our lives. In actuality, it is. To this list of Christian attitudes and characteristics, verses 12 and 13 add hope, patience, prayer, compassion, and hospitality.

In 12:14-16, Paul told his readers how they should respond to friends, neighbors, and enemies of the Gospel. In times of suffering, it is natural for believers to pray that God would afflict their persecutors with misfortune. Paul said Christians should ask the Lord to bless those who mistreated them. This reflects what Jesus taught and practiced (Matt. 5:44; Luke 23:34). It was also the practice of some in the early church (Acts 7:59-60).

When others rejoice over the good things happening in their lives, we should rejoice with them rather than be envious of them. When others grieve over some tragedy they have experienced, we should grieve with them rather than gloat over their affliction (Rom. 12:15). Regardless of whether it is the saved or the unsaved, people will see Christ in us when we respond with genuine empathy.

In trying times it is easy for believers to argue and fight with one another. Paul said God's people should promote harmony and unity, not discord and division (12:16). The apostle also said that God's people should not be swayed by one's social standing. Christians should willingly associate with others, regardless of their economic status. Believers should also freely give themselves to humble, or menial, tasks.

Paul's exhortations in Romans 12:17-21 concern how believers should relate to those who are hostile to them. He said *Do not repay anyone evil for evil, but take thought for what is noble in the sight of all* (12:17). Jesus' followers were to do their best at all times and in every circumstance to live at peace with all people (12:18). There are times, of course, when even their best intentions and efforts would fail to produce peace.

Paul urged his readers not to try to get even when others abused and exploited them. Retaliation was not the answer. Instead, Christians were to patiently wait for God to right all injustices in His time (12:19). Paul's statement agreed with Deuteronomy 32:35, which said that God would repay all wrongs and vindicate the cause of His people.

In view of this truth, Christians should heed what is written in Proverbs 25:21-22, which Paul quoted in Romans 12:20. Believers should give their hungry and thirsty enemies food to eat and liquid to drink. By doing this, God's people would heap burning coals on the heads of their opponents. In other words, it would be seen as a generous and kind act that might cause them to rethink their ways.

Paul concluded by exhorting his readers not to *be overcome by evil, but [to] overcome evil with good* (12:21). Expressed another way, they were to resist the desire to counterattack their opponents. By showing love and kindness rather than hatred and vengeance, believers might win the unsaved to Christ.

SUGGESTIONS TO TEACHERS

One of the ways we can study and apply Romans 12 is by thinking of the chapter as a new set of "Be-Attitudes," for in these verses, Paul urged believers to exhibit certain *attitudes*. There are nine Beatitudes in Matthew 5:3-11; thus for the sake of counting, we'll list nine "Be-Attitudes" drawn from Romans 12.

1. BE A LIVING SACRIFICE. Lay aside your self-centered desires and goals and follow Jesus; put all your energy and resources at His disposal for His use, and trust Him to guide you.

2. BE TRANSFORMED. Ask yourself the question, "What would Jesus do?"; then try to think as He thinks. Be one of His vessels for His loving activity in the world today.

3. BE HUMBLE. Try to see yourself through God's eyes, and try to see others through God's eyes, too. Evaluate yourself according to heaven's values, not the values of this world.

4. BE GENUINE IN LOVE. Put your love into action. Look at those who are in need as though they were Jesus Himself.

5. BE ZEALOUS. Never view the Christian life as dull or boring. Instead, get excited about being a Christian. Develop a passion and an enthusiasm for living for Christ.

6. BE HOPEFUL. Think about all that Jesus has done for you; think about all that Jesus is doing for you right now; and think about all that Jesus is going to be doing for you in the future!

7. BE PATIENT. Learn to wait and hope at the same time. Also, remember that Jesus will guide you through your troubles. Make your trust in Him your central focus when facing difficult times.

8. BE PRAYERFUL. Keep at it; persevere; don't stop praying.

9. BE PEACEFUL. As much as possible, try to live in harmony with everyone around you. Enjoy the wholesome company of others and strive to be nice even to mean people.

FOR ADULTS

■ TOPIC: Living the Christian Life

■ QUESTIONS: 1. In what ways did Paul connect belief and behavior in Romans 12? 2. What must we do to refrain from becoming conformed to the world? 3. How does God transform the believer's mind? 4. What must happen before we can *discern what is the will of God* (12:2)? 5. Of all the commands Paul listed in verses 9-21, which is the most difficult for you to obey? Why?

■ **ILLUSTRATIONS:**

So That You May Discern. A television news camera crew was on assignment in southern Florida filming the widespread destruction of Hurricane Andrew. In one scene, amid the devastation and debris stood one house on its foundation. The owner was cleaning up the yard when a reporter approached him.

"Sir, why is your house the only one still standing?" asked the reporter. "How did you manage to escape the severe damage of the hurricane?"

"I built this house myself," the man replied. "I also built it according to the

Florida state building code. When the code called for 2' x 6' roof trusses, I used 2' x 6' roof trusses. I was told that a house built according to code could withstand a hurricane. I did, and it did. I suppose no one else around here followed the code."

When the sun is shining and the skies are blue, building our lives on something other than the guidance of God's Word can be tempting. But there's only one way to be ready for a storm. Heed the teachings and admonitions of our Lord.

Not to Think of Yourself More Highly. In "Letters to Rulers of People," Francis of Assisi wrote these words:

> Keep a clear eye toward life's end. Do not forget your purpose and destiny as God's creature. What you are in His sight is what you are and nothing more. Remember, that when you leave this earth, you can take nothing that you have received—fading symbols of honor, trappings of power—but only what you have given: a full heart enriched by honest service, love, sacrifice, and courage.

Let Love Be Genuine. John Wesley Zwomunondiita Kurewa, writing for *Biblical Proclamation for Africa Today,* says he actually first heard this story in a Nazarene camp meeting when he was a child. But he had forgotten it, and it seems even better now than when he first heard it.

The story is told of a young woman who had heard people talking about an interesting book that had just been published. She took the trouble to look for the book in bookshops until she secured a copy for herself. After reading the introduction and the first chapter of the book, however, she put it away. It did not seem interesting to her.

A few months later, the young woman was traveling in a foreign country. She met a handsome young man, and she fell in love with him. To her pleasant surprise, the young man was the author of the book that she had bought and put away. Upon returning home, she found the book and started reading it from the introduction to the end. This time, it was the most interesting book she had ever read in her life.

FOR YOUTH

■ TOPIC: Living the Christian Life

■ QUESTIONS: 1. According to Romans 12:1, what is the ultimate way we can worship and serve God? 2. How is God going about the renewing of your mind right now? 3. What does genuine love look like? 4. What is the proper response, according to Paul, when someone treats us badly? 5. Of all the commands Paul listed in 12:9-21, which do you consider the toughest to obey? Why that particular one?

■ **ILLUSTRATIONS:**

Acceptable to God. In a *Power for Living* devotional, Jamie Buckingham writes about how Fred Craddock, while lecturing at Yale University, told of going back home one summer to Gatlinburg, Tennessee, to take a short vacation with his wife. One night they found a quiet little restaurant where they looked forward to a private meal—just the two of them.

While the couple was waiting for their meal, they noticed a distinguished looking, white-haired man moving from table to table, visiting guests. Craddock whispered to his wife, "I hope he doesn't come over here." He didn't want the man to intrude on their privacy. But the man did come by his table.

"Where are you folks from?" the old fellow asked amicably.

"Oklahoma."

"Splendid state, I hear, although I've never been there. What do you do for a living?

"I teach homiletics at the graduate seminary of Phillips University."

"Oh, so you teach preachers, do you. Well, I've got a story I want to tell you." And with that he pulled up a chair and sat down at the table with Craddock and his wife. Dr. Craddock said he groaned inwardly: *Oh no, here comes another preacher story. It seems everyone has one.*

The man stuck out his hand. "I'm Ben Hooper. I was born not far from here across the mountains. My mother wasn't married when I was born so I had a hard time. When I started to school, my classmates had a name for me, and it wasn't a very nice name. I used to go off by myself at recess and during lunch time because the taunts of my playmates cut so deeply.

"What was worse was going downtown on Saturday afternoon and feeling every eye burning a hole through you. They were all wondering just who my real father was.

"When I was about 12 years old, a new preacher came to our church. I would always go in late and slip out early. But one day the preacher said the benediction so fast I got caught and had to walk out with the crowd. I could feel every eye in church on me. Just about the time I got to the door I felt a big hand on my shoulder. I looked up and the preacher was looking right at me.

"'Who are you, son? Whose boy are you?' he bellowed.

"I felt the old weight come on me. It was like a big black cloud. Even the preacher was putting me down.

"But as he looked down at me, studying my face, he began to smile a big smile of recognition. 'Wait a minute,' he said. 'I know who you are. I see the family resemblance. You are a child of God!'

"With that he slapped me across the back and said, 'Boy, you've got a great inheritance. Go and claim it!'"

The old fellow looked across the table at Fred Craddock and said, "That was the most important single sentence ever said to me." With that he smiled, shook the hands of Craddock and his wife, and moved on to another table to greet old friends.

Suddenly, Fred Craddock remembered some old state history lessons. On two occasions the people of Tennessee had elected a born-out-of-wedlock individual to be their governor. One of them, he remembered, was a man by the name of Ben Hooper.

Be Patient in Suffering. In his book *Deep Down*, Tim Riter tells how George's first job as a landscape contractor was to remove a large oak stump from a farmer's field. He also was using dynamite for the first time. With the farmer watching, George tried to hide his nervousness by carefully calculating the size of the stump, the proper amount of dynamite, and where to place it.

Finally, George and the farmer moved to the detonator behind his pickup truck. With a silent prayer, George plunged the detonator. The stump gracefully rose through the air and then crashed on the cab of the truck. George gazed in despair at the ruined cab, but the farmer was all admiration.

"Son, with a little more practice, those stumps will land in the bed of the truck every time!"

DON'T JUDGE ONE ANOTHER

BACKGROUND SCRIPTURE: Romans 14:1-13; 15:5-6
DEVOTIONAL READING: James 4:7-12

KEY VERSES: May the God of steadfastness and encouragement grant you to live in harmony with one another, in accordance with Christ Jesus, so that together you may with one voice glorify the God and Father of our Lord Jesus Christ. Romans 15:5-6.

KING JAMES VERSION

ROMANS 14:1 Him that is weak in the faith receive ye, but not to doubtful disputations. 2 For one believeth that he may eat all things: another, who is weak, eateth herbs. 3 Let not him that eateth despise him that eateth not; and let not him which eateth not judge him that eateth: for God hath received him. 4 Who art thou that judgest another man's servant? to his own master he standeth or falleth. Yea, he shall be holden up: for God is able to make him stand. 5 One man esteemeth one day above another: another esteemeth every day alike. Let every man be fully persuaded in his own mind. 6 He that regardeth the day, regardeth it unto the Lord; and he that regardeth not the day, to the Lord he doth not regard it. He that eateth, eateth to the Lord, for he giveth God thanks; and he that eateth not, to the Lord he eateth not, and giveth God thanks. 7 For none of us liveth to himself, and no man dieth to himself. 8 For whether we live, we live unto the Lord; and whether we die, we die unto the Lord: whether we live therefore, or die, we are the Lord's. 9 For to this end Christ both died, and rose, and revived, that he might be Lord both of the dead and living. 10 But why dost thou judge thy brother? or why dost thou set at nought thy brother? for we shall all stand before the judgment seat of Christ. 11 For it is written, As I live, saith the Lord, every knee shall bow to me, and every tongue shall confess to God. 12 So then every one of us shall give account of himself to God. 13 Let us not therefore judge one another any more: but judge this rather, that no man put a stumblingblock or an occasion to fall in his brother's way. . . .

15:5 Now the God of patience and consolation grant you to be likeminded one toward another according to Christ Jesus: 6 That ye may with one mind and one mouth glorify God, even the Father of our Lord Jesus Christ.

NEW REVISED STANDARD VERSION

ROMANS 14:1 Welcome those who are weak in faith, but not for the purpose of quarreling over opinions. 2 Some believe in eating anything, while the weak eat only vegetables. 3 Those who eat must not despise those who abstain, and those who abstain must not pass judgment on those who eat; for God has welcomed them. 4 Who are you to pass judgment on servants of another? It is before their own lord that they stand or fall. And they will be upheld, for the Lord is able to make them stand.

5 Some judge one day to be better than another, while others judge all days to be alike. Let all be fully convinced in their own minds. 6 Those who observe the day, observe it in honor of the Lord. Also those who eat, eat in honor of the Lord, since they give thanks to God; while those who abstain, abstain in honor of the Lord and give thanks to God.

7 We do not live to ourselves, and we do not die to ourselves. 8 If we live, we live to the Lord, and if we die, we die to the Lord; so then, whether we live or whether we die, we are the Lord's. 9 For to this end Christ died and lived again, so that he might be Lord of both the dead and the living.

10 Why do you pass judgment on your brother or sister? Or you, why do you despise your brother or sister? For we will all stand before the judgment seat of God. 11 For it is written,

"As I live, says the Lord, every knee shall bow to me,
and every tongue shall give praise to God."

12 So then, each of us will be accountable to God.

13 Let us therefore no longer pass judgment on one another, but resolve instead never to put a stumbling block or hindrance in the way of another. . . .

15:5 May the God of steadfastness and encouragement grant you to live in harmony with one another, in accordance with Christ Jesus, 6 so that together you may with one voice glorify the God and Father of our Lord Jesus Christ.

Monday, April 18	James 4:7-12	*Speak No Evil Against One Another*
Tuesday, April 19	James 5:7-12	*Do Not Grumble Against One Another*
Wednesday, April 20	Romans 14:1-6	*Do Not Judge One Another*
Thursday, April 21	Romans 14:7-13	*Each Will Be Accountable to God*
Friday, April 22	Romans 14:14-18	*Do Not Ruin Another Through Food*
Saturday, April 23	Romans 14:19-23	*Do Not Make Another Stumble*
Sunday, April 24	Romans 15:1-6	*Live in Harmony with One Another*

BACKGROUND

The practical portion of Paul's letter to the Romans that he began in chapter 12 continues in chapter 14. Having listed duties that arise from the foundation of faith in chapters 12 and 13, Paul next addressed a dire issue that had come before the church at Rome. The issue revolved around the same relationship that the apostle had already devoted so many of his words to—that of the relationship between the Jewish Christians and the Gentile Christians in the church.

The issues arose within the church because of the Jewish Christians' longing to continue to observe and practice the Mosaic law and their traditions. Paul's approach toward the matter was that there was nothing at all wrong with the Jewish Christians continuing to observe their dietary and festival laws and customs; he did consider it wrong, however, when the Jewish Christians tried to press the Gentile Christians to adhere to the Jewish traditions and ceremonies. Paul knew that what his readers believed would affect how they thought and acted. Thus, the apostle tried to settle the issue in a way that would be amicable to both sides, in a way that the unity between the Jewish and Gentile Christians would be preserved and solidified rather than broken apart.

Apparently, some of the Jewish Christians in the church at Rome had misgivings—due to their adherence to certain dietary customs—about eating meat, about observing the Sabbath, and about drinking certain beverages. The temptation to stress these practices that were unique to the Jewish Christians' identity was probably both immense and intense.

Paul undoubtedly knew the teaching of Jesus in Matthew 15:11, "*it is not what goes into the mouth that defiles a person.*" That's why the apostle regarded the observance of Jewish dietary customs as being optional. Paul referred to those who felt bound by these rules as being *weak in faith* (Rom. 14:1), and he called those who felt free not to observe these customs *strong* (15:1).

Paul urged the weak in faith not to censure other believers who did not abide by their dietary restrictions. And the apostle cautioned the strong in faith not to look down on believers who felt obligated to observe particular Jewish customs (14:3). The most important matter was for each group to welcome and love the other unconditionally. They were to avoid causing their fellow Christians to stumble and aim for harmony in the church (14:13, 15-16).

Notes on the Printed Text

Paul stressed to his readers that Christians could legitimately differ over certain peripheral issues and still associate with one another. Therefore, those who recognized their full liberty in Christ should not put down other believers who were more exacting in their behavior; instead, the strong should unconditionally welcome their weaker brothers and sisters in the *faith* (Rom. 14:1).

Paul explained that some believers were confident enough in Christ to eat *anything* (14:2). They realized that the truth of the Gospel liberated them from having to observe the Old Testament dietary restrictions. There were other believers, however, who did not have the same level of assurance. They thus limited their diet to only vegetables.

Believers who recognized their freedom in Christ were not to think less of their weaker associates in the faith. Likewise, Christians who restricted their diet due to sincere personal convictions were not to censure those who did not abide by the same regulations. Each group was to accept unconditionally the other, for God equally loved and *welcomed* (14:3) all who trusted in Christ.

In 14:4, Paul asked his readers who among them had the right to evaluate and censure the morally neutral behavior of others. Clearly, none of them had such authority. The reason is that all Christians serve the same Master. Only He could legitimately and impartially determine who did what was right or wrong. Paul was confident the Lord would ensure His people did what was proper, for He loved them enough to help them do so.

Paul next directed his attention to the issue of observing certain holy days, such as the Sabbath as well as times of fasting and feasting. There were some Christians in the church at Rome who genuinely felt one day was more special than others. Contrastingly, there were believers who did not hold to such distinctions among the days of the week; instead, they viewed every day as being equally sacred. In their minds each day was to be dedicated in wholehearted service to God (14:5).

Paul said each group should act in accordance with their personal convictions. For example, the believers who were convinced that one day was more important than another did so to honor and serve *the Lord* (14:6). Likewise, Christians who were assured that it was proper to *eat* meat did so to glorify God, for they consumed the food with a heart of gratitude. Those who, out of personal conviction, refrained from eating meat also sought to *honor* God with a thankful attitude.

In 14:7, Paul explained that the strong and weak believers at Rome did not *live* only for themselves. Similarly, they did not *die* with only themselves in mind. God created them, and thus their foremost goal was to please Him in everything they did. Despite their minor differences, each group together sought to honor and serve the Lord both in life and death. Regardless of whether they lived or died, Jesus' disciples belonged to Him and thus existed to do His will (14:8).

The supreme lordship of Christ was a key issue for Paul (14:9). He stated that Jesus *died and lived again* so that He might be sovereign over all people, regardless of whether they lived or died. In light of these truths, Paul asked the weak Christians at Rome why they censured their stronger associates in the faith. Similarly, the apostle wanted to know why the strong Christians depreciated others who scrupulously observed certain requirements of the law. Both types of behavior were unacceptable because every Christian would one day *stand before the judgment seat of God* (14:10).

In 14:11, Paul quoted from Isaiah 49:18 and 45:23 to support his point. The Lord vowed that everyone would bow before Him in submission and praise His name. Thus, every person would one day give an account to God for their actions (Rom. 14:12). Believers, therefore, had no business trying to usurp God's authority as Judge.

Paul stressed the importance of believers neither denouncing nor despising their fellow Christians. What each believer did was the more important issue (14:13). They were to resolve not to upset or impede anyone's faith by their actions. The strong would be guilty of harming others if, by what they did, they encouraged the weak to become ensnared in that which they considered to be sinful.

In Romans 15, Paul stressed the importance of accommodating and accepting one another in Christ. This would foster unity and growth among believers with differing views on nonessential practices. The Lord, of course, ultimately enabled His people to be patient and joyful in the midst of difficulties.

Paul thus prayed in 15:5 that *God* would help the believers at Rome to remain united and at peace *with one another* as they followed the Savior. Paul knew there would continue to be differences of opinion over matters not specifically dealt with in Scripture; but if unity within the church at Rome prevailed, everyone in the congregation would be joined together in praising *the God and Father of our Lord Jesus Christ* (15:6).

SUGGESTIONS TO TEACHERS

Though Paul taught that the church should be uncompromising in its stand against activities that are specifically prohibited by Scripture, he did not want the church to be bound by additional rules and regulations of its own creation. Thus he called the church to be open-minded, compassionate, and accepting of the thoughts and opinions of those who trusted in Christ for salvation. We would do well to practice this compassionate understanding and openness in the church today.

1. SHARE IDEAS. Go beyond the willingness to share your ideas with others; also be open to encouraging and having others share their ideas with you. Listen carefully, and make the decision to respect what others say before they even say it. As we share our ideas and opinions, we will grow to have a fuller, more thorough understanding of what the Bible teaches.

2. ALLOW FOR DIFFERENCES OF OPINION. Of course, you'll never agree with all the opinions that others express to you. That would be impossible!

But allow for differences of opinion even when you think others are incorrect. At least try to understand the basis for the opinions of others. And respect the person even if you can't accept his or her opinion.

3. LEARN YOUR STRENGTHS AND WEAKNESSES. We all have areas of our lives in which we are "strong Christians" and other areas of our lives in which we are "weak Christians." Therefore, it is vitally important to take inventory of ourselves to find out what are our strengths and weaknesses. Our faith is strong in an area if we can survive contact with worldly people without falling into their patterns. It is weak in an area if we must avoid certain activities, people, or places in order to protect our spiritual life.

4. TAKE A SELF-INVENTORY. It is important to take self-inventory in order to find out our strengths and weaknesses. In areas of strength, we should not fear being defiled by the world; rather, we should go and serve God. And in areas of weakness, we need to be cautious. If we have a strong faith and shelter it, we are not as effective for the Lord as we otherwise could be. And if we have a weak faith but expose it, we are being extremely foolish. In each case, both wisdom and caution are important to maintain.

5. BE ACCOUNTABLE TO CHRIST. It is perfectly acceptable—and even beneficial—to be accountable to other Christians who agree to talk with us about and help us work through our serving and living for Christ. Such accountability should never slip into judgmentalism of the kind the Jewish and Gentile Christians were practicing against one another in Rome. Ultimately, all of us will give a personal account to Christ for our lives. He alone knows our hearts and our motivation, and only He knows whether we are truly committed to Him.

FOR ADULTS

■ **TOPIC:** Living in Harmony
■ **QUESTIONS:** 1. What do you think was causing disunity among the believers living in Rome? 2. Why do you think Paul referred to some of the Christians as "weak" and to others as "strong"? 3. What effect can quarreling over opinions have in the church? 4. What principles should guide us when we are dealing with differences of opinion on matters that do not violate our Christian faith and morality? 5. How does the fact that we all belong to the Lord help us to stifle the temptation to judge our fellow believers?

■ **ILLUSTRATIONS:**

To Pass Judgment on Servants of Another. A frail old man went to live with his son, daughter-in-law, and four-year-old grandson. The old man's hands trembled, his eyesight was blurred, and his step faltered.

The family ate together at the table, but the elderly grandfather's shaky hands and failing sight made eating difficult. Peas rolled off his spoon and onto the floor. When he grasped his glass, milk spilled on the tablecloth.

The son and daughter-in-law became irritated with the mess. "We must do something about Grandfather!" blurted the son. "I've had enough of the spilled milk, noisy eating, and food on the floor." So, the husband and wife set a small table in the corner. There Grandfather ate alone, while the rest of the family enjoyed dinner. Since Grandfather had broken a dish or two, his food was served in a wooden bowl.

When the family glanced in Grandfather's direction, sometimes he had a tear in his eye, especially as he sat alone. Still, the only words the couple had for him were sharp admonitions, especially when he dropped a fork or spilled food. The four-year-old watched it all in silence.

One evening, before supper, the father noticed his son playing with wood scraps on the floor. He asked the child sweetly, "What are you making?" Just as sweetly, the boy responded, "Oh, I am making a little bowl for Papa and Mama to eat their food in when I grow up." The four-year-old smiled and went back to work.

The words so struck the parents that they were speechless. Then tears started to stream down their cheeks. Though no word was spoken, both knew what must be done. That evening, the husband took Grandfather's hand and gently led him back to the family table. For the remainder of his days, he ate every meal with the family. And, for some reason, neither husband nor wife seemed to care any longer when a fork was dropped, milk was spilled, or the tablecloth was soiled.

Children are remarkably perceptive. Their eyes ever observe, their ears ever listen, and their minds ever process the messages they absorb. If they see us patiently provide a happy home atmosphere for family members, they will imitate that attitude for the rest of their lives. The wise parents realize that every day the building blocks are being laid for their child's future.

We Do Not Live to Ourselves. A Russian tradition that was neglected for decades is bringing families to Christ. The Supper of Love, which brought families together on holidays and weeknights to drink tea, give gifts, sing, pray, and talk about God, is being revived, the Slavic Gospel Association reports. It helped church members get to know each other better and helped new Christians learn more about God by talking with mature believers, the ministry said.

A Baptist church in Omsk revived the tradition and gave it an evangelistic twist. It invited 15 married couples, some of whom were not Christians, to attend a series of suppers at the church that included video seminars on married life and a lively discussion. Many questions about God came up, allowing the Christian couples to offer answers.

The meetings have grown swiftly because members invited their families and friends to attend. Four groups of 30 to 40 members meet weekly, and an outreach to the families of deaf people has 15 members. On Mother's Day of 2000, more than 300 people came to the church to hear seminars on family life, while their children attended evangelistic plays and concerts.

■ **TOPIC:** Just Because We Disagree . . .

■ **QUESTIONS:** 1. Why do you think maintaining unity is so essential in the church? 2. Instead of our fellow believers, what should occupy our time and energy? 3. What do you think are some of your "strengths" and "weaknesses"? 4. In what ways do you belong to the Lord? 5. How can you make sure that your decisions and actions are *in honor of the Lord* (Rom. 14:6)?

■ **ILLUSTRATIONS:**

Quarreling over Opinions. The story is told of a wise master strolling through the streets with his students. When they came to the city square, a vicious battle was being fought between government troops and rebel forces. Horrified by the bloodshed, the students implored, "Quick, Master, which side should we help?"

"Both," the master replied. The students were confused. "Both?" they demanded. "Why should we help both?" The master replied, "We need to help the authorities learn to listen to the people, and we need to help the rebels learn not to always reject authority."

Before Their Own Lord. Christians are finding a ready mission field at what has been called the country's wildest "party school." Louisiana State University (LSU), cited in 2000 for that dubious distinction by the *Princeton Review*, has ministries that are rising to the challenge. Campus groups at the 31,000-student school in Baton Rouge are serving students in practical ways and sharing the Gospel.

LSU is not much different than most universities, Campus Crusade for Christ's Charley Clary told *Religion Today*. "Drinking is a problem, but not more than at the other universities where I have worked for the past 19 years." Every school has its element of partygoers, but many who get involved are just following the crowd, said Kirk Priest of Chi Alpha, an Assemblies of God ministry. "It's key to reach [the second group] before they are sucked into the lifestyle," he said.

Chi Alpha runs a coffee shop on Chimes Street outside the north gate of LSU. Bars dot the area, and students crowd the streets on weekend nights, making the rounds. On Friday nights Chi Alpha members go into the streets telling people about Jesus Christ. "We find many people who really don't want to be there, but they just got sucked in," Priest said. He noted that a number of students become Christians every week.

Evangelism outside the bars is sometimes confrontational. "We tell them that they are not only hurting themselves, they are also offending God," Priest said. He noted that ministries aren't seeking only the partyers. They also reach out to athletes, residents of dorms and fraternity houses, and international students.

Chi Alpha helped hundreds of incoming freshman move into their dorms, Priest remarked. Volunteers helped carry furniture and boxes into the rooms, and distributed packets containing candy and information about the ministry. They formed relationships with the new students and invited them to a barbecue with a live band the next day.

Some students mistakenly think Chi Alpha is a Christian fraternity. The group held a "rush party" [RU Serving Him] with bands and free food and drink, Priest said. The ministry serves the approximately 3,000 international students at LSU. "They have direct needs, like where can they find financial aid, or furniture, or clothes," Priest noted. The group works with local churches.

There are about 1,000 Christian students actively participating in campus ministry in several groups at LSU, Priest reported. They meet in cell groups in their dorms and apartment complexes, and many take part in evangelistic activities, he added.

Despite their reputation as partyers, LSU students show more respect for religious beliefs than students at some other schools, several campus ministers said. Many students have a Christian background and politely listen to the message of the Gospel. Some haven't understood that they can have a personal relationship with Christ, and embrace that message when they hear it, Clary noted.

"In a given year we see more people come to Christ than on any other campus where I have worked," Clary remarked. "Every semester we see people trusting Christ." College students are "at a critical juncture" of life and need to hear about Christ, Clary reported. "They are away from Mom and Dad for the first time, they are choosing their vocations and, often, they are choosing their lifelong mates. We want to be there to give them the Gospel."

No Other Gospel

Background Scripture: Galatians 1
Devotional Reading: Acts 13:26-33

Key Verse: For I want you to know, brothers and sisters, that the gospel that was proclaimed by me is not of human origin. Galatians 1:11.

KING JAMES VERSION

GALATIANS 1:1 Paul, an apostle, (not of men, neither by man, but by Jesus Christ, and God the Father, who raised him from the dead;) 2 And all the brethren which are with me, unto the churches of Galatia:
3 Grace be to you and peace from God the Father, and from our Lord Jesus Christ, 4 Who gave himself for our sins, that he might deliver us from this present evil world, according to the will of God and our Father:
5 To whom be glory for ever and ever. Amen.

6 I marvel that ye are so soon removed from him that called you into the grace of Christ unto another gospel: 7 Which is not another; but there be some that trouble you, and would pervert the gospel of Christ. 8 But though we, or an angel from heaven, preach any other gospel unto you than that which we have preached unto you, let him be accursed. 9 As we said before, so say I now again, If any man preach any other gospel unto you than that ye have received, let him be accursed.

10 For do I now persuade men, or God? or do I seek to please men? for if I yet pleased men, I should not be the servant of Christ. 11 But I certify you, brethren, that the gospel which was preached of me is not after man. 12 For I neither received it of man, neither was I taught it, but by the revelation of Jesus Christ.

NEW REVISED STANDARD VERSION

GALATIANS 1:1 Paul an apostle—sent neither by human commission nor from human authorities, but through Jesus Christ and God the Father, who raised him from the dead— 2 and all the members of God's family who are with me,

To the churches of Galatia:

3 Grace to you and peace from God our Father and the Lord Jesus Christ, 4 who gave himself for our sins to set us free from the present evil age, according to the will of our God and Father, 5 to whom be the glory forever and ever. Amen.

6 I am astonished that you are so quickly deserting the one who called you in the grace of Christ and are turning to a different gospel— 7 not that there is another gospel, but there are some who are confusing you and want to pervert the gospel of Christ. 8 But even if we or an angel from heaven should proclaim to you a gospel contrary to what we proclaimed to you, let that one be accursed! 9 As we have said before, so now I repeat, if anyone proclaims to you a gospel contrary to what you received, let that one be accursed!

10 Am I now seeking human approval, or God's approval? Or am I trying to please people? If I were still pleasing people, I would not be a servant of Christ.

11 For I want you to know, brothers and sisters, that the gospel that was proclaimed by me is not of human origin; 12 for I did not receive it from a human source, nor was I taught it, but I received it through a revelation of Jesus Christ.

9

Monday, April 25	2 Corinthians 11:1-15	*Do Not Be Led Astray*
Tuesday, April 26	Colossians 1:15-23	*In Christ All Things Hold Together*
Wednesday, April 27	Acts 13:26-33	*We Bring You the Good News*
Thursday, April 28	Acts 13:34-41	*Everyone Who Believes Is Set Free*
Friday, April 29	Acts 13:44-49	*Bring Salvation to All*
Saturday, April 30	Galatians 1:1-7	*Do Not Turn to Another Gospel*
Sunday, May 1	Galatians 1:8-12	*Only One Gospel Directly from God*

BACKGROUND

Many Bible scholars have called Paul's letter to the Galatians the "Magna Carta of Christian Liberty." What gave rise to the apostle's stringent teaching on Christian liberty was the churches' question about whether the Gentiles must convert to Judaism and observe the Mosaic law before they could be regarded as true believers. Legalistic members of these churches accused Paul of downplaying the importance of the law in order to make his message more appealing to the Gentiles.

These opponents of the apostle became known as "Judaizers." They taught that, in order for the Gentiles to become truly Christian, they had to submit to Jewish laws and customs. Heading the list for the Judaizers was the Gentiles' need to be circumcised. Paul followed the Jewish laws and customs; nevertheless, he adamantly opposed the efforts of the Judaizers to force Gentile converts to the faith to heed these requirements. In the Letter to the Galatians, the apostle repeatedly stressed that we are saved and justified by faith, not by keeping the law.

In the time of Paul, Galatia was a large Roman province located on the central plateau of Asia Minor (present-day Turkey). The name *Galatia* was introduced in 278 B.C. when a large number of Gauls migrated to the region from Europe. The area received full provincial status in 25 B.C. Paul visited Galatia on his first missionary journey, evangelizing the sophisticated, multiracial towns of Iconium, Antioch, Lystra, and Derbe (Acts 13:14—14:23). Later, Paul returned to strengthen the faith of the converts.

Paul's first mission through the province of Galatia evidently took place while he was suffering from an illness (Gal. 4:13). The circumstances created a close bond between the churches and Paul, and they treated him like an angel of God. They were his spiritual children, and with fatherly concern he longed for them to resist false teachers and grow toward spiritual maturity. That is why he was upset with them when some of them began to turn away from him and his teachings.

Certainly none of God's servants has ever held the Gospel more faithfully in his trust than Paul. In his years of seeking to be justified through observance of the law, Paul had found no salvation; but when he trusted in Christ, he received eternal life. That's why Paul became such an ardent preacher of the Gospel, stressing its great power to change people's lives.

After Paul's initial ministry to the Galatians, a heresy arose in the churches that threatened the purity of the gospel message. False teachers wanted to enslave God's people to legalistic Judaism. The spiritual frauds won support for their teaching by discrediting the message of grace that Paul had declared. Part of the frauds' strategy was to undermine the authority of Paul and the authenticity of his message.

Paul wasted no time in dealing with the question of his authority. He declared that no mere human chose or appointed him to his work. The Father and the Son had selected Paul to be *an apostle* (Gal. 1:1). Two aspects of Paul's apostleship were unique. First, he had not received his commission to preach from any church body or from other apostles. His authority came directly from God through Christ. Second, Paul was the only apostle commissioned by Jesus after He rose from the dead. With the exception of Matthais, the Lord commissioned the others before His death. Although Matthais became an apostle after Christ's resurrection, other church leaders appointed him to that position (Acts 1:26).

During Paul's outreach into Galatia, many opposed his efforts and persecuted him. He had put his life on the line to bring the Good News to the people of that region. He understandably was concerned that those whom he had won to Christ were abandoning the doctrine of grace. In their backslidden state, the Galatians strove to maintain God's favor and peace by human effort through lawkeeping. That is why Paul and his fellow believers endeavored to defend the Gospel to *the churches of Galatia* (Gal. 1:2).

Paul's awareness of the heresy being spread prompted him to emphasize God's grace and peace, which He made available through faith in *Christ* (1:3). *Grace* refers to the Lord's unmerited favor and blessings. We have everlasting *peace* when we receive God's favor and blessings by trusting in Christ.

By emphasizing their own good deeds, the Galatians had unknowingly discredited Christ's redeeming work. To counter this situation, Paul declared that Jesus obeyed the Father by giving Himself as a sacrifice for our sins. Those who placed their trust in Christ were rescued from this *present evil age* (1:4). The implication of this truth is clear. God alone was to be glorified for the sacrifice of Christ (1:5).

God had called the believers in Galatia to follow Him, and His summons was issued through His grace in Christ. Paul accordingly was shocked that the Galatian Christians were already abandoning the Gospel for a false message about salvation (1:6). Although there was only one true message, spiritual frauds had insisted otherwise. They distorted the Gospel, and their perverted message confused the Galatian believers (1:7).

Paul declared his disgust with those who misrepresented the Good News and troubled God's people. The apostle prayed that the Lord would eternally condemn anyone who heralded an unbiblical message of salvation. It did not matter whether that person was an ordained minister or an angel from heaven (1:8).

The term *accursed* comes from the Greek word *anathema*. The term originally referred to a pagan temple offering in payment for a vow, but later came to represent a curse. The word also relates to a Hebrew word signifying something devoted to complete destruction. Paul's great concern for the advance of biblical truth led him to wish total destruction on those perverting the message.

Paul felt so strongly about the matter that he repeated his terse rebuke. It was his hope that God would punish anyone who preached anything different from the Gospel the Christians at Galatia had already believed (1:9). The apostle was saying that those who added any additional requirements to the Good News were under the Lord's condemnation. Regardless of their credentials, they did not have the authority to twist the truth.

Paul included himself among those who had no right to preach any other gospel. Because he did this, no one could level the charge that he was merely jealous of the legalists who had won the hearts of the people. Paul was not motivated by jealously when he called for exclusive acceptance of the Gospel that he preached; rather, it was because the Good News made no provision for any other message.

The frauds accused Paul of declaring a wishy-washy, easy-to-follow gospel. They also censured him for requiring neither circumcision nor obedience to any of the other laws of Moses. Finally, Paul's opponents claimed that he had rebelled against the Jerusalem apostles, who supposedly had given him his authority and message. In response, Paul declared that he was not trying to make people accept him (1:10). His primary goal was to please God through his proclamation of the Gospel. God's *approval*, not man's, was the apostle's main concern. If Paul's ambition was to *please people*, he would not be a true *servant of Christ*.

Paul wanted the Galatians to know that the message he preached did not originate with any person (1:11); also, the Good News he declared was not based on mere human logic. The apostle's message was directly revealed by Christ when He appeared to Paul (1:12). His authority was confirmed by the Jerusalem apostles.

SUGGESTIONS TO TEACHERS

Paul became an apostle through the call of God. And the Lord commissioned him to preach the Good News to the lost. Paul taught that people can only be saved through faith in Christ, not by good works; and Paul refused to deviate from this message, regardless of how much others pressured him to do so.

1. A WORRISOME DEVELOPMENT. Tragically, the churches of Galatia were guilty of turning from divine grace to good works in the hope of being justified and sanctified. Paul therefore admonished them to accept only the gospel of grace and to reject the distorted message of the false teachers.

2. SPEAKING THE TRUTH. Satan is a master of deception. He hates the gospel of Christ, and the devil will do anything he can to distort and undermine it. As believers it is our job to do just the opposite—to proclaim the true Gospel. Correspondingly, we are to speak the truth in love so that those around us will have the opportunity to hear and understand God's plan of salvation by grace through faith in Christ.

3. REMAINING COMMITTED. Both inside and outside the church the presence of commitment is seriously lacking. People shun commitment because they think it will prevent them from doing what they want. This attitude is extremely harmful among Christians who profess to believe in the vital doctrines of the faith. For example, a lack of commitment to the truth of the Gospel can lead to spiritual confusion. It is only when we, as believers, preserve the integrity of the Good News that the doctrinal foundation of the church will stand against the attacks of spiritual frauds.

FOR ADULTS

■ TOPIC: Hanging on to God's Good News

■ QUESTIONS: 1. Why did Paul emphasize the divine origin of his apostolic commission? 2. Why did Paul feel the necessity of reminding the Galatians of God's grace and peace? 3. What astonished Paul concerning his readers? 4. Why did Paul refuse to seek human approval? 5. How did Paul receive the gospel message he proclaimed?

■ **ILLUSTRATIONS:**

A Single Aim. Some time ago my daughter, Gracie, came in the house crying because someone had trimmed the tree she likes to climb so much. She calls it "Mytree." When I confessed that I was the culprit, she was none too happy with me. To her, it looked as though there was a good climbing branch or two that had been taken away, leaving the tree not quite as full as it had been.

Gracie was especially upset that I might have hurt "Mytree." When her anger had died down a bit, I took her outside to examine the tree. I showed her how dead branches needlessly sapped the tree of its strength. I explained that the tree's nourishment was being misdirected. I told her how I had cut the branches to help the tree, not to hurt it.

Then we walked around in the yard looking at the very hardy dogwood trees. We examined these trees with single, slender trunks and rich green leaves on every branch, just teeming with life. But then I took Gracie to a spot where about 18 dogwood shoots were growing all in one place. After all these years of living in the parsonage, I've never made the hard decision to trim back 17 of those shoots so that one could grow into a full tree. Right now these shoots are all bunched together; for years they have hardly grown at all. Some of them have already died. Most of the others look sickly and weak. Those dogwood shoots are too distracted to grow. They don't have a single aim. Their strength is divided up. Their purpose is self-reliant. They are not centered in a single source.

Those dogwood shoots were like the legalists in the churches of Galatia. To them, salvation came through believing in Christ *and* observing their regulations and customs. Paul reminded his readers that Christ—and Him alone—is the sole source of our salvation.

Sermon in a Carving. While in a quaint old church outside Winchester, England, a visitor was studying a Bible resting on an old carved oak lectern. He had noticed that in nearly all old English churches, the lectern was shaped like an eagle. The pulpit in this sanctuary was also shaped like a huge eagle, except that the bird had the beak of a parrot. While examining the odd beak on the eagle, the visitor more-over noticed that a small heart was carved on the head of the eagle. The perplexed tourist asked the attendant why the lectern had the parrot's beak and the little carved heart.

"You must understand," stated the attendant, "that this ancient eagle was carved this way to remind everyone who reads the holy Word to us not to do so mechanically like a parrot, but fervently from the heart." This reminds us that when we study God's Word, we must not merely mouth the words in parrot-like fashion, but read them from the heart!

FOR YOUTH
■ TOPIC: Only One Gospel
■ QUESTIONS: 1. Why did Jesus give Himself on the cross for our sins? 2. In what way had the Galatians become confused? 3. What did Paul wish for those who perverted the truth of the Gospel? 4. Why did Paul refuse to make people-pleasing his goal? 5. Why did Paul stress that he did not receive the message he preached from any human source?

■ **ILLUSTRATIONS:**

The Main Thing. The story is told of a woman who bought a parrot to keep her company. Sadly, the woman ran into trouble, and thus she decided to return the bird the next day.

"This bird doesn't talk," the woman told the pet store owner.

"Does he have a mirror in his cage?" the pet store owner asked. "Parrots love mirrors. They see their reflection and often times that helps them to start a conversation." So the woman bought a mirror and left.

The next day the woman returned; the bird still wasn't talking.

"How about a ladder? Parrots love ladders. A happy parrot is a talkative parrot." So the woman bought a ladder and left.

But the next day, the woman was back. "Does your parrot have a swing? No? Well, that's the problem. Once he starts swinging, he'll talk up a storm." So the woman reluctantly bought a swing and left.

When the woman walked into the store the next day, her countenance had completely changed. "The parrot died," she blurted.

The pet store owner was shocked. "I am so sorry, ma'am. Tell me, did he ever say a word?" he asked.

"Yes," the woman replied. "Right before he died, he did. In a weak voice, he asked me, 'Don't they sell any food at that pet store?'"

The legalists in the churches of Galatia seem to have forgotten the main thing. Salvation through Jesus Christ and Him alone is the main thing.

Not All Traditions Are Good. The frauds plaguing the Galatians wanted them to embrace the practice of legalistic traditions as a necessary requirement for being saved. This is a case where rites and rituals threatened to undermine the faith of a thriving community of believers. It should come as no surprise that even today not all traditions are good. They can hurt you and others as well.

I'm reminded of our dog, who has certain traditions. In the last couple of months, he's even picked up a new one. We now have two dogs: Bonhoeffer, our wise and thoughtful four-year-old collie, and Oreo, our wild and crazy one-year-old mutt. Bonhoeffer has always been very good about letting us know when he wants to go outside. He will casually walk up to the door that leads to the parsonage's side yard and scratch the door three times. Whenever we open the door, Oreo shoots outside like a flying flash—way ahead of Bonhoeffer, who casually walks down the steps and out into the yard.

For the sake of this story, you also need to know that sometimes Oreo drives Bonhoeffer absolutely nuts! Oreo nips at Bonhoeffer's heals and jumps up on his head and bites his ears and steals his chew bone and steps on his tail and wakes him up while he's trying to take a nap. I'm amazed that Bonhoeffer hasn't killed that little puppy. It says a lot about the patience of that dog just by mentioning the fact that he's never even hurt Oreo.

But back to Bonhoeffer's new tradition. There are times when Bonhoeffer has taken all that he can from Oreo. (In the words of Popeye, "I've stands all I can stands and I can't stands no more!") Now when Bonhoeffer reaches the limit of his patience, he walks over to the door and scratches it three times. While Bonhoeffer stands at the door waiting to go out, we open the door. Out shoots Oreo like a flying flash. Then Bonhoeffer looks up in our eyes, breathes a sigh of relief that Oreo is outside, and walks over to the couch and lays down! He's achieved his goal of getting rid of his pest, and now he can get some rest for just a little while!

ALL SAVED BY FAITH

BACKGROUND SCRIPTURE: Galatians 2:15—3:5
DEVOTIONAL READING: Galatians 3:6-14

KEY VERSE: The life I now live in the flesh I live by faith in the
Son of God, who loved me and gave himself for me. Galatians 2:20.

KING JAMES VERSION

GALATIANS 2:15 We who are Jews by nature, and not sinners of the Gentiles, 16 Knowing that a man is not justified by the works of the law, but by the faith of Jesus Christ, even we have believed in Jesus Christ, that we might be justified by the faith of Christ, and not by the works of the law: for by the works of the law shall no flesh be justified. 17 But if, while we seek to be justified by Christ, we ourselves also are found sinners, is therefore Christ the minister of sin? God forbid. 18 For if I build again the things which I destroyed, I make myself a transgressor. 19 For I through the law am dead to the law, that I might live unto God. 20 I am crucified with Christ: nevertheless I live; yet not I, but Christ liveth in me: and the life which I now live in the flesh I live by the faith of the Son of God, who loved me, and gave himself for me. 21 I do not frustrate the grace of God: for if righteousness come by the law, then Christ is dead in vain.

3:1 O foolish Galatians, who hath bewitched you, that ye should not obey the truth, before whose eyes Jesus Christ hath been evidently set forth, crucified among you? 2 This only would I learn of you, Received ye the Spirit by the works of the law, or by the hearing of faith? 3 Are ye so foolish? having begun in the Spirit, are ye now made perfect by the flesh? 4 Have ye suffered so many things in vain? if it be yet in vain. 5 He therefore that ministereth to you the Spirit, and worketh miracles among you, doeth he it by the works of the law, or by the hearing of faith?

NEW REVISED STANDARD VERSION

GALATIANS 2:15 We ourselves are Jews by birth and not Gentile sinners; 16 yet we know that a person is justified not by the works of the law but through faith in Jesus Christ. And we have come to believe in Christ Jesus, so that we might be justified by faith in Christ, and not by doing the works of the law, because no one will be justified by the works of the law. 17 But if, in our effort to be justified in Christ, we ourselves have been found to be sinners, is Christ then a servant of sin? Certainly not! 18 But if I build up again the very things that I once tore down, then I demonstrate that I am a transgressor. 19 For through the law I died to the law, so that I might live to God. I have been crucified with Christ; 20 and it is no longer I who live, but it is Christ who lives in me. And the life I now live in the flesh I live by faith in the Son of God, who loved me and gave himself for me. 21 I do not nullify the grace of God; for if justification comes through the law, then Christ died for nothing.

3:1 You foolish Galatians! Who has bewitched you? It was before your eyes that Jesus Christ was publicly exhibited as crucified! 2 The only thing I want to learn from you is this: Did you receive the Spirit by doing the works of the law or by believing what you heard? 3 Are you so foolish? Having started with the Spirit, are you now ending with the flesh? 4 Did you experience so much for nothing?—if it really was for nothing. 5 Well then, does God supply you with the Spirit and work miracles among you by your doing the works of the law, or by your believing what you heard?

BACKGROUND

The exact location of the churches addressed in Galatians is a matter of debate that centers on two prominent theories. The North Galatian theory holds that Paul wrote the epistle for believers living in the old, ethnic area called Galatia in north-central Asia Minor. Although the Book of Acts does not mention Paul's journey there, supporters of this view believe that he visited the area on his second missionary journey and wrote the Letter to the Galatians shortly afterward, about A.D. 53–57.

The Southern Galatian theory suggests that Paul wrote Galatians to churches in the southern area of the Roman province of Galatia, in the cities of Antioch, Iconium, Lystra, and Derbe. We know that Paul founded churches there on his first missionary journey (Acts 13—14). Proponents of this view disagree whether Paul wrote Galatians before the Jerusalem Council (mentioned in Acts 15:1-29) or afterward. If the apostle wrote Galatians after the Council, it is surprising that he did not mention the event, as it dealt with the same issues that are covered in the epistle.

Of particular importance is Paul's conflict with Peter over the issue of Gentiles and the law. By refusing to fellowship with Gentile believers, Peter acted hypocritically. Rather than affirm the truth of the Gospel, he preferred to appease a group of legalistic Jews from Jerusalem.

Peter's action suggested that lawkeeping made people spiritually superior to others. But Paul argued in Galatians that the believer's union with Christ in His death frees him or her from the condemnation associated with the law. The apostle also said that the power of Christ's resurrection enabled the believer to live righteously.

NOTES ON THE PRINTED TEXT

The first part of Paul's strategy was to point out to Peter the inconsistency of his actions (Gal. 2:11-14). Peter was not alone in hypocrisy. The other Jewish Christians in the Antioch church, except Paul, were hypocrites in their actions. Paul thus broadened his speech to address all those who were Jews by birth, and not *Gentile sinners* (2:15). This phrase was the way Jews commonly referred to non-Jews.

For centuries legalistic Jews had believed they could make themselves accept-able to God by obeying the law; but they were mistaken. No one can perfectly keep *the law* (2:16), so no one can be *justified* by it. In fact, that was never the law's purpose.

The Jewish Christians at Antioch had learned this lesson. In addition, they had learned that sinners can be justified only through *faith in Christ*. Paul did not hes-itate to remind them of these truths. The implication is clear. It was not just Gentiles who needed Christ; Jews needed Him too.

While the Jewish Christians of Antioch knew that obedience to the law was ineffective in producing justification, the visiting Judaizers wanted to impose the law on Gentiles. Evidently the Judaizers thought the Gospel, when on its own, reveals one's sinfulness without revealing a way to avoid sinning. Thus, to them, the Gospel seemed to make Christ promote sin. Paul denied this claim (2:17).

Moreover, for Christians to revert to the Jewish law is really to break the law, for such a use of the law is really a misuse of it (2:18). According to 2:19, *the law* was meant to show people their need for a fuller relationship with God. Then once we have been saved by trusting in *Christ* (2:20), He *lives* within us and we look to Him for direction in life. Without Jesus, none of us can be justified and recon-ciled to God.

Apparently the Judaizers claimed that Paul nullified *the grace of God* (2:21) in giving Israel *the law* when he taught that Gentiles did not have to obey all of it. Far from it, said Paul. He did not set aside the grace of God; instead, he estab-lished it by teaching that *justification* and right behavior are made possible through Christ rather than through the law.

Paul asked the Galatian believers a series of pointed questions. He prefaced the queries by using the term *foolish* (3:1). Paul meant they were not using their God-given intelligence to the best advantage. In brief, they should have known better than to believe the Judaizers. By calling his readers *Galatians* rather than *broth-ers and sisters* as before (see 1:11), the apostle adopted a more formal tone suit-ing his message.

Paul's first question was one he did not actually expect the Galatian believers to answer: *Who has bewitched you?* (3:1). He and they both knew he was refer-ring to the Judaizers. The Galatians had been deceived by the visitors among them.

Paul next reminded the Galatians they had heard him preach about Jesus' cru-cifixion. In fact, the apostle had described Christ's execution and its significance so plainly that it was as though they had seen the event with their own eyes. Here is another reason the Galatians should have known better than to be taken in by the doctrine of the Judaizers, since that teaching made Christ's death unnecessary.

Having brought the image of Christ's death to his readers' minds, Paul asked them the central question of how they had received *the Spirit* (3:2). Was it by obeying *the law* of Moses or by hearing about Christ and trusting in Him for salvation? The answer, of course, was that the Galatians had been redeemed and had received the Spirit through faith. Their belief was based on Paul's gospel of Christ crucified. The implication for the Galatians was that since faith in Jesus had been effective in starting them on the Christian life, then faith in Jesus would be effective in continuing them in that life.

The Galatians began their life in Christ by the Spirit. It thus would have been *foolish* (3:3) for them to continue it by their own power. This is because it was impossible for them to attempt by themselves to complete what God's Spirit had *started* in them.

Galatians 3:4 indicates that Paul's readers had suffered for their faith sometime prior to the apostle's writing the epistle. Paul's point in referring to this suffering would be to say that if they now abandoned the Gospel they had endured so much for, their adversity would have been *for nothing*.

Finally, Paul repeated his central question (3:5). He asserted that God had given the Galatians *the Spirit* and worked *miracles* in their lives. The apostle asked whether the Lord did this because they had obeyed *the law* of Moses or because they had heard about Christ and had faith in Him. The answer is clear. The believers in Galatia did not experience the blessings of God because they had followed the law. The Lord redeemed them and enriched their lives because they believed the good news about Christ.

SUGGESTIONS TO TEACHERS

Paul wanted to convey to the Christians throughout Galatia—including both Jewish and Gentile Christians—the centrality of the Gospel, namely, that there is only one Gospel, and that that Gospel is the gift of salvation through faith in Jesus Christ. Any other message was a perversion of the Gospel. That's why Paul preached . . .

1. ONLY ONE WAY. Paul taught that there is only one way to be forgiven of sin, and that comes through faith in Christ for salvation. All other supposed means of salvation are insufficient. No other person, no other method, and no other ritual can redeem us or give us eternal life. The only way is through faith in Jesus Christ.

2. ONLY ONE TRUTH. Paul realized that the Judaizers had some measure of the truth; but because they were attempting to add to that truth, they were in effect twisting it. They claimed to follow Christ; but by requiring Gentiles to adhere to Jewish laws and customs, the legalists were denying that Jesus' death, burial, and resurrection were sufficient for salvation. Paul retorted that the truth of the Gospel cannot be added to or taken away from.

3. ONLY ONE GIFT. The Judaizers' argument that one had to obey the law in order to be a Christian undermined the message that salvation is a gift, not a reward for good works and deeds. Paul said that through Jesus' sacrificial death on the cross, He made God's gift of salvation available to all people—regardless of their race, nationality, or cultural and religious background. Because salvation is a gift of God, there is nothing people can do to earn it. All a person can do is accept the offer of salvation.

4. ONLY ONE REQUIREMENT. Those who were causing confusion in the Galatian churches believed that Jewish practices such as circumcision and dietary restrictions were required of all believers if they were to attain salvation. Paul reminded them that salvation cannot be attained, only received. The sole requirement is to believe in God's Son for eternal life.

5. ONLY ONE JUSTIFICATION. Paul noted that observing Jewish laws can never justify us, for the law is not able to make us acceptable to God. Because Jesus took our sins upon Himself and died in our place, our trusting in Him for salvation brings us acquittal before God. It is no longer with our own righteousness that we stand before God; rather, we do so with Jesus' righteousness. This means that believing sinners are justified by grace through faith.

6. ONLY ONE LIFE. As a result of trusting in Jesus for salvation, we have been identified with His death. We have also been identified with His resurrection and share in the new life He offers. Though we were once spiritually dead in our sins, now we can proclaim with Paul that *the life I now live in the flesh I live by faith in the Son of God* (Gal. 2:20).

FOR ADULTS

■ **TOPIC:** Living on Faith

■ **QUESTIONS:** 1. Why are people not justified by the works of the law? 2. What place does faith in Christ have with respect to good works? 3. What does it mean to live by faith? 4. What place does the Spirit have in the proclamation of the Gospel? 5. What place does the Spirit have in living the Christian life?

■ **ILLUSTRATIONS:**

Faith Only in Jesus. An anonymous author made this striking comparison: "Socrates taught for 40 years, Plato for 50, Aristotle for 40, and Jesus for only 3. Yet the influence of Christ's 3-year ministry infinitely transcends the impact left by the combined 130 years of teaching from these men who were among the greatest philosophers of all antiquity. Jesus painted no pictures; yet some of the finest paintings of Raphael, Michelangelo, and Leonardo da Vinci received their inspiration from Him. Jesus wrote no poetry; but Dante, Milton, and scores of the world's greatest poets were inspired by Him. Jesus composed no music; still Haydn, Handel, Beethoven, Bach, and Mendelssohn reached their highest perfection of melody in the hymns, symphonies, and oratorios they composed in His praise. Every sphere of human greatness has been enriched by this humble Carpenter of Nazareth.

"His unique contribution is the salvation of the soul! Philosophy could not accomplish that. Nor art. Nor literature. Nor music. Only Jesus Christ can break the enslaving chains of sin and Satan. Jesus alone can speak peace to the human heart, strengthen the weak, and give life to those who are spiritually dead."

Faithful or Fizzled. A skyrocket is lovely to watch, but its beauty doesn't last long. There are people who have Christian experiences as brilliant as skyrockets or like giant Roman candles. They certainly can dazzle our eyes for a while. But then they sputter and go out. Their lives become sad, sick, and disappointing. People who faithfully maintain a spiritual glow over the years, through good times and bad, help us believe in the faithfulness of God. Their devotion to Christ is deep and constant because it is real.

I think about my aunt who for years has prayed for her brothers and sisters and their families, read and studied her Sunday school lesson each week, and generally thought of others more than herself. When I decided to go to seminary, she was one of the first persons I told, because I knew she would understand my desire to serve the Lord—and she did. Every young person should have someone like my aunt to look up to as a shining example of how a steadfast faith is lived out in everyday life.

FOR YOUTH	■ TOPIC: Free for All ■ QUESTIONS: 1. Why did Paul place so much emphasis on faith in Jesus? 2. What value are the works of the law? 3. What place do

religious traditions have in the Christian life? 4. In what sense had the Galatian Christians been bewitched? 5. What place did the working of miracles have in the Galatian congregation?

■ **ILLUSTRATIONS:**

Deny Guilt. I heard about a woman who was at a social gathering of some ladies. When it came time to leave, she found that her car door was locked and her keys were in the ignition. Knowing that she had an appointment in an hour, the woman reluctantly went in the house and called her husband. He had to leave in the middle of an important meeting at work and drive 20 miles to the house.

While the ladies were waiting, one of them went around the car and tried each of the doors when she suddenly discovered that the passenger door was unlocked. Her friend looked at her and said, "What are you going to do?" The woman replied, "I'm gonna do what any decent wife would do." So she reached in, locked the door, and slammed it shut!

Everyone deals with guilt in different ways. You can deny guilt, attempt to minimize it, rationalize it, or blame others. But the only real solution is to repent of our sin and put our faith in Christ for salvation. He alone can free us from our sin and enable us to live for God.

Get Back on the Bus. Patsy Clairmont shares the following true story about her son Jason on the tape *God Uses Cracked Pots:*

"When he was 7, I sent him off to school one day and a little while later there was a knock at the door and I opened the door and it was Jason. I said 'Jason, what are you doing here?'

"He said, 'I've quit school!'

"I said, 'Why have you quit school?'

"He said, 'Well, it was too long, it was too hard, and it was too boring.'

"I said, 'Jason, you have just described life; get back on the bus!'"

Everyone wants to get off the bus at one time or another, but steadfast faith means you stay on for the ride. You may not know exactly where the bus is going, but you have faith in the Driver.

Traditions Can Be Good. Traditions are a lot like habits: they can be very good. They can add to your life or take away from your life. They can help you. As a minister, I have had the wonderful privilege of sharing in many traditions—at least some of the good ones. As a church family we celebrate a few traditions, such as when we participate in the Lord's Supper throughout the year or when we have our footwashing service on Maundy Thursday and our Hanging of the Greens on the First Sunday of Advent. It's even traditional for me to greet as many folks as I can in the foyer before they leave to go home. Sweet traditions.

I've also had the privilege of participating in some people's personal traditions. For instance, Floyd has a tradition of sneaking off to the Cross Creek National Wildlife Refuge to watch the birds and sometimes to fish. A couple of springs ago Floyd took me with him to gaze with binoculars on the baby eaglets in their nest and the mother eagle feeding them food brought by the father eagle, who flew directly over our heads. It was magnificent! I'll never forget it.

Then there's Lyle and Marie's tradition of eating at Patti's Restaurant up in Grand Rivers. They introduced Jill and me to Patti's, and no matter where we've lived since—including Chicago—that has remained our favorite restaurant. And we'll never forget it.

Then there are the weddings. One of the most recent was Jeff and Jennifer's out at the Hewell farm in Woodlawn. We watched the horse-drawn carriage bring Jennifer over the gently rolling fields to where we were gathered for the ceremony. Don opened the door of the carriage, and there at Jennifer's feet in the carriage was her most incredibly loyal dog, Skeeter. And as I looked at Skeeter, I thought it was so sweet, and I had to fight back the tears to perform the ceremony. I'll never forget that either.

THE PURPOSE OF THE LAW

BACKGROUND SCRIPTURE: Galatians 3:19—4:7
DEVOTIONAL READING: Romans 3:27-31

KEY VERSES: But when the fullness of time had come, God sent his Son, born of a woman, born under the law, in order to redeem those who were under the law, so that we might receive adoption as children. And because you are children, God has sent the Spirit of his Son into our hearts, crying "Abba! Father!" Galatians 4:4-6.

KING JAMES VERSION

GALATIANS 3:19 Wherefore then serveth the law? It was added because of transgressions, till the seed should come to whom the promise was made; and it was ordained by angels in the hand of a mediator. 20 Now a mediator is not a mediator of one, but God is one. 21 Is the law then against the promises of God? God forbid: for if there had been a law given which could have given life, verily righteousness should have been by the law. 22 But the scripture hath concluded all under sin, that the promise by faith of Jesus Christ might be given to them that believe. 23 But before faith came, we were kept under the law, shut up unto the faith which should afterwards be revealed. 24 Wherefore the law was our schoolmaster to bring us unto Christ, that we might be justified by faith. 25 But after that faith is come, we are no longer under a schoolmaster. 26 For ye are all the children of God by faith in Christ Jesus. 27 For as many of you as have been baptized into Christ have put on Christ. 28 There is neither Jew nor Greek, there is neither bond nor free, there is neither male nor female: for ye are all one in Christ Jesus. 29 And if ye be Christ's, then are ye Abraham's seed, and heirs according to the promise. . . .

4:4 But when the fulness of the time was come, God sent forth his Son, made of a woman, made under the law, 5 To redeem them that were under the law, that we might receive the adoption of sons. 6 And because ye are sons, God hath sent forth the Spirit of his Son into your hearts, crying, Abba, Father. 7 Wherefore thou art no more a servant, but a son; and if a son, then an heir of God through Christ.

NEW REVISED STANDARD VERSION

GALATIANS 3:19 Why then the law? It was added because of transgressions, until the offspring would come to whom the promise had been made; and it was ordained through angels by a mediator. 20 Now a mediator involves more than one party; but God is one.

21 Is the law then opposed to the promises of God? Certainly not! For if a law had been given that could make alive, then righteousness would indeed come through the law. 22 But the scripture has imprisoned all things under the power of sin, so that what was promised through faith in Jesus Christ might be given to those who believe.

23 Now before faith came, we were imprisoned and guarded under the law until faith would be revealed. 24 Therefore the law was our disciplinarian until Christ came, so that we might be justified by faith. 25 But now that faith has come, we are no longer subject to a disciplinarian, 26 for in Christ Jesus you are all children of God through faith. 27 As many of you as were baptized into Christ have clothed yourselves with Christ. 28 There is no longer Jew or Greek, there is no longer slave or free, there is no longer male and female; for all of you are one in Christ Jesus. 29 And if you belong to Christ, then you are Abraham's offspring, heirs according to the promise. . . .

4:4 But when the fullness of time had come, God sent his Son, born of a woman, born under the law, 5 in order to redeem those who were under the law, so that we might receive adoption as children. 6 And because you are children, God has sent the Spirit of his Son into our hearts, crying, "Abba! Father!" 7 So you are no longer a slave but a child, and if a child then also an heir, through God.

11

Monday, May 9	Psalm 19:7-14	*God's Law Is Perfect*
Tuesday, May 10	1 Timothy 1:3-11	*Understanding the Law*
Wednesday, May 11	Matthew 5:17-22	*Jesus Fulfills the Law*
Thursday, May 12	Romans 3:27-31	*We Uphold the Law through Faith*
Friday, May 13	Galatians 3:19-23	*Why the Law?*
Saturday, May 14	Galatians 3:24-29	*The Law Was Our Disciplinarian*
Sunday, May 15	Galatians 4:1-7	*No Longer Slave but Heir*

BACKGROUND

This week's lesson stresses that believers are heirs to God's wealth and blessings. In Romans 8:17, Paul said that we are *heirs of God and joint heirs with Christ.* Similarly, in Galatians 3:1—4:7, the apostle explained our position in God's family using an illustration from the first century A.D. of a child heir before becoming an adult.

This heir, even though he will someday inherit his rich father's entire estate, is treated no differently than a slave when he is a minor child. Even if his parents were dead, he would have no control over the property until his appointed time. In the meantime, guardians would watch over him and the estate.

Under Roman law, the time for coming of age was set by the father. A sacred family festival celebrated this time of the child's maturity when the child was recognized as an adult and heir to the family estate. Paul compared the childhood state to the inferior condition of someone under the law, while the ascent into adulthood represents the freedom that both believing men and women share as co-heirs with Christ.

NOTES ON THE PRINTED TEXT

In his ongoing discussion with the Galatians, Paul asked and answered two key questions. The first is this: What purpose does *the law* (Gal. 3:19) serve? In brief, the law *was added* as a temporary provision by which God prepared people for Christ's coming. The Lord gave the law for the sake of defining *transgressions*. The law showed people their sinfulness by giving them specific decrees that they often failed to keep. Thus, when Christ came as a fulfillment of God's promise, the Jewish people should have been ready to receive the Savior.

As a means of preparing people for Christ, the law, unlike God's promise to Abraham, was temporary. Though the law came from God, it had heavenly mediators (*angels*) and an earthly *mediator* (Moses). The tradition that the law came through angels (Acts 7:38, 53; Heb. 2:2) probably was based on Deuteronomy 33:2 and Psalm 68:17.

Normally, covenants that need a mediator are those in which both parties are active (Gal. 3:20). The covenant of Moses was of this kind. God gave the law, but the people were responsible to obey it. The covenant of Abraham was not of this kind. It had only one active agent: God, who *is one* (see Deut. 6:4), He gave the promise to Abraham, and God would fulfill His pledge.

Paul's second question is this: Is the law *opposed* (Gal. 3:21) to, or against, the promises that God made to Abraham? Paul answered no. He reasoned that if any law could give life, people could become acceptable to God by obeying that law. Since *law* controls everyone, however, no one can become right with God by lawkeeping. The world is bound by sin so that God's promises would be freely given and received *through faith* (3:22).

The law controlled us and kept us under its power until the time when we would have faith in Christ (3:23). Before Jesus' advent, the law was our *disciplinarian* (3:24), or tutor. In Bible times a tutor would note and punish misbehavior in the children of his master. The law functioned as a tutor by revealing and condemning sin.

God established faith in Christ as the way to be justified. Believers thus no longer need to be under the guardianship of the law (3:25). The law prepared people for faith in Christ, who was the fulfillment of God's promises to Abraham. Because of their faith in Christ, Gentile as well as Jewish believers are God's adult *children* (3:26). Believers reach adulthood in God's family, not by keeping the law, but by trusting in Christ. As adopted children in God's family, we have all the corresponding rights and privileges.

Paul also described salvation as being *baptized into Christ* (3:27) and *clothed . . . with Christ*. The first phrase speaks of baptism by the Spirit and points to the believer's close identification with Christ. In addition, believers wear the Savior like they wear clothing; in other words, they take on His righteousness by faith.

The world is full of divisions based on race, social status, and gender. Faith in Christ Jesus, however, makes it possible for believers to be spiritually equal with one another (3:28). It does not matter whether one is a *Jew or Greek*, a *slave or free* person, a man or a woman. Such distinctions have no bearing on who can become a follower of Christ.

Paul's statement that all believers are equal in Christ regardless of ethnicity, gender, or social standing is a reversal of the traditional prayer Jewish males uttered every morning, in which they thanked God that "Thou has not made me a Gentile, a slave, or a woman." Women thanked God every morning that He made them what they were. Only in Christ were the traditional separations of first century A.D. culture broken down.

Faith in Christ is what makes someone a true child of Abraham and of God. Thus, if one belongs to Christ, he or she is also a spiritual descendant of Abraham. Believers receive all of God's blessings because of the promise that He made to *Abraham* (3:29). Included would be forgiveness of sins, a right relationship with God, and eternal life.

Paul told the Galatians that because of their faith in Christ, the days of spiritual impoverishment were behind them. Jewish legalists, however, threatened to drag many of them back into ruin under the bondage of the law. Thus it was necessary for Paul to impress his readers with the superiority of grace over law (4:1-3).

In Bible times the parents determined when it was the right moment for a child to move from the status of minor to adult. Paul said that in the *fullness of time* (4:4), God established when He would allow His children to become adult heirs, and thus able to enjoy all their rights and privileges as members of His family.

According to God's perfect plan, Christ was born of a Jewish *woman* and lived *under the law*. The Son became a sinless human being, died on the cross for the lost, and provided redemption for those who were *under the law* (4:5). Christ has set us free from the curse pronounced by the law so that we might become God's *children*. One of the associated blessings is that we have *the Spirit* (4:6) He is the seal of our adoption into God's family, and through the Spirit we share God's life in our daily experience.

Our new relationship with the Father means we can approach Him with confidence. "*Abba! Father!*" is an address of love reserved for children who are fully aware of their standing with their parents. As children of God, we no longer relate to Him as fearful slaves but as joyous family members. Whereas before we were outside of Christ, now we have the legal right as God's children to draw upon the vast riches of heaven (4:7).

SUGGESTIONS TO TEACHERS

Though Paul was addressing both Jewish Christians and Gentile Christians in the Letter to the Galatians, he took pains to make sure they understood that they were all a part of God's spiritual family. Because God adopts as His own children all who believe in His Son, *There is no longer Jew or Greek, there is no longer slave or free, there is no longer male and female; for all of you are one in Christ Jesus* (3:28). And as God's spiritual children, we have a share in all of His wonderful blessings.

1. A SHARE IN ABRAHAM'S BLESSING. As the adopted children of God, we have a great heritage that goes all the way back to Abraham. God's original promise to Abraham was that God intended to provide the means for the lost to be saved. Once Jesus Christ—the means for our salvation—had come, all those who are justified by grace through faith in Him become participants in this promise to Abraham and are eternally blessed.

2. A SHARE IN CHRIST'S SALVATION. It is actually our salvation through Christ that brings about our adoption into God's family. Through the law, we come to see our need for salvation; and through faith in Christ, we receive salvation. All who are justified by grace through faith have a share in this redemption.

3. A SHARE IN THE FAMILY OF GOD. As the adopted children of God, we are part of His family. While all of us, as believers, have a share in the family of God, none of us is better than anyone else within this family. And none of us should allow ourselves to be separated from our brothers and sisters in Christ because of differences in race, class, or gender. In fact, we would do well if we made it a point to seek out and appreciate our fellow believers who are not like us. When we do, we'll find that we have a lot in common through our faith in Christ.

4. A SHARE IN AN INTIMATE RELATIONSHIP. Because of Jesus Christ's work of salvation on the cross, He has enabled us to become the sons and daughters of God. Whereas we could not enter into God's presence with our sinfulness in tow, now that we have been forgiven, we can boldly come into the Lord's presence. Christ has opened the way for us to have a share in an intimate relationship with our heavenly Father.

5. A SHARE IN FREEDOM. Jesus' saving work on the cross not only provided the means for us to be forgiven but also redeemed us from the law. Jesus' death brought freedom for us who were enslaved to sin, and thus we also have a share in the freedom from the penalty of sin.

6. A SHARE IN CHRIST'S INHERITANCE. As the adopted children of God, we share along with Jesus—God's *only Son* (John 3:16)—all of the rights and privileges of being God's spiritual sons and daughters. We have access to God's resources; we are heirs along with Christ; and we have complete and full identity as God's children. As such, we have a share in the glory of Christ that will one day be revealed.

FOR ADULTS	■ TOPIC: From Slave to Heir

■ **TOPIC:** From Slave to Heir

■ **QUESTIONS:** 1. What purpose does the law serve for believers? 2. How is the law not opposed to the promises of God? 3. In what sense was the law our disciplinarian? 4. In what sense are believers heirs of God's promises in Christ? 5. Why is it important for believers to relate to God as His adopted children and not as slaves under the law?

■ **ILLUSTRATIONS:**

All the Things Written in the Book of the Law. A devout Christian athlete passed up the 2000 Olympics because the final of his event took place on Sunday. Chris Harmse of South Africa, a hammer thrower, withdrew from his country's team, the publication *Business Day* reported.

Harmse, who held the record on the African continent for the hammer throw, had qualified for the team during a pre-Olympic event. He "agonized over his decision before deciding that his faith took precedence," Sam Ramsamy, president of South Africa's National Olympic Committee, told *Business Day.*

Harmse was the second Olympian to withdraw from the games for religious reasons since 1924, when British sprinter Eric Liddell dropped out of the 100-meter race in Paris because the final took place on Sunday. Liddell, the son of a Scottish missionary, won the 400-meter gold medal but was preaching in a church on the day of the final, opening the way for Harold Abrahams to win the 100-meter gold medal. That story inspired the movie "Chariots of Fire."

All of You Are One in Christ Jesus. God speaks in the world's most difficult language. Tabasaran, spoken by a group of people living in the Caucasus region of southern Russia, is described by the *Guinness Book of World Records* as the most difficult language in the world to learn because of its complex grammatical structure, International Russian Radio/Television reports.

One ministry has started translating Christian television programs into Tabasaran, even though there are only a few Christians among the mostly Muslim people, IRR/TV's Hannu Haukka said. "There is no language so difficult that God does not speak it—that is why the Gospel of Jesus Christ must be presented to the Tabasaran people."

■ **TOPIC:** More than Rules

■ **QUESTIONS:** 1. How does God use the law to make people aware of their sin and their need for Christ? 2. What does it mean to be baptized into Christ? 3. In what sense are there no longer gender distinctions within the body of Christ? 4. What happened when the fullness of time came? 5. In what sense are believers children of God?

■ **ILLUSTRATIONS:**

Guarded under the Law. There are some things that only a mother can teach you. It has been said that our mothers taught us a lot about anticipation: "You just wait until your father gets home!" They teach us logic: "If you fall off that swing and break your neck, you're not going to the store with me." They teach us medicine: "If you don't stop crossing your eyes, they're going to get stuck that way." They teach us humor: "When the lawn mower cuts off your toes, don't come running to me." They teach us about genetics: "You're just like your daddy." They teach us about the wisdom of age: "When you get to be my age, you will understand." They teach us about justice: "One day you'll have kids, and I hope they turn out just like you; then you'll see what it's like." My own mother taught me the whole gist of life and living—from the Bible, of course: *All Scripture . . . is useful for teaching, for reproof, for correction, and for training in righteousness* (2 Tim. 3:16).

The Law Was Our Disciplinarian. As kids learn lessons from their mothers, they are sometimes able to pass on to other kids what they've learned. Here's some wise advice from a few kids. Fourteen-year-old Michael has learned this: "Never tell your mom her diet's not working." Mitchell, 12, says, "Don't sneeze in front of mom when you're eating crackers." Armir has learned that "You can't hide a piece of broccoli in a glass of milk." Alyesha figured this out: "When you get a bad grade in school, show it to your mom when she's on the phone." Taylia knows that "When your mom is mad at your dad, don't let her brush your hair." And Michael advises, "When your mom is mad and asks you, 'Do I look stupid?' don't answer her."

Clothe Yourselves with Christ. A good way to judge character in people is by observing how they treat those who can do them absolutely no good. So if you want to see character, watch a loving mother with her newborn. The newborn can do the mother absolutely no good. The newborn won't even remember the care and concern offered by the mother. The mother knows this, and yet, still she showers the baby with care and warmth and concern. Why? Because love is the foundation of her character. Former UCLA basketball coach John Wooden advised his players well when he told them, "Be more concerned with your character than your reputation, because your character is what you really are, while your reputation is merely what others think you are."

CHRISTIAN FREEDOM

BACKGROUND SCRIPTURE: Galatians 5:1-15
DEVOTIONAL READING: 1 Peter 2:11-17

KEY VERSE: You were called to freedom, brothers and sisters; only do not use your freedom as an opportunity for self-indulgence, but through love become slaves to one another. Galatians 5:13.

KING JAMES VERSION

GALATIANS 5:1 Stand fast therefore in the liberty wherewith Christ hath made us free, and be not entangled again with the yoke of bondage. 2 Behold, I Paul say unto you, that if ye be circumcised, Christ shall profit you nothing. 3 For I testify again to every man that is circumcised, that he is a debtor to do the whole law. 4 Christ is become of no effect unto you, whosoever of you are justified by the law; ye are fallen from grace. 5 For we through the Spirit wait for the hope of righteousness by faith. 6 For in Jesus Christ neither circumcision availeth any thing, nor uncircumcision; but faith which worketh by love. 7 Ye did run well; who did hinder you that ye should not obey the truth? 8 This persuasion cometh not of him that calleth you. 9 A little leaven leaveneth the whole lump. 10 I have confidence in you through the Lord, that ye will be none otherwise minded: but he that troubleth you shall bear his judgment, whosoever he be. 11 And I, brethren, if I yet preach circumcision, why do I yet suffer persecution? then is the offence of the cross ceased. 12 I would they were even cut off which trouble you.

13 For, brethren, ye have been called unto liberty; only use not liberty for an occasion to the flesh, but by love serve one another. 14 For all the law is fulfilled in one word, even in this; Thou shalt love thy neighbour as thyself. 15 But if ye bite and devour one another, take heed that ye be not consumed one of another.

NEW REVISED STANDARD VERSION

GALATIANS 5:1 For freedom Christ has set us free. Stand firm, therefore, and do not submit again to a yoke of slavery.

2 Listen! I, Paul, am telling you that if you let yourselves be circumcised, Christ will be of no benefit to you. 3 Once again I testify to every man who lets himself be circumcised that he is obliged to obey the entire law. 4 You who want to be justified by the law have cut yourselves off from Christ; you have fallen away from grace. 5 For through the Spirit, by faith, we eagerly wait for the hope of righteousness. 6 For in Christ Jesus neither circumcision nor uncircumcision counts for anything; the only thing that counts is faith working through love.

7 You were running well; who prevented you from obeying the truth? 8 Such persuasion does not come from the one who calls you. 9 A little yeast leavens the whole batch of dough. 10 I am confident about you in the Lord that you will not think otherwise. But whoever it is that is confusing you will pay the penalty. 11 But my friends, why am I still being persecuted if I am still preaching circumcision? In that case the offense of the cross has been removed. 12 I wish those who unsettle you would castrate themselves!

13 For you were called to freedom, brothers and sisters; only do not use your freedom as an opportunity for self-indulgence, but through love become slaves to one another. 14 For the whole law is summed up in a single commandment, "You shall love your neighbor as yourself." 15 If, however, you bite and devour one another, take care that you are not consumed by one another.

12

HOME BIBLE READINGS

Monday, May 16	John 8:31-38	*The Truth Will Make You Free*
Tuesday, May 17	1 Peter 2:11-17	*Live As Free People*
Wednesday, May 18	1 Corinthians 7:17-24	*Free in Christ*
Thursday, May 19	Hebrews 2:14-18	*Freed from Slavery by Christ*
Friday, May 20	Galatians 5:1-5	*Christ Has Set Us Free*
Saturday, May 21	Galatians 5:6-10	*Faith Working through Love*
Sunday, May 22	Galatians 5:11-15	*Love Your Neighbor As Yourself*

BACKGROUND

After Paul won the Galatians to Christ, they undoubtedly struggled to find their way. The new believers strained to grasp how grace had changed them. They also faced staggering social upheaval—the Gospel put Gentiles on an equal basis with Jews. In this explosive atmosphere a spark was struck. Judaizers introduced their brand of the Gospel. They believed God's grace was for Jews only. According to the legalists, if Gentiles wanted salvation, they first had to become Jewish.

Paul's message was quite different from that of the Judaizers. He taught that grace means freedom. To return to the law was to abandon grace. To use freedom irresponsibly was unloving, contradicting grace. Paul stressed to the Galatians that they needed to mature in Christ and live in the power of the Spirit, not the flesh. Many people today, of course, want to live godly lives, but they feel frustrated with their performance—particularly if they measure themselves against unrealistic standards.

What happens when everyday aggravations push a person to the brink? In the stress and strain of living earthbound lives, heavenly vision can become blurred. This is what happened with the Galatian believers. Consequently, Paul stressed that their relationship to God was based on faith in Christ, not observing the law. It is only as they directed their attention to the grace of God that the Galatians would become spiritually whole once again.

In this week's lesson we will learn that Paul urged the Galatians not to give up their Christian freedom for bondage to the law. If they tried to win God's favor by obeying the law, they would be denying His grace. As long as the Galatians continued in legalism, it would hinder their spiritual growth and create division among the members of their church. That's why Paul reminded them once again of their liberty in Christ, and their freedom to serve God and others out of love.

If we want to please God and obey His Word, we must trust in Christ and live by the power of the Spirit. Through the ministry of God, we will realize that all that the law says can be summed up in the command to love others as much as we love ourselves. As those who are characterized by the love of God, we are encouraged by Paul not to verbally attack one another like wild animals. Instead, we should show compassion, understanding, and kindness to our fellow Christians.

NOTES ON THE PRINTED TEXT

The liberating truth the Galatians needed to embrace is that Christ had set them free from bondage to sin and the curse pronounced by the law. Although the Savior rescued His people from spiritual slavery, it was their responsibility to resist being enslaved again. The Judaizers were burdening the Galatians with a yoke of legalistic demands. Paul urged them (and us) to stand firm as *free* (Gal. 5:1) people.

Although the Galatians were flirting with legalism, they evidently had not succumbed to being *circumcised* (5:2). If they allowed this rite to be performed on them, two negative consequences would result. First, Christ would not do them any good, for they would be looking to the *law* (5:3), not Christ, for righteousness. Second, if the Galatians got circumcised, they would be a debtor to the law and obligated to obey every aspect of it. Paul's readers had not thought of this, however. In fact, by looking to the law for righteousness they alienated themselves from Christ and abandoned the *grace* (5:4) of God.

When we trust in Christ, God declares us righteous and gives us His Holy Spirit. *The Spirit* (5:5) helps us to live for God and look with anticipation to the day when the Lord will make our salvation final. *Circumcision* (5:6), by the way, has no positive effect on the outcome. From an eternal perspective, the act of circumcision does not matter with God. Rather, it is our faith in Christ demonstrating itself in sincere acts of *love*. This implies that love is the motivating force behind practical Christianity.

Paul said the Galatians had been *running well* (5:7) until the Judaizers, like unfair competitors, had cut in on them and broken their stride. The legalists had hindered Paul's readers from obeying *the truth* of the Gospel. Despite the Judaizers' claims, they and their message did not originate from God (5:8). Quoting a popular proverb, Paul said a *little yeast* (5:9) can cause a *whole batch of dough* to rise. The false teaching of the Judaizers, like yeast, was spreading through the Galatian church and poisoning the thinking of every member. Despite the grim situation in Galatia, Paul was convinced that his readers belonged to *the Lord* (5:10). The apostle was assured they would heed his words and reject the teaching of the Judaizers. Moreover, Paul believed God would punish the legalists.

The Judaizers tried to convince the Galatians that Paul affirmed the necessity of *circumcision* (5:11). The apostle, however, asked why the Judaizers *persecuted* him if he preached circumcision. If Paul insisted on the necessity of this religious ceremony, he would be nullifying Christ's work on *the cross*. The cross was an offense to the Jewish law, yet it was the source of life for all who believe.

Paul greatly disliked the confusion and distress the Judaizers had caused for the Galatians. The apostle wished the legalists *would castrate themselves* (5:12). Paul believed that circumcision had no religious significance for Christians and that when it was forced on Gentile converts, it amounted only to bodily damage.

Paul said to his friends in Galatia that God chose them in Christ to be free.

Their liberty, however, was not an excuse for living in sin, but rather an opportunity to serve God and others in *love* (5:13). The apostle declared that everything the law said could be *summed up in a single commandment, "You shall love your neighbor as yourself"* (5:14). The legalistic mentality of the Galatians had produced a critical, self-righteous spirit among them. Consequently, they were verbally biting and devouring one another like wild animals. If this continued, it would destroy their fellowship (5:15). That is why Paul wanted them to put a stop to their bickering and begin again to love one another unconditionally.

SUGGESTIONS TO TEACHERS

The freedom we enjoy in the West was won at the cost of many lives. It would be a tragedy if we took this freedom for granted. Yet when we relate to God in a legalistic manner, we are guilty of devaluing the freedom we have in Christ. When we try to obtain God's favor by performing a long list of good deeds, we are saying that the sacrifice of Christ was insufficient to secure our righteousness. This week's lesson reminds us that the liberty we have in Christ is too precious to abandon or abuse.

1. BE FREE. We are told to *stand firm* (5:1) in the freedom that has been gained for us because of the death, burial, and resurrection of Jesus Christ. We have been set free from the constraints of the law, from our sinfulness, and from the punishment for our sinfulness. Thus we have also been set free to live unselfishly, to love others as we have been loved by God, and to obey the Savior.

2. DON'T BE CUT OFF FROM CHRIST. Seeking salvation by any other means than through faith in Christ is not only futile, but it also diminishes the significance of our faith in Him.

3. BE FAITHFUL. We are saved by faith, not by our deeds. We simply accept the gracious gift that God has offered us in Christ. In gratitude, we ought to strive to live faithfully for the one who has been so completely faithful to us.

4. BE LOVING. Compassion for others and love for God is our response for the forgiveness God offers us in Christ. Paul wrote that *the whole law is summed up in a single commandment, "You shall love your neighbor as yourself"* (5:14).

5. DON'T BE SELF-INDULGENT. In the course of living out our freedom in Christ, we are warned that our freedom is not to be exercised only for our own good. The costly freedom that Christ paid for with His own life is precious, and thus it is not to be used as we please. The apostle called upon all believers to exercise their freedom in self-sacrificing service for God and for others.

6. DON'T BE MALICIOUS. Surely we are all precious in God's sight. Therefore, we should not think of ourselves as better than or above others in the Body of Christ. When we become critical of others, when we can only see their faults, when we focus on their shortcomings, our unity as Christians is broken. Maliciousness has no place in the body of believers; it breeds destruction within a fellowship that should be operating with concern and each other's best interest at heart.

FOR ADULTS

■ **TOPIC:** Free to Serve

■ **QUESTIONS:** 1. What do you think Paul meant when he said *For freedom Christ has set us free* (Gal. 5:1)? 2. What kind of *yoke of slavery* are Christians tempted to submit themselves to today? 3. How are you supposed to live out your dependence on Christ for your salvation? 4. Why would the desire to be justified by the law cut one off from Christ? 5. How is our Christian freedom sometimes seen *as an opportunity for self-indulgence* (5:13)?

■ **ILLUSTRATION:**

Stand Firm, Therefore. On the opening day of Major League Baseball back in 1954, the Cincinnati Reds played the Milwaukee Braves. There were two rookies who started in that game. Cincinnati had a rookie who went four-for-four with four doubles. The Braves' rookie went zero-for-four.

But keep this in mind: that was just the first day. Which of these two rookies is it that people remember today? Is it the Reds' rookie who went four-for-four? I doubt it, unless you can remember the very brief baseball career of a guy named Jim Greengrass. So then it must be the Braves' rookie, the one who went zero-for-four. You've probably heard of him! His name is Hank Aaron. Hammerin' Hank surpassed Babe Ruth's lifetime record of 714 home runs, retiring with a total of 755 home runs.

The point here is that people won't remember how you started. But they will remember how you finish. Your life may be strewn with countless mistakes and blunders and even sins, but the question for today is this: Which direction is it heading now? Face the right direction; then stand firm.

FOR YOUTH

■ **TOPIC:** Freed to Love

■ **QUESTIONS:** 1. Why would anyone who had been set free want to return to slavery? 2. What exactly do you think has to happen for someone to *have fallen away from grace* (Gal. 5:4)? 3. In what ways are you, *through the Spirit, by faith* (5:5), eagerly waiting for *the hope of righteousness*? 4. How could Paul be so confident that the Galatians would accept what he had said? 5. What principles can you find in Galatians 5:13-15 to guide believers in the proper use of Christian liberty?

■ **ILLUSTRATIONS:**

Christ Has Set Us Free. George Thomas was a pastor in a small New England town. One Easter Sunday morning he came to church carrying a rusty, bent, old birdcage, and set it by the pulpit. Several eyebrows were raised and, as if in response, Pastor Thomas began to speak. . . .

I was walking through town yesterday when I saw a young boy coming toward me swinging this birdcage. On the bottom of the cage were three little wild birds, shivering with cold and fright. I stopped the lad and asked, "What you got there son?"

"Just some old birds," came the reply.

"What are you gonna do with them?" I asked.

"Take 'em home and have fun with 'em," he answered. "I'm gonna tease 'em and pull out their feathers to make 'em fight. I'm gonna have a real good time."

"But you'll get tired of those birds sooner or later. What will you do then?"

"Oh, I got some cats," said the little boy. "They like birds. I'll take 'em to them."

I was silent for a moment. "How much do you want for those birds, son?"

"Huh? Why, you don't want them birds, mister. They're just plain old field birds. They don't sing—they ain't even pretty!"

"How much?" I asked again.

The boy sized me up as if I were crazy, and then he said, "Ten dollars?"

I reached in my pocket and took out a ten dollar bill. I placed it in the boy's hand. In a flash, he was gone. So I picked up the cage and gently carried it to the end of the alley where there was a tree and a grassy spot. Setting the cage down, I opened the door, and by softly tapping the bars persuaded the birds out, setting them free. (Having explained the empty bird cage on the pulpit, the pastor then began to tell this story. . . .)

One day Satan and Jesus were having a conversation. Satan had just come from the Garden of Eden, and he was gloating and boasting. "Yes, sir, I just caught the world full of people down there. Set me a trap, used bait I knew they couldn't resist. Got 'em all!"

"What are you going to do with them?" Jesus asked.

Satan replied, "Oh, I'm gonna have fun! I'm gonna teach them how to marry and divorce each other, how to hate and abuse each other, how to drink and smoke and curse. I'm gonna teach them how to invent guns and bombs and kill each other. I'm really gonna have fun!"

"And what will you do when you get done with them?" Jesus asked.

"Oh, I'll kill 'em," Satan glared proudly.

"How much do you want for them?" Jesus asked.

"Oh, you don't want those people. They ain't no good. Why, you'll take them and they'll just hate you. They'll spit on you, curse you, and kill you!! You don't want those people!"

"How much?" He asked again.

Satan looked at Jesus and sneered, "All your tears and all your blood."

Jesus said, "Done!" Then He paid the price.

The Only Thing That Counts. When she learned that she was dying from cancer, Erma Bombeck wrote a column called "If I Had My Life to Live Over." In that column she recounted some of her life experiences that she wished she had done a bit differently. This is what Erma said:

I would have gone to bed when I was sick instead of pretending the earth would go into a holding pattern if I weren't there for the day. I would have burned the pink candle sculpted like a rose before it melted in storage. I would have talked less and listened more. I would have invited friends over to dinner even if the carpet was stained or the sofa faded. I would have eaten the popcorn in the "good" living room and worried much less about the dirt when someone wanted to light a fire in the fireplace. I would have taken the time to listen to my grandfather ramble about his youth. . . . I would never have insisted the car windows be rolled up on a summer day because my hair had just been teased and sprayed. I would have sat on the lawn with my children and not worried about grass stains. I would have cried and laughed less while watching television—and more while watching life. I would never have bought anything just because it was practical, wouldn't show soil, or was guaranteed to last a lifetime. Instead of wishing away nine months of pregnancy, I'd have cherished every moment and realized that the wonderment growing inside me was the only chance in life to assist God in a miracle. When my kids kissed me impetuously, I would never have said, "Later. Now go get washed up for dinner." There would have been more "I love yous." More "I'm sorrys." But mostly, given another shot at life, I would seize every minute— look at it and really see it, live it, and never give it back.

LIVING OUT COVENANT WITH ONE ANOTHER

BACKGROUND SCRIPTURE: Galatians 5:22—6:10
DEVOTIONAL READING: 1 John 3:14-23

KEY VERSE: Bear one another's burdens, and in this way you will fulfill the law of Christ. Galatians 6:2.

KING JAMES VERSION

GALATIANS 5:22 But the fruit of the Spirit is love, joy, peace, longsuffering, gentleness, goodness, faith, 23 Meekness, temperance: against such there is no law. 24 And they that are Christ's have crucified the flesh with the affections and lusts. 25 If we live in the Spirit, let us also walk in the Spirit. 26 Let us not be desirous of vain glory, provoking one another, envying one another.

6:1 Brethren, if a man be overtaken in a fault, ye which are spiritual, restore such an one in the spirit of meekness; considering thyself, lest thou also be tempted. 2 Bear ye one another's burdens, and so fulfil the law of Christ. 3 For if a man think himself to be something, when he is nothing, he deceiveth himself. 4 But let every man prove his own work, and then shall he have rejoicing in himself alone, and not in another. 5 For every man shall bear his own burden. 6 Let him that is taught in the word communicate unto him that teacheth in all good things. 7 Be not deceived; God is not mocked: for whatsoever a man soweth, that shall he also reap. 8 For he that soweth to his flesh shall of the flesh reap corruption; but he that soweth to the Spirit shall of the Spirit reap life everlasting. 9 And let us not be weary in well doing: for in due season we shall reap, if we faint not. 10 As we have therefore opportunity, let us do good unto all men, especially unto them who are of the household of faith.

NEW REVISED STANDARD VERSION

GALATIANS 5:22 By contrast, the fruit of the Spirit is love, joy, peace, patience, kindness, generosity, faithfulness, 23 gentleness, and self-control. There is no law against such things. 24 And those who belong to Christ Jesus have crucified the flesh with its passions and desires. 25 If we live by the Spirit, let us also be guided by the Spirit. 26 Let us not become conceited, competing against one another, envying one another.

6:1 My friends, if anyone is detected in a transgression, you who have received the Spirit should restore such a one in a spirit of gentleness. Take care that you yourselves are not tempted. 2 Bear one another's burdens, and in this way you will fulfill the law of Christ. 3 For if those who are nothing think they are something, they deceive themselves. 4 All must test their own work; then that work, rather than their neighbor's work, will become a cause for pride. 5 For all must carry their own loads.

6 Those who are taught the word must share in all good things with their teacher.

7 Do not be deceived; God is not mocked, for you reap whatever you sow. 8 If you sow to your own flesh, you will reap corruption from the flesh; but if you sow to the Spirit, you will reap eternal life from the Spirit. 9 So let us not grow weary in doing what is right, for we will reap at harvest time, if we do not give up. 10 So then, whenever we have an opportunity, let us work for the good of all, and especially for those of the family of faith.

13

Monday, May 23	Matthew 7:15-20	*A Tree and Its Fruit*
Tuesday, May 24	Matthew 18:15-20	*Where Two or Three Are Gathered*
Wednesday, May 25	1 Timothy 6:11-19	*Be Rich in Good Works*
Thursday, May 26	1 John 3:18-24	*Let Us Love One Another*
Friday, May 27	Galatians 5:22-26	*The Fruit of the Spirit*
Saturday, May 28	Galatians 6:1-5	*Bear One Another's Burdens*
Sunday, May 29	Galatians 6:6-10	*Work for the Good of All*

BACKGROUND

Paul's letter to the Galatians is a progressive argument against the idea that people are saved by adhering to the Mosaic law; rather, justification is by grace through faith. In many respects, the first four chapters are a well-assembled succession of examples and citations about the claims of the law and the claims of the Gospel. Knowing that the Judaizers had gained considerable influence over the Gentile Christians of Galatia, Paul fiercely fought to regain lost turf. The Gospel itself had been slandered and diminished because of the Judaizers' teaching that to be saved one must not only believe in Christ, but must also heed Jewish regulations and customs.

Having led the charge to reinstate and reiterate the believer's freedom in Christ, the apostle, in the closing chapters of his letter, defined what kind of freedom the believer experiences as well as what it entails. Paul warned that Christian liberty is not a freedom toward the self-indulgence of licentiousness. Instead, he pointed to the exercise of loving service as the truest mark and measure of Christian freedom. The apostle directed his readers away from their self-interest and recalled for them that loving service is measured by the way they treated other people. Love, as demonstrated through service to others, is the fruit of Christian freedom.

Although Christians are free from the condemnation of law, the apostle said they are not free from ethical responsibility. It is possible that his teaching on Christian freedom had led some to label him as a libertine. And it is also possible that Paul intended to answer and refute those who had labeled him as such. Yet, his teaching in Galatians remains the same as that throughout his other letters. The message that we are justified by grace through faith in Christ comes through clearly, but so also do the apostle's moral imperatives for the believer.

Paul, of course, never intended for us to live up to these moral imperatives in our own strength. To do so, in one sense, was similar to attempting to attain salvation by keeping the law, for such an attempt was futile. But so was trying to live up to a good moral standard based on our own resources and strength. The apostle understood that to follow God's moral imperatives, believers needed a power from outside themselves. That power, Paul explained, is the Holy Spirit. Only the Spirit of God can enable believers to live uprightly and serve one another sacrificially.

NOTES ON THE PRINTED TEXT

When the flesh is at the helm, our lives are characterized by a host of vices. In Galatians 5:19-21, Paul listed 15 sinful acts to represent all the ways people do evil. He may not have intended to list these vices in any particular order, but they seem to fall into four categories. The list includes three vices of sensuality, two vices associated with pagan religions, eight vices of interpersonal conflict, and two vices related to the misuse of alcohol. The apostle stated that no one who did these would share in the blessings of the kingdom.

Paul next talked about the godly virtues produced by those whose lives were under the Spirit's control. Like the previous list of vices, the one appearing in 5:22-23 is representative. The singular word *fruit* suggests that the virtues of the Spirit are united, not separate, qualities. This implies that all the elements of the Spirit's fruit should be found in our lives as followers of Christ.

Paul placed *love* (5:22) at the top of his list. This should not surprise us, for love is the virtue from which all the rest develop. *Joy* and *peace* come next, followed by *patience, kindness, generosity, faithfulness, gentleness, and self-control* (5:23). The apostle concluded by saying there is no law in Scripture that says these virtues are wrong to have.

When we are ruled by the flesh, our primary objective is to satisfy our sinful *passions and desires* (5:24). The cycle is broken, however, through our union with Christ. Because of our identification with His death and resurrection, our sinful nature has been put to death. It is still true, of course, that the Christian life is a daily process of saying no to the flesh and yes to the Spirit. When the Spirit is in control of us, our flesh will not regain control over us.

Paul said the Spirit was the source of our new life in Christ. This being the case, we should allow the Spirit to lead and empower us (5:25). We know we are out of step with the Spirit when such vices as conceitedness, provoking others to anger, and envy remain entrenched (5:26). By letting go of such divisive feelings, we will promote unity and harmony.

Detected (6:1) means that sin has overwhelmed a person. Paul told his readers they should restore such believers who have fallen. To restore with *gentleness* means the person should not condemn the sinner; instead, the Galatians were to encourage people while confronting their sin. In this way, the Spirit could bring conviction that leads to repentance.

Paul wanted the spiritually mature person to do the restoring. This would be someone who exhibited the fruit of the Spirit; yet even such a person should be careful not to be *tempted* by sin. When he or she helped others overcome the burden of temptation, *the law of Christ* (6:2) was fulfilled, especially the law of love.

Legalists care about the law, not about people. Thus, they refuse to carry the *burdens* of others. This shows that they deceive themselves, believing they are spiritual giants because they practice detailed ritual; but Paul said the legalists were really nothing because they missed God's love, the whole point of the law.

Each person should evaluate himself or herself without making a comparison with others (6:3).

Again Paul reminded those self-deceived people who took pride in themselves—thinking they were much better Christians than other believers—that they should look at their own work. If they were faithful to the tasks God had given them, they would have cause to rejoice, but they certainly had no cause to rejoice when others fell (6:4).

When Paul called the Galatian believers to bear one another's burdens, he was asking them to strengthen the moral resolve of their fellow Christians to resist temptation to sin; and when Paul said that everyone should carry his or her *own loads* (6:5), the apostle meant that everyone is accountable to the Lord for his or her own actions.

Paul described another way the Galatians could bear one another's burdens. With regard to their financial responsibility to the church, they could give to those who taught them God's Word (6:6). Paul also warned the Galatians about deceiving themselves into thinking that God was either unaware of or unconcerned with what they did. If they had this attitude, they were mocking God, and He would not tolerate it (6:7).

Paul borrowed a familiar saying to press home his point. He pictured the life in the body as sowing and reaping. What people *sow* (6:8) to please their sinful nature, they will *reap* from that nature; in other words, they would experience self-destruction. What people *sow* to please *the Spirit*, they will *reap* from the Spirit, which includes *eternal life*.

Paul feared that the Galatians, who had started well in their faith, were losing enthusiasm for Christian living. The Judaizers' false teachings and the Galatians' own unethical living had weakened their spiritual vitality. Thus Paul portrayed the reward awaiting the faithful—namely, an intimate relationship with God—as an incentive for the Galatians to renew their efforts at *doing what is right* (6:9).

God provides strategic opportunities for us to do good to others (6:10). We should try to discern these occasions and eagerly act on them. Helping unbelievers is an excellent way to witness without words to God's goodness; but if anything, we should be more eager to help other Christians, since we are all part of *the family of faith*.

SUGGESTIONS TO TEACHERS

Living according to our new life in the Spirit is a lot like raising a garden. There are certain little things that we need to attend to, and God abundantly blesses our efforts. From this week's lesson, we might create a to-do list that includes these three tasks:

1. WEED OUT THE WORKS. Paul said *the works of the flesh are obvious* (Gal. 5:19). The vices he listed in 5:19-21 should have no part in a life that is being led by the Spirit. Thus, if any of these weeds—vices—are cropping up in the garden of your life, seek God's help in weeding them out. Verse 24 tells us plainly that *those who belong to Christ Jesus have* nailed the passions and desires of their sinful nature to His cross and have crucified them there.

2. TEND TO THE FRUIT. The fruit of the Spirit that the apostle listed in 5:22-23 reads like a character description of the person who is wholly committed to living by the Spirit. It is the Spirit who produces these character traits in us, and these were complete in the person of Christ. Although we don't produce this fruit, we can tend to the fruit that God is producing in us by doing our part to make sure that this fruit stays in an environment conducive to growth.

3. REAP WHAT YOU SOW. It would be ridiculous for a person to plant dandelion seeds and expect to grow an apple tree! And yet we often fool ourselves into thinking that our evil deeds will still manage to somehow reap us eternal benefits. It is a natural law that we get what we plant. Such is also true in our moral and spiritual lives. Every action, thought, and attitude has a result. Each action, thought, and attitude is like a seed we are sowing. Plant to please God, and you will reap a harvest of love, joy, peace, and everlasting life!

FOR ADULTS

■ **TOPIC:** Life and Consequences

■ **QUESTIONS:** 1. What evidence from your own life do you have that you are being led by the Spirit? 2. To what extent would you say that you have *crucified the flesh with its passions and desires* (Gal. 5:24)? 3. To what extent would you say that you *Take care that you yourselves are not tempted* (6:1)? 4. In what ways is *the law of Christ* (6:2) comparable to *the whole law . . . summed up in a single commandment* (5:14)? 5. What things can you do to encourage your fellow believers to make the right choices?

■ **ILLUSTRATIONS:**

Giving Thanks to God. A family returning from an August 2000 missions trip gave thanks to God after a brush with death. Henry Anhalt, who had never piloted a plane, took control of the single-engine Piper he and his family were riding in and landed it safely in Florida after the pilot, Kristopher Pearce, had a heart attack and passed out at the controls.

A part-time flight instructor in the area managed to tell Anhalt how to fly and guided him to Winter Haven airport. Pearce, 36, of Haines City, was taken to a hospital and pronounced dead. An autopsy showed he suffered from coronary artery disease.

Anhalt, his wife, and three sons were returning from the Bahamas, where they had taught vacation Bible school. They were not injured. God "sent a flight instructor—you don't get much more help than that," Anhalt said on NBC's *Today* show. Pearce, chairman of the Northridge Christian Academy school board, had taken church members to the Bahamas in his plane several times.

You Reap Whatever You Sow. In the African-American experience, the phrase "to have church" has become synonymous with "to have a good time." Zan W. Holmes, Jr., tells why, returning to an African-American adage, "If you don't put anything in, you won't get anything out." In terms of worship, says Holmes in his book *Encountering Jesus*, that means "you have to bring something to the sermon to get something out of it."

Holmes then goes on to tell the story of a "young college student who returned home for the holidays and accompanied his mother to church one Sunday. Afterward the young man said, 'The preacher was not too good today.' His mother said, 'Well, maybe not.' He said, 'I noticed that the choir was not too good today.' His mother said, 'Well, maybe not.' Then she said to him, 'Well, son, tell me, how good were you today?'"

FOR YOUTH	■ **TOPIC:** Free to Care ■ **QUESTIONS:** 1. Since we're not under the law, what would be wrong with indulging our sinful natures every once in a while?

2. How would you go about gently restoring someone who is practicing a deep, dark sin? 3. After Paul listed the fruit of the Spirit, why do you think he had to warn his readers about becoming conceited and competing with each other? 4. What are some ways that you can *Bear one another's burdens* (Gal. 6:2)? 5. What do you do for yourself to make sure that you do not *grow weary in doing what is right* (6:9)?

■ **ILLUSTRATIONS:**

Live by the Spirit. I used to hate it whenever my dad came home during the summer and announced that he was taking a vacation. When my dad took a vacation, it meant that I was being pulled from the teenage unemployment line and being put to work in hard, manual labor—in my dad's yard. Just when the summer heat reached its peak and the humidity readings were at a record index, I'd be out pulling weeds, hoeing gardens, and shoveling and raking manure that we had picked up from the agricultural campus at the University of Tennessee, among all the other diverse forms of yard work that my dad could concoct. We'd begin at daybreak and work into the twilight. And I never remember air-conditioning feeling so good as on those nights.

Of course, I learned a lot, because as we worked along, my dad would teach me all kinds of things about gardening, landscaping, fertilizing, and small engines—not to mention the work ethic. There were phrases I remember him using every time he took one of these "summer vacations." For example, I'll always remember getting on the riding mower, heading out into the lawn, revving it up as fast as it would go to try to generate some degree of breeze on my face, and my dad stopping me to ask that infernal question: "Did you check the oil?"

Shamefully, I'd drop my head and shake it "no," reminding him that I did fill up the gas tank. Then I'd get that brief speech that I've got well memorized now: "Son, the tractor will tell you when it's out of gas. It'll just stop running. But when it tells you that its out of oil, it's already too late. You've burned up the engine."

You know what? It wouldn't hurt us to take my dad's wise advice when it comes to our spiritual lives. When was the last time you checked the "oil" of your spiritual life? Picture yourself driving along in the car when suddenly the "check oil" light appears. What do you do? If you're smart, you would pull into the nearest gas station and add a quart of oil. Without lubrication, no engine can survive for long. And we can't survive either without God's "oil." Without the constant softening of God's anointing through the Spirit, we would dry up and become unproductive and bored. We need to be constantly refilled. So get off the tractor and check the oil. The oil for your spiritual engine, of course, is the Spirit.

We Will Reap at Harvest Time. Put your life in God's hands. Let Him control it through His Holy Spirit. Let Him direct it through His Holy Spirit. It will no longer be your life to live as you will, I know; but with God, your life will go on forever and it will have everlasting significance. Just as Soren Kierkegaard wrote, "The tyrant dies and his rule is over, the martyr dies and his rule begins." In many ways, Kierkegaard's words echo those of Jesus when He said, "*If any want to become my followers, let them deny themselves and take up their cross and follow me. For those who want to save their life will lose it, and those who lose their life for my sake will find it*" (Matt. 16:24-25).

JESUS' LIFE, TEACHINGS, AND MINISTRY

I

BAPTISM AND TEMPTATIONS

BACKGROUND SCRIPTURE: Mark 1:4-13
DEVOTIONAL READING: Matthew 12:17-21

KEY VERSE: A voice came from heaven, "You are my Son,
the Beloved; with you I am well pleased." Mark 1:11.

KING JAMES VERSION

MARK 1:4 John did baptize in the wilderness, and preach the baptism of repentance for the remission of sins. 5 And there went out unto him all the land of Judaea, and they of Jerusalem, and were all baptized of him in the river of Jordan, confessing their sins. 6 And John was clothed with camel's hair, and with a girdle of a skin about his loins; and he did eat locusts and wild honey; 7 And preached, saying, There cometh one mightier than I after me, the latchet of whose shoes I am not worthy to stoop down and unloose. 8 I indeed have baptized you with water: but he shall baptize you with the Holy Ghost.

9 And it came to pass in those days, that Jesus came from Nazareth of Galilee, and was baptized of John in Jordan. 10 And straightway coming up out of the water, he saw the heavens opened, and the Spirit like a dove descending upon him: 11 And there came a voice from heaven, saying, Thou art my beloved Son, in whom I am well pleased. 12 And immediately the Spirit driveth him into the wilderness.

13 And he was there in the wilderness forty days, tempted of Satan; and was with the wild beasts; and the angels ministered unto him.

NEW REVISED STANDARD VERSION

MARK 1:4 John the baptizer appeared in the wilderness, proclaiming a baptism of repentance for the forgiveness of sins. 5 And people from the whole Judean countryside and all the people of Jerusalem were going out to him, and were baptized by him in the river Jordan, confessing their sins. 6 Now John was clothed with camel's hair, with a leather belt around his waist, and he ate locusts and wild honey. 7 He proclaimed, "The one who is more powerful than I is coming after me; I am not worthy to stoop down and untie the thong of his sandals. 8 I have baptized you with water; but he will baptize you with the Holy Spirit."

9 In those days Jesus came from Nazareth of Galilee and was baptized by John in the Jordan. 10 And just as he was coming up out of the water, he saw the heavens torn apart and the Spirit descending like a dove on him. 11 And a voice came from heaven, "You are my Son, the Beloved; with you I am well pleased."

12 And the Spirit immediately drove him out into the wilderness. 13 He was in the wilderness forty days, tempted by Satan; and he was with the wild beasts; and the angels waited on him.

HOME BIBLE READINGS

Monday, May 30	Psalm 2:7-12	*You Are My Son*
Tuesday, May 31	Mark 1:4-8	*Baptism for Repentance and Forgiveness*
Wednesday, June 1	Matthew 3:7-12	*John the Baptist's Message*
Thursday, June 2	Matthew 3:13-17	*Jesus Is Baptized*
Friday, June 3	Mark 1:9-13	*Jesus Is Baptized and Tested*
Saturday, June 4	Matthew 12:17-21	*Here Is My Servant*
Sunday, June 5	Matthew 4:1-11	*Jesus Is Tempted by the Devil*

BACKGROUND

The English word "gospel" is derived from the Anglo-Saxon word *godspell*, which can mean either "a story about God" or "a good story." The latter meaning is in harmony with the Greek word *euangelion*, which is translated "gospel" and which means "good news." The four Gospels are the good news about the life, sacrificial death, and resurrection of Jesus of Nazareth.

Like the historical writings of the Old Testament, the Gospels (and Acts) do not provide us with every historical detail we might want to know. The events included were carefully selected to present clearly and powerfully the message about Christ. Unlike what one would expect from a biography, a large portion of each Gospel is devoted to the last week of Jesus' ministry. This underscores the importance of knowing the purpose for which a particular New Testament narrative, such as the Gospels and Acts, was written. A detail that might seem insignificant at first might subsequently prove to be quite important.

It is noteworthy that God has given us four Gospels, not just one. Each author wrote from a unique perspective and for a different audience. For example, Matthew wrote primarily to a Jewish audience and presented Jesus of Nazareth as Israel's long-awaited Messiah and rightful King. Jesus' genealogy, the many Old Testament quotations, and the five lengthy teaching sections were intended to strengthen the faith of Jewish Christians. Mark targeted a Gentile audience (especially a Roman one). The second Synoptic Gospel portrays Jesus as the Servant who came to suffer for the sins of the world.

Luke addressed a broader Gentile audience. He wrote in a sophisticated literary style of Greek. He proved to be a careful researcher and historian. Luke portrayed Jesus as the Son of Man, the answer to the needs and hopes of the human race, and the Savior of the world. John predominately emphasized the deity of Christ. John wrote to strengthen the faith of believers and to appeal to unbelievers to trust in Christ. When viewed together, the four Gospels weave a complete portrait of the God-man, Jesus of Nazareth.

What factors distinguish Mark's Gospel? Compared to the other three, this one is much more action packed. It devotes much less space to Jesus' teaching and offers a simple fast-paced account of events. For instance, *immediately* (and similar terms) appear frequently throughout the narrative.

Although Mark wrote the briefest of the four Gospels, he spared no words as he painted a compelling portrait of the Savior serving others. In fact, the tone of the book is practical, written in such a way that the material would appeal to the Roman mind. These next weeks, as you study and teach Mark's accounts, may the truth about Jesus brighten the lives of those who hear and believe!

NOTES ON THE PRINTED TEXT

Mark stated at the outset that his Gospel was about *Jesus Christ* (Mark 1:1). Yet the first person Mark presented in his book was not Jesus but John the Baptist (1:2-8). That may seem odd. However, in Mark's view the Gospel of Jesus had its beginning in the ministry of John.

God chose John for an important task. He was to prepare the way for the Lord, as foretold by Malachi (Mal. 3:1) and Isaiah (Isa. 40:3). In Bible times there were no superhighways. When an important dignitary was expected to travel through the country, a messenger would go out in advance to tell the people to prepare the way for the dignitary's coming. This meant they had to improve roads by cutting down trees, leveling steep hills, and generally clearing away obstacles. Figuratively speaking, this was the ministry of John. He was a messenger preparing the hearts of people for the coming Messiah (Mark 1:2-3).

John the Baptizer (1:4) lived *in the wilderness* and was urging people to be baptized to show they had renounced their *sins* and looked to God in faith for *forgiveness.* People flowed to this desert preacher *from the whole Judean countryside* (1:5) as well as from *Jerusalem.* When people confessed their sins, John *baptized* them *in the river Jordan.* John was eccentric in his dress and behavior. He wore a garment of *camel's hair* (1:6), which he tied at his *waist* with a *leather belt.* His diet included *locusts and wild honey.*

John did not come to establish a movement or build an institution of his own. Even with all his popularity, John knew Christ was infinitely superior to him in status and work. John expressed Christ's superior status by declaring his own unworthiness to untie Christ's *sandals* (1:7). John shrank from assuming the position of even the lowliest servant to Christ. John was Christ's forerunner, not His competitor.

John went on to outline Christ's superior work by saying, *"I have baptized you with water, but he will baptize you with the Holy Spirit"* (1:8). John offered a symbol (water) that held no real power to cleanse sin. Jesus would baptize with the Holy Spirit, providing an actual cleansing from sin.

Jesus validated John's ministry by joining the crowds coming to be baptized by him (1:9). Where had John gotten the idea of baptizing? Jews, in the preceding centuries, had developed a ritual washing for pagans who wished to join the Jewish community. But John offered baptism, not to pagans, but to Jews, those who considered themselves already God's people. By this act, they admitted that they too needed to reverse their course and head in a new direction. Jesus, who had not sinned, needed no baptism. Yet from the beginning of His public ministry, He identified Himself with sinners, especially those who longed for righteousness.

At the start of Jesus' earthly ministry, God the Father and God the Holy Spirit empowered and encouraged God the Son for His ministry. Immediately after Jesus' baptism, the Spirit descended on Him *like a dove* (1:10). In what sense did Jesus need the Spirit? Hadn't Jesus remained one with the Spirit throughout the earlier years of His life? Yes, but perhaps the Father sent the Spirit to anoint the Son with even greater power for the work that lay ahead (Acts 10:38). As the Father gave Jesus His approval in action (by sending the Spirit upon Him), He also commended Jesus verbally (Mark 1:11). God affirmed Jesus for who He was (*"You are my Son"*) and what He had done (*"I am well pleased"*).

The next two verses give a terse account of Jesus' temptation. Matthew and Luke more specifically described the temptation itself, but Mark offered detail they omitted. The other writers told how the Spirit led Jesus into the wilderness; Mark said the Spirit *drove* (1:12) Jesus out. Mark left no doubt but that Jesus' temptation was part of the divine plan. God does not tempt anyone, but God evidently saw it best that His Son experience the enemy's full force right from the beginning of Jesus' ministry. During this period of temptation, Jesus was accompanied by both *wild beasts* (1:13) and *angels*. The first placed Jesus in a position of further vulnerability, but the second offered protection and encouragement.

While Matthew and Luke also mention Jesus' temptation in the wilderness for 40 days (Matt. 4:1-11; Luke 4:1-13), only Mark mentions the presence of wild animals. One reason may be that Mark wanted to emphasize the danger Jesus faced. In Christ's day, far more wild animals roamed the countryside than today, including lions that prowled the wooded areas along the Jordan River (Jer. 5:6; 49:19). The mention of wild beasts thus adds drama to Jesus' confronting of evil.

Another reason for mentioning wild animals may be that untamed beasts were associated with evil powers, thus symbolizing the cosmic struggle of good and evil in which Jesus was engaged. Perhaps the wild animals are connected with the hope of the messianic era, when animal enemies such as the wolf and the lamb will live in peace (Isa. 11:6-9).

A third reason may come from Mark's audience. If Mark was writing his Gospel for Gentile Christians about A.D. 64–67, particularly those in Rome (see 1 Pet. 5:13), they would be facing persecutions from the emperor Nero that often included being thrown to the lions for refusing to worship the emperor. The early Christians could take comfort in the fact that Jesus too had confronted wild animals.

As John disappeared from the scene, Jesus took center stage (Mark 1:14). He returned to His home area of *Galilee* and announced *the good news*. God's faithful people had waited long for the fulfillment of prophecies of a better day to come. Jesus proclaimed that God (who had always ruled) had taken a further step to bring His heavenly *kingdom* (1:15) to earth. Jesus later would instruct His followers to pray for the fuller coming of that kingdom, but, in its initial stages, the kingdom had come. Jesus called His hearers to *repent* and *believe*, just as John had done. Repentance involved a change in lifestyle, while belief involved a change in perspective.

SUGGESTIONS TO TEACHERS

Mark chose memorable incidents that would introduce Jesus to the lost. These events, from the beginning, let us know that we are not dealing with any ordinary ancient teacher or philosopher. In this week's lesson (and in the coming weeks), as you and your class members meet Jesus once again, try to encounter Him as if you were hearing about Him for the first time. Catch the excitement as you imagine what took place in ancient Palestine. Also, be sure to ask, who is this person?

1. THE ONE WHO IS FAR ABOVE US. Jesus was one whom God unconditionally praised. God willingly adopts us as His children, but only through grace. Jesus is different. He is God's Son by nature, not adoption.

2. THE ONE WHO KNOWS AND CARES ABOUT US. No matter what He did for us, Jesus would deserve our praise for who He is. But even as one who stands infinitely above us, He reaches down to us. He knew the four fishermen. In subsequent accounts, we come to know the weaknesses that Jesus may have known from the beginning. Yet He invited people He encountered to be His companions. Jesus (for example) could easily have rejected or ignored the man plagued by the demon (see Mark 1:21-28). Yet Jesus reached out to him and to other needy people with the saving truth of the good news.

3. THE ONE WHO BECAME ONE OF US. Jesus was not a phantom or apparition. Rather, He was truly human as well as truly divine. In the realm of His physical existence, Jesus was as vulnerable to wild animals as we are. And He allowed Himself to be tempted by Satan, who tempts us all. But despite Jesus' constant victory over Satan, He still identified with us in our spiritual need. Also, at Jesus' baptism, the entire Trinity was involved. The initiative of God the Father, the atoning work of God the Son, and enabling power of God the Holy Spirit were all present.

 FOR ADULTS

■ TOPIC: Preparing for Leadership

■ QUESTIONS: 1. What was the message that *John the Baptizer* (Mark 1:4) proclaimed? 2. What response did John receive from those who heard his proclamation? 3. What was unique about the way John dressed? 4. How did John distinguish himself from the Messiah? Why was this important for John to do? 5. Why was it necessary for Jesus to be tempted by Satan? 6. How can the Lord enable us to overcome enticements to sin we may experience from time to time?

■ ILLUSTRATIONS:

Trumpet Call. Every hour on the hour, in Krakow, Poland, a trumpeter blares out an oddly truncated call. The trumpet call begins sounding from the pinnacled tower of ancient Saint Mary's Church, but then abruptly stops after a few notes. Some strangers think that the trumpeter has forgotten the tune. Then the same brief fanfare blares again.

The reason behind the sudden stop to the call in mid-note lies in an historic event. In 1241, a watchman in the tower caught sight of a band of invading tartars and sounded the alarm on his bugle. He had gotten as far as the first few notes when an arrow struck him in the throat. But the warning allowed Krakow time to prepare itself.

Today, hourly, the same brief, sad call rings out over the city, and at midday it is broadcast to the nation. The trumpeter then and now reminds his people to be ready and to serve!

John the Baptist was the herald of God to call people to be ready and to serve the King whose coming was at hand. Today, John's summons to repentance and acceptance of God's rule is just as clear and compelling!

Follow the Leader. Charles Colson undoubtedly felt great pride when the new president of the United States invited him to serve on his staff. Few people ever receive this privilege—to have the opportunity to work in the White House, perhaps to impact the history of the nation or world. Colson did receive fame, but not in the way he intended, for the path down which he followed Richard Nixon. Colson ended up in prison for his part in the Watergate scandal. But in jail, Colson found a new and far superior leader to follow. Colson's Prison Fellowship organization has done far more to impact eternity than any act for which any presidential advisor ever could hope.

Making Prayer Work. Robert had been a pastor for 20 years. He had done well, at least by some standards. His church had grown. He poured himself into the work, hoping for more success. In the process, his family received little of his time. When Robert's son, in his late teens, developed a deep fear that developed into schizophrenia, Robert took time to reflect.

Hoping for help, Robert began reading a book written by a woman known for her God-given power in prayer. Robert discovered this woman lived in his own city. He visited her. She was blunt. "You preachers know all about prayer except how to make it work." She became Robert's mentor in prayer.

Together the two prayed over Robert's son, who found healing from his mental illness. When Robert subsequently suffered a heart attack (likely caused by his stressful lifestyle), he learned that prayer (and a changed lifestyle) brought healing where medical science by itself could not. Now at age 70, Robert's ministry continues to bear fruit.

Lures. To aid you as you speak this illustration, you could ask an appropriate member of your class to bring in a variety of fishing lures. Holding several where the class can see them, remind the students that most lures don't look at all like food a fish would enjoy. They merely offer shiny or colorful surfaces that catch a fish's attention. Attracted by the novelty, the fish swims over to investigate. The fisherman knows there's nothing for the fish in his lures but danger and potential death. But the fish is not smart enough to figure that out. Satan's temptations are like fishing lures. They catch our attention. But we end up getting hurt, sometimes seriously.

FOR YOUTH

■ **TOPIC:** Baptism and Temptations

■ **QUESTIONS:** 1. In what sense was John the Baptist a forerunner for the Messiah? 2. Why did John proclaim a message of repentance? 3. What is the significance of Jesus' baptism? 4. What is the significance of Jesus' temptation? 5. Why do you think it is hard for people to submit to Jesus' authority?

■ **ILLUSTRATIONS:**

Opening Act. When country music superstar Hank Williams, Jr., performed at Pittsburgh's Civic Arena, he began by singing the popular tune, "Restless Heart." The purpose of his opening act was to prepare the audience for the main attraction by building anticipation and excitement.

In a spiritual sense, John was the "opener" for Jesus. In other words, John prepared the people for Jesus' arrival by building their anticipation. John wanted to make sure that they (as well as all of us) were prepared to meet the Savior.

Where Are the Fruits? Knowing that many are afraid of talking about their spiritual problems, a well-known religious leader in Philadelphia launched a toll-free hotline in December 1998. A week-long blitz of television and radio commercials, bought at a cost of $225,000, produced floods of calls, most of which began, "Pastor, I'm in need of spiritual help."

The line, staffed Monday through Friday from 8 A.M. to 8 P.M., receives about 100 calls each day, while a message machine records calls coming in at other times. In 1999, a Spanish language line was added. More than 140 volunteers listened to people talk about their spiritual problems.

Some think the ministry does not really fulfill John's call to repentance. According to these critics, John stressed the importance of spiritual fruit that demonstrated the reality of one's faith commitment. He also emphasized that personal actions should accompany one's feelings and words.

Genuine Repentance. The members of a local church in the southern part of the United States listened to their pastor read aloud a handwritten, two-page letter from one of their members. In this document, the writer expressed his sorrow for what he had done wrong. It was clear that the person was truly repentant and wanted to get right with God and His people. Though some were skeptical, the majority of church members were responsive to the repentant believer's request and gladly received him back into their fellowship.

This forgiving spirit mirrors God's willingness to pardon those who genuinely repent. He can forgive sin because of what Christ did at Calvary.

Reward or Punishment? Picture yourself as a second string member of your school's varsity basketball team. You have been practicing hard and improving your skills. How would you feel if your coach rewarded you by sending you back to the junior varsity squad so that you could play easy games against younger opponents? Even if the coach said, "Here's your reward for hard work. I will make your life easier for a while," you would not feel rewarded but punished.

No, you would expect your coach to give you more varsity playing time or possibly even move you into the starting five. But if he did that, then you would face even more challenges than before. But through more game time, even against tough teams, you would continue to increase your abilities.

In the same way, when God wants us to grow, He does not give us an easy stretch, but allows us to face temptations that will challenge us. As we face those challenges and defeat them through the power of Christ, we grow stronger.

A New Adventure. By the time she was seven, Elizabeth had lived on three different continents. Her parents, in Christian ministry, had taken her around the world. This gave her a hunger to see more of the world and to serve people facing all kinds of needs.

As she approached her teen years, Elizabeth begged her parents, on an international flight, to stop over in a third world country. During high school, Elizabeth took a short term mission trip to Russia. Travel with a college group took her to Honduras. She's planning toward an entire semester in Tanzania. These adventures have "bitten" her. She now plans a career in international missions and relief work. Following God's way can offer the greatest of adventures!

THE MIRACLES

BACKGROUND SCRIPTURE: Mark 2:1-12; 3:1-6; 8:1-10
DEVOTIONAL READING: Mark 7:31-37

KEY VERSE: [Jesus said,] "I say to you, stand up, take your mat and go to your home." Mark 2:11.

KING JAMES VERSION

MARK 2:1 And again he entered into Capernaum after some days; and it was noised that he was in the house. 2 And straightway many were gathered together, insomuch that there was no room to receive them, no, not so much as about the door: and he preached the word unto them. 3 And they come unto him, bringing one sick of the palsy, which was borne of four. 4 And when they could not come nigh unto him for the press, they uncovered the roof where he was: and when they had broken it up, they let down the bed wherein the sick of the palsy lay. 5 When Jesus saw their faith, he said unto the sick of the palsy, Son, thy sins be forgiven thee. 6 But there were certain of the scribes sitting there, and reasoning in their hearts, 7 Why doth this man thus speak blasphemies? who can forgive sins but God only? 8 And immediately when Jesus perceived in his spirit that they so reasoned within themselves, he said unto them, Why reason ye these things in your hearts? 9 Whether is it easier to say to the sick of the palsy, Thy sins be forgiven thee; or to say, Arise, and take up thy bed, and walk? 10 But that ye may know that the Son of man hath power on earth to forgive sins, (he saith to the sick of the palsy,) 11 I say unto thee, Arise, and take up thy bed, and go thy way into thine house. 12 And immediately he arose, took up the bed, and went forth before them all; insomuch that they were all amazed, and glorified God, saying, We never saw it on this fashion.

NEW REVISED STANDARD VERSION

MARK 2:1 When he returned to Capernaum after some days, it was reported that he was at home. 2 So many gathered around that there was no longer room for them, not even in front of the door; and he was speaking the word to them. 3 Then some people came, bringing to him a paralyzed man, carried by four of them. 4 And when they could not bring him to Jesus because of the crowd, they removed the roof above him; and after having dug through it, they let down the mat on which the paralytic lay. 5 When Jesus saw their faith, he said to the paralytic, "Son, your sins are forgiven." 6 Now some of the scribes were sitting there, questioning in their hearts, 7 "Why does this fellow speak in this way? It is blasphemy! Who can forgive sins but God alone?" 8 At once Jesus perceived in his spirit that they were discussing these questions among themselves; and he said to them, "Why do you raise such questions in your hearts? 9 Which is easier, to say to the paralytic, 'Your sins are forgiven,' or to say, 'Stand up and take your mat and walk'? 10 But so that you may know that the Son of Man has authority on earth to forgive sins"—he said to the paralytic— 11 "I say to you, stand up, take your mat and go to your home." 12 And he stood up, and immediately took the mat and went out before all of them; so that they were all amazed and glorified God, saying, "We have never seen anything like this!"

Monday, June 6	Mark 5:1-13	*Jesus Heals the Demoniac*
Tuesday,, June 7	Mark 7:31-37	*He Has Done Everything Well*
Wednesday,, June 8	Mark 8:1-5	*How Many Loaves Do You Have?*
Thursday, June 9	Mark 8:6-10	*Four Thousand Are Fed*
Friday, June 10	Mark 3:1-6	*Stretch Out Your Hand*
Saturday, June 11	Mark 2:1-5	*Son, Your Sins Are Forgiven*
Sunday, June 12	Mark 2:6-12	*I Say to You, Stand Up*

BACKGROUND

As Mark continued telling his account about Jesus' ministry, he turned next to a collection of incidents involving conflict. Several of them appear in Mark 2:1—3:6, which forms the backdrop for this week's lesson. Some of the interesting contrasts among these incidents include how the opponents approached Jesus and how they responded at the conclusion of the encounters.

For instance, when Jesus forgave a sick man's sins, Jesus' opponents (in this case, the scribes) questioned this action. After Jesus physically healed the man, they evidently joined the crowd in amazement (2:1-12).

When Jesus ate with sinners, the scribes and the Pharisees went beyond silent questioning. Behind the scenes, they asked Jesus' disciples about His actions. In this case, Mark did not record how the opponents received the disciples' answer (2:13-17). Then, when Jesus' opponents saw that His disciples did not follow their customary practices regarding fasting, the religious leaders went directly to Jesus to ask why (2:18-22).

The religious leaders' opposition intensified gradually. The next confrontation involved the disciples picking grain on the Sabbath. It appears that by the time of this incident, antagonists were following Jesus and looking for actions of His to criticize. How else would they have been near a grain field on the Sabbath, unless they were watching while Jesus' disciples picked a bit of grain? After seeing Christ's followers break their rules, the opponents again asked Jesus what was happening. The response of the opponents was perhaps silence (2:23-28).

Then in the last of these incidents involving conflict, Mark noted that Jesus' opponents were watching Him so that they might bring a charge against Him. When, on the Sabbath, Jesus healed the man with a withered hand, the Pharisees no longer marveled, and they no longer remained silent. Instead, they began to plot how they would murder Jesus (3:1-6).

In each of these episodes, Jesus or His disciples acted in a way that displeased the religious leaders. Note the progression both in the way Jesus' opponents expressed their concern and in their final response. At first the antagonists appeared somewhat reluctant even to mention the problems they saw. But as the narrative progressed, they became rabid in their opposition. By the last incident, they were ready to pounce on Jesus.

How did the religious leaders become so critical? Today we easily picture them as the bad guys in the Gospel accounts. But it may help to know that the scribes and Pharisees developed out of a revival movement within Judaism.

During the time between the events recorded in the Old and New Testaments, some among God's people wanted to insure that they were paying adequate attention to God and His law. The last thing they wanted was for God to send them off into another exile. To insure that they did not break the law, they placed a "hedge" (so to speak) around it.

For example, the law instructed that the nation should honor the Sabbath. The reformers decided that people should know precisely what that meant. So they said, "Even if you were hungry, you should not pick enough grain for a small meal on the Sabbath" (the thinking behind 2:24); or, "unless the situation meant life or death, no one should give or receive medical care on the Sabbath" (the thinking behind 3:2).

If these humanly-devised regulations were stricter than God intended, the Pharisees thought that, in following them, at least everyone would be safe. People who did not break the overly strict rules certainly would not be breaking God's less strict laws.

This thinking was flawed because ordinary people needed to earn a living and raise a family. They did not have time to keep all the additional regulations. That apparent failure gave the wealthier, more legalistic members of society even more reason to look down on their poorer neighbors. Those who were keeping all the law fell into the deep sin of pride. Also, since it was easier to regulate external actions (as opposed to inner attitudes), the Pharisees focused their laws on visible actions, rather than on a person's heart.

Jesus never spoke against the law as God intended it. In contrast, He upheld it (Matt. 5:17-20). However, Jesus had no qualms about breaking the humanly devised commandments the Pharisees cherished. Likewise, Jesus condemned the way their traditions contradicted God's Word.

NOTES ON THE PRINTED TEXT

Soon after healing a leper (Mark 1:40-45), Jesus returned to *Capernaum* (2:1), which became His newly adopted headquarters. The *home* where He was staying (possibly Peter's) quickly overflowed with people. Jesus took advantage of the occasion to preach *the word to them* (2:2).

By this time the news had spread about Jesus' healing power (1:28). That's why four concerned friends hoped to bring a *paralyzed man* (2:3) to Him. But so many people gathered around Jesus that the bearers saw no hope of reaching Him in any ordinary way. This prompted them to choose an extraordinary approach. Palestinian homes usually had flat roofs and outdoor stairways. The friends could, with some effort, remove the branches (packed with dirt) that laid on crossbeams (2:4). Luke adds that the roof had tiles (Luke 5:19).

As the friends lowered the paralyzed man into the room where Jesus taught, no one needed to explain their desire. Jesus must have smiled, especially as He discerned what was happening. He saw the faith the group expressed, and spoke to the man on the pallet: *"Son, your sins are forgiven"* (Mark 2:5). Why did Jesus say this? Perhaps He wanted to dispel the notion that this illness was the direct result of sin (John 9:2).

When the crowd heard Jesus offer forgiveness, the teachers of the law shuddered. They began *questioning in their hearts* (Mark 2:6), *"Who can forgive sins but God alone?"* (2:7). To assume a privilege that belonged only to God was considered *"blasphemy."* And the punishment for blasphemy was *death* (Lev. 24:16).

Jesus heard the unspoken challenge and accepted it. The religious leaders had asked their questions in their minds and perhaps among themselves, but Jesus questioned them aloud (Mark 2:8). And He did far more than merely debate His own qualifications; He offered action.

Jesus asked whether it was easier to tell the paralyzed man he was pardoned or to enable him to stand up and walk away with his *"mat"* (2:9). Obviously the first option was easier, for it could not be verified by conventional means. After all, forgiveness takes places invisibly. In contrast, a false claim of miraculous healing can be disproved on the basis of visible evidence. In offering healing, Jesus had outwitted the religious leaders. They provided the opportunity for Him to offer proof of His *"authority"* (2:10) as the *"Son of Man."*

This phrase was Jesus' favorite designation for Himself. He wanted to teach that, as the Messiah, He combined two Old Testament roles: Son of Man (Dan. 7:13-14) and Servant of the Lord (Isa. 52:13—53:12). Daniel described a Son of Man to whom God gives an everlasting kingdom. And Isaiah described a Servant of the Lord who suffers on behalf of others. Jesus knew that He must perform the role of the suffering Servant. But He also knew that eventually He would receive glory as the Son of Man. In relation to Jesus, therefore, the expression "Son of Man" indicates both His humanity and divine authority.

When Jesus said, *"stand up, take your mat and go to your home"* (Mark 2:11), the command He issued proved effective. The man walked out under his own power (2:12). Everyone, including the religious leaders, marveled at Jesus' unprecedented power.

On the one hand, the crowd that watched Jesus heal the paralyzed man responded enthusiastically to His dramatic display of power. On the other hand, they overlooked His more significant ability to forgive sins—a power that deeply troubled the religious leaders. Scripture teaches that God alone has the authority to forgive sins (Isa. 43:25; 44:22). After all, it is against Him ultimately that people commit sin (Ps. 51:4). Because the religious leaders rejected Jesus' claim to be God, they charged Him with blasphemy.

The religious leaders, then, did not deny that God had the power to forgive people and save them. What bothered them so much in Jesus' message is the radical idea that God loves and saves "sinners" as they are, without their first having to follow the law, "clean up their act," and thus be deserving of His love and mercy.

SUGGESTIONS TO TEACHERS

Jesus offered Himself to several different groups of people. The barriers that separated them from Him and one another meant nothing to Jesus. He wanted to break down those barriers. The standards by which some saw themselves as superior meant little to Him. Some received Him with joy, at least for a while. Some stayed with Him in the long term. And some ultimately helped murder the Son of God. Nothing has changed. Our communities and even our churches are full of these same types of people today.

1. THE NEEDY. In Mark 2:1-12, a man was paralyzed by his body and evidently had no one but Jesus to turn to for help. When Jesus offered freedom, the man willingly accepted what the Savior had to offer.

2. THE FRIENDS OF THE NEEDY. The four friends who carried the paralyzed man to Jesus most likely rejoiced as their friend entered new freedom. What changes might have occurred in their lives as they watched Jesus act?

3. THE DISCIPLES. At least Simon, Andrew, James, and John had been following Jesus for a period of days or weeks. They had already watched Him perform astounding miracles. What would they have felt during the incident recorded in this week's lesson? Continued amazement? Pride in their association with Jesus?

4. THE CROWDS. At this point in Jesus' ministry, there were lots of people who accompanied Him. His amazing abilities to teach and heal attracted them to Jesus. They listened and watched. They gladly received. But were they ready to commit themselves to Jesus? Perhaps not in any depth.

5. THE OPPONENTS. Members of this group could not help but marvel at all Jesus said and did. But they wished that He would play the game by their rules. Forgiving sins? Operating with divine authority? They saw these things as questionable behavior. They also wished to restrict Jesus. He supposedly should do nothing that violated their expectations.

FOR ADULTS

■ **TOPIC:** Healed to Wholeness

■ **QUESTIONS:** 1. What do you think made Jesus so popular during the early part of His earthly ministry? 2. How did the friends of the paralyzed man try to work around the obstacle of the crowds of people? 3. Why did the religious leaders balk at the idea of Jesus being able to forgive sins? 4. What was the source of Jesus' authority to forgive sins? 5. What principles of managing conflict can be gleaned from the way in which Jesus handled the religious leaders?

■ ILLUSTRATIONS:

She Can See! David McGuire could have said a quick prayer and moved his attention to the next person. While offering baked beans and buttered bread to Romanian refugees, Elvira, a gypsy woman, asked the missionary to pray for her infant daughter, Elisabeta. David did not let racial, social, or economic differences prevent him from listening to Elvira. He soon learned that the baby held in her mother's arms was blind. He took special interest in the child. Along with a friend, he paid for an optical implant, a medical procedure performed in a nearby city. But that effort failed and all but destroyed one of Elisabeta's eyes.

David refused to give up. He contacted a church in the United States, where people began raising money. He wrangled with governments to arrange visas. An airline donated seats to get mother and daughter to the state of Washington. Paul Shenk, a surgeon, offered his expertise. During the operation, he said he "felt as if the Great Physician Himself were helping me." In the food line months before, Elisabeta's situation looked grim. Today, with the help of God and lots of people, she can see.

I've Forgotten. Craig Brian Larson tells the following story. After several years of marriage, Bert and Mary were still childless. They decided to adopt a boy they named John. Within months, Mary found herself pregnant. She gave birth to Larry. Some years later, a supposed friend was visiting the home. As the two women chatted, the visitor inquired, "Now which of these boys is yours, Mary?"

"Both of them," she quickly replied.

The friend was not satisfied. "Which of them did you adopt?"

In an answer that demonstrated overwhelming love for both her sons, Mary responded, "I have forgotten."

God, in adopting us as His children, forgave our sins. In heaven, we may ask God about one of our less desirable choices, asking how He could have forgiven that one. He may say, "Did you really do that? I don't remember that at all."

The Party. In an area of the city known for prostitution, a church in Melbourne, Australia, has named itself for the apostle Matthew. No, this church is not called St. Matthew's. Most of us would gladly bring our respected friends to a church named after a saint, but the members of this church purposely wanted something quite different. They called their church "Matthew's Party."

You guessed it right. These Christians read Mark 2:15 and said, "We can do that too." Like Matthew, they invite people of all types to their services, making sure they all feel welcome when they get there. Matthew might have gotten Jesus in trouble by inviting all his (Matthew's) friends, just as they were, to dinner with Jesus. But Jesus was undoubtedly delighted to meet them all.

When I visited Matthew's Party in Melbourne, I met people of types with whom I don't normally interact. I didn't feel all that comfortable. Many of these people still live in lifestyles of which I don't approve. But I couldn't help but rejoice in the fact that they have found a place where they feel accepted. They may still be spiritually ill (in other senses, so are we), but those at Matthew's Party soon discover that Jesus came to help those who need a spiritual physician.

<table>
<tr><td>

FOR YOUTH

</td><td>

■ **TOPIC:** Jesus' Miracles Bring Wholeness
■ **QUESTIONS:** 1. How did the four men demonstrate their faith in Jesus? 2. In what order did Jesus address the needs in the paralyzed

</td></tr>
</table>

man's life? 3. How did the religious leaders respond to Jesus? 4. For what reason did Jesus say He had come? 5. Why is it always best to respond in faith to Jesus' offer of forgiveness?

■ **ILLUSTRATIONS:**

Dad's Concern. As a child, I regularly attended church with my parents. Dad was the pastor; only occasionally, when visiting another church, did I have the opportunity to sit next to my dad.

As a little guy, I often did what some of you may have done in church. I got tired of listening! I would yawn. If I began to lean toward my father, what would he do? My father would raise his arm. To do what? To shake me back into an alert state? No, he offered grace. He raised his arm so that I could cuddle against his side and rest comfortably.

When we come to Jesus, sometimes not in the best of shape, He never pushes us away. He does not seek to shake us up. He receives us as we are. He offers His forgiveness and love, that is, if we will lean on Him.

A Difference. Several years ago, Trevor, a 12-year-old boy, traveled with his family from Philadelphia's suburbs into the city. When he encountered homeless people, he felt shocked. Perhaps you've already heard the end of this story. With the help of others, this young man established Trevor's House, a ministry to homeless families. Trevor was only one sixth grader, but he decided that he could make a difference.

Ruth, another teen, works a part-time job at a coffee shop near her home. She chose to tithe her earnings to help the poor of the world. When she entered a web site that enabled her, from a distance, to purchase essentials for less well-off people around the world, she ended up joyfully giving far more than 10 percent. She bought a goat for a family trying to establish their farm, and a bicycle and books for a new pastor in Ghana. Ruth was even able to help purify the water supply for an entire Indian village.

A Librarian's Investment. When I moved from a small elementary school to a much larger junior high, I looked for friends, both among my peers and the school staff. The librarian, Mrs. Houser, looked friendly, so I joined the Library Club, volunteering a bit of study hall time to help out with small tasks. Two years later, during my last year in that school, I was spending hours each day helping out in the library.

If God had not called me to pastoral ministry, I would have become a librarian. Why? Because Mrs. Houser took special interest in me, a chubby seventh grader. I and other members of the Library Club may have been as much of a bother as a help, but Mrs. Houser invested herself in me. We remained friends, corresponding regularly. Years later, while serving as a missionary overseas, I heard that she had died. I'm so glad I had taken many opportunities to thank her for all the friendship she had offered me.

THE TRIALS AND OPPOSITION

BACKGROUND SCRIPTURE: Mark 14:53-65; 15:1-5
DEVOTIONAL READING: Mark 14:17-21

3

KEY VERSE: Now the chief priests and the whole council were looking for testimony against Jesus to put him to death; but they found none. Mark 14:55.

KING JAMES VERSION

MARK 14:53 And they led Jesus away to the high priest: and with him were assembled all the chief priests and the elders and the scribes. 54 And Peter followed him afar off, even into the palace of the high priest: and he sat with the servants, and warmed himself at the fire. 55 And the chief priests and all the council sought for witness against Jesus to put him to death; and found none. 56 For many bare false witness against him, but their witness agreed not together. 57 And there arose certain, and bare false witness against him, saying, 58 We heard him say, I will destroy this temple that is made with hands, and within three days I will build another made without hands. 59 But neither so did their witness agree together. 60 And the high priest stood up in the midst, and asked Jesus, saying, Answerest thou nothing? what is it which these witness against thee? 61 But he held his peace, and answered nothing. Again the high priest asked him, and said unto him, Art thou the Christ, the Son of the Blessed? 62 And Jesus said, I am: and ye shall see the Son of man sitting on the right hand of power, and coming in the clouds of heaven. 63 Then the high priest rent his clothes, and saith, What need we any further witnesses? 64 Ye have heard the blasphemy: what think ye? And they all condemned him to be guilty of death. 65 And some began to spit on him, and to cover his face, and to buffet him, and to say unto him, Prophesy: and the servants did strike him with the palms of their hands. . . .

15:1 And straightway in the morning the chief priests held a consultation with the elders and scribes and the whole council, and bound Jesus, and carried him away, and delivered him to Pilate. 2 And Pilate asked him, Art thou the King of the Jews? And he answering said unto him, Thou sayest it. 3 And the chief priests accused him of many things: but he answered nothing. 4 And Pilate asked him again, saying, Answerest thou nothing? behold how many things they witness against thee. 5 But Jesus yet answered nothing; so that Pilate marvelled.

NEW REVISED STANDARD VERSION

MARK 14:53 They took Jesus to the high priest; and all the chief priests, the elders, and the scribes were assembled. 54 Peter had followed him at a distance, right into the courtyard of the high priest; and he was sitting with the guards, warming himself at the fire. 55 Now the chief priests and the whole council were looking for testimony against Jesus to put him to death; but they found none. 56 For many gave false testimony against him, and their testimony did not agree. 57 Some stood up and gave false testimony against him, saying, 58 "We heard him say, 'I will destroy this temple that is made with hands, and in three days I will build another, not made with hands.' " 59 But even on this point their testimony did not agree. 60 Then the high priest stood up before them and asked Jesus, "Have you no answer? What is it that they testify against you?" 61 But he was silent and did not answer. Again the high priest asked him, "Are you the Messiah, the Son of the Blessed One?" 62 Jesus said, "I am; and
  'you will see the Son of Man
  seated at the right hand of the Power,'
  and 'coming with the clouds of heaven.'"
63 Then the high priest tore his clothes and said, "Why do we still need witnesses? 64 You have heard his blasphemy! What is your decision?" All of them condemned him as deserving death. 65 Some began to spit on him, to blindfold him, and to strike him, saying to him, "Prophesy!" The guards also took him over and beat him. . . .

15:1 As soon as it was morning, the chief priests held a consultation with the elders and scribes and the whole council. They bound Jesus, led him away, and handed him over to Pilate. 2 Pilate asked him, "Are you the King of the Jews?" He answered him, "You say so." 3 Then the chief priests accused him of many things.

HOME BIBLE READINGS

Monday, June 13	Mark 14:26-31	*Jesus Predicts Peter's Denial*
Tuesday, June 14	Mark 14:43-50	*Jesus Is Betrayed by Judas*
Wednesday, June 15	Mark 14:53-59	*False Testimony Is Given About Jesus*
Thursday, June 16	Mark 14:60-65	*Jesus Is Condemned*
Friday, June 17	Mark 14:66-72	*Peter Denies Jesus*
Saturday, June 18	Mark 15:1-5	*Jesus Goes Before Pilate*
Sunday, June 19	Mark 15:6-15	*Pilate Hands Jesus Over to Die*

BACKGROUND

After Jesus was arrested in Gethsemane, He was taken to a series of trials, both religious and civil, supposedly to determine His guilt or innocence on some kind of charges. Only the Gospel of John records Jesus' questioning before Annas, the former high priest (John 18:12-14, 19-23). Though the Romans had deposed Annas as the high priest in A.D. 14, he still influenced the politics of his day. Caiaphas, the current high priest, was his son-in-law, while five of Annas' sons, and his grandson, all became high priest as well.

Once Annas had questioned Jesus, he sent Him on to Caiaphas and members of the Sanhedrin, who held an unusual, if not illegal, nighttime trial (see Acts 4:3, 5). If *the whole council* (Mark 14:55) was indeed present, there would have been 70 people. However, to have a legal decision only a quorum was needed. Normally the Sanhedrin would have met in the temple and not in the high priest's house. According to later Jewish law, no trials were allowed on the Sabbath or at festival times, but this did not seem to bother those present. Nor did their requirement that a day must pass before a verdict could be rendered in a capital case, which this one was.

That this was a "rigged" trial is shown by the presence of witnesses in the middle of the night. (It was probably already very early Friday morning when the trial started.) However, the witnesses could not agree in their testimonies, a point that should have invalidated the charges (Deut. 19:15-21). In fact, a person could not be put to death unless two witnesses agreed in their testimony (17:6).

Jesus remained *silent and did not answer* (Mark 14:61) while the witnesses contradicted themselves and misquoted Him. With the case against Jesus in shambles, the high priest finally got Jesus to say He was "*the Messiah, the Son of the Blessed One.*" The high priest and the council were thus satisfied that Jesus had condemned Himself, so they mocked and abused Him before taking Him to the next stage of the trial process (14:62-65).

Sometime just before dawn on Good Friday, the council reached a final, "legal" decision. Since the Romans would not consider blasphemy a crime punishable by death, the Jews had to convince the Roman governor, Pilate, that Jesus was guilty of treason against Caesar. Ironically, the man who had refused to become king and begin a revolt against Rome (John 6:15) was now charged with being a political revolutionary. Pilate, who normally stayed in the Roman capital of Caesarea, was in Jerusalem for the Passover to keep a lid on any celebrating that might turn against Rome. Now he was faced with a man who did not look or act like a traitor, but who was lumped together with someone who definitely was—Barabbas. In an incredible, almost impossible reversal of what should have happened, Pilate released the true revolutionary and sent the man who had done no evil to be crucified (18:28—19:16).

NOTES ON THE PRINTED TEXT

Jesus had been betrayed by one of His disciples and was now in the hands of His bitterest enemies, those religious leaders who were jealous of His power and angered by His criticism of them (Mark 14:53). We do not know exactly how many were part of the kangaroo court convened in the house of *the high priest* (14:54), Caiaphas, that night, but at least Joseph of Arimathea (Mark 15:43; Luke 23:50-51) was not part of the group that gathered to condemn Jesus.

Caiaphas, however, could have called this gathering in his house an "inquiry" into the facts, not a trial. The size and wealth of the house of Caiaphas is shown by the fact that the council group met in a large upstairs room above a courtyard while the servants were below (Mark 14:66). As a Sadducee, Caiaphas was kept in office by the Romans because he could keep the people under control. It was Caiaphas who first suggested that Jesus should die for the good of the nation (John 11:49-53), and Caiaphas was determined to carry out that plan.

As the religious leaders *look[ed] for testimony against Jesus to put him to death . . . they found none* (Mark 14:55). The parade of false witnesses gave testimony that did not agree (14:56-57). When they tried to remember what Jesus had said about destroying and rebuilding the temple in three days (14:58), they could not correctly quote Him (14:59). Their statements sound like a garbled combination of Mark 13:2 and John 2:19.

With no credible witnesses to make a case against Jesus, the high priest then badgered Him to say something in self-defense (Mark 14:60), *but he was silent* (14:61; see Isa. 53:7; 1 Pet. 2:23). To try to get Jesus to incriminate Himself, the high priest put Jesus *"under oath"* (Matt. 26:63) and asked Him if He was *"the Messiah, the Son of the Blessed One"* (Mark 14:61). Calling God *"the Blessed One"* kept the high priest from using God's sacred name, something Caiaphas instead wanted Jesus to do.

Jesus replied *"I am"* (14:62) the Messiah. He then went on to say He was *"the Son of Man,"* combining in His reply ideas from Daniel 7:13 and Psalm 110:1. While Caiaphas and the Sanhedrin were sitting in judgment of Jesus at that moment, He was looking to the future, when He would sit in judgment on them at His return (Mark 14:62).

Now Caiaphas *tore his clothes* (14:63), an official indication from the high priest that he had heard someone commit *"blasphemy"* (14:64). Those present now all *condemned* Jesus to death, though they themselves could not carry out that sentence. Instead they spit on Him and humiliated Him (14:65).

Abuse by His enemies must not have been as painful emotionally to Jesus as His treatment by Peter. This disciple wanted to stay close enough to Jesus to know what was going on, but not close enough to be identified with Him. Peter probably looked upon his actions as innocent self-preservation. After all, what was the sense of being arrested? That would do nothing to help Jesus.

When people recognized Peter and noticed his Galilean accent, he made a solemn oath before God that he was not a follower of Jesus. But when a rooster crowed a second time, the realization of how he had fulfilled Jesus' prophecy rushed in upon Peter. He was crushed. His devotion to Jesus had been exposed as shallow (14:66-72).

Early the next morning (15:1), the council and religious leaders took Jesus to the Roman procurator, Pontius Pilate, to convince him that he should execute Jesus, since the Jews could only execute someone for profaning the temple. Also, the Jews stoned people to death, but they wanted Jesus cursed forever by being crucified (Gal. 3:13).

Pilate held trials between dawn and noon, so the leaders were quick to bring Jesus to him. Pilate had been appointed to the post of procurator, a kind of governor, in A.D. 26. He ruled Judea in the service of the Roman governor of the province of Syria, who could have Pilate removed at any time and sent back to Rome. Other contemporary writings tell us that Pilate had seriously offended the Jews at least twice since he had been appointed, which means he did not want more "incidents" that could cost him his job.

Therefore, Pilate immediately questioned Jesus on the only charge that really mattered to the rulers in Rome: *"Are you the King of the Jews?"* (Mark 15:2). Jesus' statement *"You say so"* seems to mean that He is a king, but not in the way that Pilate thinks. The Gospel of John expands on that idea in Jesus' further reply to Pilate (John 18:33-37). The governor evidently did not consider Jesus a danger to the empire. This remained true despite the many crimes the chief priests accused Jesus of having committed against the government (Mark 15:3).

While Pilate did not want to antagonize the Jews, he was not interested in doing them any favors either, and he knew they had brought Jesus to him *out of jealousy* (15:10). To both satisfy the Jews and keep from executing an innocent man, Pilate proposed letting one prisoner, Jesus or Barabbas, free in honor of the Passover. While this particular custom is not found in writings outside the Gospels, other Roman documents mention similar practices.

Pilate presumed that the crowd that had gathered for the trial would want Jesus released to them instead of Barabbas, who was in prison because of being involved with murderers and an *insurrection* (15:7). The leaders, however, had *stirred up the crowd* (15:11) against Jesus, and the crowd was shouting, *"Crucify him!"* (15:13). Though Pilate knew Jesus had done no *"evil"* (15:14), and though

Pilate had been warned by his own wife not to harm Jesus (Matt. 27:19), Pilate sent Jesus to be crucified in order to satisfy *the crowd* (Mark 15:15).

We ought to remember that neither the Jewish leaders who sentenced Jesus to death, nor the Roman soldiers who conducted the crucifixion finally killed the Savior. He breathed His last on His own so that we might find salvation through Him. As 1 Peter 2:24 described it, *He himself bore our sins in his body on the cross, so that, free from sins, we might live for righteousness; by his wounds you have been healed.*

SUGGESTIONS TO TEACHERS

How do you react when someone accuses you of something that you did not do? Most of what we would do is just the opposite of what Jesus did. Scripture reveals that even before Jesus was arrested, He spent time in prayer with His Father, keeping His focus on what His Father wanted to happen in the coming events.

1. JESUS DID NOT GET ANGRY AND YELL. Despite the midnight arrest and false accusations, Jesus did not say anything. He did not argue. He also did not accuse His opponents of lying and false arrest. Instead, He peacefully responded to their charges. Too often we respond first with anger and later repent of what we said. Sometimes we can wind up being as sinful as the ones who attacked us.

2. JESUS DID NOT SEEK REVENGE. Jesus did not call down 10,000 angels or strike the high priest dead. Jesus allowed them to do what they were going to do. Sometimes we will not even pause when attacked. We will speak or act automatically, and make the situation worse. Instead, as someone once said, "It is better to suffer an injustice than to commit one."

3. JESUS DID NOT SINK INTO SELF-PITY. Jesus did not cry to His Father, or anyone else, about how unfair this whole ordeal was becoming. Jesus did not allow Himself the luxury of this emotion. We, on the other hand, can easily think *Why is everybody always picking on me?*

4. JESUS DID NOT RUN AWAY. Although the Messiah had the ability to avoid the situation entirely, He didn't. We can all learn from that. Whenever times get tough, we can be assured that Jesus is there, helping us face whatever is happening.

FOR ADULTS

■ **TOPIC:** The Prevailing God

■ **QUESTIONS:** 1. What was the testimony the witnesses gave against Jesus? 2. What was Jesus' response to the witnesses and the high priest? 3. What did the religious leaders claim Jesus was guilty of doing? 4. What happened when Jesus was turned over to Pilate? 5. When we are falsely accused of something, how should we respond?

■ ILLUSTRATIONS:

No Greater Opportunity. James C. Dobson has said, "There is no greater opportunity to influence our fellowman for Christ than to respond with love when we have been unmistakably wronged. Then the difference between Christian love and the values of the world are most brilliantly evident."

Jesus was "unmistakably wronged" by the religious leaders, high priests, and Pilate. Jesus had every right to respond in any way except with love. But what an impact Jesus made in this world when He showed love instead of hatred, revenge, anger, or bitterness to those who so wrongfully accused and abused Him. We need to remember Jesus' response when we are faced with those who try to harm us, either intentionally or unintentionally.

The Fugitive. A popular U.S. television series of the 1960s was *The Fugitive.* Richard Kimball, wrongfully sentenced to die for his wife's murder, was running from the law in pursuit of the one-armed man he saw murder her. Week after week the only focus was to find the criminal and clear Kimball's name. The concluding episode when Kimball finally found the one-armed man was one of the highest rated shows in television history. The story was so powerful that it was made into a movie and another television series in 2000.

Unlike Jesus, who was willing to die for our sins, Kimball would not die for something he did not do. Jesus allowed Himself to be falsely accused for the benefit of all who would trust in Him.

Under the Gallows. Back in 1738, London's main prison was called Newgate. Charles Wesley (later to be the great Christian hymn writer) frequently went there, preaching to those prisoners sentenced to death. On one occasion Charles was even locked in overnight in order to pray with and comfort prisoners.

In his *Journal*, Wesley tells about a poor man who was condemned to die for his many crimes. Wesley told him of "one who came down from heaven to save the lost and him in particular." Wesley led this man to faith in Christ. After Wesley served this man Communion, he accompanied the man to the gallows. The assurance of salvation was etched on the new convert's face. Because of his new friend's faith, Wesley penned, "That hour under the gallows was the most blessed hour of my life!"

FOR YOUTH

■ TOPIC: Jesus Faced Trials and Opposition

■ QUESTIONS: 1. What did the witnesses accuse Jesus of saying? 2. How did the witnesses and the high priest respond to Jesus' silence? 3. Who did Jesus say He was? 4. Why did Pilate, the Roman governor, release Barabbas instead of Jesus? 5. How have you benefited from Jesus' willingness to go to the cross?

■ **ILLUSTRATIONS:**

Stuck in the Middle. Being the middle child is just asking to be wrongly accused, especially according to many middle children. Sometimes parents will unconsciously believe the oldest child would just know better than to do anything wrong, and the youngest child would just be too innocent to do anything wrong, leaving the middle child to be accused.

As a middle child myself, I remember many occasions when that was the case. When the cookie jar lid got cracked, when there was a piece of cake missing, or when someone let the bathtub overflow, I always seemed to be the one blamed—even when I was not home at the time! I could have held grudges against my parents and my brothers, but instead I have forgiven them. However, in fun I do enjoy reminding them of all the things my parents did catch my brothers doing wrong when I was totally innocent.

Being wrongly accused is just part of life at times; however, how we decide to deal with it speaks volumes on our relationship with God. Jesus was able to endure false accusations and forgive those who hurt Him. That is not always easy for us to do, but it should be a goal we all strive to reach.

The Magical Mr. McBeevee. In an episode of the classic television series *The Andy Griffith Show,* Opie told his father about meeting a magical Mr. McBeevee in the woods who walked in the treetops, while jingling and blowing smoke out of his ears. Andy tried to get Opie to admit that this man was just in Opie's imagination, but Opie refused to change his story about the man being real. Opie was even willing to be punished for lying and have his father angry at him, because he knew he was telling the truth.

Thankfully, Andy came to the point where he was going to believe his son no matter how fabulous Opie's story seemed, because he believed in his son. In the end, Andy and Opie both learned lessons about believing in people from the miraculous telephone lineman who walked in the treetops with extra hands and had a shiny silver hat.

Although Opie was only a small boy, he had already learned the value of standing up for the truth when others falsely accused him of lying. Jesus also told the truth about Himself to the religious leaders, high priest, and Pilate, none of whom believed Him. In fact, Pilate asked Jesus *"What is truth?"* (John 18:38) without realizing that the answer was standing right in front of him.

The Stolen Wallet. Have you ever had a friend who was falsely accused of something and you hesitated to help or even refused to help? That is what happened to Angie. Angie and Kim, who were best friends, were going to have lunch together when Angie noticed she had forgotten her money. Telling Kim to wait a minute, Angie rushed back to the art room and grabbed her money. She hurried back down to the cafeteria, passing the art teacher, Miss James, to meet Kim in the lunchroom. Kim laughed and told Angie she had never seen anyone move so fast!

After lunch, when Angie and Kim went back to the art room, Miss James informed them that, while the class had been gone, her wallet had been taken; however, she kept glancing at Angie the whole time she said it. After class Miss James asked Angie to stay behind and started to ask her about why she had been in the art room while everyone else was gone. Angie explained why she had been in the room, and didn't even know where Miss James kept her purse.

Angie, hurt that her teacher thought she would have done such a thing, appealed to Kim to go and talk to Miss James and verify her story, but Kim did not want to get involved. Although Kim eventually went to Miss James to explain, and another person confessed to have stolen the wallet earlier that day, the friendship between Kim and Angie had been strained.

There were many people who did nothing to help Jesus on the way to the cross. Pilate's biggest crime was not so much what he did, but what he did not do. He knowingly sent a falsely accused, innocent man to His death, because Pilate was afraid to do otherwise.

THE TRIUMPH

BACKGROUND SCRIPTURE: Mark 16
DEVOTIONAL READING: Matthew 28:16-20

KEY VERSE: "Do not be alarmed; you are looking for Jesus of Nazareth, who was crucified. He has been raised; he is not here. Look, there is the place they laid him." Mark 16:6.

KING JAMES VERSION

MARK 16:1 And when the sabbath was past, Mary Magdalene, and Mary the mother of James, and Salome, had bought sweet spices, that they might come and anoint him. 2 And very early in the morning the first day of the week, they came unto the sepulchre at the rising of the sun. 3 And they said among themselves, Who shall roll us away the stone from the door of the sepulchre? 4 And when they looked, they saw that the stone was rolled away: for it was very great. 5 And entering into the sepulchre, they saw a young man sitting on the right side, clothed in a long white garment; and they were affrighted. 6 And he saith unto them, Be not affrighted: Ye seek Jesus of Nazareth, which was crucified: he is risen; he is not here: behold the place where they laid him. 7 But go your way, tell his disciples and Peter that he goeth before you into Galilee: there shall ye see him, as he said unto you. 8 And they went out quickly, and fled from the sepulchre; for they trembled and were amazed: neither said they any thing to any man; for they were afraid. . . .

12 After that he appeared in another form unto two of them, as they walked, and went into the country. 13 And they went and told it unto the residue: neither believed they them.

14 Afterward he appeared unto the eleven as they sat at meat, and upbraided them with their unbelief and hardness of heart, because they believed not them which had seen him after he was risen. 15 And he said unto them, Go ye into all the world, and preach the gospel to every creature.

NEW REVISED STANDARD VERSION

MARK 16:1 When the sabbath was over, Mary Magdalene, and Mary the mother of James, and Salome bought spices, so that they might go and anoint him. 2 And very early on the first day of the week, when the sun had risen, they went to the tomb. 3 They had been saying to one another, "Who will roll away the stone for us from the entrance to the tomb?" 4 When they looked up, they saw that the stone, which was very large, had already been rolled back. 5 As they entered the tomb, they saw a young man, dressed in a white robe, sitting on the right side; and they were alarmed. 6 But he said to them, "Do not be alarmed; you are looking for Jesus of Nazareth, who was crucified. He has been raised; he is not here. Look, there is the place they laid him. 7 But go, tell his disciples and Peter that he is going ahead of you to Galilee; there you will see him, just as he told you." 8 So they went out and fled from the tomb, for terror and amazement had seized them; and they said nothing to anyone, for they were afraid. . . .

12 After this he appeared in another form to two of them, as they were walking into the country. 13 And they went back and told the rest, but they did not believe them.

14 Later he appeared to the eleven themselves as they were sitting at the table; and he upbraided them for their lack of faith and stubbornness, because they had not believed those who saw him after he had risen. 15 And he said to them, "Go into all the world and proclaim the good news to the whole creation.

Monday, June 20	Matthew 27:62-66	*Jesus' Tomb Is Sealed*
Tuesday, June 21	Matthew 28:1-6b	*He Is Not Here*
Wednesday, June 22	Mark 16:1-8	*He Has Been Raised*
Thursday, June 23	Matthew 28:6c-10	*Jesus Appears to the Women*
Friday, June 24	Mark 16:9-13	*Jesus Appears to Other Followers*
Saturday, June 25	Matthew 28:16-20	*I Am With You Always*
Sunday, June 26	Mark 16:14-20	*Go into All the World*

Background

In Mark's description of Jesus' execution and burial, we read some grim details about first-century life. Crucifixion was a horrible death, reserved for slaves and the worst of criminals. Roman law prohibited any citizen from facing this end. The horror of any crucifixion began soon after the appropriate official pronounced the sentence.

Four soldiers carried out the assignment. The worst of the physical labor—carrying the cross-beam to the site of execution—was forced on the condemned by the soldiers. Four of the latter surrounded their victim. To warn city residents about the dangers of disobeying Rome, the tragic parade snaked through many streets, traveling further than was necessary to reach the appointed place of death.

Before His own crucifixion, Jesus had already suffered many wounds. The whipping would have left His back raw. Despite those wounds, soldiers still made Jesus carry His own cross at least part way (John 19:17). He was unable to finish that task, however; thus the soldiers forced a passer-by to assist Jesus. Roman soldiers possessed the authority to force almost anyone to carry almost anything. Often, kind women of Jerusalem softened the pain of crucifixion by offering *wine mixed with myrrh* (Mark 15:23). This combination slightly sedated the victim, making the pain less noticeable.

As if this brutal death were not enough, soldiers stripped the condemned before nailing him to the beams. Before friends, family, and strangers, the victim bore the indignity of nakedness. If the nails themselves were adequate to bring death, then the end would have come quickly. In many cases, though, the condemned suffered for two or three days before dying of suffocation. After losing strength, they could no longer raise their chests to breathe. They would pant tiny gulps of air until even that became impossible. Breaking a criminal's legs mercifully hastened suffocation. Some possessed enough strength to survive several awful days until they died of thirst.

If no one claimed the body of a crucified person, it would hang on the cross until birds finished their gruesome feast. Joseph of Arimathea received permission to take Jesus' body down from the cross and bury it in his garden tomb. Joseph, obviously a person of wealth, owned a tomb carved out of a stony hillside. After Jesus' body was wrapped in strips of cloth and laid in the tomb, Joseph rolled a large, disk-shaped stone into a ready-made groove before the tomb opening.

Jesus died at roughly three P.M. on Friday afternoon (15:34). The Sabbath began at 6 P.M. That short period barely gave Joseph enough time to perform the absolute essentials of burial. No one had adequate time to anoint Jesus' body, despite what contemporary custom mandated. Then, at 6 P.M. on Saturday evening, as the Sabbath ended, devoted women purchased spices in preparation for anointing Jesus' body. They wished to honor their Lord by offering one last service to His dead body. Neither they nor anyone else gave thought to the possibility that an executed criminal might rise again.

NOTES ON THE PRINTED TEXT

While Mark 15 records Jesus' sacrifice, chapter 16 shows God's acceptance of that sacrifice. The grand confirming act of the life and death of Jesus is His resurrection. The Savior was buried late on Friday afternoon. The Sabbath ended at sundown on Saturday. Jesus' followers were free to go to His tomb now, but of course they did not want to do so at night.

Thus, at first light on Sunday, three prominent women from Jesus' earthly ministry—Mary Magdalene, Mary the mother of James, and Salome—went to the burial site (16:1-2). Along the way the women had been discussing who would *"roll away the stone"* (16:3) from *"the entrance to the tomb"* so that they could anoint Jesus' body. This was a customary practice to mask the odor brought on by decay. It was also an act of devotion.

To the surprise of the women, they discovered someone had moved for them the stone, *which was very large* (16:4). No one needed to move the stone to allow Jesus out; rather, the stone was removed so that witnesses to Jesus' resurrection could verify the tomb's emptiness.

As the women entered the tomb, they saw a *young man* (16:5) dressed in *a white robe.* The angel assured them that they had come to the right place, but for the wrong reason. They would not need to anoint Jesus' dead body, for He was no longer dead (16:6).

As the women processed this stunning news, the angel instructed them to take the good news to *"his disciples and Peter"* (16:7). It seems the angel had received specific instructions to mention Peter. Perhaps Jesus wished him to know that their relationship would continue, despite Peter's failings. The women left the garden dumbfounded. The angel had spoken words they struggled to take in (16:8). But Mark's readers, knowing the full account, moved beyond the women's fear to celebrate Jesus' victory over sin and death.

By comparing early manuscripts, most New Testament scholars have concluded that 16:8 is the last verse in the Gospel of Mark that has survived. It is true that many early copies of Mark contain one or two additional endings. These endings differ from the rest of the Gospel in style, in vocabulary, and (some say) in theology. Of the various endings, one is brief. Another ending, which is longer, has been designated verses 9-20 of Mark 16. This passage represents ancient Christian teaching, but may not be equal in authority with the rest of the Gospel.

With respect to 16:12-13, it most likely signifies a condensed version of the episode recorded in Luke 24:13-35. Two of Jesus' disciples were walking to the village of Emmaus, which was about seven miles out of Jerusalem. According to Mark 16:12, the two were journeying into the country when they encountered the risen Lord. At first the two did not recognize Him because He had somehow changed His appearance. But when they realized they had been with Jesus, the two rushed back to tell the others. Regrettably, Jesus' disciples refused to believe the report of the Savior's resurrection (16:13).

It's possible that Mark 16:14-18 is a shortened account of Jesus' appearance to His disciples recorded in either Luke 24:36-48 or John 20:19-23. Another possibility is that Mark 16:14-18 represents a completely different post-resurrection appearance. In any case, 16:14 notes that Jesus appeared to the Eleven as they were eating together. With the demise of Judas (Matt. 27:3-5; Acts 1:16-18), the disciples were known for a while as *the eleven* (Mark 16:14). Jesus censured them for their stubborn refusal to accept the reports of other disciples who had seen the risen Lord.

Jesus then commanded His followers to herald the Good News throughout the world to everyone (16:15). This injunction parallels the Great Commission recorded in Matthew 28:18-20. The Good News is that Jesus lives to give salvation to repentant sinners, and, more than that, to give them abundance and fullness of life. Once abandoned on the cross, He lives with the Father now to intercede on our behalf and to work out His kingdom rule in our lives.

SUGGESTIONS TO TEACHERS

Someone has said Jesus' atoning sacrifice and resurrection, "Though each step to the cross was a step of agony, it was also a step of victory." Jesus was victorious over the enemy that all of us finally face—death. What happened that first Easter morning has profound implications for all Christians today. Four truths stand out.

1. THE EMPTY TOMB. There is no greater hope in this life than what comes from Jesus' resurrection. Because He lives, we can live too after the end of this lifetime. Note what Paul said: *If for this life only we have hoped in Christ, we are of all people most to be pitied. But in fact Christ has been raised from the dead, the first fruits of those who have died* (1 Cor. 15:19-20). Jesus was the "advance party" of those who will follow Him.

2. THE ETERNAL DESTINATION. Christ rose from the dead to return to heaven and to reign eternally. Heaven is also the destination of all believers. As Paul said, *We have a building from God, a house not made with hands, eternal in the heavens* (2 Cor. 5:1). That home is waiting for us even now, and that is why we long to be there one day.

3. THE DEFEATED ENEMY. While Satan may have believed that he had triumphed over the Son of God on the cross, the opposite was true. Jesus defeated Satan, and we can have victory over him as well. He cannot keep us from doing God's will unless we let him. If you *resist the devil . . . he will flee from you* (Jas. 4:7).

4. THE WONDERFUL MESSAGE. The good news about Jesus is most of all a message that must be shared. It is, Paul told the Corinthians, a message *of first importance* (1 Cor. 15:3). Every person needs to hear that Jesus rose from the dead and offers those who trust in Him eternal life. Will everyone believe the truth? No. But that does not mean we should not share it, and especially share what it means to us personally.

<table>
<tr><td>

FOR ADULTS

</td><td>

■ TOPIC: Hope in the Midst of Despair

■ QUESTIONS: 1. Why did various women come to the tomb where Jesus had been buried? 2. Why were the women alarmed at the

</td></tr>
</table>

sight of the angel? 3. How did the angel try to calm the unnerved women? 4. What was the message of hope the women were to proclaim? 5. How can the good news of Jesus' resurrection give us hope in the midst of despair?

■ **ILLUSTRATIONS:**

No Discussion, for Now. William Willimon, Dean of the Chapel at Duke University, recalled a time when the famous pastor-teacher-leader Carlyle Marney once visited the students at Duke Divinity School. A student said, "Dr. Marney, would you say a word or two about the resurrection of the dead?"

Marney replied, "I will not discuss that with people like you."

"Why not?" asked the student.

"I don't discuss such matters with anyone under 30," Marney said. "Look at you, in the prime of life—never have you known honest-to-God failure, heartburn, impotency, solid defeat, brick walls, mortality. So what can you know of a dark world that only makes sense if Christ is raised?"

Sooner or later, we humans realize this: without the living Lord, life's greatest moments are doomed to extinction. Only Christ has made eternal life a reality.

Self-Sacrifice. In 1946, Louis Slotin, a young scientist, needed to perform a crucial experiment to develop further American nuclear bomb capacities. He invited several of his colleagues to observe the process. Slotin hoped to determine the amount of uranium-235 necessary to start a chain reaction. To do this, he brought two blocks of uranium close to each other. When he sensed that a chain reaction had started, he would use a tool to separate the uranium blocks and stop the reaction.

But just at the crucial moment, he dropped the tool. A blue haze began to fill the room. Slotin made an instant choice. With his bare hands, he shoved the two blocks apart. This saved the lives of his colleagues but doomed him. As they waited for an ambulance to arrive, Slotin spoke quietly to his best friend. "You'll come through all right. But I haven't the faintest chance." Nine days later, he died in agony.

Our Experience as Well. D. T. Niles once said, "The resurrection that awaits us beyond physical death will be but the glorious consummation of the risen life that we have in Christ." I like the way F. B. Meyer said it in a sermon title: "Death— A Parenthesis in Life." He knew that Jesus' resurrection means that believers can conquer death through faith in Him. According to Ken Roscoe, the resurrection of Christ means that believers don't have to fear death. We also don't have to be entombed in doubt, anxiety, loneliness, or guilt.

Stronger than Death. Jeff Knight served as a youth pastor in Monroe, Washington. His senior pastors? His own parents, until they were killed in an airline crash off the coast of California. Suddenly, Jeff became a father figure to his 17-year-old sister and, along with his wife, co-pastor of the Rock Church.

A year later Jeff and 40 others from the church traveled to the spot nearest the crash site. They went, not to grieve, but to celebrate the life and ministry of Joe and Linda Knight. Because this son and the congregation made it through their grief through the power of Jesus' resurrection, God has enabled them to minister more effectively to others who are hurting. Although Jeff and his wife are young and did not expect to move into leadership so quickly, the church has continued to grow under their direction. They have discovered that God is stronger than death.

Crossing the River. An old saint was dying. A friend asked if he was afraid. "Do you fear crossing over the river of death?" Without hesitation, the old saint replied, "I belong to a Father who owns the land on both sides of the river."

FOR YOUTH

■ TOPIC: Jesus Is Victorious

■ QUESTIONS: 1. What did several of Jesus' disciples do when the Sabbath was over, and why? 2. Why had the stone been rolled away from the entrance to the tomb? 3. What joyous message did the angel deliver to the women? 4. Why do you think the women responded in fear to the angel's declaration? 5. What would you say is the primary significance of Jesus' various post-resurrection appearances?

■ ILLUSTRATIONS:

Special Tolling. The ancient village church in the town of Malden, England, is built from wooden beams that were part of the Norman invasion fleet that came ashore in A.D. 1066. The old building was constructed during the reign of Edward I (who died in 1199).

Before the worship service each week, the bell-ringing members of the parish gather in the room above the narthex to ring the changes. Each bell has a name, and when they are pulled in certain sequences, they do more than ring a tune; they announce news to the rest of the parish.

A bell is called a "tailor." Tailor Paul and the others have hung in the tower for centuries and are rung in times of death as well as on celebratory occasions. When someone in the parish dies, Tailor Paul leads off, followed by the others in a carefully orchestrated pattern. The ringing of the bells in certain patterns announces the age, the gender, and the location in the parish of that church member.

God doesn't need bells to tell Him the name, identity, or location of any person. Through Jesus Christ, He assures believers that He knows each by name. The resurrection of Jesus Christ signifies that God remembers and bestows new life on the faithful—just as He conferred new life on the crucified one.

He Did It for Me. One afternoon, a church youth group decided to act out the account of Jesus' trial and crucifixion. The youth leader took the role of Jesus, while the youth played the roles of Pilate, the accusers, the soldiers, and the crowds. The youthful mob shouted, "Crucify Him! Crucify Him!" Continuing their play, they led their leader toward a cross they had erected on the church lawn.

Then the one playing Jesus' role spoke. "Even though you are doing this to me, I still love you." As the youth heard those words, their drama suddenly was more than an ordinary group activity. They went silent, and a few tears appeared. Young men and women suddenly realized afresh the value of what Jesus had done for them.

Hoax? The fuzzy black-and-white photograph appeared in London's *Sunday Telegraph* in 1934. It caused enormous excitement. The picture showed a long neck and head rising from the murky waters of Loch Ness. Photographed by a physician, Robert Wilson, it appeared to be an extinct dinosaur. Some claimed the photo depicted "the Loch Ness monster." But many people remained skeptical.

Of course, it was all a hoax. And many years later, Christian Spurling confessed his role in the fake photography just before he died in November 1994. The "monster" had been fabricated from a 14-inch toy submarine upon which Marmaduke Wetherell, Spurling's stepfather, attached a long neck and a small head fashioned from plastic wood. The two floated the model out into the shallows and made the photograph. Wilson became the front man for the deception.

Were the disciples trying to deceive, as well? Were they simply trying to put one over on the authorities and the people by announcing that Jesus was alive? Is your faith simply the result of a clever deception? No. People will not die to keep a hoax alive. Far from losing their enthusiasm, Jesus' followers continued to proclaim the Resurrection at great personal risk. They willingly died for their faith. They did things that no hoax could ever inspire.

Only a Memory? As the exhibit of Egypt's King Tut toured the United States, the banner at the end of the show carried an old Egyptian proverb: "To speak the name of the dead is to make them live again."

Is this true? Do the dead live only in our memories? Do they live only so long as we, the living, recall their names or lives? It's a popular sentiment today. However, the Gospel of Mark proclaims a miraculous, bodily resurrection. Jesus wasn't merely remembered by the disciples or by those who came after them. God raised His Son from the dead. He is present with us in vibrant fellowship.

Fascination. Some psychologists say that the popularity of Brad Silberling's film *Casper* comes from the fact that it is a fable about children's fascination with death and the afterlife. Through a "friendly ghost," children can flirt with the idea of being dead. The main character, a young girl named Kate, eagerly explores death but then is forced to decide which of the dead to bring back to life, either her father or Casper, her new best friend.

The account of Jesus' resurrection is no childhood fable revisited. The Gospel of Mark announces that God has conquered death and has raised His Son to be present with us, wherever we are.

THE BEATITUDES

BACKGROUND SCRIPTURE: Matthew 5:1-16
DEVOTIONAL READING: Luke 6:17-23

KEY VERSE: "Blessed are those who hunger and thirst
for righteousness, for they will be filled." Matthew 5:6.

KING JAMES VERSION

MATTHEW 5:1 And seeing the multitudes, he went up into a mountain: and when he was set, his disciples came unto him: 2 And he opened his mouth, and taught them, saying,

3 Blessed are the poor in spirit: for theirs is the kingdom of heaven. 4 Blessed are they that mourn: for they shall be comforted. 5 Blessed are the meek: for they shall inherit the earth. 6 Blessed are they which do hunger and thirst after righteousness: for they shall be filled. 7 Blessed are the merciful: for they shall obtain mercy. 8 Blessed are the pure in heart: for they shall see God. 9 Blessed are the peacemakers: for they shall be called the children of God. 10 Blessed are they which are persecuted for righteousness' sake: for theirs is the kingdom of heaven. 11 Blessed are ye, when men shall revile you, and persecute you, and shall say all manner of evil against you falsely, for my sake. 12 Rejoice, and be exceeding glad: for great is your reward in heaven: for so persecuted they the prophets which were before you.

13 Ye are the salt of the earth: but if the salt have lost his savour, wherewith shall it be salted? it is thenceforth good for nothing, but to be cast out, and to be trodden under foot of men. 14 Ye are the light of the world. A city that is set on an hill cannot be hid. 15 Neither do men light a candle, and put it under a bushel, but on a candlestick; and it giveth light unto all that are in the house. 16 Let your light so shine before men, that they may see your good works, and glorify your Father which is in heaven.

NEW REVISED STANDARD VERSION

MATTHEW 5:1 When Jesus saw the crowds, he went up the mountain; and after he sat down, his disciples came to him. 2 Then he began to speak, and taught them, saying:

3 "Blessed are the poor in spirit, for theirs is the kingdom of heaven.

4 "Blessed are those who mourn, for they will be comforted.

5 "Blessed are the meek, for they will inherit the earth.

6 "Blessed are those who hunger and thirst for righteousness, for they will be filled.

7 "Blessed are the merciful, for they will receive mercy.

8 "Blessed are the pure in heart, for they will see God.

9 "Blessed are the peacemakers, for they will be called children of God.

10 "Blessed are those who are persecuted for righteousness' sake, for theirs is the kingdom of heaven.

11 "Blessed are you when people revile you and persecute you and utter all kinds of evil against you falsely on my account. 12 Rejoice and be glad, for your reward is great in heaven, for in the same way they persecuted the prophets who were before you.

13 "You are the salt of the earth; but if salt has lost its taste, how can its saltiness be restored? It is no longer good for anything, but is thrown out and trampled under foot.

14 "You are the light of the world. A city built on a hill cannot be hid. 15 No one after lighting a lamp puts it under the bushel basket, but on the lampstand, and it gives light to all in the house. 16 In the same way, let your light shine before others, so that they may see your good works and give glory to your Father in heaven."

5

HOME BIBLE READINGS

Monday, June 27	Luke 6:17-23	*Jesus Teaches About Discipleship*
Tuesday, June 28	Matthew 5:1-8	*Instructions on Living the Christian Life*
Wednesday, June 29	Matthew 5:9-16	*More Instructions for True Disciples*
Thursday, June 30	Matthew 5:43-48	*Love Your Enemies*
Friday, July 1	Luke 6:32-36	*Be Merciful*
Saturday, July 2	Matthew 7:1-5	*Do Not Judge*
Sunday, July 3	Luke 6:37-42	*On Judging Others*

BACKGROUND

Two primary views surface when we ask when the Gospel of Matthew was written. One group of Bible scholars dates it between A.D. 80 and 100, while a second group dates it between A.D. 50 and 65. The destruction of the Jerusalem temple in A.D. 70 and the relationship between the Gospel of Matthew and the Gospel of Mark are two pivotal issues in the debate.

Those who hold to a later date argue that Matthew used and reworked much material found in the Gospel of Mark. If Mark was written shortly after Peter's death (around A.D. 65), this would place the writing of Matthew later than A.D. 70. A second argument for the later date cites Matthew 22:7, which may refer to the fall of Jerusalem. A third argument contends that the church situation in Matthew (Matt. 16:18; 18:15-20) was more fully developed than it was in Mark, reflecting a state of affairs toward the close of the first century.

Some who hold to an early date for the first Synoptic Gospel believe it was the first written account of Jesus' life and ministry. One reason is that Matthew does not explicitly mention the destruction of the Jerusalem temple in A.D. 70. His silence would have been strange if he had written after that horrendous event. A second argument for the earlier dating is based on the writings of Irenaeus, an early church leader. He maintained that Matthew was written around the time of the Roman emperor Nero, who reigned from A.D. 54–68.

Where was Matthew written? Some think the Gospel was first penned in Aramaic and later translated into Greek. According to this view, the book would have originated in Palestine—probably in Jerusalem itself. Others think the Gospel was first written in Greek and originated from a major Near Eastern city outside Palestine with a large Greek-speaking Jewish population. Based on the history of the expansion of the early church, the city of Antioch in Syria becomes a possible place of origin.

Wherever it was written, this Gospel soon found its way into the hands of Jewish Christians. Despite the Gospel's Jewish flavor, however, Matthew did not merely focus on the people of Israel. He introduced Jesus both as the son of David (an Israelite) and as the son of Abraham (originally a Chaldean; see Gen. 11:31). Matthhew told readers how Christ must be the first priority (Matt. 6:25-34; 7:24-27) and what it means to be His true follower (10:37-39; 16:24).

NOTES ON THE PRINTED TEXT

Matthew 5—7 is called the Sermon on the Mount because Jesus delivered this series of messages on one of the gently sloping hillsides at the northwest corner of the Sea of Galilee, probably not far from Capernaum. As Jesus' popularity soared, huge crowds began to follow Him (5:1-2). His disciples could easily have been tempted to feel proud, prestigious, and possessive. Perhaps that's why Jesus warned them about the challenges they faced. He told them that instead of expecting fame and fortune, they should expect to mourn, face hunger, and be persecuted. And though their reward may not come in this life, Jesus assured them that they would reap rich heavenly rewards for embodying certain spiritual qualities (5:3-12).

The Beatitudes are the first section of the Sermon on the Mount. The Beatitudes are named from the Latin word *beatitudo,* a term that refers to a state of joy or bliss. The Beatitudes are a list of both the responsibilities and blessings of discipleship. In His discourse, Jesus implied much more than just being happy. Worldly joy is a fleeting emotion that's dependent on one's outward circumstance. Being *blessed* (5:3), however, is a deep-seated, long-lasting spiritual joy that comes from God and is independent of one's outward circumstances.

Each beatitude recorded in 5:3-12 seems to clash with some worldly value. For instance, our need for God clashes with our longing for personal independence; our mourning clashes with our desire for happiness at any cost; and the call to be gentle and lowly clashes with our innate craving for power. Clearly, Jesus neither wanted nor expected His disciples to be like everybody else. Of course, He knew that by them being different, they would face intense opposition, especially in the form of persecution. Nevertheless, those who cultivated these spiritual qualities were promised eternal blessings.

"The poor in spirit" (5:3)—those who humbly acknowledge their spiritual need—are blessed because they will receive as a gift the kingdom of heaven. *"Those who mourn"* (5:4)—those who grieve over their spiritual poverty—are blessed because God will forgive and comfort them. *"The meek"* (5:5)—those who humbly submit to God—are blessed because they are promised the earth as an inheritance.

"Those who hunger and thirst for righteousness" (5:6)—those who earnestly long for all that God offers and requires—are blessed because God will satisfy their desire for salvation. *"The merciful"* (5:7)—those who show kindness and forgiveness to the undeserving—are blessed because they will receive from God the compassion they've shown to people. *"The pure in heart"* (5:8)—those whose lives are marked by virtue and integrity—are blessed because they will enjoy an intimate relationship with the living God.

"The peacemakers" (5:9)—those who work for peace in their families, schools, churches, businesses, and communities—are blessed because they will be known as spiritual children in God's heavenly family. *"Those who are perse-*

cuted for righteousness' sake" (5:10-12)—those who suffer for truth, uprightness, and goodness—are blessed because they will receive the divine kingdom.

It is clear from this teaching of Jesus that position, authority, and money are simply not important in His kingdom. What is important is His followers' faithful and humble obedience. Such a message would have challenged the proud and legalistic religious leaders of the day.

Jesus summed up the Beatitudes by reminding His disciples that their character, integrity, and way of living should stand out from the rest of the world. As *"the salt of the earth"* (5:13) and *"the light of the world"* (5:14), they were to be a positive moral influence, that is, a reflection of God's love. Also, they were to radiate the knowledge and presence of God to people living in spiritual darkness or ignorance (5:15).

Given these statements, it's not surprising why Jesus told His disciples to *"let your light shine before others"* (5:16). He wanted the unsaved to see the good works that God's grace had produced in the lives of believers. As a result, the lost might be drawn to God's saving power.

SUGGESTIONS TO TEACHERS

Jesus longs for us to both have and demonstrate the spiritual qualities He possesses. There are some virtues that we would really like to have; yet we find them difficult to possess and express. There are other qualities that seem undesirable to us, for they run counter to our own worldly values.

In either case, Jesus still wants us to be different, to be a purifying agent in a sinful world, to be *"the salt of the earth"* (Matt. 5:13). He also yearns for us to stand out like *"a city built on a hill"* (5:14). If we accept Jesus' offer of love, grace, and mercy, He will empower us to be a source of spiritual *"light to all in the house"* (5:15). When this is consistently true for us, there are certain virtues that will become increasingly evident in our lives.

1. BE DISTINCTIVE. Living for God sometimes means being different from the people of the world. We have to be willing to love when others hate, to give when others take, and to help when others abuse. But by giving up our own rights in order to serve other people, we'll one day receive the eternal rewards God has in store for us.

2. BE HUMBLE. Reflecting Jesus' humility isn't easy, especially when the world around us is grasping for power and pride. Admittedly, though our Christian faith may make us unpopular, it sometimes can actually bring us a certain measure of attention. At those times, if we don't remember who we are and who God is, we can easily find ourselves using our Christian notoriety to promote our own personal interests.

3. BE UNPOPULAR. Surely there will be times when our Christian lifestyle will cause us to be alienated from and ostracized by others. Remember that we were forewarned; but we're also promised a heavenly reward for living for Jesus.

4. BE NOTICED. The only way we'll ever get *"persecuted for righteousness' sake"* (Matt. 5:10) is if it becomes known that we're followers of Christ. We can't always run and hide from the truth that we belong to God. In fact, our being verbally, emotionally, and even physically persecuted proves that we are being faithful to our Lord.

5. BE SALTY. In ancient times, people used salt to season and preserve their food and to bring out its flavor. In a figurative sense, we need to have a wholesomeness about us that enables us to be a blessing and a moral preservative in the world. Otherwise, if we become too much like the world, we become morally insipid.

6. BE SHINY. We are not *the* light of the world; Jesus fulfills that role. But we are lesser *lights* in the world, reflecting His presence and purity in the same way that the moon, in the dark night sky, reflects the radiance of the sun. Thus, if we live for Christ, we will shine like lights, showing others what Jesus is like. May we be beacons for the Lord, shining our light to the rest of the world!

FOR ADULTS

■ **TOPIC:** Experiencing True Happiness

■ **QUESTIONS:** 1. In what ways do all of the Beatitudes relate to each other? 2. How do each of the Christian spiritual qualities relate to the promise that follows it? 3. Which of the Beatitudes do you think is the easiest to carry out? Which is the hardest? 4. In what ways would fulfilling the Beatitudes help us to be "salt" and "light" in the world? 5. How has your Christian faith given you contentment with life?

■ **ILLUSTRATIONS:**

How to Live. A psychiatrist and a student of Sigmund Freud, James Tucker Fisher, closed his book called *A Few Buttons Missing: The Case Book of a Psychiatrist* (which he co-wrote with Lowell S. Hawley) with this final note:

"I dreamed of writing a handbook that would be simple, practical, easy to understand, and easy to follow. It would tell people how to live—what thoughts and attitudes and philosophies to cultivate and what pitfalls to avoid, in seeking mental health. I attended every symposium . . . possible, . . . and took notes on the wise words of teachers and my colleagues who were leaders in the field.

"And then quite by accident, I discovered that such a work had already been completed. . . . If you were to take the sum total of all the authoritative articles ever written by the most qualified of psychologists and psychiatrists on the subject of mental hygiene—if you were to combine them and refine them and cleave out the excess verbiage . . . you would have an awkward and incomplete summation of the Sermon on the Mount."

When People Revile You and Persecute You. During World War II, when the Nazi armies were in almost every country of Europe, King Christian of Denmark stubbornly resisted them. His country was quite small compared to the powerful Third Reich, and the king knew he could not win on the battlefield, but he still put up a valiant moral struggle.

One day he observed a Nazi flag flying above one of his public buildings. He reminded the German commander that this was contrary to the treaty between the two nations. Then he told the occupying forces, "The flag must be removed before twelve o'clock; otherwise I will send a soldier to remove it."

At five minutes before noon, the flag was flying, and the king announced that he was sending a soldier to take it down. "The soldier will be shot," the Nazi officer replied. Then King Christian calmly said, "I think I should tell you that I will be that soldier."

Blessed Are the Peacemakers. William Penn's colony of Pennsylvania pioneered two experiments. The first was the Quaker guarantee of total freedom of conscience. The second was its security system. Unguarded by fort or by soldier, the colony protected itself from attack by a just social policy that treated native Americans fairly and as friends. For 70 years the colony was absolutely safe, its borders respected and its people unharmed. But all this changed in 1756, when the British government ordered the colony to bear arms against the French, which drove the Quakers from power and the colony into the Seven Years' War.

FOR YOUTH

■ TOPIC: What Is True Happiness?

■ QUESTIONS: 1. What do you think it means to be *"poor in spirit"* (Matt. 5:3)? 2. What erroneous ideas might people have about meekness (5:5)? 3. What would you say it means to be *"pure in heart"* (5:8)? How is this possible in our age of materialism and vice? 4. Why is it possible to rejoice when we are persecuted? 5. How do the promises of the Beatitudes compare with what most people in the world really value?

■ ILLUSTRATIONS:

For Righteousness' Sake. The day after the funeral for Cassie Bernall, who was gunned down in the Columbine, Colorado, school shooting, Amy Goldstein of *The Washington Post* wrote, "For her funeral yesterday morning, friends of Cassie Bernall had stitched together a video, interspersing their remembrances of the Columbine High School junior with photographs of the young woman with long blond hair, a wide smile, and slender cross at her throat.

"'Her eyes shone with Christ's light,' one of the friends said in the video.

"'Cassie was one of the strongest Christians I've ever known,' said another friend. 'I knew that she was so willing to die for Christ.'

"Added a third: 'I just thank God she went out . . . a martyr. She went out dying for what she believed.'

"As the first jolt of tragedy has begun yielding to a deeper search for meaning, the deaths of at least a few of Littleton's dozen murdered teenagers are being understood—locally and in churches across the United States—through the prism of Christianity. As the identities of the victims began to seep out last week, it became evident that some apparently had been selected by Eric Harris and Dylan Klebold, the gun-wielding pair who rampaged the school, because of their fervent religious faith."

Salt of the Earth. A television news director says God gave her a job to do. "I have no problem seeing myself as a missionary," Paula Madison of WNBC in New York said in a 2000 interview. "I genuinely believe God put me here for a reason. I see myself as an agent of change for the better."

Madison has downplayed sensationalism. Since taking the job back in 1996, she has looked for stories about "the least among us." And she has increased religion coverage, hoping to prove that if she can set a different tone and still be successful, other stations will follow. She attained that goal in 1999 when News Channel 4 finished first among local newscasts in the ratings for the first time in 16 years.

In addition to assigning reporters, Madison, 47, selects off-screen personnel, and sets the tone, discipline, and style of the newsroom. She says she prays every day that she and the reporters she assigns to stories will exercise good judgment, wisdom, and sensitivity. "I want measured, reasonable discourse," she said.

In the Same Way They Persecuted the Prophets. When Mother Teresa first began her work among the dying on the streets of Calcutta, India, she was obstructed at every turn by government officials and orthodox Hindus, who were suspicious of her motives and used their authority to harass her and frustrate her efforts. She and her colleagues were insulted and threatened with physical violence.

One day a shower of stones and bricks rained down on the women as they tried to bring the dying to their humble shelter. Eventually Mother Teresa dropped to her knees before the mob. "Kill me!" she cried in Bengali, her arms outstretched in a gesture of crucifixion, "and I'll be in heaven all the sooner." The rabble withdrew, but soon the harassment increased with even more irrational acts of violence, and louder demands were made of officials to expel the foreigner.

One morning, Mother Teresa noticed a gathering of people outside the nearby Kali Temple, one of the holy places for Hindus in Calcutta. As she drew closer, she saw a man stretched out on the street with turned-up eyes and a face drained of blood. A triple braid denoted that he was of the Brahman caste, not of the temple priests. No one dared to touch him, for people recognized he was dying from cholera.

Mother Teresa went to him, bent down, took the body of the Brahman priest in her arms, and carried him to her shelter. Day and night she nursed him, and eventually he recovered. Over and over again he would say to the people, "For 30 years I have worshiped a Kali of stone. But I have met in this gentle woman a real Kali, a Kali of flesh and blood." Never again were stones thrown at Mother Teresa and her colleagues.

PRACTICES OF PIETY

BACKGROUND SCRIPTURE: Matthew 6:1-18
DEVOTIONAL READING: Luke 11:5-13

KEY VERSE: "Beware of practicing your piety before others in order to be seen by them; for then you have no reward from your Father in heaven." Matthew 6:1.

KING JAMES VERSION

MATTHEW 6:1 Take heed that ye do not your alms before men, to be seen of them: otherwise ye have no reward of your Father which is in heaven. 2 Therefore when thou doest thine alms, do not sound a trumpet before thee, as the hypocrites do in the synagogues and in the streets, that they may have glory of men. Verily I say unto you, They have their reward. 3 But when thou doest alms, let not thy left hand know what thy right hand doeth: 4 That thine alms may be in secret: and thy Father which seeth in secret himself shall reward thee openly.

5 And when thou prayest, thou shalt not be as the hypocrites are: for they love to pray standing in the synagogues and in the corners of the streets, that they may be seen of men. Verily I say unto you, They have their reward. 6 But thou, when thou prayest, enter into thy closet, and when thou hast shut thy door, pray to thy Father which is in secret; and thy Father which seeth in secret shall reward thee openly. 7 But when ye pray, use not vain repetitions, as the heathen do: for they think that they shall be heard for their much speaking. 8 Be not ye therefore like unto them: for your Father knoweth what things ye have need of, before ye ask him.

9 After this manner therefore pray ye: Our Father which art in heaven, Hallowed be thy name. 10 Thy kingdom come. Thy will be done in earth, as it is in heaven. 11 Give us this day our daily bread. 12 And forgive us our debts, as we forgive our debtors. 13 And lead us not into temptation, but deliver us from evil: For thine is the kingdom, and the power, and the glory, for ever. Amen. 14 For if ye forgive men their trespasses, your heavenly Father will also forgive you.

NEW REVISED STANDARD VERSION

MATTHEW 6:1 "Beware of practicing your piety before others in order to be seen by them; for then you have no reward from your Father in heaven.

2 "So whenever you give alms, do not sound a trumpet before you, as the hypocrites do in the synagogues and in the streets, so that they may be praised by others. Truly I tell you, they have received their reward. 3 But when you give alms, do not let your left hand know what your right hand is doing, 4 so that your alms may be done in secret; and your Father who sees in secret will reward you.

5 "And whenever you pray, do not be like the hypocrites; for they love to stand and pray in the synagogues and at the street corners, so that they may be seen by others. Truly I tell you, they have received their reward. 6 But whenever you pray, go into your room and shut the door and pray to your Father who is in secret; and your Father who sees in secret will reward you.

7 "When you are praying, do not heap up empty phrases as the Gentiles do; for they think that they will be heard because of their many words. 8 Do not be like them, for your Father knows what you need before you ask him.

9 "Pray then in this way:
Our Father in heaven,
    hallowed be your name.
10 Your kingdom come.
    Your will be done,
    on earth as it is in heaven.
11 Give us this day our daily bread.
12 And forgive us our debts,
    as we also have forgiven our debtors.
13 And do not bring us to the time of trial,
    but rescue us from the evil one.
14 For if you forgive others their trespasses, your heavenly Father will also forgive you.

6

HOME BIBLE READINGS

Monday, July 4	James 5:13-18	*The Importance of Prayer*
Tuesday, July 5	Mark 11:20-25	*Have Faith and Pray*
Wednesday, July 6	Matthew 7:7-11	*God Answers Prayer*
Thursday, July 7	Luke 11:5-13	*Perseverance in Prayer*
Friday, July 8	Matthew 6:1-8	*Concerning Almsgiving and Prayer*
Saturday, July 9	Matthew 6:9-15	*The Lord's Prayer*
Sunday, July 10	Matthew 6:16-21	*Concerning Fasting and Treasures*

BACKGROUND

One of the dangers of practicing a religious tradition is the desire to show off one's piety. Exhibitionists crop up in every faith community. As this week's lesson shows, the Judaism of Jesus' day had its share of people who paraded their holiness in public.

Many Jewish prayers were (and are) beautiful expressions of devotion. The problem was not always in the prayers but in the participants. In some cases, the required recitations of long prayers and short prayers three times a day became empty rote. Some who were praying these lovely petitions rattled them off without thinking. Their main desire was to be seen and heard by others. Some rabbis preached against such empty formality, but the practice continued.

Some on the Jerusalem streets also took pride in offering public prayers to God. They uttered long, windy addresses that were characterized by ornate language. One old Hebrew prayer actually began with 16 different adjectives to describe the Almighty's name. And some worshipers delighted in mumbling these words over and over, often before awed spectators.

Jesus insisted that His followers avoid any forms of egotistic piety. Part of what we know as the Sermon on the Mount records the Lord's warnings against hypocrisy in praying. The sincerity of one's heart, not the eloquence of one's words or showiness of one's actions, is what mattered to the Savior.

To aid His disciples in praying, Jesus offered a model prayer. Rabbis sometimes gave a prayer for their students, and this is apparently what Christ did too. But the so-called Lord's Prayer excelled by summarizing the kind of things a genuine worshiper of God would want to say while praying. This model prayer can be repeated in 15 seconds, but it takes a lifetime to understand fully!

NOTES ON THE PRINTED TEXT

In Matthew 5:20, Jesus warned that unless a person's righteousness exceeded that of Israel's religious leaders, one could not enter the heavenly kingdom. Christ stressed that it was inadequate to obey God outwardly but not let Him transform one's attitude and actions. Internal conformity to the spirit of the law was just as vital as an external compliance to the letter of the law.

In 6:1-18, Jesus showed how the righteousness of the scribes and Pharisees was deficient in three areas: charitable deeds (vss. 1-4), prayer (vss. 5-15), and fasting (vss. 16-18). This week's lesson focuses on the first two categories.

When certain religious leaders performed their acts of *piety* (6:1), they sought to win the praise of the people. Jesus condemned such self-serving motives. He declared that good deeds should be done with no thought of being admired. When engaging in religious activities, the motives of Jesus' followers were to remain pure. Otherwise, they could expect to receive no reward from their heavenly Father. The acclaim they obtained from others would be their only reward.

When these religious leaders performed a charitable deed, a trumpet blast would announce it to the public *"in the synagogues and in the streets"* (6:2). In this way the leaders obtained praise from the people. Jesus condemned such pretense. The term rendered *hypocrites* had its origins in Greek theater, and described a character who wore a mask. In this verse, hypocrites were those who claimed to have a relationship with God but who were self-seeking and self-deceived.

Jesus encouraged His followers to give to those who were impoverished. He cautioned, however, *"do not let your left hand know what your right hand is doing"* (6:3). This means the disciples were not to draw attention to themselves. Rather, their motive was to honor God and give Him recognition.

The Savior told His disciples to do their charitable giving *in secret* (6:4), that is, in a private and inconspicuous manner. This implies that their acts of kindness and compassion did not need to be announced to the public. Their heavenly Father was well aware of what they had done and would eternally reward them.

Many leaders prayed in such conspicuous places as *"in the synagogues and at the street corners"* (6:5). They were frauds, for they wanted as many people as possible to see them praying. Undoubtedly, the people admired what appeared to be religious devotion. But God knew it was a sham.

Jesus did not specifically condemn praying in public, for even He did so (see John 11:41-42). Rather, He censured praying with impure, self-serving motives. His followers could avoid drawing attention to themselves by praying in a private, secluded spot (Matt. 6:6).

When the Gentiles prayed, they were known for their *empty phrases* (6:7). The disciples were not to mechanically resay their words in prayer, for the Father already knew what they needed even before they asked (6:8). Jesus was not condemning lengthy or repeated prayers, for at times He prayed all night (see Luke 6:12) and on occasion repeated His prayers (see Matt. 26:44). He sought to dispel the notion that prayers could force God to respond in a certain way.

The Lord's Prayer is recorded in 6:9-13. It teaches that when believers pray, they are to acknowledge God's holiness (6:9). They are also to long for the establishment of His future kingdom and for the completion of His will on earth even though it had been fully accomplished in heaven (6:10).

Jesus encouraged His followers to pray to God about their personal needs, for He ultimately provides their daily bread (6:11). This does not mean they will get all they want. Instead, God is promising to meet their needs, not satisfy their greedy desires.

Believers are to confess their sins, or moral and spiritual debts, to God. Jesus noted that God's forgiveness of them was to be reflected in their willingness to forgive those who had wronged them (6:12). The more aware and appreciative believers are of God's forgiveness, the more inclined they will be to forgive others.

Believers should pray to God about their spiritual well-being. For example, they can petition Him to steer them away from temptation. Only the Lord can deliver them from all evil influences, including the father of wickedness, the devil (6:13; see John 8:44).

Matthew 6:14-15 may be taken in two ways. Some say that the forgiveness God extends is conditional on how much His people forgive their offenders. Others say that believers enjoy the forgiveness of their sins to the same extent that they either forgive or withhold forgiveness from others who have wronged them. In either case, Jesus' point remains clear. God has freely pardoned believers from their transgressions. And He wants His people, in turn, to freely forgive others who have sinned against them (see Eph. 4:32).

SUGGESTIONS TO TEACHERS

This week's lesson is so packed with material that you might have difficulty covering all of it. For example, Jesus' teachings on prayer cannot be easily squeezed into one class session. But don't fret. Touching on the subjects in the Sermon on the Mount relating to prayer will plant thoughts that the students can ponder during the upcoming week.

1. PLAY-ACTING POSES. Jesus warned His followers about trying to make a public spectacle of their piety. He taught that praying was not meant to impress others. That's why He admonished the disciples to find a quiet place where they could pray in private. Use this admonition to encourage your class to talk seriously about their need to set aside time each day for personal, private prayer.

2. PRETENTIOUS PRATTLE. Some have the mistaken notion that elaborate phrases and long-winded addresses to God are the key to a relationship with Him. In fact, some church leaders have given the impression that their "eloquent" prayers are the way everyone must pray. Jesus dismissed the idea that God wants us to approach Him with flowery speeches and lengthy orations. Honesty and simplicity, authenticity and humility are what counts to Him.

3. PROTOTYPE PIETY. Discuss each verse of the Lord's Prayer. An entire series of lessons could well be devoted to studying this model prayer. Nonetheless, allow ample time in this lesson to discuss the meaning of each verse.

4. PURPOSEFUL PARDONING. Highlight Matthew 6:14-15, in which Jesus emphasized the place of forgiveness. Appreciating God's mercy means being merciful to others. Invite your students to discuss the connection between receiving God's forgiveness and extending forgiveness to those who have wronged them in some way.

FOR ADULTS

■ **TOPIC:** Practicing Genuine Piety

■ **QUESTIONS:** 1. In what ways were some of Israel's religious leaders hypocrites? 2. What is the connection between God's forgiveness of believers and their willingness to forgive those who have wronged them? 3. What do you like most about praying to God? 4. What are some of your recent prayers that God has answered? 5. Who is someone you could pray for today?

■ **ILLUSTRATIONS:**

Strange Petition. A mother, while listening to her little girl's bedside prayer, heard her say, "Dear God, please make Boston the capitol of Vermont!" Astonished by the strange petition, her mother asked, "Why did you pray for that?" "Because," answered the child, "that's the way I wrote it down on my examination paper today."

We often wonder whether God hears and answers our prayers. Some people, if posed with the question, would unhesitatingly answer, "I doubt it."

Perhaps we have difficulty acknowledging the efficacy of prayer because we find that we want to set the ground rules for it. In prayer, we often bombard God with petitions for this or that, and we neglect an important aspect of prayer, namely, letting God speak to our hearts. We expect God to hear our prayers but we don't wait around for His answer. It's like the person who prayed, "God give me patience, and I demand it now!"

If we approach prayer with an attitude of openness, seeking it to be an offering of ourselves and our needs, God will answer. His response might not be when we expect it. We might not always like the answer, for God gives His blessings according to His purposes, not ours. But He will answer, especially when we listen to Him.

Eyes Open and Shut. In Christian history, there are two traditions of prayer. One is praying with the eyes shut and is called "apophatic prayer." The other is praying with the eyes open and is known as "kataphatic prayer." Apophatic praying is centering on the divine in silence, knowing that all human expressions are inadequate. In contrast, kataphatic prayer attempts to experience in a limited way the majesty of God's grace that is present. Both approaches, at their deepest level, see prayer as listening for God's peace and presence.

We should pray remembering both kinds of methods—with eyes open as well as shut. We are open to the needs of the world around us and also shut in meditation and wonder before the mysteries of God, which cannot ever be completely understood. We are open to God's summons to live in response to His love by committing ourselves to share His mercy and work for justice. And we are shut in private, personal listening to the gentle leading of the Spirit.

The Story behind the Song. Albert Malotte's is the most popular version of the musical rendition of the Lord's Prayer. You have undoubtedly heard it sung many times, and with millions of others felt thrilled by the composition.

Malotte had once been a choirboy but then he ran away from home. He tried to support himself in small town theaters by playing the piano while standing on his head, but then he realized that he could not survive this way indefinitely. He also became aware that he had hurt his parents. Finally, one day, he went to a telegraph office and sent the message: "Dad, please forgive me. Wire me money to come home."

Al Malotte's father did forgive him, and welcomed him home. The boy never forgot the meaning of his father's love and acceptance. Years later, while relying on the power of prayer, Malotte began a series of jobs. He worked as a pilot and then as a church organist. There were ups and downs. But the Lord's Prayer, along with the memory of running away and being received home by his father, remained the constant form of praying for him. In his leisure, Malotte began writing music. He wrote the music for ballets in Hollywood, which were accepted, and then music for Walt Disney films. He was accorded recognition. But Malotte wanted to express his faith in a composition, saying, "I am so grateful to God."

The root of the melody of the piece, "The Lord's Prayer," began to grow. One night, he called to his parents and said, "Listen, Mom! Listen, Pop!" And he sang to them the prayer the Lord Jesus had given to us.

Subsequently, artists such as the great John Charles Thomas performed Malotte's "The Lord's Prayer." Though G. Schirmer had already published 19 other versions of the Lord's Prayer, not one reached the popularity of Malotte's. Malotte himself modestly insisted that his musical arrangement of Jesus' prayer was simply his way of wanting to bow in grateful, forgiving prayer.

FOR YOUTH

■ TOPIC: Practicing My Faith

■ QUESTIONS: 1. Why were the religious leaders so eager for others to see their acts of piety? 2. What are the key elements of the Lord's Prayer? 3. What time of the day is best for you to pray? 4. What do your friends think about praying to God? 5. How has praying helped you?

■ ILLUSTRATIONS:

A Better Model. Wayne Lee Jones was a student of religion and languages at Harvard University. While doing research, he discovered that most children's books on prayer were similar to ones in the fifteenth or sixteenth century. All were primers, but did not satisfy a child and lacked theological and spiritual content. He thus wrote *God, Good Morning: Prayers for Children from Around the World* to introduce youngsters to 100 prayers from various religious traditions. His view was that this varied collection would enhance the prayer life of children.

Jesus offered a model prayer. It has a simple form, which suggests that God is caring and compassionate. Why buy any book on praying when God's own Son gave us a model that is free of charge?

The Shelter of Your Life. Workers excavating for Berlin's Holocaust Memorial in the winter of 1997–1998 discovered the bunker of Joseph Goebbels, Hitler's minister of propaganda. The bunker was a series of dark, cramped, concrete-lined tunnels. Even at best, living there would have been a miserable existence. It was built for protection from Allied bombers. As the Third Reich crumbled in the closing days of World War II, Goebbels urged his fellow citizens to fight to the last German, while he stayed in the protection and safety of his bombproof shelter. When the end came, Goebbels and his wife poisoned their six children and then committed suicide. Lost and forgotten in the no-man's land of the old Berlin Wall, the bunker remains a focal point of debate as to whether it should be destroyed or turned into a museum.

Jesus urged His followers to seek spiritual shelter with God. That protection came through a relationship with the Lord that was maintained through prayer. Christ urged His followers to find a place of solitude, and develop a prayer life that would enable them to experience God's enduring peace.

Challenged. In 1997, Ted Turner gave one billion dollars to the United Nations amidst great hoopla. He also challenged Bill Gates, the head of Microsoft, to do the same. Despite the media hype, isn't Turner's giving the kind that Jesus condemned? All that was lacking was the sound of trumpets! Jesus said that giving should be done in a private, quiet way, without fanfare or promotion.

No Fear of Death. One of my favorite storytellers is the author Robert Fulghum. He's written several best-selling books, beginning with one called *All I Really Need to Know I Learned in Kindergarten.* More than 15,000,000 copies of his books are in print, in more than 25 languages, and in nearly 100 countries. Needless to say, he has done very well financially.

In an interview several years ago with a Christian magazine called *The Door,* Fulghum reports that since his success, people are always saying, "Well, you must have a big house and a big car." And he responds, "No, I have the same house, same car, same friends, same wife." Fulghum admits to being on guard against all kinds of greed, and is committed to serving God, not money.

Of course, fame is a challenge, Fulghum admits, "and the challenge is to be a good steward with this kind of authority and power—especially with the economics." So one year he did a book tour, and used it to raise $670,000 for a number of good causes. "I don't think I should be given extra credit for doing that," he says. "I think you should think ill of me if I didn't do that."

Death doesn't scare Fulghum. In fact, in one of his books is a picture of the grave he has already picked out, and he likes to visit it. It reminds him to live in a way that is laying up for himself treasures in heaven. And when Fulghum sees the grave, he says to himself, "Don't get lost here. Know where you're going."

Those who find ways to serve God have discovered the right path. They don't have to fear death, for they know where they're going. Their treasure is waiting for them in heaven, not in an earthly bank account, an estate, or in stocks and bonds.

THE PURPOSE OF THE PARABLES

BACKGROUND SCRIPTURE: Matthew 13:1-23
DEVOTIONAL READING: Mark 4:10-20

KEY VERSE: [Jesus said,] "Let anyone with ears listen!" Matthew 13:9.

KING JAMES VERSION

MATTHEW 13:9 Who hath ears to hear, let him hear. 10 And the disciples came, and said unto him, Why speakest thou unto them in parables? 11 He answered and said unto them, Because it is given unto you to know the mysteries of the kingdom of heaven, but to them it is not given. 12 For whosoever hath, to him shall be given, and he shall have more abundance: but whosoever hath not, from him shall be taken away even that he hath. 13 Therefore speak I to them in parables: because they seeing see not; and hearing they hear not, neither do they understand. 14 And in them is fulfilled the prophecy of Esaias, which saith, By hearing ye shall hear, and shall not understand; and seeing ye shall see, and shall not perceive: 15 For this people's heart is waxed gross, and their ears are dull of hearing, and their eyes they have closed; lest at any time they should see with their eyes, and hear with their ears, and should understand with their heart, and should be converted, and I should heal them. 16 But blessed are your eyes, for they see: and your ears, for they hear. 17 For verily I say unto you, That many prophets and righteous men have desired to see those things which ye see, and have not seen them; and to hear those things which ye hear, and have not heard them.

NEW REVISED STANDARD VERSION

MATTHEW 13:9 Let anyone with ears listen!"
10 Then the disciples came and asked him, "Why do you speak to them in parables?" 11 He answered, "To you it has been given to know the secrets of the kingdom of heaven, but to them it has not been given.
12 For to those who have, more will be given, and they will have an abundance; but from those who have nothing, even what they have will be taken away. 13 The reason I speak to them in parables is that 'seeing they do not perceive, and hearing they do not listen, nor do they understand.' 14 With them indeed is fulfilled the prophecy of Isaiah that says:

'You will indeed listen, but never understand,
  and you will indeed look, but never perceive.
15 For this people's heart has grown dull,
  and their ears are hard of hearing,
    and they have shut their eyes;
    so that they might not look with their eyes,
  and listen with their ears,
and understand with their heart and turn—
  and I would heal them.'

16 But blessed are your eyes, for they see, and your ears, for they hear. 17 Truly I tell you, many prophets and righteous people longed to see what you see, but did not see it, and to hear what you hear, but did not hear it."

7

Monday, July 11	Psalm 78:1-7	*Truth in a Parable*
Tuesday, July 12	Isaiah 6:1-10	*Keep Looking and Listening*
Wednesday, July 13	Mark 4:1-9	*The Parable of the Sower*
Thursday, July 14	Mark 4:10-20	*The Purpose and Explanation of Parables*
Friday, July 15	Matthew 13:1-9	*Let Anyone with Ears Listen*
Saturday, July 16	Matthew 13:10-17	*Blessed Are Your Eyes and Ears*
Sunday, July 17	Matthew 13:18-23	*The Parable of the Sower Explained*

BACKGROUND

In the Gospels, the most intense opposition to Jesus came from the Pharisees. These highly respected and influential religious scholars prided themselves on being more righteous than others. Jesus looked beyond their upright appearance and saw them as frauds. Rather than respond with repentance and obedience to Jesus, the Pharisees—as a whole—actively opposed Him. When Jesus performed miracles, which proved that He was indeed the Messiah, the Pharisees refused to accept the evidence. Instead, they charged Him with working by demonic power.

In response to this malicious, false charge, Jesus used devastating logic to demonstrate the error of the Pharisees. Regrettably, they ignored the facts and rejected what Jesus had to say. The religious leaders' refusal to believe in Jesus revealed that their hearts were evil and that they had abandoned their commitment to God. As the Old Testament prophets had often described sinful Israel, so the Pharisees also were guilty of spiritual adultery against the Lord.

As Matthew 12 makes clear, the Pharisees pretended to be curious about Jesus, but they refused to consider commitment to Him. Jesus, in turn, refused to play games with them. This is evident in chapter 13, which continues the response Jesus gave to the unbelief of His opponents. A key feature of this portion of Matthew's Gospel is Jesus' use of parables.

The Savior often made use of parables when teaching His disciples and the large crowds that gathered to hear Him speak. Because of Jesus' apparent love for telling these parables and His masterful skill at doing so, author Madeleine L'Engle once briefly summed up the whole of the Savior's being by calling Him "the God who told stories." A parable, in fact, is a story that teaches a lesson. It compares something familiar to something unfamiliar. Each parable usually points out only one spiritual truth, enabling hearers to understand that truth by using everyday objects and relationships.

The story lines of Jesus' parables were easily understood by His listeners, but there were often times when He had to explain what they meant. His purpose in telling these stories was to compel those of His listeners who were truly searching for spiritual truth to discover it. For them, Jesus' simple stories were loaded with profound eternal insight. At the same time, His parables tended to conceal spiritual truth from those too lazy, stubborn, or haughty to diligently seek it out. For them, Jesus' parables were little more than stories without meaning.

Jesus' favorite subject matter for His parables was the kingdom of God. In fact, the parable of the sower is a description of *"the secrets of the kingdom of heaven"* (Matt. 13:11)—what living under God's reign looks like, sounds like, feels like, and acts like. These "kingdom parables" are usually clearly introduced by Jesus' words, *"The kingdom of heaven may be compared to"* (13:24) or *"The kingdom of heaven is like"* (13:31, 33, 44, 45, 47).

NOTES ON THE PRINTED TEXT

The parable of the sower forms the backdrop for this week's Scripture text. Jesus was at the shore of the Sea of Galilee (Matt. 13:1) when an immense crowd gathered around Him (13:2). He then *got into a boat*, where He sat and taught the listening group of people who were assembled *on the beach*. The first story Christ told concerned a farmer who scattered some seed (13:3).

In ancient times, farmers would first break up the hard soil by using wooden plows pulled by oxen or other animals. Additional workers would follow behind, carrying seed in a jar, basket, or pouch. They would grab handfuls of the seed and scatter it on the ground. After the seed had been planted, the ground would be covered up to prevent such birds as ravens and crows from consuming the seed. One method was to have animals trample the seed beneath the soil. Another method was to turn the seed under the soil using wooden hoes.

One group of seeds scattered by the farmer in Jesus' parable fell on a footpath, which *the birds came and ate* (13:4). A second group of seeds fell on shallow soil with underlying rock. Though the plants sprang up quickly, they withered in the hot sun (13:5-6). They had no staying power due to the lack of nourishment their roots found in the shallow soil. A third group of seeds *fell among thorns* (13:7), which in turn choked out the tender blades of the emerging plants.

Only the fourth group of seeds *fell on good soil* (13:8), resulting in a crop many times more abundant that what had been planted. Most first-century farmers expected an abundant harvest to yield 10 bushels of wheat for every bushel of seed planted. But in Jesus' parable, the farmer gets yields of outrageous proportions—30, 60, and even 100-fold increases!

In 13:9, Jesus urged His listeners to hear and heed what He had to say. Later, in 13:18-23, Christ explained that the parable of the sower illustrated a variety of responses to the proclamation of the Gospel. For instance, the first group of seeds signifies those who hear the Good News; but the devil prevents it from ever penetrating their hearts (13:19). The second group of seeds represents people who make an emotional commitment to the truth about Christ; but their pledge is insincere and lasts only momentarily (13:20-21). The third group of seeds illustrates people whose embracing of the Gospel is superficial; in fact, their love of the things of the world prevents them from breaking free from its enslaving grip (13:22).

The fourth group of seeds depict people who make a genuine and lasting commitment to Christ. Their response to the Good News results in spiritual abundance and eternal joy (13:23). The underlying lesson in Jesus' parable is that only divine power—only God's own hand—can bring about salvation and a changed life.

After Jesus' disciples listened to Him tell the story about the farmer scattering seed (13:9), they afterward asked, *"Why do you speak to them in parables?"* (13:10). In response, Jesus declared that God had permitted the Savior's followers to understand *"the secrets of the kingdom of heaven"* (13:11). Not everyone, however, enjoyed this privilege. Only those who were receptive to Jesus' teaching would be blessed with *an abundance* (13:12) of spiritual insight. In contrast, those who refused to hear and heed Jesus' words would lose whatever understanding they had concerning eternal issues.

Christ further explained that He used parables to clarify the truth for receptive hearts and conceal it from hardened hearts (13:13). Those in the second category failed to *understand* (13:14) and *perceive* what Jesus declared, for their hearts were *dull* (13:15) and their *eyes* were blinded to the truth (see Isa. 6:9-10).

The experience of the disciples was entirely different. God had *blessed* (Matt. 13:16) them with the ability to *hear* and heed what Jesus said. In fact, their clear grasp of eternal truths eclipsed what the Old Testament *prophets* (13:17) and other *righteous people* had understood. They *longed to see* and *hear* what Jesus' followers were privileged to know about the divine kingdom.

SUGGESTIONS TO TEACHERS

It is true that the parable of the sower points out one primary spiritual truth, namely, that through the Gospel, God actively spreads the message of His kingdom throughout the world, and people will respond to it in varied ways. Only when one *"hears the word and understands it"* (Matt. 13:23) will the message take root, grow to maturity, and bear fruit in that person's life.

Still, as sowers in God's service, Christians are called to spread the message of the kingdom, to *"make disciples of all nations, baptizing them in the name of the Father and of the Son and of the Holy Spirit, and teaching them to obey everything that I have commanded you"* (28:19-20). As such, there are a few lessons that we might glean from this farmer's approach to sowing seeds.

1. SPREAD LOTS OF SEED! The sower in Jesus' parable did not sow his seed sparingly. He sowed abundantly, fully expecting a huge harvest. Whenever we can, at every possible opportunity, we ought to plant the seeds of God's kingdom in the minds and hearts of those around us. And the more seeds we plant, the better!

2. SPREAD GOOD SEED! Much of the seed that we'll sow will not be our words or explanations, but our actions and behaviors. Are our lives so directed by the Holy Spirit that others cannot help but see Jesus living within us? Our Christian walk—the way we conduct our lives—has immeasurable potential to impact others for the kingdom of God.

3. SPREAD SEED ON GOOD SOIL! Though it is best to sow our seed thickly and abundantly, we would do well to keep our eyes open for good soil into which to sow. Some are more diligently seeking the truths of the kingdom of God than others. Are we able to recognize these seekers? May we discipline ourselves to discern the best soil in which to plant our seeds.

4. SPREAD SEED WITH OTHER SOWERS! The more sowers there are, the more seeds that will get sown. When we join with other believers to sow the seeds of kingdom truth, we cover more ground, get the message to more people, better maximize our potential, and reap a greater harvest.

FOR ADULTS

■ **TOPIC:** Learning to Listen

■ **QUESTIONS:** 1. Why did Jesus stress the importance of heeding what He declared? 2. In what sense had the knowledge of the divine kingdom been given to Jesus' followers? 3. Why was it so hard for Jesus' opponents to appropriate what He taught? 4. In what sense are believers the objects of God's love and favor? 5. How can Christians encourage the lost to accept by faith what Jesus has revealed?

■ **ILLUSTRATIONS:**

Preparing the Soil. Eugene, the pastor of a rural church, was thrilled to have Steve, the pastor of one of the denomination's largest churches, come into town. The people of Eugene's church had high regard for Steve, and Eugene felt that having the preacher speak at his church would greatly inspire his small flock.

When the renowned minister arrived late in the morning, Eugene took him to the local diner for lunch. But when the waitress, who attended Eugene's church, brought the two men the food they had ordered, Steve immediately grew upset at how the food had been prepared and arranged on his plate. Loudly voicing his disapproval to the waitress, Steve left no opening for the waitress to address his accusations. Finally, the waitress picked up Steve's plate, and with tears streaming from her eyes, hurried back into the kitchen.

Eugene was so astounded at Steve's inconsideration that, for a moment, he was speechless. Then he leaned over the table toward Steve and said, "Pastor, I dare you to witness to our waitress about the love and mercy of Jesus when she comes back."

Sometimes our actions and behaviors prepare the soil into which we will plant the seeds of God's grace. At times, we have the potential to make the soil harder or softer, more or less willing to accept the message of God's kingdom.

Becoming Good Soil. Laura Schlessinger, the host of her own radio program called "Dr. Laura," states the following in her book *How Could You Do That?:*

"What's the number one, most typically asked question on [my] internationally syndicated show? The caller usually wants to know this: 'Now that I've done all these things I shouldn't have done, how can I avoid the consequences I knew, but denied, and just hoped would not happen?'"

Schlessinger confesses that her pet peeve is "when callers protest that they are 'only human.' Only human? As if one's humanness were a blueprint for instinctive, reflexive reactions to situations, like in the rest of the animal kingdom. I see being 'human' as the unique opportunity to use our minds and wills to act in ways that elevate us above the animal kingdom."

Schlessinger then closes her point with an illustration from the film classic *The African Queen*. Humphrey Bogart as Charlie, the solitary sailor, tries to invoke the "only human" excuse when he attempts to explain his prior drunken evening. Katharine Hepburn as Rosie, the missionary, peers over her Bible and aptly retorts, "We were put on the earth to rise above nature."

It is time to allow the Holy Spirit to work in us to become "good soil," and then let the seeds that God has planted in our hearts take root, grow to maturity, and bear fruit.

Scattering Gospel Seeds. In May of 2000, a pastor in Russia scattered seeds for the kingdom of God by setting up a large tent in a Muslim region of the country. Within a few weeks, the services he was leading were drawing 3,000 people. Vladimir Silchuk then began preaching nightly, and most of the people who attended became Christians, he told *Religion Today*.

Silchuk's tent held about 1,000 people and was filled to capacity each night with many sitting outside. The meetings, which took place in the city of Ufa, in the Bashkortostan region, continued throughout the summer.

The region is home to the Tartar and Bashir people, who are of Mongolian descent and largely unreached with the Gospel. The region "has been an Islamic stronghold for many years," said Perry Hubick of Saskatchewan, Canada, a church elder who has ministered with Silchuk. "Many heard the Gospel for the very first time and responded to Christ."

 FOR YOUTH ■ TOPIC: Earthly Stories, Heavenly Meanings
■ QUESTIONS: 1. Why do you think Jesus used parables as His chief teaching method? 2. What is Jesus really saying in the parable of the sower? 3. How might this parable help you understand what is happening in your own ministry? 4. Why is it that when it comes to understanding the kingdom of God, *"to those who have, more will be given, and they will have an abundance; but from those who have nothing, even what they have will be taken away"* (Matt. 13:12)? 5. In what ways can you encourage others to heed Jesus' teachings?

God's Employee. Russ Blowers is a minister who is active in his local Rotary Club. Each week at the Club's meetings, one of the members gives a brief statement about his job. When it was his turn, Russ told, in essence, a modern-day parable describing his role as a Christian under God's employ: "I'm with a global enterprise. We have branches in every country in the world. We have our representatives in nearly every parliament and boardroom on earth. We're into motivation and behavior alteration. We run hospitals, feeding stations, crisis pregnancy centers, universities, publishing houses, and nursing homes.

"We care for our clients from birth to death. We are into life insurance and fire insurance. We perform spiritual heart transplants. Our original Organizer owns all the real estate on earth plus an assortment of galaxies and constellations. He knows everything and lives everywhere. Our product is free for the asking. (There's not enough money to buy it.)

"Our CEO was born in a hick town, worked as a carpenter, didn't own a home, was misunderstood by His family, hated by enemies, walked on water, was condemned to death without a trial, and arose from the dead—and I talk with Him every day."

Sowing Abundantly. When a lot of seeds are scattered abundantly over a plot of ground, some of the seeds will fall on good soil. An Indonesian evangelist was trying to scatter seeds abundantly in May of 2000, when a couple of bandits tried to rob him. But the robbers ended up giving their lives to Christ.

The evangelist and his associates were returning from a conference in Jayapura, Indonesia, when the two gunmen stopped them. When the evangelist rolled down the window of the car to hand over their money, one of the associates told the bandits that they had just come from leading a seminar "about the kingdom of God."

"Why don't you hold a seminar here?" one of the bandits said. "Then we can be freed from our drinking." The evangelist got out of the car and explained what sin is and the need to trust in Christ for forgiveness and to be freed from alcoholism. The young man knelt in the middle of the road to pray, and when he stood, "his deliverance was visible," the evangelist said. "His body relaxed noticeably." Another member of the gang also asked to become a Christian.

Seeds of Revival. During one week back in the year 2000, more than 27,100 people were baptized by Christians in Peru. The baptisms, performed throughout the country, accompanied the Impacto 2000 outreach program held at San Marcos Stadium in Lima by evangelist Alejandro Bullon. The program appeared live on television, cable, and satellite broadcasts in Peru and in the Spanish-speaking areas of South and Central America.

"This shows that no one knows what God will do," said pastor Raul Gomez, the leader of a local church in Peru. "Jesus just said go and make disciples. That's what we as pastors and lay members are continuing to do through small groups studying the Bible together."

"This event well illustrates the amazing church growth here in Peru and throughout South America," said Jan Paulsen, president of a large church organization. "For my wife, Kari, and myself, this has been a truly astonishing experience to see the Holy Spirit working in so many ways."

Bullon, a native of Peru, said the baptisms were a result of the whole church working together to reach friends and neighbors. "Christ is waking us up, and the Holy Spirit is preparing His church," he said. "This is the result of the personal enthusiasm of lay members. Even my 75-year-old mother is out looking for people to study with and to invite to the meetings. I can't give 50,000 Bible studies, but the members can. I just preach and give the call. Together we can do great things for God."

The Unforgiving Servant

Background Scripture: Matthew 18:21-35
Devotional Reading: 2 Corinthians 2:5-11

Key Verse: "Out of pity for him, the lord of that slave released him and forgave him the debt." Matthew 18:27.

KING JAMES VERSION

MATTHEW 18:21 Then came Peter to him, and said, Lord, how oft shall my brother sin against me, and I forgive him? till seven times? 22 Jesus saith unto him, I say not unto thee, Until seven times: but, Until seventy times seven. 23 Therefore is the kingdom of heaven likened unto a certain king, which would take account of his servants. 24 And when he had begun to reckon, one was brought unto him, which owed him ten thousand talents. 25 But forasmuch as he had not to pay, his lord commanded him to be sold, and his wife, and children, and all that he had, and payment to be made. 26 The servant therefore fell down, and worshipped him, saying, Lord, have patience with me, and I will pay thee all. 27 Then the lord of that servant was moved with compassion, and loosed him, and forgave him the debt. 28 But the same servant went out, and found one of his fellowservants, which owed him an hundred pence: and he laid hands on him, and took him by the throat, saying, Pay me that thou owest. 29 And his fellowservant fell down at his feet, and besought him, saying, Have patience with me, and I will pay thee all. 30 And he would not: but went and cast him into prison, till he should pay the debt. 31 So when his fellowservants saw what was done, they were very sorry, and came and told unto their lord all that was done. 32 Then his lord, after that he had called him, said unto him, O thou wicked servant, I forgave thee all that debt, because thou desiredst me: 33 Shouldest not thou also have had compassion on thy fellowservant, even as I had pity on thee? 34 And his lord was wroth, and delivered him to the tormentors, till he should pay all that was due unto him. 35 So likewise shall my heavenly Father do also unto you, if ye from your hearts forgive not every one his brother their trespasses.

NEW REVISED STANDARD VERSION

MATTHEW 18:21 Then Peter came and said to him, "Lord, if another member of the church sins against me, how often should I forgive? As many as seven times?" 22 Jesus said to him, "Not seven times, but, I tell you, seventy-seven times.

23 "For this reason the kingdom of heaven may be compared to a king who wished to settle accounts with his slaves. 24 When he began the reckoning, one who owed him ten thousand talents was brought to him; 25 and, as he could not pay, his lord ordered him to be sold, together with his wife and children and all his possessions, and payment to be made. 26 So the slave fell on his knees before him, saying, 'Have patience with me, and I will pay you everything.' 27 And out of pity for him, the lord of that slave released him and forgave him the debt. 28 But that same slave, as he went out, came upon one of his fellow slaves who owed him a hundred denarii; and seizing him by the throat, he said, 'Pay what you owe.' 29 Then his fellow slave fell down and pleaded with him, 'Have patience with me, and I will pay you.' 30 But he refused; then he went and threw him into prison until he would pay the debt. 31 When his fellow slaves saw what had happened, they were greatly distressed, and they went and reported to their lord all that had taken place. 32 Then his lord summoned him and said to him, 'You wicked slave! I forgave you all that debt because you pleaded with me. 33 Should you not have had mercy on your fellow slave, as I had mercy on you?' 34 And in anger his lord handed him over to be tortured until he would pay his entire debt. 35 So my heavenly Father will also do to every one of you, if you do not forgive your brother or sister from your heart."

HOME BIBLE READINGS

BACKGROUND

The rule of revenge still applies in many societies. Lest we feel smug, we should note how retaliation is often uppermost in the minds of those injured or affronted in our culture. Getting even may not always take the form of going after another with a weapon (although it often does in our gun-crazy world). Sometimes getting revenge means taking someone to court. Ours is an increasingly go-to-court society, observers point out.

The ancient practice of avenging oneself meant inflicting terrible slaughter on the other party and his family. If the guilty person could not be found, his kinfolk would suffer. The Hebrew code was a giant step forward. The Law in the Old Testament carefully spelled out what steps could be taken by an aggrieved party. Not even the Code of Hammurabi came near the Mosaic Law. Humane treatment was prescribed by the Hebrew Scriptures (see Exod. 21–22, Lev. 19 and 24, and Deut. 17, 19, 21, and 25) and through the institution of the cities of refuge (see Num. 35:6-9). The same rules for justice applied for everyone: king and commoner, native and stranger. Throughout the Scriptures was a call for mercy, echoing the mercy the Lord showed Israel.

By the first century, the rabbis had further refined the rules of conduct. But these teachers taught that there were limits to mercy. A person was expected to extend forgiveness to another three times and no more. Jesus claimed the authority to improve on rabbinic teaching, and even to amend the ancient rules regarding retaliation. That meant the sky was the limit for forgiveness! God's people were to show the same kind of mercy that the Lord showed everyone.

When Peter self-righteously asked about forgiving a person seven times, he probably expected Jesus to pat him on the back. Instead, Jesus startled him by giving him the 7 times 70 statement! Our model, the forgiving Lord who suffered on the cross, means that we never tally the number of times we extend mercy. The arithmetic of love never keeps score.

NOTES ON THE PRINTED TEXT

As Jesus instructed the disciples about disciplining and forgiving members, Peter raised a question. *Then Peter came and said to him, "Lord, if another member of the church sins against me, how often should I forgive? As many as seven times?"* (Matt. 18:21). Peter had been generous in his estimate. The rabbis taught that forgiveness should be limited to three times. Peter had more than doubled that stipulation.

Jesus surprised everyone by answering that there were no limits to forgiveness. *Jesus said to him, "Not seven times, but, I tell you, seventy-seven times"* (18:22). (The King James Version's 490 is derived from later Greek manuscripts.) Jesus' reply to Peter probably alluded to the stories of Cain and Lamech (Gen. 4:1-24). When Cain murdered Abel, God put on Cain a mark of some kind and said that anyone who killed Cain would *"suffer a sevenfold vengeance."* (4:15). Cain and his wife later had their first child, Enoch, and a descendant of Enoch was Lamech.

Lamech is credited in Scripture with humanity's second known murder. He proclaimed to his wives, *"I have killed a man for wounding me"* (4:23). Then he proudly told them that if *"Cain is avenged sevenfold, truly Lamech seventy-sevenfold"* (4:24). In some way Lamech believed that by taking vengeance into his own hands he had outdone God.

To teach the disciples the unlimited scope of forgiveness, Jesus told a parable. *For this reason the kingdom of heaven may be compared to a king who wished to settle accounts with his slaves* (Matt. 18:23). In the course of an audit, a king decided to collect his outstanding debts. *When he began the reckoning, one who owed him ten thousand talents was brought to him* (18:24). The disciples would have smiled at Jesus' exaggeration. A talent was a large piece of silver about the size of a dinner plate and was worth 6,000 denarii. An ordinary working man earned one denarius per day for his labor. The thought of a slave's owing that kind of a debt and a master's willingness to have made such a loan was absurd. Consider also that the combined taxes for the Roman provinces of Judea, Samaria, Galilee, Perea, and Idumea produced only 800 talents. Jesus described a slave in the ridiculous position of owing the king more than 10 times the national budget!

And, as he could not pay, his lord ordered him to be sold, together with his wife and children and all his possessions, and payment to be made (18:25). Since executing the man would yield nothing, the king ordered the slave, his family, and his possessions to be seized and sold. A partial payment was better than nothing.

So the slave fell on his knees before him, saying, "Have patience with me, and I will pay you everything" (18:26). The panicked slave pleaded for mercy, promising that he would repay the king. His promise was absurd and would have had the disciples chuckling. The king, however, was moved by the man's request and agreed to forgive the debt. *And out of pity for him, the lord of that slave released him and forgave him the debt* (18:27).

Exiting the king's palace, the servant met a fellow servant, perhaps also called as a result of the king's audit. The first servant grabbed the startled man by his throat and demanded payment for a relatively modest amount of money (18:28). Nearly choking, the second servant gasped out the same request for mercy that the first servant had used. *Have patience with me, and I will pay you* (18:29).

The borrowing and lending done in Jesus' parable seem to go beyond the restrictions the Old Testament placed on lending to ensure that no one took advantage of the borrower. Among the Israelites, lending was supposed to be a means of showing mercy to the poor. As a result, an Israelite could not charge interest on a loan made to a fellow Israelite (Lev. 25:35-38). However, interest could be collected from a Gentile (Deut. 23:20).

A lender who took a borrower's cloak as collateral could not keep it overnight but had to return it at sunset (Exod. 22:26-27). Nor could a lender take a borrower's millstone as security for a loan because that would also be taking away the borrower's means for repaying the debt (Deut. 24:6). Every seven years, as part of the year of Jubilee, all debts were supposed to be forgiven (15:1-2). We might draw the application that for the Christian every year is one of Jubilee when it comes to forgiveness of our unpayable debt of sin.

In Jesus' parable, the first servant refused to be merciful, in spite of having received mercy himself (Matt. 18:30). He had the poor servant thrown into debtors' prison, where he would remain until the debt was satisfied. The tightly knit group of royal servants were outraged at the injustice. As a group, they spoke with the king. *When his fellow slaves saw what had happened, they were greatly distressed, and they went and reported to their lord all that had taken place* (18:31).

The furious king summoned the first servant and angrily lectured him on forgiveness. *Then his lord summoned him and said to him, "You wicked slave! I forgave you all that debt because you pleaded with me. Should you not have had mercy on your fellow slave, as I had mercy on you?"* (18:32-33). The irate king ordered the servant to be imprisoned and tortured until his debt was repaid (18:34).

The ungrateful servant should have treated others as he himself had been treated. In Jesus' application, the Savior pointed out that this is also what God expects of those who have experienced His forgiveness (18:35). Even more disturbing, Jesus' words imply that God will treat similarly those who refuse to forgive. They will be shown the same measure of mercy that they have extended to others.

SUGGESTIONS TO TEACHERS

A woman dropped out of her Bible class on Wednesday evenings in order to attend a course on assertiveness training. To her surprise, she discovered that the course's emphasis was on standing up for one's rights and contriving to get redress for any slights. "I thought the course would help me get over my shyness," she later related. "But they tried to get me to leave [behind] what they called my religious hang-ups, like being a forgiving person."

This woman learned how radical Jesus' demands are on members of His community. She also found that Jesus' way runs counter to the world's way. This lesson should help your class to discover what this perceptive woman now knows.

1. MATHEMATICAL APPROACH. Start by looking at the way Peter thought he was being magnanimous by offering to forgive a person for the same offense a total of seven times. By the standards of his time and background, Peter was generous indeed. But Jesus put no limits on forgiveness. Peter's careful calculation of seven times was thrown out. Mercy has no mathematics.

2. MOUNTAINOUS DEBT. Have the class look hard at the parable of the unforgiving servant. This sneaky, big-time embezzler had chiseled the ruler out of a fortune, breaking trust with the monarch and making off with an enormous amount which he could never hope to pay back. Discuss how the mountainous debt the servant owed is equivalent to the mountainous debt a sinner owes God.

3. MAGNANIMOUS KING. The king's fury turned to pity when the guilty ex-official pleaded for mercy. Instead of exercising his right to ship the criminal and his family off to the slave mart, the king forgave the man and erased the entire debt. Jesus' parable hints at the extraordinary mercy of God toward us. Instead of exercising His rights to demand payment of us, God has acted through Jesus Christ to extend mercy to us.

4. MERCILESS SCOUNDREL. The big-time cheat promptly accosted a small-time debtor. Refusing to show pity on the poor debtor, the previously pardoned embezzler had the hapless man thrown into jail. The official failed to extend the same mercy toward another that the king had extended toward him. Forgiveness, the parable teaches, must be shared with others—or else! Save the bulk of lesson time to talk over what it means to receive forgiveness, and how it is imperative for Christians to be forgiving toward others.

FOR ADULTS

■ **Topic:** Free to Forgive

■ **Questions:** 1. What was the background for Jesus' parable about the king settling accounts with the dishonest servant? 2. Can a person receive God's forgiveness without showing forgiveness to others? 3. What was the hardest occasion for you to extend forgiveness to someone? 4. Have you ever known forgiveness from someone? 5. Why is forgiving others sometimes difficult?

■ **ILLUSTRATIONS:**

True Forgiveness? The entertainment industry knows that when a celebrity is in trouble, he or she can turn to Barbara Walters. A spot on the newsmagazine show *20/20,* a few confessions, some tears to wash away iniquities, and he or she is as good as new.

Is Walters the mother confessor? Is this all that constitutes repentance? Is this true forgiveness? True forgiveness starts with sincere repentance for the wrong and a resolution not to repeat the action. True repentance means a new direction. True forgiveness is given to the individual by others and Jesus Christ, not Barbara

Walters. Have class members reexamine Jesus' parable to understand true forgiveness.

Finding Forgiveness. On June 8, 1972, John Plummer, a gung-ho young helicopter pilot and operations officer in the Vietnam War, ordered an air strike on the village of Trang Bang. He had been twice assured that there were no civilians in the area. Shortly after the strike, he saw the Pulitzer Prize-winning photograph of a little nine-year-old Vietnamese girl, her clothes incinerated by napalm and her body horribly burned, running naked from Trang Bang. The brutal image of the American assault on that village and the suffering the little girl and other children experienced haunted John Plummer.

"My heart was wracked with guilt," Plummer admitted. "I realized that it was I who was responsible for her injuries; it was I who had sent bombs into her village."

For decades Plummer struggled with his conscience. He drank and suffered through a divorce. Although he could concede to himself that he'd done everything possible to make sure the area was clear of civilians, he felt new pain every time he saw the picture. Eventually, John Plummer was led by his third wife, Joanne, to commit his life to the Lord. He left his job with a defense contractor and accepted God's call to go to seminary. After theological studies, he was ordained as a Methodist minister and became pastor of a United Methodist congregation. But the guilt over the little girl in the photo remained.

In June 1996, Plummer once more saw the famous photo, this time on television. The program's announcer spoke about the girl in the photograph. Plummer learned that the photo had been taken by Huynh Cong ("Nick") Ut, a 21-year-old Associated Press photographer. This man had poured water from his canteen onto the girl's burns and rushed her to a hospital 15 miles away. Plummer finally heard the girl's name: Kim Phuc. She had not been expected to survive the napalm burns. But after 14 months in various hospitals, she had finally been discharged. Ut had set up a bank account to provide for the long, expensive medical treatments.

At the time of the TV program Kim Phuc was an adult with a child of her own. Plummer saw for the first time the thick white scars the napalm had left on her neck, arms, and back, and learned she had survived 17 operations.

While at a reunion of helicopter pilots, Plummer met a man who knew Kim Phuc. Plummer was stunned to learn that she lived in Toronto. The man, Linh Duy Vo, agreed to put Plummer in touch with Kim Phuc, if possible.

On November 11, 1996, Kim Phuc made a rare public appearance by coming to Washington, D.C., to the Vietnam Veterans Memorial. Plummer knew that he had to meet her. With 15 friends from the Vietnam Helicopter Flight Crew Network, and their families, Plummer finally met Kim Phuc.

"She saw my grief, my pain, my sorrow," Plummer reported. "She held out her arms to me and embraced me. All I could say was, 'I'm sorry, I'm sorry' over and over again. At the same time, she was saying, 'I forgive; I forgive.' " Later, the two were able to spend two hours together at Kim's hotel with their respective families. Plummer discovered that Kim Phuc had become a Christian in 1982. The two prayed together, and now frequently talk on the telephone. Forgiven and forgiving, the two celebrate the new life Christ gave them both.

<table>
<tr><td>■ FOR YOUTH</td><td>■ Topic: The Unforgiving Servant
■ Questions: 1. What did Jesus' answer to Peter's question mean?
2. Why did the king cancel his servant's debt? 3. How did the ser-</td></tr>
</table>

vant respond to the king's compassion? 4. What did the king do when he learned about the forgiven servant's behavior? 5. How is our relationship with God affected when we refuse to forgive someone who has wronged us?

■ **ILLUSTRATIONS:**

Incomplete Peace. Diane Anton was born on Christmas Eve in 1941, just as Manila fell to the Japanese. She was interned with her parents in Santo Thomas Camp in the Philippines. She remembered being so hungry that she ate a pudding her mother had made from laundry starch, sugar, and water.

Another girl, 17-year-old Carmen Leffler, was also interned in the same camp. Carmen had recently graduated from high school and recalled standing and crying as the survivors of the Bataan Death March stumbled by as the Japanese guards beat and bayoneted the men. She vividly recalled the viciousness of the Japanese, the communicable diseases, the starvation, and the random acts of brutality.

Neither woman has ever forgotten her treatment. Both are part of the Miami-based Center for Internee Rights, formed in 1990 to represent the 47,000 former prisoners of the Japanese (33,000 military POWs and 14,000 British, Dutch, and Australian civilian internees). The group filed a suit in 1995 in Tokyo's District Court. The suit asks for an official apology and $22,000 per person in individual compensation for Japan's wartime brutality. Both women agree that the money is unimportant. In spite of all that these women have been through, they say that they can forgive. They carry no grudges or hatred. They feel that they can come to terms with what has taken place if an apology is offered. However, until that time, they live in an incomplete peace.

Jesus reminded His followers of the importance of forgiveness. He challenged believers to hear His words and to forgive others. Once forgiveness is made, the believer will find a more complete peace.

"Into" Forgiveness. Fred Rogers, the former host of TV's *Mister Rogers's Neighborhood* once spoke of a teenage boy from New Jersey named Tony. Tony was never cared for by his biological parents. They never even bought him a bed or a winter coat, although they could afford them both. He was verbally, physically, and sexually abused. Some nights, Tony rode the subway rather than go home. Eventually Tony's parents were discovered, charged with child abuse, and sent to jail after nearly killing him following one beating. A couple became his adoptive parents. After being cured of malnutrition and his bones healed, Tony began to grow. Tragically, he also discovered that the abuse had left him with AIDS.

Tony is writing a book about his life. The book is dedicated to Fred Rogers, whose show he watched when his biological parents were not looking. Mr. Rogers, who took a personal interest in the boy, once asked him about forgiveness. Tony responded that if he forgave, then he could be forgiven.

Then Tony stated that if forgiveness meant that what his parents had done to him when he was little was all right, then he was not "into" forgiveness. If it meant letting go of all that happened to him and putting it behind him, then he was into forgiveness. Tony is a young man with a firm grasp of forgiveness. Are you "into" or "out of" forgiveness?

FINAL ACCOUNTING

BACKGROUND SCRIPTURE: Matthew 25:31-46
DEVOTIONAL READING: Luke 6:27-31

KEY VERSE: The king will answer them, "Truly I tell you, just as you did it to one of the least of these who are members of my family, you did it to me." Matthew 25:40.

KING JAMES VERSION

MATTHEW 25:31 When the Son of man shall come in his glory, and all the holy angels with him, then shall he sit upon the throne of his glory: 32 And before him shall be gathered all nations: and he shall separate them one from another, as a shepherd divideth his sheep from the goats: 33 And he shall set the sheep on his right hand, but the goats on the left. 34 Then shall the King say unto them on his right hand, Come, ye blessed of my Father, inherit the kingdom prepared for you from the foundation of the world: 35 For I was an hungred, and ye gave me meat: I was thirsty, and ye gave me drink: I was a stranger, and ye took me in: 36 Naked, and ye clothed me: I was sick, and ye visited me: I was in prison, and ye came unto me. 37 Then shall the righteous answer him, saying, Lord, when saw we thee an hungred, and fed thee? or thirsty, and gave thee drink? 38 When saw we thee a stranger, and took thee in? or naked, and clothed thee? 39 Or when saw we thee sick, or in prison, and came unto thee? 40 And the King shall answer and say unto them, Verily I say unto you, Inasmuch as ye have done it unto one of the least of these my brethren, ye have done it unto me. 41 Then shall he say also unto them on the left hand, Depart from me, ye cursed, into everlasting fire, prepared for the devil and his angels: 42 For I was an hungred, and ye gave me no meat: I was thirsty, and ye gave me no drink: 43 I was a stranger, and ye took me not in: naked, and ye clothed me not: sick, and in prison, and ye visited me not. 44 Then shall they also answer him, saying, Lord, when saw we thee an hungred, or athirst, or a stranger, or naked, or sick, or in prison, and did not minister unto thee? 45 Then shall he answer them, saying, Verily I say unto you, Inasmuch as ye did it not to one of the least of these, ye did it not to me. 46 And these shall go away into everlasting punishment: but the righteous into life eternal.

NEW REVISED STANDARD VERSION

MATTHEW 25:31 "When the Son of Man comes in his glory, and all the angels with him, then he will sit on the throne of his glory. 32 All the nations will be gathered before him, and he will separate people one from another as a shepherd separates the sheep from the goats, 33 and he will put the sheep at his right hand and the goats at the left. 34 Then the king will say to those at his right hand, 'Come, you that are blessed by my Father, inherit the kingdom prepared for you from the foundation of the world; 35 for I was hungry and you gave me food, I was thirsty and you gave me something to drink, I was a stranger and you welcomed me, 36 I was naked and you gave me clothing, I was sick and you took care of me, I was in prison and you visited me.' 37 Then the righteous will answer him, 'Lord, when was it that we saw you hungry and gave you food, or thirsty and gave you something to drink? 38 And when was it that we saw you a stranger and welcomed you, or naked and gave you clothing? 39 And when was it that we saw you sick or in prison and visited you?' 40 And the king will answer them, 'Truly I tell you, just as you did it to one of the least of these who are members of my family, you did it to me.' 41 Then he will say to those at his left hand, 'You that are accursed, depart from me into the eternal fire prepared for the devil and his angels; 42 for I was hungry and you gave me no food, I was thirsty and you gave me nothing to drink, 43 I was a stranger and you did not welcome me, naked and you did not give me clothing, sick and in prison and you did not visit me.' 44 Then they also will answer, 'Lord, when was it that we saw you hungry or thirsty or a stranger or naked or sick or in prison, and did not take care of you?' 45 Then he will answer them, 'Truly I tell you, just as you did not do it to one of the least of these, you did not do it to me.' 46 And these will go away into eternal punishment, but the righteous into eternal life."

9

Monday, July 25	Psalm 14	*God Wants Us to Do Good*
Tuesday, July 26	Proverbs 3:27-33	*Do Not Withhold Good*
Wednesday, July 27	Luke 6:27-31	*The Golden Rule*
Thursday, July 28	1 Timothy 6:13-19	*Do Good, Be Generous, Share*
Friday, July 29	1 John 3:11-17	*Help Your Brother or Sister*
Saturday, July 30	Matthew 25:31-40	*You Did It to Me*
Sunday, July 31	Matthew 25:41-46	*You Did It Not to Me*

BACKGROUND

At the close of Matthew 24, Jesus, while teaching His disciples on the Mount of Olives, told a parable contrasting the reward given to a master's faithful servants with the punishment meted out to his unfaithful servants. As Jesus continued teaching His disciples about His second coming, Matthew recorded three more parables on the same theme: that the faithful will be rewarded and the unfaithful punished.

In Jesus' parable of the 10 bridesmaids, the wise young women who remain prepared for the bridegroom's return take part in the marriage feast, while the foolish young women who fail to prepare themselves are excluded from the feast (25:1-13). In Jesus' parable of the talents, the two servants who invest and make gains on their talents are rewarded with more, while the worthless servant who buried his talent is thrown into the outer darkness (25:14-30). And in Jesus' parable of the sheep and the goats, those who respond to the needs of people around them inherit the kingdom, while those who fail to respond suffer the condemnation awaiting the devil and his angels (25:31-46).

The clear-cut distinction between each of the two groups reminds us of the parable with which Jesus closed His Sermon on the Mount, namely, about the wise man who built his house on a rock and the foolish man who built his house on the sand (7:24-27). The distinction also reminds us of Jesus' frequent warning: *"For the Son of Man is to come with his angels in the glory of his Father, and then he will repay everyone for what has been done"* (16:27).

The separation of sheep and goats would have sounded quite familiar to anyone in Palestine who had worked with both kinds of animals. During the day, sheep and goats were allowed to graze together; but at nightfall they were usually separated because sheep prefer the open night air while goats need the warmth of shelter. Of course, the shepherd stayed with the sheep through the night to protect them, and because he spent more time with them than he did the goats, his fondness for the sheep typically rose above that of his fondness for the goats. The sheep had a way of becoming familiar to him, and they depended on him for their safety. Thus would Jesus say, *"The one who enters by the gate is the shepherd of the sheep. The gatekeeper opens the gate for him, and the sheep hear his voice. He calls his own sheep by name and leads them out. When he has brought out all his own, he goes ahead of them, and the sheep follow him because they know his voice"* (John 10:2-4).

NOTES ON THE PRINTED TEXT

Sheep are mentioned more often in the Bible than any other animal. Kept more for their milk and wool than for their meat, they needed pasture and water, so the shepherd and his household moved with the sheep from place to place. Goats, of course, are also mentioned frequently in the Bible. These animals were an important source of milk and meat. Their hair was made into clothing and their skins into containers for water and wine.

Goats were viewed as a lesser animal than sheep perhaps because the Old Testament law prescribed that people's sins be placed upon a goat—the scapegoat—and sent away from the camp into the wilderness (Lev. 16:8-10). In the parable recorded in Matthew 25:31-46, the sheep represent the righteous, who demonstrate the reality of their faith by their actions. The goats, in contrast, represent the wicked, who demonstrate the reality of their unbelief by their actions.

Jesus was emphatic about the certainty of His second coming. He declared that He would come *"in his glory, and all the angels with him, [and] then he will sit on the throne of his glory"* (25:31). Following Jesus' return, all the nations will be gathered into His presence for a time of judgment, which will take place *"as a shepherd separates the sheep from the goats"* (25:32).

When this judgment will take place is debated, but two views are worth mentioning. One group says this judgment will occur at the end of the age at the great white throne (Rev. 20:11-15). At that time, the determination will be made as to who will enter the eternal kingdom of the saved and who will be relegated to eternal punishment in hell. Another group says this judgment will occur when Jesus comes to set up a kingdom on earth. At that time, the determination will be made as to who will enter His kingdom based on the way they treated *"these who are members of my family"* (Matt. 25:40) during the preceding time of great distress (24:15-22).

Who are these members of the King's family? Some say they are all Christians; others say they are the Jews; still others say they are suffering people everywhere. But debating the identity of these members of the King's family is similar to the lawyer's testing Jesus with the question, *"And who is my neighbor?"* (Luke 10:29). The point of the parable of the sheep and goats, like the point of the parable of the good Samaritan, is not so much concerned with the "who" but rather with the "what." In other words, God wants us to reach out to others in need.

For the sheep on Jesus' right-hand side (the place of honor; Matt. 25:33), the King will offer an invitation to *"inherit the kingdom prepared for you from the foundation of the world"* (25:34). The reason the King will give for His invitation is that the righteous loved and took care of Him when He was in need. But those who are rewarded won't be able to recall a time when they did this for the King

(25:35-39). Then the King will tell them that "*just as you did it to one of the least of these who are members of my family, you did it to me*" (25:40). Thus the divine blessing will be given to those who served with no thought of getting a reward. Their service arose out of their love and concern for others.

For the goats on Jesus' left-hand side (the place of dishonor), the King will send them away "*into the eternal fire prepared for the devil and his angels*" (25:41). The reason the King will give for this decision is that they failed to look after Him when He was in need. The condemned, however, won't be able to recall a time when they failed to help Him (25:42-44). Then the King will tell them that "*just as you did not do it to one of the least of these, you did not do it to me*" (25:45). The wicked will be sentenced to eternal punishment because they showed by their actions that they worshiped and served themselves (25:46).

SUGGESTIONS TO TEACHERS

Though we may be unaware of it at the time, when we minister to the deprived and dispossessed, we are, indeed, ministering to the Lord. Still, even ministering to the Lord does not earn us our salvation. The New Testament teaches that our deeds of kindness in and of themselves cannot secure us everlasting life. Yet Scripture also teaches that when faith is real, it must, of necessity, express itself through a lifestyle of concern for others. For example, the Book of James reminds us that *faith by itself, if it has no works, is dead* (2:17). Thus, if our commitment to God is real, it will show in our actions. Clearly, then, our serving and meeting the needs of others is not a substitute for our faith in Christ, but rather an affirmation of our trust in Him.

1. ACTS OF MERCY. Jesus' parable of the sheep and the goats describes acts of mercy we all can do every day—feeding the hungry, giving drinks to the thirsty, welcoming strangers, clothing the naked, taking care of the sick, and visiting the imprisoned. None of these deeds of kindness depend on our being wealthy, skillful, or intelligent. They are simple acts of mercy and compassion that are freely received just as much as they are freely given.

2. ACTS OF BELIEF. The most genuine evidence of our belief in Christ is in the way we act, especially toward those who can use our help. Jesus calls us to treat others as if they were Him. Of course, carrying out this mandate is no easy task. But what we do for others demonstrates what we really think about Jesus' words: "*Truly I tell you, just as you did it to one of the least of these who are members of my family, you did it to me*" (Matt. 25:40).

3. ACTS OF CONCERN. God looks for us to have sincere, heartfelt concern for our fellow human beings, and especially so for our brothers and sisters in Christ. Because of the command to "*love your neighbor as yourself*" (22:39), we have no excuse to neglect those around us who have deep needs. And we cannot hand over the responsibility of caring and helping to our government or even to our church. Jesus demands our personal involvement in caring for others' needs.

■ **TOPIC:** Meeting Human Needs

■ **QUESTIONS:** 1. Do you consider Jesus' story more of a parable or more of a prophecy? Explain your answer. 2. Why do you think the King waited until the scene of the judgment to separate the sheep from the goats? 3. In what ways are those who carry out these acts of mercy similar to those who don't? In what ways are they different? 4. Who do you think are *"the least of these"* (Matt. 25:40) mentioned in Jesus' parable? 5. What does His parable teach us about our Christian responsibility to others in need?

■ **ILLUSTRATIONS:**

I Was Thirsty, and You Gave Me Milk. Dan West, a Christian relief worker in Spain during the Spanish Civil War, was handing out cups of powdered milk to a long line of hungry children on both sides of the conflict. All too often, the milk ran out before the line ended. As a farmer, Dan's response was practical. "Wouldn't it be better," he reasoned, "to supply families with an ongoing source of nutritious milk so that parents could feed their children themselves without having to depend on powdered milk from abroad?"

When Dan shared his idea back home in Indiana, his friends agreed. "I'll give a calf, if someone else will raise her," one person said. Soon afterward, the first boatload of heifers sailed in 1944, not to Spain, because the war there was soon over, but rather to Puerto Rico. And right from the start, families who received the heifers made a commitment to pass on their gift animal's first female offspring to another family in need.

In the 57 years since then, a parade of animals—some familiar (like goats, cows, chickens, sheep, and rabbits) and some exotic (like camels, water buffalo, llamas, and guinea pigs)—has circled the world. The oldest U.S. hunger organization, Heifer Project International, has helped more than 23 million people in 110 countries move toward self-reliance.

Showing That We Care. In one of the uplifting stories in *Chicken Soup for the Soul at Work*, Rick Phillips, a management trainer for the Circle K Corporation, tells about how hard it is to retain quality employees. During the management seminars that he leads, he asks the participants, "What has caused you to stay long enough to become a manager?" At one of his seminars, Cynthia, a new manager, slowly answered with her voice almost breaking, "It was a $19 baseball glove."

Cynthia told the group that she originally took a Circle K clerk job as an interim position while she looked for something better. On her second or third day behind the counter, she received a phone call from her nine-year-old son, Jessie. He needed a baseball glove for Little League. She explained that as a single mother, money was very tight, and her first check would have to go for paying bills. Perhaps she could buy his baseball glove with her second or third check.

When Cynthia arrived for work the next morning, Patricia, the store manager, asked her to come to the small room in back of the store that served as an office. Cynthia wondered if she had done something wrong or left some part of her job incomplete from the day before. She was concerned and confused.

Patricia handed her a box. "I overheard you talking to your son yesterday," she said, "and I know that it's hard to explain things to kids. This is a baseball glove for Jessie because he may not understand how important he is, since you have to pay bills before you can buy gloves. You know we can't pay good people like you as much as we would like to; but we do care, and I want you to know you are important to us."

The thoughtfulness, empathy, and love of this convenience store manager demonstrates vividly that people remember more how much an employer cares than how much the employer pays. And what an important lesson to be learned for the price of a Little League baseball glove!

God Blesses the Cheerful Giver. Some years ago a church in northern California decided to give away its building fund—and it received an even bigger blessing. The congregation had raised $120,000 toward its multimillion dollar sanctuary when pastor David heard about the needs of another ministry in Los Angeles, California. The center had bought the former Queen of Angels Hospital in the city and was refurbishing nine buildings as a massive center for its ministry.

David sensed that God wanted the building fund money to go to that undertaking, not to his church. So he received approval from his congregation in 1997, and soon afterward he was presenting a check for $120,000 to pastor Tommy, who was developing the center along with his son Matthew.

But soon after David gave away the building fund money, new and more money began pouring into his church's building project. Donations came in from unexpected sources, such as nonprofit foundations, other ministries, as well as private individuals. David and his congregation dedicated their new multimillion dollar facility to the Lord on Easter Sunday of 2000. And they moved into the facility debt-free!

Starting to Get Better. Pastor Duane Windemiller tells about how years ago he was conducting a funeral at a church in New Hampshire. The funeral was for an old family physician who had lived 102 years. A woman stood up in the middle of the service and, with tears making tracks down her face, said, "Whenever we heard his old Model T turning into our yard, we started to get better."

"Yes!" In a 1998 *Our Daily Bread* devotional, it was noted that "on April 19, 1995, a bomb destroyed the federal building in Oklahoma City, killing 169 people. On the same day, an Ohio couple, Julie and Bruce Madsen, set out on a cross-country odyssey to write a book about hope and goodness in America.

"In their search, the Madsens found stories of hope in the lives of ordinary people responding to adversity and tragedy. For example, a minister leads prayer vigils at the site of every murder in his midwestern city, and a physician has devoted his career to helping the homeless. 'By their fruits you will know them,' Julie wrote in one of her stories. She wondered, 'Do we leave people feeling uplifted, or drained and downhearted?'

"If the Madsens had met you or me, would they have discovered a story of hope? If Christ is at work in and through us, the answer can be a resounding 'Yes!'"

■ **FOR YOUTH** ■ **TOPIC:** Final Accounting

■ **QUESTIONS:** 1. What do you think was the King's reason for separating the sheep from the goats? 2. How are the sheep and the goats alike? How are they different? 3. Why do you think Jesus called those needing help *"the least of these who are members of my family"* (Matt. 25:40)? 4. How might the thought of serving Jesus help you serve people you wouldn't normally reach out to? 5. How have those whom you've helped with acts of kindness reminded you of Jesus?

■ **ILLUSTRATIONS:**

Seeing the Face of Christ. In a 1997 *Sojourners* article, Jim Forest writes how for six years Dorothy Day looked for a way to connect her social conscience with her religious conversion. Finally, her search gave birth to a relief movement in May 1933.

Originally it was just a newspaper, but within weeks of the paper's publication, the first house of hospitality—her apartment—came into being simply because Dorothy couldn't turn away a homeless woman who had seen the paper and came asking for help. Today there are nearly 175 houses of hospitality, not to mention the many more places of welcome that wouldn't exist had it not been for Dorothy Day's struggle to live her faith with directness and simplicity.

At the core of Dorothy's life was her experience of ultimate beauty—Christ's face hidden in the faces of America's human castoffs. "Those who cannot see the face of Christ in the poor," she used to say, "are atheists indeed."

Pass on the Kindness. In a little poem called "Pass It On," Henry Burton wrote:

Have you had a kindness shown?
Pass it on;
'Twas not given for thee alone,
Pass it on;
Let it travel down the years,
Let it wipe another's tears,

'Till in Heaven the deed appears—
Pass it on.

Aim at Heaven. C. S. Lewis knew that for us to be effective Christian servants, we must keep our eyes on Jesus and we must keep as our goal the kingdom of heaven. He has been quoted as saying, "If you read history, you will find that the Christians who did the most for the present world were just those who thought most of the next. The apostles themselves, who set on foot the conversion of the Roman Empire, the great people who built up the Middle Ages, the English evangelicals who abolished the slave trade, all left their mark on earth, precisely because their minds were occupied with heaven. It is since Christians have largely ceased to think about the other world that they have become so ineffective in this one. Aim at heaven and you will get earth 'thrown in.' Aim at earth and you will get neither."

Being Happy with God. Mother Teresa taught those who joined her in her mission to minister to the destitute and dying of India that "being happy with God means loving as He loves, helping as He helps, giving as He gives, serving as He serves, rescuing as He rescues, being with Him 24 hours, touching Him in His distressing disguise."

LUKE'S MISSION STATEMENT

BACKGROUND SCRIPTURE: Luke 4:14-30
DEVOTIONAL READING: Matthew 13:54-58

KEY VERSE: "The Spirit of the Lord is upon me, because he has anointed me to bring good news to the poor." Luke 4:18.

KING JAMES VERSION

LUKE 4:16 And he came to Nazareth, where he had been brought up: and, as his custom was, he went into the synagogue on the sabbath day, and stood up for to read. 17 And there was delivered unto him the book of the prophet Esaias. And when he had opened the book, he found the place where it was written, 18 The Spirit of the Lord is upon me, because he hath anointed me to preach the gospel to the poor; he hath sent me to heal the brokenhearted, to preach deliverance to the captives, and recovering of sight to the blind, to set at liberty them that are bruised, 19 To preach the acceptable year of the Lord. 20 And he closed the book, and he gave it again to the minister, and sat down. And the eyes of all them that were in the synagogue were fastened on him. 21 And he began to say unto them, This day is this scripture fulfilled in your ears. 22 And all bare him witness, and wondered at the gracious words which proceeded out of his mouth. And they said, Is not this Joseph's son? 23 And he said unto them, Ye will surely say unto me this proverb, Physician, heal thyself: whatsoever we have heard done in Capernaum, do also here in thy country. 24 And he said, Verily I say unto you, No prophet is accepted in his own country. . . . 28 And all they in the synagogue, when they heard these things, were filled with wrath, 29 And rose up, and thrust him out of the city, and led him unto the brow of the hill whereon their city was built, that they might cast him down headlong. 30 But he passing through the midst of them went his way.

NEW REVISED STANDARD VERSION

LUKE 4:16 When he came to Nazareth, where he had been brought up, he went to the synagogue on the sabbath day, as was his custom. He stood up to read, 17 and the scroll of the prophet Isaiah was given to him. He unrolled the scroll and found the place where it was written:

18 "The Spirit of the Lord is upon me,
   because he has anointed me
      to bring good news to the poor.
He has sent me to proclaim release to the captives
   and recovery of sight to the blind,
      to let the oppressed go free,
19 to proclaim the year of the Lord's favor."

20 And he rolled up the scroll, gave it back to the attendant, and sat down. The eyes of all in the synagogue were fixed on him. 21 Then he began to say to them, "Today this scripture has been fulfilled in your hearing." 22 All spoke well of him and were amazed at the gracious words that came from his mouth. They said, "Is not this Joseph's son?" 23 He said to them, "Doubtless you will quote to me this proverb, 'Doctor, cure yourself!' And you will say, 'Do here also in your hometown the things that we have heard you did at Capernaum.' " 24 And he said, "Truly I tell you, no prophet is accepted in the prophet's hometown. . . . 28 When they heard this, all in the synagogue were filled with rage. 29 They got up, drove him out of the town, and led him to the brow of the hill on which their town was built, so that they might hurl him off the cliff. 30 But he passed through the midst of them and went on his way.

10

BACKGROUND

The Gospel accounts were not written as mere biographies; rather, they were evangelistic tracts. Biographers usually delve into the childhood of their subjects. But the Gospel writers mostly skipped over the years when Jesus was growing up, except for one reference in Luke to Jesus accompanying His parents to the temple (2:41-50).

Like the other Gospel writers, Luke's main intent was to show what Jesus' life, death, and resurrection meant to believers. Luke thus proceeded quickly in his narrative to the start of Jesus' ministry. First, we learn about the preparatory work of John the Baptist (3:1-22). Then we find information about the genealogy of Christ (3:23-38).

The next section concerns Jesus' encounter with the devil and how the Savior resisted Satan's repeated enticements to sin (4:1-13). Following this, Christ returned to Galilee, being filled with the Spirit's power. Soon Jesus became well known throughout the surrounding country, and He won acclaim from those who heard Him teach in their synagogues (4:14-15).

Jesus then returned to His hometown of Nazareth to deliver His manifesto. It is important to note that He worshiped regularly as part of God's people, and was no soloist purposely separating Himself from the faith community. Likewise, Jesus was quite familiar with Scripture, and readily found the passage from the scroll of Isaiah, which He read to those in the Nazareth synagogue.

Synagogues served a key role in Jewish life in the time of Jesus. Wherever 10 Jewish families lived, they formed a synagogue (literally, "congregation" or "assembly"). Sacrifices could be made only at the temple, but from the time of the Exile, teaching of the law and worship took place in synagogues situated wherever Jews had been scattered throughout the world.

After recitation of the Shema ("Hear, O Israel, the Lord is our God, the Lord is One"), prayers, Scripture readings, and teaching followed. Since there was no professional clergy (rabbis held secular trades to earn their living), the synagogue leader could invite anyone considered qualified to teach.

Typically, seven members of the congregation would stand to read Scripture. The designated teacher would then sit down to teach. In this week's lesson, we find that Jesus' reading from Isaiah 61:1-2 caused quite a stir in Nazareth.

NOTES ON THE PRINTED TEXT

Jesus' initial preaching took place in Galilee. After returning to His childhood home, the Savior went to worship in the synagogue, *as was his custom* (Luke 4:16). While attendance was stipulated for every devout Jew, worship for Jesus was more than a mere formality. He longed to commune with and give praise to His heavenly Father.

During the period of the Exile, after the temple in Jerusalem was destroyed, the Jews started meeting in places called synagogues. The synagogue served as a substitute for the temple, where the Jews always worshiped before the Exile in 586 B.C. Synagogues allowed Jews outside of Israel to gather for divine instruction. We don't know exactly how many synagogues there were in Israel in the first century A.D., but we know nearly 400 synagogues existed in Jerusalem when the Romans burned the city in A.D. 70.

Those taking a lead role in a synagogue worship service often varied. While any devout Jewish male was allowed to participate, usually a priest, Levite, or visiting rabbi would have been the most likely choice. In this case, Jesus was asked to read from the Hebrew Scriptures.

Jesus was given a scroll containing the Book of Isaiah (Luke 4:17). He unrolled the document to Isaiah 61:1-2, which says, *"The Spirit of the Lord is upon me, because he has anointed me to bring good news to the poor. He has sent me to proclaim release to the captives and recovery of sight to the blind, to let the oppressed go free, to proclaim the year of the Lord's favor"* (Luke 4:18-19).

Isaiah pictured the deliverance of Israel from exile in Babylon as a year of Jubilee when all debts were cancelled, all slaves were freed, and all property was returned to its original owners (Lev. 25:8-23). Of course, the release from Babylonian exile did not bring the fulfillment the Jews had expected, for they were still a conquered and oppressed people.

Jesus understood this, which makes His declaration all the more profound. After rolling up the scroll, handing it back to the attendant, and sitting down, Jesus declared to His audience that He fulfilled the messianic prophecies made by Isaiah (Luke 4:20-21). In other words, Jesus would bring this good news to pass, though in a way that many of His fellow Jews were not yet able to grasp.

At first those in attendance were amazed by the *gracious words that came from [Jesus'] mouth* (4:22). But then some began to get suspicious. They asked, *"Is not this Joseph's son?"* In other words, how is it possible for the son of an ordinary carpenter to be the Messiah?

Jesus bluntly responded by quoting the maxim, *"Doctor, cure yourself!"* (4:23) This proverb underscored the people's demand that Jesus repeat the type of miracles He had performed in Capernaum (Mark 1:21-27). It was not enough for them to believe what Jesus had claimed in the synagogue. Perhaps this is why He declared that prophets are usually not accepted by the residents in their hometown (Luke 4:24).

Jesus next cited examples of two Gentiles whom God chose to help in Old Testament times, namely, the widow of Zarephath (1 Kings 17:8-16) and Naaman the Syrian (2 Kings 5:1-14). In the case of the widow, she was miraculously taken care of during a severe famine because she trusted God and sheltered Elijah. The prophet came to Israel at a time when the people were heavily involved in worship of idols and were falling away from their devotion to the Lord. God sent Elijah to them, but because they did not believe, God's blessings fell to a Gentile woman who did believe in God.

Tragically, the Jews of Jesus' day believed that being God's children meant no other group of people could be welcomed into the Lord's spiritual family. By referring to the account of the widow of Zarephath and Naaman the Syrian, Jesus was trying to teach the people of His day that it is not those who are descendants of Abraham who are true children of God, but instead, those who truly believe in the Lord are His children. Jesus was telling the residents of Nazareth that because they did not embrace Him as the Messiah, God's blessings—especially His salvation—would be offered to others.

In summary, Jesus made it clear that God had anointed Him to bring salvation to all people, whether Jews or Gentiles (Luke 4:25-27). Jesus' comments enraged His listeners (4:28). In fact, *they got up, drove him out of the town, and led him to the brow of the hill on which their town was built* (4:29). The intent of the mob was to push Jesus over the cliff. Amazingly, however, this didn't happen, for Jesus *passed through the midst of them and went on his way* (4:30). Though the biblical text doesn't say this escape was a miracle, it probably was.

Why did Jesus' comments so enrage the people of Nazareth? They were upset because Jesus claimed that God sometimes chose to reach Gentiles rather than Jews. The Savior implied that His hearers were as unbelieving as the citizens of the northern kingdom of Israel in the days of Elijah and Elisha, a time notorious for its widespread injustice and immorality.

Apparently those in Jesus' audience were concerned with preserving the ethnic reputation and customs of their religious tradition. If so, Jesus' words might well have represented a threat to the image they wanted to project to the watching world. Once Jesus' neighbors realized what He was really saying, they determined to reject Him. In a sense, the reaction of the people of Nazareth foreshadowed the reaction of the crowd at the end of Jesus' public ministry. The latter took Him outside of town and did kill Him, on the cross. Jesus' rejection also foreshadowed the coming rejection of all who would follow Him, including Stephen, who would be stoned outside of Jerusalem's gates (Acts 7:54-60).

The reaction of Jesus' hometown crowd moves us to ask whom we are reaching out to with the good news about Christ. Also, what issues does Jesus' Gospel address in our times? Are we, like the Nazareth listeners, so committed to preserving the status quo that the Lord has to go around us to accomplish His work? Perhaps nothing could be more tragic than this!

SUGGESTIONS TO TEACHERS

Some congregations in the United States have the custom of making a cross out of the Christmas tree they displayed during the holidays. They then place it in the front of their sanctuary during Lent. The purpose is to show the tie between the manger of Bethlehem and the cross of Calvary. In other words, the infant Jesus eventually grew up and sacrificed Himself for others.

Realizing this truth helps us to note that, from the start of Jesus' ministry, He was aware that God had anointed Him to bring the good news of the Kingdom to all people, regardless of their race, nationality, gender, or social status. We also learn from Jesus that God wants us to be His ambassadors to the lost.

1. CUSTOMARY PRACTICE. Jesus studied God's Word and gathered regularly with the community of faith. Though He was the perfect Son of God and His local synagogue was far less than perfect, Jesus attended services every week. His example underscores how important it is for us to make regular worship a part of our lives (Heb. 10:25).

2. CLEAR PROCLAMATION. Take a few moments to discuss Isaiah 61:1-2 with your students, and be sure to consider ways in which this passage applies to them. For instance, ordained clergy are not the only ones whom God wants to accomplish His work. All of God's people are to do whatever they can to serve Him. This includes reaching out to the poor and homeless in the community with the good news of salvation and compassionate involvement.

The unconditional love of God is at the heart of such ministry. It's easy, of course, to talk about love, but it's much harder to do the tough work of living it. Love as God intended it is more than just passion, romantic feelings, or sentimental expressions. It involves commitment, sacrifice, and service—the kind of things that benefit both the giver and the receiver.

3. COMMANDING PERSONAGE. Jesus went against popular expectations in His Nazareth sermon and stirred up such severe opposition that His townsfolk wanted to murder Him. Despite this, He had the courage to speak up for and show compassion to those whom society despised. Even when threatened, Jesus didn't sidestep issues. This high level of trust in God, which was evident from the start of Jesus' ministry, should also be characteristic of our lives.

4. CONTEMPTIBLE PATRIOTISM. At first we might think that the fury of the people of Nazareth was an extreme example from the dark ages of the past. The sad truth, however, is that such rage still exists today among those who are unbelieving and wicked. This is not surprising, for Jesus said in John 15:18, *"If the world hates you, be aware that it hated me before it hated you."*

FOR ADULTS

■ **TOPIC:** What Is My Calling?

■ **QUESTIONS:** 1. Why do you think Jesus accepted the invitation from the leader of the synagogue to read the Scriptures? 2. What did Jesus say that caused the people of Nazareth to reject Him? 3. How do you think Christ handled the rejection He experienced? 4. Why are we sometimes surprised when our Christian life and faith are not easily understood or accepted by those who know us well? 5. What are some things we can do when others reject us because of our faith?

■ **ILLUSTRATIONS:**

The Negative Spirit of Rejection. H. B. London has written a book titled *Your Pastor Is an Endangered Species: A Wake-up Call to the Local Church.* In it he says he has talked with numerous ministers and church leaders across the country. London reports hearing about clergy and laypeople who, because of a negative, complaining attitude, spread a contagious spirit that keeps congregations in the desert for years.

From this we see that a sour disposition is like a deadly pollutant. Though it harms everyone, it usually harms the person who expresses it the most. Imagine how much their lives would have been changed had the people of Nazareth accepted their own, hometown Messiah, instead of adopting a negative spirit of rejection toward Him!

Reminder of Mission. In the old House of Representatives in the capitol in Washington, D.C., there once stood a clock made by an elderly New Englander. Prominent in the decoration of the clock was a large carving of the "gatekeeper of history." The people in the House of Representatives were reminded constantly by the clock's carving that history would judge what they said and did. They came to see that more important than the time of day was whether their lives and actions in that chamber would stand the scrutiny of time.

Today there is no such symbol in the House of Representatives. Now there is only the television camera. This prompts many leaders to pose and perform before a fickle public. What reminders of God's mission do we as believers have in our daily lives?

Pleasing God. In *Sold Out*, Promise Keepers founder Bill McCartney wrote the following:

> Recently I spoke at a large arena. The moment I stepped off the stage, I began asking friends and associates how I'd done. There were high fives, back slaps, and encouraging compliments to the effect that I'd "hit a home run." I went back to the hotel quite pleased with myself.
>
> The next morning, early, I went to my knees. God wasn't to be found. I asked, "Lord, where are You? I rose early to meet with You. I spoke of Your wonder and glory last night. I praised You with all of my heart. I thought You would be pleased. What have I done? Where are You?"
>
> In that very instant, I sensed God was asking me a direct question:

"Last night, when you finished your message, why didn't you ask *Me* how you did? You came to Me for anointing to speak, but you went to your friends seeking their opinions. Why did you not seek *Mine* first?"

It broke my heart to hear. But it was true. I'd spent weeks seeking God's heart for that message. And it *was* a home run; the power of the Holy Spirit fell upon that arena—not because of anything I said, but because *God* showed up. And yet I didn't seek *God's* affirmation first. I sought the approval of people. I confessed my sin and repented. Immediately God's sweetness returned. It shocked me into seeing that the only one I've ever needed to please is God.

Challenged to Serve. God wants us to make the good news of salvation known throughout the world, especially among the impoverished of our planet. But few of us really know what these people have to endure on a daily basis. One reason is that their living conditions are beyond what most of us have ever experienced.

In *Nine Steps to Third World Living*, John Nelson made the following observations about the reality of life among the poor:

> First, take out the furniture. Leave a few old blankets, a kitchen table, and maybe a wooden chair. You've never had a bed, remember? Second, throw out your clothes. Each person in the family may keep their oldest suit or dress and a shirt or blouse. The head of the family has the only pair of shoes. Third, all kitchen appliances have vanished. Keep a box of matches, a small bag of flour, some sugar and salt, a handful of onions, and a dish of dried beans. Rescue the moldy potatoes from the garbage can, for those are tonight's meal.
>
> Fourth, dismantle the bathroom, shut off the running water, and take out the wiring and the lights and everything that runs by electricity. Fifth, take away the house and move the family into the tool shed. Sixth, no more letter carrier, firefighters, or government services. The two-   classroom school is three miles away, but only two of your seven children attend anyway, and they have to walk.
>
> Seventh, throw out your bankbooks, stock certificates, pension plans, and insurance policies. You now have a cash hoard of only $5. Eighth, get out and start cultivating your three acres. Try hard to raise $300 in cash crops because your landlord wants one-third and your moneylender 10 percent. Ninth, find some way for your children to bring in a little extra money so you have something to eat tomorrow. But it won't be enough to keep your family healthy, so lop off 25 to 30 years of your life.

Contrast the above with the percentage of American adults who say this is what they would spend money on first, especially if they suddenly became wealthy:

their house, 31%; education for kids and/or self, 30%; a vacation, 10%; a new car, 9%; help for kids and extended family, 3%; charity, 2%; household help, 2%; paying off debt, 2%; boat, 2%; investments, 1%; clothes/jewelry, 1%; other miscellaneous items, 7%.

This reminds us that virtually every American is already wealthy compared to the impoverished people of the world. Given the conditions in which hundreds of millions of people live, it's scandalous that only two percent of Americans would first give to charity, while the vast majority would spend their wealth only on themselves.

FOR YOUTH ■ **TOPIC:** Jesus Declares His Mission
■ **QUESTIONS:** 1. What point was Jesus making by reading from Isaiah 61:1-2? 2. What was Jesus' point by mentioning the widow of Zarephath? 3. How was Jesus able to slip away from the angry mob? 4. How can we make regular worship a part of our lives? 5. How do people sometimes show their rejection of Christians?

■ **ILLUSTRATIONS:**

Strange Irony. A 64 million-dollar project, financed by American donations, is rapidly transforming modern Nazareth—a congested city of 60,000—into a biblical era village. Nazareth draws on its connection to the past and its obvious tourist appeal.

Visitors to the heart of the city now can stroll along donkey paths into a replica of the ancient village in which Jesus lived. One-room stone houses and courtyards have actors playing the part of first-century peasants and laborers. The actors describe the news of Jesus as if He were a contemporary. And storytellers take tourists on the "parable walk." For the truly devout, there are communion services, foot washings, and Bible readings. The hope is to draw millions of visitors to the city over the next few years.

What a strange irony that modern Nazareth is capitalizing on its association with Jesus. The Gospel of Luke reminds us that the ancient residents of the city rejected the Messiah. His contemporaries refused to listen to anything He had to say.

Hometown Boy at Death. Andy Warhol is best remembered for his parodies of the consumerism and pop culture of the 1960's. His revolutionary silk-screened likenesses of Jackie Kennedy, Chairman Mao, and Marilyn Monroe are well known, as are the Campbell's Soup cans, Brillo Pads, and the Coca-Cola bottles. Lesser known are his religious paintings that reflect his strict spiritual upbringing.

Warhol preferred to live and work in New York City. In fact he died there at age 58 due to an infection he received after undergoing routine surgery. But it was his hometown of Pittsburgh that created the Andy Warhol Museum. The city, which has a blue-collar outlook, and which abhorred his outlandish outfits and lifestyle, nonetheless wanted the museum within its boundaries.

Jesus, too, was initially rejected and abhorred by the people of Nazareth. Sadly, the city's residents were negative toward Him when He ministered among them centuries ago.

Heard Call to Free the Captives. Barbara Vogel's fifth grade American history class at a public school in Colorado had finished a unit on slavery when the students were shocked to discover that the slave trade still continued in the Sudan. One student wanted to stop the trade in human lives. He convinced the class to start collecting change in jars with the hope of buying the freedom of two slaves.

The local newspaper heard about the project and ran a story on it. Soon other newspapers and radio and television stations were sharing the story. The checks began pouring in to the class. Within the first year, the students sent over $50,000 to a charitable organization, which in turn arranged for over 1,000 people to be set free.

These students are just a few of those who are striving to improve the lot of others around the world. Jesus had even loftier goals not only for His hometown of Nazareth but also for the rest of the world. As His faithful followers, we are given the task of fostering hope, peace, and joy through the liberating message of the Gospel.

RESTORATION AND HEALING

BACKGROUND SCRIPTURE: Luke 8:40-56
DEVOTIONAL READING: Matthew 9:18-26

KEY VERSE: "Daughter, your faith has made you well; go in peace." Luke 8:48.

KING JAMES VERSION

LUKE 8:40 And it came to pass, that, when Jesus was returned, the people gladly received him: for they were all waiting for him. 41 And, behold, there came a man named Jairus, and he was a ruler of the synagogue: and he fell down at Jesus' feet, and besought him that he would come into his house: 42 For he had one only daughter, about twelve years of age, and she lay a dying. But as he went the people thronged him. 43 And a woman having an issue of blood twelve years, which had spent all her living upon physicians, neither could be healed of any, 44 Came behind him, and touched the border of his garment: and immediately her issue of blood stanched. 45 And Jesus said, Who touched me? When all denied, Peter and they that were with him said, Master, the multitude throng thee and press thee, and sayest thou, Who touched me? 46 And Jesus said, Somebody hath touched me: for I perceive that virtue is gone out of me. 47 And when the woman saw that she was not hid, she came trembling, and falling down before him, she declared unto him before all the people for what cause she had touched him, and how she was healed immediately. 48 And he said unto her, Daughter, be of good comfort: thy faith hath made thee whole; go in peace. 49 While he yet spake, there cometh one from the ruler of the synagogue's house, saying to him, Thy daughter is dead; trouble not the Master. 50 But when Jesus heard it, he answered him, saying, Fear not: believe only, and she shall be made whole. 51 And when he came into the house, he suffered no man to go in, save Peter, and James, and John, and the father and the mother of the maiden. 52 And all wept, and bewailed her: but he said, Weep not; she is not dead, but sleepeth. 53 And they laughed him to scorn, knowing that she was dead. 54 And he put them all out, and took her by the hand, and called, saying, Maid, arise. 55 And her spirit came again, and she arose straightway: and he commanded to give her meat. 56 And her parents were astonished: but he charged them that they should tell no man what was done.

NEW REVISED STANDARD VERSION

LUKE 8:40 Now when Jesus returned, the crowd welcomed him, for they were all waiting for him. 41 Just then there came a man named Jairus, a leader of the synagogue. He fell at Jesus' feet and begged him to come to his house, 42 for he had an only daughter, about twelve years old, who was dying.

As he went, the crowds pressed in on him. 43 Now there was a woman who had been suffering from hemorrhages for twelve years; and though she had spent all she had on physicians, no one could cure her. 44 She came up behind him and touched the fringe of his clothes, and immediately her hemorrhage stopped. 45 Then Jesus asked, "Who touched me?" When all denied it, Peter said, "Master, the crowds surround you and press in on you." 46 But Jesus said, "Someone touched me; for I noticed that power had gone out from me." 47 When the woman saw that she could not remain hidden, she came trembling; and falling down before him, she declared in the presence of all the people why she had touched him, and how she had been immediately healed. 48 He said to her, "Daughter, your faith has made you well; go in peace."

49 While he was still speaking, someone came from the leader's house to say, "Your daughter is dead; do not trouble the teacher any longer." 50 When Jesus heard this, he replied, "Do not fear. Only believe, and she will be saved." 51 When he came to the house, he did not allow anyone to enter with him, except Peter, John, and James, and the child's father and mother. 52 They were all weeping and wailing for her; but he said, "Do not weep; for she is not dead but sleeping." 53 And they laughed at him, knowing that she was dead. 54 But he took her by the hand and called out, "Child, get up!" 55 Her spirit returned, and she got up at once. Then he directed them to give her something to eat. 56 Her parents were astounded; but he ordered them to tell no one what had happened.

HOME BIBLE READINGS

Monday, August 8	Luke 7:1-10	*A Centurion's Servant Is Healed*
Tuesday, August 9	Matthew 9:18-26	*A Girl Restored, A Woman Healed*
Wednesday, August 10	Matthew 9:27-31	*Two Blind Men Healed by Faith*
Thursday, August 11	Mark 5:24b-34	*A Hemorrhaging Woman Is Healed*
Friday, August 12	Mark 5:35-43	*A Girl Is Restored to Life*
Saturday, August 13	Luke 8:40-48	*A Sick Woman Is Healed*
Sunday, August 14	Luke 8:49-56	*Jairus' Daughter Is Alive*

BACKGROUND

From the day they occurred, these two incidents—the restoring of Jairus' daughter to life and the healing of the woman plagued by hemorrhages—have been linked. The two accounts contrast in several ways, but also share many features.

The major contrast involved the social status of the two people who approached Jesus for help. Synagogue leaders were key figures in each village. These leaders administered the affairs of the local religious community, organizing worship services and religious education for children, as well as superintending care for the synagogue building. Men in the community elected these leaders, likely from their wealthier members.

On the other extreme, the woman needing healing was an outcast, and on the social ladder nearly as low as lepers. Her ongoing bleeding made her, in a ritual sense, continually unclean. This prevented her from gathering with her neighbors for worship. Anyone who touched her became unclean; thus, she was isolated from all local gatherings. No man would marry such a woman. In addition to these religious and social stigmas, her condition left her physically weak and financially destitute. She *had spent all that she had* (Luke 8:43).

Both Jairus and the unnamed woman felt desperate. In coming to Jesus, they both opened themselves to potential humiliation. Jairus could have played it safe, sending a servant to invite Jesus to his home. Instead, Jairus not only went to Jesus, but also *fell at [His] feet* (8:41). A person did this only before someone having great status.

As Jairus bowed before Jesus, he publicly confessed his respect for someone whom other religious leaders had already rejected. If Jesus had not healed his daughter, Jairus would have looked like a fool. Regarding the woman, she came to Jesus, believing He could help, but desired to sneak in and out of the crowd unnoticed. She knew her touching Jesus' clothing would make Him ceremonially unclean. But the woman was willing to risk Jesus' rebuke.

Both Jairus and the woman were surrounded by those who could not help them. Jairus had friends, but they may not have trusted Jesus to the degree that he did. When the daughter of Jairus died, the professional mourners gathered quickly and entered their role of *weeping and wailing for her* (8:52). They, too, held no hope that Jesus could offer any real help (8:53). Regarding the woman, she had few friends (if any). But, for money, physicians would attend to her. They had done their best to help, but offered no cure. In fact, she grew worse (8:43).

In desperation, both Jairus and the woman approached Jesus. To both, Jesus reached out in compassion. Notice the way Jesus thought about Jairus' daughter. He kept the crowds away from her so that she would not be unduly startled when she awoke. Although Jesus likely knew Greek and Hebrew, He spoke in Aramaic, the local language that the girl would understand. He reached out and touched her, even though touching a corpse made a person ceremonially unclean. After she got up, Jesus even thought to remind her family to prepare food for her (8:54-55).

Jesus could merely have ignored the woman who had just received healing from Him; that way, no one would ever have known that the woman had made Him unclean. Or, Jesus could have rebuked her for covertly receiving His healing power. Instead, Jesus spoke gently and affirmed her faith (8:48).

NOTES ON THE PRINTED TEXT

Jesus had been ministering in *the country of the Gerasenes* (Luke 8:26), which was predominantly Gentile in population. After the episode involving the healing a demon-possessed man (8:27-39), Jesus *returned* (8:40) to territory that was predominantly Jewish in population. What follows in the Luke's narrative are two intertwined events involving sickness and death.

The anxious father of a 12-year-old girl introduced the problem of death. This parent was *Jairus* (8:41), a man of influence among the Jews in his area. He was a ruler of a local *synagogue*, perhaps the one in Capernaum. Jairus knew that his daughter's condition was grave and that if things took their normal course, she might die. Thus, Jairus came to Jesus, *fell at [His feet]*, and began to beg the Savior *to come to his house*. The synagogue ruler's request was simple. He wanted Jesus to place His hands on the girl and heal her so she could live (8:42).

Jesus had been sitting (Matt. 9:19), which was the normal posture of a Jewish teacher while giving instruction. The Savior promptly got up and went with Jairus. Jesus had been moved with compassion by the ruler's request. Accompanied by His disciples and a large crowd, Jesus began to follow the official to his home.

It was at this time that Jesus encountered the problem of illness. He met a woman in the throng who had been *suffering from hemorrhages for twelve years* (Luke 8:43). This was some form of uncontrollable internal bleeding, probably chronic bleeding from the womb. The woman had endured a wretched existence. She had spent all her money seeing numerous physicians. But her condition had worsened, not improved (Mark 5:26).

The woman's physical discomfort wasn't the only pain she had to endure. She also had to withstand rejection from her fellow Jews. This is because the law excluded someone with her sickness from religious ceremonies and social events. Added to the problem of isolation and loneliness was the financial drain of medical bills.

The woman's hope was not yet gone. Somehow she had heard about Jesus' miracles. Thus, in desperation, the woman sought Him out (Mark 5:27). But she did so secretly, perhaps fearing that her condition would bring shame upon herself or upon Jesus. If she was aware that Jesus was going on a lifesaving mission to the home of an important synagogue official, this might have added to her reluctance.

Despite these potential factors, the woman cautiously approached Jesus anyway. The woman *came up behind him and touched the fringe of his clothes* (Luke 8:44), thinking that doing this would heal her. (The verse refers to either the edge of Jesus' long outer garment or to the tassel of His prayer shawl.) As a result of the woman's action, her hemorrhaging *immediately . . . stopped*. She could tell that her physical afflictions had been cured.

The woman evidently thought no one would notice. But someone did. The Savior knew instantly that healing power had *gone out* (Luke 8:46) from Him. He thus turned around in the crowd and asked who had touched His clothes (8:45). Jesus' query seemed ridiculous to His disciples, for they were all being pressed on every side by people. But Jesus knew that the woman's touch was unique, for it expressed great need and great faith.

The woman could see that there was no way out short of a confession. So she came forward, frightened and *trembling* (8:47) at the realization at what had happened to her. Perhaps the woman thought that such an important person as this well-known rabbi would be upset at what she had done.

The woman first prostrated herself at the feet of the Savior. Then, *in the presence of all the people*, the woman explained why she had *touched* Jesus and that she had been *immediately healed*. Jesus, far from delivering the rebuke the woman anticipated, put her fears to rest by addressing her as *"Daughter"* (8:48). The Messiah praised her faith and urged her to *"go in peace,"* enjoying her newfound wholeness.

The woman had touched Jesus' garment because she believed that doing so would heal her. Jesus, however, brought about more than just physical healing. He also brought spiritual vitality and wellness to the woman—all because she dared to believe in Him. Jesus was concluding His conversation with the woman He had healed when a messenger arrived from the home of Jairus. The synagogue official learned that his *daughter* (8:49) had died. Thus, at least from a human perspective, it seemed pointless to trouble Jesus any further with the matter.

Jairus and other loved ones had hoped to receive help from Jesus, especially if He had arrived while the girl was still alive; but now that she was *dead*, the case appeared to be hopeless. Jesus was not discouraged, however, by the report. He thus reassured Jairus not to *fear* (8:50); moreover, the Savior encouraged the synagogue official to simply put his faith in Jesus, believing that He would somehow heal the official's daughter.

When the entourage arrived at the home of Jairus, the Savior would not *allow anyone to enter with him, except Peter, John, and James* (8:51), along with the young girl's parents. Peter, James, and John seem to have been an inner circle within the band of disciples. Jesus chose them to witness the miracle He was about to perform.

Jairus' house was filled with mourners who were providing a great deal of noise and ritual signs of grief (8:52). The hired mourners at the home of Jairus may have been chanting and clapping, or pulling their hair, tearing their clothes, and beating their chests. We know their grief was feigned by their response to Jesus' announcement that the girl was asleep—the mourners *laughed at him* (8:53). Jesus did not deny that the girl was dead, but only wanted the onlookers to understand that her condition was not final; tragically, the mourners thought they knew better.

Jesus, after sending the mourners out, took the girl's hand and *called out, "Child, get up!"* (8:54). At that moment the *spirit returned* (8:55) to the girl and she immediately stood up. Jesus then directed the girl's parents to give her something to eat. Understandably, Jairus and his wife were *astounded* (8:56) to see their previously dead daughter get up and walk (Mark 5:42). The parents learned that the hopeless case was not hopeless at all.

Luke 8:56 relates that Jesus didn't want anyone else to know what He had done. The reason is that, while news of the miracle would have attracted some people to Jesus, it also would have fueled the hatred of His enemies.

SUGGESTIONS TO TEACHERS

Some critics of Western culture claim that most Americans and Europeans are obsessed with death. Pointing to the high statistics of teenage suicide and rampant violence, these observers portray our society as being filled with people having little hope for a fulfilling life. They compare our times to the grim fourteenth and fifteenth centuries, when the *danse macabre*—skeletons dancing in graveyards—symbolized an era of death and futility.

God counteracted death once and for all on the first Easter by raising Jesus Christ to life. This week's lesson demonstrates that the Savior forever remains the Lord of life. Here is another bounteous helping of scriptural material that could serve up a dozen class sessions! This lesson should give you so much for the students to feast on that you might find yourself quickly running out of time to discuss everything.

1. THE LEADER WHO INCONVENIENCED JESUS. A frantic father, Jairus, pushed his own agenda on Jesus. Despite the fact that Jairus was head man of the Capernaum synagogue and perhaps had witnessed others berating Jesus for breaking the Sabbath, Jesus went with him to the dying daughter's bedside. Jesus heeded cries for help, setting aside His plans to meet human concerns. Through this gracious Savior, we may be certain that God heeds our every cry.

2. THE WOMAN WHO INTERRUPTED THE LORD. The account of the woman with a long-lasting medical problem comes in the middle of the Jairus account. The poor woman was desperate, for her problem had persisted despite the best medical help. But Jesus healed her immediately. Ask your students to tell about times when they have been desperate for God's help and comfort. What happened?

3. THE TEACHER WHO IGNORED THE EXPERTS. On the way to Jairus' house, messengers announced that the girl had died. They knew the signs of death; they acted like experts in detecting the hopeless case. *"Do not trouble the teacher any longer"* (Luke 8:49), they remarked. Although they and everyone saw only futility, Jesus saw life. To whom do we listen today? To the "experts" who tell us that all is hopeless? Or to the Lord of life, who claims to have power greater than any other?

4. THE SAVIOR WHO INSTILLS LIFE. Comment on Jesus' tender concern for the young girl. Remind your students that Jesus broke all the rules for ceremonial cleanness by coming near a corpse. Even today Jesus reverses the effect of death in every form. Ask your group members to comment on the forms of resurrection Jesus brings in our day. Raising a person from the grave of guilt? from the pit of substance abuse? Rescuing us from various death traps in our society?

■ TOPIC: Hope for Healing

FOR ADULTS

■ QUESTIONS: 1. What do you think motivated Jairus to seek Jesus for help? 2. What do you think prompted the Savior to take the time to help Jairus? 3. Why would the woman with a hemorrhage think that Jesus could help her any more than the physicians she had previously consulted? 4. In what ways were the faith of Jairus and the woman similar and different? 5. Why is Jesus worthy of our faith and devotion?

■ ILLUSTRATIONS:

Keep Looking to Jesus. During the 1940s, Robert Schuller, pastor of the Crystal Cathedral, had just returned home to the farm after a year's college studies in Michigan. One afternoon, the family knew a big storm would soon break. In the distance, Schuller's dad picked out a tornado. Everyone piled into the car to see whether they could escape its terror. They did, but their farm did not. The powerful storm cleared the property, not leaving even any debris.

As the family returned to the site, Schuller's father wept. He remembered the family's years of hard work, especially through the decade of the Depression. They had struggled not merely to build up the farm, but even to keep it. What was left of the family house was found a half-mile away in a pasture. Among the wreckage there, they found the top half of a plaster plaque that had hung in the kitchen. Originally, it had said, "Keep looking to Jesus." Even the half that remained, "Keep looking . . ." seemed to speak a message from God.

From scraps of another house being torn down, the Schullers built a new house. They gradually rebuilt the farm buildings. God proved Himself faithful to this family who looked to Him.

God Uses Medical Science Too! Faith does conquer fear, and God employs faith as He offers healing to His people. But the faithful God often uses medical science in bringing healing.

David Seamands told the story of a brilliant young missionary in India. God was using this man powerfully to speak His Word. But no Christian is totally immune to illness. Appendicitis attacked this young man. Just as he was leaving for the hospital, some well-meaning, but foolish friends convinced him that God would receive more glory if they all prayed for a miraculous divine healing. Within hours, his appendix had burst. Within days, he was dead. God brings glory to Himself through all forms of healing.

God Does Not Always Heal as We Wish. When Catherine Marshall contracted tuberculosis, she prayed for healing. For two years she asked for God to change her circumstances. Then she reached the point of submission, asking God to change her. She admitted that she did not understand what He was doing, but if, for any reason, He saw fit to leave her ill, she would still rejoice in His love. After that prayer, both physical and spiritual health gradually returned.

Fear of Death. One morning, a man named Alfred read his own obituary in the daily paper. Obviously he had not yet died, but some reporter hearing that Alfred's brother had died, somehow became mixed-up and printed news of Alfred's death. Alfred received the rare opportunity to see how the world might remember him. The article highlighted Alfred's fame. He was proclaimed the "King of Dynamite," for he had invented this deadly explosive. That one invention had made him quite wealthy.

But Alfred then and there decided that he did not want to be remembered as the rich inventor of destruction. What could he do with the years he had left to change his reputation? He chose to put his wealth to good use. With his will, he established a foundation that would reward other great scientific discoverers. You have heard of Alfred's prizes; his last name was Nobel. Over the last century, his foundation has awarded the Nobel prizes in such fields as chemistry and medical science, as well as the much coveted Nobel Peace Prize—all because of Alfred's healthy fear of death.

Jesus' Compassion. When Jesus went with Jairus to heal the official's daughter, He was doing something highly unusual for that time. Jesus showed concern for the health of a little girl. Tragically, caring about young females was almost unheard of in the first century A.D. One example of this callousness toward little girls can be seen in a letter written in A.D. 10 by a Greek businessman named Hilarion on a trip in Egypt. He sent the following message to his wife in Greece.

"Hilarion to Alis his wife, heartiest greetings, and to my dear Berous and to Apollonarion. I want you to know that we are still in Alexandria. Don't worry that when all the others come back, if I stay on in Alexandria. . . . If—good luck be with you—you bear a child, if it is a boy, let it live; if it is a girl, throw it out. You told Aphrodisias to say to me not to forget you. How can I forget you? So I beg you not to worry."

In the midst of the affection expressed toward his wife and to Berous and Apollonarion, this man also displayed a shockingly calloused attitude toward female babies. In contrast, Jesus cared about the welfare of a young girl whom He had never seen before.

■ TOPIC: Restored and Healed

■ QUESTIONS: 1. Why was Jairus feeling so desperate? 2. Why was the woman with the hemorrhage feeling so desperate? 3. How did Jesus resolve the woman's problem? 4. How did Jesus resolve Jairus' problem? 5. What kinds of needs do you bring to the Lord? What are your expectations of the Lord regarding those needs?

■ ILLUSTRATIONS:

Troubles Are Over. While still a child, Cleveland Amory read *Black Beauty*. It became his desire to build a ranch for animals where they could be free to end their days, like the fictional horse. Amory fulfilled his dream by starting *The Fund for Animals* and by building the *Black Beauty Ranch* in Murchison, Texas. This ranch has become a sanctuary for many animals who have been mistreated.

A cat, the ranch's first animal, literally dragged itself to the gate. Its foot had been seized by a hunter's leghold trap. The leg was so badly damaged that it had to be amputated. Now there are numerous three-legged animals, cats, foxes, coyotes, and a deer. The ranch also houses elephants, horses, wild burros, buffaloes, prairie dogs, and Nim (the talking chimp). All are animals that had been mistreated, experimented upon, or simply considered inconvenient to keep, and were subsequently abandoned or abused. Amory has proven to be compassionate to these creatures.

If an individual can be so compassionate to animals, how much more should people demonstrate compassion to their fellow human beings.

Disbelief. In the late nineteenth century, a bishop speaking from his pulpit made the flat statement, "No vehicle heavier than air could ever fly. Anyone who tried to invent such a contraption would obviously be going against the will of God." This particular bishop had two sons. Their first names were Orville and Wilbur. In this case, Bishop Wright was wrong. Thankfully, both the needy people studied in this week's lesson believed that Jesus could perform what seemed impossible.

Receiving Help in Order to Give Help. This week's Scripture passage speaks of two people who were willing to seek help from Jesus. Today Susan Booth asks people to help her help others. Susan earns her living taking tickets on a commuter train between Connecticut and New York City. But Susan finds meaning in ministering to orphans in Romania.

A number of years ago, Susan saw a television documentary portraying the plight of these children. After a trip to Romania, where she found that many orphans lived in sewers, she took action. Susan started by describing the problem to people on her train route. With their help, she founded ARCHWAY—Abandoned Romanian CHildren's WAY.

Here in the U.S., this organization runs out of Susan's apartment and a post-office box. In Romania, ARCHWAY has built two houses, and employs eight Romanians, including a young physician. With the help of North Americans, these eight feed, clothe, and help house young people whose lives otherwise would have little hope.

Black Bart. Jairus, not wanting his daughter to die, was only a normal human being. We all have a natural fear of death. A fascinating story from the nineteenth century illustrates this fact.

Between 1875 and 1883, a thief named Black Bart robbed 29 Wells Fargo stagecoach crews. Black Bart became well known. All Western travelers feared what such a man could do to them. Despite the fact that no one remembered Black Bart ever shooting anyone, many people feared for their lives. He did it with a hood that covered his face. No one could see him. No one knew his face. His very unknowability gave him his reputation. Black Bart sounds a lot like death itself.

People Need People. None of us can face life alone. We need each other. Melissa was almost three the night she spoke a profound truth. From the top of the stairs, she called down to her mom. She wanted some help getting ready for bed. Her mom, in the middle of a task, and not wanting to come upstairs quite yet, shouted back up to Melissa, "You know how to put on your pajamas, don't you?" "Of course I do, but sometimes people need people anyway, even when they could do something all by themselves."

THE GOOD SAMARITAN

BACKGROUND SCRIPTURE: Luke 10:25-37
DEVOTIONAL READING: Matthew 22:34-40

KEY VERSE: "You shall love the Lord your God with all your heart, and with all your soul, and with all your strength, and with all your mind; and your neighbor as yourself." Luke 10:27.

KING JAMES VERSION

LUKE 10:25 And, behold, a certain lawyer stood up, and tempted him, saying, Master, what shall I do to inherit eternal life? 26 He said unto him, What is written in the law? how readest thou? 27 And he answering said, Thou shalt love the Lord thy God with all thy heart, and with all thy soul, and with all thy strength, and with all thy mind; and thy neighbour as thyself. 28 And he said unto him, Thou hast answered right: this do, and thou shalt live. 29 But he, willing to justify himself, said unto Jesus, And who is my neighbour? 30 And Jesus answering said, A certain man went down from Jerusalem to Jericho, and fell among thieves, which stripped him of his raiment, and wounded him, and departed, leaving him half dead. 31 And by chance there came down a certain priest that way: and when he saw him, he passed by on the other side. 32 And likewise a Levite, when he was at the place, came and looked on him, and passed by on the other side. 33 But a certain Samaritan, as he journeyed, came where he was: and when he saw him, he had compassion on him, 34 And went to him, and bound up his wounds, pouring in oil and wine, and set him on his own beast, and brought him to an inn, and took care of him. 35 And on the morrow when he departed, he took out two pence, and gave them to the host, and said unto him, Take care of him; and whatsoever thou spendest more, when I come again, I will repay thee.
36 Which now of these three, thinkest thou, was neighbour unto him that fell among the thieves? 37 And he said, He that shewed mercy on him. Then said Jesus unto him, Go, and do thou likewise.

NEW REVISED STANDARD VERSION

LUKE 10:25 Just then a lawyer stood up to test Jesus. "Teacher," he said, "what must I do to inherit eternal life?" 26 He said to him, "What is written in the law? What do you read there?" 27 He answered, "You shall love the Lord your God with all your heart, and with all your soul, and with all your strength, and with all your mind; and your neighbor as yourself." 28 And he said to him, "You have given the right answer; do this, and you will live."

29 But wanting to justify himself, he asked Jesus, "And who is my neighbor?" 30 Jesus replied, "A man was going down from Jerusalem to Jericho, and fell into the hands of robbers, who stripped him, beat him, and went away, leaving him half dead. 31 Now by chance a priest was going down that road; and when he saw him, he passed by on the other side. 32 So likewise a Levite, when he came to the place and saw him, passed by on the other side. 33 But a Samaritan while traveling came near him; and when he saw him, he was moved with pity. 34 He went to him and bandaged his wounds, having poured oil and wine on them. Then he put him on his own animal, brought him to an inn, and took care of him. 35 The next day he took out two denarii, gave them to the innkeeper, and said, 'Take care of him; and when I come back, I will repay you whatever more you spend.' 36 Which of these three, do you think, was a neighbor to the man who fell into the hands of the robbers?" 37 He said, "The one who showed him mercy." Jesus said to him, "Go and do likewise."

12

BACKGROUND

Racial prejudice and a history of animosity fueled an intense rivalry between the Jews and Samaritans. The Samaritans, who lived in the province of Samaria between Judea and Galilee, considered themselves proper; but Jews living in the province of Judea did not think the Samaritans were following the true Jewish religion. Thus the rivalry bred a deep hatred between the two groups—a hatred that was present at least 400 years before Christ. The bitterness between them was so fierce that Jews traveling between Judea and Galilee tried never to go through Samaria, even if it meant an extra day's journey.

The history of this rivalry goes back to 722 B.C., when Assyria conquered the northern kingdom of Israel and sent many of the people from Samaria into exile. The Assyrians also relocated foreigners into this region. Eventually some of these immigrants married the Israelites whom the Assyrians left behind in Samaria.

In 586 B.C., Babylon overran the southern kingdom of Judah and deported many of its people to Babylon. Then, in 538 B.C., the first group of Jewish exiles were allowed to return to their homeland to rebuild the Jerusalem temple. Their presence initiated the conflict between the people of Judah (the Jews) and the people of Samaria (the Samaritans), for each group viewed the other with suspicion. The Jews (who prided themselves on their "pure" Jewishness) came to hate the Samaritans, and the Samaritans reciprocated with bitterness and resentment.

The detestation reached a point of no return when the Samaritans built their own temple on Mount Gerizim, a sanctuary meant to rival the Jews' temple in Jerusalem. Additionally, the two groups despised each other for what they considered the other's hybrid religion. Samaritans accepted only their Torah—the five books of Moses—as the true law of God, whereas the Jews considered the entire Old Testament as the inspired message of the Lord.

NOTES ON THE PRINTED TEXT

Jesus' parable of the good Samaritan is one of several that are recorded solely in the Gospel of Luke. Jesus told the story in response to a question. Rather than answering the query by granting a succinct definition of "neighbor," Jesus decided to illustrate His reply by spinning a tale about some familiar territory, some familiar characters, and their very unfamiliar actions.

Jesus had been praying and blessing His disciples when an expert in the Jewish law stood up in the crowd to test Him by asking Him a question: *"Teacher, . . . what must I do to inherit eternal life?"* (Luke 10:25). The lawyer was trying to discredit Jesus, perhaps thinking he could outwit the Savior in public debate. But Jesus immediately turned the tables on the legal expert. Instead of saying something that might sound like a contradiction of the law, Jesus asked the official, *"What is written in the law? What do you read there?"* (10:26).

The lawyer quoted two Old Testament passages (10:27): Deuteronomy 6:5, which emphasizes our love for God, and Leviticus 19:18, which emphasizes our love for humankind. Jesus affirmed the lawyer's response: *"You have given the right answer; do this, and you will live"* (Luke 10:28). But the lawyer asked an additional question to show that he knew what he was talking about: *"And who is my neighbor?"* (10:29).

Jesus responded with a story about a man who traveled from Jerusalem to Jericho. Those listening would have been familiar with that notorious stretch of road. The route was known for the beggars and thieves who camped nearby. They plundered travelers along the narrow, winding mountain road. In fact, that's what happened to the traveler in Jesus' story. He *"fell into the hands of robbers, who stripped him, beat him, and went away, leaving him half dead"* (10:30).

As the traveler lay on the ground fighting for his life, a Jewish priest came along. But seeing the beaten and bloodied victim, the priest made the decision not to help him; instead, the clergy-type walked to the other side of the road and passed by the injured man. A temple assistant (a Levite) also noticed the man, but he, too, decided not to get involved (10:31-32).

Finally, a Samaritan came along. Because of the Jewish-Samaritan rivalry, the Samaritan could have rationalized failing to assist the wounded traveler more easily than did the Jewish priest and temple assistant. But unlike them, the Samaritan, *"when he saw him, he was moved with pity"* (10:33), and took extensive action to help the hapless victim. The Samaritan bandaged the man's injuries, pouring on oil to ease the pain and wine to cleanse the wounds. He then *"put him on his own animal"* (10:34) and transported the man to an inn. Moreover, the Samaritan arranged to pay all the man's expenses for a lengthy stay at the inn (10:35).

In telling this story, Jesus did not answer the lawyer's question. Rather, the Savior presented him with an entirely different query: *"Which of these three, do you think, was a neighbor to the man who fell into the hands of the robbers?"* (10:36). The answer, of course, was clear: *"The one who showed him mercy"* (10:37). Jesus then told the lawyer to *"Go and do likewise."*

SUGGESTIONS TO TEACHERS

One of the Pharisees asked Jesus, *"Teacher, which commandment in the law is the greatest?"* He said to him, *"'You shall love the Lord your God with all your heart, and with all your soul, and with all your mind.' This is the greatest and first commandment. And a second is like it: 'You shall love your neighbor as yourself.' On these two commandments hang all the law and the prophets"* (Matt. 22:36-40). Jesus wants us to apply the principle of love to our lives—love both for God and for our fellow human beings. To be a good neighbor, we should look for opportunities to do the following.

1. GET LOVE. Love is both a choice and an attitude. Without it, selfishness takes control of our hearts, and we become more concerned about what might happen to us than about helping those who are in need. We should remember that *"No one has greater love than this, to lay down one's life for one's friends"* (John 15:13). God's love is the driving force that gets a good neighbor to take action.

2. GET INVOLVED. Our society is plagued with a lack of involvement. Like the priest and the temple assistant in Jesus' parable, there is a growing tendency to go out of our way to avoid getting involved. A good neighbor cannot cross to the other side of the road and leave a truly needy person without help. A good neighbor gets involved. A good neighbor stoops to help. A good neighbor sacrifices. And a good neighbor eases the pain.

3. GET MERCIFUL. There's never been, nor will there ever be, a human being for whom God did not show some measure of mercy. We're all the recipients of His mercy, so let's pass a little of it on! May we strive to offer compassionate treatment to those around us. And may God grant us and develop within us a disposition to be kind.

4. GET HELP. None of us can do all that needs to be done by ourselves. So when the task seems overbearing or too much to accomplish on our own, we should enlist the help of other good neighbors who, out of the love of their hearts, are more than willing to get involved and to show mercy.

5. GET NEIGHBORLY. A combination of love, involvement, mercy, and help makes for a good neighbor. And that's what Jesus has called us to be. We cannot become hermits and adequately love our neighbors. We have to get to know them. The lesson that Jesus taught—and the lesson that we must live—is that we become good neighbors by showing compassion and kindness to everyone we encounter.

FOR ADULTS

■ **TOPIC:** Stretching Our Love
■ **QUESTIONS:** 1. How might the priest and the temple assistant justify—or rationalize—not getting involved with the injured traveler? 2. What did the Samaritan sacrifice to get involved with the wounded traveler? What might the Samaritan have potentially sacrificed? 3. How do you think Jesus' hearers might have reacted when they learned that a Samaritan was the hero of the story, and not the priest or the Levite? 4. Do you think the lawyer's attitude was changed after he had heard Jesus' parable? Explain your answer. 5. In what ways can you show mercy to your fellow human beings?

■ ILLUSTRATIONS:

Good Samaritans at the Battlefront. Although over the years Russian soldiers stationed in Chechnya have been suspicious and leery of practically everyone other than their fellow soldiers, there is one group of people that they have learned to trust: the Salvation Army. Surly Russian soldiers in Chechnya have been polite to Salvation Army aid workers and have even pinned the organization's emblems to their own lapels.

The Salvation Army has been among the few international religious groups working in the war-torn region, according to a report from the Religion News Service. And the Salvation Army aid workers have a big job. The state-sponsored religious organization, which has backed the Russian invasion of Chechnya, has made little effort to send humanitarian aid. Even the United Nations has typically considered the area too dangerous to enter, and instead has helped some 215,000 refugees in neighboring Ingushetia.

In the meantime, the Salvation Army has acted as good Samaritans by delivering $100,000 in baby food every month to Chechen mothers and infants in devastated villages. A package containing juice, dry milk, porridge, and puree has been enough to feed a child for three weeks. Chechen children often are born underweight, and mothers traumatized by the war aren't producing breast milk, the Salvation Army's Geoff Ryan explained.

Nearly all the Salvation Army staff in Chechnya are Muslim. Ryan is the only Christian, and he is determined to make sure people know about the Salvation Army's religious identity. "I want to make sure it is clear right up front that we are a Christian organization," he said. More than 40,000 pocket calendars clearly stating the organization's Christian principles have been given out.

Trashing Overlooked Human Beings. In an Indianapolis newspaper some years ago was this headline: "Homeless Woman Crushed with Trash." It seems that a homeless woman crawled into a dumpster to sleep, was loaded into a truck, compressed with the trash, and arrived at the incinerator, dead. They found her by her white tennis shoes and red windbreaker. Nearby residents had seen her climb into the dumpster, but when they heard the truck begin to grind, they did not warn the driver in time.

Accounts of the homeless being crushed—even crushed to death in trash bins—have actually become commonplace. It happened in Denver at least twice during the 1990s, in Washington once, in Los Angeles once, and in Atlanta once (just to name some incidents). How tragic it is that overlooked human beings are being gathered up with the trash!

Do Something. Theodore Roosevelt, the twenty-sixth president of the United States, seemed to always display a vigorous determination to get involved. He was Assistant Secretary of the Navy in 1898 when the Spanish-American War broke out, and he resigned that post to form the Rough Riders, a volunteer cavalry group that was to become famous for its charge up San Juan Hill in Cuba. An advocate of a venturesome foreign policy, Roosevelt effected the construction of the Panama Canal, won the Nobel Peace Prize for his successful intervention in the Russo-Japanese War, and dispatched the U.S. Fleet on a round-the-world tour.

Roosevelt's famous motto was "Speak softly and carry a big stick." But he had another motto that he wrote as advice to himself and others but that sounds as if it could have come from the mouth of the good Samaritan: "In a moment of decision, the best thing you can do is the right thing to do. The worst thing you can do is nothing."

FOR YOUTH

■ TOPIC: The Merciful Enemy

■ QUESTIONS: 1. Why did Jesus respond to the lawyer's question with a story instead of a straight answer? 2. What might have caused the Samaritan to stop and help, while the others "*passed by on the other side*" (Luke 10:31-32)? 3. What is it that really made the Samaritan good? 4. How does your conscience feel when you avoid helping someone who might really need assistance? How does it feel after you've stopped to help? 5. Who are the people that might classify as your "neighbors"?

■ **ILLUSTRATIONS:**

Keeping to Ourselves. Our lack of involvement is showing up on a lot of fronts. Back in the 1970s, we bemoaned the death of Kitty Gennovese, who was murdered on the streets of New York in plain view of scores of people in a nearby apartment building. During the incident, no one tried to stop the murder or even call the police.

Still today many scholars worry that we're becoming more and more isolated. One professor illustrates our increasing seclusion by pointing out what is happening to bowling. In his book, *Bowling Alone: America's Declining Social Capital,* Harvard political scientist Robert D. Putnam tells how more Americans are bowling than ever before. But bowling in organized leagues has plummeted. According to his statistics, "Between 1980 and 1993, the total numbers of bowlers in the United States increased by 10 percent, while league bowling decreased by 40 percent."

Putnam uses bowling only as an analogy of what is happening throughout our society. Fewer people are volunteering their time to work with churches and social agencies; fewer people are becoming members of social clubs; and more people are keeping to themselves. "Where once we played together, ate pizza together, kept score together, drank Coke together, while building up the social capital and trust necessary among members of a community that could bring about greater civic involvement, today we bowl alone."

Stranger in Need. In his book, *The Samaritan's Imperative*, Michael J. Christensen cites a story about two monks walking back to their monastery in the freezing cold. As they cross a bridge, the two monks hear a man calling for help in the ravine below. They want to stop, but they know they must reach the monastery before sunset or they will freeze to death. The first monk chooses to risk the danger of the cold in order to help another to safety. He climbs down into the ravine, gathers the wounded man into his arms, and slowly makes his way back to the monastery. The second monk has already gone on ahead, determined to get back safely before sunset.

Night comes, and with it, the bitter cold. As the first monk nears the monastery, he stumbles over something in the middle of the road. To his sorrow, it is the body of his spiritual brother who had gone on alone and had frozen to death. In seeking to save his life, he had lost it. But the compassionate monk, willing to lose his life, was kept warm by the heat exchanged from carrying the stranger in need.

Whom Shall I Send? Both Bob and Deloris are very active at the church I attend, but if the truth be told, Deloris is more active than Bob. In fact, Deloris is more active than just about anyone else I know! When someone is needed to lead a Bible study for the kids, Deloris is there with an open Bible. When someone needs food, Deloris collects it and delivers it. When someone needs good Christian counsel, Deloris is there to give it in a heartbeat. When someone desires prayer, Deloris is on her knees beside him or her, praying fervently for that person. She is the perennial good Samaritan.

Just watching Deloris go sometimes saps Bob—and the rest of us—of energy. So you can imagine our stares when we were asking for volunteers to help with our children's church, and we saw Bob's hand shoot up before Deloris's. With his hand still in the air and our eyes glued on him, Bob, quoting his own version of Isaiah 6:8, said, "Here am I, Lord. Send Deloris!"

HUMILITY AND HOSPITALITY

BACKGROUND SCRIPTURE: Luke 14:7-24
DEVOTIONAL READING: 1 Peter 5:3-10

KEY VERSE: "Go out into the roads and lanes, and compel people to come in, so that my house may be filled." Luke 14:23.

KING JAMES VERSION

LUKE 14:7 And he put forth a parable to those which were bidden, when he marked how they chose out the chief rooms; saying unto them, 8 When thou art bidden of any man to a wedding, sit not down in the highest room; lest a more honourable man than thou be bidden of him; 9 And he that bade thee and him come and say to thee, Give this man place; and thou begin with shame to take the lowest room. 10 But when thou art bidden, go and sit down in the lowest room; that when he that bade thee cometh, he may say unto thee, Friend, go up higher: then shalt thou have worship in the presence of them that sit at meat with thee. 11 For whosoever exalteth himself shall be abased; and he that humbleth himself shall be exalted. . . .

15 And when one of them that sat at meat with him heard these things, he said unto him, Blessed is he that shall eat bread in the kingdom of God. 16 Then said he unto him, A certain man made a great supper, and bade many: 17 And sent his servant at supper time to say to them that were bidden, Come; for all things are now ready. 18 And they all with one consent began to make excuse. The first said unto him, I have bought a piece of ground, and I must needs go and see it: I pray thee have me excused. 19 And another said, I have bought five yoke of oxen, and I go to prove them: I pray thee have me excused. 20 And another said, I have married a wife, and therefore I cannot come. 21 So that servant came, and shewed his lord these things. Then the master of the house being angry said to his servant, Go out quickly into the streets and lanes of the city, and bring in hither the poor, and the maimed, and the halt, and the blind. 22 And the servant said, Lord, it is done as thou hast commanded, and yet there is room. 23 And the lord said unto the servant, Go out into the highways and hedges, and compel them to come in, that my house may be filled. 24 For I say unto you, That none of those men which were bidden shall taste of my supper.

NEW REVISED STANDARD VERSION

LUKE 14:7 When he noticed how the guests chose the places of honor, he told them a parable. 8 "When you are invited by someone to a wedding banquet, do not sit down at the place of honor, in case someone more distinguished than you has been invited by your host; 9 and the host who invited both of you may come and say to you, 'Give this person your place,' and then in disgrace you would start to take the lowest place. 10 But when you are invited, go and sit down at the lowest place, so that when your host comes, he may say to you, 'Friend, move up higher'; then you will be honored in the presence of all who sit at the table with you. 11 For all who exalt themselves will be humbled, and those who humble themselves will be exalted." . . .

15 One of the dinner guests, on hearing this, said to him, "Blessed is anyone who will eat bread in the kingdom of God!" 16 Then Jesus said to him, "Someone gave a great dinner and invited many. 17 At the time for the dinner he sent his slave to say to those who had been invited, 'Come; for everything is ready now.' 18 But they all alike began to make excuses. The first said to him, 'I have bought a piece of land, and I must go out and see it; please accept my regrets.' 19 Another said, 'I have bought five yoke of oxen, and I am going to try them out; please accept my regrets.' 20 Another said, 'I have just been married, and therefore I cannot come.' 21 So the slave returned and reported this to his master. Then the owner of the house became angry and said to his slave, 'Go out at once into the streets and lanes of the town and bring in the poor, the crippled, the blind, and the lame.' 22 And the slave said, 'Sir, what you ordered has been done, and there is still room.' 23 Then the master said to the slave, 'Go out into the roads and lanes, and compel people to come in, so that my house may be filled. 24 For I tell you, none of those who were invited will taste my dinner.'"

13

HOME BIBLE READINGS

Monday, August 22	Ephesians 4:1-6	*Bear with One Another in Love*
Tuesday, August 23	Philippians 2:1-8	*Imitate Christ's Humility*
Wednesday, August 24	1 Peter 5:3-10	*Clothe Yourself with Humility*
Thursday, August 25	Matthew 22:1-10	*Parable of the Wedding Banquet*
Friday, August 26	Luke 14:1-6	*Jesus Heals the Man with Dropsy*
Saturday, August 27	Luke 14:7-14	*Humility and Hospitality*
Sunday, August 28	Luke 14:15-24	*Parable of the Great Dinner*

BACKGROUND

The Gospel of Luke (as well as the Book of Acts) is addressed to someone named Theophilus. The author called the recipient of his book *"most excellent"* (Luke 1:3), possibly indicating that Theophilus was an important government official. Perhaps Theophilus, whose name means "lover of God," was a convert to Christianity who yearned to learn more about his new faith. Or perhaps Theophilus was a spiritual seeker who wanted to explore the facts about Christ so he could decide for himself what to believe. Either scenario might explain why Luke paid close attention to historical details.

Luke's purpose in writing this Gospel seems to have been to create an accurate, dependable account of the works, teachings, and life of Jesus. Luke's own Gentile roots and his Gentile audience explain why his Gospel has a universal perspective. It speaks to the condition of the entire human race, not just to Jews. Luke either omitted Jewish phrases and practices found in the other Gospels or explained them carefully, making his Gospel helpful and readable for those less familiar with Jewish ways. Perhaps Luke, even though he addressed the book specifically to Theophilus, expected that his Gospel would be read by many others.

Luke's main interest was what God had done through the Messiah to save sinners. Luke concerned himself with many people who would be neglected by most writers of his day—children, women, and the poor. Though ancient Roman society regarded these people as having no great significance, Luke demonstrated Jesus' special concern for them.

Prominent in the literary structure of the third Synoptic Gospel is Luke's description of Jesus' journey to Jerusalem and His sacrifice on the cross. The sovereignty of God in Christ's life and ministry is clear as He made His way to His eternally appointed goal. Another major emphasis of Luke's account is that the Good News is not for a select nation. Jesus offers forgiveness and salvation freely to all humanity, regardless of race, gender, or social merit.

In stepping back from this last thought, we should note that one common thread between people of the first century A.D. and people living today is their need for a Savior. Men and women are bruised and battered by life's disappointments and society's injustices. So were the people of the first century. People today must face the awfulness of their own sin, just as people had to do in the first century. And people today can find strength and hope through trusting in Jesus, just as Luke's first reader, Theophilus, may have done when he read the Gospel of Luke.

Notes on the Printed Text

Luke 14:1 states that on one *sabbath*, Jesus was dining in the home of a highly respected Pharisee. The occasion, however, was rather tense, for the attendees were watching Jesus closely. They wanted to see how He would deal with a man in His presence who suffered from *dropsy* (14:2).

When Jesus questioned the religious leaders in attendance at the meal about the legality of healing someone *on the sabbath* (14:3), *they were silent* (14:4). More than likely, they were enraged when Jesus healed the man and sent him away. Their continued silence, despite Jesus' efforts to reason with them, should be seen as a disapproval of the Savior's action (14:5-6).

Jesus noticed the dinner guests endeavored to sit in *the places of honor* (14:7). Jesus stated that it was unwise to do so (14:8). An occasion could arise in which someone with more respect might afterward show up at the banquet. Imagine the embarrassment felt by the presumptuous attendee when the host asked him or her move to some other spot at the end of the table to make room for the more distinguished guest (14:9).

Jesus' recommendation, as recorded in Luke 14:10, must have seemed counterintuitive to His listeners. Nevertheless, it resonated with the divine priority to cultivate humility, rather than pride. Thus, Jesus encouraged sitting *"down at the lowest place"* of the table and then being invited by the host to *"move up higher."*

The issue was much broader than maintaining good etiquette at a social function. At stake were eternal matters related to the kingdom of God. In 14:11, Jesus explained that in the day of judgment those who were proud in this life *"will be humbled"*; in contrast, those who were humble *"will be exalted."* The context strongly suggests that it is God who does the exalting or humbling.

Jesus next told His host whom he should invite to his banquets (14:12-14). This was followed by another guest declaring to Jesus that those who get to *"eat bread in the kingdom of God"* (14:15) are *blessed*. In response, Jesus told a story illustrating how the guests who eventually will attend the heavenly banquet are not necessarily the ones who were expected.

On the surface Jesus' parable is simple. A man plans *"a great dinner"* (14:16) and makes certain that his friends are notified beforehand. When the time comes for the actual meal, he sends *his slave* (14:17) to alert the guests. In the ancient world, meals were often major social events. It was important who was invited and who was not, who accepted and who declined. Even where the guests sat the table when the meal was finally served was important.

The words used in 14:16 for *"great dinner"* indicate that this event was no ordinary meal. It was a special occasion, and it would have been an honor to receive an invitation. It was customary at that time (and still is, in some parts of the Middle East) for a second invitation to be given once the meal was ready. And so a servant would be dispatched to remind the guests of their earlier commitment.

Amazingly, one invited guest declined because he wanted to check out a new *"piece of land"* (14:18). Another preferred to test his *"five yoke of oxen"* (14:19). And the third chose to stay with his bride (14:20). None of these excuses was adequate to justify breaking a commitment to attend the feast.

With this story Jesus was suggesting to the Pharisees around the table that they had much in common with the three guests. Although they expressed their devotion at every opportunity and heartily endorsed the prospect of an eternity with God, Jesus knew that they were, at the same time, finding reasons why they would not be able to attend His own banquet—the feast of salvation.

When the host learned from his servant that his guests would not be coming, he *"became angry"* (14:21). If they had no desire to be with him, he would open his doors to those who would welcome his invitation. After all, the food was prepared and the table set. It should not go to waste.

Thus, instead of leading a dinner party for well-known and well-to-do people, the host called in *"the poor, the crippled, the blind, and the and the lame."* Yet even after his new guests were gathered, still there was enough room at the banquet (14:22). And so the host gave a second call, inviting whoever he might gather from *"the roads and lanes"* (14:23). Persuasion rather than brute force is implied in the phrase *"compel people to come in."* Food, drink, and fellowship would be powerful tools of persuasion for needy people. The Lord offers us blessings greater than anything the world has to offer.

Jesus was speaking quite clearly to His host and the other guests. They were the ones who should have embraced Him—the ones who were best equipped to understand exactly who He was and what His coming meant for Israel and the world. But they would not have Him. Thus Jesus would invite those who were willing to come when He called (14:24).

SUGGESTIONS TO TEACHERS

We can all identify with someone who tries to get out of attending a wedding, funeral, or some other event with a lame excuse. Although the three excuses given in Jesus' parable of the great feast were all inadequate, they reflect the kinds of excuses adults often give to God when He invites them to be a part of His spiritual family.

1. PRETEXT #1. The first excuse in the parable is that the individual had purchased some land and needed to go see it. This is an excuse because the landowner had undoubtedly looked the property over before buying it. The adults who give this type of excuse are too tied to their possessions.

2. PRETEXT #2. The second excuse is that the individual had just purchased some oxen and needed to try them out. In a manner similar to the landowner, the oxen's owner no doubt had tried out the beasts before purchasing them. This type of excuse is common among adults who are too absorbed in their occupations.

3. PRETEXT #3. The third excuse is a groom's desire to stay with his bride. Yet the groom had certainly known about his upcoming marriage at the time he had accepted the banquet invitation. This third excuse represents all excuses by adults who are too occupied with domestic cares and responsibilities.

Be sure to stress to the class members that such activities as buying land, purchasing oxen, and getting married are not morally wrong in isolation by themselves. They become problematic, however, when they are used as excuses to avoid trusting in and submitting to the Messiah. While giving lame excuses to the Lord is an all-too-common tendency with many adults in our society, things can (and should) be different with the students in your class.

FOR ADULTS

■ TOPIC: Building Community

■ QUESTIONS: 1. Why did the guests at the banquet seek the places of honor? 2. Why did Jesus discourage seeking the places of honor? 3. Why do you think Jesus responded to the man's comment with a story rather than by speaking to him directly? 4. If it is good to take care of one's business affairs and one's spouse, why did Jesus treat the three responses like excuses rather than good reasons? 5. Who do the guests who attended the banquet in the parable represent?

■ **ILLUSTRATIONS:**

Is Jesus First? A stunned husband whose wife had filed for divorce said to his pastor, "I gave her everything a woman could want." Wrong! It's true that he gave her *possessions* in abundance. But what she wanted was *him*. She wanted attention from and a relationship with a husband who, unfortunately, was so immersed in his business that he had no time for his family. He learned too late the penalty of misplaced priorities.

So what's first in your life? Jesus said that when God is first and others are second, He will give us all we need from day to day (see Phil. 4:19). But if our priorities are out of order, our emotional and spiritual lives will ultimately wind up in chaos.

Faithful Family. For years, one could always count on singing the hymn entitled "Faith of Our Fathers" during the Father's Day recognition at church. The song celebrates the positive influence of a faithful father on his family. Sadly, this hymn isn't sung as often these days. Perhaps it's because faithful fathers and mothers are becoming rare.

Faithful parents are a blessing. Children raised in a home where mom and dad lead them in Christian spiritual development are more likely to become believers themselves. Of course, this is not always true. As faithful as parents might be, their belief cannot save their children. The decision of parents to follow Christ is not a package deal that ushers the family into heaven. But the parents' faith can create a predisposition within the family toward believing in Christ. In the families of most faithful parents, it is natural for the children and grandchildren to become believers (1 John 2:12-14).

While the Christian faith is one that's lived within a community of believers (namely, the local church), there are other crucial issues worth remembering. For instance, every individual must decide whether to reject or accept Christ. And everyone must deal with the sin issues in their life. Though the faith of a parent can spiritually unite his or her family, the children remain accountable to God for their actions.

Aspiring to Greatness. Many years ago there was a young man named Bill who was a great football running back at the former Lee Edwards High School. When game time arrived on Fridays, the crowds would pour out to watch Bill almost single-handedly defeat the opponents.

Bill's younger brother, Charlie, didn't play football. Why try? Who could ever live up to his older brother's greatness? Charlie would languish in Bill's shadow. It seemed easier not even to make the effort.

However, a wise football coach named Lee Stone went to Charlie and said, "Son, I think you have the speed and skills to play this game. Why don't you try out for the team?" After some cajoling and encouraging, the coach convinced the reticent younger brother to give it a shot. The rest is history. Charlie "Choo Choo" Justice went on to become an All-American at the University of North Carolina and one of the leading rushers and scorers in the history of the Washington Redskins.

God is still in the business of doing what seems most unlikely. Paul reminded his readers that not many of them were wise in the world's eyes, or powerful, or even wealthy (1 Cor. 1:26). Nevertheless, the Lord redeemed them for His glory. Who is to say what God can do with unlikely folks, if He so chooses? Though our dreams may seem foolish to the world (1:27), in God's hands they can become tomorrow's realities. Don't give up on yourself or on God's power to make something exciting out of your life (1:28).

For Youth

■ **TOPIC:** Humility and Hospitality

■ **QUESTIONS:** 1. What was the point of the parable Jesus told regarding the wedding banquet? 2. In what sense will the humble one day be exalted? 3. Why do you think one of the dinner guests, upon hearing Jesus' remarks, responded as he did? 4. When you first heard God's invitation, did you truly understand what it meant to be a Christian? Explain. 5. What things should we as Christians say to make sure people truly understand God's invitation to them?

■ ILLUSTRATIONS:

A Child's Faith. Some years ago, I was sharing my faith in Christ with a former high school friend. Following college she had become successful financially, and she was very self-sufficient.

This person had many intellectual questions. After trying to answer them, I finally explained that no matter how much one tries to understand God, it still takes simple faith to become a Christian. That statement stunned her. "I don't think there is anything such as simple faith," she replied.

A child comes to Christ the same way as an adult—by grace through faith. Few children understand deep theological issues. They've not experienced all of the complexities of life. They simply take God at His word.

Trusting in Christ represents two sides of a fence. Each side gives us a different perspective. One side is a worldly and intellectual view. The other side is a transformed view of worldly and intellectual issues. Christ creates a new world view in the life of a Christian. Hope replaces hopelessness. Possibilities replace impossibilities. Love replaces hate. Trust replaces mistrust. Faith replaces skepticism. It's a world a child could love!

Keeping Our Priorities Straight. Several years ago, there was a cartoon in *The New Yorker* magazine that depicted an American couple dashing up the steps of the Louvre in Paris shouting "Where's the Mona Lisa? We're double-parked!" So often we approach faith in this same hurry. We know that it is important, but we just don't have time to spend on it, so we make our dash at faith as if we are double-parked.

As a young boy, I learned that if I could not devote myself to a task or a project, I had to be honest, say "I cannot do it," and leave it alone. The choice for many young people is to give no attention or a little attention to anything that lies outside of what they consider to be the immediate needs for survival or success, as defined by their culture.

Jesus taught that how we see ourselves in relation to our peers is secondary to loving and obeying Him. When our priorities are in proper order, our lives are pleasing to Him.

A Humble Admission. When I was young, baseball was important to me. I loved the game so much that I studied it and played it everyday. I even hustled when I played, for baseball was my life.

You can imagine the excitement I felt when my oldest son began playing baseball. This would be one of our main bonding mechanisms. I didn't know beans about soccer, so baseball would be a mentoring vehicle. Plus, he has more talent than I ever had. My love for the game has far exceeded my ability.

If my son would just listen to me, I could help him be a great baseball player. Reading curve balls, shifting body weight with the swing, stealing bases, turning double plays . . . it's the little things that separate the amateurs from the pros.

A pattern developed in our relationship. Because of my familiarity with the game, I saw every mistake that my son made. In addition, I knew how to correct them. So post-game drives home became a critique of how to improve his game. It soon got old for my son. One night he finally said, "Dad, could you not start by telling me everything I did wrong? Tell me what I did right first."

My mobile "coaching clinic" wasn't helping. My son had become discouraged. I was anxious to help, but I had become a hindrance. He was becoming bitter toward me. It caused me to think. Was my childhood obsession with baseball worth risking a relationship with my son? It was time to deemphasize a game and refocus on the person (Col. 3:21).